Architectural Theory

ARCHITECTURAL THEORY

Volume II
An Anthology from 1871 to 2005

Edited by Harry Francis Mallgrave and
Christina Contandriopoulos

Blackwell
Publishing

Editorial material and organization © 2008 by Harry Francis Mallgrave and Christina Contandriopoulos

BLACKWELL PUBLISHING
350 Main Street, Malden, MA 02148-5020, USA
9600 Garsington Road, Oxford OX4 2DQ, UK
550 Swanston Street, Carlton, Victoria 3053, Australia

The right of Harry Francis Mallgrave and Christina Contandriopoulos to be identified as the authors of the editorial material in this work has been asserted in accordance with the UK Copyright, Designs, and Patents Act 1988.

The publisher and the authors make no representations or warranties with respect to the accuracy or completeness of the contents of this work and specifically disclaim all warranties, including without limitation warranties of fitness for a particular purpose. No warranty may be created or extended by sales or promotional materials. The advice and strategies contained herein may not be suitable for every situation. This work is sold with the understanding that the publisher is not engaged in rendering legal, accounting, or other professional services. If professional assistance is required, the services of a competent professional person should be sought. Neither the publisher nor the author shall be liable for damages arising herefrom. The fact that an organization or website is referred to in this work as a citation and/or a potential source of further information does not mean that the author or the publisher endorses the information the organization or website may provide or recommendations it may make. Further, readers should be aware that Internet websites listed in this work may have changed or disappeared between when this work was written and when it is read.

First published 2008 by Blackwell Publishing Ltd

1   2008

Library of Congress Cataloging-in-Publication Data

Architectural theory, volume II: an anthology from 1871 to 2005 /
edited by Harry Francis Mallgrave and Christina Contandriopoulos.
p. cm.
Includes bibliographical references and index.
ISBN: 978-1-4051-0259-9 (hard cover: alk. paper)
ISBN: 978-1-4051-0260-5 (pbk.: alk. paper)
1. Architecture–Philosophy. I. Mallgrave, Harry Francis.

NA2500.A7115 2005
720′.1–dc22
2004030886

A catalogue record for this title is available from the British Library.

Set in 10/13pt Dante
by SPi Publisher Services, Pondicherry, India
Printed and bound in Singapore
by Fabulous Printers Pte Ltd

The publisher's policy is to use permanent paper from mills that operate a sustainable forestry policy, and which has been manufactured from pulp processed using acid-free and elementary chlorine-free practices. Furthermore, the publisher ensures that the text paper and cover board used have met acceptable environmental accreditation standards.

For further information on
Blackwell Publishing, visit our website at
www.blackwellpublishing.com

The image on the title page and all part and chapter opening pages © Travelwide / Alamy.

CONTENTS

C. Reforms in the United States   43

D. Conceptual Underpinnings of German Modernism: Space, Form, and Realism   63

D. German Expressionism and the Bauhaus   195

E. European Modernism: 1925–32   211

Part IV: The Politics of Modernism: 1930–45   **233**

A. Totalitarianism in Europe   **235**

Part V: High Modernism in the Postwar Years 273

A. Postwar Theory in the United States 275

B. Postwar Theory in Europe 293

C. The Rise and Fall of CIAM   313

C. Critiques of Modernism 368

Part VII: The Prospect of a Postmodern Theory: 1969–79   393

A. Rationalism and the IAUS   395

Part VIII: The 1980s   457

A. Poststructuralism and Deconstruction   459

B. Postmodernism and Historicism   481

C. Regionalism and Traditionalism   505

Part IX: Millennial Tensions   **533**

A. Tectonics and Geometry   **535**

B. The End of Theory?   562

PREFACE

This second volume follows the format and style of the first. There we made the decision to include a greater, rather than fewer, number of texts, which of course limits the length of a cited text. This decision, we believe, also says something about the nature of anthologies in general – that is, they are capable only of underscoring general theoretical tendencies, and they do not replace the need, in some cases, to read the texts in their entirety. Anthologies are also best used as companion volumes with history textbooks. If anthologies, for instance, point out when and where significant debates occurred, they cannot substitute for a visual understanding of buildings themselves.

The proliferation of published materials in the last forty or fifty years also presents its special problems. The great complexity of theory during this period again limits what slices of thought we are able to present. Nuanced positions on complex issues tend to be overshadowed by the larger trends, which often, by nature, are ephemeral. Thus a historian writing a history of theory in the 1970s, for instance, will paint a quite different and more complete picture of events than an anthology is able to present. We apologize to those who may feel slighted by our necessarily limited choice of texts.

Our textual conventions are as follows. The use of simple ellipses, "...", denotes the omission of words or phrases within a sentence. Square brackets, [...], indicate the omission of a sentence, sentences, or several short paragraphs, and are also employed at the beginning and end of a text. Asterisks, * * *, appear as in the original text. We have left all English texts in their original punctuation, spelling, and style. Book titles are italicized and the use of quotation marks indicates shorter writings.

GENERAL INTRODUCTION

Although the association of theory with practice in architecture is at least as old as the first book of Vitruvius in classical Roman times, the two notions do not run in parallel. The sketch or construction of a building may in fact precede the understanding of the novel idea contained within, and similarly, ideas may be put forth in speculation far in advance of the day when they are realized in practice. This is an important point to make with respect to twentieth-century practice and theory. Whereas historians since the 1920s have generally (and somewhat correctly) tended to see the first experiments with modern forms as beginning in the years surrounding the turn of the twentieth century, the theoretical underpinnings of these forms are another matter. This book will argue that modern forms can no more be disassociated from the reforms of the Arts and Crafts movement, the numerous discussions with respect to the use of iron, or German psychological and physiological theories of perception any more than the Enlightenment can be detached from the physical speculations of Isaac Newton or the Renaissance from the invention of perspective. We have thus defined the beginning of this volume with the year 1871 in order to provide the intellectual context for modern design.

There are other reasons, also, for selecting this date: political, social, and technological. If the conclusion of the Franco-Prussian War helped to give birth to the national states of Germany and Italy, and more expansively to the desire for national identities elsewhere in Europe, the years following the American Civil War also saw the accelerated growth of the United States as a political and economic power. The Western world thus changed quite dramatically in the years between 1871 and 1900. Many of the inventions and time-saving devices we associate with modern life – from the telephone and transcontinental railways to indoor plumbing, refrigeration, automobiles, Alpine tunnels, and steel structural systems, to name but a few – came into existence well before the turn of the century. The rise of new nations also took place alongside the creation of an educated and relatively affluent middle class and general improvements in health, education, and living conditions. The phenomenon of the modern department store, miraculous in its day, was but one of many harbingers of the prosperity to come. Architects naturally perceived these changes and were quick to speculate on the forms that would house this new world, leading to a discourse in the closing decades of the nineteenth century almost entirely devoted to change.

By contrast, the first half of the twentieth century seems to be more a period guided by actual events. Albert Einstein's theories of relativity and European avant-gardism belong to the cultivation of modernity to be sure, but even more so do two world wars, the Great Depression, and concentration camps. Thus the period of the first great flowering of "modern architecture" – the 1920s – was limited in a Europe still recovering from the war to five or six years of actual practice at best, that is, before the economic downturn halted things once again. And between 1933 and 1950 theory virtually ceased to exist in Europe.

If the decades immediately following World War II offered a recovery in the form of optimism and increasing prosperity (the Cold War notwithstanding), the year 1968 defines another major turning point in architectural thought. This time it was the "event" of the political and social unrest that dominated the decade, and architects and their now changing perceptions of the world naturally responded to the charged atmosphere of events. The forms of high modernism did not succumb overnight (indeed they still remain a part and parcel of our vocabulary), but theory did undergo a profound shift in direction as well as an intensification of interests. Not only were the tenets of modernism – from its beneficent social mission to its minimalist aesthetics – overtly and in some cases mercilessly challenged on several fronts, but practical and technical deliberations fell victim to a conscious separation of theory from practice. As theory prospered in exploring tenets of sociological and philosophical abstraction (from structuralism, Marxism, and phenomenology to ecology, semiotics, and poststructuralism), the one issue that seemingly united all parties was the belief that we had indeed entered a new postmodern era.

Yet the shelf-life of popular labels in our day and age tends to be relatively short, and by the early 1990s the euphoria with the "postmodern" had clearly passed over to a nervous concern for and fascination with the built world. The impulses affecting change were varied. If climatologists and ecologists pointed to systemic aberrations that were threatening human existence, new digital tools were at the same time allowing architects to explore wholly new forms and solutions. The pace and scale of building dramatically increased in the 1990s, as the profession for the first time became a true global union of practitioners. The issue of technology and its capacity to solve certain problems again pushed itself to the fore after nearly three decades of dormancy.

Nevertheless, we want to stress that architectural theory and practice do not just respond to any given course of events. As the intellectual framework and quintessential art of building the world in which we inhabit, architecture has the very serious obligation to contribute to the shape of history itself. A historical understanding of architecture's past can only facilitate the understanding of the environmental, technological, and aesthetic issues yet to be confronted.

PART I EARLY MODERNISM

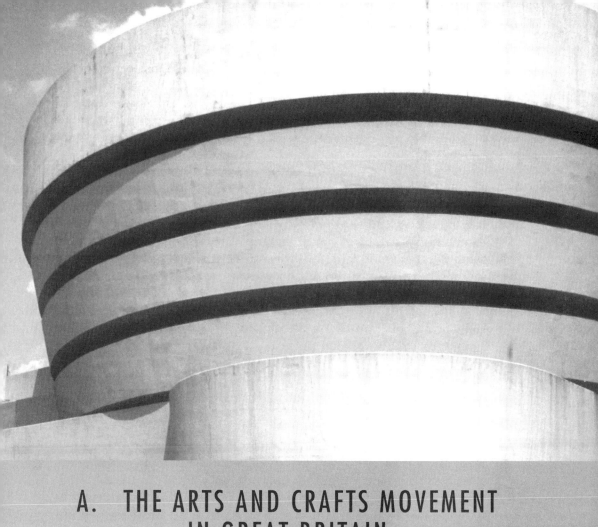

A. THE ARTS AND CRAFTS MOVEMENT
IN GREAT BRITAIN

Introduction

The Arts and Crafts movement was among the most prominent and influential of the European movements of the last three decades of the nineteenth century. Its roots, as we saw in the previous volume, extend back several decades: to the writings of Augustus Welby Pugin and John Ruskin, to the Great London Exhibition of 1851, to the reorganization of the Department of Practical Art, and to the artisanal example of Morris, Marshall, Faulkner and Company, founded in 1861.

The movement was also a response to the rapidly maturing Industrial Age – the passage from a system of handicraft production to a society predicated on wages and the machine. Over the preceding decades hundreds of thousands of workers (and their families) had migrated from rural areas to cities and formed a working class, while large and small entrepreneurs, from factory owners to shopkeepers, became the regulators of society and its burgeoning economy. Major advances in transportation, communications, and the national infrastructure were empowering the individual and opening the world to many to whom it formerly lay closed, even those of modest means. Universal education enhanced literacy rates and created the value system of the new "middle class." And of course numerous social ills also came to be associated with industrialization as well, from unemployment to urban poverty, slums, crime, economic disparities, and rising friction between the classes. Reformers in Britain, which among the European nations had pushed fastest down the path of industrialization, reacted most sharply to this time of social upheaval.

One of the hallmarks of the British Arts and Crafts movement was therefore its social conscience or near-universal condemnation of existing social conditions. For many (and this includes the movement's godfather John Ruskin), the critique took the form of contempt for the machine and industry, as well as a pious nostalgia for medieval living conditions. For others, the argument assumed a political cast: the socialist desire to overturn the economic system of laissez-faire capitalism and share equally the growing economic wealth. For others still, there resided the belief that social conditions, while seemingly spiraling in no clear way, were in a natural process of transformation or evolution, beyond which a new and happier society would emerge, a new "modern" world. What should not be overlooked in these widely shared reactions to the "ugliness" of industrial society was the strong desire by all to enhance artistically and architecturally the living conditions of people.

1 JOHN RUSKIN
from *Fors Clavigera* (1871)

Although the name William Morris is today synonymous with the founding of the Arts and Crafts movement in Britain, Morris himself always proclaimed John Ruskin as his spiritual "master." Since his early writings, Ruskin's reputation continued to expand, and in 1870 he was appointed the first Slade Professor at the University of Oxford, a post that he would hold for the next seventeen years. In 1871 Ruskin began another long-term involvement with a project that was perhaps closer to his heart – the writing of *Fors Clavigera*. The book assumed the form of letters addressed "To the Workmen and Labourers of Great Britain." The ninety-six letters, written over fourteen years, are perhaps the most unique of his writings from the perspective of both style and content. They are unmeasured, fanciful, and unconventional in their language, as well as meandering in their mixing of politics, satire, and artistic criticism. The letters were also connected with another of Ruskin's ventures – the founding of the St. George's Company, later known as the Guild of St. George. This new feudal or communistic society of masters and servants was conceived as a protest against the industrial age, and Ruskin, from his own purse, put up the first £7,000 for its foundation. The idea was to create an endowment from whose interest land could be purchased and turned over to tenants, who in turn would build their homes and cultivate the land without machinery. These new serfs owned their production (save for a tithe to the company), and a class of carpenters and smiths would round out the self-sufficient community. Every aspect of communal life – from education to costume – was to be regulated.

The project, which he describes below, was a failure and a keen disappointment to Ruskin, who over the next several years pleaded for donations but with little success. Nevertheless, the seed was sown, and the idea of a "guild," in another form, would become quite popular throughout Britain in the 1880s.

John Ruskin, from *Fors Clavigera: Letters to the Workmen and Labourers of Great Britain*. Chicago and New York: Belford, Clarke & Co., n.d., pp. 72–3.

I am not rich; (as people now estimate riches), and great part of what I have is already engaged in maintaining artworkmen, or for other objects more or less of public utility. The tenth of whatever is left to me, estimated as accurately as I can, (you shall see the accounts) I will make over to you in perpetuity, with the best security that English law can give, on Christmas Day of this year, with engagement to add the title of whatever I earn afterwards. Who else will help, with little or much? the object of such fund being, to begin, and gradually – no matter how slowly – to increase, the buying and securing of land in England, which shall not be built upon, but cultivated by Englishmen, with their own hands, and such help of force as they can find in wind and wave.

I do not care with how many, or how few, this thing is begun, nor on what inconsiderable scale, – if it be but in two or three poor men's gardens. So much, at least, I can buy, myself, and give them. If no help come, I have done and said what I could, and there will be an end. If any help come to me, it is to be on the following conditions: – We will try to make some small piece of English ground, beautiful, peaceful, and fruitful. We will have no steam-engines upon it, and no railroads; we will have no untended or unthought-of creatures on it; none wretched, but the sick; none idle, but the dead. We will have no liberty upon it; but instant obedience to known law, and appointed persons: no equality upon it; but recognition of every betterness that we can find, and reprobation of every worseness. When we want to go anywhere, we will go there quietly and safely, not at forty miles an hour in the risk of our lives; when we want to carry anything anywhere, we will carry it either on the backs of beasts, or on our own, or in carts, or boats; we will have plenty of flowers and vegetables in our gardens, plenty of corn and grass in our fields, – and few bricks. We will have some music and poetry; the children shall learn to dance to it and sing it; – perhaps some of the old people, in time, may also. We will have some art, moreover; we will at least try if, like the Greeks, we can't make some pots. The Greeks used to paint pictures of gods on their pots; we, probably, cannot do as much, but we may put some pictures of insects on them, and reptiles; – butterflies, and frogs, if nothing better. There was an excellent old potter in France who used to put frogs and vipers into his dishes, to the admiration of mankind; we can surely put something nicer than that. Little by little, some higher art and imagination may manifest themselves among us; and feeble rays of science may dawn for us. Botany, though too dull to dispute the existence of flowers; and history, though too simple to question the nativity of men; – nay – even perhaps an uncalculating and uncovetous wisdom, as of rude Magi, presenting, at such nativity, gifts of gold and frankincense.

Faithfully yours,
JOHN RUSKIN.

2 CHRISTOPHER DRESSER
from *Studies in Design* (1874–6)

The work of Henry Cole and Richard Redgrave at South Kensington can be viewed as a second front of the handicraft movement when it blossomed in the 1870s and 1880s, and certainly one of the more gifted designers to emerge from this institution was Christopher Dresser. Born in Glasgow, Dresser entered the London School of Design at Somerset House in 1847 and he was still taking his studies in 1853, when Cole and Redgrave moved it (temporarily) to the Marlborough House. Dresser at this time was influenced by the work of Owen Jones and he even prepared a plate for Jones's *Grammar of Ornament* (1856). Shortly before this book's appearance, Dresser was appointed a lecturer on botany at the reorganized Department of Art and Industry. Dresser quickly distinguished himself as a designer, and over the course of a lengthy career he designed an array of products that today could still be seen as "modern" for their lack of ornamentation and simple functional lines. Among Dresser's numerous writings was his *Studies in Design*. This collection of articles was written to assist "those who desire to decorate houses in a manner that shall reveal their knowledge," and the work forms an early volume to a body of books written in these years to improve the level of interior design. This short passage on "repose" is typical of those in the Cole circle to put forward principles.

But how are we to achieve the necessary amount of repose in our rooms? We need not paint the walls of our apartments grey, nor of mud-colour, neither need we make them black; indeed, the highest sense of repose – *i.e.*, dreamy, soothing repose, may be realised where the brightest colours are employed. Repose is attained by the absence of any want. A plain wall of dingy colour reveals a want; it does not then supply all that is necessary to the production of a sense of quiet and rest. A wall may be covered with the richest decoration, and yet be of such a character that the eye will rest upon it and be satisfied.

If strong colours are used upon walls and ceilings, it is usually desirable that they be employed in very small masses; thus blue, red, and yellow may be used upon a wall (the three primary colours), either alone, or together with white, gold, or black, and be so mingled that the general effect will be perfectly neutral, and an effect so produced may induce the highest sense of repose. There will, however, be a glow, or radiance, about such a wall; yet this radiance will only give richness to neutrality, and this is desirable.

Those effects which are "subtle" – which are not commonplace – which are attained by the expenditure of special skill or knowledge, are the best, provided that the end which is most desired is attained by them. A tertiary colour which is formed of two parts of yellow and one of red and one of blue – in fact, a citrine – is neutral. But a wall covered with a well-designed pattern of minute parts, with the separate members coloured red, blue, and yellow – the yellow being in relation to the blue and the red as two is to one – would be neutral, yet it would be refined and glowing in effect, and thus it would exceed in merit the mere tertiary tint on the wall.

The white ceilings which we have in our rooms are almost fatal to the production of those qualities which yield the sense of repose or rest. A harmony between walls and a ceiling of

Christopher Dresser, from *Studies in Design*. London: Cassell, Petter & Galpin, 1874–6, pp. 11–12.

cream tint is much more easily attained than between walls and a white ceiling; but there is no reason whatever why a ceiling should not be blue, or any dark colour. No satisfactory room, of dark general aspect, can look well if the ceiling is white, and rooms which are somewhat dark in tone are often desirable. Furniture looks best on a dark ground, unless it be white and gold, when it is invariably execrable. Persons always look better against a somewhat dark background, and pictures on light strongly-figured walls are rarely sufficiently attractive to call to themselves the least attention. If it can be had, I like much window-space, to let in light, but the walls I prefer of darkish hue.

If the room is dark through lack of light, the walls may be light above, and have a dark dado – that is, the lower third, or any desired portion, may be dark, and the upper portion light. If this arrangement is adopted, and the upper part of the wall and the ceiling are each of cream tint, while in the cornice there is a rather broad line of deep blue, and one or more lines of pale blue, and perhaps a very fine line of red, these colours being all separated from each other by white – or, in the absence of a cornice, if the ceiling is surrounded by a border in blue and white – the effect will appear to be lighter and brighter than if the room were all white, and yet there will be a certain amount of repose about the general effect such as could not be easily attained were the ceiling white.

By our decorations we must ever seek to achieve repose, but we must always remember that repose is compatible with richness, subtlety, and radiance of effect.

3 RICHARD REDGRAVE
from *Manual of Design* (1876)

Richard Redgrave, as we saw in the first volume (197), wrote the highly influential "Report on Design" for the Great Exhibition of 1851, which was sharply critical of the British goods displayed. The following year he and Henry Cole were appointed as co-directors of the national Schools of Design (Cole in charge of administration; Redgrave of the curriculum). The two men eventually reorganized into the Department of Art and Industry at the South Kensington Museum. In his capacity as co-director, Redgrave established the general principles to be taught at the various design schools and wrote several governmental reports on artistic education. His son Gilbert assembled these writings in 1876, shortly after his father's retirement. They truthfully convey his teachings, and the following passage on style, from the American edition of the book, encapsulates his views regarding architectural style. The emphasis on construction and utility reveals the influence of Augustus Welby Pugin.

In considering the elements of *style*, it must be remembered, that style does not merely relate to decoration, as is too often supposed, but originates in construction, to which decoration is only subsidiary. All the great æras of style have been notedly æras of changed construction. The mound-like temples of Egypt, the horizontal constructions of Greece, the arched vaultings of Rome, the vertical aspirings of Gothic buildings, contain elements of STYLE as

Richard Redgrave, from *Manual of Design* (1876). New York: Scribner, Welford & Armstrong, 1877, p. 15.

marked in their *bare walls*, as when, in their completed state, they are covered with the rich decorative treatments peculiar to them.

These preliminary arguments being admitted, it will follow, first, that style implies some dominating influence reflecting the mind of the age in all its works, and therefore presumes a certain unity of character throughout.

Secondly, that the primary elements of style are constructive, and that the design of a work must have regard to construction, and consequently to proper use of materials, prior to the consideration of its ornamental decoration.

Thirdly, that as construction necessarily implies a purpose, *utility* must have the precedence of decoration.

Fourthly, as construction necessitates a proper consideration of materials, and as each material has its own mode of manipulation, and is wrought by separate and varied processes; design must be bad which applies indiscriminately the same constructive forms or ornamental treatments to materials differing in their nature and application.

Fifthly, that as the greater regulates the lesser, the building should determine the style, and all which it contains of furniture or decoration should conform to its characteristics; and thus there would be a proper uniformity of style throughout, and a subordination of all the inferior objects to one another and to the whole.

4 WILLIAM MORRIS
from "The Prospects of Architecture in Civilization" (1881)

M orris's writings specifically devoted to architecture were few, but they were nevertheless highly influential within Britain. This particular lecture may well have served as an architectural manifesto to the Arts and Crafts movement. The themes are quintessentially Morris: the carelessness and "ugliness" wrought by modern industrial society and its "progress," the confusion of luxury with art, the slavery of the worker to mechanical toil, and the scarring of the physical environment with a pervasive disregard for the beauty of nature and simple living. At one point in the lecture, Morris points to a common laborer's cottage built of Cotswold limestone — "a work of art and a piece of nature" — as the architectural ideal to be opposed to the speculative creations of suburban London. The following passage of the lecture of 1881, which appears near the conclusion of his talk, wraps these themes up in a philosophy of simplicity and respect for nature.

I believe that what I am now saying will be well understood by those who really care about art, but to speak plainly I know that these are rarely to be found even among the cultivated classes: it must be confessed that the middle classes of our civilization have embraced luxury instead of art, and that we are even so blindly base as to hug ourselves on it, and to insult the

William Morris, from "The Prospects of Architecture in Civilization" (1881), in *Hopes and Fears for Art*. Boston: Roberts Bros., 1882, pp. 212–14.

memory of valiant peoples of past times and to mock at them because they were not encumbered with the nuisances that foolish habit has made us look on as necessaries. Be sure that we are not beginning to prepare for the art that is to be, till we have swept all that out of our minds, and are setting to work to rid ourselves of all the useless luxuries (by some called comforts) that make our stuffy art-stifling houses more truly savage than a Zulu's kraal or an East Greenlander's snow hut.

I feel sure that many a man is longing to set his hand to this if he only durst; I believe that there are simple people who think that they are dull to art, and who are really only perplexed and wearied by finery and rubbish: if not from these, 'tis at least from the children of these that we may look for the beginnings of the building up of the art that is to be.

Meanwhile, I say, till the beginning of new construction is obvious, let us be at least destructive of the sham art: it is full surely one of the curses of modern life, that if people have not time and eyes to discern or money to buy the real object of their desire, they must needs have its mechanical substitute. On this lazy and cowardly habit feeds and grows and flourishes mechanical toil and all the slavery of mind and body it brings with it: from this stupidity are born the itch of the public to over-reach the tradesmen they deal with, the determination (usually successful) of the tradesman to over-reach them, and all the mockery and flouting that has been cast of late (not without reason) on the British tradesman and the British workman, – men just as honest as ourselves, if we would not compel them to cheat us, and reward them for doing it.

Now if the public knew anything of art, that is excellence in things made by man, they would not abide the shams of it; and if the real thing were not to be had, they would learn to do without, nor think their gentility injured by the forbearance.

Simplicity of life, even the barest, is not misery, but the very foundation of refinement: a sanded floor and whitewashed walls, and the green trees, and flowery meads, and living waters outside; or a grimy palace amid the smoke with a regiment of housemaids always working to smear the dirt together so that it may be unnoticed; which, think you, is the most refined, the most fit for a gentleman of those two dwellings?

So I say, if you cannot learn to love real art, at least learn to hate sham art and reject it. It is not so much because the wretched thing is so ugly and silly and useless that I ask you to cast it from you; it is much more because these are but the outward symbols of the poison that lies within them: look through them and see all that has gone to their fashioning, and you will see how vain labor, and sorrow, and disgrace have been their companions from the first, – and all this for trifles that no man really needs!

5 CHRISTOPHER DRESSER

from *Japan: Its Architecture, Art, and Art Manufacturers* (1882)

One of the cultural influences to appear across Europe and North America in the second half of the nineteenth century was Japanese art and architecture, examples of which were viewed with increasing interest at the various international exhibitions. Christopher Dresser first discussed his fascination with the theme in a paper he read before the Royal Society of Arts in 1874, "Eastern Art and its Influence on European Manufactures and Taste." In displaying several objects to his audience, he noted that Asian art was at heart an expression of a "poetic thought or a beautiful idea." Two years later Dresser departed London for a lecture tour of the United States, which he extended with a three-month tour of Japan at the beginning of 1877. In the Preface to this chronicle of this visit, Dresser admits to being "an earnest student of Oriental art for nearly thirty years." What follows in the passage below, from a book heavily illustrated with woodcuts, is one of the first attempts to explain the principles of Japanese architecture from a sympathetic Western perspective.

Before we begin to consider Japanese architecture itself we must look at one or two of those circumstances which have always modified the architecture of a nation, as the climate, the materials at command for the erection of edifices, and the wants which have consequently to be met by the production of a building.

Although Japan has a considerable rainfall, the rain is almost exclusively confined to one season of the year (about six weeks, between the end of April and the early part of June), and this wet period is followed by a continuance of hot weather.

This is a general statement, but the climate is by no means the same throughout the whole of Japan. In the central portion cold is intense on some winter days, while the heat is great in summer; but the long and severe frosts of the north are unknown at the Satsuma end of the country.

The Japanese seek shelter from the rain, and they desire houses which give shade from the sun. They also require buildings which allow of the freest circulation of air. They are a hardy people, and can stand cold, and in the warmer season lead what is practically an outdoor life. At this period of the year, and indeed through most of the winter days, the window-like surroundings of their houses are removed, when all that remains is a roof supported on uprights.

But although a Japanese house is a building intended to afford shelter from rain and sun, the nature of the building is influenced by other causes.

Japan is a land of earthquakes. And this brings us to one of the most singular facts connected with the structure of Japanese buildings; – a method adopted with the special view of insuring safety during these periods of the earth's vibration.

Japanese houses and temples are put together in a solid and simple manner, each work being complete in itself, and having an altogether independent existence. Thus a Japanese

Christopher Dresser, from *Japan: Its Architecture, Art, and Art Manufacturers*. London: Longmans, Green & Co., 1882, pp. 234–5, 237–8.

house is in no way built upon foundations, or fixed to the ground on which it rests. It stands upon a series of legs, and these legs usually rest on round-topped stones of such a height as will, during the rainy season, support the timber uprights above any water that may lie upon the ground.

It is obvious that while an object fixed to the earth might, if rocked, be broken off from the ground or become strained and destroyed, that that which is loose would simply oscillate and settle down again after the cause of its vibration had ceased. For instance, we may cause a chair or a table to rock by jolting it, but in a very short time it will become stationary and will be uninjured; whereas, were the legs fixed, the application of a small amount of pressure on the upper part (especially if the top was heavy), or any upheaving of a portion of the ground on which it rests, would be likely to injure or destroy it.

[. . .]

A notable instance of the Japanese understanding of the conditions under which they exist occurs in the manner of giving security to pagodas. Pagodas are often of great height, yet many have existed for seven hundred years, and have withstood successfully the many vibrations of the ground, which must have inevitably achieved their overthrow had they been erections of stone or brick.

When I first ascended a pagoda I was struck with the amount of timber employed in its construction; and I could not help feeling that the material here wasted was even absurdly excessive, But what offended my feelings most was the presence of an enormous log of wood, in the centre of the structure, which ascended from its base to its apex. At the top this mass of timber was nearly two feet in diameter, and lower down a log equally large was bolted to each of the four sides of this central mass.

I was so surprised with this waste of timber that I called the attention of my good friend Sakata to the matter; and especially denounced the use of the centre block. To my astonishment he told me that the structure must be strong to support the vast central mass. In my ignorance I replied that the centre part was not supported by the sides, but upon reaching the top I found this monstrous central mass suspended, like the clapper of a bell; and when I had descended I could, by lying on the ground, see that there was an inch of space intervening between it and the earth which formed the floor of the pagoda.

The pagoda is to a Buddhist temple what a spire is to a Christian church; and by its clever construction it is enabled to retain its vertical position even during the continuance of earthquake shocks: for by the swinging of this vast pendulum the centre of gravity is kept within the base.

I now understood the reason for that lavish use of timber which I had so rashly pronounced to be useless; and I see that there is a method in Japanese construction which is worthy of high appreciation. In the absence of any other instance the employment of this scientific method of keeping the pagoda upright shows how carefully the Japanese have thought out the requirements to be met.

6 OSCAR WILDE
from "Art and the Handicraftsman" (1882)

One of the young artists to be drawn into the Arts and Crafts movement was the writer and playwright Oscar Wilde. A native of Dublin, Wilde attended Trinity College in his hometown before attending Oxford between 1874 and 1879. There he was first attracted to the lectures of the artistic critic Walter Pater, who advocated "art for art's sake," but after a chance encounter on High Street with John Ruskin – "going up to his lecture in cap and gown" – Wilde was also challenged by his suggestion to "do good to other people." This challenge soon entailed building a road between two neighboring villages. Wilde would later be drawn into the artistic circle known as the "Decadents" (notable for the work of Aubrey Beardsley and Arthur Symons), but for a few years at least he was strongly attracted to the teachings of Ruskin and Morris. In 1882 Wilde embarked on an extended lecture tour of the United States and Canada, where he was one of the first to take forth the message to the New World. In this particular lecture, likely given in Philadelphia, he not only paraphrases the ideas of Ruskin and Morris but also encourages his American listeners to join the new movement and create a new American art.

Ours has been the first movement which has brought the handicraftsman and the artist together, for remember that by separating the one from the other you do ruin to both; you rob the one of all spiritual motive and all imaginative joy, you isolate the other from all real technical perfection. The two greatest schools of art in the world, the sculptor at Athens and the school of painting at Venice, had their origin entirely in a long succession of simple and earnest handicraftsmen. It was the Greek potter who taught the sculptor that restraining influence of design which was the glory of the Parthenon; it was the Italian decorator of chests and household goods who kept Venetian painting always true to its primary pictorial condition of noble colour. For we should remember that all the arts are fine arts and all the arts decorative arts. The greatest triumph of Italian painting was the decoration of a pope's chapel in Rome and the wall of a room in Venice. Michael Angelo wrought the one, and Tintoret, the dyer's son, the other. And the little 'Dutch landscape, which you put over your sideboard to-day, and between the windows to-morrow, is' no less a glorious 'piece of work than the extents of field and forest with which Benozzo has made green and beautiful the once melancholy arcade of the Campo Santo at Pisa,' as Ruskin says.

Do not imitate the works of a nation, Greek or Japanese, Italian or English; but their artistic spirit of design and their artistic attitude to-day, their own world, you should absorb but imitate never, copy never. Unless you can make as beautiful a design in painted china or embroidered screen or beaten brass out of your American turkey as the Japanese does out of his grey silver-winged stork, you will never do anything. Let the Greek carve his lions and the Goth his dragons: buffalo and wild deer are the animals for you.

Golden rod and aster and rose and all the flowers that cover your valleys in the spring and your hills in the autumn: let them be the flowers for your art. Not merely has Nature given

Oscar Wilde, from *Essays and Lectures* (1888). London: Methuen & Co. Reprinted New York: Garland, 1978, pp. 185–8, 190–1.

you the noblest motives for a new school of decoration, but to you above all other countries has she given the utensils to work in.

You have quarries of marble richer than Pentelicus, more varied than Paros, but do not build a great white square house of marble and think that it is beautiful, or that you are using marble nobly. If you build in marble you must either carve it into joyous decoration, like the lives of dancing children that adorn the marble castles of the Loire, or fill it with beautiful sculpture, frieze and pediment, as the Greeks did, or inlay it with other coloured marbles as they did in Venice. Otherwise you had better build in simple red brick as your Puritan fathers, with no pretence and with some beauty. Do not treat your marble as if it was ordinary stone and build a house of mere blocks of it. For it is indeed a precious stone, this marble of yours, and only workmen of nobility of invention and delicacy of hand should be allowed to touch it at all, carving it into noble statues or into beautiful decoration, or inlaying it with other coloured marbles: for 'the true colours of architecture are those of natural stone, and I would fain see them taken advantage of to the full. Every variety is here, from pale yellow to purple passing through orange, red, and brown, entirely at your command; nearly every kind of green and grey also is attainable, and with these and with pure white what harmony might you not achieve. Of stained and variegated stone the quantity is unlimited, the kinds innumerable. Were brighter colours required, let glass, and gold protected by glass, be used in mosaic, a kind of work as durable as the solid stone and incapable of losing its lustre by time. And let the painter's work be reserved for the shadowed loggia and inner chamber.'

[. . .]

This is the spirit of our movement in England, and this is the spirit in which we would wish you to work, making eternal by your art all that is noble in your men and women, stately in your lakes and mountains, beautiful in your own flowers and natural life. We want to see that you have nothing in your houses that has not been a joy to the man who made it, and is not a joy to those that use it. We want to see you create an art made by the hands of the people to please the hearts of the people too. Do you like this spirit or not? Do you think it simple and strong, noble in its aim, and beautiful in its result? I know you do.

7 ARTHUR H. MACKMURDO
from ''Arbitrary Conditions of Art''
(1887)

One of the defining moments for the Arts and Crafts movement was the founding of the Century Guild in 1882 by Selwyn Image, Arthur Mackmurdo, and his former pupil Herbert Horne. The purpose of the guild was twofold: first to counter the influence of the Royal Academy and its concern for the ''high arts,'' and second to raise the so-called minor arts to an equal footing. Whereas Image was an illustrator, Mackmurdo was

Arthur H. Mackmurdo, from ''Arbitrary Conditions of Art,'' in *Hobby Horse* II (1887), pp. 58–60.

trained as an architect, and his first house on Private Road, Enfield was built in 1876. Most important in shaping his outlook was John Ruskin, with whom Mackmurdo traveled to Italy in 1874 and for whom he later taught. In his important essay written for the Century Guild's mouthpiece, *Hobby Horse*, Mackmurdo pens another manifesto to the new movement. If the first of his architectural requisites ("ornament should be a finish of finished construction") traces its lineage back to Pugin, his other two points ("appeal to the sense" and "interesting and appropriate in symbolism") herald Art Nouveau sensibilities already taking formation.

The choice completion of things necessary: this is the function of the decorative Arts, those Arts that, beginning in the endowment of the platter with simple imagery, find their end in the glorification of the temple walls. "Look that thou make them after their pattern shewed thee in the mount." How then shall we follow this pattern in architecture? If we answer this, we answer for all the Arts; for this Art comprehends all others, inasmuch as it is architecture that builds up the inner formal world in which all actual imagery lives, and which all imagery makes interesting: a world as self-contained and as fully informed by the Creative Genius as that outer world wherein Nature reigns; one also to be as much reverenced, since it is the joint creation of all peoples and of all ages: the soul treasury of all remaining from the inner life of the human past. For our purpose, however, we will take it part by part, dismissing architecture proper by saying it should be the Scholarship of Construction informed with character and with purpose; or to use our old definition, the choice completion of skilful building. If we understand this, it is sufficient for its service and for its symbolism. For that music of proportion which comes from the delicate adjustment of space to space in window and wall is one of the grandest elements of Beauty, and it is the highest compliment the artist can pay to their necessity that he makes them lovely in their mere disposition and measure. But in the sculptured or pictorial ornament of these features, this is the authoritative pattern after which the artist must work, would he be guided, and would he have his Art adequate in interest. In order, the requisites are these: –

   I. His ornament should be a finish of finished construction.

  II. It should make a direct appeal to the sense.

 III. It should be interesting and appropriate in symbolism.

Thus, the first is a test of the simplicity of an ornament's application; the second is a test of its power in sensuous effect; the third is a test of its subjective force.

By saying that it should be a finish of finished construction, it is meant that the ornament should be not the embellishment of ill-bound books, but the gracing of exquisite workmanship. This implies that it should claim for itself no necessity of structure, so that were the ornament omitted the construction would suffer no change. Now to allow but the slightest departure from this frank simplicity of application, or technical rightness, is inevitably to doom the artistic result of any work, as may be seen in the case of turrets, gables, and other features built up solely for picturesque effect in our suburban villas. To confine this condition within a more restricted limit, as some have tried to do, is unnecessary for the architect, since that "sentiment exquis de la service," so strong in the artist, will safely guide in matters of detail, making it impossible for him to exceed the limits of artistic propriety. Now the best example of this simple application of ornament, is to be found in the decoration of structural points chosen for that purpose by the early Gothic builders, and in the directness of treatment employed by the metal workers and furniture workers of the fifteenth century. By saying that ornament should directly appeal to the sense, is meant that the general aspect of ornament should before all else be decorative and full of *taste*. And since the decorative aspect depends largely on a certain inevitableness of disposition in the parts, as in the case of musical intervals, the ornament should have movement, and this movement should be rhythmic. Only by insistence on this "tastefulness" or "sympathy" of arrangement in his ornament, by means of symmetry or by means of repetition that is, can the artist hope to be successful in exciting the sensuous nature to the degree required of Art. And in evidence of this decorative quality, we may study the Attic vases, the ornaments of Byzantine buildings, the carpets and the cretonnes of William Morris.

8 WILLIAM MORRIS
from "The Revival of Architecture" (1888)

I n one of Morris's later writings on architecture, his views on the prospects of architecture are somewhat rosier than those of six years earlier. The theme of the lecture is a brief history of the present architectural "revival," which he traces to the Anglo-Catholic reform movements of the 1840s and to the writings of John Ruskin (*Stones of Venice* and his essay "On the Nature of Gothic"). Of the evolution of medieval forms into the Queen Anne style in the late 1860s and 1870s, Morris is less sanguine, although not entirely disapproving. He concludes that the reformers are simply too few in number to have much of an impact on society as a whole, and it is indeed society that must first change if genuine architectural reform is to take place. The concluding passage to his talk was first published in the *Fortnightly Review* of May 1888.

There I say some of the Gothic feeling was left, joined to forms, such as sash windows, yet possible to be used in our own times. The architects in search of a style might well say:

> We have been driven from ditch to ditch; cannot we yet make a stand? The unapproachable grace and loveliness of the fourteenth century is hull down behind us, the fifteenth-century work is too delicate and too rich for the commonplace of to-day; let us be humble, and begin once more with the style of well-constructed, fairly proportioned brick houses which stand London smoke well, and look snug and comfortable at some village end, or amidst the green trees of a squire's park. Besides, our needs as architects are not great; we don't want to build churches any more; the nobility have their palaces in town and country already (I wish them joy of some of them!); the working man cannot afford to live in anything that an architect could design; moderate-sized rabbit-warrens for rich middle-class men, and small ditto for the hanger-on groups to which we belong, is all we have to think of. Perhaps something of a style might arise amongst us from these lowly beginnings, though indeed we have come down a weary long way from Pugin's *Contrasts*. We agree with him still, but we are driven to admire and imitate some of the very things he cursed, with our enthusiastic approbation.

William Morris, from "The Revival of Architecture" (1888), in Nikolaus Pevsner, *Some Architectural Writers of the Nineteenth Century*. Oxford: Clarendon Press, 1972, pp. 322–4.

Well, a goodish many houses of this sort have been built, to the great comfort of the dwellers in them, I am sure; but the new style is so far from getting under way, that while on the other hand the ordinary builder is covering England with abortions which make us regret the brick box and slate lid of fifty years ago, the cultivated classes are rather inclined to return to the severity (that is to say, the unmitigated expensive ugliness) of the last dregs of would-be Palladian, as exemplified in the stone lumps of the Georgian period. Indeed I have not heard that the 'educated middle classes' had any intention of holding a riotous meeting on the adjacent Trafalgar Square to protest against the carrying out of the designs for the new public offices which the Aedileship of Mr. Shaw-Lefevre threatened us with. As to public buildings, Mr. Street's Law Courts are the last attempt we are likely to see of producing anything reasonable or beautiful for that use; the public has resigned itself to any mass of dulness and vulgarity that it may be convenient for a department to impose upon it, probably from a half-conscious impression that at all events it will be good enough for the work (so-called) which will be done in it.

In short we must answer the question with which this paper began by saying that the architectural revival, though not a mere piece of artificial nonsense, is too limited in its scope, too much confined to an educated group, to be a vital growth capable of true development. The important fact in it is that it is founded on the sympathy for history and the art of historical generalization, which, as aforesaid, is a gift of our epoch, but unhappily a gift in which few as yet have a share. Among populations where this gift is absent, not even scattered attempts at beauty in architecture are now possible, and in such places generations may live and die, if society as at present constituted endures, without feeling any craving for beauty in their daily lives; and even under the most favourable circumstances there is no general impulse born out of necessity towards beauty, which impulse alone can produce a universal architectural style, that is to say, a habit of elevating and beautifying the houses, furniture, and other material surroundings of our life.

All we have that approaches architecture is the result of a quite self-conscious and very laborious eclecticism, and is avowedly imitative of the work of past times, of which we have gained a knowledge far surpassing that of any other period. Meanwhile whatever is done without conscious effort, that is to say the work of the true style of the epoch, is an offence to the sense of beauty and fitness, and is admitted to be so by all men who have any perception of beauty of form. It is no longer passively but actively ugly, since it has added to the dreary utilitarianism of the days of Dr. Johnson a vulgarity which is the special invention of the Victorian era. The genuine style of that era is exemplified in the jerry-built houses of our suburbs, the stuccoed marine-parades of our watering-places, the flaunting corner public-houses of every town in Great Britain, the raw-boned hideousness of the houses that mar the glorious scenery of the Queen's Park at Edinburgh. These form our true Victorian architecture. Such works as Mr. Bodley's excellent new buildings at Magdalen College, Mr. Norman Shaw's elegantly fantastic Queen Anne houses at Chelsea, or Mr. Robson's simple but striking London board-schools, are mere eccentricities with which the public in general has no part or lot.

This is stark pessimism, my readers may say. Far from it. The enthusiasm of the Gothic revivalists died out when they were confronted by the fact that they form part of a society which will not and cannot have a living style, because it is an economical necessity for its existence that the ordinary everyday work of its population shall be mechanical drudgery;

and because it is the harmony of the ordinary everyday work of the population which produces Gothic, that is, living architectural art, and mechanical drudgery cannot be harmonized into art. The hope of our ignorance has passed away, but it has given place to the hope born of fresh knowledge. History taught us the evolution of architecture, it is now teaching us the evolution of society; and it is clear to us, and even to many who refuse to acknowledge it, that the society which is developing out of ours will not need or endure mechanical drudgery as the lot of the general population; that the new society will not be hag-ridden as we are by the necessity for producing ever more and more market-wares for a profit, whether any one needs them or not; that it will produce to live, and not live to produce, as we do. Under such conditions architecture, as a part of the life of people in general, will again become possible, and I believe that when it is possible, it will have a real new birth, and add so much to the pleasure of life that we shall wonder how people were ever able to live without it. Meantime we are waiting for that new development of society, some of us in cowardly inaction, some of us amidst hopeful work towards the change; but at least we are all waiting for what must be the work, not of the leisure and taste of a few scholars, authors, and artists, but of the necessities and aspirations of the workmen throughout the civilized world.

9 WALTER CRANE
from *The Claims of Decorative Art* (1892)

Walter Crane, together with William Morris, represents the more militant wing of the Arts and Crafts movement in Great Britain. The son of an artist, he was initially trained in wood engraving by William James Linton, but soon branched out into watercolors and painting. Already well established as an illustrator of children's books in the 1860s, Crane came under the influence of Ford Madox Brown and Edward Burne-Jones, and in the following decade he added the design of wallpapers, fabrics, and ceramics to his repertoire of artistic interests. He drew close to Morris and his socialist politics in the 1880s and with him joined the Social Democratic Federation, an early Marxist group. Crane later followed Morris in departing the organization to form the Socialist League, and he became active within Fabian circles as well. *The Claims of Decorative Art* (1892) is a collection of talks delivered over the previous decade, perhaps more political than artistic in their overall tone. The leading theme is the new art under the new socialism – "A religion and a moral code as well as an economic system" – which Crane repeatedly contrasts with the evils of commercialism.

Through the columns of the colossal architecture of time we look back down the long vista of ages and epochs, and read their spirit in the unmistakable language of art, coloured as it is by the human systems and beliefs of which it is the monument; whether as in the wall-paintings and reliefs of ancient Assyria, Egypt, and Persia, art is devoted to the glorification of military or sacerdotal despotism; or the systematised symbolism of an ancient nature

Walter Crane, from *The Claims of Decorative Art*. London: Lawrence & Bullen, 1892, pp. 12–15.

worship, humanised and made beautiful by the Greek, informed by freedom and life; decaying amid the corruption of ancient Rome, or graced with a new splendour from the East, rising in the solemn magnificence of Byzantine art; and so through the vivid imagination of the Middle Ages, absorbed in the new mysticism, yet through the Church linked to the hopes as well as the fears of humanity. Then with the new thoughts and hopes of the Renaissance it rekindles its lamp at the shattered shrine of classical sculpture and learning, until choked with artifice and pedantry in succeeding centuries, it is forced back to nature and life again on the threshold of our own time. But again it is in danger from a new tyranny in that unscrupulous commercialism, which is not less dangerous because less tangible, and not less despotic because it is masked under the form of political liberty. Steam machinery, like a many-headed, many-handed dragon, rules industry literally with a rod of iron, and fain would it make art prisoner too, for its profit, but that its touch is death. Intended for the service of man and for the saving of human labour, it has under our economic system enslaved humanity instead, and become an engine for the production of profits, an express train in the race for wealth, only checked by the brake of what is called over-production. Who can tell what will be the end of the journey?

Thus we are driven to the conclusion that the whole force of our economic system is against spontaneous art, and it is in spite of it that there is any life left in it yet. As William Morris has so strikingly pointed out, the system of producing all things for profit, which has succeeded the old one of producing for use; the necessity of selling in the big world market, division of labour, and lastly, machine labour, have rapidly destroyed the art of the people, and are fast vulgarising and destroying all local characteristics in art, as in costume and the surroundings of common life throughout the world. The system of absolute individual ownership of land, which, with the advance of commercialism, has displaced the older systems of tenure, and defrauded the people of their common rights wholesale, naturally leads to much destruction of natural beauty, and when not destroyed it is made inaccessible. It is also answerable, with the causes already named, for that other great disaster both to architecture and art already alluded to, the abnormal growth of the big towns, which year by year throws out its long and aimless feelers that feed upon the green country. When we speak of an advance in education, we too often forget that no education of the schools can compensate for life passed amid hills and woods, and by the sea, itself an education in a lore never to be forgotten.

Overshadowed by such conditions of life, what wonder is it that we should get our art by accident, that it should be in great measure the Art of Accident, which is really what modern realism or naturalism comes to, in spite of elaborate systems of art training, and the elaborate unlearning of them which follows? The sense of beauty may be stunted, but Nature cannot be altogether suppressed under the most perverse social conditions. It is sometimes urged in defence of the artistic aspects of modern life that strange and wonderful momentary effects are seen, in London smoke-fogs, for instance, or amid the fiery eyes of railway signals, and our blackened Stygian rivers, where the Charon of the coal-wharf plies his trade. I have even heard an apostle of beauty defend those monuments of commercial effrontery and theatrical competition, our advertisement hoardings, covered with vari-coloured posters, as in certain lights becoming transfigured so as to rival the tints on a Japanese fan. But it is one thing to find accidental beauties in the midst of monstrosities, jewels on dung-hills as it were, and quite another to defend the monstrosities for the sake of accidental beauties. The glow, the light fades, and with it the momentary exaltation of spirit; the north-east wind succeeds the south-west, and there being no dignity of form or beauty of proportion in our streets, they are apt to look more sordid and miserable than before. Grace and spirit may be shown by a child dancing to a barrel-organ in a smoky, squalid street, but one would rather see her on a village green dancing to a shepherd's pipe. We should aim at a condition of things which would not keep beauty at a distance from common life, or on the footing of an occasional visitor. No artist should be satisfied with such a cold relationship.

Art is not the mere toy of wealth, or the superficial bedizenment of fashion, not a revolving kaleidoscope of dead styles, but in its true sense, in a vital and healthy condition, the spontaneous expression of the life and aspirations of a free people.

10 JOHN D. SEDDING
from "Design" (1891)

John Sedding was another architect attracted to the Arts and Crafts movement, one whose influence remains today much underappreciated. He was trained by George Street in the late 1850s, and later set up an office with his brother in London. After his brother's death and a period in Bristol, Sedding returned to London in 1874, where he rented an office next door to Morris and Company. His Holy Trinity Church, London (1885–9), became an early showcase for the talents of many Arts-and-Crafts designers, but perhaps more important were his polemics, which at times were critical of the movement. In a speech given to a Liverpool audience in 1888, he attacked Morris's anti-industrial bias in artistic reform, and in the following year in Edinburgh he did the same – this time opposing Ruskin. Sometime before his death in 1891, Sedding wrote a short essay entitled "Design." Although the theme of the piece is needlepoint or embroidery, it stands as an early polemical masterpiece on behalf of modernism, and its architectural significance becomes all the more important for the attention it would soon receive from Charles Rennie Mackintosh (see next selection).

We have, I said, realised our ideals. We can do splendidly what we set ourselves to do – namely, to mimic old masterpieces. The question is, What next? Shall we continue to hunt old trails, and die, not leaving the world richer than we found it? Or shall we for art and honour's sake boldly adventure something – drop this wearisome translation of old styles and translate Nature instead?

Think of the gain to the "Schools," and to the designers themselves, if we elect to take another starting-point! No more museum-inspired work! No more scruples about styles! No more dry-as-dust stock patterns! No more loathly Persian-tile quilts! No more awful "Zoomorphic" table-cloths! No more cast-iron-looking altar cloths, or Syon Cope angels, or stumpy Norfolk-screen saints! No more Tudor roses and pumped-out Christian imagery suggesting that Christianity is dead and buried! But, instead, we shall have design *by* living men *for* living men – something that expresses fresh realisations of sacred facts, personal broodings, skill, joy in Nature – in grace of form and gladness of colour; design that shall recall Shakespeare's maid who

John D. Sedding from "Design" (1891), in *Arts and Crafts Essays*. London, 1893. Reprinted New York: Garland, 1977, pp. 409–12.

> " . . . with her neeld composes
> Nature's own shape, of bud, bird, branch, or berry,
> That even Art sisters the natural roses."

For, after all, modern design should be as the old – living thought, artfully expressed: fancy that has taken fair shapes. And needlework is still a pictorial art that requires a real artist to direct the design, a real artist to ply the needle. Given these, and our needlework can be as full of story as the Bayeux tapestry, as full of imagery as the Syon Cope, and better drawn. The charm of old embroidery lies in this, that it clothes current thought in current shapes. It meant something to the workers, and to the man in the street for whom it was done. And for our work to gain the same sensibility, the same range of appeal, the same human interest, we must employ the same means. We must clothe modern ideas in modern dress; adorn our design with living fancy, and rise to the height of our knowledge and capacities.

11 CHARLES RENNIE MACKINTOSH
from "Architecture" (1893)

Charles Rennie Mackintosh was born in Glasgow and trained in architecture under John Hutchinson, and at the firm Honeyman and Keepie. In 1889, while working in the latter's office, he enrolled at the Glasgow School of Art, where he soon found prominence as a designer – forming the nucleus of "The Four," which included Margaret and Frances Macdonald and Herbert McNair. They were influenced by Pre-Raphaelitism in Britain and early Art Nouveau tendencies on the Continent. Mackintosh's architectural sensibilities, however, developed somewhat more slowly. He toured Italy in 1891, and in the following year (while still working as an apprentice) he gave his first talk on architecture. The talk was scarcely original and drew heavily on the ideas of Gerard Baldwin Brown and John Ruskin. One year later, in 1893, Mackintosh delivered another talk on architecture before the Glasgow Architectural Association. Here he strikes new ground, again with some help from others. References to Ruskin are still apparent in this talk (as are references to Lethaby and César Daly), but what is new is how Mackintosh invokes the cited passage from Sedding (on modern ideas and modern dress) and transposes it into architecture. The conclusion to this passage predates by one year Otto Wagner's famous embrace of the same polemic in his inaugural address before the Vienna Academy of Fine Arts (see 51). It also precedes Mackintosh's design for the Glasgow School of Art by three years.

Old architecture lived because it had/a purpose. Modern architecture, to be real, must not be a mere envelope without contents.

As Cesar Daly says, if we would have architecture excite an interest real & general, we must have a symbolism immediately comprehensible by the great majority of spectators. But this message cannot be that of the past terror, mystery, splendeour. Planets may not circle nor thunder roll in the temple of the future. No barbaric gold with ruddy bloom; no jewels,

Charles Rennie Mackintosh, from "Architecture" (1893), in *Charles Rennie Mackintosh: The Architectural Papers*, ed. Pamela Robertson. Cambridge, MA: MIT Press, 1990, pp. 206–7.

emeralds half a palm over, rubies like an egg, and crystal spheres, can again be used more for majic that for beauty. No terraced temples of Babylon to reach the skies no gold plated palaces of Ecbatana seven walled. no ivory palaces of Ahab. nor golden houses of Nero with corridors a mile long: no stupendeous temples of Egypt at first/all embracing then court and chamber narrowing and becoming lower, closing in on the awed worshipper and crushing his imagination; these all of them can never be built again, for the manner and the materials are worked out to their final issue. Think of the Sociology and Religion of all this, and the stain across it "each stone <u>cemented</u> in the blood of a human creature. These colossal efforts of labor forced on by an irresistable will, are of the past, and such an architecture is not for us nor for the future.

What then will this art of the future be?

The message will still be of nature & man, of order and beauty, but all will be sweetness, simplicity, freedom, confidence, and light: the other is past and well is it, for its aim was to crush life: the new, the future, is to aid life/and train it, "so that beauty may flow into the soul like a breeze".

This much about ancient architecture will (and although I have only instanced one period and that very early, all architecture in successive ages up till the end of the 15th Century when we may say architecture ceased to be – was as vividly & inseperably the expression of the religious or social thoughts of the times) – I hope prove two things firstly that what are called Architectural styles were not made purposely as many people imagine – some say I like gothic – some I like classic – but you cannot surely believe that Architecture changed from classic to gothic because the old architects were sick of classic. No Architecture changed or rather evolved because the religious & social needs & beliefs changed, and when you consider as I said before how no change can be definitely pointed out you will understand how the/changes of Architecture were only the expression & embodiment of the natural unconcious evolution of mans thoughts caused by the changes of civilization and things around him.

And this leads on to the second point which I hope this essay so far will help to emphasize – namely all great & living architecture has been the direct expression, of the needs & beliefs of man at the time of its creation, and how if we would have great architecture created this should still be so. How absurd it is to see modern churches theatres, Banks, Museums, Exchanges Municipal Buildings, Art Galleries &c &c made in imitation of greek temples. I am quite concious of the dignity of greek temples when built in greece 1000 years ago as temples, but to be imported into this country and set up for such varied purposes, they must/surely loose all their dignity. And yet these are the modern buildings most people admire – perhaps even some of you dispute the loss of dignity – well let us admit that an art gallery copied from a greek temple has the same charm & dignity as its original I would ask whether the dignity is still retained if we reduplicate the design and make it into a small black marble clock & put it on a black marble chimney piece as is so often done. There are many such buildings in Glasgow but to me they are as could & lifeless as the cheek of a dead chinaman Dignity in architecture is the same as natural dignity – the very frankness of some natures is the essence of all thats dignified – which frankness if copied by one not natually frank immediately becomes impudence not dignity. It is absurd to think it is the duty of the modern architect to make believe he is living 4 – 5 – 6 hundred or even 1000/years ago – and that his mission is to exercise on the forms found associated with a certain decade – no all the past is one art and all for us. And I am glad to think that now there are men such as Norman Shaw – John Bentley, John Belcher Mr Bodley Leonard Stokes and the late John D Sedding – names most of you will never have heard before but for all that quite as great if not greater artists than the best living painters men who more & more are freeing themselves from correct antiquarian detail and who go streight to nature. We must clothe modern ideas, with modern dress – adorn our designs with living fancy. We shall have designs by living men for living men – something that expresses fresh realization of sacred fact – of personal broodings of skill – of joy in nature in grace of form & gladness of colour.

12 CHARLES ROBERT ASHBEE
from *A Few Chapters in Workshop Re-Construction and Citizenship* (1894)

The last of the major Arts and Crafts architects and reformers to be associated with a guild was Charles Robert Ashbee. After attending King's College, Cambridge, he became articled to the London architect G. F. Bodley in 1883. During this tenure he resided in the East End of London at Toynbee Hall, an experiment in socialist living and continuing education founded by Canon Samuel Barnett. Ashbee soon came under the influence of Morris and at Toynbee Hall he began a reading class on Ruskin, which evolved into an art class. In 1888 he transformed this experiment into the School of Handicraft, alongside which he also created the Guild of Handicraft, which flourished in the early 1890s. During this decade he emerged as one of the international leaders of the Arts and Crafts movement, and on a lecture tour of the United States in 1900 he became quite enamored with the designs of Frank Lloyd Wright. Ashbee was slightly more accepting of the machine than many of his colleagues; nevertheless he shared the socialist beliefs of Morris and Crane that the Arts and Crafts movement was revolutionizing art (by a return to the medieval workshop) and the social fabric of society itself. This "humanising of the citizen," as he puts it, forms the very heart of the movement.

It is well that in our constructive citizenship we should bear this constantly in mind. Let us remember it when we hold in our hands anything made to-day for our service. "The commercial article," for instance, made not to use but to sell. Let us ask ourselves where was the producer, and what manner of man was he? It is well that we should bear this in mind when we walk these streets of London. Every now and then through this wilderness of brick and stone we come upon a reminiscence of other happier conditions, but only in name, for looking to the corners of the nearest brickwork, or asking some inhabitant, we mockingly learn that it is Bethnal Green, or Hackney Downs, Bow Common, Cambridge Heath, Mile End Waste or Stepney Green: a whiff of the fresh fields of a hundred years ago comes back to us. Let us remember, then, that sweeter conditions of life are an essential to better production.

None of the themes in the following chapters lay claim to novelty in themselves. To the founder of Christianity, to the Athenian Citizen, to the mediæval state builders, and to the

Charles Robert Ashbee, from *A Few Chapters in Workshop Re-Construction and Citizenship*. London: Guild and School of Handicraft, 1894, pp. 12–13.

modern exponents of socialistic economics, they might all be traced, but my effort has been to point to a few newer applications and to make clearer, positions often misunderstood by thoughtful men, whose experience and sympathies lie elsewhere. I believe that there are two movements going on in our midst which are tending to the expression of the new citizenship, and they are the *Re-construction of the Workshop* and the *humanising of the citizen*. I would ask for a closer study of the former and a more generous encouragement of the latter. In the former we have, on the part of the workman, the producer, an unconscious reversion to the mediæval state, the central idea of which was the maintenance of a moral code and an economic standard of life conformably with it. In the latter, we have through the educationalist, and the citizen himself, a readiness to enter again into that culture as it was understood by the great thinkers, poets and painters of the 15th and 16th centuries – we have, potentially, the spirit of the Renaissance.

The wave of revolutionary socialism that broke over us in the years 1880–90, has spent its force, done its work, and the result has been a variety of efforts in social re-construction throughout the country, and a strengthening and amplifying, owing to the new impulse, of older institutions already in existence. The points of view of the constructive and the revolutionary socialist, are, as I understand them, much the same, only the former makes for his end the reconstruction of society by little pieces of work here and there; while the latter says, it is no use tinkering, we must clear the old society away first before we can reconstruct the new. English love of order and constitutionalism will inevitably, indeed has already, given judgment in favour of the former, and we find the collectivist ideal, if not accepted, certainly compromised with, and often acted upon in every department of the State, whether under the guidance of the so-called Conservative or the so-called Liberal. The socialistic propaganda has, in other words, bitten into modern English political philosophy until we conceive it within the bounds of possibility that a Conservative Government shall, some day, give us land nationalization, even as it has given us factory acts and free education.

But apart from its political or semi-political aspects, the new thought has an due influence and is daily exerting a greater influence upon life, upon our relations towards one another, upon our way of regarding labour, upon the morale that underlies our conduct either in individual or collective citizenship.

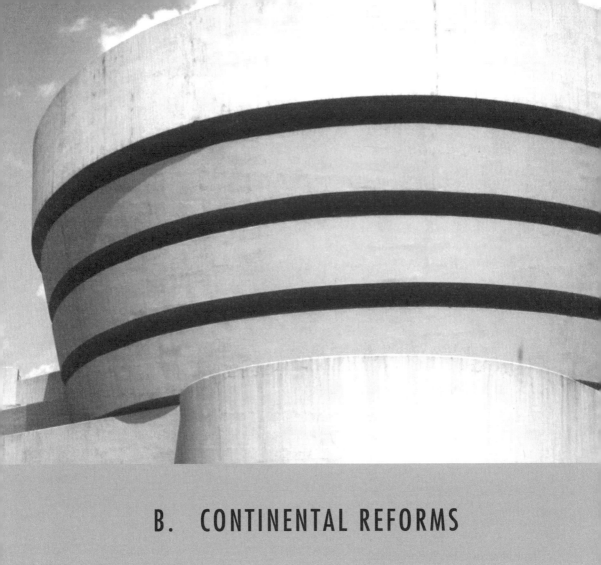

B. CONTINENTAL REFORMS

Introduction

The desire for reform so evident in Great Britain was also quite visible on the Continent, where national boundaries in the last decades of the century were in a state of flux. Both Germany and Italy, for instance, were only unified as countries in 1871. Stirrings of nationalism, or more correctly the desire for a national state and the trappings of modern culture, were also evident among the Spanish, Portuguese, Belgian, Dutch, Czech, Polish, and Scandinavian peoples.

Architecturally, Germany and France remained at the forefront in their scale of reforms. Traditional historical accounts once viewed Germanic developments through the lens of Hermann Muthesius's turn-of-the-century fascination with the "English House," and therefore as a movement largely derived from Britain. But in fact a domestic reform movement in Germany and Austria was well underway during the 1870s, and these efforts are perhaps better seen as running parallel with developments in England. The one qualification is that much of the impetus for reform in Germany and Austria was carried out by the newly founded industrial-art museums, many of which were in fact inspired by Henry Cole's efforts at South Kensington. By the end of the century, Germanic tendencies to reform not only compete with those in Britain but even surpass them, particularly with the attention being paid to industrial development and machine-made products. Hence architectural development in Germany at the start of the twentieth century plots its very specific course of modernism.

In France, the quest for reform also takes a somewhat different path – in part owing to France's lead in engineering and the use of iron, in part owing to political and psychological causes. The defeat by Germany was emotionally devastating, and the collapse of the government in 1870–1 led to another vicious civil war – the Paris Commune – in which as many as 30,000 Communards died. The Third Republic was not officially formed until 1879, and politically it remained highly unstable down to World War I. Within the arts, the reform movement was driven first by the great international expositions of 1878 and 1889, and second by a government-led reform movement in the decorative arts (again aimed at exportation of goods). The importance of the development of iron as a new building material during the French international expositions has long been recognized, most notably by Sigfried Giedion. Yet this paradigmatic modernist perspective leaves aside other aspects that also shaped the French architectural discourse of this period. One is the strong Oriental influence in the development of interior design. Forms, colors, and patterns from Japan, Turkey, and India were mixed with eighteenth-century French rococo, and strangely enough were seen as a natural contribution to the development of a national French style. Whereas the spirit of reform in the decorative arts culminates in the 1890s in Art Nouveau, the great engineering structures of the two major expositions herald the long-span technology of the twentieth century.

13 JACOB VON FALKE
from *Art in the House* (1871)

The reform movements in the domestic arts throughout Germany and Austria begin in the 1860s and have much to do with the founding of the Bavarian National Museum in Munich (1853), the Museum for Art and Industry in Vienna (1863), and the Applied Arts Museum in Berlin (1867). Perhaps the leading voice calling for reform in Vienna was the art historian Rudolf von Eitelberger, who since the 1850s (often in concert with the architect Heinrich von Ferstel) had been demanding better living conditions for the city's residents in the midst of its explosive growth. Eitelberger was able to act upon his pleas in 1863 when he was appointed the director of the newly created Museum for Art and Industry. He appointed Jacob von Falke as one of the curators, and the latter (who later became the museum's director) responded by introducing stylized rooms into the museum as a way of educating the public into the manners of tasteful and practical appointments. Falke outlined his strategy in his book *Die Kunst im Hause* (Art in the house), which again was directed to the general public and again put an emphasis on simple and elegant design. The emphasis on color and form as the primary ingredients of good interior design signals an early desire in Austria to move away from the traditional historical styles.

Artistic harmony depends upon two things, color and form. In both there must be unity, that is to say, a union and blending together of many dissimilar things.

Jacob von Falke, from *Die Kunst im Hause* (1871), trans. Charles C. Perkins as *Art in the House*. Boston: L. Prang & Co., 1878, pp. 170–2.

Ordinarily, and one may say absolutely, color is of more importance in the decorative appointments of a house than form. Color makes the first and strongest impression; it gives the general tone; it may be used, if not to conceal faults and incongruities of form, at least to divert attention from them. Although a perfect eye for color is a rare gift, the power of perceiving defects and dissonances in color is much less uncommon than that of perceiving defects in form, which cannot be appreciated without a certain amount of education. It is color which chiefly gives character to a house, and by its help we may produce any desirable effect. A room may be made to look narrower or broader, lower or higher, by means of color. If we desire to make it grave or cheerful, bare or rich, simple or splendid; if we would impart to it a cosey and attractive or a poetic aspect, make it look warm or cool; if we would fashion for ourselves a place to dream in, or one fitted for serious and solitary meditation, or one suited to social enjoyment, our first and last medium is color. Color is a fairy, an enchantress who brings good and evil, joy and sunshine, or mourning and melancholy in her train, but she is always positive in her effect, and never allows herself to be treated with indifference. She repels and attracts, satisfies or disturbs, raises enjoyment to rapture or deepens discomfort into horror and *ennui*. He who covets her must not play the coward as we generally do nowadays, but must bear himself with that courage which wins beauty. Courage is needed chiefly at the outset, in the choice of the pervading tone. This is decisive, and it involves the artist in certain unavoidable consequences. Nevertheless, his freedom in the choice of colors and shades is so great that the possibilities of working out a rich scale of melodious hues are almost unlimited.

But although we are to depend mainly upon colors and colored decoration for effect, it will not do to neglect unity and harmony in form, because their absence is less generally observed. By unity of form, as I have before said, I do not mean any one of those definite historic styles which have been important in the history of art. We may expressly give up any idea of the Greek, the Gothic, the Renaissance, or any other style, no matter by what name it may be called, and yet insist upon unity; we may even demand a style, or, more properly speaking, style in the abstract. A design, a form of decoration, a piece of furniture, may have style without belonging in style to any one of the famous art-epochs either as original or copy, just as a painting may have style without following the taste of any master, time, or school. Style is the idealization of an object, the harmonious adaptation of form to means and end, the identification of the object with itself and its idea. A piece of furniture has style when it is exactly what it ought to be, when it is suited to the purpose for which it was intended, and has that purpose unmistakably inscribed upon it. From this point of view the simplest and the richest furniture, the humblest and the stateliest dwelling, may alike be full of style.

14 GEORG HIRTH
from *The German Renaissance Room* (1880)

A ligned with the work of Falke in Vienna were the efforts of Georg Hirth in Munich. After serving as a political editor of the *Allgemeine Zeitung*, Hirth began the publishing firm of Knorr and Hirth in 1875, which specialized in high-quality art books. The following year he lent objects from his collection of domestic furnishings to the Munich Exhibition of the Applied Arts, and from this time forward his interest in reform only grew. His book of 1880, *Das deutsche Zimmer der Renaissance* (the German Renaissance room), is beautifully illustrated and an intelligent plea for tasteful design and furnishings in the home. The use of the German Renaissance period, or sixteenth century, was embraced throughout Germany in the 1870s as a way to simplify and reform design, that is, through the use of clean lines, neutral tones (unstained woods), and built-in furniture with a few harmonious parts. The following excerpts from the introduction echo two themes that will be paramount in German literature from the 1880s onward: the need to educate the new German middle class in the correct principles of taste, and the desire to simply design in keeping with the spirit of the new bourgeois era. It is likewise a challenge thrown out to the German people to embrace the ideals of its new democratic form of government.

For years I have been growing more and more convinced that among the many things that must work together for the enhancement of our economic life, the cultivation of a good national taste occupies a prominent, if not the leading place. It is an economic question to the extent to which it is assuredly transformed by the magic of art and removed as far as possible from the unpleasant conflict of interests between free trade and protective tariffs.

Even more relevant for industry and the economy in general is its meaning for our private lives. The older among our esteemed readers will understand me well if I say that there are hours and days in which we are completely soured by the world and its disappointments, in which we, tired and burdened with the troubles of life, see the bustle of humanity in tones of gray. Few are the happy people who get over such depression with a strong belief in God or simply out of necessity of mind. We "humanity" almost always seek out sensual impressions to help us chase off such gloomy thoughts. One person finds solace in the heights of mountains or in the scent of a forest, another in the harmony of musical tones, a third in the images of art. It may well be that the comforts that we thus create for ourselves, like our entire lives, rest only on a happy illusion; but it is not an *empty* illusion if we gain with it new vigor and new hope. Yes, this capacity for illusion for civilized man, if I might say, forms a likewise necessary protection against the unkindness of fortune, similar to assurance against the dangers of fire or impoverishment.

In this circle of magic, to which a good upbringing directs us and which can domesticate our troubles, the *artistic design of our household* should form, in a manner of speaking, the focus – the warming heart. In the house we rest from the burdens of the day; here we live with the ones who we love most in the world; here we plant nothing but good seeds into

George Hirth, from *Das deutsche Zimmer der Renaissance* (1871), trans. Harry Francis Mallgrave. Munich: G. Hirth's Verlag, 1880, pp. 1–2.

the hearts of our children. Even if it were just this one thing – a matter of playfully introducing our *small ones* into the sphere of beauty, of making their eyes susceptible to harmonies of artistic forms and color – then it would be enough to lead each father of a family to apply himself to domestic furnishings with the greatest care. Unfortunately, this happens only in the rarest or most exceptional of cases, and the reason for this sin of omission is certainly not superficial or pecuniary; it resides rather in the inner inability to seek, that is, in the lack of good taste.

15 ROBERT DOHME
from *The English House* (1888)

By the start of the 1880s the domestic reform movement in Germany had assumed a well-defined life of its own. But Germany, with its economy bustling forward, was also looking carefully at the trends of its neighbors, especially France and Great Britain. Robert Dohme was a custodian of art at the Prussian court of Frederick III and in 1887 he published a comprehensive history of German architecture. He followed this publication with a semi-official trip to England in order to observe new developments there, and he was impressed in particular with the work of Richard Norman Shaw and the Queen Anne Revival. What resulted, then, was the first major study to bear the title *The English House*. Dohme championed the Queen Anne not as a style to be emulated, but rather as an approach to design with the functional attributes of privacy, light, and ventilation, and also the emotional attributes of cheerfulness, comfort, convenience, and fastidiousness – the last four of which he left in their English spelling in his German text. His metaphor of "modern wagons and ships" was – following Horatio Greenough – an early paradigm for design that would be frequently repeated in Germanic literature in the 1890s, and of course it later becomes central to the polemics in the 1920s.

More unconditionally in England than in Germany is the principle that the value of a dwelling is to be sought more in its practicality than in its aesthetic appearance. In the eyes of the Englishman the desirability of a house is found not in its size and monumentality, nor in its richness and luxury, but in the harmony of the individual rooms and their skillful grouping, in short, in fulfilling that sum of demands that practical sense and the refined needs of life have shown to be prerequisites for a comfortable existence. The English architect will give to the small and simple cottage – which in its limits well corresponds to those demands – the honorary title of a "gentleman's house," a title he refuses to give to the badly disposed palace. For this reason one no longer finds in present-day English architecture those academically correct villas striving toward monumentality, conventionally laid out inside, developed as canons of classical periods, whereas with us they are indeed still the fashion. Less monumentality and more comfort, less classicism and more individuality – this can be the motto of modern English domestic architecture in contrast to our German counterpart.

★ ★ ★

Robert Dohme, from *Das englische Haus*, trans. Harry Francis Mallgrave. Braunschweig: George Westermann, 1888, pp. 28, 42.

I see in this movement (at the acme of which are the Queen Anne men, and especially their leader R. Norman Shaw) nothing of a fashion statement. It seems to me – in contrast to the creations on the Continent that at first glance today also seem so striking – that herein lies the beginning of *a new period of cultural evolution*, a period that moves away from the ornamentally lavish artistic character of the Renaissance, and toward new and still concealed goals lying before us. On the Continent we still do not recognize the impulses of this new spirit in the field of architecture; yet for a number of our utensils, however, it has already appeared to us, found sympathy, and been accepted – if indeed also arising from the examples of England and America. One thinks, for example, of our modern vehicles and ships, whose beauty, in fulfilling their task, we have to a great extent achieved by limiting any and all decorative ornaments merely to graceful lines, in seeking the object's greatest functionality and simplicity of form, and in divesting it of all superfluities. In a similar way, England has achieved the same today in architecture.

16 CORNELIUS GURLITT
from *Inside the Middle-Class House* (1888)

If Dohme looked to England to provide examples for artistic reform in Germany, Cornelius Gurlitt looked to his native country. A prolific author of ninety-seven books (including the first great history of the Baroque period), Gurlitt was a shrewd critic. An architect by training, he was appointed a curator at the Dresden Museum for the Applied Arts in 1879 and later became a professor at that city's famed technical university. His book is addressed not to architects but to the public, and the word *Bürger* in the title (related to the English word "burgher") connotes not only the middle-class, but also the attributes of honest, simple, and functional design. His book is therefore a primer for modern home design, although he also rewards the reader with a learned discourse on the aesthetic principles of neoclassicism and romanticism as well as the more recent reform movement in Germany, which he traces back to Gottfried Semper. Gurlitt, although appreciative of recent English design, discounts the possibility of too closely mimicking a sensitivity that is at heart English, and in these closing remarks he challenges his countrymen to draw upon their own native instincts. Gurlitt was an early and, as we will see, articulate champion of modernism.

Enough! One could still speak on many things, but it is impossible to treat exhaustively every aspect of domestic interiors without composing a series of volumes that would be of no use to anyone. Before the pen of the last volume would be put down, the first would already have changed. For fashion, like style, marches inexorably forward. It transforms not only the form of things but also our eyes. The table that appears so charming to us today will seem ungainly in five years. Are there laws for such changes? Are there rules of beauty for how thick a table leg should be? Surely not. Each man makes it according to his own judgment following what he has seen before, following the images of similar things living in his

Cornelius Gurlitt, from *Im Bürgerhaus*, trans. Harry Francis Mallgrave. Dresden: Gilbers'sche Königl. Hof-Verlagsbuchhandlung, 1888, pp. 227–9.

memory. Each man experiences beauty differently and no one can convey his perception to another in full. All attempts to create a unified concept of beauty will be in vain. For beauty lies not in the nature and in things, but resides in each of us.

[...]

True art, however, is the expression of our time. All the looking backward that has characterized our works for decades belonged to the time in which the German people had to seek their greatness in past centuries. In my view, this time has past. The march of our nation goes ever forward. We no longer live in the realm of dreams and history; our actions and thoughts direct themselves first to what is going on around us, in which we have to take an active part, in which we have to maintain our position. Let us turn our heads forward in order to view truly the continuing greatness of our nation. Then our art will be modern and only modern.

17 LOUIS-CHARLES BOILEAU
from "Shops of the Bon Marché in Paris – Grand Staircase" (1876)

Louis-Charles Boileau was the son of Louis-Auguste Boileau. The father was trained as a woodcarver, but early in his career made the transition into architecture. In 1854 he created a sensation by building a Gothic church – Saint-Eugène, Paris – with a light-weight iron structure. His design was controversial, but at the same time it helped to foster a debate regarding the architectural limits of iron, that is, whether its use should be restricted to utilitarian structures or whether it could be used in more traditional building types. In 1869 the elder Boileau was commissioned to design the Paris department store "Au Bon Marché," but the interior was designed by his son Louis-Charles in the 1870s, with the help of the engineer Gustave Eiffel. This design reverberated through Parisian circles because of its open atriums, iron staircases, and surrounding galleries – all illuminated by three colossal skylights. In this discussion of its conception, Louis-Charles goes far beyond the abstract theorizing of many of his colleagues by insisting that the architecture of iron and glass differs fundamentally from the architecture of stone. Architecture is no longer the shaping of form in daylight but rather the sculptural shaping of light itself.

It is always somewhat unrewarding to show the details of an iron and glass structure with engravings. The metallic tightness of columns and trusses offers little possibility of rendering the different planes of the transparent surfaces, and the geometric drawing does not permit the picturesque expression of atmosphere and light, in which resides almost all the charm of this type of building. We must also beg of our readers that if they cannot go and judge with their own eyes that part of the department store for which we give some drawings, they should at least not consider these drawings in an isolated way; rather, they should try to reassemble them in their minds in order to deduce the artistic effect of the executed work.

Louis-Charles Boileau, from "Magasins du Bon Marché, à Paris – grand Escalier," trans. Christina Contandriopoulos and Harry Francis Mallgrave, in *Encyclopédie d'architecture*. Paris: V. A. Morel, 1876, p. 120.

If the rendering of such a work is difficult, the design is no less so and the typical training of the architect provides very little help. What is the use of having to learn to design and proportion moldings or ornaments on stone surfaces, on which we find the easy projections of friezes, cornices, bosses, or panels – in a word, all the architectural clichés that we have tirelessly put forth to rejuvenate art through new combinations – when there are no more surfaces available to receive them? Of course I do not consider these small-diameter shafts or some thin cast-iron details as columns or entablatures. Therefore I do not believe that they should play a prominent decorative role in these retail galleries.

In this regard, I am uncompromising and I know that one could cite some eminent architects who, having to deal with an analogous problem, have been delighted to treat the necessary meagerness of metal as a decorative material by resorting to a profusion of cuttings and embellishments. Well, I am sure that if these masters would have compared their efforts with the results they produced, they would also have to admit that this type of building cannot be seriously compared with stone building, and that they should refrain from all their imitation and consider the problem from an altogether different point of view.

If I may use an almost paradoxical exaggeration to express my thought, I would say that this viewpoint should consist in no longer designing the building surfaces but rather the void that they envelop, that is to say, instead of trying to play with light on plastic forms, we should rather consider the atmosphere that circulates throughout the structure and, by its profusion or economy, creates radiance, half-lights, or reflections, which endow a space with brilliance in the same way that we endow crystal chandeliers with a luster by sculpting them into differently shaped prisms.

In this luminous concert, architectural solids should play the role of being the setting for a fine stone. It exists just enough to make this full interior daylight vibrate with the greatest possible intensity, in such a way that the broad glass surfaces and semi-bright depth that surround it will render the stone happier, more resonant, and more expansive than, say, the pure and simple daylight of the outdoors.

18 CHARLES BLANC
from *The Fine Arts at the Universal Exposition of 1878* (1878)

If the idea of an international exhibition was a creation of the British in 1851, it was an idea nowhere embraced with greater enthusiasm during the following decades than in France. Paris followed the London example with its first international exposition in 1855, and continued with ever more lavish fairs in 1867, 1878, 1889, and 1900. The events were meant to put French goods on display, but also to entertain and bolster French pride.

Charles Blanc, from *Les Beaux-Arts à l'Exposition Universelle de 1878*, trans. Christina Contandriopoulos and Harry Francis Mallgrave. Paris: Librairie Renocard, 1878, pp. 39–41.

With France's excellent engineering schools, they too became showcases for structural innovation. The exposition of 1878 came at a particularly low point in French confidence, as earlier in the decade French armies had been routed by German forces and the country had subsequently endured another bloody civil war. In his competition proposal for this event of 1878, the engineer Gustave Eiffel responded with a bold design for an iron exhibition structure that would run from the site of his later tower across the Seine to the Place du Trocadéro, supported on a colossal arched truss. Although this proposal was not accepted, Eiffel did engineer the largest of the iron structures that were eventually built on the Champ de Mars, measuring 350 meters by 700 meters in length. The iron, glass, and sheet-metal structures of this event were so impressive that they were seen by the historian Charles Blanc as inaugurating a new era of human history. This former director of the École des Beaux-Arts was appointed professor of aesthetics and art history at the Collège de France in 1878, and his color theories published in *Grammaire des arts du dessin* (1867) had greatly influenced the first generation of Impressionist painters. Here he speculates on the future of architecture.

Since antique times, two great innovations have been introduced into architecture. The first one is that which was invented during the twelfth century, which Viollet-le-Duc has called genuinely French because it was born in France and specifically in the Île-de-France. This admirable innovation consisted in having a whole building supported by a framework, in other words by a system of thin isolated piers, supporting the ribbed springing vaults. The vertical force of these vaults pressed down on pillars and the diagonal force or thrust was projected outside to be resolved in the buttresses. In the interior, this system lent itself to very poetic effects, for the walls merely played a very secondary role. The panels of the ribbed vaults were only a veil of light masonry and the partitions of the building – having nothing to bear, for even the rafters of the roof were supported by the vaulting – could be transformed into glass panels. In ancient architecture, the wall was a thick support whose function was to resist both compression and lateral thrust; in Gothic architecture, the wall was but a divider whose only purpose was to resist horizontal stress.

This wonderful innovation, which then limited the usefulness of the wall, was succeeded in this century by other, no less astonishing innovations deriving from the introduction of iron into all parts of the building, as both supporting and supported elements. The ability to cover immense spaces without obstructing them with intermediary supports, and the power to remove the interior walls (whose only function is to enclose) by pushing them to the boundaries of the building – these are, we have to admit, novelties that collectively announce a civilization very different from the one preserved in the monuments and by history. For the masses who wish to assemble, for the people who would rather unite and live amicably, instead of struggling against one another, new buildings were necessary. They are temples whose construction corresponds to sentiments that exist only as germs within humanity, to needs that humanity has not known until now, to ideas that could develop only under the very protection of these temples. When these newly invented wonders receive their baptism of art, when grace consents to marry with the useful, we will be able to say truly that architecture reveals and sanctifies a new order of things. *Novus aedium et rerum narcitur ordo.*

19 EUGÈNE-EMMANUEL VIOLLET-LE-DUC
from "The Buildings of the Universal Exposition of 1878" (1878)

Although a somewhat embittered Viollet-le-Duc spent much of this decade in his Alpine retreats at Chamonix, and later near Lausanne, he was by no means retired from letters. During this time he finished the last four of his *Lectures on Architecture* and the final five volumes of the *Dictionnaire raisonné*. In addition, he wrote on a score of other subjects, ranging from the geology of Mont Blanc to the origin of Russian art. This short excerpt from a report on the architecture of the Exposition of 1878 also demonstrates his undiminished capacity to discern a new development: the advantages of prefabrication and the organizational complexity of the modern building project, where every element is designed prior to the start of construction.

In this regard, let us report something that deserves our attention today, when our habits and our needs require the rapid construction of buildings but cannot accept the congestion of a busy city produced by construction sites.

Apart from the foundation and grading, all the parts of the buildings on the Champ de Mars were made in factories and workshops. The advantages of this system speak for themselves. If the different parts of a building are thus able to be fabricated in many places, there is no reason to fear congestion. When they are ordered at the right time, the parts arrive from these places on the appointed day and are put in place. Generally it is the division of labor that is most advantageous and truly useful. But it should also be understood that such an approach requires absolute precision from the project manager, because if it happened that some pieces were a centimeter too long or too short it would cause the greatest difficulties during installation. Simple dimensional drawings no longer suffice and the manager must send the manufacturer perfectly calibrated measurements for the cast or shaped pieces. It is thus understandable how this demands both organization and a method, because any part of the work that arrives too soon would cause congestion, while any part arriving too late would bring the regular run of the work to a halt.

Eugène-Emmanuel Viollet-le-Duc, from "Les bâtiments de l'Exposition Universelle de 1878," trans. Christina Contandriopoulos and Harry Francis Mallgrave, in *L'art, Revue hebdomadaire illustrée*. Paris: Ballue, 1878, p. 140.

20 ÉMILE ZOLA
from *The Ladies' Delight* (1884)

Wcat e have already seen this novelist of realism and his exaltation of the new iron architecture (vol. 1, 216), and in this later novel he returns to the same theme in a more dramatic fashion. The scene here is the opening of the fictional department store, based in part on the recently completed Bon Marché. Over many pages, Zola describes the experiences of Madame Desforges as she makes her way into the new building on its crowded opening day. The spectacular novelty of the iron and glass structure, bathed in white light streaming down from a colossal skylight above, cannot be suppressed. It is a classic homage to the new era of modernity, and, interestingly, Zola, in composing this passage, was advised by Frantz Jourdain, the later architect of the Samaritaine department store.

At that moment, Madame Desforges, who had almost had her coat pulled off in the crowd, finally got in and was crossing the first hall. Then, once she got to the main gallery, she looked up. It was like the concourse of a railway station, surrounded by the balustrades of the two upper storeys, cut by suspended stairways and crisscrossed with bridges. The iron stairways, in double spirals, formed daring curves with many landings. The iron bridges hung high up in straight lines across the void. And all this cast iron beneath the white light of the glass roof composed an airy architecture of complicated lacework which let the daylight through – a modern version of a dream palace, a Tower of Babel with storey piled on storey and rooms expanding, opening on vistas of other storeys and other rooms reaching to infinity. Moreover, iron reigned on all sides, the young architect having had the honesty and courage not to disguise it beneath a coat of whitewash or to imitate stone and wood. Downstairs, so as not to detract from the goods, the décor was sober, with large expanses of the same, neutral colour. Then, as the metal framework rose upwards, so the capitals of the columns grew richer, the rivets formed rosettes, the brackets and the corbels were laden with moulded sculptures. Finally, at the top, the painting shone out green and red, in the midst of a profusion of gold: streams of gold, harvests of gold, even on the windows where the panes were enamelled and encrusted with gold. Beneath the covered galleries, the visible bricks on the vaults were also enamelled with bright colours. Mosaic and faience were incorporated in the décor, brightening up the borders and adding a fresh note to moderate the severity of the whole; while the staircases with their banisters of red velvet were decked out with a strip of moulded, polished iron, shining like the steel on a breastplate.

Although she was already acquainted with the new building, Madame Desforges had stopped, struck by the bustling life that seethed that day beneath the huge vault. On the ground floor, around her, the crowd continued to flow in the same double current from the entrance or towards the exit, and this was perceptible as far as the silk department – a very mixed crowd, though in the afternoon there were more ladies among the petty bourgeoises and the housewives, many women in mourning, with their large veils, and errant wet nurses protecting their charges with their broad elbows. And this sea, these many-coloured hats,

Émile Zola, from *Au Bonheur des Dames* (1884), trans. and ed. Robin Buss as *The Ladies' Delight*. London: Penguin, 2001, pp. 245–6.

these bare heads, blonde or black, flowed from one end of the gallery to the other, blurred and drab amid the sharp, vibrant colours of the materials. Madame Desforges could see nothing but huge placards everywhere with enormous figures on them, standing out as garish stains against the bright Indian prints, the lustrous silks and the dark woollens. Piles of ribbons gashed across heads, a wall of flannel spread out like a promontory and everywhere the mirrors extended the shops, reflecting displays with fragments of the public, faces reversed, portions of shoulders and arms, while to the left and to the right the side galleries opened up vistas, snowy depths of white linens or the speckled pits of hosiery, far-away, vanishing, lit by the rays of light shining through some glazed bay, where the crowd was no more than a dust of humanity. Then, when Madame Desforges looked up, she could see along the stairways and on the suspended bridges, around the banisters on every floor, a continuous, humming, upward flow, a whole tribe suspended in the air, travelling past the spaces in this enormous metal frame and silhouetted black against the diffuse glow from the windows.

21 JORIS-KARL HUYSMANS
from *Against Nature* (1884)

Against the backdrop of escalating modernity in the 1880s – with its cold iron forms – stands the odd and seeming contrary French fascination with the pre-revolutionary period of Louis XV. Huysmans's novel, in fact, helps to inaugurate a trend in French art that finds its culmination a decade later in the artistic phenomenon of Art Nouveau. The novel itself is highly symbolic. A misanthropic aristocrat and former dandy, with especially acute senses and nervous excitability, takes refuge in posh surroundings, where he indulges his cravings for the luxurious pomp of the past. His self-imposed retreat and isolation represent not only a withdrawal from the world of changing tastes but also a desire to return to something genuinely French in the face of growing cosmopolitanism and excessive "mental stimulation." The novel may seem remote from architectural theory, but this passage, in fact, was crafted concurrently with Paul Sédille's construction of the Printemps department store, where the Paris architect wrapped his dazzling iron interiors with rococo towers and ornamental motifs on the outside.

There were, in his opinion, only two ways of arranging a bedroom: you could either make it a place for sensual pleasure, for nocturnal delectation, or else you could fit it out as a place for sleep and solitude, a setting for quiet meditation, a sort of oratory.

In the first case, the Louis-Quinze style was the obvious choice for people of delicate sensibility, exhausted by mental stimulation above all else. The eighteenth century is, in fact, the only age which has known how to develop woman in a wholly depraved atmosphere, shaping its furniture on the model of her charms, imitating her passionate contortions and spasmodic convulsions in the curves and convolutions of wood and copper, spicing the

Joris-Karl Huysmans, from *À Rebours* (1884), trans. Robert Baldick as *Against Nature*. London: Penguin, 2003, pp. 61–2.

sugary languor of the blonde with its bright, light furnishings, and mitigating the salty savour of the brunette with tapestries of delicate, watery, almost insipid hues.

In his Paris house he had had a bedroom decorated in just this style, and furnished with the great white lacquered bed which provides that added titillation, that final touch of depravity so precious to the experienced voluptuary, excited by the spurious chastity and hypocritical modesty of the Greuze figures, by the pretended purity of a bed of vice apparently designed for innocent children and young virgins.

In the other case – and now that he meant to break with the irritating memories of his past life, this was the only one for him – the bedroom had to be turned into a facsimile of a monastery cell. But here difficulties piled up before him, for as far as he was concerned, he categorically refused to put up with the austere ugliness that characterizes all penitential prayer-houses.

After turning the question over in his mind, he eventually came to the conclusion that what he should try to do was this: to employ cheerful means to attain a drab end, or rather, to impress on the room as a whole, treated in this way, a certain elegance and distinction, while yet preserving its essential ugliness. He decided, in fact, to reverse the optical illusion of the stage, where cheap finery plays the part of rich and costly fabrics; to achieve precisely the opposite effect, by using magnificent materials to give the impression of old rags; in short, to fit up a Trappist's cell that would look like the genuine article, but would of course be nothing of the sort.

He set about it in the following way: to imitate the yellow distemper beloved by church and state alike, he had the walls hung with saffron silk; and to represent the chocolate-brown dado normally found in this sort of room, he covered the lower part of the walls with strips of kingwood, a dark-brown wood with a purple sheen. The effect was delightful, recalling – though not too clearly – the unattractive crudity of the model he was copying and adapting. The ceiling was similarly covered with white holland, which had the appearance of plaster without its bright, shiny look; as for the cold tiles of the floor, he managed to hit them off quite well, thanks to a carpet patterned in red squares, with the wood dyed white in places where sandals and boots could be supposed to have left their mark.

22 SAMUEL BING
from *Artistic Japan* (1888)

Yet another thematic and formal wellspring for the development of Art Nouveau in France was the artistic influence of Japan. Although this interest initially ran in parallel with that in other European countries and North America, over the course of the 1880s it takes a surprising turn in French art. Louis Gonse, in his book *L'art Japonais* (1883), first establishes the tone for this discussion by applauding the functionalism of Japanese architecture and the fact that every Japanese architect is a "Le Nôtre" in his love and appreciation of nature. Samuel Bing's lavishly illustrated journal of 1888, *Le Japon Artistique* (issued simultaneously in German and in

Samuel Bing, from *Artistic Japan*. London, 1888, pp. 1–4.

English as *Artistic Japan*), now views Japanese art as indeed a possible source for fresh artistic inspiration. Bing was a German by birth and he moved to Paris in the 1850s to oversee a family porcelain business. He not only became increasingly more Francophile in his outlook (eventually switching his citizenship and changing his first name from Sigfried to Samuel) but he also thrived as the owner of several Parisian shops dealing in objects of decorative art. By the mid-1880s, after a year-long visit to Japan, he came to embrace Japanese art as a way to resuscitate or revitalize French design. He therefore speaks in this "Programme" as a Frenchman, a dilettante, an entrepreneur, and most importantly as an aesthetician of modern life.

In presenting to the public ARTISTIC JAPAN, I lay no claim to the addition of a fresh chapter to the many works upon the history of Japanese Art already in existence. Its aim is not that of a guide to unexplored regions, or the examination of recondite theories. These have already been treated of by masters of æsthetics, who have subjected them to the keenest analysis, to the most careful verification, classification, and comparison.

But the section of the public which has been thus catered for is a comparatively small one: the inquiring spirit who is never satisfied unless he is admitted behind the scenes, and receives certificates of authenticity for every one of his much-prized objects as he acquires them, is only to be met with now and then. These have had, as I have already said, their requirements met. To them this publication is addressed, but not in the first instance. It is primarily intended for the instruction of the general public in the real and rare beauties of an Art which has hitherto attracted chiefly through its superficial qualities. How, indeed, could this be otherwise? In almost every country in Europe (England perhaps excepted) the great State collections, in which marvels of all styles, all epochs, and all lands are included, have disdainfully closed their doors to Japanese Art. In the shop and the bazaar only has Japanese Art been represented, and there merely in its least refined and elevated form.

There its productions, in picturesque disorder, have appealed to the undiscriminating glance of the passer-by, who, indeed, could not help being fascinated by the undeniable charm of nicknacks made only for exportation, but who did not consider that what he saw was no more than the vague reflection of an art which was formerly vigorous and sound. He could not know that the sculptured groups whose effeminate forms he admired had some masterpiece of life and expression for their prototype; he has not been told that yonder garish vase is but a feeble imitation of a piece of pottery marvellous in colour and technical perfection. It is not surprising that he admired a sample of tissue woven in the period of decadence, for he has never seen any of those sumptuous stuffs which the artist in embroidery of the feudal times covered with harmonious tints in a style of lordly grandeur. Even the artist, when he stopped to admire the drawings and engravings sketched with the cleverness of the race by some draftsman of modern Japan, knew naught of the wonderful albums in which the genius of the famous masters of the bygone time was matched by that of the engravers who interpreted and multiplied their works.

It is in the power of but very few, when first they are privileged to see side by side two phases of Japanese art – one in its prime, the other in its decadence – to recognise at a glance the vast distance that divides them. It is by degrees only that the eye can distinguish between them. It is only as we begin to examine them with closer attention that we arrive at some knowledge of the subject, and come to see that precisely the same distinction which there is in the case of the productions of our own country, exists between the masterly works of Japanese art which were creations, and the current products of a modern industry, in which the mighty genius of ancestral artists has been frittered away under the mercantile influence of a later epoch.

This truth was, however, immediately recognised by that limited number of connoisseurs who in every age devote themselves to the study of the beautiful, and it came with especial force to the few well-informed collectors who were so fortunate as to meet at the onset with specimens of a superior order. Unfortunately, such specimens are rare, and are becoming more so every day, and it is within the means of but few to acquire them. To the great majority therefore the only way of instructing them as to what is really choice in Japanese Art is by placing before them faithful reproductions of the original objects. This is the task to which I am about to devote myself. I propose to furnish the lovers of Japanese Art, by the aid of the best processes of engraving, with a continuous series of diversified specimens, taken from every branch of that art, at all its various epochs. The work will constitute a sort of graphic encyclopædia, for the use of all those students of Japanese Art who are desirous of tracing the course of its development.

The present publication has yet another object. It is especially addressed to those persons who, on any grounds, are interested in the future of the industrial arts, and especially to those who, whether as manufacturers or as artizans, have an active share in their production. In the new forms of art which have come to us from the uttermost parts of the East, we see something more than a Platonic feast set before our contemplative dilettanti, we find in them examples worthy to be followed in every respect, not, indeed, worthy to uproot the foundations of the old æsthetic edifice which exists, but fitted to add a fresh force to those forces which we have appropriated to ourselves in all past time, and brought to the support and aid of our national genius. How could the vitality of that genius have been maintained had it not been recruited from fresh sources from time to time? Where is the civilized country, ancient or modern, from which we have not at some time borrowed some of its artistic culture?

23 JOSEPH EUGÈNE ANATOLE DE BAUDOT from "The Universal Exposition of 1889 – first visit to the Champs de Mars" (1889)

B oth the interest in Japanese art and the fascination with the rococo were evident in the Paris International Exposition of 1889, and can be found in the work of the young Art Nouveau designer Émile Gallé. But Gallé's exotic designs were for the moment overtaken by the two compelling architectural events of the exposition: the Galerie des Machines and the Eiffel Tower. The last phenomenon, still standing as the preeminent symbol of the city, created a furor, as artists and architects, government officials, and the public lined up to voice their support or – more generally – opposition to its presence on the Paris skyline. The architect Anatole de Baudot

Joseph Eugène Anatole de Baudot, from "The Universal Exposition of 1889 – first visit to the Champs de Mars", in *Encyclopédie d'architecture* 4. 1888–9, trans. Christina Contandriopoulos and Harry Francis Mallgrave, pp. 9–10.

opposed its erection, although he was one of the more moderate voices in dissent. As a youth Baudot had been one of those protesting students who in 1856 petitioned Eugène-Emmanuel Viollet-le-Duc to open his atelier to students, and he, with his Gothic predilections as a designer, remained a close associate of the master. In the 1880s, after Viollet-le-Duc's death, he began to take a more original architectural course, particularly with his later experiments of reinforced concrete. As the founding editor of the *Encyclopédie d'architecture*, Baudot here voices his opposition on the grounds that iron, as a material, had yet to find its appropriate artistic form.

In comparing the appearance of these metallic forms to those of works in stone, many artisans and amateurs deplore their sparse and light character and refuse to assign any artistic value to these modern productions. This way of viewing the architectural question is very unfortunate and somewhat small-minded. Such criticism hinders greatly the efforts being made in the ordering of modern ideas, because it leads builders to search for a compromise or to depart from the true path indicated by the design principle, which science lays out in a very clear way.

Instead of accepting frankly and without reservations this light appearance, the designing architect, in searching for the solution, believes he is obliged to increase the size of the supports, shorten the purlins or trusses that link them, and design the general form in such a way as to introduce elements into the composition that are in contradiction with the general principles of using metal. Once the general composition is designed, in comes the engineer who, through the aid of calculations, gives to each of the elements of the structure the section and strength requiring the least possible use of metal. Is this reasonable from an economic point of view? It is doubtful, but surely we can say that art gains nothing from compromises, and that if metallic construction were designed with no other concern than to satisfy its purpose and structural requirements it would take on a surprising new look and striking expression, and this spindly aspect reminiscent of scaffolding would disappear. I know well that one could object to the Eiffel Tower because, even though its appearance seems to answer my program, it possesses neither the artistic value nor the arresting character of a new work.

Nevertheless, the objection would not be serious if one did not take the trouble to reflect on it. Indeed, while the famous tower rather candidly proceeds from science and from the skillful calculations of the engineer, we should not forget that it does not answer any purpose or idea, and it therefore loses the spiritual value and attraction of a work of art. Moreover, this work, which is nothing but a vain symbol of the modern builder, has the great failing of bearing no comparison with any high-rise building. From antique columns to the minarets of the Orient to the towers of the Middle Ages, there are conceptions whose practical utility may be debatable, but whose idea is superb and great. In these works of the past, the idea intervenes and satisfies the imagination while it charms the eyes. But piling up several hundred meters of iron supports on top of each other without any other reason than to satisfy the pretension that we know how to do it is not sufficient to charm the skeptical spirits of the nineteenth century. Is iron, whose plastic quality has not yet been given its artistic note, ready for this kind of endeavor? Certainly not, and it was, then, rather audacious for an art in its initial stages to raise the highest structure that the world has seen since the Tower of Babel. However that may be, this error increases daily and today it reaches around 140 meters in height, and we must be resigned to see it going up the whole way. We must do so because if it were to stop it would mean the failure of our international exposition, one that, for my part, I would be far from wishing.

24 LOUIS GONSE

from "The Architecture of the Universal Exposition of 1889" (1889)

Taking a very different position from Baudot on the issue of the Eiffel Tower was Louis Gonse. This well-known critic was the influential editor of the *Gazette des Beaux-Arts*, a vice-president of the Commission des Monuments Historiques, and a close friend of Samuel Bing, and it was he who first sparked interest in France over Japanese art – a subject on which he wrote in both the expositions of 1867 and 1878. He organized the first major exhibition on Japanese art in 1883, the same year in which his influential book *L'Art japonais* (Japanese art) appeared. In turning his attention to the controversial subject of the Eiffel Tower, he reveals a different perspective by writing a very positive review of its mathematical engineering and architectonic order, and thereby underscoring its psychological pleasure.

Within minutes, the Decauville light rail takes us to the base of the Eiffel tower. The metallic colossus, next to which the tallest buildings in the world are only pigmies, rises on four gigantic feet at the entrance to the Champ de Mars. It should not be necessary to describe it, for its design is today known to the entire universe. At first glance, everyone has understood and admired its lightness, audacity, and the perfection of its structure; everyone has divined that the constructional and structural problems were resolved with incomparable expertise. As a work of science and industry, nobody contests that the Eiffel Tower is a prodigious monument that has brought fame to the name of someone who had both the courage to conceive it and the talent to carry it through. Is, however, the iron tower to an equal degree, or to any degree, a work of art? Despondent spirits and those who fear novelty, the finicky, the quibblers, the shrewd – all answered "no" well before the tower was finished. As for me and many artists, we do not hesitate to say "yes," if it can be conceded that an impression of art, or at least a visual pleasure akin to art, can be had by the sight of great lines engendered by the calculation of forces and resistances, impeccably suited to their functions.

There are for me, in certain scientific discoveries and in certain creations belonging to the mathematical order, such as a suspension bridge or a warship, a harmonious perfection that attains beauty and awakens sensations in the soul analogous to those that we experience in standing before a beautiful tree or a large mountain. Note that the forms, lines, and proportions of the Eiffel Tower did not arise from engineering caprice. The tower, as we know, is not connected with the foundations; it poses, rather, it stands firmly on feet planted wide apart, like a man who opens his legs to resist the wind. Its weight, its equilibrium of forces holds it in this state of inert stability. Therefore it is the calculation of thrusts and resistances alone that created the building's profile; calculations gave the curve of the positioning of the bases, the relative height of the platforms, the diameter of the rise.

Louis Gonse, from "The Architecture of the Universal Exposition of 1889," in *Gazette des Beaux-Arts*, trans. Christina Contandriopoulos and Harry Francis Mallgrave. Paris, 1889, pp. 476–8.

Whereas some (not without reason) have criticized the work of M. Eiffel on some small points, such as the dryness intrinsic to a network of metallic construction whose main quality must be lightness, nobody can remain insensible to the greatness of its lines, the boldness of the curves, the majesty of the great base-arches that almost span a hundred meters. These arches are marvelous, especially in the evening, when they are illuminated with a string of lights and the accentuation of the large shadow enhances them even more. These horseshoe arches are the largest that have ever been built and we know that among all arch shapes the semicircular is that which best corresponds to the laws of eurhythmy. In summary, thanks to mathematical calculations, the proportions of the Eiffel Tower, without our knowing it, provide us with a feeling of security or fullness, which is one of the mysterious sources of aesthetic pleasure in architecture.

25 EDMOND DE GONCOURT
from *Journal: Mémoires de la vie littéraire* (1895)

In late December 1895 Samuel Bing opened his newly expanded and renovated shop in Paris, the Maison de l'Art Nouveau, which can be seen as a culmination of the French artistic reform of the previous two decades. Bing, as we have seen, was an articulate advocate of Japanese art and the lessons it holds for the West; he was also a strong supporter of the various activities of the Union of Decorative Arts, the state bureaucracy charged with promoting French goods. In 1894 Bing had made a visit to the United States on behalf of the French government in order to gauge artistic developments there, and he was particularly impressed with the large workshops and studio of Louis Comfort Tiffany. Bing then hired the architect Louis Bonnier to enlarge his Japanese shop in Paris, and he conceived his new private venture as an international studio and workshop that would support the leading modern artists in their cultivation of a new art. One of the centerpieces to his new shop was the work of the Belgian artist and architect Henry van de Velde, whom Bing had recently "discovered" in Uccle, Belgium. Van de Velde designed and built several rooms of furnishings, in which he first displayed the forms of his popular "Art Nouveau" style.

These rooms stand behind the criticisms of Edmond de Goncourt, which he penned in his diary just a few days after the shop's opening. Goncourt had been close to Bing's circle and, like him, was an art historian, collector, and aesthete of long prominence and distinction. He was born into aristocratic and bourgeois circumstances and, financially secure, developed both an appreciation for and historical knowledge of the eighteenth century and its rococo style. From his rococo-inspired mansion in Auteil Edmond preached the message of "art for art's sake" (coined in 1830 by Théophile Gautier) and naturalistic objectivity. In the 1880s Edmond chimed in with the enthusiasm for Japanese art, and later in this decade he began collecting the glassware of the modern artist from Nancy, Émile Gallé. Thus his artistic tastes inclined both forward and to the past, but always from the protective shelter of his comfortable aristocratic bearing. These brief remarks from his journal portray French art at an

Edmond de Goncourt, from Edmond and Jules de Goncourt, *Journal: Mémoires de la vie littéraire, 1895–1896*, vol. 4, trans. Christina Contandriopoulos and Harry Francis Mallgrave. Monaco: Fasquelle & Flammarion, 1956, pp. 156–7.

interesting crossroads. On the one hand the exposition of 1889 had a few years earlier demonstrated to the world France's mastery of engineering and technology, fields that would soon become the hallmark of twentieth-century modernity. On the other hand, the nationalist and artistic impulses of the decorative art movement often became essentially a conservative reaction to a rapidly changing world.

Monday, 30 December 1895

Bing Exhibition. I do not find fault with the idea of the exhibition, I find fault with the exhibition of the day, today.

What! Is this country, which in the eighteenth century had stylish and curving furniture for idleness, now threatened by hard and angular furniture that seems to be designed for a rude cave or lake dweller? Will France be condemned to prizewinning shapes crowned for their ungainliness, to bay sections, windows, and dressers borrowed from the portholes of a ship? To the backs of sofas, seats, and chairs that have the look of sheet metal, covered with fabric on which gosling-green birds fly over a soapy, dingy blue, to washstands and other furniture that share a kinship with the washbasin of a dental office in the vicinity of the morgue? And will Parisians eat in this dining room in the midst of these tinted panels of false mahogany, decorated with these arabesques of gold powder, near this chimney serving as the heater for the towels of a public bath? And will Parisians sleep in this bedroom between these two chairs of horrifying taste, in this bed consisting of a mattress laid on a tombstone?

Really, have we become *denationalized*? Conquered morally in a conquest worse than war? Is this a time when there is no longer any place in France except for the Muscovite, Scandinavian, or Italian writer, and maybe soon a Portuguese one? Is this a period in which it also seems there is no longer any place in France except for Anglo-Saxon or Dutch furniture?

No! Is this the new furniture of France? No! No!

C. REFORMS IN THE UNITED STATES

Introduction

The intellectual and architectural traditions established around mid-century by Ralph Waldo Emerson, Horatio Greenough, Alexander Jackson Davis, and Andrew Jackson Downing slowly but quite persuasively colored American architectural practice over the last third of the nineteenth century. At the same time, influences from abroad — particularly from England and France — continued to make themselves felt. The American private house, to take but one specific example, truly began to come of age in the 1870s with timber techniques based on the "balloon frame" and Shingle style. Yet these forms, at times, also betrayed in part the influence of Richard Norman Shaw and the Queen Anne style. By the mid-1880s, however, a very unique American housing naissance was in full swing throughout the Northeast and Midwest, as documented by the photographic studies of such critics as George William Sheldon.

Another national transformation taking place within American architecture was the westward expansion of the country in the second half of the century, fostered by the first transcontinental railroad lines. Almost overnight a number of new urban centers sprang up in Cleveland, Detroit, Chicago, Minneapolis, and San Francisco. The new hub of the Midwest – Chicago – literally rose from the ashes of the great fire of 1871 and it rapidly became an urban center known for its civic bluster and high-rise experimentation. The dominance of the generally European-inspired, established styles of the East Coast thus came to be challenged by the likes of William Le Baron Jenny, John Root, Holabird and Roche, and Adler and Sullivan – nearly all of whom had some architectural training in France while at the same time remaining committed to creating an original American style. Technological and economic developments were feeding this growth. Between the Philadelphia Centennial Exhibition of 1876 and the Columbian Exposition in Chicago in 1893, the United States in many ways came of age as a country, and was rivaling Great Britain and Germany in terms of industrial production. The accompanying bravado, too, would soon foster a few unique and sizable American architectural talents.

26 HENRY HUDSON HOLLY
from "Modern Dwellings: Their Construction, Decoration, and Furniture" (1876)

Within the tradition of such pattern-book writers as Alexander Jackson Downing and Calvert Vaux fall the efforts of Henry Hudson Holly. This New York City architect first became a champion of American design with *Holly's Country Seats*, which appeared in 1863 in the middle of the Civil War. Holly had long been attracted to English architecture and to the picturesque movement in particular, and though he spoke of the need for a uniquely American architecture he, like Downing before him, was heavily dependent on English examples for his models. In this particular essay of 1876 – the first in a series of articles for *Harper's New Monthly Magazine* – Holly again pleads for the need for a vernacular style for the young country, but once again he follows up by recounting the latest fashion from Britain, the Queen-Anne movement, which he feels is superior to the Gothic style. This passage nevertheless underscores the desire of many American architects to pay lip service, at least, to the creation of a new American style, even if this meant a tentative importation of ideas from abroad. Holly's magazine articles were later collected and appeared under the title *Modern Dwellings in Town and Country Adapted to American Wants and Climate* (1878).

In this way we are doubtless building up an architecture of our own, profiting, as other founders of styles have done, by precedents in older countries. Our materials, climate, and habits differ enough from those of Europe to demand a distinctive change in their use and arrangement. For example, in European countries, wood, a most valuable building material, is rare and expensive, while in most sections of our own it is very abundant. But instead of

Henry Hudson Holly, from "Modern Dwellings: Their Construction, Decoration, and Furniture," in *Harper's New Monthly Magazine* 52 (December 1875–May 1876), pp. 855–6.

using this in accordance with its nature and capacities, we have stupidly employed it in copying, as exactly as we can, details of foreign architecture which were designed with reference to the constructive capacities of brick and stone. Hence we see rounded arches, keystones, and buttresses of wood; wood siding is sanded and blocked off to represent stone; and the prosperous American citizen with a taste for feudal castles, like Horace Walpole, may live and see three sets of his own turrets decay. Fortunately our people are beginning to recognize the folly of such unmeaning shams, and when stone or brick is adopted, it is treated as such; and when wood is employed, we are properly commencing to show details adapted to its nature. Until, however, we come to possess a vernacular style, we must content ourselves with copying; and the question arises, Which of the innumerable systems is best suited to our requirements? [. . .]

But the Gothic revival, started by the masterly hand of Pugin, glorified and made national by such men as Street and Ruskin, seemed to have decided the matter, and both England and America have rested with unmolested satisfaction for the past half-century until within the last three years, when suddenly it has been discovered that the Gothic, however well adapted to ecclesiastical purposes, is lacking in essential points for domestic use; and Norman Shaw, J. J. Stevenson, and others have openly advocated the heresy. Their argument was that the Gothic meant the development of the arched construction in the pointed work, vaulting, and traceried windows, and that while these features were suited to churches and great halls, they were unfitted for modern domestic structures, divided as they are into comparatively low stories; therefore that even in the dwellings of the Middle Ages, when this style reached its highest perfection, its characteristic features could not be displayed. In fact, Gothic architecture was not originally intended to meet domestic wants.

These writers, then, exempt themselves from a slavish conformity to the Gothic, admirable as it may be in its proper sphere on the ground that it is manifestly inadequate to meet all modern requirements. One of the principles upon which the promoters of the Gothic revival insisted with energy and eloquence was *"truth in architecture"* – that the construction should not be hidden under some fair-seeming mask, which had no affinity with it, and often represented something very different from it, but should be made apparent, and the basis of whatever adornment should be employed. But these new reformers say that truth is not the peculiar possession of Gothic architecture; and, indeed, *modern* Gothic has often found the temptations of an age that loves to be deceived too strong for it, and has fallen into the errors of the system it has attempted to replace. What, then, do they propose as a substitute for this in domestic architecture? They claim that in what is loosely called the "Queen Anne" style we find the most simple mode of honest English building worked out in an artistic and natural form, fitting with the sash windows and ordinary doorways, which express real domestic needs (of which it is the outcome), and so in our house building conserving truth far more effectively than can be done with the Gothic.

27 ROBERT SWAIN PEABODY
from "Georgian Homes of New England" (1877)

Robert Swain Peabody was one-half of the highly successful Boston firm of Peabody and Stearns. A native of Bedford, Massachusetts, Peabody attended Harvard University before taking his architectural training in Paris at the École des Beaux-Arts and in the office of Ware and Van Brunt. In 1870 he formed a successful partnership with John Stearns. Although the firm's designs for larger buildings often reflected Peabody's Beaux-Arts training, its houses were much more relaxed and influenced by British developments, and in keeping with the American idea of a Shingle style. This relatively early essay of Peabody, written in the aftermath of the 1876 Philadelphia Centennial Exhibition, responds at least in part to Holly's penchant for the Queen Anne, and it becomes the first instance of the American "Georgian," or American architecture from the colonial period, being proposed as a model – a source of inspiration almost chronologically paralleling the Queen Anne in England.

The English Queen Anne designers have a way of justifying their many vagaries as follows. They say: In the seventeenth century men had rather ceased to think of style. Classical detail as introduced in Renaissance days had become completely naturalized, and gradually it had ceased to be used in a servile way, or with great regard for precedent; but it simply made things seem attractive without much thought of purity of style, or style at all. Following this came the successive revivals, – of Palladian art, then of Grecian work, then of all the phases of Gothic, – all these lifeless imitations of the antique. From this study of archaeology the Queen Anne men profess to rebel, and to turn to the point where our art was before all this direct imitation of obsolete forms began. They find more of the spirit of independence and carelessness for precedent which they seek for in the work of the seventeenth century than elsewhere; so they study and work on that basis, but are ready to combine any thing with it which is attractive. They say they have red bricks and white mortar for their walls, tiles for their roofs, and white sash frames for their windows; and of these the house shall be made.

All this sounds like good reasoning, although in practice the antiquarian spirit makes the movement seem much like other revivals. In fact, we really know that reasoning is not at the bottom of it at all, but that Mr. Norman Shaw and others like him admired and studied and sketched all the quaint old work they could find, and that this work enlivened by their talent has set a quietly imitated example to other designers. If we follow their lead without any native Jacobean or Queen Anne models of importance to inspire us, we shall but be adding one more fashion to our already rather long list. A neo-Jacobean table can join the Eastlake chairs, the American rococo mantel, and the Puginesque sideboard in our dining-rooms; but there is nothing in this but an additional fashion. Now, however, that this wave is felt along our shores, can it not be directed into more fitting channels here even than it has worn for itself in England? We too have had our revivals; and if we go behind them we find in the Georgian days men working without thought of style, simply, delicately, beautifully. Many

Robert Swain Peabody, from "Georgian Homes of New England," in *The American Architect and Building News* II (1877), p. 338.

a choice wooden cornice, many a stiff mantel in our farm-houses, attest to this. Plancia, fascia, and soffit still are Yankee words in spite of our mediaeval period. With our Centennial year have we not discovered that we too have a past worthy of study? – a study, too, which we can subsequently explain and defend by all the ingenious Queen Anne arguments, strengthened by the fact that our colonial work is our only native source of antiquarian study and inspiration.

28 CLARENCE COOK
from *The House Beautiful* (1877)

The architectural pattern books that proliferated in the 1850s and 1860s were followed in the 1870s by a spate of American books devoted to the relatively new field of interior design. And in the forefront of this new movement was Clarence Cook, a long-time journalist for the *New York Tribune* with a keen eye for trends abroad. In writing his essays for *Scribner's Monthly* magazine in the 1870s, Cook was following the lead of the British writer Charles Eastlake, whose *Hints on Household Taste* (first appearing in London in 1868, and in an American edition in 1872) was one of the first primers of interior design directed to the middle class. Both Eastlake and Cook are sometimes associated with the "aesthetic movement," that is, as reformers reacting to the entrenched Victorian taste of the middle decades of the nineteenth century. Adherents to the aesthetic movement included the American artist James Whistler (living in London) and Louis Comfort Tiffany, who first gained success as an interior designer in the early 1880s. Cook, however, was of a more practical bent and he was preaching the ethic of good taste in a simple and straightforward manner.

Among the smaller facts that must be taken note of in drawing the portrait of these times is the interest a great many people feel in everything that is written on the subjects of house-building and house-furnishing. There never was a time when so many books written for the purpose of bringing the subject of architecture – its history, its theory, its practice – down to the level of the popular understanding, were produced as in this time of ours. And, from the house itself, we are now set to thinking and theorizing about the dress and decoration of our rooms: how best to make them comfortable and handsome; and books are written, and magazine and newspaper articles, to the end that on a matter which concerns everybody, everybody may know what is the latest word.
[. . .]
    The best plan is to know first, as near as may be, how we ought to live externally, and then to surround ourselves with the things best suited for that mode of life, whatever it may be. This, however, commonplace as it sounds, is so seldom done, that it must be thought a thing extremely difficult to do. Look about you, reader, and ask yourself, how many people you know who live as they really like to live, and let the world go by. There are such people. I know such in my own circle, but there are not many of them, and it certainly is not the way of the world at large. But, whoever will try the experiment will find the reward in peace, and serenity, and real comfort, so abounding, that it will be no longer a query with him whether

Clarence Cook, from *The House Beautiful: Essays on Beds and Tables, Stools and Candlesticks* (1877). New York: Charles Scribner's Sons, 1895, pp. 19, 20.

he shall continue it or not. And he will find that the question of furniture will disappear from the catalogue of vexations, because there is always provision in the world for every reasonable want. Every country, too, has its own models, and was at one time satisfied with its own – that is, the mass of the people were satisfied, though in every country, at all times, the rich have preferred something borrowed and exotic.

> "I would give thilke Morpheus
> *   *   *   *   *
> If he woll make me sleepe alite,
> Of downe of pure doves white
> I woll give him a feather bed,
> Raied with gold, and right well cled
> In fine black sattin *d'outremere*;
> And many a pillow, and every bere,
> Of *cloth of raines* to slepe on soft,
> Him there not need to turne oft."

Their satins must come from over seas, and homespun will not do, but they must go for cloth to some foreign town of Rennes, else they cannot rest in their beds. But the charm of every house is to find the people in it self-contained, and taking their pleasure and their comfort where they can, in the things that come to them, rather in what they have had to seek painfully and far.

29 LEOPOLD EIDLITZ
from *The Nature and Function of Art: More Especially of Architecture* (1881)

The American Transcendental movement – the legacy of Ralph Waldo Emerson and Henry David Thoreau – continued to flourish in the second half of the nineteenth century but along a somewhat different course. Among those enthused by its powerful spiritual inspiration was Leopold Eidlitz, one of the more underappreciated architects of the century. Eidlitz was born in Prague and trained in Vienna, before he immigrated to the United States in the 1840s. There he became one of the first practitioners of the Germanic *Rundbogen* (rounded-arch) style, which was a functionally oriented reform movement emanating from Heinrich Hübsch and Friedrich von Gärtner. But Eidlitz's ideas were also evolving. He was drawn to philosophical issues, and he combined his interest in Emerson with German Romantic idealism and the recent development of German psychological aesthetics (see next

Leopold Eidlitz, from *The Nature and Function of Art: More Especially of Architecture*. New York: A. C. Armstrong & Son, 1881, pp. 223–4.

section). The result – following Horatio Greenough – was an involved organic theory of architecture and another formulation of the form-follows-function thesis. Architecture, for Eidlitz, was a highly expressive art, and like all human expression it must also be a truthful expression.

We find in nature that the human frame does mechanical work, sometimes with the labor of the carrier of burdens, and then again with the ease of the athlete. It is these gradations of ease, grace, directness, and expression with which labor is performed, or with which mechanical work is done by the human frame, which furnish to the architect the elements of art expression in his structures.

Like the elements of all natural combinations which serve the purpose of artistic or natural expression, they are but few in number, but capable of an infinite series of artistic combinations.

When we enumerate strength, elegance, and repose, we have probably stated the whole range of the architectural gamut; but if we consider that each of these qualities may be endowed with an endless range of quantity, we can readily imagine that these mechanical conditions of matter may express endless varieties of ideas, from the dungeon keep to the tabernacle which contains the Sacraments in the church of St. Laurence at Nuremberg.

All natural organisms are possessed of the mechanical ability to perform certain functions. This ability we find more or less clearly expressed in their forms as a whole, or in their crystallization. In this way they convey to the mind an expression of these functions, and thus they tell the story of their being. The architect, in imitation of this natural condition of matter, so models his forms that they also tell the story of their functions; and these functions are always mechanical conditions of strength, elegance, and repose, in combinations of various quantities of these properties. The fundamental principle of the modelling of architectural forms is therefore mechanical.

30 LOUIS SULLIVAN
from "Characteristics and Tendencies of American Architecture" (1885)

The transcendental legacy that moved Eidlitz acquired another energetic devotee in the 1880s in the person of Louis Sullivan. The architect was born in Boston, and briefly trained at the Massachusetts Institute of Technology and in the Philadelphia office of Frank Furness. The economic Panic of 1873 ended his job there and he migrated to Chicago, where he joined the office of William Le Baron Jenney. Another brief period of training at the École des Beaux-Arts in Paris concluded his formal training. In 1880, back in Chicago, he joined the office of Dankmar Adler, but their celebrated partnership was not formed until 1883, and Sullivan's better designs would not appear until the 1890s. Thus the decade of the 1880s was still a period of intellectual fermentation for the romantically inclined ornamentalist, as he immersed himself in the writings of Emerson and Whitman and struggled

Louis Sullivan, from "Characteristics and Tendencies of American Architecture," in *The Inland Architect and Builder* VI:5 (November 1885), pp. 58–9.

with the question of how modern architects could create a new American style. The issue was intensely considered during this period in Chicago and Sullivan's address to the Western Association of Architects meeting in Saint Louis in 1885 becomes historically important as an initial contribution to the debate.

The ability to develop elementary ideas organically is not conspicuous in our profession. In this respect, the architect is inferior to the business man and financier, whose capacity to expand a simple congenial idea once fixed, into subtle, manifold and consistent ramifications, is admirable, and a shining example which we have often ignored, creating thereby an undesirable impression.

This view leads us to a consideration of the element of power. Until this element is widely introduced into our work, giving it the impress of brilliancy, intuition and great depth of feeling, that work, exhaustively considered, will remain but little more than a temporary expedient.

The presence of power, as a mental characteristic in one class of our people, augurs well for the belief that it may pervade our ranks. The beginnings of power are usually so crude and harsh as to be revolting to a refined taste, and hence it is instinctively shunned; but once subtilized, flushed with emotion and guided by clear insight, it is a worker of miracles. Responsive to its ardent wooings, Nature yields up her poetic secrets.

We surely have in us the germ of artistic greatness. No people on earth possessing more of innate poetic feeling, more of ideality, greater capacity to adore the beautiful, than our own people; but architects, as a professional class, have held it more expedient to maintain the traditions of their culture than to promulgate vitalizing thought. Here, then, we are weak, and should sentiment gain a pronounced ascendency, we may remain weak.

On us rests partially the responsibility, and partially on the public. We have at times individually sought to lead the public, when we, more wisely, should have followed it, and have, as a body, often followed, when, with beneficent results, we could have led. While we may compromise for a time, through a process of local adaptation, no architectural style can become a finality than runs counter to popular feeling. The desire at once to follow and to lead the public should be the initial attitude of our profession toward the formation of a national style. For while we conduct the technical operations, the shaping and controlling process is mainly in the hands of the public, who are constantly watching us, constantly criticising us, and constantly keeping us within bounds. We cannot wholly escape this control while we are without a national architecture fully representing the wishes of the public, and ministering to its conceptions of the beautiful and the useful. This can evidently not come to pass forthwith, for the public itself can only partially and imperfectly state its wants. Responding readily, however, to the intuition of those who anticipate its desires, it accepts provisionally, year by year, all the satisfaction it can get, so that while one recognized style after another shall pass through our hands to be tried and finally rejected in the search for permanent satisfaction, a modified residuum from each will doubtless be added to a fund representing our growth in emotional and spiritual wealth. The progress of this growth toward consummation in a national style involves the lives of many generations, and need be of but little practical concern to us of today. We work at short range and for immediate results. Perhaps, however, there would be infused into our profession an abiding *esprit de corps*, should consideration of this subject and its associated themes lead to a substantial agreement upon our status, our tendencies and our policy.

If the conclusions set forth in this paper be accepted as correct, it becomes clearly evident, however, that the formative beginnings of this national style, now in progress, are of the utmost immediate interest to us, in part through feelings of patriotism, in part because of a surmise that those who approach most nearly in the substance of their work and administration to the qualities inherent to our race and potential to a national style, will come nearest to the hearts of our people.

Harassed though the architect may be, by the cares and responsibilities of his daily life, there exists nevertheless within him, in the midst of this turmoil, an insuppressible yearning toward ideals. These delicate promptings should be both protected and nourished, that, like the flowering plants springing by the sun's gentle persuasion from little seeds buried in the coarser elements of the soil, they also, because of the warmth of human feeling, may bloom at times by the wayside, yielding refreshing odors and the joy of color to the plodding wayfarer.

The soft beams of the full-orbed moon fall with pathetic caress upon the slumbering life of the world; paling with the dawn, her tender vigil ended, she melts into the infinite depths when the ruddy herald of day proudly summons the workers. So does the soul watch over its greater ideals until the thrilling radiance of power shall awaken them to action.

Ideal thought and effective action should so compose the vital substance of our works that they may live with us and after us, as a record of our fitness, and a memorial of the good we may have done. Then, in the affluence of time, when a rich burden of aspiring verdure may flourish in the undulating fields of thought, wrought into fertility through the bounty of nature and the energy of the race, the mellowed spontaneity of a national style, reaching its full and perfect fruition, shall have come from out the very treasury of nature.

31   GEORGE WILLIAM SHELDON
from *Artistic Country-Seats* (1886)

Like Clarence Cook, George Sheldon was a critic for a New York newspaper. He was, in addition, a prolific writer on artistic themes and the author of numerous books on the state of American art. He first ventured into architecture with his *Artistic Houses* (1883–4), a profuse compendium of 203 photographs that documented the interiors of some of the more lavish American estates. In his follow-up *Artistic Country-Seats*, he turned to home exteriors and, as fortune would have it, documented American residential architecture at the moment it was achieving its first great flowering, under the lead of such talented designers as Peabody and Sterns, Bruce Price, Stanford White, and William R. Emerson. The house of Mary F. Stoughton in Cambridge, Massachusetts, designed by Henry Hobson Richardson in 1883, was once lauded by Vincent J. Scully as "perhaps, the best suburban wooden house in America." Sheldon's more modest description of the design nevertheless fully recognizes its architectural importance. It was an early manifestation of the mature "Shingle Style" – the fulfillment of the legacy of Alexander Jackson Davis and Andrew Jackson Downing.

George William Sheldon, from *Artistic Country-Seats: Types of Recent American Villa and Cottage Architecture*. New York: D. Appleton & Co., 1886, p. 157.

One of the simplest private residences designed by the late Henry Hobson Richardson is Mrs. STOUGHTON's cottage, in Cambridge, Massachusetts; and few cottages of equal dimensions were ever planned, in this country or abroad, which show better results in point of convenience, spaciousness, and architectural purity. The architect has used on the external walls, as well as on the roofs, cypress shingles of a size somewhat larger than usual, and has caused them to be painted a deep olive-green. The hall runs through the center of the building, and on the left are the parlor and library, and on the right the dining-room, with kitchen, china-closet, and pantry adjoining. The finishing of the interior is in harmony with the simplicity of the exterior, and the effect is that of a comfortable country-house, without ostentation, and yet at the same time with a pervasive and stimulating sense of the organizing presence of an artist.

When Mr. Richardson built this house, he set the style, so to speak, for many other country-houses; and since its erection, the use of shingles instead of clapboards has greatly increased, while the entire absence of all frivolous ornamentation of scroll-work, and other souvenirs of the "Vernacular" architecture of former years, set hundreds of architects to thinking; and if any one will compare it with the country-house built for Mr. Frederick L. Ames, at North Easton, Massachusetts, in 1859, he will note to what extent Mr. Richardson's own taste was capable of change.

32 JOHN ROOT ET AL.
from "What Are the Present Tendencies of Architectural Design in America?" (1887)

A symposium was sponsored by the Illinois Association of Architects on March 5, 1887, in which the above question was posed to the attendees. John Root, whose masterful design for the Rookery was nearing completion, delivered a short lecture on the theme, which was followed by both prepared and non-prepared responses to Root's remarks. Among those participating were Dankmar Adler, Clarence L. Stiles, W. W. Boyington, Louis Sullivan, and Frederick Baumann. The discussion about style reflects the fermentation underway, as the outlines of a Chicago commercial style of building were indeed taking shape. The reference of Baumann to the theory of Gottfried Semper reflects the influence of this theorist making its way into Chicago through the large community of German émigrés in the city.

John Root et al., from "What Are the Present Tendencies of Architectural Design in America?," in *The Inland Architect and News Record* 9:3 (March 1887), pp. 23–4, 26.

JOHN W. ROOT

[. . .]

Probably in no age was it so difficult to determine such a question as now. All movements are now so rapid; thought is so lightning-like, so rapidly changing; transmission of ideas and news is so instantaneous that each one of us today realizes, not only the accomplishments of all other men, but is enabled, within limits, to think their very thoughts. The consequence of this is, that we are somewhat like Sancho Panza, in that many of the dishes thus rapidly presented to our lips must be taken away untasted; while much of the pabulum with which we load our stomachs remains unassimilated.

Before every one of us has passed a kaleidoscopic panorama of styles, for whose original development three thousand years were required. To what extent may we call any of these rapidly dissolving architectural impressions our own? To what extent will architects of today leave enduring impressions upon any one of the various styles in which they have rendered their buildings? Note some of the changes of the last twenty years. Nowhere today do we find academic productions in Neo-Grec so common a decade since; nowhere those pseudo Gothic designs, to whose production were consecrated the talents of Burges and Street and Scott. In high stays, and crisp, unyielding ruffs, Queen Anne has taken coach and driven off, and now only the rumble of her distant wheels, and the lingering perfume of her lavender remain; the Neo-Jacobean has lost its royal state; the Dutch have come to London, and, like William of Orange, holds silent sway in Cadogan square; here in America the present vogue is a style called "Romanesque."

In recalling this series of swift changes we can but ask, "What in heaven's name are the present tendencies of architectural design in the world? What are they in America?"

In striving to reach some answer to this question, we will find it useless to waste time over the great mass of imitations, or the host of mere imitators. In no one of these quickly born and quickly dead art movements has anything been vitally done by the heedless throng who blindly followed the masters of their school. In each case the first apostle has made converts, among whom were a few, not content with the study of his work alone, but who went back to those original sources from which their master gained inspiration. These have added to the permanent value of his work. But how few have been their number. The vast mass of converts have been satisfied to follow where he led, to repeat what he has said, to devote lives to that mere industry of pencil which covered original and strong work with the killing vine of meaningless affectation.

Thus, in the so-called Romanesque work of today, how much comes freshly studied from France, and how much from New England? Which are commoner sources of modern inspiration, Ste. Croix, in Bordeaux, or Trinity Church, in Boston? St. Pierre, in Angoulême, or Harvard Law School? To the really creative minds of our day, and to those students whom they have inspired to imitate, but not copy them, must we look for the tendencies of our day. In considering these men and their work, we may see reflected in them something of the influences operating upon architecture in America. The creative artist must always be a man in whom are especially focalized these influences, which are different from those which move other men of his time, not in kind; but in degree alone. Thus, in one such man will be manifestations, not only through his work; but through the mere attitude of his mind, which will clearly indicate what forces are in play about him.

But apart from questions of architectural styles, as commonly understood, and quite distinct from the study of examples in these styles, or of the men who revived them, are considerations of national characteristics in non-architectural directions. These will, perhaps, after all, give us the best answer to what American architecture must soon be, and therefore what its present tendencies are. Judged by the character of the American people, in as far as this character has been developed, some qualities which we may assume of American architecture will be:

First. It will be *Catholic*. The American people do not tend toward narrow views of things, nor have they yet developed sufficient conservatism to retain things merely because they exist. They rather tend to the adoption of any new thing, provided it merely seem better than the old, which often leads to a too sudden abandonment of older modes, cutting off slow and yet promising developments, and inflicting the newer fashion with certain harshness and crudity. What conservatism the nation may acquire when it is older is wide of the question. It is the present condition which is creating the architectural tendencies we are striving to discover; and these conditions being what they are, it does not seem that there is immediate prospect of a single national style, or of adherence to single lines of development. On the contrary, it seems more likely that each architectural style will, in its turn, be taken and Americanized, – that is acclimatized and modified by local conditions.

Second. It will be *Grave*. No student of the American people can doubt their essential gravity. Even their humor is often a mere cover for an underlying seriousness, and the sober view of things is frequently disguised beneath what, to the careless observer, seems a trifling jest. Though Americans are really grave, the gravity is not of a somber sort, nor of the quality which marks our English brother. The gravity, essentially American, has a humorous complement, strongly marked, which will give to the architecture of the future a certain *Lightness*. This lightness may, in certain buildings, express itself in grace of detail, or in delicacy of parts, or in occasional touches of fancy or even *whimsicalness*. But underlying this lightness will still remain the essential and national gravity.

Third. Our architecture will probably remain *Practical*.

This means not only that structures of purely decorative character will be few in number, but that each important detail of a building must have some immediate, easily recognized and practical use. This is made likely by the strength in American character of the "commercial instinct, which involuntarily shrinks from what it considers a 'waste of money.'" Not that Americans are mean, for they are on the contrary, generous; but it is to be feared that long time must pass before we will as a nation, consider with equanimity large expenditures for buildings whose sole function is æsthetical, and whose sole beauty is to make the public mind more sensitive to beauty. At the same time there will come in America, and that very soon, an architecture of the greatest splendor.

The tremendous and rapidly acquired wealth, not only of individuals, but of the nation as a whole, coupled as it is by no national indifference to display, and by no national parsimony, will inevitably lead to the erection of buildings, both of private, commercial and public character, whose splendor will be phenomenal in the history of the world. We see many indications of this even now, not only in the magnificent palaces erected as dwellings for millionaires, but in the gorgeous trade-palaces which have already become typically American.

Thus, we may assume that architecture tends today in several widely different directions: toward *Catholicity*, toward *Gravity*, with its modifying *Grace*, toward *Utility*, and toward

Splendor. Other tendencies there are, arising from the tastes and needs of that chief element in all republics, the vast middle class; but this class is with us so unstable, so quickly passing from a middle state to great wealth or great poverty, so influenced by boundless ambition which seems to be cognizant of all possibilities; so imitative in cheap ways of the splendor of great wealth, that these tendencies seem difficult to estimate.

DANKMAR ADLER

[...]

The truly good features of the higher class of buildings cannot be effaced in reproduction, while the meretriciousness and "whimsicalness" that may be found in buildings upon which large sums of money have been expended, and which in such buildings may derive from their association with better work, and execution in the best material, and with the best workmanship, a certain dignity of effect which, when imitated in cheaper buildings, in cheaper materials, in inferior workmanship, become grotesque, and carry with them their own condemnation – a condemnation which will then reflect upon their prototype in better buildings. The danger, therefore, of finding salient features of good buildings travestied and caricatured in inferior structures, will make the projectors and designers of the better buildings all the more careful to exclude from them all features that are not subject to this danger.

I therefore believe that to the tendencies of modern American architecture enumerated by Mr. Root, there should be added another, namely, that of the gradual elimination of all whimsical and trivial features.

CLARENCE L. STILKS

[...]

Taking into consideration the acknowledged lack of conservatism and the independence of American thought, may not the formation of a distinctively American architecture be among the possibilities of the near future? By this is meant an order or style which shall be the outgrowth of American thought and feeling, and the result of conditions under which that thought and feeling has been developed. Not an American edition of any existing style, not even a combination of them, but a style of architecture which shall be as distinctive as any of the already recognized styles of other countries.

[...]

DISCUSSION

[...]

Mr. Baumann said that he thought *utility* one of the most salient points, and that it had not been as fully emphasized as it ought to be; that in this modern age *utility* was the true base of architectural art. We have spoken of *style*. What do we call style? What is style in architecture? He concluded by quoting from Professor Gottfried Semper, the great German architect, in his work published on the subject: *"Stile ist die Uebereinstimmung eines Bauwerkes mit den Bedingungen seines Enstehens"* – Style is the coincidence of a structure with the conditions of its origin.

Mr. Sullivan: I think we are starting at the wrong end entirely. We are taking the results of what has already passed, examining on the surface, and from that are searching for the source of impulse. I do not believe the origin of style is outside, but within ourselves, and the man who has not the impulse within him will not have the style. But the more he thinks, the more he reflects, observes and assimilates, the more style he will have. So, therefore, it seems to me that the eventual outcome of our American architecture will be the emanation of what is going on inside of us at present, the character and quality of our thoughts and our observations, and above all, our reflections. If I were to forecast the outcome of American architecture I should search for it by the study of my own generation; not by studying the architecture of the past. We are in a vast ferment at present, and like most of them, the top of the liquor is covered with scum, but the real process is down below; and it is from this gradual clarifying of the fermentation of thought that the style will result, but the impulse must come first. Therefore, I think that to arrive at the style it is a great deal more important that we should be good observers and good reflectors rather than good draughtsmen.

33 MARIANA GRISWOLD VAN RENSSELAER
from *Henry Hobson Richardson and His Works* (1888)

A lthough H. H. Richardson's residential designs were highly influential, this architectural genius was best known within Chicago architectural circles by the design of his "Field Building," also known as the Marshall Field Wholesale Store, designed and erected in Chicago between 1885 and 1887. Here Richardson strengthened his earlier style with a more Spartan character and reduced the volume to a rectangular block enlivened with a rhythmic sequence of arched and flat openings. The building particularly impressed Louis Sullivan, and is often credited with advancing him toward his mature style, as seen first in his Auditorium Building, Chicago (1887–90). Richardson's Field Building impressed others as well, including Richardson's first biographer, Mariana Griswold Van Rensselaer. For many years she had excelled as a literary critic, but in the mid-1880s she turned her attention to architecture and produced her series "Recent American Architecture" for *Century Magazine*. Her biography of Richardson, published two years after his death, is a masterpiece of facts and analysis, so much so that she was made an honorary member of the American Institute of Architects in 1890.

Mariana Griswold Van Rensselaer, from *Henry Hobson Richardson and His Works* (1888). Reprint edition, New York: Dover Publications, 1969, p. 97.

The Field Building is the vast rectangular box in its most uncompromising estate. The site measures three hundred and twenty-five feet by one hundred and ninety feet, and every foot of it is covered by a solid mass which rises to a height of one hundred and twenty-five feet. The roof is invisible, the doorways are inconspicuous, and decoration is very sparingly used. The whole effect depends upon the structure of the walls themselves. No building could more frankly express its purpose or be more self-denying in the use of ornament. Yet the most elaborately massed, diversified, and decorated structure could not be more truly a design; and its prime virtues of a solidity commensurate with its elevation and a dignity equal to its bulk are secured in such a way that even a high degree of beauty is not wanting. The material is fine in color – red sandstone in the upper parts and red Missouri granite in the lower. The tone of the two differs only slightly, but they are unlike, of course, in quality and are differently finished – the sandstone is cut and the granite is rock-faced. Each detail of the reticent sculptured decoration tells strongly against the general severity, and the hand of a careful, skillful artist is as plainly visible in that varied disposition of the plain units of construction which gives interest to every foot of the surface. It is visible, too, in the beautiful profile of the angles, and in that alternation of heavier with lighter piers which inconspicuously yet effectively relieves the monotony of the upper range of windows. In short, this vast, plain building is as carefully studied as the smallest and most elaborate could be, and is a text-book of instruction in treatment no less than in composition.

34   FRIEDRICH BAUMANN
from "Thoughts on Architecture" (1889)

Baumann's remarks regarding Gottfried Semper earlier in this section are echoed in this address delivered before the American Institute of Architects convention in October 1889 in Washington, DC. Baumann at this time was a senior fellow with the Institute. He had emigrated from Germany to Chicago in 1851, and had built much in the city before the great fire of 1871. In 1873 he published a very important structural manual on footings in Chicago's loamy soil, and he was again quite active in the style discussions of the late 1880s. What makes this particular reiteration of Semper's "dressing" or "curtain" thesis so interesting is its coincidence with the evolving notion of a curtain wall. The question of whether theory was influencing practice or practice theory has no clear answer.

Architecture has its own special language. Its works narrate their history. Were this possible in a language which has not been transmitted from generation to generation?

Architectural construction, according to Semper, bases on four constituent parts: The fireside as center; the protecting roof; the circumvallation; the substruction. From these originally very modest parts the temple bases its origin. It starts with the simplest wood to become the finest marble structure. The sacredness of the purpose demanded the

Friedrich Baumann, "Thoughts on Architecture," from "Thoughts on Style," in *The Inland Architect and News Record* XVI:5 (November 1890), p. 59.

best material at command. And this did not suffice. Even the finest and at the time the most appreciated of wood materials, the cedar of Lebanon, had to be ornamented and wholly covered with metal, precious gold not excepted. To this fashion, which must have been at the time thousands of years old, we find the tabernacle gorgeously ornamented as related in scripture.

Its partitions were mere curtains of the most precious kind. This most original fashion of partitioning off was retained by Solomon in the gorgeous construction of his stable temple. Palaces in olden times had partitions merely fashioned in this style. The king was equal at least to a demi-god and was entitled to fashion his domicile accordingly. Even in later times we find partitions thus made. Think of Polonius stabbed by Hamlet when listening behind a partition made of cloth.

But partitions were, with the process of culture, made of solid material. Yet, wherever they thus appear, they are not artistically treated as structural parts. They are decorated in a manner to represent curtains, and at no time become an expressed mechanical element. Do we not at the present day decorate the entire within parts of an edifice exclusively in this fashion?

35 LOUIS SULLIVAN
from "Ornament in Architecture" (1892)

I n the heyday of functionalist thinking in the mid-twentieth century, the first point made by Sullivan in this essay – that a building could be "well formed and comely in the nude" – was generally interpreted as a precocious statement of his later axiom regarding form following function. What was seldom mentioned regarding this essay is the second point made here by Sullivan – that ornamental treatment endows a building both with life and individuality. This point also better characterizes Sullivan's own approach to design in the 1890s, when his most prolific period as an architect was also his most profuse in terms of his ornamentation of the building fabric.

I take it as self-evident that a building, quite devoid of ornament, may convey a noble and dignified sentiment by virtue of mass and proportion. It is not evident to me that ornament can intrinsically heighten these elemental qualities. Why, then, should we use ornament? Is not a noble and simple dignity sufficient? Why should we ask more?

If I answer the question in entire candor, I should say that it would be greatly for our aesthetic good if we should refrain entirely from the use of ornament for a period of years, in order that our thought might concentrate acutely upon the production of buildings well formed and comely in the nude. We should thus perforce eschew many undesirable things, and learn by contrast how effective it is to think in a natural, vigorous and wholesome way.

Louis Sullivan, from "Ornament in Architecture," in *Louis Sullivan: The Public Papers*, ed. Robert Twombly. Chicago: University of Chicago Press, 1988, pp. 80–1.

This step taken, we might safely inquire to what extent a decorative application of ornament would enhance the beauty of our structures – what new charm it would give them.

If we have then become well grounded in pure and simple forms we will reverse them; we will refrain instinctively from vandalism; we will be loath to do aught that may make these forms less pure, less noble. We shall have learned, however, that ornament is mentally a luxury, not a necessary, for we shall have discerned the limitations as well as the great value of unadorned masses. We have in us romanticism, and feel a craving to express it. We feel intuitively that our strong, athletic and simple forms will carry with natural ease the raiment of which we dream, and that our buildings thus clad in a garment of poetic imagery, half hid as it were in choice products of loom and mine, will appeal with redoubled power, like a sonorous melody overlaid with harmonious voices.

I conceive that a true artist will reason substantially in this way; and that, at the culmination of his powers, he may realize this ideal. I believe that architectural ornament brought forth in this spirit is desirable, because beautiful and inspiring; that ornament brought forth in any other spirit is lacking in the higher possibilities.

That is to say, a building which is truly a work of art (and I consider none other) is in its nature, essence and physical being an emotional expression. This being so, and I feel deeply that it is so, it must have, almost literally, a life. It follows from this living principle that an ornamented structure should be characterized by this quality, namely, that the same emotional impulse shall flow throughout harmoniously into its varied forms of expression – of which, while the mass-composition is the more profound, the decorative ornamentation is the more intense. Yet must both spring from the same source of feeling.

I am aware that a decorated building, designed upon this principle, will require in its creator a high and sustained emotional tension, an organic singleness of idea and purpose maintained to the last. The completed work will tell of this; and if it be designed with sufficient depth of feeling and simplicity of mind, the more intense the heat in which it was conceived, the more serene and noble will it remain forever as a monument of man's eloquence. It is this quality that characterizes the great monuments of the past. It is this certainly that opens a vista toward the future.

To my thinking, however, the mass-composition and the decorative system of a structure such as I have hinted at should be separable from each other only in theory and for purposes of analytical study. I believe, as I have said, that an excellent and beautiful building may be designed that shall bear no ornament whatever; but I believe just as firmly that a decorated structure, harmoniously conceived, well considered, cannot be stripped of its system of ornament without destroying its individuality.

36 MONTGOMERY SCHUYLER
from "Last Words about the World's Fair" (1894)

Among the foremost architectural critics of the late nineteenth century was Montgomery Schuyler, who in 1891 was active in starting the *Architectural Record*. He wrote essays on a range of themes, from Leopold Eidlitz to the Romanesque Revival to Chicago Architecture, but here he turns his eye to the Columbian Exposition in Chicago in 1893. Although later critics, led by Louis Sullivan, strongly criticized the buildings at the Exposition, this was not the impression shared by most architects or observers at the time. Henry Adams, for instance, noted that the exhibition was "the first impression of American thought as a unity," while Charles Eliot Norton, President of Harvard University, saw the "magnificent structures" as producing a "superb effect." Schuyler follows these two men in his praise, but with one very interesting qualification. Earlier in this review he had lauded the buildings (he was critical only of Louis Sullivan's Transportation Building) as "the most admired group of buildings ever erected in this country." In further analysis, he goes on to explain what he means by this statement. He praises the unity of their formal (Renaissance) language, again their magnitude or colossal scale, but above all he lauds their theatricality or power of fanciful illusion. If an embittered Sullivan (in 1924) saw the buildings only as "naked exhibitionism of charlatanry," Schuyler views the spectacle in a quite different and perhaps more revealing light. The effect of the event of 1893 on the collective American psyche, in fact, was not unlike that of the Great Exhibition on the British psyche in 1851. The new inventions, the automobiles, the Bessemer furnaces, the rapidly constructed rows of exhibition palaces – all documented not only a growing industrial and economic might but also the future possibilities of the young country.

There is still another cause for the success of the World's Fair buildings, a cause that contributes more to the effect of them, perhaps, than both the causes we have already set down put together. It is this which at once most completely justifies the architects of the Exposition in the course they have adopted, and goes furthest to render the results of that course ineligible for reproduction or for imitation in the solution of the more ordinary problems of the American architect. The success of the architecture at the World's Fair is not only a success of unity, and a success of magnitude. It is also and very eminently a success of illusion.

What the World's Fair buildings have first of all to tell us, and what they tell equally to a casual glimpse and to a prolonged survey is that they are examples not of work-a-day building, but of holiday building, that the purpose of their erection is festal and temporary, in a word that the display is a display and a triumph of occasional architecture. As Mr. Burnham well described it, it is a "vision" of beauty that he and his co-workers have presented to us, and the description implies, what our recollections confirm, that it is an illusion that has here been provided for our delight. It was the task of the architects to provide the stage-setting for an unexampled spectacle. They have realized in plaster that gives us the illusion

Montgomery Schuyler, from "Last Words about the World's Fair" (1894), in *American Architecture and Other Writings*, ed. William H. Jordy and Ralph Coe. Cambridge, MA: Harvard University Press, 1961, pp. 571–3.

of monumental masonry a painter's dream of Roman architecture. In Turner's fantasias we have its prototype much more nearly than in any actual erection that has ever been seen in the world before. It is the province and privilege of the painter to see visions and of the poet to dream dreams. They are unhampered by material considerations of structure, of material or of cost. They can imagine unrealizable centaurs and dragons, gorgons, hydras and chimeras dire and in turn affect our imaginations with these.

[. . .]

Such a pleasure and such an illusion the architects of Jackson Park have given us. The White City is the most integral, the most extensive, the most illusive piece of scenic architecture that has ever been seen. That is praise enough for its builders, without demanding for them the further praise of having made a useful and important contribution to the development of the architecture of the present, to the preparation of the architecture of the future. This is a praise that is not merely irrelevant to the praise they have won, but incompatible with it. It is essential to the illusion of a fairy city that it should not be an American city of the nineteenth century. It is a seaport on the coast of Bohemia, it is the capital of No Man's Land. It is what you will, so long as you will not take it for an American city of the nineteenth century, nor its architecture for the actual or the possible or even the ideal architecture of such a city. To fall into this confusion was to lose a great part of its charm, that part which consisted in the illusion that the White City was ten thousand miles and a thousand years away from the City of Chicago, and in oblivion of the reality that the two were contiguous and contemporaneous. Those of us who believe that architecture is the correlation of structure and function, that if it is to be real and living and progressive, its forms must be the results of material and construction, sometimes find ourselves reproached with our admiration for these palaces in which this belief is so conspicuously ignored and set at naught. But there is no inconsistency in entertaining at the same time a hearty admiration for the Fair and its builders and the hope of an architecture which in form and detail shall be so widely different from it as superficially to have nothing in common with it. Arcadian architecture is one thing and American architecture is another.

37 LOUIS SULLIVAN
from "Emotional Architecture as Compared with Intellectual" (1894)

I n one of Sullivan's more revealing essays, the architect speaks of intuition, imagination, inspiration, and the "Great Spirit" that should animate the work of the architect. The essay is explicitly pantheistic or Emersonian in its worldview. If the classical and Gothic styles for Sullivan represent the objective and subjective sides of human imagination, the new "Poetic Architecture" now arising shall transcend these limitations and partake of that

Louis Sullivan, from "Emotional Architecture as Compared with Intellectual: A Study in Subjective and Objective," in *The Inland Architect and News Record* 24:4 (November 1894), p. 34.

larger organic wellspring of Nature. This essay strikes to the core of Sullivan's personal philosophy, and it is particularly relevant in that it was written shortly before he began work on the Guaranty Building (1894–5) in Buffalo, NY.

It was a pure, it was a noble art, wherefore we call it classic; but after all it was an apologetic art, for while possessing serenity it lacked the divinely human element of mobility. The Greek never caught the secret of the changing of the seasons, the orderly and complete sequence of their rhythm within the calmly moving year. Nor did this self-same Greek know what we now know of nature's bounty, for music in those days had not been born; this lovely friend, approaching man to man, had not yet begun to bloom as a rose, to exhale its wondrous perfume.

That the Gothic architecture, with somber, ecstatic eye, with its thought far above with Christ in the heavens, seeing but little here below, feverish and overwrought, taking comfort in gardening and plant life, sympathizing deeply with nature's visible forms, evolved a copious and rich variety of incidental expressions, but lacked the unitary comprehension, the absolute consciousness and mastery of pure form that can come alone of unclouded and serene contemplation, of perfect repose and peace of mind.

I believe, in other words, that the Greek knew the statics, the Goth the dynamics of the art, but that neither of them suspected the mobile equilibrium of it – neither of them divined the movement and stability of nature. Failing in this, both have forever fallen short, and must pass away when the true, the *Poetic Architecture* shall arise; that architecture which shall speak with clearness, with eloquence and with warmth of the fullness, the completeness of man's intercourse with nature and with his fellow men.

Moreover, we know, or should by this time know, that human nature has now become too rich in possessions, too well equipped, too magnificently endowed that any architecture hitherto can be said to have hinted at its resources, much less to have exhausted them by anticipation.

It is this consciousness, this pride, that shall be our motive, our friend, philosopher and guide in the beautiful country that stretches so invitingly before us.

In that land, the schools, having found the object of their long, blind searching, shall teach directness, simplicity, naturalness; they shall protect the young against palpable illusion. They shall teach that, while man once invented a process called composition, nature has forever brought forth organisms. They shall encourage the love of nature that wells up in every childish heart, and shall not suppress, shall not stifle the teeming imagination of the young.

They shall teach, as the result of their own bitter experience, that conscious mental effort, that conscious emotionality, are poor mates to breed from, and that true parturition comes of a deep instinctive, subconscious desire. That true art, springing fresh from nature, must have in it, to live, much of the glance of an eye, much of the sound of a voice, much of the life of a life.

That nature is strong, generous, comprehensive, fecund, subtile; that in growth and decadence she continually sets forth the drama of man's life.

That, thro' the rotating seasons, thro' the procession of the years, thro' the march of the centuries, permeating all, sustaining all, there murmurs the still, small voice of a power that holds us in the hollow of its hand.

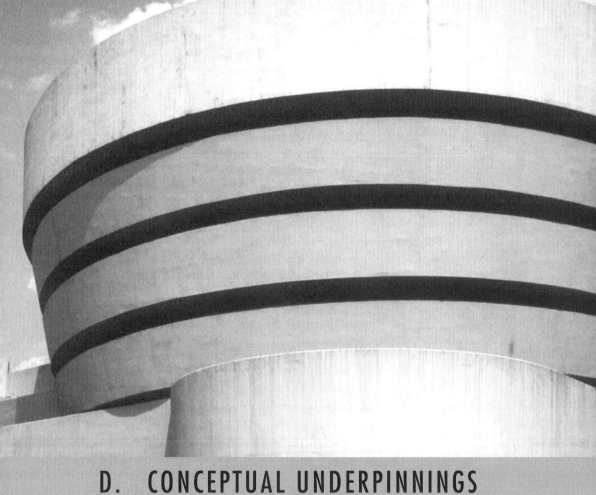

D. CONCEPTUAL UNDERPINNINGS OF GERMAN MODERNISM: SPACE, FORM, AND REALISM

Introduction

Throughout much of the twentieth century, German architectural theory of the last decades of the nineteenth century remained an area virtually untouched by historians. Various reasons led to this vacuum of research. One was the destruction of the German university system (and its famed scholarship) during the 1930s, as nearly every major German art historian of the period fled into exile. Another reason was Germany's military aggression and the massive destruction wrought by World War II, which for many decades made the study of German thought unpopular in both Europe and North America. The result was that most histories of modern architecture were written without citing any Germanic contributions prior to the twentieth century, and even the

German "pioneers" at the start of the century were viewed simply as pioneers, that is, as scouts operating without any prepared intellectual terrain.

A more critical examination of the matter will reveal that just as Britain, France, and North America provided significant contributions to the fostering of an international modern movement, so too did Germanic theory. The German contribution, however, formed somewhat differently and unfolded in three areas. First, there was a particular Germanic fascination (throughout the arts) with psychology and in particular a psychology of form – how the eye and brain perceive and interpret form. Such an approach intuitively strips forms of their symbolic content, where they may then be seen as "pure form" or forms acting without stylistic trappings. This abstraction of form, secondly, leads one to focus on other elements of the architectural experience, such as light and space, which in German architectural theory become other favorite themes of deliberation. The rich German heritage in this regard goes back to Immanuel Kant and German philosophy in general. Thirdly, in Germany – and here we have the legacy of Karl Friedrich Schinkel, Carl Bötticher, and Gottfried Semper – there had also been a long tradition of theorizing about iron as a new building material. This interest, in parallel with theorizing in France, rapidly accelerated in the last three decades of the nineteenth century, as Germany expanded economically and grew into a world power. When these three variables are taken as a whole, it is clear that the so-called German pioneers of the early twentieth century were scarcely pioneers in their formal innovations, but in fact were architects working upon a substantially developed theoretical basis. Saying this another way, there is a quite discernible line of theoretical development in German thought that runs from Karl Friedrich Schinkel through Gottfried Semper to Peter Behrens or Walter Gropius.

38 RICHARD LUCAE
from "On the Aesthetic Development of Iron Construction, especially its Use in Spaces of a Significant Span" (1870)

In Volume I we saw Richard Lucae present a lecture in 1869 on the meaning and significance of space in architecture (229). This address, given to the Berlin Association of Architects in 1870, follows on the same theme, but now frames it specifically with regard to iron. The question posed to the profession is: What are the aesthetic possibilities of iron, and how has the use of the material affected contemporary architecture? Lucae's response is ambivalent. On the one hand, he greatly admired the audacious structural feats of the new material and its roof trusses, as well as the overall spatial effects of "suspension" or "soaring." On the other hand – both conceptually and perceptually – he could not get used to the unfamiliar thinness or slightness of the material. As he notes below, his generation was raised on the aesthetics of stone or mass, that is, forms shaped by superfluous mass. Iron, by virtue of its mathematical precision and economy of form, disallows superfluity and demands in fact a whole

Richard Lucae, from "Über die ästhetische Ausbildung der Eisen-Konstruktionen," trans. Harry Francis Mallgrave, in *Deutsche Bauzeitung* (January 13, 1870), pp. 10–13.

new aesthetics of form. Lucae, however, also realizes that this issue is at heart a generational issue born of visual habits. And like Gottfried Semper, he commends this aesthetic issue to the succeeding generation of younger architects to explore — those who will be raised upon and therefore who will be accustomed to iron's thinner proportions.

If we pose the question of whether the use of iron has until now exerted a decisive influence on the development of our architecture, we cannot unconditionally answer it with a "no," nor can we answer it with a "yes!" Aesthetically, perhaps we can say "no," because I believe that in the nature of iron itself there are a number of factors that make it extraordinarily difficult to treat artistically.

One of its main properties in this regard is the costliness of the material, which in many cases forces us to be content with the least weight for constructional purposes, and this seems to preclude the beauty of mass from the start. For, Gentlemen, as I have remarked earlier in another forum, *the purely mathematical construction is no more a finished artistic result than is the human body with its muscles and ligaments lying open, or even as the skeleton is a living creature of nature*, and therefore I maintain that the beauty of an architectural system is partly due to the fact that there is a surplus of mass beyond the material necessary for support. [. . .]

The second reason why the aesthetic cultivation of iron construction is difficult is the slight corporeality of iron itself. Iron lacks, as it were, the materiality by which we can display beauty, and if we give it greater corporeality than it must have in order to fulfill its functions, then we will not only be lacking in the principles of art but we will also commit an untruth. We improve it (analogous to stone architecture) in suitable places to achieve an art form, but when we do so we rob iron of a characteristic property of its aesthetic appearance that we should protect under all circumstances – namely that it remains delicate and yet must evoke the impression of strength. [. . .]

But the introduction of iron into monumental building in many respects also meets with a prejudice. I will concede the fact, gentlemen, that with our generation the eye must first become accustomed to the new visual proportions related to the use of iron. A succeeding generation that has grown up with iron construction, just as we have grown up with stone construction, will in many cases have that fully undisturbed sense of beauty that still today leaves our generation unfulfilled, because we feel the tradition of beauty so dear to us is under attack.

39 FRIEDRICH NIETZSCHE
from "The Use and Abuse of History" (1872)

I f the nineteenth century can be seen in architectural terms as the century of industrialization – as the power of the machine to redefine or reshape society and its forms – it should also be seen in a complementary sense as the century of history. The second half of the eighteenth century "rediscovered" Greece as the wellspring of Western civilization, but the nineteenth century not only extended the historical panorama to the Middle East, Egypt, and Asia, but it also filled in the details of Western culture by providing the first great histories of the Middle Ages, the Renaissance, and the Baroque periods. The result architecturally was the phenomenon of historicism or the symbolic use or sanctioning of historical forms for contemporary usage – be it a Gothic church or a Neoclassical Parliament building. But this great dependence of history also had its critics, among them the young philosopher Friedrich Nietzsche. In his view, history in the second half of the nineteenth century had become a destructive or inhibiting factor stifling contemporary artistic development and crushing the modern spirit. He wrote this essay at a time when he was still close to the artistic circle of Richard Wagner and Gottfried Semper, but in a forceful way this polemic serves as a mighty declaration of independence from the historical past. The great menaces here are the over-reliance of the present generation on historical models as well as the growing monopoly of the middle-class's "good taste" over artistic matters. The result is the first manifesto to view modernism as an ideological creed.

What is the use to the modern man of this "monumental" contemplation of the past, this preoccupation with the rare and classic? It is the knowledge that the great thing existed and was therefore possible, and so may be possible again. He is heartened on his way; for his doubt in weaker moments, whether his desire is not for the impossible, is struck aside. Suppose one should believe that no more than a hundred men, brought up in the new spirit, efficient and productive, were needed to give the deathblow to the present fashion of education in Germany; he will gather strength from the remembrance that the culture of the Renaissance was raised on the shoulders of such another band of a hundred men.

[. . .]

Consider the simplest and commonest example, the inartistic or half-artistic natures whom a monumental history provides with sword and buckler. They will use the weapons against their hereditary enemies, the great artistic spirits, who alone can learn from that history the one real lesson how to live, and embody what they have learned in noble action. Their way is obstructed, their free air darkened by the idolatrous – and conscientious – dance round the half-understood monument of a great past. "See, that is the true and real art," we seem to hear; "of what use are these aspiring little people of today?" The dancing crowd has apparently the monopoly of "good taste," for the creator is always at a disadvantage compared with the mere onlooker, who never put a hand to the work; just as the armchair politician has ever had more wisdom and foresight than the actual statesman. But if the custom of democratic suffrage and numerical majorities be transferred

Friedrich Nietzsche, from *The Use and Abuse of History* (1872), trans. Adrian Collins. New York: Macmillan, 1967, pp. 14, 16–17.

to the realm of art, and the artist put on his defense before the court of aesthetic dilettanti, you may take your oath on his condemnation; although, or rather because, his judges had proclaimed solemnly the canon of "monumental art," the art that has "had an effect on all ages," according to the official definition. In their eyes there is no need nor inclination nor historical authority for the art which is not yet "monumental" because it is contemporary. Their instinct tells them that art can be slain by art: the monumental will never be reproduced, and the weight of its authority is invoked from the past to make it sure. They are connoisseurs of art primarily because they wish to kill art; they pretend to be physicians when their real idea is to dabble in poisons. They develop their tastes to a point of perversion that they may be able to show a reason for continually rejecting all the nourishing artistic fare that is offered them. For they do not want greatness to arise; their method is to say, "See, the great thing is already here!" In reality they care as little about the great thing that is already here as that which is about to arise; their lives are evidence of that. Monumental history is the cloak under which their hatred of present power and greatness masquerades as an extreme admiration of the past. The real meaning of this way of viewing history is disguised as its opposite; whether they wish it or no, they are acting as though their motto were: "Let the dead bury the – living."

40 ROBERT VISCHER
from "On the Optical Sense-of-Form: A Contribution to Aesthetics" (1873)

The science of psychology was yet another creation of the nineteenth century. Although its roots in Germanic philosophy lay with Immanuel Kant, Arthur Schopenhauer, and above all Johann Friedrich Herbart, it receives a clearer definition as a science in the second half of the century with the appearance of Karl Albert Scherer's *Das Leben des Traums* (The life of the dream, 1861), Eduard von Hartmann's *Philosophie des Unbewussten* (Philosophy of the unconscious, 1869), and Wilhelm Wundt's *Grundzüge der physiologischen Psychologie* (Principles of physiological psychology, 1874). One of the first individuals to apply these new theories to art was Robert Vischer, the son of the noted aesthetician Friedrich Theodor Vischer. The father, in fact, set up the problem in 1866 by discussing the "buoyant life" inherent in architecture: its linear and planar suspension of bodies, the movement of lines rising and falling in space, and its capacity "to express the whole outer and inner life of nations." Robert follows by developing a theory that could be applied to all the visual arts, which he encapsulated under the new concept of *Einfühlung*. Literally "in-feeling," the term is difficult to translate in the sense that Vischer intended, but it is generally rendered by the term "empathy." For Vischer, the concept of empathy is not a casual transference of emotions toward the object of artistic contemplation, but a more thoroughgoing transference of the metaphysical self into the object, that is, a pantheistic urge to merge with the world. The psychological problem, as Vischer first

Robert Vischer, from *Über das optische Formgefühl: Ein Beitrag zur Aesthetik* (1873), trans. Harry Francis Mallgrave and Eleftherios Ikonomou, in *Empathy, Form, and Space: Problems in German Aesthetics, 1873–1893*. Santa Monica, CA: Getty Publication Programs, 1994, pp. 91–2.

formulates it, is how artistic form comes to be perceived as symbolic, how it is that we invest a building, for instance, with certain emotions. His reference to the "association of ideas" of course underscores the affinity of "empathy theory" with earlier picturesque theory. And, like its eighteenth-century counterpart, Vischer's short dissertation would spawn volumes of research that would have a profound effect on architectural thinking.

The term "symbolism of form" was first defined and applied to aesthetics in a systematic way by Karl Köstlin; he based it in particular on the notion of "associations of ideas." The author began his analysis by referring to music, where the aural forms evoke a living, "reminiscent" visualization of "themes," which "in themselves specifically characterize" these (aural) forms, so that upon hearing them "we can believe that we can see and perceive these themes together with the sound" ("sweet, mild" tones are conducive to mental tranquillity). Further, music "indirectly imitates the theme symbolically through allusions to the imagined theme." With regard to spatial phenomena, we are also conscious that "one form can remind us of another, can be a symbol for another form, as when body size becomes a symbol of spiritual greatness, significance, and maturity." "All quantitative characteristics of form recall their corresponding qualitative ones; all sensuous character-istics remind us of the corresponding mental characteristics of form." "Just as the human mind is sufficiently active to be reminded of something by seeing something similar, it is also sufficiently occupied with, directed toward, and conscious of itself to find everywhere resemblances between external things and its own mental states, experiences, sensations [*Empfindungen*], moods, emotions, and passions. It finds in everything a counterpart to itself and a symbol of its humanity."

The longer I concerned myself with this concept of a pure symbolism of form, the more it seemed to me possible to distinguish between ideal associations and a direct merger of the imagination [*Vorstellung*] with objective form. This latter possibility became clear to me with the help of Karl Albert Scherner's book *Das Leben des Traums* (The life of the dream). This profound work, feverishly probing hidden depths, contains a veritable wealth of highly instructive examples that make it possible for any reader who finds himself unsympathetic with the mystical form of the generally abstract passages to arrive at an independent conclusion. Particularly valuable in an aesthetic sense is the section on "Die symbolische Grundformation für die Leibreize" (Symbolic basic formation for bodily stimuli). Here it was shown how the body, in responding to certain stimuli in dreams, objectifies itself in spatial forms. Thus it unconsciously projects its own bodily form – and with this also the soul – into the form of the object. From this I derived the notion that I call "empathy" [*Einfühlung*]. Soon, however, I realized that this notion would only in part explain the symbolism of form, for the effect of light and color, the contour, and the pure line cannot be described by empathy. Here one can only assume a direct continuation of the external sensation into an internal one, a direct mental sublimation of the sensory response. At the same time I became aware of the all-important distinction between sensory and kinesthetic stimuli. I placed this distinction at the head of my basic scheme, from which I distinguished between a sensory "immediate feeling" and a kinesthetic "responsive feeling" – analogously, between a sensory and kinesthetic empathy.

41 CONSTANTIN LIPSIUS
from "On the Aesthetic Treatment of Iron in Tall Buildings" (1878)

As psychology was laying the basis for a new understanding of architectural form, industrialization was advancing forward in the 1870s and defining form in its own way. Among those excited about the new formal and spatial possibilities of iron was Constantin Lipsius, a native of Saxony. Lipsius was trained at the Dresden Academy of Arts under Georg Hermann Nicolai, but he was a self-styled Semperian and in fact wrote an important biography of Semper in which he praised his master's realism. Later, Lipsius was also the architect of the (much underappreciated) Dresden Academy of Fine Arts (1883–94). In 1878 Lipsius delivered a major address to the union of German architects and engineers, in which he picked up the theme earlier raised by Richard Lucae. The talk is a classic expression of the idea that form follows function, but at the same time Lipsius acknowledges that work remains to be done. It also underscores the anxiety of architects who were witnessing the proliferation of new scientific inventions while feeling inadequate to respond architecturally in a way equal to the efficiencies of modern times.

The powerfully developed natural sciences have impressed their signature on our times. Their demands have transformed our living conditions and influenced our views on lives in significant ways. And just as science – metaphysics aside – strives for tangible results, the whole direction of our time is primarily pointed toward the functional. With unswerving energy, we are seeking to deny hindrances contrary to the fulfillment of modern needs; with the aid of the many resources offered by the progressive and exact sciences, we are seeking to overcome the limits of space and time. We see this rather conspicuously and convincingly in the practical uses of physics and chemistry, in the telegraph (mail delivery by air pressure), and in all the utilities that facilitate commerce, such as spectral analysis and the telephone. It is simply astonishing how audaciously and fearlessly the present time acts, ventures, and investigates. Thus we can maintain that there has never been a time that has displayed such a wealth of intelligence in these areas!

Among the technical sciences, engineering powerfully distinguishes itself as a true child of our time. Standing on thoroughly modern and real soil, it is entirely functional in its orientation; it strives with a ruthless logic to create the most naked, relentless truth, leaving aside everything aesthetic to other fields. The slighter the expense of material, the more minimal the dimensions in achieving maximum loads – all the greater the triumph! And because purely technical purpose does not need the clarification of beauty, because its appearance is only the expression of the function that it fulfills, the form has become function. Because its purely purposeful structure finds its self-clarification and its necessity in the construction itself, it is therefore often convincing and to a certain degree aesthetically satisfying. The distinct clarity of a bridge ... with its iron arches spanning free of supports

Constantin Lipsius, from "Ueber die ästhetische Behandlung des Eisens in Hochbau," trans. Harry Francis Mallgrave, in *Deutsche Bauzeitung* 12 (1878), pp. 360–3.

over hundreds of meters, accords us the convincing certainty of its functionality and a certain joy with its victorious overcoming of large difficulties and with the mathematics that calculated the load-bearing capacity of the construction so beautifully in advance.

[...]

And through the use of iron, which in a technical sense allows the wildest dreams of the engineer to become reality and which, as a supported and supporting material, permits roofs and room dimensions of a scale that no previous human generations could have imagined, we now expect talented results in an aesthetic sense, that is, the promise and immediate blossoming of a new, strange art. I am also of the opinion that this material, with its incalculable properties and with its inherent formal laws, will and must be influential in the development of a new architectural style. But the use of a new constructional resource, whose logic in a practical sense is still not fully recognized and become dominant, will not give birth to a new era of architecture without something more. And if Semper thought that architects were unjustifiably blamed for the lack of invention because nowhere had a world-historical idea pursued with force and vigor announced itself, and if he was convinced that if such an idea did appear that someone among the younger colleagues would be capable of giving it a suitable architectural expression – we should still not accept it yet as a positive certainty.

Our view of the world has changed, and the ideas that ruled the world of Rousseau and the French Revolution have fallen into ruins. Yet the dawn of a new art has still not broken. We have sought much, and out of the efforts to impose a past style we have at least gained an understanding of the nature of each style, of making clear what is enduring and transient in them. But just as our time is one of seeking and struggling, so also is our art. A new style cannot be invented overnight. Through the work of generations it forms itself in and with the spiritual content of the time; it is bound to the known and given. [...] And how wrong is the expectation that a new constructional idea can *ex abrupto* be transformed into a finished gown. First and foremost we must learn to understand and grasp the new material in its particularity before we can determine the limits of its aesthetic appearance. And therefore engineers are right when they make the structural functions of iron the object of their investigations, when they construct from a functional perspective. On the basis of these functional experiences with iron, we architects, however, have the task of countering with a formal aesthetic viewpoint.

42 CONRAD FIEDLER
from "Observations on the Nature and History of Architecture" (1878)

I n 1878 the second edition of Gottfried Semper's *Style in the Technical and Tectonic Arts* appeared, which put his great study before a new generation of readers. Conrad Fiedler found himself to be "astounded again and again by his revelations"; at the same time he was puzzled by how a book of such "originality and daring" could be written by an architect whose buildings "tediously wind their way through their historically prescribed course." Fiedler had just published his first important book, *Über die Beruteilung von Werken der bildenden Kunst* (*On judging works of visual art*, 1876), which put forward his psychological theory of "visibility" (*Sichtbarkeit*). With it, Fiedler attempted to upend idealist aesthetics by underscoring the personal or cognitive nature of art, that is, art as a medium that can be understood only through a psychology of perception. When Fiedler read Semper's book, he was attracted to Semper's discussion of the spatial development of Roman architecture (vol. 1, 228). In this review of Semper's study, Fiedler attempts to advance the architect's model by pointing out that not only was "space" a new aspect of Roman architectural development but space, as a conscious idea, was more fully developed during Romanesque times. Thus architects now can escape from the current plague of historicism by studying Romanesque buildings, where "space" emerges for the first time as an abstract component of the design. Architects can thereby dismiss the historicist "dressing" (*Bekleidung*) of walls and explore this new medium for its own creative values, "the new evolution in architecture."

A tendency toward the vertical has often been termed the distinguishing characteristic of medieval architecture, in contrast to a tendency toward the horizontal in the architecture of antiquity. Certainly the structural idea of the Middle Ages was not based on the union of supporting and nonsupporting parts but rather on the possibility (arising from the new structural use of stone) of letting the spatial shell – unified, uninterrupted, coherent – rise from the ground, or rather, letting it be borne by the ground. The vaulting does not seem to be supported by the wall; rather, the walls seem to join together at the crown of the vault; or alternatively, the vault appears to continue through the walls down to the ground. This is the simple starting point of the new evolution in architecture.

The earliest Romanesque buildings, preserved only in their vaulted crypts, convey the impression that the new idea of spatial enclosure had as yet taken only a very rudimentary form; the few articulations of form are unwieldy and awkward, and the massive material seems to have been reluctant to accept even the most general features of the new formulation. Soon, however, we recognize by individual signs the intrinsic and continuous development of that original idea: material and construction are progressively made to deny their identity and are reduced to a mere means of expressing the form. We first become aware of this through the peculiar form of wall construction. From the outset, the Romanesque wall was not what walls had been in the architectural system of antiquity. The tapestry-dressed [*bekleidete*] stone wall of antiquity must be seen as the monumental art-form for a concept of

Conrad Fiedler, from "Observations on the Nature and History of Architecture" (1878), trans. Harry Francis Mallgrave and Eleftherios Ikonomou, in *Empathy, Form, and Space: Problems of German Aesthetics 1873–1893*. Santa Monica, CA: Getty Publication Programs, 1994, p. 142.

spatial enclosure derived from the use of textile hangings for the purpose of shutting off inner space from the outside world. Here, by contrast, the idea of enclosing space seems to have been planned in stone from the beginning. It was a matter of expressing the idea of a continuous enclosure by means of a wall and at the same time of elevating the heavy material into a free expression of that idea.

43 HANS AUER
from "The Development of Space in Architecture" (1883)

B uilt upon the spatial insights of Gottfried Semper and Conrad Fiedler was this essay by Hans Auer. A Swiss citizen by birth, Auer studied architecture in Zurich under Semper, before moving to Vienna to join the office of Theophil von Hansen. He became one of Hansen's most trusted designers and worked on the design of the Vienna Academy of Fine Arts, the Vienna Stock Exchange, and the Austrian Parliament. But Auer's architectural career was defined by his winning the international competition for the new Swiss Parliament, built between 1894 and 1902. Few historians today, however, recognize his important contributions to theory with three lengthy essays in the early 1880s. In the first, "The Influence of Construction on the Development of Architectural Styles" (1881), Auer breaks somewhat with Semper by insisting that construction should take priority in modern architectural theory, although he too stresses the importance that should be given to space in design. In the third, "Modern Style Questions" (1885), Auer considers at length the whole issue of style and its cultural ramifications. In between these two writings lies this pivotal essay of 1883, in which Auer becomes the first theorist to sketch out the notion that spatial development is not only the "soul" of architectural creation but also the generative force in the development of a new style. The two selections are from the beginning and concluding pages of his essay.

Architecture has two souls. One relates to the earth and is subordinate to practical purpose; the other, like a free angel, reaches up into the higher regions and is self-sufficient in her service to free beauty. This dualism is seen also in the cultivation of space. The form of its basic surfaces, their length and breadth, is ordered by practical demands and is directly conditioned by purpose. But height goes far beyond human needs and it is that which affects the soul of the spectator with pleasant, imposing, uplifting, and all-powerful effects. The more those in the past wanted to emphasize the sanctity of a space, the more they sought greater height. In the proportions of height to extension lies one of the most beautiful moments of spatial creation, which the architects of antiquity as well as of the Renaissance sought to explore, even by the establishment of defined proportional ratios.

Through the activity of the ordering human mind and under the force of practical necessity the required columns and pillars were grouped in series and rhythmic regularity within the spaces. In this way space received its articulation, its proportional division, like every other work of art and nature. From it arises that painterly beauty, that perspectival

Hans Auer, from "Die Entwickelung des Raumes in der Baukunst," trans. Harry Francis Mallgrave, in *Allgemeine Bauzeitung* 48 (1883), pp. 66, 74.

charm, that variation in levels of illumination, in short, that wealth and richness of inner form that is able to impress space as a true work of art – all of which we describe as the *poetry of space*.

Whereas space is created from the discussed factors by artistic activity, the demands of *purpose, construction*, and *beauty* should be completely in balance, so that none of these elements dominates the other. Space at the same time impresses a definite form on its veil, namely the exterior appearance of the building.

Space is the soul of the building, which fills out the body and characterizes it from without. Just as the soul is bound to the body and likewise the body to the soul, both dependent on the other, so space affects not only the exterior appearance of the body but it also, for its part, is conditioned by the interior constructive organism. The selected or traditionally prescribed way of building conditions both the physiognomy of the space and the combined exterior appearance down to the smallest detail.

★ ★ ★

We live with a seeming chaos of artistic concepts, with a confusion of the most varied artistic viewpoints, such as probably have never existed. This condition characterizes our time as a *transitional period*. The traditional ways of building have lost their rationale; through them the spatial art has nowhere to go. We live today in a period in which a new style is forming under the unstoppable influence of a material that shakes its brazen fist at all past traditions – namely, *iron*. We live in one of those moments in which intensified needs put new demands on techniques, which have always (as noted above) prepared and created a new style. In our century the production and preparation of iron have made such an impact that they have called forth significant social upheavals. In connection with them are the tasks that have been put to architecture, which now, with the help of iron, can be solved. Architecture has not everywhere grasped its firm feet, but it is striding from victory to victory in such a way that most modern buildings more or less wear the stamp of the iron century itself.

44 JOSEF BAYER
from "Modern Building Types" (1886)

Another of the unsung theorists of the 1880s was the Austrian Josef Bayer. A shrewd critic, he was a close friend of Johannes Brahms as well as being a self-styled Semperian, and, even though he was not an architect, he devoted much of his attention to discerning the architectural trends of his day. Bayer felt strongly that the new style – modernity – was indeed taking shape in all the arts, if in fact it had not already appeared. It is found, he argued, not in the decorative language of the traditional styles but rather in the whole "social" direction of bourgeois society: in its horizontal, multifunctional buildings, functionally articulated in parts, built close to the ground. Bayer's critique is a classic statement of the time, and it is indicative of the great optimism found in the earlier stages of Germanic modernism.

Josef Bayer, from "Modernene Bautypen," trans. Harry Francis Mallgrave, in *Baustudien und Baubilder: Schriften zur Kunst*. Jena: Eugen Diederichs, 1919, pp. 282–3, 286–7.

Whoever is a complete, living architect and a true son of his time will also find today that it is a joy to build. The straightforward element that brings the needs of the present into our building practices will on the other hand be offset by the size of the projects, and a creative architectural talent will understand how to master this matter-of-factness with an energetic composition and a meaningful layout. Architecture must once again understand how to fall in with the so-called "materialist" age, which incidentally spends large sums on building, just as literature has long since done. The task of architecture, like literature, is to represent the characteristics of the age; it has, in general, to design the artistic image of space, just as literature is called upon to express the spiritual image of life in its particulars, following its changing and moving multiplicity.

The architecture of the present is *social*, just as in the past it was monarchical, aristocratic, and religious. This also completely defines the design of the new building types, to the extent that they have already developed or at least been prepared.

★ ★ ★

No! We no longer live in the age of tower building. [...] Not only in art but also in politics, in society, in practical efforts, in scientific research – everywhere we ask more of an outlook than an outlook; we ask for a perspective, a point of view. Our living direction is likewise subject to horizontal laws; it is gauged, it fixes its goal in a straightline way – and this must above all define the spatial-symbolic art of building in its composition. Our entire modern direction necessarily leads to the visual perspective, to the powerfully emphasized rhythm of the masses, and no more upward to the romantic tower-realm of the jackdaw nester. This also particularly conditions the floor plans of our public buildings. Their principle is spatial articulation, clear arrangement, and integrating unity once that arrangement has been clearly and forcefully expressed. Multiple functions need also – as it is easy to understand – a multi-articulated, monumental housing. The great modern buildings that fully bear the stamp of our age are *groupings of buildings*.

45 HEINRICH WÖLFFLIN
from ''Prolegomena to a Psychology of Architecture'' (1886)

Building fast upon the psychological aesthetics of Robert Vischer and Conrad Fiedler was this doctoral dissertation of Heinrich Wölfflin. The task here is specifically to write the outline for a psychology of architecture, or to answer the question with which he opens the dissertation – "How is it possible that architectural forms are able to express an emotion or a mood?" Wölfflin was keen to eliminate kinetic or excerpt

Heinrich Wölfflin, from ''Prolegomena zu einer Psychologie der Architektur'' (1886), trans. Harry Francis Mallgrave and Eleftherios Ikonomou, in *Empathy, Form, and Space: Problems of German Aesthetics 1873–1893*. Santa Monica, CA: Getty Publication Programs, 1994, pp. 151, 182–3.

physiological explanations. He prefers to base his psychological answer entirely on the notion of "empathy," and thus turns (as the first shows) to a recent theory of musical form to explain how and why we respond to architectural forms in the way we do. Taking the analogy of musical form, however, leads Wölfflin into difficulties, and in the end his analysis of architecture becomes quite conventional (classical) in that he goes on to find pleasing architectural forms in such attributes as symmetry, regularity, and numerical proportions. Although architects such as Henry van de Velde and August Endell would later be attracted to Wölfflin's theory, they would also seek to construct an empathetic theory of architectural form outside of these classical parameters.

Yet toward the end of his dissertation (see the second excerpt), Wölfflin seeks a breakthrough in another regard: by transposing his empathetic psychology of form (discerned by an individual) into a collective psychology of form (the formal attitude of a culture). In essence, he follows the lead of Gottfried Semper in arguing that architectural styles follow very directly from the "attitude and movement of people" of a given period. The Gothic style, for instance, reflected a more general Scholastic outlook that stressed precise (pointed) concepts. This became the basis of Wölfflin's famous methodology of artistic "formalism," which dominated art history throughout the early part of the twentieth century. But such formalism also carries with it an important architectural implication. Germanic architectural theory since Semper had largely been in open revolt against the Hegelian idea that styles operate in fixed cycles determined by the intellectual development of a culture. Wölfflin essentially transposes Hegel's philosophical idea into a psychological guise, thus allowing the notion of historical destiny once again to be reclaimed. Historical determinism becomes, in fact, one of the central premises of the German Modern Movement in the first part of the twentieth century.

If we did not have the ability to express our own emotions in sounds, we could never understand the meaning of sounds produced by others. We understand only what we ourselves can do.

So here, too, we must say: *Physical forms possess a character only because we ourselves possess a body.* If we were purely visual beings, we would always be denied an aesthetic judgment of the physical world. But as human beings with a body that teaches us the nature of gravity, contraction, strength, and so on, we gather the experience that enables us to identify with the conditions of other forms. Why is no one surprised that the stone falls toward the earth? Why does that seem so very natural to us? We cannot account for it rationally: the explanation lies in our personal experience alone. We have carried loads and experienced pressure and counterpressure, we have collapsed to the ground when we no longer had the strength to resist the downward pull of our own bodies, and that is why we can appreciate the noble serenity of a column and understand the tendency of all matter to spread out formlessly on the ground.

[. . .]

We have seen how the general human condition sets the standard for architecture. This principle may be extended still further: any architectural style reflects the *attitude and movement of people* in the period concerned. How people like to move and carry themselves is expressed above all in their costume, and it is not difficult to show that architecture corresponds to the costume of its period. I would like to emphasize this principle of historical characterization all the more energetically because I am unable here to pursue the idea in any detail.

The Gothic style will serve as an example.

Lübke saw it as the expression of spiritualism. Semper called it lapidary scholasticism. According to what principles has it been judged? The *tertium comparationis* is not exactly clear, even though there may be a grain of truth in both descriptions. We will find firm ground only by referring these psychological observations to the human figure.

The mental fact in question is the tendency to be precise, sharp, and conscious of the will. Scholasticism clearly reveals this aversion to anything that is imprecise; its concepts are formulated with the greatest precision.

Physically, this aspiration presents itself in precise movements, pointed forms, no relaxation, nothing bloated, and a will that is everywhere most decisively expressed.

Scholasticism and spiritualism can be considered the expression of the Gothic period only if one keeps in mind this intermediate stage, during which a psychological feeling is directly transformed into bodily form. The sophisticated subtlety of the scholastic centuries and the spiritualism that tolerated no matter divested of will can have shaped architectural form only through their bodily expression.

Here we find the Gothic forms presented in principle: the bridge of the nose becomes narrower; the forehead assumes hard vertical folds; the whole body stiffens and pulls itself together; all restful expansiveness disappears. It is well known that many people (especially university lecturers) like the feeling of rolling a sharply angled pencil between their fingers in order to sharpen their thoughts. A round pencil would not serve the same purpose. What does roundness want? Nobody knows. And the same is true with the Romanesque rounded arch; no definite will can be recognized. It ascends, but this upward impulse finds a clear expression only in the pointed arch.

46 ADOLF GÖLLER
from "What is the Cause of Perpetual Style Change in Architecture?" (1887)

V ery much in line with the psychological formalism of Wölfflin is this exceptionally important tract by Adolf Göller. This little known theorist and architect taught at the Stuttgart Polytechnikum in the early 1880s, where he became much attracted to the psychological models put forth by Hermann Helmholtz and Wilhelm Wundt. His application of perceptual theories to architecture here yields some very dramatic results. His thesis revolves around two concepts: the cultivation of a cultural "memory image" and the baneful effect of psychological "jading." In essence, each generation is reared with a collective image of the architectural forms with which it is familiar, and over time these forms and proportions become jaded, that is, architects tire of using the same forms and begin to pursue proportional deviations (explaining, for instance, the passing of the high Renaissance into mannerism). Thus over a period of time a style becomes used up, as it were, and a new style is created with a new memory image. Taking his model one step further, Göller chooses to disregard entirely the historical and symbolic

Adolf Göller, from "Was is die Ursache . . ." (1887), trans. Harry Francis Mallgrave and Eleftherios Ikonomou, in *Empathy, Form, and Space: Problems of German Aesthetics 1873–1893*. Santa Monica, CA: Getty Publication Programs, 1994, pp. 194–5, 198.

content of style (e.g., the spirituality of a pointed arch), and focus his analysis on what he calls "pure form," or the simple visual play of forms, lines, light and shade. The result is a remarkable analysis of abstract architecture stripped of all historical associations. This appreciation of abstract forms, Göller concludes, is in fact the "noblest or the richest" source of aesthetic pleasure for the art of architecture. The short excerpts cited here reveal this small treatise to be one of the most important of nineteenth-century theory.

I would like to make this phenomenon – this law – the subject of my address, in which I will venture to offer the fruit of some reflections on our attitude toward the beauty of form. I shall endeavor to identify the psychological causes from which our sensibility to the beauty of the decorative forms of any architectural style changes with time and to show how the individual's attitude to individual form accounts for the inevitability of perpetual style change in architecture. The path no doubt leads through a distant field, but permit me to reach out beyond the framework of our curriculum – so that we at the Technische Hochschule, in responding to an academic question, can express our grateful and happy participation in today's national celebration.

I

The impression that works of architecture and the fine arts make on us is the product of numerous individual effects, which separate themselves distinctly into two main groups. The first is a series of feelings that are based more or less on clear thoughts about the work of art in question, the second is a pleasure of a more external kind that has nothing to do with thoughts but arises directly out of viewing the form or image. The former impression is based on the *intellectual content* of the work of art, the second on its *beauty of form*. This latter, perhaps less valued aspect of beauty – this beauty of pure visible form, considered free of any ideal content – will be the subject of my address. It is defined as *an inherently pleasurable, meaningless play of lines or of light and shade.*
[. . .]
Certainly the content of architecture is not restricted to the expression of its structural achievement. Many works also have the capacity to touch the depths of our soul. Architecture can endow its creations with the expression of soaring aspiration, solemn gravity, festive joy, and splendid power. Even a utilitarian work can wear its rank and character, judiciously expressed, on its face. How we arrive at a feeling of sublimity or gravity or festive cheerfulness from viewing abstract forms and ornaments will probably for a long time to come remain a deep psychological mystery. Only a lengthy chain of unconscious ideas can lead us from one notion to the other. Especially the powerful impression of great masses and the elevating effect of a high, wide space flooded with light give a feeling whose causes may well be active in the deepest reaches of the human soul.

Yet even without pursuing the trail of such impressions, we can conclude directly from experience that our feeling for such an expression, and likewise our pleasure in any building with a well-defined character, does not in the least prevent us from judging and appreciating the beauty of pure form in and of itself. Here, as with the structure, it is possible to show by focusing on the small parts that beautiful architectural form would not altogether cease to be pleasing if the expression were not present or if the building were deprived of its character.

Architecture is, after all, the true decorative art, the true *art of visible pure form*. The beauty of pure form is not the noblest or the richest, emotionally speaking; but it is the first and often the only source of aesthetic pleasure in works of architecture.

47 CORNELIUS GURLITT
from "Göller's Aesthetic Theory" (1887)

Göller's remarkable model for explaining the aesthetics of architecture did not go unnoticed. The perspicacious critic Cornelius Gurlitt wrote a book review of Göller's writings for the German architectural journal *Deutsche Bauzeitung*. Gurlitt was ebullient over the ramifications of Göller's argument. He likened it to the relativism espoused by Claude Perrault in the seventeenth century, because Göller had essentially reduced all historical styles to the particular period's "memory's image" — hence no one style could be deemed superior. More importantly, as the first excerpt shows, Gurlitt felt that Göller's model would end the Hegelian hegemony underpinning architectural historicism, by shifting the emphasis from purposeful content (a historical style) to pure form. In the end, Gurlitt chides the Stuttgart theorist for only one thing — his restriction of pure form's aesthetic pleasure simply to architecture. For by extending the same model to painting and sculpture, Gurlitt (in his own act of great originality) now argues that, we have the rationale for abstract art! Gurlitt reduces this tendency to the term "realism," a word that was to gain increasing currency in Germany in the 1890s and become an early synonym for modernism.

Göller shows that there is also a beauty of pure form, which he altogether opposes to Hegelian aesthetics. He says that there are certain combinations of lines, light, and shadow that, although indeed meaningless, nevertheless please our eye and mind. Thus he cites the "purely decorative" ornament, the play of lines and light on a cornice, which is applied *not* for functional reasons (that is, the functions have nothing to say), but is perceived by us to be beautiful simply for its form. How is it that one column can be beautiful and another ugly if both express their functions very well? Can we, then, infer the mass of details from their purpose, or from those proportions that give us pleasure? The Ionic column, whose volutes no one has been able to explain, whose spiritual content was perhaps unknown even to the Greeks and completely meaningless for us, is yet beautiful because of the form. It is therefore not true to say, as Hegel wants, that a work of art must be ugly if it lacks the spiritual content that determines this beauty. How else could the very meaningless ornament of a Persian carpet or arabesque be beautiful?

★ ★ ★

Cornelius Gurlitt, from "Göller's ästhetische Lehre," trans. Harry Francis Mallgrave, in *Deutsche Bauzeitung* 21 (1887), pp. 603, 606.

But what is important is not only what can be read in Göller's books. A far greater booty will be reserved for him who logically applies the theory of the beauty of pure form to painting and sculpture – that is, for he who demonstrates that the world of form, to a great extent now removed from intellectual content, can also greatly affect our sense of beauty in these arts. He will also show by this how proper it was for German art to pass from the content-laden manner of [Peter] Cornelius to realism, or from the world of ideas to that of the sensuously felt form.

48 FERDINAND TÖNNIES
from *Community and Society* (1887)

Modernism in architecture was not simply an aesthetic preference for certain forms or approaches to design; it was a more deep-seated shift in how one looks at the world, one carrying both psychological and sociological implications. One of the first sociologists to ponder this issue of modernity was Ferdinand Tönnies, who received his doctorate in classical philology at Tübingen in 1877 and ten years later produced this ground-breaking study. The title of the book plays off the German words *Gemeinschaft* (community) and *Gesellschaft* (society). The former is the union of people found in agrarian life, that is, a knowing relationship or social bond formed with each member of the community, based on trust and rural neighborliness. Society or life in the large city, by contrast, is an artificial union, one predicated on social conventions and laws and presuming a measure of anonymity in social relations. Not only are human personalities affected by these respective lifestyles (and not always for the better), Tönnies argues, but so are human outlooks on a range of issues, including aesthetics.

This whole development, from its primary to its subsequent manifestations, can also be conceived as a transition from an original, simple, family communism and village-town individualism based thereon, to an independent, universal, urban individualism and, determined thereby, a socialism of state and international type. The latter is inherent in the concept of Gesellschaft, although in the beginning it exists only as an actual interrelation between all capitalistic powers and the state, which maintains and promotes order in the social organization. Gradually attempts are made to impose a uniform regulation on the social organization and labor itself through the mechanism of the state, but success in this would necessarily dissolve the entire Gesellschaft and its civilization. This same tendency necessarily implies a dissolution of all those ties which bind the individual through his natural will and are apart from his rational will. For these ties restrict his personal freedom of movement, the salableness of his property, the change of his attitudes, and their adaptation to the findings of science. They are restrictions on the self-determined rational will and on the Gesellschaft in so far as trade and commerce tend to make property or property rights as mobile and divisible as possible and require unscrupulous, irreligious,

Ferdinand Tönnies, from *Gemeinschaft und Gesellschaft* (1887), trans. Charles P. Loomis as *Community and Society*. New Brunswick, NJ: Transaction Books, 1988, pp. 234–5.

easygoing people. The state, too, feels the restrictive influence of these ties, and hastens the tendency toward their dissolution, and considers enlightened, greedy, and practical people its most useful subjects.

The development of these forces and contrasts and their struggle for supremacy are common to the two spheres of culture and their people of which we may believe ourselves to have definite knowledge. One is the South-European classic culture which reached its acme in Athens and came to an end in Rome, the other is the North-European modern culture which followed it and, in many respects, was influenced and furthered by it. We discover these similar developments under an enormous variety of historical facts and conditions. Within the general uniform process to which all elements contribute, each of these has its own hidden history, which is determined partly by the general development, partly by causes of its own, and which, impeding or furthering, interferes with the whole.

The concepts and findings which have been presented in this book will help us to understand the tendencies and struggles which have come down from earlier centuries to the present period and will reach out into the future. To this end, we conceive the whole development of Germanic culture, which rose upon the ruins of the Roman Empire and, as its heir, expanded under the beneficial influence of the Church, as in a state of constant progress as well as decay.

49 CAMILLO SITTE
from *City Planning According to Its Artistic Principles* (1889)

Walter Benjamin called Paris the "capital of the nineteenth century," and the city, as a symbol of modernity and progress, was redefined in the 1860s and 1870s through the new boulevards and urban changes of Georges-Eugène Haussmann. Thus when Vienna decided to tear down the old city walls and ramparts (the walls that had saved the city from Ottoman conquest in 1689), city officials looked to Paris for inspiration. They replaced the old walls and broad glacis separating the old town from the suburbs with a new boulevard – the *Ringstrasse* (Ring Street) – and connected it with a series of traffic arteries and squares. The regularity of the new urban forms differed radically from the irregularity of the old town, and here Tönnies's issues of community versus society meet head on. The person to step forward to challenge the new urban model was Camillo Sitte. He was the son of an architect, trained in the applied arts, and his home was very much a hub of Viennese cultural life. His book on city planning quickly became the Bible of those opposing the newer "straight streets," but Sitte's theory is not so succinctly summarized. His book is replete with numerous plans of old irregular streets and squares (mainly taken from Italy), but he argues that they should not be copied for their own sake. They should be studied, rather, for the psychological lessons they exemplify with their urban scale, diverse and comfortable pedestrian spaces, and overall urban vitality.

Camillo Sitte, from *Die Städtebau nach seinen künstlerischen Grundsätzen* (1889), trans. George R. Collins and Christiane Crasemann Collins, in *Camillo Sitte: The Birth of Modern City Planning*. New York: Rizzoli, 1986, pp. 224–5.

Straight lines and right angles are certainly characteristic of insensitive planning, but are apparently not decisive in this matter, because Baroque planning also used straight lines and right angles, achieving powerful and truly artistic effects in spite of them. In the layout of streets it is true that rectilinearity is a weakness. An undeviating boulevard, miles long, seems boring even in the most beautiful surroundings. It is unnatural, it does not adapt itself to irregular terrain, and it remains uninteresting in effect, so that, mentally fatigued, one can hardly await its termination. An ordinary street, if excessively long, has the same effect. But as the more frequent shorter streets of modern planning also produce an unfortunate effect, there must be some other cause for it. It is the same as in the plazas, namely *faulty closure of the sides of the street*. The continual breaching by wide cross-streets, so that on both sides nothing is left but a row of separated blocks of buildings, is the main reason why no unified impression can be attained. This may be demonstrated most clearly by comparing old arcades with their modern imitations. Ancient arcades, nothing short of magnificent in their architectural detail, run uninterruptedly along the whole curve of a street as far as the eye can see; or they encircle a plaza enclosing it completely; or at least they run unbroken along one side of it. Their whole effect is based on continuity, for only by it can the succession of arches become a large enough unity to create an impact. The situation is completely different in modern planning. Although occasional outstanding architects have, in their enthusiasm for this magnificent old motif, succeeded in providing us with such covered walks – as, for instance, in Vienna around the Votive Church and at the new Rathaus – these hardly remind us of the ancient models, because their effect is totally different. The separate sections are larger and much more sumptuously carried out than almost any ancient predecessors. Yet the intended effect is absent. Why? Because each separate loggia is attached to its own building block, and the cuts made by the numerous broad cross-streets prevent the slightest effect of continuity. Only if the openings of these intersecting streets were spanned by a continuation of the arcade could any coherence result that might then create a grandiose impression. Lacking this, the dismembered motif is like a hoe without a handle.

For the same reason a coherent effect does not come about in our streets. A modern street is made up primarily of corner buildings. A row of isolated blocks of buildings is going to look bad under any circumstances, even if placed in a curved line.

These considerations bring us close to the crux of the matter. In modern city planning the relationship between the built-up and open spaces is exactly reversed. Formerly the empty spaces (streets and plazas) were a unified entity of shapes calculated for their impact; today building lots are laid out as regularly shaped closed forms, and what is left over between them becomes street or plaza.

50 AUGUST SCHMARSOW
from *The Essence of Architectural Creation* (1893)

With Heinrich Wölfflin having put forth the outline for a psychology of architecture and having advanced, more broadly, his methodology of formalism, it was perhaps inevitable that an alternative model should be proffered – both for architecture and in opposition to Wölfflin's emphasis on form. That a young rival of Wölfflin should also put forward this challenge is hardly coincidental. In 1893 August Schmarsow won a professorial chair from the University of Leipzig over the applications of both Wölfflin and Robert Vischer. For his inaugural lecture, Schmarsow chose to challenge Wölfflin's formalism with a lecture that carried the intriguing title "The Essence of Architectural Creation." Schmarsow, like Wölfflin before him, returned to Gottfried Semper for the start of his deliberations on space, and in this regard he seems to have been unfamiliar with the earlier theories of Conrad Fiedler and Hans Auer. Schmarsow, however, went further than his two immediate predecessors in constructing what was essentially a phenomenology of the human spatial experience and its centrality to architectural design. Although Schmarsow's lecture was widely read within art-historical circles, it scarcely resonated among architects. And there is the additional historical irony in that when Sigfried Giedion and Bruno Zevi – a half-century later – came also to define architecture in identical terms, they seem to have been unaware of Schmarsow's earlier effort.

Let us now try to bring within a single historical perspective the varied phenomena that immediately suggest themselves when we first consider this theme. From the troglodyte's cave to the Arab's tent; from the long processional avenue of the Egyptian pilgrimage temple to the Greek god's glorious column-borne roof; from the Caribbean hut to the German Reichstag building – we can say in the most general terms that they are all without exception *spatial constructs* [*Raumgebilde*], whatever their material, duration, and construction, and whatever the configuration of their supporting and supported parts. "The one essential feature is the enclosure of space," says Eduard von Hartmann; but his qualification – "for a specific purpose" – overshoots the mark. The reference to the human need for protection against the hardships of the external world, or indeed any other reference to a specific purpose, is premature as long as we are pursuing an aesthetic investigation. External stimuli provide only the contingent cause, the occasion for the exercise of human skill. Yet even the smallest human attempt to make a spatial enclosure presupposes that the person has some notion of the intended spatial construct. Thus we come to the final precondition: the predisposition to the intuited form [*Anschauungsform*] that we call space.

* * *

Psychologically, the intuited form of three-dimensional space arises through the experiences of our sense of sight, whether or not assisted by other physiological factors. All our visual

August Schmarsow, from *Das Wesen der architektonischen Schöpfung* (1893), trans. Harry Francis Mallgrave and Eleftherios Ikonomou, in *Empathy, Form, and Space: Problems of German Aesthetics 1873–1893*. Santa Monica, CA: Getty Publication Programs, 1994, pp. 286–7.

perceptions and ideas are arranged, are ordered, and unfold in accordance with this intuited form; and this fact is the mother lode of the art whose origin and essence we seek.

The intuited form of space, which surrounds us wherever we may be and which we then always erect around ourselves and consider more necessary than the form of our own body, consists of the residues of sensory experience to which the muscular sensations of our body, the sensitivity of our skin, and the structure of our body all contribute. As soon as we have learned to experience ourselves and ourselves alone as the center of this space, whose coordinates intersect in us, we have found the precious kernel, the initial capital investment so to speak, on which architectural creation is based – even if for the moment it seems no more impressive than a lucky penny. Once the ever-active imagination takes hold of this germ and develops it according to the laws of the directional axes inherent in even the smallest nucleus of every spatial idea, the grain of mustard seed grows into a tree and an entire world surrounds us. Our sense of space [*Raumgefühl*] and spatial imagination [*Raumphantasie*] press toward spatial creation [*Raumgestaltung*]; they seek their satisfaction in art. We call this art architecture; in plain words, it is the *creatress of space* [*Raumgestalterin*].

PART II THE FORMATION OF THE MODERN MOVEMENT: 1894–1914

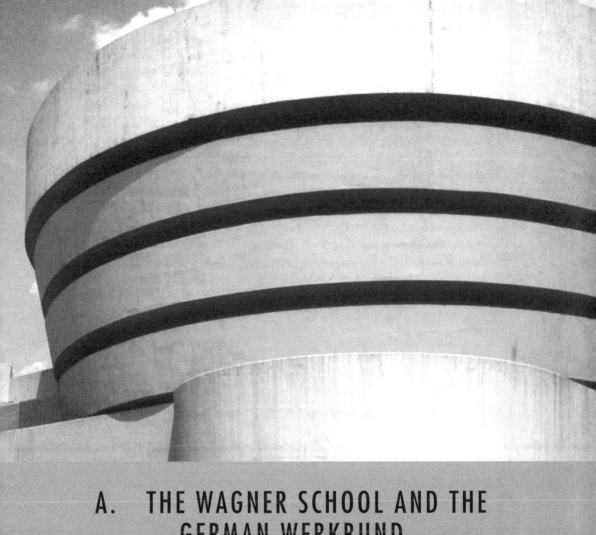

A.   THE WAGNER SCHOOL AND THE
GERMAN WERKBUND

Introduction

The theoretical activities of the German-speaking lands in the last half of the nineteenth century came to a head in the two decades surrounding the start of the twentieth century, as an identifiable "modern movement" now took shape. In the christening of this new movement, two events stand out. First was Otto Wagner's appointment as a professor of architecture at the Academy of Fine Arts in Vienna in 1894; second was the founding of the German Werkbund in 1907.

The Wagner appointment instigated a pivotal change within the architectural curriculum. The Vienna Academy of Fine Arts had long been the premier architectural school of the Habsburg Empire, and for several decades it operated essentially as two schools: one offering instruction in the Gothic tradition and the other led by an architect teaching the Renaissance style. Wagner – a self-proclaimed practitioner of a "certain Free Renaissance" – was hired to teach the latter, but he seized the occasion of his inaugural address in 1894 to announce his break from the past and his commitment to teach "modern" design. His comments exhilarated an already impatient student body, but his words, more importantly, reverberated throughout every other academy, university, and polytechnical school in Austria, Germany, and beyond. That one of the most respected architectural schools in Europe should commit itself to modernism was, in retrospect, a death knell to historicist curricula elsewhere, and the newly formed "Wagner School" now stood in the forefront with its embrace of modernity.

The German Werkbund — initially a coalition of 300 architects, artisans, museum directors, and industrialists — represented a similar palace coup on behalf of modernism, but on a governmental and professional front. The idea for such an organization had been floating since the late 1890s, and behind its foundation was the energy and commitment of Hermann Muthesius, an official within the Ministry of Trade and an activist on several organizational fronts. Muthesius was the first to articulate clearly the Werkbund's mission to foster the practice of modern design, both industrial and craft-based, and his intention was to align the fruit of such an approach with an enhancement of German exports. Inevitably these artistic and economic interests would collide, but the showdown that came at the German Werkbund Exhibition of 1914 also demonstrates, in a vivid way, just how fully modernism had now insinuated itself within German architecture by this date. It did so, as well, with a new sense of historical determinism that presaged the ideological spirit of the 1920s.

51 OTTO WAGNER
from "Inaugural Address to the Academy of Fine Arts" (1894)

Otto Wagner was born in the year of Karl Friedrich Schinkel's death, and he graduated from the Academy of Fine Arts in Vienna in 1863. For nearly thirty years his practice was scarcely revolutionary. He specialized largely in speculative apartment buildings in a well-accepted baroque or *Ringstrasse* guise, although he also participated in several international competitions — all without success. In the late 1880s, however, his work begins to evolve. In the first volume of his self-published monograph, *Sketches, Projects and Executed Buildings* (1889), in which he identifies himself as a practitioner of a "certain free Renaissance," he also speaks of an "utility style" as having relevance for the future. Indeed, his practice in the early 1890s moves away, in part, from his former baroque sensibilities and toward what was then referred to as the "Empire" fashion, that is, French design of the early 1800s. Also in 1894 he was appointed the architect of the city's new rail system, which would entail the design of more than forty stations, bridges, and viaducts. Although these designs were generally more Spartan in character, they scarcely indicate the work of one who has broken from the past. All of this, of course, makes his revolutionary words of October 1894 all the more startling. He begins his historic pronouncement, in fact, by apologizing for his former "*practical trend.*"

Perhaps you have heard from hearsay or have your own view that I am the representative of a certain *practical trend*. My explanation may seem to you rather prosaic at first, or suggest

Otto Wagner, from "Inaugural Address to the Academy of Fine Arts," trans. Harry Francis Mallgrave as *Otto Wagner: Modern Architecture*. Santa Monica, CA: Getty Publication Programs, 1988, pp. 159–60.

ideas that you associate with a kind of decline of the school or the dampening of your youthful ideals, but this is not the case. If you will follow my train of thought, I believe I can in a few words prove the contrary to be true.

● The exteriors of almost all modern buildings, whether they are more or less happily arranged, attempt to be as accurate *copies of stylistic trends* as possible. Such good copies of styles, to which as a rule much is sacrificed, are then considered stylistically pure and usually provide the standard of value according to which an architectural work is judged. Certain architectural styles are granted a monopoly for certain purposes, and the public, and unfortunately many artists too, go along with this opinion. The matter has even gone so far that architectural styles almost change like fashions, and works of art are intentionally made "old" in order to give them the appearance of dating from past centuries. Form and style are truly abused in this way, and if the matter were not much too sad it could be looked upon as a kind of architectural comedy. That this cannot possibly be the right approach scarcely needs further proof.

● In contrast to this, let us look at the works of art of past centuries. From antiquity to the Renaissance – even to the "Empire" of our century – the work has always been a reflection of its time.

● And precisely herein lies the secret. Art and artists should and must represent their time. The salvation of the future cannot lie in racing through every stylistic trend, as has happened in the last decades. With skill and taste we can no doubt use and improve all forms handed down to us, whether they are simple supports, towers, or crowns, or have to do with surface treatment. Yet the starting point of every artistic creation must be the need, ability, means, and achievements of *our* time.

● *Artis sola domina necessitas* (Art knows only one master – the need).

● Thus, when you are about to solve a task, always ask yourself this: how will this solution relate to modern man, to the assignment, to the *genius loci*, the climatic conditions, the materials at hand, and the financial means? Only thus can you hope to elicit true appreciation, and only then will the works of architecture that today are met for the most part with incomprehension or a certain tentativeness become generally understandable, original, and even popular.

● Our living conditions and methods of construction must be fully and completely expressed if architecture is not to be reduced to a caricature. The realism of our time must pervade the developing work of art. It will not harm it, nor will any decline of art ensue as a consequence of it; rather it will breathe a new and pulsating life into forms, and in time conquer new fields that today are still devoid of art – for example, that of engineering. Only thus can we speak of a real improvement in art. I would even maintain that we must force ourselves in this way to reach a characteristic style representative of us.

● You see therefore that I, in proceeding from such principles, do not preach anything like giving up your ideal goals, but, on the contrary, consider it my task to train you to become children of our time, among whom I also count myself.

● There you have, as it were, my credo.

52 MAX FABIANI
from "Out of the Wagner School" (1895)

The response among students to Wagner's inaugural address can be measured by this recapitulation of Wagner's ideas that appeared in the new journal *Der Architect* early in 1895. Its author was the Slovenian architect Max Fabiani, who had trained in Wagner's office. Fabiani was also a member of the Siebener Club, an informal coalition of young artists and architects that included Joseph Olbrich and Josef Hoffmann. They were the forerunners to the Vienna Secession that officially formed in 1897, although this passage demonstrates that the move was already contemplated at this time. Fabiani here marshals Wagner's tectonic principles under the "battle cry" of realism, and at the conclusion of his manifesto he even apologizes for Wagner's earlier historicist tendencies. Thus Wagner's better students, it seems, were encouraging their master's rebellion at this time, and Fabiani, as an important architect in Wagner's office, may even have contributed to the writing of Wagner's *Modern Architecture* (1896). In any case, the enthusiasm for change was high.

Realism, truth, this was the battle cry. A closer observation of nature, a deeper recognition of its laws created the foundation – today a completely new art is forming.

Poets and sculptors, painters and musicians have long recognized their new ideals; they have long found a popular feeling.

Yet the art that is most involved with the real needs of life, which should accompany us every step of the way, still today searches in vain for understanding and popularity.

Architecture.

At the beginning of our century the tired forms of the late Baroque and Empire periods no longer pleased but were rashly seized; indeed everywhere there was the tendency to rejuvenate these forms through studies of antiquity and the Renaissance, in short, of past periods of art.

A half-century was given over to it.

The storehouse of forms of whole ages (styles) were often mastered in a wonderful way in their details.

It may have been necessary.

Undoubtedly between our cultural epoch and many past ones there lie many points of contact and parallels; several things can be taken over with advantage and be understandable.

But what lies in between are the needs of modern life, our century's much advanced constructional knowledge, and the technology of wholly new materials.

During these studies and style experiments the natural sciences pushed ahead; the skill of engineers proceeded with giant strides. Whereas earlier an accommodation was possible, in this period of historicism there arose a cleft, a scarcely bridgeable distance from the past.

Architecture lacked the truth of form, realism in expressing materials and construction.

★ ★ ★

Accordingly, the first principle is the creation of form out of the tectonic task. Our premise of an artistic total conception is the goal of the architectural Secession.

Max Fabiani, from "Aus der Wagner Schule," trans. Harry Francis Mallgrave, in *Der Architekt* 1 (1895), pp. 53–4.

In fact the complete output of master Wagner shows this double striving: first toward development of the clearest possible architectural idea supported by salient, constructional factors, and secondly toward a creative disposition of practical demands. A surprising mastery of all technical means and a powerful creative force are evident in the truth and invention of his main motives.

Nowhere a template. An unbiased, courageous spirit, which always has a liberating and stimulating effect on his surroundings, speaks through each of his words and works.

In adhering to this directive within this most exalted, simple, and clear system is the greatest freedom. That is the Wagner School!

53   JULIUS LESSING
from "New Paths" (1895)

While Wagner was seizing the initiative in Vienna, another center of German modernism was forming in Berlin, as seen in this article by Julius Lessing, the long-time curator of the Applied Arts Museum there. Lessing had been active in the German reform movement in the 1870s, but this particular article shows him to be – by the 1890s – a vocal partisan for what soon would be called "tectonic realism," that is, creating artistic forms solely from the new material and constructional techniques. He thus arrives at an identical position to that of Otto Wagner, but from his applied arts perspective. The condemnation of the buildings of the Columbian Exposition in Chicago was relatively widespread in Germany during these years. Many German architects, very familiar with the work of Chicago architects in the 1880s, believed that the United States had the lead in the cultivation of modernism, but the classical forms employed by Daniel Burnham and others were perceived as a disappointment in view of the strides made in Paris in 1889. The reference here to modern ships and wagons of course picks up on Robert Dohme's polemics of a decade earlier.

Is it conceivable that instead of a gradual development taking place from the historical tradition, these technical factors will create a completely new form? Can we consider the newly invented, purely constructional form of a modern steel girder to be a creation similar to the Greek column, whose hallowed form has ruled all artistic periods until today?

Certainly we can and we must.

Even the old Greek column was in essence a result of a structural calculation of support and loads: bearing capacity and the spanning capacity of the stone. Its height and spans, which we perceive as rules of beauty, were based on technical limits. The Gothic style created a new structural principle with its taut, pointed arch, and the columns disappeared. How can the iron engineer of our day begin with columnar architecture? He can treat it like a luxurious coulisse, like an occasional ornament pasted onto his halls (as on the exhibition palaces of Chicago), but the living core of iron construction no longer points him in this direction. We see in our railway stations, the exhibition buildings of Paris, and the art palaces of 1889 that iron construction has achieved a fully independent artistic life!

Julius Lessing, from "Neue Wege," trans. Harry Francis Mallgrave, in *Kunstgewerbeblatt* 6 (1895), pp. 1–5.

This same movement toward new ideals is already evident in other fields in which construction likewise dominates, and it has achieved a complete victory. The beauty of a ship earlier consisted in the decoration of the carving or the gilding; today we perceive the pure constructional lines of the trout-shaped rowboat as a thing of beauty, which an applied ornament would only destroy. The same is true with the modern, flexible, smoothly glazed wagons [. . .]

★ ★ ★

Like it or not, our work has to be based on the soil of the practical life of our time; it has to create those forms that correspond to our needs, our technology, our materials. If taking this lead we fashion a form of beauty in the manner of our scientific age, it will resemble neither the pious beauty of the Gothic nor the opulence of the Renaissance, but will perhaps appear as the somewhat austere beauty of the late nineteenth century, and that is all anyone can ask of us.

54 RICHARD STREITER
from "Out of Munich" (1896)

I n 1896, in the new artistic journal *Pan*, there appeared this article by Richard Streiter, which surveyed new architectural developments taking place in Munich. Streiter was an architect who had worked for several years in the Berlin office of Paul Wallot, the architect of the German Reichstag building. In 1894 Streiter left Wallot's office to pursue doctoral studies in Munich, where he was attracted to psychological aesthetics and in particular to the theory of "Empathy." Under the noted psychologist Theodor Lipps he wrote a dissertation on Karl Bötticher, in which he concluded that psychological aesthetics had provided models for modern theory that had, in effect, superseded all past efforts. The following short excerpt is crucial to the deliberations of the 1890s in two ways. First Streiter, in surveying the architectural school led by the Bavarian Gabriel Seidl, provides an alternative definition to Lessing's formulation of realism, one that exalts not only functionality but also takes into account regional and historical nuances. Second, he compresses this definition of realism into the single word *Sachlichkeit*. This word, which literally means "thingness," cannot be easily translated into English, but here it means the most simple and most practical architectural solution to a problem. This term would shortly be embraced by German modernists and, in fact, replace "realism" as the banner for the new modern movement.

Realism in architecture is the most extensive consideration of the real conditions in the creation of a building, and the most perfect fulfillment of the demands of functionality, comfort, health – in a word, *Sachlichkeit*. But this is not all. Just as realism in poetry focuses on the relation of the characters to their milieu, realism in architecture sees the principal goal of artistic truth as residing in the character of a building based not only on its purpose but also on its milieu, local building materials, the landscape, and the historical characteristics of the region.

Richard Streiter, from "Aus München," trans. Harry Francis Mallgrave, in *Pan* 2:3 (1896), p. 249.

Such healthy realism is found in the group of architects whose main master is Gabriel Seidl, the most sensitive and consistent representative of the Munich tendency toward unpretentious architecture and applied arts. The affiliation of this group with the old vernacular ways of building of the southern German unpretentious baroque is therefore more than a fashion. It means, in more than one respect, a return to *Sachlichkeit*, simplicity, good design without ostentation, and simple solidity without empty chatter or false appearance.

55   OTTO WAGNER
from *Modern Architecture* (1896)

In 1895 Otto Wagner followed his inaugural address by writing the first great manifesto of the new movement. When this polemical masterpiece appeared in 1896, it reverberated once again across European architectural circles. Wagner's interpretation of "realism" in the book follows the lead of Fabiani and Lessing by attempting to define a "modern architecture" entirely out of the fulfillment of modern needs and in the detailing of constructional materials and techniques. Any artistic treatment, which he refers to as "art-form," should be derived entirely from these constructional motifs. Interestingly, he begins this passage by referring to Gottfried Semper's four motives, but he also criticizes Semper for his (un-Darwinian) clinging to the symbolic dimension of architecture. It should also be noted that the polemics of Wagner at this stage were far in advance of his architectural practice, which in its stylistic or symbolic motifs was still largely historicist. In the second of the two passages, however, he points precisely to how a new modern style may be achieved. Wagner first proposed this "modern way of building" in the design for the Capuchin Church in Vienna in 1898, and again in his designs for the Vienna City Museum, beginning in 1900 – neither of which was built. Thus it was not until the construction of his Postal Savings Bank (1903) that he was able to implement his ideas.

- The first human building form was the roof, the protective covering, surely a substitute for the lack of the cave. The roof preceded the supports, the wall, even the hearth. After the roof came the supports, artificially built of tree trunks and stones, and finally the wickerwork, the partition, the bearing wall.
- These building elements received further development in permanent settlements through the use of tools and natural circumstances. After an immeasurably long evolution, traditions (a continuous addition of new purposes and means of production) together with art (born of the human sense of beauty) gradually elevated the basic forms of supports, walls, and rafters to art-forms [*Kunstformen*].
- Only in such a way could art have arisen. There can scarcely be any doubt of the correctness of what I have said.
- Moreover, if one examines all the art-forms from historical periods, an almost unbroken series of gradual developments from the date of their CONSTRUCTIVE origin until today can easily be proven, notwithstanding all the stylistic epochs.

Otto Wagner, from *Moderne Architektur* (1896), trans. Harry Francis Mallgrave as *Otto Wagner: Modern Architecture*. Santa Monica, CA: Getty Publication Programs, 1988, pp. 92–3, 96. The capitalization appeared in the original and in the 1902 edition, used here.

- Logical thinking must therefore convince us that the following tenet is unshakable: "EVERY ARCHITECTURAL FORM HAS ARISEN IN CONSTRUCTION AND HAS SUC- CESSIVELY BECOME AN ART-FORM." This principle withstands all analyses and explains every art-form.

Earlier, in the chapter "Style" and just now, it was emphasized that art-forms undergo change. Apart from the fact that the form had to correspond to the ideal of beauty of each epoch, these changes arose because the mode of production, the material, the tools, the means available, and the need were different, and further, forms came to fulfill different purposes in different places. IT IS THEREFORE CERTAIN THAT NEW PURPOSES MUST GIVE BIRTH TO NEW METHODS OF CONSTRUCTION, AND BY THIS REASONING ALSO TO NEW FORMS.

- Our modern epoch has, like none earlier, produced the greatest number of such new methods of construction (one need only consider the success of iron).
- If today all of these forms have not yet developed into perfect art-forms, it is for the reason indicated earlier – namely, that utility first prepares these forms for art.
- It might again be emphasized that every shaping of form always proceeds slowly and imperceptibly.
- It is Semper's undisputed merit to have referred us to this postulate, to be sure in a somewhat exotic way, in his book *Der Stil*. Like Darwin, however, he lacked the courage to complete his theories from above and below and had to make do with a symbolism of construction, instead of naming construction itself as the primitive cell of architecture.

Construction always precedes, for no art-form can arise without it, and the task of art, which is to idealize the existing, is impossible without the existence of the object.

- Thus the formation of our very own art-forms, corresponding to modern construction, lies within ourselves; the possibility of creating them is offered and facilitated by the rich legacy that we have inherited.
- The useful result of this way of looking at things is very simple.
- "THE ARCHITECT ALWAYS HAS TO DEVELOP THE ART-FORM OUT OF CONSTRUCTION."

[...]

- A colonnade with an entablature was designed as the principal architectural motif of the upper story of a prominent monumental building. The building was constructed in courses of stone and the material was procured with a great expenditure of time and money. Immense stone blocks, reminiscent of the old Roman method of construction, were employed for the lower members of the main cornice; it was even structurally necessary to carve the modillions of the main cornice out of the same stone. The preparation and procurement of these blocks required great temporal and pecuniary sacrifice.
- This type of production should be called "the Renaissance way of building" and may be compared next with a "modern way of building."
- For the exterior cladding of a building (based, of course, on the same premises) a panel system will be used for the planar surfaces. Since these panels can be assumed to have significantly less cubic volume, they can be designed for a nobler material (for example, Laase marble). They are to be fastened with bronze bolts (rosettes). For the support of the

deeply projecting cornice, divided into small courses, iron anchor bolts will be used, which are sheathed in a bronze console-like casing, etc., etc.

- The result of this comparison might be approximately the following:
- The cubic volume of the stone will be reduced by from one-eighth to one-tenth of that in the original case; the number of components will be fewer; the monumental effect will be enhanced by the nobler material; the money spent will decrease enormously, and the production time will be reduced to the normal and desired amount.

- Certainly the advantages are sufficient to prefer the modern way of building in such cases. But the list of advantages is not exhausted; the greatest advantage is that IN THIS WAY A NUMBER OF NEW ARTISTIC MOTIFS WILL EMERGE, whose development the artist not only will find very desirable, but also that which he must seize with alacrity and enthusiasm so as to make genuine progress in art.

56 RICHARD STREITER
from "Contemporary Architectural Questions" (1898)

The importance of Wagner's ideas and the generally happy reception they received can be seen from this 96-page review of the book by Richard Streiter. This review, in fact, stands by itself as one of the most important theoretical documents of early modernism – if only for the acumen with which Streiter places all the design issues on the table. Streiter begins his review by noting the "sensation" created by Wagner's book, and he speaks very highly of Wagner's "extremely progressive program," which has already found many emulators across Germany and Austria. With that, Streiter embarks on a lengthy recapitulation of the "style" problem over the course of the twentieth century (beginning with Schinkel and Heinrich Hübsch), as well as a history of the realist movement, which in architectural theory he traces back to Jean-Louis de Cordemoy, Marc-Antoine Laugier, and Friedrich-August Krubsacius. Streiter is particularly impressed with the similarity of Wagner's argument with Robert Dohme's remarks concerning modern vehicles and ships, and he comes to label Wagner's theory a "tectonic realism," because of its artistic reliance on constructional motifs. Competing against Wagner's theory, however, is another strand of modernism, one of "mannerism, affectation, and thoughtless profundity." Streiter is referring to recent *Jugendstil* and Art Nouveau tendencies, which he casts here simply as an "episode." Thus French and German theory effectively part company at this critical juncture, but it is important to note that Streiter, a few pages later, will also counter Wagner's tectonic realism with his own plea for a regional realism, tempered by artistic consciousness.

But even if one were inclined to view the newest fashion in painting and literature as more than an "episode," it would be unfair to play this direction as a trump card against Wagner's

Richard Streiter, from "Architektonische Zeitfragen: Eine Sammlung und Sichtung verschiedener Anschauungen mit besonderer Beziehung auf Professor Otto Wagners Schrift 'Moderne Architektur'" (1898), trans. Harry Francis Mallgrave, in *Richard Streiter: Ausgewählte Schriften zur Aesthetik und Kunst-Geschichte*. Munich: Delphin, 1913, pp. 81–2.

demand for honest realism in architecture. The architect does not create in seclusion like the painter or poet, following the whim of his imagination. Unlike these artists, his creations often depend on the very prosaic and constrained demands of practical life. And his creations are generally not enjoyed in the lonely solitude of the evening house, like a picture book, but in the hustle and bustle of everyday life that surrounds them. Architecture forms the artistic framework for the total image of the life of individuals as well as of the masses. It has to suit the basic mood of this image. A strong realist current runs through our public and private lives. Both today and earlier the task of this art is to ennoble and to embellish the forms and creations springing from practical needs with a breath of poetry. It can scarcely be argued that such an ennoblement of our exterior forms of life should be characterized by excessive imagination or by an artificially reawakened romanticism.

If ever a time, more so than any other, was ready to accept the principle of artistic truth, conciseness, and *Sachlichkeit* in architecture and the applied arts – the most perfect fulfillment of purpose with the simplest means – it is ours. Our grandly developed modern technology, whose huge array of products passes hourly and daily through our hands, is ruled by one supreme principle: maximum performance with minimum means. By repeatedly viewing and using these products, our eyes and sense of touch have grown more and more accustomed to this structural–technical *Sachlichkeit*, and our tectonic sense-of-form has likewise be influenced by it. Our corporeal feeling has also become receptive to greater mobility through the extraordinary increase in the means of transportation, and it is therefore very sensitive to any restraining or burdening ballast. This psychological fact – the influence of modern technology and changed living conditions on our corporeal sense, and therefore also on our structural feeling and sense-of-form – alone supplies the key to understanding the specific modern way of conceiving tectonic tasks.

57 FRITZ SCHUMACHER
from "Style and Fashion" (1898)

Streiter's hostility toward *Jugendstil* tendencies, as well as his plea for regional realism predicated on *Sachlichkeit*, would also attract many followers, and arguably would become the dominant position of German theory in the first decade of the twentieth century. Close to this viewpoint in 1898 was Fritz Schumacher. The son of a German diplomat, Schumacher was raised in South America and New York City, before he returned to Germany to study architecture in Berlin and Munich. In the latter city he worked for Gabriel von Siedl; in 1896 he obtained a municipal position in Leipzig. Schumacher's essay consigns both the Arts and Crafts movement and Art Nouveau to the category of fashions, which he opposes with his vision of a regional or vernacular realism. This position is important because in 1901 Cornelius Gurlitt would secure for him a chair at Dresden's Technical

Fritz Schumacher, from "Stil und Mode" (1898), trans. Harry Francis Mallgrave, in *Im Kampfe um die Kunst*. Strasbourg: J. H. Heitz, 1902, pp. 23, 28–9.

University, from which base Schumacher would later help to coordinate the founding of the German Werkbund. Schumacher, in fact, gave the keynote address at the first Werkbund meeting in Munich in 1907.

Connected with the group of artists gathered around Morris in England and those in Belgium and France with their headquarters in Bing's "L'Art Nouveau," we saw everywhere in Germany in the last decades new forms emerging that – sometimes in the pose of being revolutionary, sometimes in a quieter and more modest way – sought to create new values for the market of our artistic forms. What these precursors had in mind, and in particular what became the battle cry of the rapidly emerging journals, was the impulse to discover a new style.

A new style! Every age before our century had its style. Why should we suddenly doubt our ability to develop one of our own? The demand has something engaging about it, a fomenting kernel; it conceals within it a certain booty for our scribbling time. Here is finally a program worth getting excited about, and we ceremoniously hear all the high-sounding manners of speech that the augurs of art place on this catchphrase. We must therefore not be surprised that the idea quickly aroused enthusiasm in every quarter – but unfortunately good intentions alone do not create a style, and the blessed awareness that we are fully justified in going our own way does not in itself provide us with a direction.

★ ★ ★

We must get used to the fact that the different tasks of our time require essentially different stylistic characters. What can unite and hopefully serve as a common bond may be a certain commonality of taste, and perhaps it is nothing more than the artistic recognition that the basis for solving tasks means going back to the nature of practical purpose, to the nature of the material, to the nature of the organic world of forms, to the nature of the vernacular. As different as individual cases may be, this could, then, be described as the achievement of an epoch of *realist* architecture.

58   AUGUST ENDELL
from "On the Possibility and Goal of a New Architecture" (1898)

I f Henry van de Velde was the principal theorist of the Art Nouveau movement in Belgium and France, the principal representative of the parallel *Jugendstil* movement in Germany was August Endell. After university studies at the University of Tübingen, Endell transferred to the University of Munich in 1892, where he, like so many others of his generation, became attracted to the new psychological aesthetics. Like Streiter, he took doctoral studies on the notion of "empathy" (*Einfühlung*) under the psychologist Theodor Lipps. But whereas Streiter dismissed the decorative sensitivities of *Jugendstil* art in favor of his realist outlook, Endell sought to support

August Endell, from "Möglichkeit und Ziele einer neuen Architektur," trans. Harry Francis Mallgrave, in *Deutsche Kunst und Dekoration* 1 (March 1898), pp. 143–5.

Jugendstil aesthetics with the new psychological theories. Endell's application of empathy theory to architecture came in two essays he wrote in 1898, and thus his aesthetic reasoning precedes van de Velde's articulation of similar ideas by a few years. But whereas van de Velde's penchant for curvilinear lines and forms are reflected in his writings on art, Endell's theory, with its preference for rectilinear or rectangular forms, in a curious way presages the De Stijl movement of the 1920s.

A cultivated and refined sense-of-form is the basic premise of all architectural creation, and it cannot be intellectually learned. [. . .]

A sense-of-form is the basic premise for the person enjoying the work of art and for the creator, but the creator needs more. His imagination must be so full of forms that for a specific purpose they tirelessly stream toward him in abundance, forms from which he selects, out of which he creates the formal design. For *formal creations* are the goal of all decorative arts, not, however, stylized plants or animals. [. . .]

The architect must be a form-artist; the path to new architecture leads only through the art of pure form. We have now still very few works of the art of pure form, that is, formal creations that are nothing and that signify nothing, but that have a direct effect on us without any intellectual mediation, like the tones of music. This way of working, this new art is almost unknown, and the few examples that do exist are discarded with a shrug, and for this reason the present state of our architecture should not surprise us. Therefore the architect should be primarily a form-artist. But the goal is not to create any kinds of forms, but forms that at the same time serve a specific purpose. It is generally a matter of creating living spaces or interior spaces, and thus for technical and pecuniary reasons there is a preference for straight lines and planes, as well as for the vertical and horizontal directions. [. . .]

Yet this limitation does not hinder the effect, because countless planar designs can be composed from straight lines. Simple rectangles exhibit all possible characters following the proportions of their sides and whether their longer sides are horizontal or vertical. And likewise simple rectangular rooms can have infinitely different characters, according to the relation of length, width, and height. The possibilities of the effect are not lacking, but one should be clear about the goal to be achieved.

59 ADOLF LOOS
from ''Potemkin City'' (1898)

Although living and working in Vienna in the shadow of Otto Wagner, Adolf Loos was not part of his circle of students. This Moravian had studied architecture in Dresden in the early 1890s and he famously visited the United States between 1893 and 1896. There he worked at odd jobs and acquired his fondness for the United States and all things Anglo-Saxon. When Loos returned to Europe to live in the capital of the Habsburg Empire, he was an outsider. Because he had not attended the Academy of Fine Arts, he was essentially precluded

Adolf Loos, from ''Die Potemkin'sche Stadt'' (1898), trans. Jane O. Newman and John H. Smith as ''Potemkin City,'' in Adolf Loos, *Spoken into the Void: Collected Essays 1897–1900.* Cambridge, MA: MIT Press, 1982, pp. 95, 96.

from higher state service in architecture, and thus he made his living with a small architectural practice (mostly remodeling apartments) and as a newspaper critic. In the last regard he was noted for his sarcasm and acerbic wit, which he took great delight in directing at the cultural pretensions of the capital. In this early essay, which in fact appeared in 1898 in the Secession journal *Ver Sacrum*, Loos attacks architectural historicism by criticizing the Renaissance-inspired apartment buildings of Vienna's *Ringstrasse*. It was one of his earliest salvos in a war that he would wage on behalf of modernism over the next two decades.

Who does not know of Potemkin's villages, the ones that Catherine's cunning favorite built in the Ukraine? They were villages of canvas and pasteboard, villages intended to transform a visual desert into a flowering landscape for the eyes of Her Imperial Majesty. But was it a whole city which that cunning minister was supposed to have produced?

Surely such things are only possible in Russia!

But the Potemkin city of which I wish to speak here is none other than our dear Vienna herself. It is a hard accusation; it will also be hard for me to succeed in proving it. For to do so I need listeners with a very fine sense of justice, such listeners, unfortunately, as are scarcely to be found in our city nowadays.

Anyone who tries to pass himself off as something better than he is is a swindler; he deserves to be held in general contempt, even if no one has been harmed by him. But if someone attempts to achieve this effect with false jewels and other imitations? There are countries where such a man would suffer the same fate. But in Vienna we have not yet come so far. There is only a small circle of people who would feel that in such a case an immoral act has occurred, that they have been swindled. But today it is not only by means of the fake watch chain, not only by the furnishings of one's residence (which consist of outright imitations), but also by one's residence itself, the building in which one lives, that everyone wants to make himself out to be something more than he is.

Whenever I stroll along the Ring, it always seems to me as if a modern Potemkin had wanted to carry out his orders here, as if he had wanted to persuade somebody that in coming to Vienna he had been transported into a city of nothing but aristocrats.
[. . .]

Poverty is no disgrace. Not everyone can come into the world the lord of a feudal estate. But to pretend to one's fellow men that one has such an estate is ridiculous and immoral. After all, should we be ashamed to live in a rental apartment in a building with many others who are our social equals? Should we be ashamed of the fact that there are materials that are too expensive for us to build with? Should we be ashamed to be nineteenth-century men and not men who want to live in a building whose architectural style belongs to an earlier age? If we ceased to be ashamed, you would see how quickly we would acquire an architecture suited to our own times. This is what we have anyway, you will object. But I mean an architectural style that we will be able to pass on to posterity in good conscience, an architectural style that even in the distant future will be pointed to with pride. But we have not yet found this architectural style in our century in Vienna.

Whether one tries to create out of canvas, pasteboard, and paint the wood huts where happy peasants dwell, or to erect out of brick and poured cement would be stone palaces where feudal lords seem to reside, it is the same in principle. Potemkin's spirit has hovered over Viennese architecture in this century.

60 HERMANN MUTHESIUS
from "New Ornament and New Art" (1901)

The first major German theorist of the twentieth century was Hermann Muthesius, whose contribution to modern theory resides in the synthesis he brings to the ideas that had been percolating over the previous twenty years. Muthesius was a student of art history and philosophy at the University of Berlin before he began his architectural studies at the Berlin Technische Hochschule in 1883. In this same decade he worked for the Prussian government, the architect Paul Wallot (narrowly missing Richard Streiter there), and for a firm that was building in Japan and the Far East. In 1891 he returned from Asia to Germany and resumed his service in the Prussian Ministry of Public Works, which – together with the Ministry of Trade – arranged his appointment to the German Embassy in London as a cultural attaché. There he was asked to study the situation of the British decorative arts. Out of this mission came his first two books on English architecture and the contemporary English house. Muthesius is known to Anglo-Saxon readers primarily for these two titles, but his theoretical approach has its grounding in other sources, principally in the German reform movement of Robert Dohme, Cornelius Gurlitt, Alfred Lichtwark, Richard Streiter, and Fritz Schumacher. Another person influencing Muthesius here is Julius Meier-Graefe, one of the original founders of the *Jugendstil* journal *Pan* and the editor of the journal *Dekorative Kunst*. Meier-Graefe had resigned his position at *Dekorative Kunst* in 1897 to open a shop in Paris, "La Maison Moderne," designed by Henry van de Velde. But Meier-Graefe by 1900 was distancing himself from the Jugendstil movement, and it is the acknowledgment of this fact with which Muthesius opens this essay – a sharply worded condemnation on all *Jugendstil* and Secessionist tendencies (which he interestingly equates with William Morris's love of medieval ornaments). Muthesius counters with "common sense" and the newly coined term *Sachlichkeit*. His polemics are not only brilliant, but they define the mission of which he will take charge over the coming decade.

Already thirteen years ago a very observant Robert Dohme, in his writing on the English house, directed the eyes of the German reader to a whole new field of art, which his studies of the English dwelling had opened to him. The results of his observations can be summarized in the axiom "the person of greater sensitivity no longer decorates (for decoration is a superficiality); he transfigures from the inside out." It is a grand and highly interesting statement, in which probably lies concealed the whole artistic problem of the future. It is therefore of little importance whether our new carpets are decorated with "object-less" lines or naturalistic roses or with stylized sea waves (I personally would prefer them to be without patterns). These trivialities do not address themselves to the artistic tasks of our time. The elegantly built sailing vessel shooting across the water's surface, the electric lamp, and the bicycle – these seem to capture the spirit of our time more closely than the erstwhile new furniture or wallpaper in the *Jugendstil* or Secession style.

Art supports itself on the life of its time. In the end it also has to give prominence to another consideration that until now has only dimly shown itself in the recent artistic outbursts on the Continent – sanitary concerns. If we were to distinguish the true achievements of our

Hermann Muthesius, from "Neues Ornament und neue Kunst," trans. Harry Francis Mallgrave, in *Dekorative Kunst* 4:9 (1901), pp. 364–5.

very changed living habits from earlier times, they would incontestably belong to the field of health. A great need for light and air, for physical comfort, for care of the body in general, the absolute exclusion of all dust from our environment, the flawless plumbing of our houses, effective ventilation of our living spaces – these are the achievements that modern man recognizes as his own. The small washbasin the size of a large sauce dish, placed on our great-grandmother's small wooden stand, served as a cleaning tool; our modern marble washroom and bathroom make the distinction immediately clear. Yet this achievement has to show itself in the other parts of our surroundings. We need bright and clean rooms without clutter or dust catchers, with smooth and simple furniture that is easy to clean and move; we need a room that is airy and open in plan, which gives us the self-evident awareness that here light, air, and cleanliness are at home. We unify these ideas today under the notion of comfort. These demands have not the slightest thing to do with lyrical lines and ornamental art. The more these demands are fulfilled, the more today's room furnishings will make a modern impression, that is, a truly modern one that is not just to be seen as the newest fashion.

61   HERMANN MUTHESIUS
from *Style-Architecture and Building-Art* (1902)

I f Otto Wagner's *Modern Architecture* can be deemed the first polemic of the Modern Movement, Muthesius's *Style-Architecture and Building-Art* can be seen as its first theoretical tract. The theme of the book is contained in its German title, which positions the German word *Baukunst* (building-art) against the imported terms *Stilarchitektur* (style-architecture, or the architecture of styles). If the former is an old (and therefore good) German word for straightforward, practical, or *sachliche* construction, the Greek/Latin terms "style" and "architecture" signify for Muthesius the high or pretentious historical styles of the nineteenth century. In part one of his study, Muthesius (as the first excerpt demonstrates) condemns this period as a whole as the "inartistic century" – the first of the great "myths" of the Modern Movement that would be endlessly repeated. But Muthesius's vision of modernism should also be qualified. Whereas the second of the cited passages announces his commitment to "scientific objectivity," or *Sachlichkeit* in design – the functional elegance of a ship or bicycle – he goes on, in later remarks, to temper this industrial realism with a "Nordic-Germanic spirit," that is, plead for a regional and national modernism based on the principles of simple and unpretentious design. His vision of modernism thus remains close to that of Richard Streiter and actually somewhat hostile to the tectonic realism of Otto Wagner. And these two different interpretations of *Sachlichkeit* would now become the competing camps of German modernism in the first decade of the twentieth century.

As we crossed the threshold of the new century, we were not lacking in reflections that sought to capture in a few words the significance of the passing century. The nineteenth

Hermann Muthesius, from *Stil-Architektur und Baukunst* (1902), trans. Stanford Anderson as *Style-Architecture and Building-Art*. Santa Monica, CA: Getty Publication Programs, 1994, pp. 50, 79.

century was termed the century of transportation, of electricity, of the natural sciences, of historical research, the century of the national armies, of labor, of machines. Each of these labels is of little value, but taken collectively we notice that no one has dared to call the nineteenth century the century of art. Every acclaimed accomplishment is scientific in nature – those that devolve from the intellectual activity of mankind. Nothing is said of the arts; they obviously played no role in the nineteenth century. And indeed in this century every field was forcefully reshaped: the civilized world has been overtaken with a desire for practical application, with earnestness for the comprehension of life, and with a compulsion for research and acquisition that were unknown in earlier times. This activity was, however, very one-sided: purely intellectual or technically oriented. Yet with regard to art, especially the plastic arts, we can think of no better way to designate this period than as the "inartistic century."

[. . .]

From this point of view, a great part of contemporary architectural production fails completely, for its creators remain imprisoned in their efforts at a style. If we wish to seek a new style – the style of our time – its characteristic features are to be found much more in those modern creations that truly serve our newly established needs and that have absolutely no relation to the old formalities of architecture: in our railway terminals and exhibition buildings, in very large meeting halls, and further, in the general tectonic realm, in our large bridges, steamships, railway cars, bicycles, and the like. It is precisely here that we see embodied truly modern ideas and new principles of design that demand our attention. Here we notice a rigorous, one might say scientific objectivity [Sachlichkeit], an abstention from all superficial forms of decoration, a design strictly following the purpose that the work should serve. All things considered, who would deny the pleasing impression of the broad sweep of an iron bridge? Who is not pleased by today's elegant landau, trim warship, or light bicycle? Since such works stand before us as the products of our time, we see a modern sensitivity recorded in them. They must embody an expressive modern form; they must mirror the sensibility of our time, just as the richly acanthusladen cannon barrel did the seventeenth century or the carved and gilded sedan chair the eighteenth century.

In such new creations we find the signs indicating our aesthetic progress. This can henceforth be sought only in the tendency toward the strict matter-of-fact [Sachlichen], in the elimination of every merely applied decorative form, and in shaping each form according to demands set by purpose.

62 FRITZ SCHUMACHER
from "The Reconquest of a Harmonious Culture", inaugural address to the German Werkbund (1907)

The culmination of the efforts of Muthesius and others in the first decade of the new century was the creation of the German Werkbund. The founding meeting took place in October 1907, in Munich. The association was formed of twelve artists and twelve industrial firms, in what was yet another attempt (after Henry Cole) to align artists with industrial chieftains, but there were also key differences. Not only would the efforts of many of the leading German architects of the early modern movement be united (among them Peter Behrens, Joseph Hoffmann, Joseph Olbrich, and Richard Riemerschmid), but the association dedicated to the reform of industrial production would, over the next seven years, exercise a profound influence on all artistic matters in Germany. From the founding of the Werkbund town of Hellerau to the tumultuous debate at the 1914 congress in Cologne – the Werkbund became the face of German modernism. The Semperian theme annunciated in Fritz Schumacher's keynote address at the first conference – the desire to bridge the estrangement between the creative artist and the industrial producer – also became a leading polemic of the day.

We wish to create an association to further and promote the applied arts. Why is this necessary? To the many organizations that pursue artistic goals, why add a new one?

Within the development of cultural questions, gentlemen, there is always a moment when specific forces must be combined anew, when the old premises that drove earlier events, which may at one time also had pursued similar goals, are no longer viable. And thus when we must begin anew in order to be able to express through actions a definite, necessary, and apparent idea, completely and clearly.

This is our situation. We need an association that is based on the premise of a close and above all trusting relationship between artist and producer. We need an organization that brings these same forces together not only locally but also in the whole of Germany, an organization that seeks a bridge from city to country, from country to country. [. . .]

The truth seems simple, and yet within it lies something new that has to be explained. The separation between creator and producer that we have today did not exist earlier. The power of old creation in the applied arts lay in this unity, and many of its best characteristics developed out of the fact that the separation was not there. Nevertheless the separation has inescapably come to pass. And though we all recognized this process earlier, no one has been able to prevent what has transpired.

Fritz Schumacher, from excerpts published by Kurt Junghanns in *Der Deutsche Werkbund: Sein erstes Jahrzehnt*, trans. Harry Francis Mallgrave. Berlin: Henschelverlage Kunst und Gesellschaft, 1982, pp. 140–2.

It came about because the machine began to compete with the hand, because an industry developed alongside handiwork, in which the quantity and the tempo of production far exceeded that of the individual artisan. [...]

Thus out of unobstructed economic and technical development of the time a great danger has formed at the root of the handicrafts, the danger of an estrangement between the producer and the creative spirit. This danger cannot be disguised, nor will we be able to banish it so long as there is industry. We must try to overcome it by bridging over the existing separation.

That is the great goal of our association. [...]

63   ADOLF LOOS
from "Ornament and Crime" (1908)

I n 1909 Adolf Loos would become embroiled in the famous controversy surrounding his design of the "Looshaus" in Vienna – the starkly white, unornamented, commercial and residential building that would turn him overnight into something of an architectural celebrity. One year earlier he penned his equally famous essay, "Ornament and Crime," which in its own way would be enshrined as a manifesto for the modern movement. Loos, as usual, pulled no verbal punches. If a primitive human aboriginal has a right to tattoo his own body, if a local cobbler has a right to apply tassels to a pair of shoes of his creation, the modern man of culture – the man who attends a Beethoven concert – has forsaken this right. For him the purchase of a machine-made product with ornamental tattooing etched on its casing is tantamount to a criminal act.

The urge to ornament one's face, and everything within one's reach is the origin of fine art. It is the babble of painting. All art is erotic.

The first ornament that came into being, the cross, had an erotic origin. The first work of art, the first artistic action of the first artist daubing on the wall, was in order to rid himself of his natural excesses. A horizontal line: the reclining woman. A vertical line: the man who penetrates her. The man who created it felt the same urge as Beethoven, he experienced the same joy that Beethoven felt when he created the Ninth Symphony.

But the man of our time who daubs the walls with erotic symbols to satisfy an inner urge is a criminal or a degenerate. It is obvious that this urge overcomes man; such symptoms of degeneration most forcefully express themselves in public conveniences. One can measure the culture of a country by the degree to which its lavatory walls are daubed. With children it is a natural phenomenon: their first artistic expression is to scrawl on the walls erotic symbols. But what is natural to the Papuan and the child is a symptom of degeneration in the modern man. I have made the following observation and have announced it to the world:

The evolution of culture is synonymous with the removal of ornament from objects of daily use. I had thought to introduce a new joy into the world: but it has not thanked me for it. Instead the idea was greeted with sadness and despondency.

Adolf Loos, from "Ornament und Verbrechen" (1908), trans. Wilfried Wang, in *The Architecture of Adolf Loos.* London: Arts Council Exhibition, 1985, pp. 100, 103.

My shoes are covered all over with ornaments, which result from notches and holes: work which the cobbler carried out and which he was not paid for. I go to the cobbler and say to him: 'For a pair of shoes you are asking thirty crowns. I will pay you forty crowns'. By doing this I have made him happy and he will thank me for it by the work and materials which will not bear any relation in terms of quality to the extra amount. He is happy because rarely does fortune enter his house and he has been given work by a man who understands him, who appreciates his work and who does not doubt his honesty. He already imagines the finished pair in front of him. He knows where the best leather is to be found today, he knows which worker he will entrust with the shoes, and that they will display notches and holes, as many as there is space for on an elegant pair of shoes. And now I say: 'But there is one condition which I have. The shoes must be completely smooth.' By that, I have plunged him from the height of happiness to the depths of Tartarus. He has less work to do, I have robbed him of all pleasures.

I preach to the aristocrats. I allow decoration on my own body, if it provides a source of pleasure for my fellow men. Then they are also my pleasures. I suffer the ornament of the Kafir, that of the Persian, that of the Slovak farmer's wife, the ornaments of my cobbler, because they all have no other means of expressing their full potential. We have our culture which has taken over from ornament. After a day's trouble and pain, we go to hear Beethoven or Wagner. My cobbler cannot do that. I must not rob him of his pleasures as I have nothing else to replace them with. But he who goes to listen to the Ninth Symphony and who then sits down to draw up a wallpaper pattern, is either a rogue or a degenerate.

The absence of ornament has raised the other arts to unknown heights. Beethoven's symphonies would never have been written by a man who walked around in silk, velvet and lace. The person who runs around in a velvet suit is no artist but a buffoon or merely a decorator. We have become more refined, more subtle. Primitive men had to differentiate themselves by various colours, modern man needs his clothes as a mask. His individuality is so strong that it can no longer be expressed in terms of items of clothing. The lack of ornament is a sign of intellectual power. Modern man uses the ornament of past and foreign cultures at his discretion. His own inventions are concentrated on other things.

64 JOSEPH AUGUST LUX
from *Engineer-Aesthetic* (1910)

Opposing the *sachliche* modernism of Muthesius and the German Werkbund was the competing vision of the Austrian Joseph August Lux. This historically somewhat neglected architect published the first biography of Otto Wagner in 1914, and it was Wagner's brand of tectonic realism (artistic motives must arise out of construction) that he championed in numerous writings over the course of this decade. Lux in some ways went

Joseph A. Lux, from *Ingenieur-Aesthetik*. Munich: Gustav Lammers, 1910, pp. 14, 38, trans. Harry Francis Mallgrave.

farther than Wagner: both in his opposition to all handicraft production and in the great esteem in which he held the engineer. Lux is thus the first modern historian to see the engineer as the most uncompromising representative of modernity and to view the "engineer aesthetic" as a mandate for architects to follow. Time, he felt, would ease the disquietude felt by many laypersons in perceiving the new engineered forms. And while this uncompromising position of historical determinism was still the minority view in 1910, Lux's ideas would be embraced in the 1920s, especially by the historical school led by Sigfried Giedion.

I have previously said somewhere that the true architect of modern times is the engineer. It is clear that the exacting engineer does not labor under stylistic-historical influences. But this should also not lead to the false view that technical genius operates without regard to aesthetic or, if one will, artistic appearance. Many parts of construction and machines are owed not merely to mathematical calculation but also to empirical experience. Their design is imparted with a sense-of-form. For example, the size of a thrashing chord of a steam engine is owed less to mathematical calculation than to aesthetic sensitivity; its thickness is approximate and determined by the desire for a certain visual harmony. Even if inspired by material and technique, the idea of form is the precursor and pathfinder for mathematically hardened construction. And this idea of form is the artistic element that also blesses the birth of engineering works. The new style was officially born in 1851, when the Crystal Palace was erected in London for the World Exhibition.

65 PETER BEHRENS
from "Art and Technology" (1910)

This clash between technology and more traditional conceptions of art, which forms so much of the Germanic debate at the start of the twentieth century, is represented in the ever-evolving writings and designs of Peter Behrens. Trained as a painter in the 1880s, Behrens enjoyed the fashion of the *Jugendstil* in the 1890s, and in 1900 he accepted an invitation to the Darmstadt artists' colony, where he first cultivated an interest in architecture and the crafts. Within a year or two, however, his views began to change. In 1903 he joined with the efforts and program of Muthesius, and it was with the blessing of the latter that Behrens became the director of the Dusseldorf School of Arts and Crafts. Behrens at this time was still struggling with his design sensibilities, but his mature style was reached shortly after 1907, the year that Behrens joined the AEG as the artistic director. This large corporation not only provided the machinery and equipment for electrical generation in Germany, but it also supplied a line of electrical products (such as lamps, toasters, fans, vacuum cleaners, and clocks) for use in the newly electrified German homes. Hence Behrens became a designer on the frontline of advancing technology, and he put together a staff that included such young architects as Walter Gropius and Mies van der Rohe. Behrens's signature design as an architect was the AEG Turbine Factory in Berlin (1908–9). Although this factory building, with its exposed glass and steel, later became one of the first paradigms of German modernism, we should also point out that Behrens's collaborating engineer on this project – Karl Bernhard – actually wanted a greater use of glass and

Peter Behrens, from "Kunst und Technik" (1910), trans. Iain Boyd Whyte, in *Industriekultur: Peter Behrens and the AEG 1907–1914*. Cambridge, MA: MIT Press, 1984, pp. 215, 219.

steel, but he was opposed by Behrens and his desire for battered concrete pylons at the corners and the concrete gable atop the main façade. This wish to soften technology with (traditional) artistic concerns was central to Behrens's design philosophy, as this excerpt shows. What Behrens also brings to the table, like Lux, is a sense of historical (Hegelian) determinism and, like Muthesius, a keen nationalism. Art is now placed almost solely in service to the larger economic and political life. Such words, certainly not unique within the deteriorating political situation of Europe at this time, were voiced just a few years before the outbreak of World War I.

One often hears that we are approaching an iron and steel style. But, as already noted, no style derives from construction or materials alone. There is no materialistic style, and there never has been. The all-embracing unity of an age stems from a much broader complex of conditions than can be represented by these two factors alone. Technology cannot permanently be understood as an end in itself, but gains in value and significance just at that point at which it is recognized as the most refined means of achieving a culture. A mature culture, however, speaks only through the language of art.

From the side of the art lover, there are great hopes of achieving a style linked to the highly individual development of the applied arts as they have evolved in Germany since the end of the 1890s. And although the talent behind these most diverse artistic statements should in no way be underestimated, it must nevertheless be asserted that there can be no individual style. An individual and personal artistic inclination cannot create the all-embracing unity of forms that in history has made an exact and eternal monument to a particular age. This formal unity will rather be derived from the preconditions of our age, among which technology and economics are the most important. Our most serious task, therefore, is to help technology to achieve artistic quality, at the same time helping art to great achievements through contact with technology.
[. . .]

Even though it must be conceded that, by their nature, art and technology are quite different, this in no way lessens the legitimacy of the view that they still belong together. Art should no longer be regarded as a private matter in which one indulges at will. We do not want an aesthetic system that looks for its rules in romantic dreaming, but one that is based on the full legitimacy of bustling life. Nor, however, do we want a technology that goes its own way, but one that is receptive to the artistic will of our age. In this way, German art and technology will work toward one goal: toward the power of the German nation, which reveals itself in a rich material life ennobled by intellectually refined design.

66 HERMANN MUTHESIUS AND HENRY VAN DE VELDE
from "theses" and "counter-theses" presented at the Cologne Werkbund Congress (1914)

B y far the largest and most significant of the prewar German Werkbund exhibitions was held in Cologne in the spring and summer of 1914. With great circumstance, the first architectural fruits of German modernism were put on display, as represented, for instance, by Henry van de Velde's theater and the model factory of Walter Gropius and Adolf Meyer. But more significant for the direction of modernism was the debate that transpired at the Werkbund's annual congress, which was held in the exhibition's main assembly hall in early July. Here Hermann Muthesius, the keynote speaker, was rudely confronted by Henry van de Velde over the issues of "stylization" (*Typisierung*) and artistic freedom — a dispute that would resonate within the German modern movement for more than a decade to come. The issues were complex and in fact had much to do with the personalities involved. Muthesius had been the guiding force behind the German Werkbund over the previous seven years, and his power had consolidated itself to the point where he had alienated many Werkbund members with his heavy-handed direction. Van de Velde, by this date, had become one of Europe's best-known architects, and since 1904 he had served as the director of the arts and crafts school in Weimar. A few days before the opening of the congress, Muthesius issued ten "theses," which he circulated in order to be approved by voice vote at the congress. Their content could not have been surprising to many. From the Werkbund's inception, Muthesius (also an official within the German Ministry of Trade) had always viewed the association as the semi-official arm of his governmental agency, in service to the exportation of German goods abroad. By "stylization" he probably had in mind such rationally designed products as the electric tea kettles, toasters, and lamps that Peter Behrens had introduced at the AEG. But opposition to Muthesius's theses quickly formed. Before speaking, Muthesius became aware that a group of younger artists, led by van de Velde, would present ten counter-theses to his proposals, and he thus toned down his rhetoric. Van de Velde, nevertheless, followed him to the podium and framed the debate not as the alliance of art with governmental trade policies but as one of artistic freedom. What was really at stake, however, was the power and influence of Muthesius within the association.

The showdown proved disastrous to both individuals, as July also saw the mobilization of the German and Austrian armies for the outbreak of World War I. Van de Velde, as a Belgian national, was eventually placed under house arrest within Germany and effectively marginalized within the modern movement. Muthesius saw his control of the Werkbund broken forever, and the anger of a defeated Germany (in four years) would be directed toward him for attempting to align art with governmental policies. He survived the war as a prolific writer on residential design, but from a position outside of the movement he had been so instrumental in creating.

Hermann Muthesius and Henry van de Velde, from *Hermann Muthesius, Die Werkbund-Arbeit der Zukunft*. Jena: Eugen Diederichs, 1914, pp. 32, 49–50, trans. Harry Francis Mallgrave.

[Hermann Muthesius]

1. Architecture, and with it all the creative activity of the Werkbund, strives toward stylization [*Typisierung*], and only in this way can it again achieve that universal significance that it had in times of harmonious culture.

2. Only through stylization, which should be conceived as the result of a healthy concentration [of forces], can a universally valid and sure taste again be achieved.

3. As long as a universally high level has not been achieved, we cannot count on the German applied arts making its influence felt abroad.

4. The world will demand our products only when they speak with a convincing expression of style. The basis for this has been laid by the earlier German movement.

[. . .]

6. Proceeding from the conviction that it is a matter of life and death for Germany always to advance its production, the German Werkbund, as an association of artists, industrialists, and businessmen, must direct its attention to the creation of the preconditions for the export of its industrial arts.

[. . .]

[Henry van de Velde]

1. So long as there are artists in the Werkbund and so long as they exercise some influence over its destiny, they will protest against any suggestion of a canon or stylization. In his innermost essence the artist is a burning idealist, a free spontaneous creator; with his free will he will never submit himself to a discipline that forces him into a type or a canon. Instinctively he mistrusts anything that could sterilize his actions or anyone who preaches a rule that could hinder him from pursuing his thoughts to their own free end, or that attempts to direct him to a universally valid form, in which he sees only a mask that might make a virtue out of a lack of ability.

[. . .]

B.   MODERNISM ELSEWHERE IN EUROPE

Introduction

Although no other European country created the unified front or matched the scope of discussion that transpired in Germany in the first decade of the twentieth century, similar demands for modernism were heard everywhere throughout Europe. Again, as in the last decades of the nineteenth century, much of the debate was connected with the formation of national cultural entities. Italy, Belgium, and the Netherlands, each in their own way, became centers for modernism. In northern Italy's case, the long-standing cultural dominance of the Hapsburgs actually hastened the advent of modernism, in that the influence of the Wagner School and architects such as Joseph Marie Olbrich and Joseph Hoffmann rapidly erased the vestiges of the Renaissance and Gothic traditions and set Italian architects on the course that would soon be defined by "Futurism," an uniquely Italian interpretation of modernism overlaid with a fascination for advanced industrial technologies. Belgium, especially through the efforts of Henry van de Velde, became one of the centers of the Art Nouveau movement, which was driven by both rationalist currents and a new fascination with the psychological aesthetics emanating from Germany. The Netherlands, which saw its historical borders shrink in the nineteenth century, quickly embraced the modern movement. Hendrik Berlage did for Holland what Otto Wagner accomplished for Austria – he became a determined and highly influential champion of modernism, and roughly during the same years. The Netherlands, in fact, would become one of the leading centers for European modernism at the conclusion of World War I.

Both Britain and France too had their spokesmen for modernism. If British theory at the turn of the century was still largely driven by the handicraft restraints of the Arts and Crafts movement, Ebenezer Howard's concept of a "garden city" demonstrated how such thinking could be transposed into an influential modern concept. France, another center for Art Nouveau, still had its legacy of technological accomplishment, and the work of Auguste Perret and Charles Garnier continued the tradition of experimentation with new materials.

67   CAMILLO BOITO
from "On the Future Style of Italian Architecture" (1880)

The high tradition of twentieth-century Italian theory arguably has its origins in Camillo Boito. This native of Rome had studied in Venice but established his practice in Milan, where he combined his predilection for the Italian Gothic style with teaching and historical writings on medieval architecture. Boito's thought in this regard runs parallel with the rationalist ideas of Eugène-Emmanuel Viollet-le-Duc, and, like the latter, Boito was also much concerned with the course of future developments. Thus this 1880 study of medieval Italian architecture concludes with this remarkable chapter, in which Boito raises the theme of mediating Italy's rich architectural tradition with the needs and necessities of modern life. It is a theme that would resonate in Italian theory throughout the twentieth century. And this country's concern for regional or specifically Italian solutions to differing cultural and landscape conditions will often set Italian theory apart from more cosmopolitan visions of modernism evident elsewhere in Europe.

The newly discovered sciences and their new methods can ignore the past and start from scratch, but for literature and the arts, which are not based on mathematical reasons or experimental matters, to break entirely with tradition means losing a living, obvious, and compelling voice, and thereby losing their moral and civil effectiveness. A language cannot be rebuilt in one stroke, and the arts are also a language. As Italian architecture manifestly must have a national appearance and temperament, it should be connected in some way to one or more Italian architectures of the past; and because presently this connection does not exist, they are in effect all there.

Should it be connected to more than one style? Each style of architecture is an organic living system, more or less complex, more or less perfect in relation to others, but complete and perfect in itself. Unions between analogous architectural styles give birth to hybrid ones; unions between different architectural styles produce abortions or monsters. We hope

Camillo Boito, from *Architettura del Medio Evo in Italia*. Milan: Hoepli, 1880, pp. 26–7, trans. Maria Pia Smargiasso.

this brief architectural history, which we believed was necessary to recount, has shown how renewals and improvements in art have never come from mixing, composing, or superimposing two or more past arts, but rather from the aesthetic and social development of an art that was either in decline or in recovery. It is one thing to get a lesson, a concept, a form, or inspiration from an architectural past, but it is something else again to try to merge it with a different one to get a new style. Must one cling to one past style in order to mimic it? Let's not dream of it, for imitation makes everything colder, poorer, more shriveled, and renders everything unbearable. Besides, there can be no architecture in the past that presently serves our specific needs. Therefore? We do not believe that old styles can be adapted to today's buildings in a useful and expressive way when they are copied in their organism and symbolism. We believe, nonetheless, that one must take a given Italian style from past centuries and modify it so that it can represent the temperament of our society and respond to our needs and customs. Naturally that style should lose its archaeological character and preserve the fecundity of its own aesthetic seeds, from which the new culture could spring – and herein lies the problem – one suitable, unique, and of a fully modern beauty.

To the three essential qualities previously mentioned, we can thus add the following negative and positive attributes of a new architecture. If history, in which we have great faith and reason but little faith, does not mislead us, the new architecture:

(1) cannot be created by one architect;
(2) cannot be totally new;
(3) cannot be composed of several old styles mixed together;
(4) must not mimic one style;
(5) must be national;
(6) must clearly be tied to one Italian style of the past;
(7) must lose the archaeological character of that style in order to become a totally modern one.

68 HENDRIK P. BERLAGE
from "Architecture and Impressionism" (1894)

Hendrik Berlage was born in Amsterdam, but he trained in the early 1870s at the ETH in Zurich – in a program of instruction that still carried the imprint of Gottfried Semper, who had moved to Vienna in 1869. Other influences on Berlage were the rationalist writings of Eugène-Emmanuel Viollet-le-Duc, the Dutch Gothic style of P. J. H. Cuypers, and the theosophy of J. L. M. Lauweriks and K. F. C. De Bazel. Combine these forces

Hendrik Berlage, from "Baouwkunst en impressionisme" (1894), trans. Iain Boyd Whyte as "Architecture and Impressionism," in *Hendrik Petrus Berlage: Thoughts on Style 1886–1909*. Santa Monica, CA: Getty Publication Programs, 1996, pp. 119–20.

with a commitment to socialism inherited from his readings of William Morris, and the stage is set for Berlage to emerge as an architect committed to revolutionary change. Like Wagner, his commitment begins to become evident in the 1890s, and this essay, which in fact precedes his heralded revised design for the Amsterdam Exchange by a few years, signals his first tentative steps. In the opening pages Berlage speaks of the Impressionist movement in painting and the lessons it might hold for architecture. The transposition of this term from painting to architecture is, however, not entirely a happy one, as by Impressionism Berlage intends a general simplification of masses and less attention to details. Time and money are given as two of the practical reasons for this change, but behind it is his socialist vision for society that no longer needs what he deems to be the false pretense and empty luxury of high art.

The architect should become an impressionist!

I have given practical reasons why, in my opinion, the age compels us to do so. There are, however, also ideal reasons that are even more important.

The already-mentioned fact that it is possible to design a good building that meets all requirements without art implies an age in which, because of both economic and various other special considerations, we shall be forced to cut expenditure, in which we will give up all luxury and will in fact do without any art. Architecture will be in bad shape if there is no impulse to prove that one can also make something beautiful without extra expense. Despite man's innate desire for art, one fears that a more democratically governed society will have a cooler attitude toward art, for everything that is not of immediate use and does not benefit the prosperity of the community is considered to be criminal.

Well, let the architects make sure that by that time they are ready with their art, which should in short be an art that will cost no money. Should they be unprepared, we will see the architect's work taken over by the engineer, whose job it already is to make the actual functional buildings [*Nutzbauten*]. This word sounds harsh to today's architects but will no longer do so in the future, for then we shall be able to call all architecture by that name. If the architects are not ready with their great impressionistic art, their work in this world will have come to an end; *sic transit gloria mundi*. If they are ready, the coming generations will be able to distinguish the artist from the scientific builder, the architect from the engineer. The architect will then have a splendid future, for mankind cannot do without an artistic ideal.

The architect should prove himself able to keep abreast of his times, for only then will his work be guaranteed in the future.

A further ideal reason compels us to develop the great impressionist concept in architecture. After the Middle Ages, architecture gradually lost its leading place among the arts; no longer were sculpture and painting subservient to it, no longer did it lead. Later, the three arts each went their separate ways, and architecture, now lowered in status, had the reputation of being the least [important] of the three. Today, architecture, which in classical and medieval times was the most important, beautiful, proud, and respected of all arts, is considered by many people not to be an art at all.

In the second half of the nineteenth century, through the efforts of a large number of capable architects, this opinion has been changed completely in favor of architecture. Even painters and sculptors (as biased as they were for a long time) no longer doubt that architecture is an art.

We can again see the great coming together of all the arts, which should lead to collaboration, the artistic ideal of all times.

Talented architects and sculptors are already working on large paintings and reliefs, no longer created as isolated museum pieces, but as building decorations – as in the times of the great monumental frescos. These paintings respect the architecture and keep in mind the purpose of the decoration of large surfaces, which means complementing rather than ignoring the architecture. These painters and sculptors, who understand the great art of lines and surfaces, hold out their hands to the architects; let the latter not decline the offer out of ignorance.

Understanding the new art, the most capable architects should make sure that their work shows great simplicity. Then, and only then, will they be able, as before, to take upon themselves the leadership of the great art of the future.

69 EBENEZER HOWARD
from *To-morrow: A Peaceful Path to Real Reform* (1898)

With this short but highly influential book, Ebenezer Howard first puts forward the idea of a "garden city." The idea had been somewhat long in its nurturing. Howard was an Englishman who immigrated to Nebraska in 1871 with the intention of becoming a farmer, and when his farm failed he eventually moved back to England. In between, however, he lived for some years in Chicago, where he witnessed and pondered the birth of the American suburb. Although many utopian thinkers in the late nineteenth century made proposals for alternative modes of living (with alternative political systems) to the large industrial centers, Howard's garden city was conceived from the beginning as a realistic proposal that combined the incentives of the capitalist system with the socialist sense of communal land protection. The garden city was in essence a satellite town of 30,000 residents, comprising urban, industrial, and agricultural sectors, and functioning semi-autonomously with other garden cities in free trade. Two garden cities – Letchworth and Welwyn – were eventually built in England in the first few decades of the new century, but Howard's effect on theory was far more expansive and extended.

The town of Garden City, which is to be built near the centre of the 6,000 acres, covers an area of 1,000 acres, or a sixth part of the 6,000 acres, and is of circular form, 1,240 yards (or nearly three-quarters of a mile) from centre to circumference. [. . .]

Six magnificent boulevards – each 120 feet wide – traverse the city from centre to circumference, dividing it into six equal parts or wards. In the centre is a circular space of 185 yards in diameter, and containing about five and half acres, laid out as a beautiful and well-watered garden; and, surrounding this garden, each standing in its own ample grounds, are the larger public buildings – town hall, principal concern and lecture hall, theatre, library, museum, picture-gallery, and hospital.

Ebenezer Howard, from *To-morrow: A Peaceful Path to Real Reform*. London: Swan Sonnenschein & Co., pp. 14–16. Republished in 1902 as *Garden Cities of To-morrow*.

The rest of the large space encircled by the "Crystal Palace" is a public park, containing 145 acres, which includes ample recreation grounds within very easy access of all the people.

Running all round the Central Park (except where it is intersected by the boulevards) is a wide glass corridor called "Crystal Palace." This building is in wet weather one of the favorite resorts of the people, whilst the knowledge that its bright shelter is ever close at hand tempts people into Central Park, even in the most doubtful of weathers. Here manufactured goods are exposed for sale, and here most of that class of shopping which requires the joy of deliberation and selection is done. The space enclosed by the Crystal Palace is, however, a good deal larger than is required for these purposes, and a considerable part of it is used as a Winter Garden – the whole forming a permanent exhibition of a most attractive character, whilst its circular form brings it near to every dweller in the town – the furthest removed inhabitant being within 600 yards.

Passing out of the Crystal Palace on our way to the outer ring of the town we cross Fifth Avenue – lined, as are all the roads of the town, with trees – fronting which, and looking on to the Crystal Palace, we find a ring of very excellently-built houses, each standing in its own ample grounds; and as we continue our walk, we observe that the houses are for the most part built either in concentric rings, facing the various Avenues (as the circular roads are termed), or fronting the boulevards and roads, which all converge to the centre of the town. Asking the friend who accompanies us on our journey what the population of this little city may be, we are told about 30,000, and that there are in the town 5,500 building lots of an average size of 20 feet by 130 feet – the minimum space allotted for the purpose being 16 by 125. Noticing the very varied architecture and design which the houses and group of houses display – some having common gardens and cooperative kitchens – we learn that general observance of street line or harmonious departure from it are the chief points as to house-building over which the municipal authorities exercise control, for, though proper sanitary arrangements are strictly enforced, the fullest measure of individual taste and preference is encouraged.

Walking still toward the outskirts of the town, we come upon "Grand Avenue." This avenue is fully entitled to the name it bears, for it is 420 feet wide, and forming a belt of green upwards of three miles long, divides that part of the town which lies outside Central Park into two belts. It really constitutes an additional park of 115 acres – a park which is within 240 yards of the furthest removed inhabitant. In this splendid avenue six sites, each of four acres, are reserved for public schools and their surrounding play-grounds and gardens, while other sites are reserved for churches of any denominations which the religious feelings of the people may select, and which they are prepared out of their own funds to erect and maintain. [...]

In the outer ring of the town are factories, warehouses, dairies, markets, coal yards, timber yards, etc., all fronting on the circle railway, which encompasses the whole town, and which has sidings connecting it with the main line of railway which passes through the estate.

70   HENRY VAN DE VELDE
from "The New Ornament"
(1901)

The painter, furniture designer, and architect Henry van de Velde created a sensation in Europe in 1895 with the three rooms he designed for Samuel Bing's Maison de l'Art Nouveau in Paris. A native of Antwerp, van de Velde had begun his career as a painter, and had been influenced by Vincent Van Gogh and Georges Seurat. In the early 1890s he became disaffected with what he perceived to be the elitism of high art and he redirected his interests to the decorative arts, now enthused with the socialist calling of William Morris. The design of his own "cottage" in Uccle, near Brussels, led to Bing's invitation to display his "new art" in Paris, and by the end of this decade the much-in-demand van de Velde had moved his base of operations to Berlin, and later Weimar. There he ran a furniture workshop and began a promising career in architecture. Sometimes called an Art Nouveau designer, van de Velde and his approach to art were more complex. For one thing he saw his non-naturalistic attempts at a new style to be grounded in the contemporary currents of realism, and in his writings – as here – he often championed the rationality and clean lines of the engineer as worthy of emulation. For another thing van de Velde, like August Endell, was much attracted to the recent theories of psychological aesthetics. His notion of ornament is divorced from any historical connection with the past and refers to the abstract harmony and balances of lines and colors. This is an early but succinct statement of his theory.

It was born in the same hour as the logic of this unique beauty was revealed, and it was the idea that a composition of lines could have the same logical and constant relationships as numbers and musical tones. It thus led me to search for an abstract ornamentation that creates harmony out of the constructions, and out of the regularity and balance of the forms that compose an ornament.

I have wanted to create a form of ornament that allows the willfulness of artistic imagination no more freedom than might be permitted for the design of a locomotive, an iron bridge, or a hall.

The same laws that guide the works of engineers should also guide ornament, which I want to make one and the same with technology. To the new architecture belongs a new ornament. The deliberation and ingenuity that is a characteristic of the former must also be a characteristic of the latter.

Henry van de Velde, from "Das neue Ornament," trans. Harry Francis Mallgrave, in *Die Renaissance im modernen Kunstgewerbe*. Berlin: Bruno & Paul Cassirer, 1901, pp. 97–8.

71 HENRY VAN DE VELDE
from "Clarification of Principles" (1902)

These two excerpts from his "Clarification of Principles," penned one year later, reveal further the intellectual depth of van de Velde's design theory. Not only is his definition of architecture firmly rooted in rational purpose or functionality, but he now grounds his search for new ornament forms within the current theories of empathy.

22. Yet it seems that beauty arises in a natural way from these normal and logical creative processes, and thus we are led to proclaim – following Plato's conception – that the essential character of architectural beauty is what it has always been: the perfect accord of means with purpose. [...]

31. The task of ornament in architecture seems to me to be twofold. It resides in part in supporting the construction and indicating its means. It also in part resides, as I explained with regard to Greek ornament, in the play of light and shadow, in bringing life into an otherwise too regularly illuminated space. [...]

33. The laws that define the forms of such ornament are new and still not sufficiently studied; someday, however, they will be more exactly defined. To my knowledge, science has almost completely neglected this field, and today we understand lines no better than the painter Eugène Delacroix divined the scientific theories of colors before Chevreul, Helmholtz, and Rood defined its laws. Today every painter must know that a stroke of color influences another, following definite laws of contrasts and mutual complements. He must know that he cannot proceed freely or arbitrarily. I am convinced that we will soon have a scientific theory of lines and forms.

34. A line is force that, like all elementary forces, is active; when several opposing lines are brought together, they react in the same way as several opposing elementary forces. This truth is crucial; it is the basis of the new ornament, but not its only principle. I have several times before stated my belief that we will soon discover complementary lines, but I want you not to feel bound to follow my hypotheses, and I want to explain here only what must be unconditionally conceded. If I now say that a line is a force, I am saying something entirely factual; it borrows its force of energy from what it has drawn. This force and this energy affect the mechanism of the eye in the way that they force it – the eye – into directions. These directions complement each other, combine with one another, and in the end create definite forms.

Henry van de Velde, from "Principielle Erklärungen," trans. Harry Francis Mallgrave, in *Kunstgewerbliche Laienpredigten*. Leipzig: Hermann Seemann, 1902, pp. 175–6, 186–8.

72 HENDRIK BERLAGE
from *Thoughts on Style* (1905)

Between the years 1897 and 1903 Berlage built his famous Amsterdam Exchange, one of the first European attempts to define a new style. In 1904 Berlage delivered two lectures in Germany, in which he begins to outline the themes of his mature theory. Published in 1905, his book displays interesting parallels and contrasts with Otto Wagner's modern manifesto. Contrary to Wagner, Berlage did not see the modern movement as in any way a rejection of the immediate past, but rather as vindication of the ideas of the two nineteenth-century apostles of truth — the "mighty Gottfried Semper" and the "highly talented Eugène-Emmanuel Viollet-le-Duc." Berlage's socialism also played prominently into his cause, as he viewed the "sham" architecture of the nineteenth century as a direct result of unbridled capitalist forces, and thus a new style would be intimately related to the new social order. The hallmark of the architecture of this new order is repose, unity, and order (geometry). Still, Berlage's theory also shows one surprising similarity with that of Wagner. In alluding to his design for the Amsterdam Exchange, Berlage — as the first extract shows — encourages architects to devise the new decorative motifs directly out of the construction itself, that is, to exalt the new constructional materials and techniques in a simple and honest way. At the end of the book, Berlage becomes the first architect since Hans Auer to speak of modern architecture as the art of "spatial enclosure."

Semper says something very original at the beginning of his observations on "the seam" [*die Naht*] as a necessary element in the joining together of various parts. He asks if there is an etymological link between the word "necessity" [*die Not*], as in the phrase "making a virtue out of necessity," and the word "seam"; and whether the phrase should really mean "making a virtue out of the seam." In other words, in assembling constructional elements, one should not attempt to eliminate the necessary "seam." On the contrary, one should make it into a virtue, that is to say, a decorative motif. You artists should exploit, therefore, the various constructional difficulties as decorative motifs.

In these words Semper paid tribute to true stylistic rationalism, even though he has little good to say about medieval or Gothic art.

But does not this sentence correspond to Viollet-le-Duc's principal tenet, "Every form that is not determined by the structure should be rejected."

The passages I have taken from Semper's book might not seem to be related, yet they do connect and can serve as the basis of style. We ask ourselves why earlier works give an impression of repose that is lacking in our restless creations. Repose is the chief quality, not itself the cause, but the result of a number of qualities that are immediately striking and allow us to distinguish an old building from a new one at a thousand meters' distance. [. . .]

The true principle of architecture has been dominant at the beginning of every great cultural epoch — the principle of good, honest construction.

Hendrik Berlage, from *Gedanken über Stil in der Baukunst* (1905), trans. Iain Boyd Whyte as *Thoughts on Style in Architecture*, in *Hendrik Petrus Berlage: Thoughts on Style 1886–1909*. Santa Monica, CA: Getty Publication Programs, 1996, pp. 139–40, 152.

This has also been the leading principle in my own work. In accordance with the observations developed above, I have limited myself to the greatest possible simplicity and in matters of structure and decoration looked for those solutions that seemed to me the most natural.

The following comments might serve as an interpretation of this general principle. Since architecture is the art of spatial enclosure, we must emphasize the architectonic nature of space, in both a constructive and decorative sense. For this reason a building should not be considered primarily from the outside.

Spatial enclosure is achieved through walls, and the space or the various spaces are expressed on the outside as a more or less complex arrangement of walls.

Thus the prime importance falls on the wall, which in accordance with its nature should remain flat, for a too strongly modeled wall loses its intrinsic character.

The architecture of the wall is therefore limited to decoration on the plane. Projecting elements remain limited to those that are suggested by the construction, such as window lintels, water spouts, gutters, single cornices, and so on. It follows from this "architecture of the wall," in which the vertical articulation falls away of its own accord, that the possible supports, such as pillars and columns, are not given projecting capitals, but rather that the transition is accomplished within the plane of the wall.

73 HENDRIK BERLAGE
from *Foundations and Development of Architecture* (1908)

In 1908 Berlage returned to Zurich, the city of his professional schooling, to give four lectures on his vision of the new style, which he also published as a book. He reiterates his earlier views, but now presents them in a more compelling way. The essential preconditions for the new architecture are a geometric approach to design, the absence of any historical motifs, and design predicated on the principle of *Sachlichkeit*. The last theme, as he notes, is drawn from Hermann Muthesius's *Style-Architecture and Building-Art*, but Berlage goes on to give his own definition of what this term should mean.

Therefore, if the modern artists work in a *sachlich*, clear way under the preconditions that I have tried to develop, they will be striving toward the modern spiritual ideal, the principle of the economic equality of all men. In doing so, they will breathe life into the formal beauty that has already been developed but which, in the last resort, needs a style in order to rise to new heights. By *sachlich*, clear work I mean a renewed awareness that architecture is the art of spatial enclosure, and, for this reason, prime value, both constructionally and decoratively,

Hendrik Berlage, from *Grundlagen und Entwicklung der Architektur* (1908), trans. Iain Boyd Whyte as *Foundations and Development of Architecture*, in *Hendrik Petrus Berlage: Thoughts on Style 1886–1909*. Santa Monica, CA: Getty Publication Programs, 1996, pp. 249–50.

should be laid on space. It follows from this that a building should not be essentially an external manifestation.

The art of architecture resides in the creation of spaces, not in the design of facades. A spatial enclosure is produced by walls, and thus the space or the various spaces find external expression in a more or less complex arrangement of walls. It is also important in this sense that the walls should remain flat, for an overarticulated wall loses its intrinsic, wall-like character. By *sachlich*, clear work I mean that the architecture of the wall remains two-dimensional decoration, that the projecting elements are limited to those offered by the construction, such as window supports, water spouts, gutters, single cornices, and so on. It follows from this so-called wall architecture, in which vertical articulation disappears of its own accord, that the vertical supports such as piers and columns are not given projecting capitals, but rather that the development of the transitions are developed within the wall. The windows form the true decoration of the wall plane; they are installed only where necessary, and then in appropriate sizes.

By *sachlich*, clear work I mean work in which the pictorial decorations do not dominate and are employed only in those places that have shown themselves, after the most careful study, to be the correct ones.

Following the principle above, the pictorial decoration should remain surface decoration, in other words sunk into the wall, and the figures should ultimately form decorated areas of the wall.

Above all, one should once again display the naked wall in all its smooth and simple [*schlicht*] beauty.

By *sachlich*, clear work I mean a work in which all excess is most scrupulously avoided, in which there are no useless cornices and moldings, pedestals and pilasters, shoulder pieces and fixtures – in short no architecture of a parasitic nature.

By *sachlich*, clear work I mean, finally, an intelligible work that will stimulate interest as only natural simplicity and clarity can, whereas unnatural complexity and ambiguity remain misunderstood. Such complexity startles but does not evoke any interest, which explains why architecture was excluded from the realm of cultural progress in the nineteenth century. The *sachlich*, rational, and therefore clear construction can become the basis of the new art but only when this principle has penetrated deeply enough and been applied widely enough, will we stand at the door of a new art. And at the same moment the new, universal spirit [*Weltgefühl*] – the social equality of all men – will be revealed, a spirit whose ideals are located not in the beyond but here on earth, confronting all of us. In the final analysis, however, does this not represent a step nearer to the ultimate goal of all religions, a realization of the Christian idea? Or is it wrong to ascribe the entire Christian doctrine exactly to this principle of human equality – the first condition of an idealist endeavor?

74 CHARLES-EDOUARD JEANNERET (LE CORBUSIER)

from *Study of the Decorative Art Movement in Germany* (1912)

C harles-Edouard Jeanneret, who would later change his name to Le Corbusier, makes his presence known at this early date with this short study of the German decorative arts. Born in the Swiss town of La Chaux-de-Fonds, Jeanneret was trained in the decorative arts. Yet he traveled extensively throughout Europe and even worked briefly in 1909 for Auguste Perret in Paris. After accepting a teaching position back in La Chaux-de-Fonds, Jeanneret was asked in the following year by his school to tour Germany and write a report on the German applied arts. In Munich he attempted to find architectural work with Theodor Fischer, but was unsuccessful; through contacts that he made, however, he went to Berlin, where he was eventually accepted into the office of Peter Behrens in a minor capacity. Thus not only did he become familiar with German architecture at first hand, but he also gained an awareness of the still intensifying German debate on modernism. After taking another tour of the Balkans, Turkey, Greece, and Italy, Jeanneret settled back in his home town in 1911 and penned the results of his German research. Written a few years before World War I, the book is decidedly Francophilic in its tone, and Jeanneret is still a very immature architect. But, as this passage shows, he is quite aware that Germany was posing a serious challenge to France's traditional artistic leadership, and that the German Werkbund had already radically transformed the terms of the debate.

Germany is now organized. Our second chapter, "German Initiatives and Creations," reveals the nation's collective economy. As a result of this process (already well underway), German industry has taken a privileged position in relation to other nations. This is also its rehabilitation; the expression "it is German" can no longer have disdainful connotations.

But in considering which part of this is due to art and which part is due to context, it seems that this great renewal of the applied arts in Germany has everything to do with the spread of this nation's energy and organizational genius. The role of art is diminished in this process. Art was the pretext, means, and springboard. It was not, it seems to me, the goal. Thus, the creative forces that were momentarily exalted by the violent push of external factors now seem weaker. Artistic genius, having acquired the privilege of authority, suddenly feels its smallness within the immense field that these last years have given it to exploit. Worried, art looks around for itself; it has lost his faith and is disdainful of the past. The enthusiasm of the Secession has worn off and in the last few years in particular Germany is rapidly returning to the arts of France. The champions of this fight seem to want to bridle their personalities in a premature capitulation.

Are we not witnessing in France the contrary phenomenon? It is undeniable that enormous energies were consumed in stifled efforts, but the painful growth might perhaps strengthen the roots of the plant. The applied arts in France, humiliated by Germany, might

Charles-Edouard Jeanneret, from *Étude sur le mouvement d'art décoratif en Allemagne* (1912). New York: Da Capo, 1968, pp. 73–4, trans. Christina Contandriopoulos and Harry Francis Mallgrave.

be emerging from their lethargy. Signs of the future were apparent in the last two "Salons d'Automne." The first innovators of forty years ago might finally be finding recognition.

One may think that I reveal here too many of the national rivalries, but they are in fact ethnic. They exist, nevertheless, in both countries. Being French, I suffered from them in Germany and I was choked by them in Paris, where they were intensifying as the German invasion was expanding. After all, each nation is for the other a precious stimulant.

An investigation, such as that given me by the Commission de l'École d'Art, should be pursued by others as well. The marvelous Germany of industrial art wants to be known. In this time of international competition, information should also move across borders. Germany is a book of the present. If Paris is the foyer of art, Germany remains the great workshop of production. Experiments were made there; the battles proved effective. The building has been raised and its rooms, with their historicized walls, recount the triumph of order and tenacity.

75 ANTONIO SANT'ELIA
from the "Messaggio" (1914)

Of all the prewar movements committed to the creation of a new art and architecture, certainly the most radical in its intentions was the Italian Futurist movement. The force behind the movement was the poet Filippo Tommaso Marinetti, whose manifesto to the cause first appeared in 1909. It was an apocalyptical text of alienation and social contempt, which spoke of such things as the beauty of speed and the purification of war. In a follow-up manifesto of one year later, the painter Umberto Boccioni turned this rebelliousness toward art and condemned all forms of imitation or any attempt at "good taste." The architectural transposition of such ideas came in 1914 through the efforts of Antonio Sant'Elia. Born in Como, Sant'Elia was trained at the Brera Academy in Milan, but in 1911 he left school early to focus on competitions. Soon thereafter he began to work privately on his "Dinamismi" – sketches of his "New City," taking their cue from silos, power stations, and factories. At the beginning of 1914 he joined the Futurist movement and published his "Messaggio" (message), which was redrafted as the *Manifesto of Futurist Architecture*. He followed Marinetti in several respects by insisting that all the elements of the old architecture must be thrown out and a fresh start had to be made. The new city and its architecture must forgo all historical forms and emulate the world of machines and fast-paced technology. His brilliant drawings became his only legacy, for – also embracing Marinetti's love of warfare – Sant'Elia enlisted in the army and was killed at the Italian front in October 1916.

And I oppose:

Fashionable architecture of every country and of every kind;

Classical, solemn, hieratic, scenographic, decorative, monumental, graceful, and pleasing architecture;

Antonio Sant'Elia, from "Messaggio" (1914), trans. Esther da Costa Meyer, in *The Works of Antonio Sant'Elia: Retreat into the Future*. New Haven, CT: Yale University Press, 1995, p. 212.

Embalming, rebuilding, reproducing monuments;

Perpendicular and horizontal lines, cubical and pyramidal forms that are static, grave, oppressive, and wholly incompatible with our ultra-new sensibility;

The use of massive, voluminous, lasting, antiquated, and costly materials that are not consonant with modern culture and technical expertise as a whole.

And I declare:

That the new architecture is the architecture of cold calculation, of fearless audacity, and of simplicity; the architecture of reinforced concrete, of iron, glass, cardboard, textiles, and all those surrogates of wood, stone, and brick that allow us to obtain the maximum elasticity and lightness;

That real architecture is not for these reasons an arid combination of practicality and utility, but remains art, that is, synthesis, expression;

That decoration, as something overlaid or appended to architecture, is absurd, and that the decorative value of a truly modern architecture depends exclusively on the use and original orchestration of rough, naked, or violently colored materials.

And finally I declare that, just as the ancients took their artistic inspiration from the elements of nature, so too must we – [who are] materially and spiritually artificial – find our inspiration in the elements of the new mechanical world that we have created, of which architecture must be the most beautiful expression, the most complete synthesis, the most effective artistic integration.

76 TONY GARNIER
from *An Industrial City* (1917)

Although not published until after the war, Tony Garnier's vision of an "industrial city" has its origin much earlier. He began working on the project as a student in Rome, in fact after winning the *Prix de Rome* at the Académie des Beaux-Arts in 1899. The intellectual and cultural forces behind the futurist vision are disparate. There are the utopian and positivist traditions of Charles Fourier and Saint-Simon, as well as the more recently published urban ideas of Frédéric Le Play and Ebenezer Howard. There are also his socialistic ideals of a public ownership of all land and basic services, which he inherited in part from his great fascination with the writings of Émile Zola. His published vision of 1917 also owes much to his own experiments as a municipal architect working in Lyon during the war years. But where Garnier stands out from many other utopian thinkers is in his clear delineatory concept of a modern industrial city, built entirely of concrete, and uncompromising in its clean or unornamented modern forms.

Tony Garnier, from *Cité Industrielle* (1917), trans. Dora Wiebenson, in *Tony Garnier: The Cité Industrielle*. New York: George Braziller, 1969, pp. 107, 112.

The principal factories are situated in the plain at the confluence of the river and its tributary. A main-line railroad passes between the factories and the town, which is located above the factories on a plateau. Higher still are placed the hospitals; they, as well as the city, are sheltered from cold winds, and have their terraces oriented to the south. Each of these main elements (factories, town, hospitals) is isolated so that it can expand; allowance has been made for this growth although the study has been pursued from a more general point of view.

Investigation of the most satisfactory program for the material and moral needs of the individual has resulted in the creation of rules concerning road use, hygiene, and so on; the assumption is that a certain progress of social order resulting in an automatic adoption of these rules already has been realized, so that it will not be necessary to enact actual laws. Distribution of land, everything related to the distribution of water, bread, meat, milk, and medical supplies, as well as the reutilization of refuse, will be given over to the public domain.

[. . .]

The materials used are concrete for the foundations and walls, and reinforced concrete for the floors and ceilings. All the important buildings are constructed of reinforced concrete.

These two materials are prepared in molds made for this purpose. The simpler the molds, the easier will be the construction, and consequently the less the cost. This simplicity of means leads logically to a great simplicity of expression in the structure. Let us note also that, if our structure remains simple, unadorned, without molding, bare, we are then best able to arrange the decorative arts so that each object of art will retain its purest and clearest expression because it will be totally independent of the construction. Besides, who would not see that the use of such materials results in the obtaining of the horizontals and verticals that are proper to give to the construction that calm and equilibrium that will harmonize with the lines of nature? Other systems of construction, other materials, lead, without doubt, to other forms which it would also be interesting to study.

C. THE CHICAGO SCHOOL AND THE AMERICAN WEST

Introduction

A s we have seen, the last three decades of the nineteenth century in America had produced two world fairs, the settling of the West, and unparalleled economic and industrial expansion. The tempo of these changes did not slow down by the end of the century; in fact they continued to accelerate. Thus when Theodore Roosevelt, in the first years of the new century, reaffirmed the Monroe Doctrine and began construction of the Panama Canal, a new world power was being born, just at the moment when the country was edging past Great Britain as the world's leader in economic and industrial output.

The new metropolis of Chicago, of course, had for some years exemplified this unparalleled growth. The architectural legacy to Richardson's Marshall Field Wholesale Store (completed in 1887) was succeeded by the golden years of Louis Sullivan, who in the decade of the 1890s (until 1895 with Denkmar Adler) would produce such masterpieces as the Wainwright Building, St. Louis (1890–1); the Guaranty Building, Buffalo (1894–6); the Bayard

Building, New York City (1897–8); and the Schlesinger & Mayer department store, Chicago (1898–1903). The majestical star of Sullivan was, however, soon to be eclipsed by that of his one-time office manager – Frank Lloyd Wright – who by 1900 had moved well past his Arts-and-Crafts beginnings and evolved the geometric and formal elements of his "Prairie Style." The spatial innovations of this gifted, seemingly godlike designer defy easy description, and by the end of the decade Wright, after putting together one of the most extraordinary portfolios of built works in modern history, was almost everywhere seen as the country's leading modern architect. And his influence on the development of modern architecture in Europe was, if anything, more extensive than that at home.

Around 1900 also came the first stirrings of another new center for design and innovation destined to leave its imprint – the West Coast. San Francisco defined the northern pole with its first experiments in what later would be called the "Bay Region Style," developed by such talented newcomers to the area as Bernard Maybeck, Ernest Coxhead, and John Galen Howard. The southern pole of Los Angeles almost concurrently saw the appearance of such gifted designers as Irvin Gill and the Greene brothers. If many architects on the American East Coast were still looking to Europe for its design cues, the West Coast architects in their experiments drew upon a bevy of new sources of inspiration: native timbers and unpainted woods, adobe and reinforced concrete, more relaxed spatial planning, and even the newly discovered charm of the Far East. They laid the basis for what would become, by the late 1920s and 1930s, one of the most innovative architectural regions of modernism in the world.

77 LOUIS SULLIVAN
from "The Tall Office Building Artistically Considered" (1896)

I n 1890 – as Frank Lloyd Wright later recounted – Louis Sullivan rushed into his office within the firm of Adler and Sullivan and, holding his design for the Wainwright building in his hand, proudly announced to his chief draftsman that he had solved the problem of the tall building. The Wainwright Building in St. Louis was, in fact, the first of thirteen tall buildings that Sullivan (either alone or with Adler) designed over the next decade. The formula for the Wainwright Building is that which he summarizes a few years later in the opening pages of his classic essay, "The Tall Building Artistically Considered." But in this essay Sullivan also goes on to make another very interesting statement that would soon resound within the annals of modern theory. The axiom "form ever follows function" certainly owes something to the earlier formulation of Horatio Greenough in the first half of the century, but Sullivan now centers it within his highly idealized, organic philosophy of design. The slight irony here is that he, in his design propensities, was a supreme ornamentalist.

It is my belief that it is of the very essence of every problem that it contains and suggests its own solution. This I believe to be natural law. Let us examine, then, carefully the elements, let us search out this contained suggestion, this essence of the problem.

The practical conditions are, broadly speaking, these:

Louis Sullivan, from "The Tall Office Building Artistically Considered," first published in *Lippincott's Magazine* (1896), cited here from Robert Twombly, *Louis Sullivan: The Public Papers*. Chicago: University of Chicago Press, 1988, pp. 105–6, 110–11.

Wanted – 1st, a story below-ground, containing boilers, engines of various sorts, etc. – in short, the plant for power, heating, lighting, etc. 2nd, a ground floor, so called, devoted to stores, banks, or other establishments requiring large area, ample spacing, ample light, and great freedom of access. 3rd, a second story readily accessible by stairways – this space usually in large subdivisions, with corresponding liberality in structural spacing and expanse of glass and breadth of external openings. 4th, above this an indefinite number of stories of offices piled tier upon tier, one tier just like another tier, one office just like all the other offices – an office being similar to a cell in a honeycomb, merely a compartment, nothing more. 5th, and last, at the top of this pile is placed a space or story that, as related to the life and usefulness of the structure, is purely physiological in its nature – namely, the attic. In this the circulatory system completes itself and makes its grand turn, ascending and descending. The space is filled with tanks, pipes, valves, sheaves, and mechanical etcetera that supplement and complement the force-originating plant hidden below-ground in the cellar. Finally, or at the beginning rather, there must be on the ground floor a main aperture or entrance common to all the occupants or patrons of the building.

[. . .]

This view let me now state, for it brings to the solution of the problem a final, comprehensive formula.

All things in nature have a shape, that is to say, a form, an outward semblance, that tells us what they are, that distinguishes them from ourselves and from each other.

Unfailingly in nature these shapes express the inner life, the native quality, of the animal, tree, bird, fish, that they present to us; they are so characteristic, so recognizable, that we say, simply, it is "natural" it should be so. Yet the moment we peer beneath this surface of things, the moment we look through the tranquil reflection of ourselves and the clouds above us, down into the clear, fluent, unfathomable depth of nature, how startling is the silence of it, how amazing the flow of life, how absorbing the mystery. Unceasingly the essence of things is taking shape in the matter of things, and this unspeakable process we call birth and growth. Awhile the spirit and the matter fade away together, and it is this that we call decadence, death. These two happenings seem jointed and interdependent, blended into one like a bubble and its iridescence, and they seem borne along upon a slowly moving air. This air is wonderful past all understanding.

Yet to the steadfast eye of one standing upon the shore of things, looking chiefly and most lovingly upon that side on which the sun shines and that we feel joyously to be life, the heart is ever gladdened by the beauty, the exquisite spontaneity, with which life seeks and takes on its forms in an accord perfectly responsive to its needs. It seems ever as though the life and the form were absolutely one and inseparable, so adequate is the sense of fulfillment.

Whether it be the sweeping eagle in his flight or the open apple-blossom, the toiling work-horse, the blithe swan, the branching oak, the winding stream at its base, the drifting clouds, over all the coursing sun, form ever follows function, and this is the law. Where function does not change form does not change. The granite rocks, the ever-brooding hills, remain for ages; the lightning lives, comes into shape, and dies in a twinkling.

It is the pervading law of all things organic, and inorganic, of all things physical and metaphysical, of all things human and all things superhuman, of all true manifestations of the head, of the heart, of the soul, that the life is recognizable in its expression, that form ever follows function. This is the law.

78 DENKMAR ADLER
from "Function and Environment" (1896)

The contribution that Denkmar Adler made to the success of his partnership with Louis Sullivan has often been understated. Adler, like so many of his generation of Chicago architects, was born in Germany and as a child immigrated to the American Midwest in the early 1850s, following the political unrest in Germany. He fought in the Civil War and afterwards was apprenticed as an engineer. In 1879 he established his own office and shortly thereafter hired the young Sullivan as a draftsman. In the early 1880s the partnership was officially formed, but it did not thrive until the second half of the decade, when the firm secured the commission for the Auditorium Building in 1886. Whereas Sullivan handled the aesthetics of design, Adler's contributions included his areas of expertise: structural engineering, illumination, ventilation, and acoustics. He was therefore the true functionalist behind Sullivan's gifted hand. In this particular essay, written shortly after the dissolution of the partnership of Adler and Sullivan, Adler credits Sullivan with the formula "form follows function," but now modifies it into an environmental adage.

Every architectural work has a "function," a purpose which has called it into being, and its success is measured by the degree of approximation to fulfilment of "functions" which characterizes its "form."

From this one might infer that it is only necessary to divide into a few classes the functions to be served by architectural structures and to determine the form best adapted to each, and thus develop an infallibly correct system of architectural design from which none may deviate without incurring the reproach of ignorance and lack of culture.

We would then have an architecture somewhat more scientific and vastly more practical, but as trite and as devoid of the interest imparted by the creative impulse, as is the architecture founded upon the principle, *Form follows historic precedent*, which stamps as barbaric every structure for which the architect has failed to provide an academically and historically correct mask and costume, and which treats as heresy an attempt to do, not as the Romans did in the year 1, but to do as one thinks the Romans might have done in the year 1896.

Returning to Mr. Sullivan's aphorism, we find that he bases it upon studies and observations of nature, which, carried a little further, show that although the common function of all organic creation is to maintain and propagate the various species, yet an ever changing environment has produced an infinite number of species and innumerable differences in individuals of each species.

Therefore, if "form follows function," it does not follow in a straight line, nor in accordance with a simple mathematical formula, but along the lines of curves whose elements are always changing and never alike; and if the lines of development and growth of vegetable and animal organisms are infinitely differentiated, the processes of untrammeled

Denkmar Adler, from "Function and Environment" (1896), in *Roots of Contemporary American Architecture*, ed. Lewis Mumford. New York: Dover, 1972, pp. 243–4.

human thought and human emotions are even more subtle in the differences and shadings of their manifestations, while the natural variations in conditions of human environment are as great as those which influence the developments of form in the lower organisms; and human work is further modified by necessary artificial conditions and circumstances.

Therefore, before accepting Mr. Sullivan's statement of the underlying law upon which all good architectural design and all true architectural style is founded, it may be well to amend it, and say: "function and environment determine form," using the words environment and form in their broadest sense.

79   OSCAR LOVELL TRIGGS
from "A Proposal for a Guild and School of Handicraft" (1901)

The British Arts and Crafts movement began to make its presence felt in the United States in the 1890s, and by the turn of the century an organized movement was underway across America. Perhaps the strongest center of the movement in America was Chicago. Already in 1888 the social activist Jane Addams had visited the educational center Toynbee Hall in London, and in the following year she and Ellen Gates Starr founded the Hull House in Chicago, aimed at improving the lot of immigrants. The Hull House offered social and cultural services, such as daycare, employment assistance, an art gallery, library, and classes in art and music. It was here that the Chicago Arts and Crafts Society held its first meeting in October 1897 – a meeting attended by Frank Lloyd Wright, among others. Also a founding member was Oscar Lovell Triggs, a professor at the University of Chicago and the local secretary of the William Morris Society. A few years later, in 1902, Triggs published the first history of the Arts and Crafts movement, which he saw emanating from John Ruskin, Thomas Carlyle, and William Morris. Following the example of the British guilds, Triggs founded the Industrial Art League in 1899, which offered workshops and course instruction in the arts and crafts; two years later he advanced his thinking with a proposal for a Guild and School of Handicraft. As the following passage demonstrates, Triggs accepted many of the premises of the British Arts and Crafts movement, but at the same time did not see these ideals as being incompatible with industrialization. This was the key distinction between the British and American movements that Frank Lloyd Wright was at the same time exploiting.

James Russell Lowell once said that the ideal school would be a place where nothing useful should be taught. The transcendental view of education has long been abandoned by educators, but the practical view that the ideal school would be a place where nothing useless should be taught has not yet come into full acceptance. The tendency, however, to discard the useless and to develop the useful is quite marked in recent years, and it is not impossible that the school I have in mind to describe, which is essentially a workshop and

Oscar Lovell Triggs, from "A Proposal for a Guild and School of Handicraft," in *Chapters in the History of the Arts and Crafts Movement* (1901). Reprinted New York: Benjamin Blom, 1971, pp. 189–90.

not simply a place of instruction, will be the ultimate result of the modern trend toward the practical. The rapid development of the manual training school is evidence of the vitality of this movement.

The industrial factor co-operating also to this end is known as the Arts and Crafts movement. As the name given to the new industrialism implies, its supporters propose the association of art and labor – in which association, of course, art is to give up something of its special and "fine" character and become practical, and labor is to rise above its drudgery and become pleasurable. By emancipating and individualizing labor it tends to become artistic. By subduing art and rendering it useful it tends to become real and vital. By applying the principles of both art and labor to either an artist or workman the ideal craftsman is formed – a craftsman that is a new kind of artist and a new kind of workman. Such a craftsman satisfies all the life conditions that economists like Ruskin and Morris demand, and he is indeed the product of their teaching.

And now the query rises whether, by combining the new educational tendency and the new industrial tendency, a new sort of institution may not be established, which shall serve the ends of the industrial commonwealth now forming in this country, better than any existing institution. Might it not be possible to turn the school into an actual factory, and transform the factory into a genuine school? Even now some manual training schools approximate the factory in appearance, and some factories, with slight modification, could easily be made into ideal communities, entirely self-subsisting, in which an individual, while "earning his living," might also be educated by the self-same work.

80   GUSTAV STICKLEY
from foreword to *The Craftsman* (1901)

Among American designers strongly influenced by the Arts and Crafts movement was the furniture maker Gustav Stickley. Originally based in Wisconsin, he moved to the state of New York in the early 1880s, where he embarked on several furniture ventures that replicated historical styles. In 1898 he undertook a trip to England to scout activities there, and he met both Charles Robert Ashbee and C. F. A. Voysey. The trip changed everything and in 1900, with two brothers, Stickley started a new company that specialized in simple and original designs based on handicraft methods. To promote these ideals further, he launched the magazine *The Craftsman*, which became a powerful voice in promoting the creed of "simplicity, individuality and dignity of effect." The magazine would also later document many of the American innovations in residential design. The first two issues were devoted to William Morris and John Ruskin. This short passage is from the Foreword to the first issue.

With the initial number of "The Craftsman," The United Crafts of Eastwood, N. Y., enter upon a work for which they hope to gain the sympathy and the co-operation of a wide

Gustav Stickley, from foreword to *The Craftsman* 1:1 (1901), p. i.

public. The new association is a guild of cabinet makers, metal and leather workers, which has been recently formed for the production of household furnishings. The Guild has had but one parallel in modern times, and this is found in the firm organized in London, in 1860, by the great decorator and socialist, William Morris, together with his not less distinguished friends, Burne-Jones, Rossetti and Ford Madox Brown, all of Pre-Raphaelite fame.

The United Crafts endeavor to promote and to extend the principles established by Morris, in both the artistic and the socialistic sense. In the interests of art, they seek to substitute the luxury of taste for the luxury of costliness: to teach that beauty does not imply elaboration or ornament; to employ only those forms and materials which make for simplicity, individuality and dignity of effect.

In the interests of the workman, they accept without qualification the proposition formulated by the artist-socialist:

"It is right and necessary that all men should have work to do which shall be worth doing, and be pleasant to do; and which should be done under such conditions as would make it neither over-wearisome, nor over-anxious."

81 FRANK LLOYD WRIGHT
from "The Art and Craft of the Machine" (1901)

In one of his most important addresses of his lengthy career, Frank Lloyd Wright also made known his views on the Arts and Crafts movement – in a way that no doubt startled many in his audience. The address was given in March 1901 at the Hull House, and it is nothing less than his confession of apostasy from the movement. His address coincided with the perfection of his "Prairie Style," hence at a critical moment in his development. As an architect, Wright was very much raised on the movement and its ideals. In the 1880s he had been a keen student of Bruce Price and Stanford White, and in the 1890s began a series of experiments in residential design that were in sympathy with the British Arts and Crafts movement. He attended the first meeting of the Chicago Arts and Crafts Society in 1897 and Charles R. Ashbee, on his visit to Chicago in 1900, singled out Wright's work as the best he had seen in the country. Wright even begins this address with praise and admiration for the efforts of William Morris and John Ruskin, but then (in reiterating a theme he had been rehearsing for a while) he proffers a contrary thesis: however praiseworthy their efforts were, they (and the handicraft ideals they represented) were decidedly a thing of the past. In this passage from his extraordinary conclusion to his address, Wright – waxing poetic on a nighttime image of Chicago from above, with the furnaces of Gary whirling in the distance – pays his homage to the future and to the machine.

Upon this faith in Art as the organic heart quality of the scientific frame of things, I base a belief that we must look to the artist brain, of all brains, to grasp the significance to society

Frank Lloyd Wright, from "The Art and Craft of the Machine," in *Frank Lloyd Wright: Collected Writings*, vol. 1, ed. Bruce Brooks Pfeiffer. New York: Rizzoli, 1992, pp. 68–9.

of this thing we call the Machine, if that brain be not blinded, gagged, and bound by false tradition, the letter of precedent. For this thing we call Art is it not as prophetic as a primrose or an oak? Therefore, of the essence of this thing we call the Machine, which is no more or less than the principle of organic growth working irresistibly the Will of Life through the medium of Man.

Be gently lifted at nightfall to the top of a great downtown office building, and you may see how in the image of material man, at once his glory and menace, is this thing we call a city.

There beneath, grown up in a night, is the monster leviathan, stretching acre upon acre into the far distance. High overhead hangs the stagnant pall of its fetid breath, reddened with the light from its myriad eyes endlessly everywhere blinking. Ten thousand acres of cellular tissue, layer upon layer, the city's flesh, outspreads enmeshed by intricate network of veins and arteries, radiating into the gloom, and there with muffled, persistent roar, pulses and circulates as the blood in your veins, the ceaseless beat of the activity to whose necessities it all conforms.

Like to the sanitation of the human body is the drawing off of poisonous waste from the system of this enormous creature; absorbed first by the infinitely ramifying, threadlike ducts gathering at their sensitive terminals matter destructive to its life, hurrying it to millions of small intestines, to be collected in turn by larger, flowing to the great sewer, on to the drainage canal, and finally to the ocean.

This ten thousand acres of fleshlike tissue is again knit and interknit with a nervous system marvelously complete, delicate filaments for hearing, knowing, almost feeling the pulse of its organism, acting upon the ligaments and tendons for motive impulse, in all flowing the impelling fluid of man's own life.

Its nerve ganglia! – the peerless Corliss tandems whirling their hundred ton fly-wheels, fed by gigantic rows of water-tube boilers burning oil, a solitary man slowly pacing backward and forward, regulating here and there the little feed valves controlling the deafening roar of the flaming gas, while beyond, the incessant clicking, dropping, waiting – lifting, waiting, shifting of the governor gear controlling these modern Goliaths seems a visible brain in intelligent action, registered infallibly in the enormous magnets, purring in the giant embrace of great induction coils, generating the vital current meeting with instant response in the rolling cars on elevated tracks ten miles away, where the glare of the Bessemer steel converter makes a conflagration of the clouds.

More quietly still, whispering down the long, low rooms of factory buildings buried in the gloom beyond, range on range of stanch, beautifully perfected automatons, murmur contentedly with occasional click-clack, that would have the American manufacturing industry of five years ago by the throat today manipulating steel as delicately as a mystical shuttle of the modern loom manipulates a silk thread in the shimmering pattern of a dainty gown.

And the heavy breathing, the murmuring, the clangor, and the roar! – how the voice of this monstrous thing, this greatest of machines, a great city, rises to proclaim the marvel of the units of its structure, the ghastly warning boom from the deep throats of vessels heavily seeking inlet to the waterway below, answered by the echoing clangor of the bridge bells growing nearer and more ominous as the vessel cuts momentarily the flow of the nearer artery, warning the current from the swinging bridge now closing on its stately passage, just in time to receive in a rush of steam, as a streak of light, the avalanche of blood and metal hurled across it and gone, roaring into the night on its glittering bands of steel, ever faithfully encircled by the slender magic lines tick-tapping its invincible protection.

Nearer, in the building ablaze with midnight activity, the wide white band streams into the marvel of the multiple press, receiving unerringly the indelible impression of the human hopes, joys, and fears throbbing in the pulse of this great activity, as infallibly as the gray matter of the human brain receives the impression of the senses, to come forth millions of neatly folded, perfected news sheets, teeming with vivid appeals to passions, good or evil; weaving a web of intercommunication so far-reaching that distance becomes as nothing, the thought of one man in one corner of the earth one day visible to the naked eye of all men the next; the doings of all the world reflected as in a glass, so marvelously sensitive this wide white band streaming endlessly from day to day becomes in the grasp of the multiple press.

If the pulse of activity in this great city, to which the tremor of the mammoth skeleton beneath our feet is but an awe-inspiring response, is thrilling, what of this prolific, silent obedience?

And the texture of the tissue of this great thing, this Forerunner of Democracy, the Machine, has been deposited particle by particle, in blind obedience to organic law, the law to which the great solar universe is but an obedient machine.

Thus is the thing into which the forces of Art are to breathe the thrill of ideality! A SOUL!

82   LOUIS SULLIVAN
from "What is Architecture? A Study in the American People of Today" (1906)

If the relationship of form and function (with both emotional and spiritual sides) forms one of the leitmotifs of Sullivan's architectural philosophy, the idea of a new American style – one suited to the American democracy – defines another. His notion of American architecture, however, is not a simple one. Through much of his life he shared with the poet Walt Whitman the optimistic sense that the American democracy was destined to make its mark on the development of human culture. He too shared with Ralph Waldo Emerson the importance of "self-reliance" – that is, the necessity of the American people to cease imitating European traditions and define itself anew with invigorating and spiritualizing principles. To these forces must be added the fact that Sullivan's architectural practice began to undergo a slow but steady decline after 1900, and with it, a strong hint of pessimism began to color Sullivan's effusive prose. He was particularly critical of American architectural schools, for instance, which he believed were suppressing individuality and originality. This essay captures Sullivan's thought at its full maturation, at war with the pessimism that was slowly assuming the upper hand.

Thus will you make of Democracy a religion – the only one the world will have developed – befitting freemen – free in the integrity of their bodies, free in the integrity of their thought.

Louis Sullivan, from "What is Architecture? A Study in the American People of Today" (1906), originally published in *The Craftsman*, cited here from Robert Twombly, *Louis Sullivan: The Public Papers*. Chicago: University of Chicago Press, 1988, pp. 195–6.

So doing, all aspects of your activities will change, because your thoughts will have changed. All of your activities will then take on organic and balanced coherence, because all of your thoughts will have a common center of gravity in the integrity of individual Man.

And, as the oak-tree is ever true to the acorn from which it sprang, and propagates true acorns in its turn, so will you then give true expression and form to the seed of Democracy that was planted in your soil, and so spread in turn the seeds of true Democracy.

Thus, as your thoughts change, will your civilization change. And thus, as Democracy takes living and integral shape within your thought, will the Feudalism, now tainting you, disappear. For its present power rests wholly upon your acquiescent and supporting thought. Its strength lies wholly in you, not in itself. So, inevitably, as the sustaining power of your thought is withdrawn, this Feudalism will crumble and vanish!

So have you no need of Force, for force is a crude and inefficient instrument. THOUGHT is the fine and powerful instrument. Therefore, HAVE THOUGHT FOR THE INTEGRITY OF YOUR OWN THOUGHT. For all social power, for good, or for ill, rests upon the thought of the People. THIS IS THE SINGLE LESSON IN THE HISTORY OF MANKIND THAT IS REALLY WORTH THE WHILE.

Naturally, then, as your thoughts thus change, your growing Architecture will change. Its falsity will depart; its reality will gradually appear. For the integrity of your thought, as a People, will then have penetrated the minds of your architects.

THEN, TOO, AS YOUR BASIC THOUGHT CHANGES WILL EMERGE A PHILOSOPHY, A POETRY, AND AN ART OF EXPRESSION IN ALL THINGS: FOR YOU WILL HAVE LEARNED THAT A CHARACTERISTIC PHILOSOPHY, POETRY AND ART OF EXPRESSION ARE VITAL TO THE HEALTHFUL GROWTH AND DEVELOPMENT OF A DEMOCRATIC PEOPLE.

As a People you have enormous latent, unused power.

Awaken it.

Use it.

Use it for the common good.

Begin now!

For it is as true today as when one of your wise men said it: – "THE WAY TO RESUME IS TO RESUME!"

83 FRANK LLOYD WRIGHT
from "In the Cause of Architecture" (1908)

Wright's enormous intellectual debt to Sullivan is acknowledged in many of his writings, but his several references to Sullivan in this particular essay, written for the *Architectural Record*, stand out because this is also his first attempt to summarize his design philosophy as it had matured over the previous decade. The eighty-seven illustrations of Wright's work, published along with this essay, established his reputation nationally

Frank Lloyd Wright, from "In the Cause of Architecture" (1908), in *Frank Lloyd Wright: Collected Writings*, vol. 1, ed. Bruce Brooks Pfeiffer. New York: Rizzoli, 1992, pp. 89–90, 100.

and even in Europe. It was the moment of his coming-out, as it were, and Wright craved the limelight as far as it illuminated the considerable extent of his architectural imagination. Wright spoke of many of his design elements: the nature of materials, the elimination of rooms, openings as integral features of form, and colors ("soft, warm optimistic tones of earths and autumn leaves"). But he also addressed the issue of style, American self-reliance, and the simplification of forms that lay in the near future – all themes inherited from Sullivan.

In the hope that some day America may live her own life in her own buildings, in her own way, that is, that we may make the best of what we have for what it honestly is or may become, I have endeavored in this work to establish a harmonious relationship between ground plan and elevation of these buildings, considering the one as a solution and the other an expression of the conditions of a problem of which the whole is a project. I have tried to establish an organic integrity to begin with, forming the basis for the subsequent working out of a significant grammatical expression and making the whole, as nearly as I could, consistent.

What quality of style the buildings may possess is due to the artistry with which the conventionalization as a solution and an artistic expression of a specific problem within these limitations has been handled. The types are largely a matter of personal taste and may have much or little to do with the American architecture for which we hope.

From the beginning of my practice, the question uppermost in my mind has been not "what style?" but "what is style?" and it is my belief that the chief value of the work illustrated here will be found in the fact that if in the face of our present-day conditions any given type may be treated independently and imbued with the quality of style, then a truly noble architecture is a definite possibility, so soon as Americans really demand it of the architects of the rising generation.

I do not believe we will ever again have the uniformity of type which has characterized the so-called great "styles." Conditions have changed; our ideal is Democracy, the highest possible expression of the individual as a unit not inconsistent with a harmonious whole. The average of human intelligence rises steadily, and as the individual unit grows more and more to be trusted we will have an architecture with richer variety in unity than has ever arisen before; but the forms must be born out of our changed conditions, they must be *true* forms, otherwise the best that tradition has to offer is only an inglorious masquerade, devoid of vital significance or true spiritual value.

[. . .]

As for the future – the work shall grow more truly simple; more expressive with fewer lines, fewer forms; more articulate with less labor; more plastic; more fluent, although more coherent; more organic. It shall grow not only to fit more perfectly the methods and processes that are called upon to produce it, but shall further find whatever is lovely or of good repute in method or process, and idealize it with the cleanest, most virile stroke I can imagine. As understanding and appreciation of life matures and deepens, this work shall prophesy and idealize the character of the individual it is fashioned to serve more intimately, no matter how inexpensive the result must finally be. It shall become in its atmosphere as pure and elevating in its humble way as the trees and flowers are in their perfectly appointed way, for only so can architecture be worthy its high rank as a fine art, or the architect discharge the obligation he assumes to the public – imposed upon him by the nature of his own profession.

84 GUSTAV STICKLEY
from *Craftsman Homes* (1909)

O ver its first decade of publication, Stickley's journal *The Craftsman* underwent an evolution as it came to identify less with socialist aims of the British Arts and Crafts movement and more with the artistic reforms underway in the United States. The fact that Sullivan's last major essay was published in this journal is but one indication that Stickley understood that the architectural events transpiring in Chicago and elsewhere were equally if not more compelling in their ramifications. Stickley too came to embrace the machine, and more and more of his design efforts became focused on architecture. In 1909 Stickley published his first book, *Craftsman Homes*, and in it, as a concluding chapter, the designer set out his views on the reform movement and its connection with the sweeping changes within American social, political, and industrial attitudes. The influence of Wright has made its way into these feelings, but so has the nineteenth-century tradition of Andrew Jackson Downing and Calvert Vaux.

In this book we have endeavored to set forth as fully as possible the several parts which, taken together, go to make up the Craftsman idea of the kind of home environment that tends to result in wholesome living. We have shown the gradual growth of this idea, from the making of the first pieces of Craftsman furniture to the completed house which has in it all the elements of a permanently satisfying home. But we have left until the last the question of the right setting for such a home and the conditions under which the life that is lived in it could form the foundation for the fullest individual and social development.

There is no question now as to the reality of the world-wide movement in the direction of better things. We see everywhere efforts to reform social, political and industrial conditions; the desire to bring about better opportunities for all and to find some way of adjusting economic conditions so that the heart-breaking inequalities of our modern civilized life shall in some measure be done away with. But while we take the greatest interest in all efforts toward reform in any direction, we remain firm in the conviction that the root of all reforms lies in the individual and that the life of the individual is shaped mainly by home surroundings and influences and by the kind of education that goes to make real men and women instead of grist for the commercial mill.

That the influence of the home is of the first importance in the shaping of character is a fact too well understood and too generally admitted to be offered here as a new idea. One need only turn to the pages of history to find abundant proof of the unerring action of Nature's law, for without exception the people who lives are lived simply and wholesomely, in the open, and who have in a high degree the sense of the sacredness of the home, are the people who have made the greatest strides in the development of the race. When luxury enters in and a thousand artificial requirements come to be regarded as real needs, the nation is on the brink of degeneration. So often has the story repeated itself that he who runs may read its deep significance. In our own country, to which has fallen the heritage of all the older civilizations, the course has been swift, for we are yet close to the memory of the primitive pioneer days when the nation was building, and we have still the crudity as well as

Gustav Stickley, from *Craftsman Homes* (1909), in facsimile edition. New York: Dover, 1979, pp. 194–5.

the vigor of youth. But so rapid and easy has been our development and so great our prosperity that even now we are in some respects very nearly in the same state as the older peoples who have passed the zenith of their power and are beginning to decline. In our own case, however, the saving grace lies in the fact that our taste for luxury and artificiality is not as yet deeply ingrained. We are intensely commercial, fond of all the good things of life, proud of our ability to "get there," and we yield the palm to none in the matter of owning anything that money can buy. But, fortunately, our pioneers days are not ended even now and we still have a goodly number of men and women who are helping to develop the country and make history merely by living simple natural lives close to the soil and full of the interest and pleasure which come from kinship with Nature and the kind of work that calls forth all their resources in the way of self-reliance and the power of initiative. Even in the rush and hurry of life in our busy cities we remember well the quality given to the growing nation by such men and women a generation or two ago and, in spite of the chaotic conditions brought about by our passion for money-getting, extravagance and show, we have still reason to believe that the dominant characteristics of the pioneer yet shape what are the salient qualities in American life.

85 DANIEL BURNHAM AND EDWARD H. BENNETT
from *Plan for Chicago* (1909)

Although Ebenezer Howard's concept of a garden city would eventually have a significant following in the United States, the idea influencing the development of the American city in the first decades of the new century was the "City Beautiful" movement led by Daniel Burnham. This Chicago architect first achieved prominence through his partnership with John Root in the 1870s and 1880s. In large part due to the firm's success, Burnham was placed in charge of the planning of Chicago's Columbian Exposition in 1893, and it was through the popular success of the "White City" – the Beaux-Arts-inspired layout of the exposition buildings – that Burnham decided to turn much of his attention to city planning. His principal model was Haussmann's changes for Paris, but he adapted its park-and-boulevard theme to American cities, beginning with his baroque plan for Washington, DC (1901), worked out with the assistance of Frederick Olmsted, Jr. and George McKim. Burnham followed with plans for downtown Cleveland (1903), San Francisco (1905), and Manila (1905), but his most exhaustive planning venture was for Chicago, which he published in 1909 with Edward H. Bennett. Much of his park scheme along Lake Michigan was later realized, and Burnham's City Beautiful movement, by any gauge, radically altered the American urban landscape. These excerpts also reveal something of the scope of his high ambition.

The tendency of mankind to congregate in cities is a marked characteristic of modern times. This movement is confined to no one country, but is world-wide. Each year Rome, and the

Daniel Burnham, from Daniel Burnham and Edward H. Bennett, *Plan for Chicago* (1909), cited from the reprint edition. New York: Da Capo, 1970, pp. 1, 4.

cities of the Orient, as well as Berlin, New York, and Chicago, are adding to their population at an unprecedented rate. Coincident with this urban development there has been a widespread increase in wealth, and also an enlarged participation on the part of the people in the work of government. As a natural result of these causes has come the desire to better the conditions of living. Men are becoming convinced that the formless growth of the city is neither economical nor satisfactory; and that overcrowding and congestion of traffic paralyze the vital functions of the city. The complicated problems which the great city develops are now seen not to be beyond the control of aroused public sentiment; and practical men of affairs are turning their attention to working out the means whereby the city may be made an efficient instrument for providing all its people with the best possible conditions of living.

Chicago, in common with other great cities, realizes that the time has come to bring order out of the chaos incident to rapid growth, and especially to the influx of people of many nationalities without common traditions or habits of life. Among the various instrumentalities designed to accomplish this result, a plan for a well-ordered and convenient city is seen to be indispensable; and to the task of producing such a plan the Commercial Club has devoted its energies for the past three years.

[. . .]

If many elements of the proposed plan shall seem familiar, it should be remembered that the purpose has not been to invent novel problems for solution, but to take up the pressing needs of to-day, and to find the best methods of meeting those requirements, carrying each particular problem to its ultimate conclusion as a component part of a great entity – a well-ordered, convenient, and unified city.

This conception of the task is the justification of a comprehensive plan of Chicago. To many who have given little consideration to the subject, a plan seems to call for large expenditures and a consequent increase in taxation. The reverse is the case. It is certain that civic improvement will go on at an accelerated rate; and if those improvements shall be marshaled according to a well-ordered plan great saving must result. Good order and convenience are not expensive; but haphazard and ill-considered projects invariably result in extravagance and wastefulness. A plan insures that whenever any public or semi-public work shall be undertaken, it will fall into its proper and predetermined place in the general scheme, and thus contribute to the unity and dignity of the city.

The plan frankly takes into consideration the fact that the American city, and Chicago pre-eminently, is a center of industry and traffic. Therefore attention is given to the betterment of commercial facilities; to methods of transportation for persons and for goods; to removing the obstacles which prevent or obstruct circulation; and to the increase of convenience. It is realized, also, that good workmanship requires a large degree of comfort on the part of the workers in their homes and their surroundings, and ample opportunity for that rest and recreation without which all work becomes drudgery. Then, too, the city has a dignity to be maintained; and good order is essential to material advancement. Consequently, the plan provides for impressive groupings of public buildings, and reciprocal relations among such groups. Moreover, consideration is given to the fact that in all probability Chicago, within the lifetime of persons now living, will become a greater city than any existing at the present time; and that therefore the most comprehensive plans of to-day will need to be supplemented in a not remote future. Opportunity for such expansion is provided for.

The origin of the plan of Chicago can be traced directly to the World's Columbian Exposition. The World's Fair of 1893 was the beginning, in our day and in this country, of the orderly arrangement of extensive public grounds and buildings. The result came about quite naturally. Chicago had become a commercial community wherein men were accustomed to get together to plan for the general good.

86 FRANK LLOYD WRIGHT
from *Executed Buildings and Designs of Frank Lloyd Wright* (1911)

Wright's earlier essay, "In the Cause of Architecture," was written at a time when his life was nearing a crisis. The previous ten years had been extremely productive, yet Wright was at the same time growing uneasy with the limitations of his residential practice. At the same time his marriage was failing and Wright was unhappy and having an affair with Mamah Cheney, the wife of a former client. Thus when Wright also received a letter from the Berlin publisher Ernst Wasmuth, who offered to publish a monograph of his works, Wright jumped at the opportunity. He sold some of his Japanese prints and quit Chicago, abandoning his wife and family. He also made arrangements to rendezvous with Mamah Cheney for a trip abroad. After a visit to Berlin to define the parameters of his project, Wright joined Cheney in Fiesole, where Wright prepared the drawings for his monograph. The book was a stunning success in Europe and became a veritable Bible for many German and Dutch modernists. Wright's introductory essay also differs from his earlier writings in that he – mimicking Sullivan's pessimism – now adopts a far more critical attitude toward his American colleagues. He views the influence of Ruskin and Morris, as well as Beaux-Arts influences from France, as having long stifled American design, and in particular he is scornful of the tendency of the American East Coast always to look to Europe for cultural inspiration. The more authentic American spirit of innovation, Wright argues, thrives in the American Midwest and West – a polemic that Wright would repeatedly make over the coming decades. This argument represents an important turning point in Wright's development, and it is one, combined with the notoriety of his scandalous adultery, that would forever change his practice.

The ideals of Ruskin and Morris and the teaching of the Beaux Arts have hitherto prevailed in America, steadily confusing, as well as in some respects revealing to us our opportunities. The American, too, of some Old World culture, disgusted by this state of affairs and having the beautiful harmony in the architecture of an English village, European rural community, or the grandiloquent planning of Paris in view has been easily persuaded that the best thing we could do was to adopt some style least foreign to us, stick to it, and plant it continually; a parasitic proceeding, and in any case futile. New York is a tribute to the Beaux Arts, so far as surface decoration goes, and underneath a tribute to the American engineer.

Other cities have followed her lead.

Frank Lloyd Wright, from *Ausgeführte Bauten und Entwürfe von Frank Lloyd Wright*, Berlin: Wasmuth, 1911, cited here from *Frank Lloyd Wright. Collected Writings: Vol. 1,1894–1930*, ed. Bruce Brooks Pfeiffer. New York: Rizzoli, 1992, p. 108.

Our better-class residences are chiefly tributes to English architecture, cut open inside and embellished to suit; porches and "conveniences" added: the result in most cases a pitiful mongrel. Painfully conscious of their lack of traditions, our get-rich-quick citizens attempt to buy tradition ready-made and are dragged forward, facing backwards, in attitudes most absurd to those they would emulate, characteristic examples of conspicuous waste.

The point in all this is the fact that revival of the ideals of an organic architecture will have to contend with this rapidly increasing sweep of imported folly. Even the American with some little culture, going contrary to his usual course in other matters, is becoming painfully aware of his inferiority in matters of dress and architecture and goes abroad for both, to be sure they are correct. Thus assured, he is no longer concerned and forgets both. That is more characteristic of the Eastern than the Western man. The real American spirit, capable of judging an issue for itself upon its merits, lies in the West and Middle West, where breadth of view, independent thought, and a tendency to take common sense into the realm of art, as in life, are more characteristic. It is alone in an atmosphere of this nature that the Gothic spirit in building can be revived. In this atmosphere, among clients of this type, I have lived and worked.

87 IRVING GILL
from "The Home of the Future: The New Architecture of the West" (1916)

Whereas Wright's and Sullivan's influence on the American East Coast was minimal at best, this was not the case on the West Coast, which around the turn of the century was enjoying a booming development of its urban centers. Irving Gill is indicative of the kind of architect who was attracted to this area. A native of Syracuse, NY, he migrated to the office of Adler and Sullivan in 1890 without any previous architectural training. There he worked under the supervision of Wright, but in 1893, because of failing health, he set out for the warm climate of San Diego to make his mark. He struggled at first at finding himself or his style, but in 1907, with his designs for the Klauber and Laughlin houses, he devised a system of concrete and hollow-tile construction that created smooth surfaces without planar articulation. The result was a startling clean and "modern" solution to the house, a solution that he subsequently advanced with the precast concrete tilt-slab system that he devised for the Banning House, Los Angeles (1912), and the Women's Club, La Jolla (1913). Gill's stunning modern masterpiece, however, was his Dodge House, Los Angeles (1916), whose aesthetic of cubic elegance and white concrete surfaces (not to mention sun-drenched roof terraces) was extremely innovative for this period. This excerpt is from his lone aesthetic statement.

Irving Gill, from "The Home of the Future: The New Architecture of the West," in *The Craftsman* 30:2 (May 1916), pp. 141–2.

The West has an opportunity unparalleled in the history of the world, for it is the newest white page turned for registration. The present builders have the advantage of all the wisdom and experience of the ages to aid them in poetically inscribing today's milestone in the progress of humanity. The West unfortunately has been and is building too hastily, carelessly and thoughtlessly. Houses are springing up faster than mushrooms, for mushrooms silently prepare for a year and more before they finally raise their house above the ground in proof of what they have been designing so long and secretly. People pour out here as on the crest of a flood and remain where chance deposits them when the rush of waters subsides, building temporary shacks wherein they live for a brief period while looking about for more permanent anchorage. The surface of the ground is barely scraped away, in some cases but a few inches deep, just enough to allow builders to find a level, and a house is tossed together with little thought of beauty, and no thought of permanence, haste being the chief characteristic. The family of health- or fortune-seekers who comes out here generally expects to camp in these poor shacks for but a short time and plans to sell the shiftless affair to some other impatient newcomer. Perhaps such temporary proceedings are necessary in the settling of a new land; fortunately such structures cannot endure, will never last long enough to be a monument for future generations to wonder at. Such structures cannot rightly be called homes, so do not justly deserve notice in a consideration of Western domestic architecture.

If we, the architects of the West, wish to do great and lasting work we must dare to be simple, must have the courage to fling aside every device that distracts the eye from structural beauty, must break through convention and get down to fundamental truths. Through force of custom and education we, in whose hands much of the beauty of country and city is entrusted, have been compelled to study the style of other men, with the result that most of our modern work is an open imitation or veiled plagiarism of another's idea. To break away from this degradation we must boldly throw aside every accepted structural belief and standard of beauty and get back to the source of all architectural strength – the straight line, the arch, the cube and the circle – and drink from these fountains of Art that gave life to the great men of old.

PART III   THE 1920S

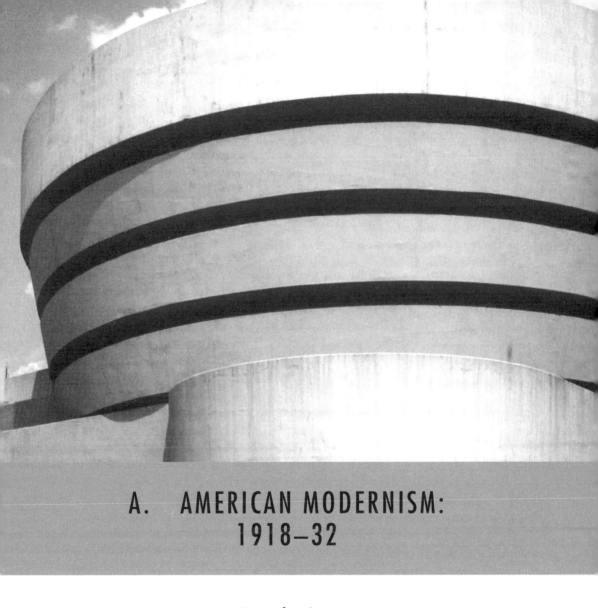

A. AMERICAN MODERNISM: 1918–32

Introduction

World War I – "the war to end all wars" – put over fifty million men and women into uniform and placed over ten million soldiers in cemeteries. The savage conflict, which was largely played out on European soil, also had the effect of creating an economic divide between Europe and North America. Not only was the United States (a hesitant and belated player within the conflict) spared all of the material and much of the personal devastation that would destabilize Europe politically during the 1920s (and arguably for the next thirty years), but the pace of American industrial expansion was, if anything, accelerated by the conflict. As a result, the "American Decade" of the 1920s was an intensely active period: intellectually and architecturally. The economic power that the country had assumed prior to the war mushroomed after the event, commensurate with the extraordinary pace of building. The birth of the "skyscraper" for many symbolized this new-found capitalist might, while at the same time it called into practice a score of technological issues that otherwise might not have been raised. Then there was the success of such industrial entrepreneurs as Henry Ford, who based his assembly line on the ideas of Frederick Winslow Taylor. This new system of production demanded a sense of efficiency and tooled precision unmatched elsewhere in the world.

Another distinction of American architectural practice in the 1920s was its growing sense of independence and geographical variety. Whereas the Northeast remained an important center for discussion and ideas, the population of the country was continuing to shift westward and southward. The centers of the Midwest and West were still expanding, but so were such cities as Atlanta, Miami, Portland, and Dallas. Hence the idea of a regional modernism, first given credence by the so-called Prairie School in Chicago, found a larger rationale in the distinct topographies and climates of these regions. Frank Lloyd Wright's relocation of his practice to Los Angeles in the 1920s, for example, had an immediate and pronounced impact on his approach to design. And whereas these new centers, with supreme American confidence, exalted in their regional independence and innovations, talented European immigrants, such as Rudolf Schindler and Richard Neutra, brought to them a knowing solidarity with experimentation elsewhere, while simultaneously having their own ideas transformed by the native spirit. In this sense, the famous exhibition at the Museum of Modern Art in 1932, with its insistence that American architects awaken from their slumber and adopt European models of modernism, could be viewed as an uninformed and somewhat effete betrayal of American culture — if the Great Depression had not already made this point moot.

88 FREDERICK WINSLOW TAYLOR
from *The Principles of Scientific Management* (1911)

If one were to define one of the two or three ideas permeating the intellectual atmosphere of the 1920s, one would have to start with this small book by Frederick Winslow Taylor. This American engineer devoted most of his working life to managing a shift in two steel mills, but little by little he came to recognize the need for "scientific management" in the production cycle. His method was to break down each particular phase of the assembly or production process, analyze and time the workers' movements (with the aid of a stopwatch, cameras, and small lights attached to workers' limbs), and devise manufacturing strategies that would minimize or eliminate movements. His aim, as this passage shows, was not just to maximize production for the employer, but just as importantly to ease the labor spent by the employee, and ultimately provide shorter working hours, higher wages, and such amenities as paid breaks and vacations. Taylor's book appeared in 1911, around the same time that Henry Ford was completing a new assembly plant in Highland Park, Michigan. When Ford adopted Taylor's methods for production and subsequently, over the course of a decade, reduced the cost of a Model T from $950 to $260 (while at the same time making Ford's three shifts of workers some of the highest paid in the world, as well as the first to purchase automobiles), Taylor and his methods were suddenly thrust upon the international stage. They were methods of efficiency that appealed equally to capitalists, socialists, or communists.

The principal object of management should be to secure the maximum prosperity for the employer, coupled with the maximum prosperity for each employé.

Frederick Winslow Taylor, *The Principles of Scientific Management* (1911), cited from the reprint edition. Mineola, NY: Dover, 1998, p. 1.

The words "maximum prosperity" are used, in their broad sense, to mean not only large dividends for the company or owner, but the development of every branch of the business to its highest state of excellence, so that the prosperity may be permanent.

In the same way maximum prosperity for each employé means not only higher wages than are usually received by men of his class, but, of more importance still, it also means the development of each man to his state of maximum efficiency, so that he may be able to do, generally speaking, the highest grade of work for which his natural abilities fit him, and it further means giving him, when possible, this class of work to do.

It would seem to be so self-evident that maximum prosperity for the employer, coupled with maximum prosperity for the employé, ought to be the two leading objects of management, that even to state this fact should be unnecessary. And yet there is no question that, throughout the industrial world, a large part of the organization of employers, as well as employés, is for war rather than for peace, and that perhaps the majority on either side do not believe that it is possible so to arrange their mutual relations that their interests become identical.

The majority of these men believe that the fundamental interests of employés and employers are necessarily antagonistic. Scientific management, on the contrary, has for its very foundation the firm conviction that the true interests of the two are one and the same; that prosperity for the employer cannot exist through a long term of years unless it is accompanied by prosperity for the employé, and *vice versa*; and that it is possible to give the workman what he most wants – high wages – and the employer what he wants – a low labor cost – for his manufactures.

89 CLAUDE BRAGDON
from *Architecture and Democracy*
(1918)

The spirit of Ralph Waldo Emerson found still another prophet in the postwar years in Claude Bragdon. A mystic and theosophist by inclination, Bragdon began his architectural practice in 1901 in Rochester, New York, a practice that remained modest in its scope. He gained prominence, however, as a lecturer and essayist and is known today chiefly for his championing of the work of Sullivan. *Architecture and Democracy* is an interesting three-part historical study of American architecture before, during, and after the war. This passage, which opens part three by distinguishing between organic and arranged architecture, has a specific context. Architectural education within American universities in 1918 was based almost entirely on Beaux-Arts methods of training, and Bragdon in this passage voices a loud protest against what he views as a contrived and antiquated approach to instruction. He counters with a plea for creativity in design, tempered with the democratic spirit of self reliance.

He whom the World-Soul "forbids to despair" cannot but hope; and he who hopes tries ever to imagine that "fairer world" yearning at birth beyond this interval of blood and tears.

Claude Bragdon, from *Architecture and Democracy before, during and after the War. Part III: After the War* (1918), cited from *Architectural Record* 44:3 (September 1918), pp. 253–4.

Prophecy, to all but the anointed, is dangerous and uncertain; but even so, the author cannot forbear attempting some prevision of the architecture likely to arise from the wrecks and sediment left by the war.

As a basis for this forecast it is necessary, first of all, briefly to analyze the expression of the building impulse from what may be called the psychological point of view.

Broadly speaking, there are not five orders of architecture – nor fifty – but only two: *Arranged* and *Organic*. These correspond to the two terms of that "inevitable duality" which bisects life. Talent and genius, reason and intuition, bromide and sulphite are some of the names we know them by.

Arranged architecture is reasoned and artificial; produced by talent, governed by taste. Organic architecture, on the other hand, is the product of some obscure inner necessity for self-expression which is sub-conscious. It is as though Nature herself, through some human organ of her activity, had addressed herself to the service of the sons and daughters of men.

Arranged architecture in its finest manifestations is the product of a pride, a knowledge, a competence, a confidence staggering to behold. It seems to say of the works of Nature. "I'll show you a trick worth two of that." For the subtlety of Nature's geometry, and for her infinite variety and unexpectedness. Arranged architecture substitutes a Euclidian system of straight lines and (for the most part) circular curves, assembled and arranged according to a definite logic of its own. It is created, but not creative; it is imagined, but not imaginative. Organic architecture is both creative and imaginative. It is non-Euclidian, in the sense that it is higher-dimensional – that is, it suggests extension in directions and into regions where the spirit finds itself at home, but of which the senses gives no report to the brain.

To make the whole thing clearer it may be said that Arranged and Organic architecture bear much the same relation to each other that a piano bears to a violin. A piano is an instrument that does not give forth discords if one follows the rules. A violin requires absolutely an ear – an inner rectitude. It has a way of betraying the man of talent and glorifying the genius, becoming one with his body and his soul.

Of course it stands to reason that there is not always a hard and fast differentiation between these two orders of architecture, but there is one sure way by which each may be recognized and known. If the function appears to have created the form, and if everywhere the form follows the function, changing as that changes, the building is Organic; if, on the contrary, "the house confines the spirit," if the building presents not a face but however beautiful a mask, it is an example of Arranged architecture.

The Gothic cathedrals of the "Heart of Europe" – now the place of Armageddon – represent the most perfect and powerful incarnation of the Organic spirit in architecture. After the decadence of Medieval Feudalism – synchronous with that of Monasticism – the Arranged architecture of the Renaissance acquired the ascendant; this was coincident with the rise of Humanism, when life became increasingly secular. During the post-Renaissance, or Scientific period, of which the war probably marks the close, there has been a confusion of tongues; architecture has spoken only alien or dead languages, learned by rote.

But in so far as it is anything at all, esthetically, our architecture is Arranged, so if only by the operation of the law of opposites, or alternation, we might reasonably expect the next manifestation to be Organic. There are other and better reasons, however, for such expectancy.

Organic architecture is ever a flower of the religious spirit. When the soul draws near to the surface of life, as it did in the two mystic centuries of the Middle Ages, it *organizes* life;

and architecture, along with the other arts, becomes truly creative. The informing force comes not so much *from* man as *through* him. After the war that spirit of brotherhood, born in the camps (as Christ was born in a manger) and bred on the battlefields and in the trenches of Europe, is likely to take on all the attributes of a new religion of humanity, prompting men to such heroisms and renunciations, exciting in them such psychic sublimations, as have characterized the great religious renewals of times past.

If this happens, it is bound to write itself on space in an architecture beautiful and new; one which "takes its shape and sun-color" not from the niggardly mind, but from the opulent heart. This architecture will of necessity be organic; the product not of self-assertive personalities, but the work of the "Patient Daemon" organizing the nation into a spiritual democracy.

90 IRVING K. POND
from "Zoning and the Architecture of High Buildings" (1921)

I n 1916 the city of New York – in response to increasingly taller, boxlike buildings rising vertically from the street – reformulated its zoning regulations. The new statutes put forward the idea of a "zoning envelope," that is, a building that could rise to any height but whose walls had to step back at an angle determined by a line drawn from the center of the street, and whose final tower could occupy no more than 25 percent of the lot area. Architects and critics generally reacted favorably to the pyramidal form that this change imposed: some because they saw it as a way of bringing much-needed sunlight and order into the city, some because they saw the law as a prompt to a uniquely American style. The Chicago architect Irving K. Pond, who in his own designs for tall buildings had favored the pyramidal form, fell into the second camp. This passage from his essay, which he published in the journal *Architectural Forum*, follows from his discussion of his designs for the City Club in Chicago and the Michigan Union in Ann Arbor, and it articulates both his psychological preference for pyramidal forms and his desire to move away from Greek and Gothic-inspired styles and elaborate a truly modern American architecture.

The critical observer will note in both these buildings that setbacks and modified corners are used to enforce another element of the design, which is a direct appeal to sentiment and understanding on the part of the beholder. Horizontality and verticality are introduced into the structures in such manner that each may make its own appeal to the emotions and be held in restraint by the other only when it tends to step beyond the bounds of the larger unity which is determined upon in advance and which it is sought in every way to preserve. In the latter instance there was a study of college life and environment and a knowledge of the college constituency which gave the designer a clue to his larger masses and lesser details and permitted him through the medium of form and color to make an appeal which should find response in the mind and heart of the beholder, for both mind and heart were appealed to and not in vain.

Irving Pond, "Zoning and the Architecture of High Buildings," in *Architectural Forum* 35:4 (October 1921), p. 133.

Every work of art, every building into which the designer has put vital feeling, will produce a definite psychological reaction in a sensate beholder – and just about in the same ratio in which the designer has expended himself. It goes without saying that the designer and the beholder must have had community of background and experience that the reaction may be commensurate with the action; that there must have been on the part of both sender and recipient of the message some similar knowledge of the past, some appreciation of the reaction of the race to physical and spiritual environment, of reaction to atmospheric, geographic, climatic and geologic surroundings – to social, political and religious conditions. And this community of apprehension and appreciation should extend to and embrace modern categories and conditions, and include a community of idealism. The potentialities of feeling and expression within us have been implanted by the age-long contact of our ancestry with these conditions, physical and spiritual, and it is for us to release them in unstinted creative and appreciative effort.

What has this to do with setback walls and tower office building? It has this: that some beneficent power, embodied at present in a zoning law, has given architects a chance to create beautiful and appropriate buildings, not Greek temples nor mediæval cathedrals, but something modern, born of a new spirit which is neither Greek or Gothic nor Roman or classic renaissance, but which is intensely of today. There is a chance for the expression of poise, serenity and restraint controlling emotionalism and exuberance of spirit. All are factors of the modern age and all are to be considered and all, at times, in one composition. The tower office building under zoning laws would seem to furnish an opportunity for the latter.

91   HUGH FERRISS
from "The New Architecture" (1922)

Another architect who attempted to interpret the new zoning regulations for New York City from the perspective of changing American architectural design was Hugh Ferriss. Trained as an architect, Ferriss made his living as a brilliant delineator with a unique chiaroscuro style. In 1922 he began working with the architect Harvey Wiley Corbett in making sketches to explicate the design implications of the new ordinance. His four sketches depicting the step-by-step sculpting of a building from the abstraction of the pyramidal lines quickly became a classic interpretation of the new law, but Ferriss, in his fascination with the novel forms, went much further. In this newspaper article, which included his futuristic sketch of New York City in 1942, Ferriss first explains the law, but then goes on to speak of its potential to create a new American style altogether. During the 1920s Ferriss became one of the leading voices in his futuristic commitment to architectural design and innovation.

The recent enaction of the New York zoning laws creates a unique situation – "restricting" in nature, they are producing a profound evolution in architecture. They not only open a wider vista to the architectural designer, but actually force him to proceed into this vista.

The laws, briefly, regulate all buildings in the city in three respects – their use, area and height.

Hugh Ferriss, from "The New Architecture," in *The New York Times* (March 19, 1922), pp. 8, 27.

The use, regulations require that in specified streets only residences be allowed; in others, only certain businesses (in addition to residences). A third group is unrestricted – that is to say, industries, &c., are allowed to occupy buildings therein.

The area, regulations require that in specified zones open spaces of stated dimensions be allowed on the lot. The maximum occurs in residence zones, the minimum in warehouse zones.

It is the third, the height regulations, with which we are now concerned. Under these regulations buildings may rise on their lot lines to only specified heights; above this they must slant backward within a line drawn from the centre of the street through the top of the wall on the lot line.

The height of this wall is based on the width of the street which it faces. There are five zones in New York of varying height allowance. In the tallest a building may rise two and one-half times the width of the street before it begins to slant backward; in the lowest only once the width of the street.

In addition to this basic requirement, a tower may be erected to any height, provided that it does not occupy more than one-fourth of the area of the lot. Dormers also are allowed within considerable restrictions.

[. . .]

The most fascinating potentiality of the new laws may lie in their ability to finally bring forth the much-debated "new style" in architecture. Aside from those who seek a "new style" simply because they naïvely want something new, or naïvely want something national, there are designers who for sound reasons have found past styles inadequate to clothe present-day facts. Many efforts have been made to produce a new style on the part of individual designers. The result has usually been based on nothing more profound than their individuality. Now, the styles of the past came into being simply because they naturally and inevitably grew from unique structural conditions; and it is precisely that with which we are faced – a unique structural condition. A new era commences.

If the matter were local, even to New York, it would be one thing. Zoning, however, has been adopted in other cities throughout the country. Its sound principles indicate that it will become universal. We are not contemplating the new architecture of a city – we are contemplating the new architecture of a civilization.

92 *CHICAGO DAILY TRIBUNE*
Announcement of an Architectural Competition (1922)

S hortly after Hugh Ferriss published his vision of the skyscraper based on New York City's new ordinance, Robert R. McCormick, the owner of the *Chicago Tribune*, announced a major international competition to design the new corporate headquarters for "the world's greatest newspaper." Two hundred and sixty-three architects from around the world submitted entries, many from Europe, where virtually no work was on the boards. Ten American firms

Chicago Daily Tribune (June 10, 1922), p. 11.

were also invited to participate, and in the end — as judged largely by a lay jury — the scheme of John Mead Howells and Raymond Hood was selected over the second-place design of the Finnish architect Eliel Saarinen (seemingly drawing upon on Ferriss's sketches). Much has been made, both then and now, about the controversy surrounding the winning "gothic" design, but the event and its outcome is more complex in its parameters. Many of the "modern" schemes in fact had little understanding of the technologies of tall buildings in general and those available in 1922, while the event also prompted a vigorous debate within American architecture and indeed shifted the ground in a near-dramatic way. Almost immediately the search would be on to find a solution for the skyscraper apart from historical forms.

$100,000.00

IN PRIZES TO ARCHITECTS

Seventy-five years old today, The Tribune seeks surpassing beauty in new home on Michigan Boulevard

THE TRIBUNE herewith offers $100,000.00 in prizes for designs for a building to be erected on its vacant lot at North Michigan Boulevard and Austin Avenue. Commemoration of our Seventy-fifth Birthday is made in this manner for three reasons:

—*to adorn with a monument of enduring beauty this city, in which The Tribune has prospered so amazingly.*

—*to create a structure which will be an inspiration and a model for generations of newspaper publishers.*

—*to provide a new and beautiful home worthy of the world's greatest newspaper.*

The contest will be under the rules of the American Institute of Architects. Competition will be open and international. Each competitor will be required to submit drawings showing the west and south elevations and perspective from the southwest, of a new building to be erected on The Tribune's property at the corner of North Michigan Blvd. and Austin Ave. Architects desiring complete information are requested to write to

Robert R. McCormick, Joseph M. Patterson, Editors and Publishers

The Chicago Tribune
The World's Greatest Newspaper

SEVENTY-FIVE YEARS OLD TODAY

93 LEWIS MUMFORD
from *Sticks and Stones* (1924)

Owing both to the profusion of his writings and to the impact of his words, Lewis Mumford may be rightly called the most important American architectural critic of the twentieth century. He was also the most longstanding. Born in Manhattan, by the early 1920s he moved within a New York literary circle that included Van Wyck Brooks, Waldo Frank, Margaret Sanger, and Walter Lippmann. Informing this group during these resurgent years were the pragmatic theories of William James (seeking a balance of theory and practice), the instrumentalism of John Dewey (an integration of theory with action), the socialism of Thorstein Veblen, and the Women's Suffrage movement. Mumford's first book, *The Story of Utopias* (1922), dealt broadly with the theme of a better society, and by this date he was already including architecture within his literary interests. Architecture became the focus of *Sticks and Stones: A Study of American Architecture and Civilization*, which was the first book to chart a history of American architecture within the context of American culture. Its inspirational sources were many: from the Emersonian tradition recently exalted by Claude Bragdon to the Garden City of Ebenezer Howard, as expanded in the ecological theory of Patrick Geddes. Still another influence was an essay by Van Wyck Brooks, "On Creating an Usable Past," which sought to extract from the American literary past a tradition that could support a creative movement for the present. Mumford, in invoking here the American Puritanical tradition of the Village Green, seeks to connect a usable past with the modern notion of a Garden City, a position that first signals his lifelong aversion to large, high-density cities. Mumford wants a more peaceful, more humane, more ecologically sound world — a goal that would transform itself into an activist crusade in 1923 with the founding of the Regional Planning Association of America (RPAA) by Mumford, Clarence Stein, Henry Wright, Benton MacKaye, and others.

In essentials, however, both the life and the architecture of the first provincial period are sound. While agriculture is the mainstay of life, and the medieval tradition flourishes, the New England village reaches a pretty fair pitch of worldly perfection; and beneath all the superficial changes that affected it in the next century and a half, its sturdy framework held together remarkably well.

Consider the village itself. In the center is a common, a little to one side will be the meeting-house, perhaps a square barnlike structure, with a hipped roof and a cupola, like that at Hingham; and adjacent or across the way will be the grammar school. Along the roads where the houses are set at regular intervals is a great columnar arcade of elm trees. All these elements are essential to our early provincial architecture, and without them it would be a little bare and forbidding. The trees, above all, are an important part of New England architecture: in summer they absorb the moisture and cool the air, besides giving shade; in the winter their huge boles serve as a partial windbrake; even the humus from their leaves keeps the soil of the lawns in better order. The apple trees and kitchen-garden, giving food and beauty, are not less essential. Would it be an exaggeration to say that there has never been a more complete and intelligent partnership between the earth and man than existed, for a little while, in the old New England village? In what other part of the world has such a harmonious balance between the natural and the social environment been preserved?

Lewis Mumford, from *Sticks and Stones: A Study of American Architecture and Civilization* (1924), cited from the reprint edition. New York: Dover, 1955, pp. 9–10.

Nowadays we have begun to talk about garden-cities, and we realize that the essential elements in a garden-city are the common holding of land by the community, and the coöperative ownership and direction of the community itself. We refer to all these things as if they represented a distinct achievement of modern thought; but the fact of the matter is that the New England village up to the middle of the eighteenth century was a garden-city in every sense that we now apply to that term, and happily its gardens and its harmonious framework have frequently lingered on, even though the economic foundations have long been overthrown.

This is a medieval tradition in American architecture which should be of some use to our architects and city planners; for it is a much more substantial matter than the building of perpendicular churches or Tudor country-houses in painfully archaeological adaptations. If we wish to tie up with our colonial tradition we must recover more than the architectural forms: we must recover the interests, the standards, the institutions that gave to the villages and buildings of early times their appropriate shapes. To do much less than this is merely to bring back a fad which might as well be Egyptian as "colonial" for all the sincerity that it exhibits.

94 LEWIS MUMFORD
from "The Search for 'Something More'" (1928)

T he debate over the tall building that was prompted by the *Chicago Tribune* competition of 1922 received a full hearing in the second half of the decade, as an awareness of European developments was joined with the high pace of building activity. Raymond Hood, the designer of the Chicago building, departed from strict historical forms in his next design for the American Radiator Building (1924), and his New York Daily News Building (1928) took this abstraction one step further with a design altogether devoid of ornament. Among those also pondering the problem of the tall building was Lewis Mumford, whose architectural horizons had considerably broadened over the previous four years. Here he has since become aware of, and developed an attraction for, European modernism (although not to the "extreme" austerity of Walter Gropius and Le Corbusier); at the same time, with his humanist outlook, he was drawn to the organic and geometric work of Wright. Mumford therefore sought to have some middle ground in his reasoning, which he found in the 120 Park Avenue Building, New York City, designed by Jacques Ely Kahn – an Art Deco masterpiece of terracotta with accentuating tiles of red, green, and blue. The "something more" is precisely this use of an abstract ornamental palette.

Mr. Kahn's decoration is the exact opposite of this. In the building that strikes the boldest and clearest note among all our recent achievements in skyscraper architecture, the Park Avenue Building, he has kept the exterior and the interior in unity: the first has become more warm, the second has become more rigorous and geometrical – and handsome. With

Lewis Mumford, from "The Search for 'Something More'" (1928), cited from *Architecture as a Home for Man: Essays for Architectural Record*, ed. Jeanne M. Davern. New York: Architectural Record Books, 1975, pp. 15, 18.

a warm buff brick as a foundation, the Park Avenue Building works up into bands of sunny terra-cotta, broken and accentuated with red, green, bright sky-blue. The pattern is abstract; and every part, down to the lighting fixtures, has the same finish, rigor, swiftness, perfection. In this building, structure and feeling are at last one: the directness and simplicity of the first have not been forfeited in the decoration; the warmth and human satisfaction of the decorative forms have not been overpowered in the structure itself, for they are expressed there, too. This building seems to me an answer both to the Europeans who, despairing of synthesis, have sought to enjoy the grimness and inflexibility of modern forms by sitting hard on their organic feelings, and to those who, equally despairing of synthesis, have permitted the human, sensuous note to break out irrelevantly – either in stale archæology, in fussy handicraft, or in unrelated bursts of modern decoration.

One swallow may not make a summer; but one building like this, which faces the entire problem of design, and has a clean, unflinching answer for each question, may well serve to crystallize all the fumbling and uncertain elements in present-day architecture. The success of the Park Avenue Building is not due to the fact that it is a tall tower or that it is a setback building. It is not a tower and the setback is trifling. Its success is due to its unique synthesis of the constructive and the feeling elements: its method is as applicable to a two-story building as to one of twenty stories: it is in the line of that rule Louis Sullivan was seeking – which would admit of no exceptions. The Park Avenue Building shows the limit of the architect's skill, to date, under urban conditions, where the programme is inflexibly laid down by the business man and the engineer, and where the site is too costly to be played with. With the part of American architecture that has been favored by more sufficient sites, a more flexible programme, and a broader schedule of resources, I shall deal in another article.

95   HUGH FERRISS
from *The Metropolis of Tomorrow* (1929)

I n 1929 Hugh Ferriss brought together many of the visionary drawings he had produced over the previous decade in what must be called one of the best visual extravaganzas of this period. While these drawings – the artist's conception of the future city – stand with little need of words in their vivid speculation of what is to come, Ferriss did provide commentary throughout the text, in which he elaborated upon his overall conception. This passage on the "Lure of the City" can be seen as his response to the skyscraper issue. It also displays his fascination with the metropolis and with the nervous energy it excites. Ferriss was a New Yorker and it was New York's urban scale against which he measured himself and felt most comfortable. It was written on the eve of such dramatically taller projects as the Rockefeller Center and the Chrysler Building. It was also the eve of the Great Depression.

Hugh Ferriss, from *The Metropolis of Tomorrow*. New York: Ives Washburn, 1929, pp. 59–60.

"The lure of the city" is the romantic way of phrasing it: imagination sketches the rural youth who is ever arising to his dream of "the big city" – the unformulated yet gleaming metropolis. Call it what you will: gregarious instinct or economic necessity: the primary trend, with which we must deal in any formulation of the future city, is the trend toward centralization.

The opinion is frequently and forcefully expressed, by sincere critics, that our sole hope lies, on the contrary, in decentralization. But, if by the term is meant the dispersal of large centers of population, this must be dismissed as a mere dream. For the imagination, it paints a lovely picture – just as a memory of Colonial towns is lovely; but in all that is actually going on about us, there is nothing to be seen which gives the slightest substance to it.

The first tendency, then, with which the following sketches will deal will be the tendency toward concentration. This will lead us at once to the tendency to build higher and higher structures: and we must notice, at the same time, the various proposals to care for the accompanying traffic congestion. Thereupon, we shall have to study, in our drawings, the more recent inclination to modify and vary this rising mass – exhibited in the movement to "step back" the buildings as well as in other proposals which seek, by various means, to limit or distribute volumes. In all this, we will note the growing desire for light and air, the increasing realization of the value of direct sunlight, the utilization of terraces and even the planting thereon of shrubs and trees. We should notice the tendency to assemble larger plots as bases for single towering structures. And a few lines, at least, must be drawn in reference to the development of materials – concrete, steel, glass.

But before illustrating these points, I must speak of a trend, with which it is quite impossible to deal in pictures – a trend, moreover, which will, perhaps more than any other, determine the appearance of the future city.

About the middle of June of every year, the streets of New York – especially in the vicinity of the Architects' Building – become appreciably enlivened by the presence of some five hundred young men most of whom are in the city for their first time. They have just graduated from the architectural schools of various Universities. They seek jobs! They go in – and out – of architects' reception rooms; secretaries get to know them by name, and sometimes sympathize. Judging by their behavior, as well as by their words, they are all on fire to deal with the problems which are now facing us.

But what, precisely, are they thinking? In what spirit is the coming generation of architects and city planners entering the arena?

We may safely say, in the first place, that this coming generation will move to abandon the practice, still current among designers, of evasion and deception concerning material fact. Of the architect who proposes to put a masonry column in the façade of a steel building in such a way as to suggest that it is serving as a support (when, in fact, support is provided by the steel, and the column supports nothing) they will say: "This is an untruth – as definitely as though he stated he is supporting some cause when, in fact, he is a slacker."

The whole custom of employing forms which no longer serve functions – the whole frame of mind which conceives that structural beauty can exist without truth – they will view as decadence; just as they will dismiss, as sentimentality, the notion that architectural beauty was once and for all delivered to the builders of ancient times. The employment of modern construction to support what are little more than classic or medieval stage sets, they will look upon as, at its most harmless, a minor theatrical art, but no longer as being Architecture.

On the other hand, they will without hesitation or embarrassment assemble and have before them every item of contemporary scientific research, and with these units they will build. Though the public continues, through habit, to conceive structural strength in terms of masonry, they will not continue to misinterpret, for the public's indulgence, the new language of steel; in a building where the load is carried more on the interior than the exterior column, they will not place a façade which states, falsely, that the greatest load is carried on the corners. Certainly, they will employ such materials as the recently developed forms of translucent glass over areas appropriate, not to the masonry wall, but to the steel grill. They will see in the grill itself not a means whereby to support some preconceived end, but something which is an end in itself. Briefly, they will take the architectural problem to be not the denying, disguising or superimposing upon the material fact – but the admitting, fashioning and reveling of the material fact.

Many people believe that the novel forms which are just now emerging are devoid of "beauty." Yet when the necessary time has elapsed for the younger architects to formulate their accurate statement – and for the public to comprehend accuracy – it will again appear that a new truth is inevitably attended by a new beauty.

But in addition to these material factors, we may look for the architects of Tomorrow to open what has for long, apparently, been a practically closed book – precisely that psychological importance of Architecture in the lives of people which was referred to on an earlier page.

Broadly speaking, it has been our habit to assume that a building is a complete success if it provides for the utility, convenience and health of its occupants and, in addition, presents a pleasing exterior. But this frame of mind fails to appreciate that architectural forms necessarily have other values than the utilitarian or even others than those which we vaguely call the æsthetic. Without any doubt, these same forms quite specifically influence both the emotional and the mental life of the onlooker. Designers have generally come to realize the importance of the principle stated by the late Louis Sullivan, "Form follows Function." The axiom is not weakened by the further realization that Effect follows Form.

96 R. BUCKMINSTER FULLER
from "The Dymaxion House" (1929)

No stronger sign of the vibrant intellectual atmosphere of the 1920s can be found than in the work of Buckminster Fuller. Yet this Massachusetts native and descendant of Margaret Fuller (a transcendentalist and close friend of Emerson) struggled in the beginning. Living in Long Island since the war, he had gone through a number of business ventures and all had ended in failure. Finally in 1927 he moved to Chicago and promised to devote all of his time to his inventions. By February of the following year he had arrived at his concept of "Lightful Houses": lightweight prefabricated houses suspended from a central mast. He continued to refine this

R. Buckminster Fuller, from "The Dymaxion House" (1929), in *Your Private Sky: Discourse*, ed. Joachim Krausse and Claude Lichtenstein. Zurich: Lars Müller, 2001, pp. 89–90.

idea and by the end of 1928 had arrived at his conception of a "Dymaxion" house, an invention of extraordinary technological refinement. Even today its design seems futuristic. Drawing upon his background in mechanical, chemical, and structural engineering, Fuller tackled the problem of economical and ecologically friendly housing by designing every component of its infrastructure — employing solar, wind, and waste-recycling technologies. Yet this extraordinary creation scarcely resonated with architects, even the most "avant-garde" designers in Europe or North America. This description of the Dymaxion house is taken from a lecture he gave to the New York Architectural League in July, 1929.

Now, to get some idea of what we are getting at here, this house that I am discussing is just a minimum house, forty feet high and fifty feet in diameter. These tubular spars, as you would see them in the regular house, would weigh just one hundred and seventy-eight pounds. So that a strong man could lift them without any trouble. You might ask, "What is the advantage of the weight?" But remember that the Ford car is sold on the basis of twenty-two cents a pound and that all industrial products get down to a weight basis; and weight is going to be the controlling factor of whether you have done well, after you have followed the dynamic problem.

The next thing that happens in this housing, having arranged this compression arch here, this hexagonal compression arch, to give me a support for the floor, we come to the problem of the floors themselves.

Flooring to date has been the heaviest single factor in building. In our present flooring we deal only with solids. In fact, all architecture deals with solids. It takes no consideration of the fact that molasses may be liquid or frozen.

In this floor we have concentric hexagons of piano steel wire every meter in here, the load emanating from the outside. You follow these lines around here.

This spider wire of piano steel wire cable is of tremendous strength. We have always known the strengh of the catenary net. You have seen people jump out of ten-story windows into the firemen's net. It is tremendously strong.

We haven't been able to use it in our solid floors of flooring because of the motion of the catenary net; because the minute this floor sets up real motion and it gives to my load, the floor is finished as far as the concrete members go. There is a theoretical flow. We all know how fast concrete flows. So that if it really gives, it is going down.

To make up for this catenary net, which is naturally strong and gives me natural strength, we have six triangular duralumin pieces, of equilateral triangles. That fits in on this catenary net. This triangular duralumin unit is a bladder. It is blown up something similar to the pneumatic mattress that you see in the surf.

This duralumin, which is an alloy of aluminium, has very much higher tensile strength than the equivalent gauge of steel and very much more elasticity. It has such high elasticity that, when they put it in the same presses as they have for mudguards on automobiles, it springs back much into its original shape.

These bladders are inflated. As you inflate the metal bladder, it is thrown into tension and it tends to knit together. You know how it is when you punch an automobile tire of perishable rubber, in view of the fact that the fibers tend to knit together. This is relatively puncture-proof.

What happens is that my load is immediately distributed, due to the elasticity of the air, to all of the tensile surface of the metal and to all of the tensile surface of the catenary net.

Further, like the automobile tire, it goes "plop, plop" when it goes soft; and when you kick it and it makes no more sound, it is getting hard.

A child can fall on these floors and not hurt itself. The shock is immediately absorbed by the elasticity of the air. You have very fine fabric covers on the floors, such as modifications of this oilcloth, etc., because they no longer pound in like an anvil.

The next thing to consider here is the extraneous covering of the building. You see these triangular forms, the windows here. These triangular forms are made out of casein. They are made as triangular flasks, vacuumized from one corner, like an electric light, so as to kill all heat transfer.

These triangular window plates are not set as are the usual rigid window plates we have here. You are using nothing rigid in this building. They are set down tension cables, like the cables of suspension bridge, pulling straight instead of trying to push straight. These are, again, piano steel wire cables. These flasks fit loosely into that cable. The edges of the flask are beveled to allow their fitting loosely in the bevel of the caging. A pneumatic tire, blown up, is put around that, giving air-tight and water-tight joint and flexibility.

Everything in that whole window assembly is flexed in tension, and you can virtually run an aeroplane into it without busting it. The whole window assembly, these six units, is made up at the service station. They are brought to the job. They are hung up. They fall down into position. They are batted down, and a pneumatic tire goes around those. We find that that pneumatic tire, where you are not pounding it long like an automobile tire, can be blown up every two years, and it will last about ten years before you have to replace it.

The next thing you will notice is that that same triangular proceeds inward in my design. In fact, this whole design is done in terms of triangles, distances from the center out; but this triangular proceeds inward. So over the whole top of the house and the bottom go these triangular vacuum plates. We will have very little heat loss in that covering.

By the way, that casein is the natural solid residue. You take cheese and remove the butterfat, and you will have casein left. And, being such, it lets all the valuable light rays through it. The reason for this thermos bottle cover is so that I can arrive at some economy of operation inside of the house in heating, ventilating, lighting, etc. We combine in this house the lighting and the heating.

In the central mast, these three little triangles here are for the heat and light passage. I will later show you how we add bathrooms and grills, etc., to this mast with manifold coupling like the coupling on railroad cars. But what I am discussing at the moment is the lighting and the heating.

In our best industrial ovens we can go up to 150 degrees with the illuminating bulb, which is the only proper element where you have no heat loss. So there is no need to use anything else but heating bulbs for proper ventilation.

97 HENRY-RUSSELL HITCHCOCK
from *Modern Architecture:*
Romanticism and Reintegration (1929)

Henry-Russell Hitchcock was a graduate of Harvard and he had initially wanted to study architecture at the École des Beaux-Arts in Paris. Instead he returned to graduate school, took a degree in Fine Arts in 1927, and joined the faculty at Vassar College (later he moved to Wesleyan University). His early writings on architecture, pretentious in tone, are of little value, but he was slowly acquiring the knowledge and experience needed to become an important historian. Thoroughly Europhilic in his outlook, he traveled regularly to the Continent and in 1927 he visited the housing exhibition at Stuttgart and became familiar with the work of Le Corbusier. Further travel fortified his appreciation for European modernism and his book in general is a brilliant survey of the contemporary European scene. But *Modern Architecture* purports to survey architecture in Europe and America (since 1750), and the problem is one of reconciling the different interpretations of modernism on the two continents. Hitchcock resolves it by dividing modernism into two chapters: "New Tradition" and "New Pioneers." Otto Wagner, Hendrik Berlage, Peter Behrens, and (most importantly) Frank Lloyd Wright fall into the first group. By contrast, the "New Pioneers" of the 1920s are solely European: led by Le Corbusier, J. J. P. Oud, Walter Gropius, and Mies van der Rohe. Hence the book is, in the end, a rude rebuke of American architects for their cultural backwardness. This passage on the Weissenhof Exhibition in Stuttgart is indicative of Hitchcock's attitude and critical style.

The Stuttgart Exposition of 1927 was in many ways symbolical. It was arranged by Germans, but among them only Gropius and Miës van der Rohe were able to offer work at all comparable to that of Oud, Stam and Le Corbusier. Visitors already familiar with the ideals of the New Pioneers could not but be astounded by the simplified New Tradition apartment house of Behrens and the modified Expressionistic constructions of Scharoun and the Tauts, at the same time they were bored with the purely conventional *Neue Sachlichkeit* of Hilberseimer and Döcker, and bewildered by the technical curiosities in the way of new building materials that were displayed. But there was no country besides Germany which could have organized such a demonstration in 1927, and none besides France and Holland which could offer single works to compare with those of Gropius and Miës van der Rohe. The publications which the constructions at the Stuttgart Weissenhofsiedling engendered – cement hardly drying in Germany before buildings there are published in illustrations and text – presented to the world more completely than any previous books both the accomplishments and the dangers of the manner of the New Pioneers. The innumerable other works in which the Germans have provided a full documentation of the new manner already have their influence, particularly in Eastern Europe. Doubtless they will in time replace even in America the documents of the Paris Exposition of 1925, as those have replaced the handbooks of the styles of the past. But this is a matter of the future. The results may, however, already be surmised by examining such work as essentially or nominally subscribes to the æsthetic of the New Pioneers in other countries than France, Holland and Germany, where its earliest and finest expressions have appeared.

Henry-Russell Hitchcock, from *Modern Architecture: Romanticism and Reintegration* (1929), cited from the reprint edition. New York: Hacker Art Books, 1970, pp. 195–6.

98 FRANK LLOYD WRIGHT
from ''The Cardboard House''
(1930)

Frank Lloyd Wright, for one, was not happy with Hitchcock's cocky analysis, even though he was unable to argue from a position of strength. He had enjoyed a second flowering of his career – briefly in Los Angeles in the first years of the 1920s. Since then, embroiled in financial and personal problems, his career had virtually shut down, although he had made valiant designs to resurrect it on the eve of the Great Depression. Nevertheless, he deeply resented Hitchcock's characterization of him in 1929 as a ''New Traditionalist.'' In one unpublished essay of 1930, he sarcastically referred to Hitchcock as someone who ''occasionally comes over from Paris to teach young ladies at Vassar what they should think about Architecture,'' and then enjoined that it is ''useless to ask why men will strike attitudes about things they know only haphazard.'' In another series of lectures given at Princeton University in 1930, he channeled his anger into a spirited defense of his conception of organic architecture – lectures that, in addition to refuting Hitchcock's characterization of him, took aim at the ''modernistic'' architecture of Europe, which he felt to be technologically much inferior to that of American practice. In this lecture entitled ''The Cardboard House,'' his target is Le Corbusier and the adage that a house is a machine-for-living-in. This passage is vintage Wright: pointed, incisive, and not without his touch of arrogance.

Any house is a far too complicated, clumsy, fussy, mechanical counterfeit of the human body. Electric wiring for nervous system, plumbing for bowels, heating system and fireplaces for arteries and heart, and windows for eyes, nose, and lungs generally. The structure of the house, too, is a kind of cellular tissue stuck full of bones, complex now, as the confusion of bedlam and all beside. The whole interior is a kind of stomach that attempts to digest objects – objects, ''objects d'art'' maybe, but objects always. There the affected affliction sits, ever hungry – for ever more objects – or plethoric with over plenty. The whole life of the average house, it seems, is a sort of indigestion. A body in ill repair, suffering indisposition – constant tinkering and doctoring to keep alive. It is a marvel we its infestors do not go insane in it and with it. Perhaps it is a form of insanity we have put into it. Lucky we are able to get something else out of it, though we do seldom get out of it alive ourselves.

But the passing of the cornice with its enormous ''baggage'' from foreign parts in its train clears the way for American homes that may be modern biography and poems instead of slanderous liars and poetry-crushers.

A house, we like to believe, is *in status quo* a noble consort to man and the trees; therefore the house should have repose and such texture as will quiet the whole and make it graciously at one with external nature.

Human houses should not be like boxes, blazing in the sun, nor should we outrage the machine by trying to make dwelling-places too complementary to machinery. Any building for humane purposes should be an elemental, sympathetic feature of the ground, complementary to its nature-environment, belonging by kinship to the terrain. A house is not going

Frank Lloyd Wright, from ''The Cardboard House,'' in *Collected Writings, 1930–1932*, ed. Bruce Brooks Pfeiffer. New York, Rizzoli, 1992, pp. 51–2.

anywhere, if we can help it. We hope it is going to stay right where it is for a long, long time. It is not yet anyway even a moving-van. Certain houses for Los Angeles may yet become vans and roll off most anywhere or everywhere, which is something else again and far from a bad idea for certain classes of our population.

But most new "modernistic" houses manage to look as though cut from cardboard with scissors, the sheets of cardboard folded or bent in rectangles with an occasional curved cardboard surface added to get relief. The cardboard forms thus made are glued together in box-like forms – in a childish attempt to make buildings resemble steamships, flying machines, or locomotives. By way of a new sense of the character and power of this machine age, this house strips and stoops to conquer by emulating, if not imitating, machinery. But so far, I see in most of the cardboard houses of the "modernistic" movement small evidence that their designers have mastered either the machinery or the mechanical processes that build the house. I can find no evidence of integral method in their making. Of late, they are the superficial, badly built product of this superficial, new "surface-and-mass" aesthetic falsely claiming French painting as a parent. And the houses themselves are not the new working of a fundamental architectural principle in any sense.

They are little less reactionary than was the cornice – unfortunately for Americans, looking forward, lest again they fall victim to the mode. There is, however, this much to be said for this house – by means of it imported art and decoration may, for a time, completely triumph over "architecture." And such architecture as it may triumph over – well, enough has already been said here, to show how infinitely the cardboard house is to be preferred to that form of bad surface-decoration. The simplicity of nature is not something which may easily be read – but is inexhaustible. Unfortunately the simplicity of these houses is too easily read – visibly an attitude, strained or forced. They are therefore decoration too. If we look into their construction we may see how construction itself has been complicated or confused, merely to arrive at exterior simplicity. Most of these houses at home and abroad are more or less badly built complements to the machine age, of whose principles or possibilities they show no understanding, or, if they do show such understanding to the degree of assimilating an aspect thereof, they utterly fail to make its virtues honorably or humanly effective in any final result. Forcing surface-effects upon mass-effects which try hard to resemble running or steaming or flying or fighting machines, is no radical effort in any direction. It is only more scene-painting and just another picture to prove Victor Hugo's thesis of Renaissance architecture as the setting sun, eventually passing with the cornice.

99 ALFRED H. BARR, JR.
from preface to *Modern Architecture: International Exhibition* (1932)

I n 1929 Henry-Russell Hitchcock met and befriended a fellow Harvard alumnus, Alfred H. Barr. In the same year the two men became acquainted with the Harvard student Philip Johnson and a mutual friendship was formed. This crimson coterie became significant a few months later when Barr, a young academic and specialist on the new European art, was appointed the first director of the newly formed Museum of Modern Art in New York. Both Hitchcock and Johnson were invited to join the staff and a triumvirate thus took charge of the institution. The first architectural fruit of their alliance was the exhibition *The International Style: Architecture Since 1922*, which took place in the winter of 1932.

The idea for the exhibition is generally conceded to be the brainchild of Barr. Johnson, who in 1929 had no knowledge of modern architecture, initially needed grooming and he traveled to Europe that summer to start his education, and in the following year he made another tour — this time with Hitchcock serving as his guide. Upon returning to New York in 1930, Johnson placed the formal proposal before the museum board and planning preparations were soon underway. The event was not without internal controversy, as all three men were committed Europhiles and had little familiarity with American practice. Frank Lloyd Wright, in particular, presented a problem. None wanted him in the exhibition, but then again excluding the most prominent American modernist was a delicate matter for the success of an event staged on American soil. Wright, with his animosity toward Hitchcock still unappeased, scarcely wanted to be shown alongside the work of Le Corbusier and others, and he twice pulled out of the show, only to be lured back. In the end the event opened with Wright, Le Corbusier, Mies van der Rohe, and J. J. P. Oud being given featured exhibition areas, with a number of other projects from around the world being shown in adjacent rooms. All in all, the exhibition was a success and later toured several other cities. It also spawned two books: the exhibition catalogue and the coinciding publication of Hitchcock and Johnson, *The International Style* (see next chapter).

Barr's Preface to the exhibition catalogue officially christens the "International Style" and it is the first attempt to lay down its stylistic principles. Barr follows with his apology for including the work of Wright and Raymond Hood, and then concludes with the pronouncement that Gropius, Le Corbusier, Oud, and Mies van der Rohe are the "four founders of the International Style." Such a bias on the part of Barr represents the first attempt by an American institutional director to change the course of architecture.

The present exhibition is an assertion that the confusion of the past forty years, or rather of the past century, may shortly come to an end. Ten years ago the Chicago Tribune competition brought forth almost as many different styles as there were projects. Since then the ideas of a number of progressive architects have converged to form a genuinely new style which is rapidly spreading throughout the world. Both in appearance and structure this style is peculiar to the twentieth century and is as fundamentally original as the Greek or Byzantine or Gothic. In the following pages Mr. Hitchcock and Mr. Johnson have outlined its

Alfred H. Barr, Jr., from preface to *Modern Architecture: International Exhibition* (1932), cited from the reprint edition. New York: Arno Press, pp. 13–16.

history and its extent. Because of its simultaneous development in several different countries and because of its world-wide distribution it has been called the International Style.

The aesthetic principles of the International Style are based primarily upon the nature of modern materials and structure and upon modern requirements in planning. Slender steel posts and beams, and concrete reinforced by steel have made possible structures of skeleton-like strength and lightness. The external surfacing materials are of painted stucco or tile, or, in more expensive buildings, of aluminum or thin slabs of marble or granite and of glass both opaque and transparent. Planning, liberated from the necessity for symmetry so frequently required by tradition is, in the new style, flexibly dependent upon convenience.

These *technical* and *utilitarian* factors in the hands of designers who understand inherent aesthetic possibilities have resulted in an architecture comparable in integrity and even in beauty to the styles of the past. But just as the modern architect has had to adjust himself to modern problems of design and structure so the modern public in order to appreciate his achievements must make parallel adjustments to what seems new and strange.

First of all, the modern architect working in the new style conceives of his building not as a structure of brick or masonry with thick columns and supporting walls resting heavily upon the earth but rather as a skeleton enclosed by a thin light shell. He thinks in terms of *volume* – of space enclosed by planes or surfaces – as opposed to *mass* and solidity. This principle of volume leads him to make his walls seem thin flat surfaces by eliminating moldings and by making his windows and doors flush with the surface.

Two other principles which are both utilitarian and aesthetic may be called *regularity* and *flexibility*. The architects of the Classical and Renaissance, and often of the Medieval periods, designed their façades and plans in terms of bilateral symmetry, that is of balanced masses on either side of a central axis. They also usually divided their façades horizontally in three parts: the bottom or base, the wall or middle section and the top or cornice. In the International Style these arbitrary conventions of symmetry and triple division are abandoned for a method of design which accepts, first, both vertical and horizontal repetition and, second, flexible asymmetry, for both are natural concomitants of modern building. The modern architect feels it unnecessary to add an elaborate ground floor and an elaborate crowning decoration to his skyscraper, or a gabled porch in the center and at either end of his school or library. He permits the horizontal floors of his skyscraper and the rows of windows in his school to repeat themselves boldly without artificial accents or terminations. And the resulting *regularity*, which may in itself be very handsome, is given accent by a door or ventilator, electric sign, stair tower, chimney, or fire escape, placed asymmetrically as utility often demands, and the principle of *flexibility* permits. The Bauhaus at Dessau in the present exhibition is a clear illustration of these principles of design.

A fourth comprehensive principle is both positive and negative: positive quality or beauty in the International Style depends upon technically perfect use of materials whether metal, wood, glass or concrete; upon the fineness of proportions in units such as doors and windows and in the relationships between these units and the whole design. The negative or obverse aspect of this principle is the elimination of any kind of ornament or artificial pattern. This lack of ornament is one of the most difficult elements of the style for the layman to accept. Intrinsically there is no reason why ornament should not be used, but modern ornament, usually crass in design and machine-manufactured, would seem to mar rather than adorn the clean perfection of surface and proportion.

These principles are not as dogmatic as they must necessarily seem in so brief a discussion: on the contrary they have been derived from the evolution and intrinsic character of the architecture itself. A study of these principles in relation to most of the models and photographs in the present exhibition will enable the visitor to understand what is meant by the International Style and how it differs from the modernistic or half-modern decorative style, which with the persistence of the revived styles of the past, has added so much to the confusion of contemporary architecture.

In this exhibition the International Style is illustrated by the work of its leading exponents in Europe and in America. One very great architect, however, is included who is not intimately related to the Style although his early work was one of the Style's most important sources. Mr. Hitchcock explains how fundamental was Frank Lloyd Wright's influence upon the important Dutch architect J. J. P. Oud. The Germans, Gropius and Miës van der Rohe, also seem to have studied his work at some time in their careers. But Wright while he does not precisely disown these architectural nephews remains, what he has always been, a passionately independent genius whose career is a history of original discovery and contradiction. While he is much older than the other architects in the exhibition his role is not merely that of "pioneer ancestor." As the embodiment of the romantic principle of individualism, his work, complex and abundant, remains a challenge to the classical austerity of the style of his best younger contemporaries.

Another exception, Raymond Hood, is included because, of all the megalopolitan architects, he seems the most straightforward as well as the most open to new ideas. It is true that his work in retrospect appears somewhat inconsistent, but he must be credited with having designed the finest skyscraper in the vertical style and, a year later, the finest New York skyscraper with a horizontal emphasis (which suggests the definite influence of the International Style). Time will shortly reveal whether his inclusion in the exhibition is a prophecy that a brilliant future awaits our commercial architecture or whether as in the past fifty years our best building will be designed by non-conformists and rebels.

The four founders of the International Style are Gropius, Le Corbusier, Oud and Miës van der Rohe. It happens that one is a Parisian of Swiss birth, another a Dutchman, the other two Germans; but it would be very difficult to find in their work any national characteristics. For Le Corbusier is perhaps the greatest theorist, the most erudite and the boldest experimenter, Gropius the most sociologically minded, Miës van der Rohe the most luxurious and elegant, while Oud of Rotterdam possesses the most sensitive and disciplined taste. These four masters prove not only the internationalism of the Style but also, as Mr. Hitchcock makes clear, the wide personal variations possible within what may seem at first glance a restricted range of possibilities.

100 HENRY-RUSSELL HITCHCOCK AND PHILIP JOHNSON

from *The International Style: Architecture since 1922* (1932)

The aspect of the MoMA exhibition that had the greatest impact on architectural theory in the United States was this book of Hitchcock and Johnson, which appeared with the exhibition's opening. It begins with the pronouncement that "a single new style" has come into being, created by a few exceptional European pioneers. Subsequent chapters didactically discuss the principles of the new style – often taking the form of axioms intended to tutor (unschooled) American architects. But what is also interesting are the secondary polemics of the text. For the American audience, Hitchcock and Johnson are eager to strip the new European style of its political (socialist and communist) premises, and thus they try to present their version of European modernism as a moderate stylistic mean between two extremes. One is the politically inspired movement they name "functionalism," such as practiced by architects like Ernst May, Mart Stam, or Hannes Meyer. The other is what they perceive to be the nostalgic and sentimental approach of most American architects, still hidebound to tradition. In short, aesthetics or a formalistic approach to design trumps all, as the two historians approach architectural design as a two-dimensional discipline, as a purely visual discipline akin to working on a canvas. At the same time their sense of American inferiority with regard to the new European paradigm recalls, in the absence of any national confidence, the darkest days of the early nineteenth century.

Today a single new style has come into existence. The æsthetic conceptions on which its disciplines are based derive from the experimentation of the individualists. They and not the revivalists were the immediate masters of those who have created the new style. This contemporary style, which exists throughout the world, is unified and inclusive, not fragmentary and contradictory like so much of the production of the first generation of modern architects. In the last decade it has produced sufficient monuments of distinction to display its validity and its vitality. It may fairly be compared in significance with the styles of the past. In the handling of the problems of structure it is related to the Gothic, in the handling of the problems of design it is more akin to the Classical. In the preëminence given to the handling of function it is distinguished from both.

The unconscious and halting architectural developments of the nineteenth century, the confused and contradictory experimentation of the beginning of the twentieth, have been succeeded by a directed evolution. There is now a single body of discipline, fixed enough to integrate contemporary style as a reality and yet elastic enough to permit individual interpretation and to encourage general growth.

The idea of style as the frame of potential growth, rather than as a fixed and crushing mould, has developed with the recognition of underlying principles such as archæologists discern in the great styles of the past. The principles are few and broad. They are not mere

Henry-Russell Hitchcock and Philip Johnson, from *The International Style: Architecture since 1922* (1932), cited from the paperback edition. New York: W. W. Norton & Co., 1966, pp. 19–20, 93–4.

formulas of proportion such as distinguish the Doric from the Ionic order; they are fundamental, like the organic verticality of the Gothic or the rhythmical symmetry of the Baroque. There is, first, a new conception of architecture as volume rather than as mass. Secondly, regularity rather than axial symmetry serves as the chief means of ordering design. These two principles, with a third proscribing arbitrary applied decoration, mark the productions of the international style.

This new style is not international in the sense that the production of one country is just like that of another. Nor is it so rigid that the work of various leaders is not clearly distinguishable. The international style has become evident and definable only gradually as different innovators throughout the world have successfully carried out parallel experiments.

In stating the general principles of the contemporary style, in analysing their derivation from structure and their modification by function, the appearance of a certain dogmatism can hardly be avoided. In opposition to those who claim that a new style of architecture is impossible or undesirable, it is necessary to stress the coherence of the results obtained within the range of possibilities thus far explored. For the international style already exists in the present; it is not merely something the future may hold in store. Architecture is always a set of actual monuments, not a vague corpus of theory.

[. . .]

Too often in European *Siedlungen* the functionalists build for some proletarian superman of the future. Yet in most buildings the expressed desires of a given client are the most explicit and difficult functions. Architects whose discipline is æsthetic as well as functional are usually readier to provide what is actually needed. Their idealism is satisfied by raising their *Siedlungen* to the level of architecture by effective general planning and distinctive composition. The idealism of the functionalists too often demands that they provide what ought to be needed, even at the expense of what is actually needed. Instead of facing the difficulties of the present, they rush on to face the uncertain future.

There is a reverse side to this question of function in housing projects. It is frequently demanded by local critics that architects should cater to peculiar wants unknown in other communities. Windows arranged for strange forms of ventilation, or so subdivided that they may be opened without disarranging flower pots on the sill, rooms catering to special methods of drying clothes indoors, solid shutters on upper storeys to which no burglar could climb, certainly are needless unless local traditions insist upon them. In America, local traditions are further complicated by an excessive sentimentality about the "homes" of the past.

The architect has a right to distinguish functions which are major and general from those which are minor and local. In sociological building he ought certainly to stress the universal at the expense of the particular. He may even, for economic reasons and for the sake of general architectural style, disregard entirely the peculiarities of local tradition unless these are soundly based on local weather conditions. His aim is to approach an ideal standard. But houses should not be functionally so advanced that they are lived in under protest.

B.   SOVIET CONSTRUCTIVISM

Introduction

The two major powers of the defeated Axis – Germany and Austria – suffered greatly with the aftermath of World War I, but the country that would be most deeply affected in its political coloration was Russia. Since 1914 its military forces had suffered heavy casualties at the hands of the invading German armies, and it could do no more than create a stalemate along its western front. This situation became unacceptable to the Germans as the war dragged on, and Berlin hatched a scheme to remedy the situation. It placed Vladimir Ilich Lenin, living in exile in Zurich, on a train to Saint Petersburg, along with many of his "Bolshevik" followers. He had promised to foster a communist revolution within Russia, which indeed proved successful in 1917 when the regime of Czar Nicholas II collapsed violently and the successor government failed to control the deteriorating situation. Thus began a vast political experiment in human governance.

Lenin came to power with high expectations of transforming Russia into a modern industrial state. As promised, he sued for peace with Germany, but he struggled mightily with the devastation of the war, with a civil war, and with economic conditions that were still largely feudal in character. Soviet architects nevertheless embraced the promise of change and industrialization, and they quickly formed a vanguard of theory that would eventually be brought together under the banner of Constructivism. Predicated on the new industrial technologies and utopian ideals, Soviet architecture in the early 1920s produced some of the most advanced images of what modernism might become – albeit nearly all of which was limited to the medium of paper. This work, nevertheless, had an enormous influence on a war-battered Europe that also had become radicalized in its political sensibilities. If this architectural experimentation was also doomed to end abruptly in the early 1930s under the iron fist of Joseph Stalin, it nevertheless would leave its indelible mark on modernism and even later on movements such as Deconstruction.

101   VLADIMIR ILICH LENIN
from *The State and Revolution* (1917)

The direction that Frederick Winslow Taylor gave to economic theory of the 1920s was matched on a political front by the ideas of Karl Marx. The German revolutionary came to prominence in the middle of the nineteenth century, and the first volume of his principal work, *Das Kapital*, appeared in 1867. Marx's influence continued to grow after his death in 1883, and we find its reach, for instance, in the socialism of William Morris. It remained for Lenin, however, to transpose Marxism into a genuine political revolution. After returning to Russia, Lenin led the successful communist uprising of October 1917 and quickly consolidated command of essential forces. The new Soviet government began the process of appropriating land and ownership of industrial production, the central economic thesis of Marxism. Lenin's best-known book, *The State and Revolution*, was written during these tumultuous events. One can read in this passage both the benign promise and oppressive potential of Soviet-style "democracy," in which the state now assumed complete authority in nearly all matters of existence. This writing, nevertheless, had tremendous appeal in an economically ravaged, postwar Europe, and many architects of the 1920s chose to align modernism in architecture with communist ideals.

Democracy for the vast majority of the people, and suppression by force, *i.e.*, exclusion from democracy, of the exploiters and oppressors of the people – this is the change democracy undergoes during the *transition* from capitalism to communism.

Only in communist society, when the resistance of the capitalists has been completely broken, when the capitalists have disappeared, when there are no classes (*i.e.*, when there is no difference between the members of society as regards their relation to the social means of production), *only then* does "the state ... cease to exist," and it *"becomes possible to speak of freedom."* Only then will really complete democracy, democracy without any exceptions, be possible and be realized. And only then will democracy itself begin to *wither away* owing to the simple fact that, freed from capitalist slavery, from the untold horrors, savagery, absurdities and infamies of capitalist exploitation, people will gradually *become accustomed* to observing the elementary rules of social life that have been known for centuries and repeated for thousands of years in all copy-book maxims; they will become accustomed to

V. I. Lenin, from *The State and Revolution* (1917), in *Essential Works of Lenin*, ed. Henry M. Christman. New York: Bantam Books, 1966, pp. 338–9.

observing them without force, without compulsion, without subordination, without the *special apparatus* for compulsion which is called the state.

The expression "the state *withers away*" is very well chosen, for it indicates both the gradual and the spontaneous nature of the process. Only habit can, and undoubtedly will, have such an effect; for we see around us millions of times how readily people become accustomed to observing the necessary rules of social life if there is no exploitation, if there is nothing that causes indignation, that calls forth protest and revolt and has to be *suppressed*.

Thus, in capitalist society we have a democracy that is curtailed, wretched, false; a democracy only for the rich, for the minority. The dictatorship of the proletariat, the period of transition to communism, will, for the first time, create democracy for the people, for the majority, in addition to the necessary suppression of the minority – the exploiters. Communism alone is capable of giving really complete democracy, and the more complete it is the more quickly will it become unnecessary and wither away of itself.

In other words: under capitalism we have a state in the proper sense of the word, that is, a special machine for the suppression of one class by another, and of the majority by the minority at that. Naturally, the successful discharge of such a task as the systematic suppression of the exploited majority by the exploiting minority calls for the greatest ferocity and savagery in the work of suppression, it calls for seas of blood through which mankind has to wade in slavery, serfdom and wage-labor.

Furthermore, during the *transition* from capitalism to communism, suppression is *still* necessary; but it is the suppression of the exploiting minority by the exploited majority. A special apparatus, a special machine for suppression, the "state," is *still* necessary, but this is now a transitory state; it is no longer a state in the proper sense; for the suppression of the minority of exploiters by the majority of the wage-slaves *of yesterday* is comparatively so easy, simple and natural a task that it will entail far less bloodshed than the suppression of the risings of slaves, serfs or wage-laborers, and it will cost mankind far less.

102 VLADIMIR TATLIN, T. SHAPIRO, I. MEYERZON, AND PAVEL VINOGRADOV
from "The Work Ahead of Us" (1920)

The impetus to the revolutionary changes in Soviet art in the 1920s was given by a small group of abstract painters and sculptors, who first carried out their experiments with abstraction during World War I. Among them was the painter Vladimir Tatlin, who was trained at the Moscow College of Painting, Sculpture, and Architecture. Inspired by a visit to Paris in 1913, Tatlin began to experiment with three-dimensional reliefs and

Vladimir Tatlin, T. Shapiro, I. Meyerzon, and Pavel Vinogradov, from "The Work Ahead of Us" (1920), trans. Troelis Andersen, in *The Tradition of Constructivism*, ed. Stephen Bann. New York: Viking Press, 1974, pp. 12–13.

counter-reliefs, the latter of which became synonymous with his "constructivist" approach. His most important work in this regard, his celebrated Monument to the Third International, was designed in 1919, and in the following year he was invited to Moscow to reconstruct his model of the Monument to the Third International at a larger scale. This proposed 400-meter spiral tower, which was to feature rotating legislative, administrative, and propaganda chambers, was not built, but it nevertheless perfectly symbolized the lofty technological ambitions of the early Soviet Revolution.

What happened from the social aspect in 1917 was realized in our work as pictorial artists in 1914, when "materials, volume and construction" were accepted as our foundation.

We declare our distrust of the eye, and place our sensual impressions under control.

In 1915 an exhibition of material models on the laboratory scale was held in Moscow (an exhibition of reliefs and counter-reliefs). An exhibition held in 1917 presented a number of examples of material combinations, which were the results of more complicated investigations into the use of material in itself, and what this leads to: movement, tension, and a mutual relationship between [them].

This investigation of material, volume and construction made it possible for us in 1918, in an artistic form, to begin to combine materials like iron and glass, the materials of modern Classicism, comparable in their severity with the marble of antiquity.

In this way an opportunity emerges of uniting purely artistic forms with utilitarian intentions. An example is the project for the monument to the Third International (exhibited at the Eight Congress).

The results of this are models which stimulate us to inventions in our work of creating a new world, and which call upon the producers to exercise control over the forms encountered in our new everyday life.

103 ALEXANDER RODCHENKO
from "Slogans" (1921)

Another artist to have a large influence on the formation of Soviet Constructivism was Alexander Rodchenko. He was associated with the circle of Vladimir Tatlin, and he contributed to the cause by writing much of the curriculum for the newly founded Moscow school VKhUTMAS, the Higher Artistic and Technical Workshops, where Rodchenko taught from 1920 to 1930. VKhUTMAS quickly became internationally recognized as the center of the constructivist movement, and many of the leading Soviet artists and architects of the 1920s – among them Kasamir Malevich, El Lissitzky, Nikolai Ladovsky, Moisei Ginzburg – taught there.

Slogans

(The discipline of construction, chief director Rodchenko)

Construction = organization of elements.

Alexander Rodchenko, from "Slogans" (1921), trans. S.-O. Khan Magomedov, in *Rodchenko: The Complete Work*. London, 1986, pp. 315–16.

Construction is a modern concept.

Art is a branch of mathematics, like all sciences.

Construction is the modern requirement for organization and utilitarian use of material.

Constructivist life is the art of the future.

Art which does not enter into life will be put under a No. of the archaeological museum of *antiquity.*

It is time that art entered into life in an organized fashion.

Life organized along Constructivist lines is superior to the delirious magic art of the sorcerers.

The future will not construct monasteries for the priests, prophets and minstrels of art.

Down with art as a beautiful patch on the squalid life of the rich.

Down with art as a precious stone in the midst of the dismal and dirty life of the poor.

Down with art as a means of escaping from a life that is not worth living.

Conscious and organized life, that knows how to see and build, is contemporary art.

The man who has organized his life, his work and himself is a genuine artist.

Work for life and not for palaces, cathedrals, cemeteries and museums.

Work in the midst of everything and with everybody; down with monasteries, institutes, studios, ateliers and islands. Awareness, experience, purpose, construction, technique and mathematics, these are the companions of contemporary art.

104   ALEKSEI GAN
from "Constructivism" (1922)

Paralleling the lead of VKhUTMAS in spawning the Constructivist movement was the Institute of Artistic Culture – INKHUK – which was founded in Moscow in 1920 as a center for artistic research. The first director of INKHUK was the painter Wassily Kandinsky, but his spiritualist program was soon rejected by hard-line revolutionaries. In November 1921 the center was reorganized and its ideology redefined by the "Productivist Manifesto," which stressed the materialist vision of "production" art in service to the revolution. This program was further elaborated in the following year by Aleksei Gan's book *Constructivism*. This spirited preamble to the book captures the early constructivists at their most ideological turn, but at the same time they lay the basis for an architectural theory founded on three notions of tectonics, fracture (material selection), and construction.

WE DECLARE UNCOMPROMISING
WAR ON ART!

The 1st Working Group of Constructivists

1920,

Moscow

Aleksei Gan, from "Constructivism" (1922), trans. Troelis Andersen, in *The Tradition of Constructivism*, ed. Stephen Bann. New York: The Viking Press, 1974, pp. 33–6.

LONG LIVE
>THE COMMUNIST EXPRESSION
>OF MATERIAL
>CONSTRUCTIONS!

The 1st Working Group of Constructivists

1921,

Moscow

From: Revolutionary-Marxist Thought in Words and Podagrism
in Practice

. . . But the victory of materialism in the field of artistic labor is also on the eve of its triumph.

The proletarian revolution is not a word of flagellation but a real whip, which expels parasitism from man's practical reality in whatever guise it hides its repulsive being.

The present moment within the framework of objective conditions obliges us to declare that the current position of social development is advancing with the omen that artistic culture of the past is unacceptable.

The fact that all so-called art is permeated with the most reactionary idealism is the product of extreme individualism: this individualism shoves it in the direction of new, unnecessary amusements with experiments in refining subjective beauty.

>ART
>**IS INDISSOLUBLY LINKED:**
>**WITH THEOLOGY,**
>**METAPHYSICS,**
>**AND MYSTICISM.**

It emerged during the epoch of primeval cultures, when technique existed in "the embryonic state of tools" and forms of economy floundered in utter primitiveness.

It passed through the forge of the guild craftsmen of the Middle Ages.

It was artificially reheated by the hypocrisy of bourgeois culture and, finally, crashed against the mechanical world of our age.

>**DEATH TO ART!**
>>**IT AROSE NATURALLY**
>>**DEVELOPED NATURALLY**
>**AND DISAPPEARED NATURALLY.**

MARXISTS MUST WORK IN ORDER TO ELUCIDATE ITS DEATH SCIENTIFICALLY AND TO FORMULATE NEW PHENOMENA OF ARTISTIC LABOR WITHIN THE NEW HISTORIC ENVIRONMENT OF OUR TIME.

In the specific situation of our day, a gravitation toward the technical acme and social interpretation can be observed in the work of the masters of revolutionary art.

CONSTRUCTIVISM IS ADVANCING – THE SLENDER CHILD OF AN INDUS-TRIAL CULTURE.

FOR A LONG TIME CAPITALISM HAS LET IT ROT UNDERGROUND.

105   MOISEI GINZBURG
from *Style and Epoch* (1924)

The foremost theoretician of Soviet rationalism and Constructivism was the architect and historian Moisei Ginzburg. He had been schooled before the war in Toulouse, Paris, and most importantly in Milan at the height of futurist activity. During the war he received a degree in engineering at the Riga Polytechnical Institute and in 1921 came to teach history and theory at VKhUTMAS. Already in his first book *Ritm v arkhitekture* (Rhythm in Architecture, 1923) he noted his preference for dynamic forms in rhythmic motion, but his follow-up study *Style and Epoch* was a far more ambitious book in that he proposed a new evolutionary scheme for architecture, in which Constructivism becomes the first "constructive" stage of a radically new era of modernism. The two passages reflect two aspects of the view he wants to encompass with Constructivism: the first the businesslike, dynamic, sober, mechanized tempo of American life, which he feels is indicative of the future of human society. Second the metaphor of the machine and its motion: a model precise, accurate, and dynamic in its parts, displaying an animism that owes something to the German theory of empathy. Constructivist architecture must be equally dynamic.

But if Europe, with its vast size, presents a picture of complete decline, America, primarily the United States of North America, offers a more instructive view.

A new national power that has not yet had the time to accumulate its own traditions and artistic experience quite naturally turns to Europe for assistance; Europe, true to the stodgy ideals of its classical system, begins transporting its products across the ocean. However, the life of North America as a vital new power cannot, despite its own wishes, proceed along a course well trodden by other cultures. An American tempo of life is emerging, utterly different from that of Europe – businesslike, dynamic, sober, mechanized, devoid of any romanticism – and this intimidates and repels a placid Europe. Nevertheless, wishing to be "as good as" Europe, America continues to import European aesthetics and romanticism as though they were commodities that had stood the test of time and been "patented," as it were. Thus, there emerges a single aspect of America: a horrifying mechanical mixture of new, organic, purely American elements with the superficial envelopes of an outlived classical system "made in Europe." The frightful forty-story Renaissance marvels and other similar nonsense perpetrated by the young America have already been judged, seemingly by everyone, on their own merits.

Yet at the same time, in those instances when the American genius permitted itself the luxury of doing without Europe's help, when the crude and sober but nonetheless

Moisei Ginzburg, from *Style and Epoch* (1924), trans. Anatole Senkevitch, Jr., in *Moisei Ginzburg: Style and Epoch*. Cambridge, MA: MIT Press, 1982, pp. 70, 92.

potentially vigorous spirit of the new pioneers manifested itself, brilliant structures teeming with unexpected poignancy and force were created spontaneously in an absolutely organic manner. I have in mind the industrial structures of America, and we shall have more to say about them later.

The America emerging at the beginning of the twentieth century thus generally presents a rather different picture. Along with the downfall of the classical system, we see flashes of a new idea, though for the time being not in "art" but in utilitarian buildings whose role and significance transcend the structures themselves.

[...]

The analysis of this kind of motion in a machine reveals new aspects of its character. Since motion occurs in the direction of an axis that lies outside the machine, with the possibility of reaching it (the axis) constituting the machine's very objective, this motion thus gives rise to a certain *unfulfillment, an unfeasible tendency,* a certain tension whose specific character is wholly at the root of the concept of the new organism. Indeed, just as the most poignant aspects of the Baroque lie in those elements which reveal an obvious unfulfillment of movement (such as, for example, broken, gouged-out cornice lines which cannot reach the axes located in their midst, or elements that are dispersed and striving to unite with their axis), so precisely all the force and poignancy embodied in the tension of purely modern organisms derive from the incompleteness and perpetual unfeasibility of dynamic tendencies, a condition keenly emphasized by the fact that the position of the axis of movement is perceived to lie either outside the general composition or within its outermost boundaries. Thus, the machine naturally gives rise to a conception of entirely new and modern organisms possessing the distinctly expressed characteristics of movement – *its tension and intensity, as well as its keenly expressed direction.* Both of these characteristics give rise to concepts of new forms, whereby the tension and concentration inherent in this movement will unwittingly – irrespective of the author's own desires – become one of the fundamental moments of artistic conception.

The other consequence resulting from the overall thrust of our discourse consists of a new definition of the machine and the new forms derived from it. An examination of movement in the architectural monuments of various historical styles indicates that the axis of movement within them always coincides with the axis of symmetry for the overall silhouette of the architectural organism; quite frequently, these monuments even represent a combination of several axes of symmetry and axes of movement. Naturally, this phenomenon cannot exist in the machine, where the axis of movement generally occurs or strives to occur beyond the machine itself. The question of symmetry in a machine is thus an altogether secondary one and not subordinated to the main compositional idea. Hence, we come to the final conclusion imposed upon us by the machine – namely, *that it is possible and natural for the modern architect's conceptions to yield a form that is asymmetrical or that, at best, has no more than a single axis of symmetry, which is subordinated to the main axis of movement and does not coincide with it.*

106 EL LISSITZKY
from "Element and Invention"
(1924)

E

l Lissitzky was another major theorist of the constructivist movement – both in Russia and on his travels in Europe. After taking his initial university studies in Germany before the war, he returned to Russia to take his degree in architecture from Riga Technical University. He then joined the Suprematist circle of Kasamir Malevich, and soon thereafter began developing his famous *Prouns*: two and three-dimensional painting/sculptures that earned him an international reputation as an artist. In 1921 Lissitzky began teaching architecture at VKhUTEMAS, but later in the year he was sent to Germany on a cultural mission of the new Soviet government. Here he became extremely influential as a theorist and ambassador for the new Russian art. He worked within Dada circles of Berlin and helped to found a new journal there; he joined forces with Dutch De Stijl artists and – perhaps most importantly – influenced the pedagogy of the Bauhaus. But in 1923, after a highly successful showing of his work in a Berlin gallery, Lissitzky came down with tuberculosis and traveled to Switzerland for treatment. While there he collaborated with the Dutch architect Mart Stam and the Swiss architect Hannes Meyer in founding yet another new avant-garde journal, *ABC*. In the first issue he published this summary of the principles of Constructivist architecture.

1.   Element

The modern designer examines the task at hand according to the functions that it has to fulfill. He therefore selects for each function the appropriate element. The elements are

For plastic Elements:

A) *Cube* – it contains flat surfaces, the edge, and the right angle in three basic directions. When viewed standing on one of its surfaces, its outline will be squared-static; when placed on a corner, its outline appears hexagonal-dynamic.

B) *Cone* – it arises on the basis of the circle, the ellipse with the outline of the triangle, the parabola, the hyperbola, the spiral. If we place the apex in infinity, it becomes a cylinder.

C) *Sphere* – the crystallization of the universe.

Plastic elements are thus given for everything that is built closed or open.

Closed: Building (cube). Silos, grain elevators (cylinder). Air balloon (sphere). Billboard. An antique sculpture, etc.

Open: Eiffel Tower, Bridges. Airplane. Luminous advertisements made out of individually illuminated letters. Counter-relief (Tatlin), etc.

If two or more elements are combined, there arises a tension. The manner in which the tensional forces are brought into balance defines the building. Against the compressive forces of load and support, the tensional forces of modern times appear as a new expression.

El Lissitzky, "Element und Erfindung" (1924), trans. Harry Francis Mallgrave, from the facsimile edition of *ABC: Beiträge zum Bauen*. Baden: Lars Müller, 1993.

Thus arises the rib, openness. Modern design separates the parts in tension from the demarcating, enclosing parts. It does not want to cover, mask, or decorate. It is the soundness of nakedness.

The Elements for the Material:

Following the resistance: concrete (compression), iron (tension), etc.

Following the kind of preparation: aluminum (rolling), glass (pouring), etc.

Following the demand of load or of demarcation: demarcating materials are glass, vulcanized materials, laminated wood panels. From these come the external qualities of surfaces: rough or smooth, grainy or polished, shiny, transparent, etc. Thus an optical and tactile effect arises at the same time. This fact has been developed in modern painting in particular, which has prepared the way for many other fields.

The Elements for Color:

It is a matter of unbroken colors, therefore not the value or the tone (the material itself possesses these), but of the color striving for a direct physiological effect. That with the full beating pulse = red. The color of hygiene and space = white. That which denies volume = black. In the modern city colors fulfill the function of indicating directions: all streets of the same direction receive the same color (e.g. the upper floors). With that the demand of the fifth facade, the view from above, will also correspond to the orientation.

In this way we possess a number of design elements that should be organized into a table, like a table of chemical elements. These elements *in themselves alone* already yield a material, equal to everything until now employed by historical traditions. In the best cases, a loose composition of elements alone can yield aesthetically pleasing means, but we do not need this today. More important is the kind of composition and therefore we demand two components for modern design.

2. Invention

The modern designer examines the task at hand according to the functions that it has to fulfill. Therefore he finds for the given function the simplest "self-evident" composition of appropriate Elements. This "self-evident quality" is invention; we must always be inventers. Thus the form arises as a result of the task, which is element and invention. We know no form in and of itself. The inventor himself places new demands on the elements, and he creates new materials, new colors, etc.

Technology, under the great pressure of life reshaping itself, has taken the path of element-invention. For several centuries now art has received no pressure from life; it has become "free" and with its "freedom" it is on the path of parasitism and is turning out booty from the storehouse of history. Thus we stand between radio and air travel on one hand and Egyptian-Greek-Roman-Gothic masquerades on the other hand. The modern designer is forced, in expectation of new life tasks, to devote himself to such things. We therefore achieve today the most important things in the laboratory. There the rule of "number" is formed out of the logic of the building. The inventor need not calculate;

he knows only that one is equal to one. But his nature itself contains the clear and simple mathematical formula. Thus modern design, for example the airplane, achieves universal standards, which are not just German, French, or American. Invention is the universal force, the biomechanical force that propels everything forward and lets it overcome all the hindrances.

The two elements of modern design – element and invention – are inseparable.

107   NIKOLAI LADOVSKY AND EL LISSITZKY
from *ASNOVA: Review of the Association of New Architects* (1926)

One of the first rallying groups for Constructivist architects in the 1920s was the Association of New Architects or ASNOVA, founded in 1923. The group was formed at the Moscow school VKhUTEMAS by Nikolai Ladovsky, who was promoting the rationalism and formal abstraction taught in his design studios there. In 1925, El Lissitzky returned to Moscow and joined the faculty at VKhUTEMAS. In addition to his teaching and practice, Lissitzky also became coeditor (with Ladovsky) of the group's new journal, the first issue of which was published in the spring of 1926. This manifesto, printed in this format on the front cover, is the most concise state of constructivist principles to appear and represents Soviet Constructivist theory in all of its revolutionary enthusiasm. For the buoyant optimism exhibited here would within a few years give way to the reality of failed economic programs and the increasing brutality and tyranny of Joseph Stalin. Several articles within the journal deal with the skyscrapers: both as buildings in the United States and as projects for the new Soviet Union.

USSR – Building a new way of life.
USSR – Energising the masses for a classless society.
USSR – Setting forth new goals for architecture.
USSR – Rationalizing work in union with science and highly developed technology.

ASNOVA believes its role is to materialize architecturally the principles of the USSR.
ASNOVA believes it is urgent to equip architecture with the tools and methods of modern science.
ASNOVA, in seeking the progress of modern architecture, believes that today's strategic moment requires the mutual creative efforts of architects-producers on one hand and of the working masses of consumers on the other hand. Today's practical work will conclude tomorrow in a theoretical system.
ASNOVA, proceeding from the rhythm of modern invention and the fact that each day the architect must face new technological systems, believes it is crucial to establish general architectural principles and free it from atrophying form.

Nikolai Ladovsky and El Lissitzky, from *ASNOVA: Review of the Association of New Architects* (1926), trans. Irina Nazarova.

ASNOVA works toward the creation of precise and scientific terms for modem architecture, and believes they are a significant tool for its progress.

This printed page **ASNOVA** is:

1. The rallying point for those establishing the parameters of modern architecture.
2. A loudspeaker for those creating these parameters.
3. An information source for the science and technology of modern architecture (theory and practice).
4. A bridge for those coming into architecture from others fields of the plastic and technical arts.
5. ....

FOR WHOM DOES ASNOVA WORK?
ASNOVA works for the masses who demand:

a. architecture that has a single meaning, like an automobile or a boot;
b. housing that is more than simply a machine for satisfying physical needs;
c. a rational validation of architecture's qualities;
d. not dilettantism but skill.

WHO WORKS WITH ASNOVA?
ALL ARCHITECTS who recognize their role in the expanding scale of construction, which otherwise threatens to turn into anarchy.

ALL ENGINEERS striving for structures than rise to the level of a work of art.

ALL BUILDERS of everything new, whose paths intersect with architecture.

REPRESENTATIVES ABROAD: GERMANY – ADOLF BEHNE; FRANCE – LE CORBUSIER; HOLLAND – MART STAM; UNITED STATES – LUNDBERG HOLM; SWITZERLAND – EMIL ROOT; CZECHOSLOVAKIA – KAREL TEIGE; YUGOSLAVIA – LUBOMIR MITSICH; JAPAN – MURAYAMA

C. DE STIJL AND PURISM

Introduction

The artistic situations in the Netherlands and France differed greatly from that in Russia just prior to and in the early 1920s. The Netherlands was one of the few European countries that did not participate in World War I, and thus it displays a greater continuity of theory and practice than elsewhere. The office of Hendrik Berlage, for instance, was active during the war, and significant building initiatives were undertaken in Amsterdam and Hilversum. Partly owing to this activity, the Netherlands became the first country in Western Europe to spawn an avant-garde theory of art and develop it consistently in practice.

The De Stijl movement, which bears a clear kinship to Russian Suprematism, was founded by the painters Theo van Doesburg and Pieter Mondrian. One inspiration for its development was Wassily Kandinsky's book *Concerning the Spiritual in Art* (1910); another was a group of Dutch mystics and mathematicians, chiefly the theophist and Christophist Mathieu Schoenmaekers. Van Doesburg was also interested in nurturing an architectural dimension to the De Stijl movement, and among the early architects to participate in the development of its ideas were J. J. P. Oud, Cornelis van Eesteren, and Garrit Rietveld. As a result, the Netherlands in the early 1920s moved to the forefront of the modern movement in Europe.

The situation in France was less defined. Although France and its Allies were victorious in the military conflict, much of the fighting (and therefore destruction) had taken place on French soil and the country's economic affairs had suffered greatly. Building activity had been brought to a halt by the war and the problems of governmental stability and monetary inflation were nearly as severe and long-standing in France as in defeated Germany. As a result, little building took place in France in the first half of the 1920s, and architectural activity was again confined largely to paper. The new prophet to emerge on the stage was the Swiss architect Le Corbusier, who moved to Paris in 1917. Le Corbusier was enamored with the principles of Taylorism, but the guiding impetus to his new outlook was Purism. The idea for Purism was put forward by the painter Amédée Ozenfant, in whose studio Le Corbusier now took instruction in painting. The two men next collaborated in founding the journal *L'Esprit Nouveau*, which quickly became one of the leading avant-garde journals on the Continent. In these pages Le Corbusier first put together the writings that he would compile in 1923 as *Toward an Architecture*, one of the most important theoretical statements of this decade.

108   THEO VAN DOESBURG ET AL.
from "Manifesto 1" (1918)

The De Stijl group was founded in the Netherlands in 1917, arising from within the climate of pessimism induced by the war. It brought together a number of artists from different disciplines under the mutual desire to create a new synthesis of the arts. Mysticism (rational, plastic, and mathematical) formed one part of the group's early ideology, while a Spenglerian dread of the present and future formed another. Hence, in this initial manifesto published by the group in 1918, there is the dichotomy between the individual (egoism) and the universal (collectivism), as well as the emphasis placed on the new consciousness and the need to turn a new page of human history. Van Doesburg, the principal theorist of the group, came to this philosophical position while serving as a border guard during the war. The manifesto was also signed by Pieter Mondrian, Robert van't Hoff, Jan Wils, Vilmos Huzar, Antony Kok, and Georges Vantongerloo.

1   There is an old and a new consciousness of time.
    The old is connected with the individual.
    The new is connected with the universal.
    The struggle of the individual against the universal is revealing itself in the world war as well as in the art of the present day.
2   The war is destroying the old world and its contents; individual domination in every state.
3   The new art has brought forward what the new consciousness of time contains: a balance between the universal and the individual.
4   The new consciousness is prepared to realize the internal life as well as the external life.
5   Traditions, dogmas, and the domination of the individual are opposed to this realization.
6   The founders of the new plastic art, therefore, call upon all who believe in the reformation of art and culture to eradicate these obstacles to development, as in the new plastic art

Theo van Doesburg et al., from "Manifesto 1" (1918), trans Nicholas Bullock, in *The Tradition of Constructivism*, ed. Stephen Bann. London, 1974, p. 65.

(by excluding natural form) they have eradicated that which blocks pure artistic expression, the ultimate consequence of all concepts of art.

7   The artists of today have been driven the whole world over by the same consciousness, and therefore have taken part from an intellectual point of view in this war against the domination of individual despotism. They therefore sympathize with all who work to establish international unity in life, art, culture, either intellectually or materially.

8   The monthly editions of *De Stijl*, founded for that purpose, try to set forth the new comprehension of life in a clear manner. Cooperation is possible by:

9   i.   Sending, as an indication of approval, name, address, and profession to the editor of *De Stijl*.

    ii.   Sending critical, philosophical, architectural, scientific, literary, musical articles or reproductions.

    iii. Translating articles in different languages or disseminating ideas published in *De Stijl*.

109   AMÉDÉE OZENFANT AND CHARLES-EDOUARD JEANNERET (LE CORBUSIER)
from the preface to the first issue of *L'Esprit Nouveau* (1920)

In 1917 Charles-Edouard Jeanneret moved to Paris and soon thereafter met the painter Amédée Ozenfant. It was the start of a collaboration highly beneficial to both men, but especially to Jeanneret. Ozenfant introduced the Swiss architect to the artistic circles of Paris, and Jeanneret began to study painting in Ozenfant's studio. In return, Jeanneret supplied the painter with ideas, energy, and organizational skill. The first product of their partnership was the book *After Cubism* (1918), which broached Ozenfant's growing dissatisfaction with many of the aesthetic premises of Cubism. The two eventually joined forces to define the contrary aesthetic of "Purism," a stage at which they arrived around the time they teamed up with Paul Dermée to start the journal *L'Esprit Nouveau* ("The New Spirit"). Jeanneret, at Ozenfant's urging, would now change his name to Le Corbusier, and the journal itself became the springboard for the architect's early fame. This preface from the first issue of 1920 states their high ambition for the project.

There is a new spirit; it is a spirit of construction and synthesis guided by a clear conception.

Regardless of what we think, today it enlivens the greatest part of human activity.

Born in some strong personalities of the nineteenth century – epoch of preparation and thus epoch of trouble – the new spirit now guides all the elites: the elites of arts and letters as well as the elites of science and industry. Society tends finally to organize itself in line with the new spirit.

Amédée Ozenfant and Charles-Edouard Jeanneret, from the preface to *L'Esprit Nouveau* 1 (1920), pp. 3–4, trans. Christina Contandriopoulos and Harry Francis Mallgrave.

As history shows, the forces liberated by centuries of agitation and disorder are now uniting and orientating themselves in a common effort. Thus, we see looming a great epoch.

A great epoch has just begun, because all forms of human activity are finally organizing themselves according to the same principle.

The spirit of construction and synthesis, of order and conscious will are again manifesting themselves; it is no less indispensable to display it in the arts and letters, in the pure or applied sciences, and even in philosophy.

What would a genius be without a constructive spirit? He could not realize any of his inspirations! He would not leave masterpieces behind. He would pass through life without leaving a trace.

We want, on the contrary, to affirm forcefully that the constructive spirit is as necessary to create a picture or a poem as it is to build a bridge.

Better yet, we affirm the necessity of an aesthetic system for creators.

Art, like science or philosophy, is an order created by man in his representations. No work of art exists without a more or less conscious aesthetic system, without being more or less elaborated by that which has created it, just as there is no scientific or philosophic work to which some systematic conceptions are not more or less avowed, for which a hypothesis has not been more or less advanced. Aesthetic, scientific, and philosophical systems are buildings, constructions that put determinate material at work.

The reflection of the creator must convey as much of the construction that he wants to raise as of the material that he wants to put into the work.

★ ★ ★

But this new spirit, that exists only with a few, the very best in arts and literature on the one hand, and the world of science and industry (applied science) on the other. One is able to hasten the evolution by a well calculated intervention. We must leave behind certain truths of the half-light and allow them to act with all of their efficacious force by placing them in full light.

Because we are especially concerned here with aesthetics, here is what we propose to do for our part:

State first of all the proper position and the directing ideas of each of today's innovators. Analyze them by emphasizing their strength or weakness, reveal what makes them exceptional or general. Therefore put a little order into our aesthetic panorama.

Analyze today's works by highlighting the ever more confirmed existence of the constructive spirit; again, clarify what the constructive spirit is by revealing its most striking characteristics in the masterpieces of the past.

Finally, to make known the results of the experimental aesthetic that everyday shows more clearly the close relationship between man and nature.

In this way again, the arts and sciences are closely related.

It is thus important that a possible and indispensable contact be established between the world of the art and letters on one hand, and the world of science and industry (applied science) on the other hand. The "New Spirit" makes rapprochement one of the most important articles of its program.

To work toward the syntheses of today's diverse activities is to work for the advent of the new spirit.

"The New Spirit"

110 AMÉDÉE OZENFANT AND CHARLES-EDOUARD JEANNERET (LE CORBUSIER)
from ''Purism'' (1920)

This lengthy article by Ozenfant and Jeanneret summarizing the principles of Purism did not appear until the fourth issue of *L'Esprit Nouveau*. What is striking in this brief passage is that the leading ideas of Purism are not at all dissimilar to those of the De Stijl artists – although the art produced by these two groups was entirely different. Whereas van Doesburg and Mondrian generally structured their abstract patches of primary colors around controlling grids, Ozenfant and Jeanneret painted prototypical manufactured objects, such as bottles and musical instruments, in much more subdued tones. These principles of painting nevertheless affected Le Corbusier and the sensibilities of his still emerging architectural conception.

Purism

The highest delectation of the human mind is the perception of order, and the greatest human satisfaction is the feeling of collaboration or participation in this order. The work of art is an artificial object which lets the spectator be placed in the state desired by the creator. The sensation of order is of a mathematical quality. The creation of a work of art should utilize means for specified results. Here is how we have tried to create a language possessing these means:

Primary forms and colors have standard properties (universal properties which permit the creation of a transmittable plastic language). But the utilization of primary forms does not suffice to place the spectator in the sought-for state of mathematical order. For that one must bring to bear the associations of natural or artificial forms, and the criterion for their choice is the degree of selection at which certain elements have arrived (natural selection and mechanical selection). The Purist element issued from the purification of standard forms is not a copy, but a creation whose end is to materialize the object in all its generality and its invariability. Purist elements are thus comparable to words of carefully defined meaning; Purist syntax is the application of constructive and modular means; it is the application of the laws which control pictorial space. A painting is a whole (unity); a painting is an artificial formation which, by appropriate means, should lead to the objectification of an entire 'world.' One could make an art of allusions, an art of fashion, based upon surprise and the conventions of the initiated. Purism strives for an art free of conventions which will utilize plastic constants and address itself above all to the universal properties of the senses and the mind.

Amédée Ozenfant and Charles-Edouard Jeanneret (Le Corbusier), from ''Purism,'' in *L'Esprit Nouveau* 4 (1920), trans. R. L. Herbert, in *Modern Artists on Art*, Englewood Cliffs, NJ: Prentice-Hall, 1964, p. 240.

111 J. J. P. OUD

from "On Future Architecture and its Architectural Possibilities" (1921)

The first major architect to emerge from the De Stijl movement in Holland was J. J. P. Oud. In the prewar years he collaborated with Willem Dudok and H. P. Berlage, before joining forces with van Doesburg around 1915 to plan the journal *De Stijl*. Oud later collaborated with van Doesburg (who provided the color scheme) on two architectural projects, the second of which – the Sprangen housing estate in Rotterdam (1921) – led to the split between the two men. Since his appointment as a city architect for Rotterdam in 1918, Oud had been moving away from van Doesburg's emphasis on primary colors and toward a more rational architecture predicated on the new materials of concrete and glass. This essay, written around the time of his breakup with van Doesburg, articulates Oud's vision of modernism, and it in fact serves as the first major theoretical statement of the 1920s in Europe. Curiously, Oud's polemics here echo the notion of *Sachlichkeit* (simple straightforward design) as earlier championed by Hermann Muthesius, but with a new appreciation of technology's aesthetic possibilities. Hence the older fascination of Muthesius and others for modern vehicles and ships is resurrected, but with the architectural acceptance of that strict or rigorous *Sachlichkeit* from which Muthesius had backed away. The essay precedes by three years Oud's famous design for the housing estate at Hook of Holland (1924–7), where the vision he puts forward here is enacted.

Architecture, unlike the free arts, is not exclusively the result of a spiritual process but rather of material factors: purpose, material, and construction. Its goal is a double one: utility and beauty at the same time. Just as spiritual factors affect it over the course of time, so too material factors continually affect it, and architecture at times can be hampered in its development. This is true for architectural as well as industrial objects. Yet when the aesthetic possibilities of an object become smaller and its useful value greater, resistance diminishes and its purely formal purpose becomes the dominant artistic conception. Thus it is possible that objects having chiefly practical purpose and possessing only a small aesthetic value can escape artistic attention and be formed in the most suitable and purely technical manner. Then it becomes apparent that the human urge for beauty is so great that these objects, as if on their own volition, overcome their purely technical purpose and acquire elementary aesthetic form.

Initially such objects – such as automobiles, steamships, yachts, men's clothing, sport clothing, electrical and sanitary articles, utensils, etc. – acquire, as a pure expression of their time, the elements of a new aesthetic design and can be considered as visual starting points for the forms of the new art. Through their lack of decoration, their taut form and flat unbroken color, through the relative perfection of their material and proportions – to a large

J. J. P. Oud, from "Über die zukünftige Baukunst und ihre architektonischen Möglichkeiten" (1921). The essay originally appeared in *Bouwkundig*, and this is cited from the German version published in *Holländische Architektur*. Dessau: Bauhaus Press, 1926, pp. 67–8, 75–6, trans. Harry Francis Mallgrave.

extent the result of a new (machine) mode of production – they come to have an indirect and stimulating affect on architecture. They bring to bear on architecture (also by more direct causes) a pressure toward abstraction... [...]

★ ★ ★

In conclusion, it follows that when architecture is based rationally on today's conditions of life, it will in every respect form itself in opposition to the architecture of the past. Without falling into a hard rationalism, it will be above all *sachlich*, but at once a higher *Sachlichkeit*. In the sharpest possible opposition to the non-technical, formless, and colorless productions of momentary inspiration with which we are familiar, it will approach the tasks posed to it with a more perfect regard for the goal, and in an almost impersonal, technical approach to design that shapes organisms with clear forms and pure proportions. Instead of the natural attractiveness of unprocessed materials – the small panes of glass, fractured surfaces, cloudy colors, fused glazes, weathered masonry, etc. – it will exhibit the charm of processed materials: clear sheets of glass, glittering and rounded surfaces, shiny and sparkling colors, gleaming steel, etc.

Thus there is a tendency in architectural development toward an architecture that in its essence is bound more so than earlier to materials, but that in its appearance will go far beyond them. It will be an architecture free of all impressionistic and sentimental design, one whose purity of proportions will be seen in the fullness of light, in a brightness of color, and in an organic clarity of form that, through the absence of anything secondary, will far exceed classical purity.

112 LE CORBUSIER
from *Toward an Architecture* (1923)

Beginning in the fourth issue of *L'Esprit Nouveau*, Le Corbusier and Amédée Ozenfant (under the pseudonym Le Corbusier-Saugnier) began to co-author a series of essays related to architecture. In 1923 Le Corbusier assembled and published these articles under his new name as *Vers une architecture* ("Toward an architecture") – arguably the most influential book of the first half of the twentieth century. The themes of the various articles are nearly related. A few of the earlier ones attempt to transpose a purist aesthetic to architecture and discuss such issues as geometry and the use of regulating lines. Increasingly, however, the essays dwell on the themes of the engineer's aesthetic, industrial production (with strong support for Taylorism), and the need for mass-produced housing in postwar France. In the book's middle chapter, "Eyes which do not see," Le Corbusier takes the engineering prototypes of ocean liners, airplanes, and automobiles as models for architectural production. The use of such metaphors for architectural design, as we have seen, is scarcely new to architectural theory, but what is original is the single-minded way in which Le Corbusier turns the problem of architectural design effectively into a problem of engineering – "A house is

Le Corbusier, from *Vers une Architecture* (1923), trans. Frederick Etchells as *Towards a New Architecture*. London: The Architectural Press, 1946, pp. 89, 104–5.

a machine for living in." If engineers, Le Corbusier argues in another place, are healthy, virile, active, and useful to society, architects are by contrast disillusioned, unemployed, boastful, and peevish.

A house is a machine for living in. Baths, sun, hot-water, cold-water, warmth at will, conservation of food, hygiene, beauty in the sense of good proportion. An armchair is a machine for sitting in and so on.

Our modern life, when we are active and about (leaving out the moments when we fly to gruel and aspirin) has created its own objects: its costume, its fountain pen, its eversharp pencil, its typewriter, its telephone, its admirable office furniture, its plate-glass and its "Innovation" trunks, the safety razor and the briar pipe, the bowler hat and the limousine, the steamship and the airplane.

Our epoch is fixing its own style day by day. It is there under our eyes.

Eyes which do not see.

[. . .]

The architecture of to-day does not fulfil the necessary and sufficient conditions of the problem.

The reason is that the problem has not been stated as regards architecture. There has been no salutary war as in the case of the airplane.

But you will say, the Peace has set the problem in the reconstruction of the North of France. But then, we are totally disarmed, we do not know how to build in a modern way – materials, systems of construction, THE CONCEPTION OF THE DWELLING, all are lacking. Engineers have been busy with barrages, with bridges, with Atlantic liners, with mines, with railways. Architects have been asleep.

113 LE CORBUSIER
from *Toward an Architecture* (1923)

The penultimate chapter of *Toward an Architecture* deals with the matter of mass-produced housing, and summarizes Le Corbusier's belief that housing design and construction should be standardized and factory-produced in the same way, for instance, that automobiles are assembled in a factory. Le Corbusier follows this argument with a final chapter that carries the title "Architecture or Revolution." The polemic seemingly carries with it the force of a threat: if politicians do not step in and solve the housing problem in France along the lines that he is suggesting, revolution – that is, political revolution – will be the result. Yet this demand of Le Corbusier does not issue from a socialist perspective but rather from a position of technocratic positivism harking back to Saint-Simonism. In Le Corbusier's scenario, the leaders of the new society are not the working proletariat but rather the economic system's intellectual elites, of which architects should form a prominent part. Hence the architect through his power of design becomes an instrument of social change; living is to be reorganized upon fundamentally new principles.

Le Corbusier, from *Vers une Architecture* (1923), trans. Frederick Etchells as *Towards a New Architecture*. London: The Architectural Press, 1946, pp. 268–9.

Disturbed by the reactions which play upon him from every quarter, the man of to-day is conscious, on the one hand, of a new world which is forming itself regularly, logically and clearly, which produces in a straightforward way things which are useful and usable, and on the other hand he finds himself, to his surprise, living in an old and hostile environment. This framework is his lodging; his town, his street, his house or his flat rise up against him useless, hinder him from following the same path in his leisure that he pursues in his work, hinder him from following in his leisure the organic development of his existence, which is to create a family and to live, like every animal on this earth and like all men of all ages, an organized family life. In this way society is helping forward the destruction of the family, while she sees with terror that this will be her ruin.

There reigns a great disagreement between the modern state of mind, which is an admonition to us, and the stifling accumulation of age-long detritus.

The problem is one of adaptation, in which the realities of our life are in question.

Society is filled with a violent desire for something which it may obtain or may not. Everything lies in that: everything depends on the effort made and the attention paid to these alarming symptoms.

Architecture or Revolution.

Revolution can be avoided.

114 THEO VAN DOESBURG
from "Towards Plastic Architecture" (1924)

The years 1921–2 were crucial to the development of De Stijl theory. In 1921, after his break-up with Oud, Van Doesburg took his (nearly) one-man show on the road and met El Lissitzky and others in Berlin. Out of these meetings came his artistic alliance with Soviet Constructivism and German Dadaist circles. The Dutch artist shortly thereafter relocated his journal and studio to Weimar – again in search of disciples – where he gave a series of lectures opposing the Bauhaus's original curriculum of crafts-based studies. While in Weimar, van Doesburg met the Dutch architect Cornelius van Eesteren, who was touring Germany in 1922. The result was a new collaboration, in which the two men began a series of axonometric drawings of three-dimensional planes suspended in space. In Paris in the following year, they collaborated again on the design of three houses for a De Stijl exhibition in Paris. The models for these projects were made by Garrit Rietveld, who had been active in De Stijl circles since 1917. The gallery drawings, in turn, became the basis for Rietveld's famous design for the Schröder House. All of this activity led a reformulation of De Stijl thought in 1923–4, as seen in this statement penned by van Doesburg. This melding of De Stijl and constructivist theory marks the first great synthesis of postwar European theory. Van Doesburg's characterization of the new architecture as "anti-cubic," for instance, would offer a formal alternative to the frontally-conceived villas of Le Corbusier, while his emphasis on "space-time" introduces a concept into modern theory that also would be later seized by others.

Theo van Doesburg, from "Towards Plastic Architecture," *De Stijl* 12:6–7 (1924), trans. Joost Baljeu, in *Theo van Doesburg*. New York: Macmillan, 1974, pp. 142, 144–5, 147.

1 *Form.* The basis for a healthy development of architecture (and of art in general) is the suppression of all *form-ideas* insofar as this concept implies a *predetermined type*.

Instead of using earlier style types as models and thus imitating previous historical styles, one necessarily must pose the problem of architecture entirely anew.

2 The new architecture is *elementary,* which signifies that it develops from the elements of construction as understood in the most comprehensive sense. These elements are for example, function, mass, plane, time, space, light, colour and material, and they are, moreover, also *plastic elements.*

3 The new architecture is *economical,* which signifies that the elementary means are organized either as efficiently and economically as possible or by wasting neither these means nor the material.

4 The new architecture is *functional,* which signifies that it develops from the precise determination of practical necessities which it embodies in a clear groundplan.

5 The new architecture is *formless,* yet defined, which signifies that it is not characterized by any predetermined aesthetic form-type or mould (like those used by pastry-cooks) into which it casts the functional spaces derived from practical living demands.

In contrast to all earlier historical styles, the new architectural method imposes no standard or *basic type.*

The division of functional spaces is strictly determined by rectangular planes which possess themselves no individual shapes, since, although defined (one plane by the other), they can be extended infinitely by the imagination. Thus they can create a coordinated system in which all points correspond to an equal number of points in universal, unlimited open space.

It follows that the planes possess a direct relationship with open (exterior) space.

6 The new architecture has rendered the concept of *the monumental* independent of largeness and smallness (since the word 'monumental' has been abused, it is replaced by the word 'plastic'). This architecture has demonstrated that everything exists in terms of relationships, through the principle of interrelationship.

7 The new architecture possesses no *passive moment.* It has abandoned the use of 'dead spaces' (holes in the wall). The *openness* of the window has an *active* meaning as against the *closure* of the wall-surface. Nowhere does a hole or a void issue forth, everything is strictly determined by means of contrast. See the various counter-constructions, in which the elements of architecture, such as, plane, line and mass, have been freely arranged into a three-dimensional relationship. [...]

8 *The groundplan.* The new architecture has *opened* the walls, thus eliminating the *separateness* of the *interior* and the *exterior.*

The whole wall no longer carries, it is reduced to points of support. The result is a new, open groundplan, which is completely different from the traditional usage, since interior and exterior space interpenetrate.

9 The new architecture is *open.* The whole consists of one space, which is divided according to the various functional demands. This division is accomplished through the use of *separating planes* (in the interior) or by *projecting planes* (on the exterior).

The former planes, which separate the different functional spaces, can be *mobile,* which means that the separating planes (formerly the interior walls) can be replaced by movable screens or slabs (doors can also be treated in this manner). In the following phase of this development in architecture, the groundplan must disappear completely. The principle of two-dimensionally projected space-composition, as *fixed* by a groundplan, will be replaced by exact *calculation of the construction*, a calculation which must transfer the carrying capacity to the simplest but sturdiest points of support. Euclidean mathematics will no longer serve this purpose; yet by using Non-Euclidean calculations in four dimensions, this calculation can be accomplished quite easily.

10 *Space and time.* The new architecture calculates not only with space but also with time as an architectural value. The unity of space and time will give architectural form a new and completely plastic aspect, that is, a four-dimensional, plastic space–time aspect.

11 The new architecture is *anti-cubic*, which specifies that it does not attempt to combine all functional space-cells into one closed cube, but *projects the functional space-cells* (as well as overhanging planes, the volumes of balconies and so forth) centrifugally, or from the core of the cube outward, thereby giving a completely new plastic expression in open space to the dimensions of height, width, depth + time.

In this manner architecture takes on a more or less hovering aspect (insofar as this is feasible from a structural point of view, which is a problem for the engineer!). This aspect, so to speak, challenges the force of gravity in nature.

12 *Symmetry and repetition.* The new architecture has suppressed symmetry's monotonous repetition as well as the rigid equality which results from division into two halves or the use of the mirror image.

It employs neither repetition in time, street walls, nor standardized parts. A block of houses is as much a whole as a single house. The laws governing single houses apply also to both blocks of houses and the city as a whole. In place of symmetry, the new architecture proposes *a balanced relationship of unequal parts*; that is to say of parts which, because of functional characteristics, differ in position, size, proportion and situation.

The equivalence of these parts is gained through an equilibrium of unequality rather than of equality. In addition, the new architecture has granted equal value to the 'front', 'back', 'right', and possibly also to the 'above' and 'below'.

13 In contrast to *frontalism*, which was born out of a rigid, static concept of life, the new architecture offers the plastic richness of an all-sided development in space–time.

14 *Colour.* The new architecture has suppressed painting as a separate, illusory expression of harmony, whether as embodied indirectly in representational art or directly in an art of coloured planes.

The new architecture *employs* colour *organically* as a direct means of expression of relationships in space and time. Without colour, these relationships are devoid of the aspect of living reality; they are *invisible*. The equilibrium of the architectural relationships becomes a visible reality only through the use of colour. The task of the modern painter is to integrate colour into a harmonic whole (by placing it not on a plane-surface of two dimensions, but within the new realm of four-dimensional space–time). In a succeeding phase of development, colour might also be replaced by synthetic materials which possess their own specific colours (this is a problem for the chemical scientist), but only if practical demands require such materials.

15 The new architecture is *anti-decorative*. Colour – and colour-shy people must strive to realize this – is not a decorative or ornamental part of architecture but its organic means of expression.

16 *Architecture as the synthesis of Neo-Plasticism.* Construction is only one part of the new architecture; by including all the arts, in their most elementary appearance, the new architecture manifests its very essence.

This architecture presupposes a capacity for thinking in four dimensions, so that the plastic architect, who might also be a painter, must construct in the new realm of space–time.

Since the new architecture prohibits representation (such as easel-painting or sculpture as separate elements), its purpose of creating a harmonic whole from all the above mentioned essential means is inherent in its *very nature*. In this manner every architectural element contributes to the maximum vitality of plastic expression, accomplished on a practical and logical basis, without prejudice to utilitarian demands.

Paris 1924

115 MART STAM
from "Collective Design"
(1924)

Van Doesburg's synthesis of Dutch and Russian theory finds a resonance in the near contemporary words of Mart Stam, an architect with ties to both the De Stijl and constructivist movements. Stam acquired his architectural training in his native Holland before moving to Berlin in 1922, where he collaborated with both El Lissitzky and Theo van Doesburg. In 1923 Stam moved to Zurich to join the office of Karl Moser, and in the following year he, together with the Swiss architect Hans Schmidt, founded the avant-garde journal *ABC: Beiträge zum Bauen* (Contributions to Building). It was inspired, at least in part, by Lissitzky's involvement with the Berlin journal *G*, and Lissitzky in fact worked closely with Stam and Meyer on the journal. In the first issue, which sadly announces the death of Swiss culture and architecture (not to mention architecture in the United States), Stam issues his proclamation on "Collective Design." It reiterates the views of Le Corbusier regarding the engineer but from a more militantly political stance in sympathy with the Soviet Revolution. Functionalism, as with Lissitzky's article, is the leitmotif, and this is the basis for Henry-Russell Hitchcock and Philip Johnson's later characterization of functionalism as a politically extreme version of modernism. Stam was a talented designer and his important contributions to the modernism of the 1920s have often been overlooked.

The struggle for survival is becoming more and more acute, and the supreme, united efforts of all peoples are required as never before. Production, the main issue in this struggle, is intimately bound up with the steadily increasing populations of the world; the path of the future is a progressive economy, i. e. better exploitation of materials and greater production in less time. Production is to be understood above all as the manufacture of foodstuffs, and further, of utensils and shelter – the house.

Mart Stam, from "Kollektive Gestaltung" (1924), trans. Catherine Schelbert and Michael Robinson, in the facsimile edition of *ABC: Beiträge zum Bauen*, vol. 1. Baden: Lars Müller, 1993, p. 10.

To ensure speedy and profitable labor, the engineer organizes the mechanical forces and, with the help of science, seeks to maximize efficiency, to discover the most economic combinations of effort in all areas. In this organizational task, artists must stand side by side with engineers. In addition to a scientific knowledge of materials and their economic demands, the former must dispose of an inner insight, an awareness of the pure, elemental value of materials.

The engineer for his part will invest his rational powers in improving the system of production down to the finest details; he will construct his machines with ever greater consistency and expediency. On the other hand, he will create new technical potential for public and domestic life. As this work progresses, the scientific achievements of each generation will in turn serve as points of departure for the studies and developments of the next. In this way, the machine, the entire process of production, the technical universe will approach greater and greater perfection through the support of research conducted by thousands of brains.

Next to the engineer, who is rationally concerned with the properties of materials, with their scientific application and with the discovery of new modes of application through the combination of new properties – next to the engineer stands the artist.

The artist must acquire knowledge, must master scientific facts, but after that he must understand the materials, he must understand the larger organic context that redeems all things from their status as isolated objects, thus placing them in and subordinating them to the totality of laws that dominate the cosmos.

Artists must discover in each object the essence of these laws in order to acquire the ability to organize things even better than the engineer. They will find the most elemental expression for the essence of the task at hand, the expression of the task itself, formed by means of suitable materials in their most suitable form.

Thus design will emerge that is removed from any formalistic tendency, that is not born of a particular artist's disposition or the fantastic inspiration of the moment but is instead solidly based on the general, the absolute.

Thus design will emerge that turns to collective means for every form of expression.

The engineer and the artist should be able to build on what their comrades have succeeded in bringing about before them –

Thus development will be possible.

116 LE CORBUSIER
from *The City of To-morrow and its Planning* (1925)

L e Corbusier's concern with housing was only a part of his larger interest in urban planning, the principal focus of his early career. In the prewar years he had been much influenced by the ideas of Camillo Sitte, but after 1917, upon viewing Tony Garnier's *Industrial City*, he began to rethink his approach. Le Corbusier eventually brought together Garnier's vision of modernity with the theories of Frederick Winslow Taylor and Ebenezer Howard, as well as images of American skyscrapers, among other things. In 1922 he arrived at his proposal for a "Ville contemporaine" (Contemporary city), which he exhibited that year at the Salon d'Automne. It consisted of a series of central traffic axes converging under twenty-four, sixty-story towers, surrounded by parkland and smaller housing complexes, with industry and a garden city for workers beyond. Aspects of the design were published in *L'Esprit Nouveau*, and in 1925 Le Corbusier used these articles as a foundation for his first book on urban theory, *Urbanisme*. Here he begins to lay out his vision of a modern city that would not fundamentally change over the next forty years. The opening discourse on the "pack-donkey's way" sets the thematic stage for his proposals.

Man walks in a straight line because he has a goal and knows where he is going; he has made up his mind to reach some particular place and he goes straight to it.

The pack-donkey meanders along, meditates a little in his scatter-brained and distracted fashion, he zigzags in order to avoid the larger stones, or to ease the climb, or to gain a little shade; he takes the line of least resistance.

But man governs his feelings by his reason; he keeps his feelings and his instincts in check, subordinating them to the aim he has in view. He rules the brute creation by his intelligence. His intelligence formulates laws which are the product of experience. His experience is born of work; man works in order that he may not perish. In order that production may be possible, a line of conduct is essential, the laws of experience must be obeyed. Man must consider the result in advance.

But the pack-donkey thinks of nothing at all, except what will save himself trouble.

*

The Pack-Donkey's Way is responsible for the plan of every continental city; including Paris, unfortunately.

[...]

But a modern city lives by the straight line, inevitably; for the construction of buildings, sewers and tunnels, highways, pavements. The circulation of traffic demands the straight line; it is the proper thing for the heart of a city. The curve is ruinous, difficult and dangerous; it is a paralyzing thing.

The straight line enters into all human history, into all human aim, into every human act.

Le Corbusier, *Urbanisme* (1925), trans. Frederick Etchells (1929) as *The City of Tomorrow and its Planning*, cited from 3rd edn. Cambridge, MA: MIT Press, 1971, pp. 5–6, 10–12.

We must have the courage to view the rectilinear cities of America with admiration. If the æsthete has not so far done so, the moralist, on the contrary, may well find more food for reflection than at first appears.

★

The winding road is the Pack-Donkey's Way, the straight road is man's way.

The winding road is the result of happy-go-lucky heedlessness, of looseness, lack of concentration and animality.

The straight road is a reaction, an action, a positive deed, the result of self-mastery. It is sane and noble.

A city is a centre of intense life and effort.

A heedless people, or society, or town, in which effort is relaxed and is not concentrated, quickly becomes dissipated, overcome and absorbed by a nation or a society that goes to work in a positive way and controls itself.

It is in this way that cities sink to nothing and that ruling classes are overthrown.

D. GERMAN EXPRESSIONISM AND
THE BAUHAUS

Introduction

With its defeat in World War I, Germany also lost its initiative in architectural theory. The immediate postwar years were difficult ones for the country in every respect. Faced with wartime mutinies in the military and famine and rioting in many of its cities, Germany sued for peace in the fall of 1918, just before the government collapsed under a socialist revolution. The Treaty of Versailles, signed in the spring of 1919, resulted in the loss of much territory (especially key coal-producing areas) and high war indemnities. Chronic inflation led to the collapse of the German Mark, and it was only through the infusion of American money that the country was saved from complete economic collapse. National morale was equally slow to recover, in part because through the first half of the 1920s almost no building activity took place. The appreciation for technical progress and industrial might (with its concomitant bravado) that was so strong prior to the war was now rejected by nearly all, particularly those influenced by Oswald Spengler's book, *The Decline of the West*. German architects largely retreated from the perceived perils of industry and embraced art for its own sake as well the cause of handicraft production.

The middle years of the decade, however, saw a profound change in architectural thinking. Now becoming influenced by the artistic movements in Russia, Holland, and France, as well as by the phenomenon of Henry Ford in America, many German architects once again embraced technology as the centerpiece of modernity. The Bauhaus, initially based in craft production, signaled this change with its curricular reforms of 1923, and with its move to Dessau in 1925 its transformation was complete. Fiscal stability in the middle years of the decade also led to a return of building activity, particularly in addressing the critical shortages of housing. Thus by the time of the famed Weissenhof housing exhibition in Stuttgart in 1927, Germany was once again vying for the lead in European architectural theory with varied schools and interpretations of modernism.

117   OSWALD SPENGLER
from *The Decline of the West* (1918)

The most popular book in Germany in the postwar years was Oswald Spengler's *Decline of the West*, a book that reflected perfectly the intellectual temper of the times. The emphasis that architects like Hermann Muthesius had placed on industrialization prior to the war was interpreted later by many as the cause of the war's tragic mistake. Spengler concurred in arguing that industrialization and economic interests had essentially created the present spiritual crisis, which was the culmination of a long spiritual decline in Western civilization. He interpreted the Faustian tenor of "modern" civilization not as something new but as something that was born in the tenth century and that presently, in the darkest winter of its historical life, was nearing its inevitable collapse. The war merely finalized the outcome; the battle for socialism in the future must be fought on different terrain and be concluded in a conflict involving imperialism, Caesarism, and blood.

The dictature of money marches on, tending to its material peak, in the Faustian Civilization as in every other. And now something happens that is intelligible only to one who has penetrated to the essence of money. If it were anything tangible, then its existence would be for ever – but, as it is a form of thought, *it fades out as soon as it has thought its economic world to finality*, and has no more material upon which to feed. It thrust into the life of the yeoman's countryside and set the earth a-moving; its thought transformed every sort of handicraft; to-day it presses victoriously upon industry to make the productive work of entrepreneur and engineer and labourer alike its spoil. The machine with its human retinue, the real queen of this century, is in danger of succumbing to a stronger power. But with this, money, too, is at the end of its success, and the last conflict is at hand in which the Civilization receives its conclusive form – the conflict *between* money and blood.

The coming of Cæsarism breaks the dictature of money and its political weapon democracy. After a long triumph of world-city economy and its interests over political creative force, the political side of life manifests itself after all as the stronger of the two. The sword is

Oswald Spengler, from *The Decline of the West*, trans. Charles Francis Atkinson. New York: Alfred A. Knopf, 1926, reprinted as a one-volume edition in 1934, pp. 506–7.

victorious over the money, the master-will subdues again the plunderer-will. If we call these money-powers "Capitalism," then we may designate as Socialism the will to call into life a mighty politico-economic order that transcends all class interests, a system of *lofty* thought-fulness and duty-sense that keeps the whole in fine condition for the decisive battle of its history, and this battle is also the battle of money and law. The *private* powers of the economy want free paths for their acquisition of great resources. No legislation must stand in their way. They want to make the laws themselves, in their interests, and to that end they make use of the tool they have made for themselves, democracy, the subsidized party. Law needs, in order to resist this onslaught, a high tradition and an ambition of strong families that finds its satisfaction not in the heaping-up of riches, but in the tasks of true rulership, above and beyond all money-advantage. *A power can be overthrown only by another power*, not by a principle, and no power that can confront money is left but this one. Money is overthrown and abolished only by blood.

118 HANS POELZIG
from "Address to the Werkbund" (1919)

P artly in response to Spengler's analysis, architects in the postwar years turned against any strategies involving industrialization. Thus one of the first acts of the reconstituted German Werkbund in 1919 was to reject its earlier policies and return to the ideals of craftsmanship. At least this was the direction given to the organization by Hans Poelzig, who was elected president of the organization in 1919. After completing his architectural studies at the Technical University in Berlin in the 1890s, Poelzig moved to Breslau to teach at the School of Art and Applied Art, where he became the director in 1903. He was active in the founding of the Werkbund, and in his writings he always emphasized good construction and taking into account regional elements. He designed several notable factories prior to the war, but he would find a measure of considerable fame in 1919 for his expressionist renovation of the Berlin Playhouse, whose fanciful forms captivated a war-weary city. This new Werkbund policy effectively annuls all earlier efforts by Hermann Muthusius to enlist art into the service of trade.

The Werkbund must bear in mind that it was engendered by a spiritual not an economic movement. This spiritual aspect has been buried under the diverse political and economic activities of the Werkbund and it is time to reinstate it in all its purity. Fine art and crafts are the foundations on which the work of the Werkbund must be built. They are in effect one and the same thing. . . .

By craftsmanship I mean something absolutely spiritual, a basic attitude of the mind, not technical perfection in some sector or other. What we should understand by craftsmanship, which is in fact absolutely identical with artistic work, is the will to dedicate great love and

Hans Poelzig, from "Address to the Werkbund" (1919), trans. Christine Charlesworth and cited from Julius Posener, *Hans Poelzig: Reflections on His Life and Work.* New York: Architectural History Foundation, 1992, p. 130.

devotion to creating forms, a task during which no thought at all is given to the economic exploitation of the work, or perhaps in the very last instance only. That is the basic difference between this kind of work and all purely industrial activities.

Industry in the broadest sense of the term is concerned only with technical things and is guided primarily by economic considerations. Fine art and crafts, on the other hand, flourish only when economic considerations merely indicate how far the creative processes, in which form plays the decisive role, can go.

It goes without saying that transitional stages do exist, that certain craftsmen might as well be called entrepreneurs and that some factory owners put their whole heart and soul into the goods they manufacture. So when we talk of craftsmanship we mean a spiritual, an ethical concept. We mean the practice of a craft – or an art – for its own sake, industrialism of any kind being something basically different.

Nor should thoughts of export possibilities guide our work in any way. This kind of consideration implies compromise and adaptation to demand, to the wishes of interested parties. We must work free from any consideration of this kind, following nothing but our artistic and craftsman's conscience, and leaving all other considerations to industry.

119 MANIFESTO
"Work Council for Art" (1919)

The collapse of the German Reich in the waning days of the war led to a revolution and a socialist government formed under Friedrich Ebert in 1918. The political nature of the revolution, however, was as yet undecided. Many argued for a parliamentary form of socialism within the limited bounds of capitalism, and this was the nature of the so-called Weimar Republic, which was formally declared in February 1919. The more radical German communists – the Spartacists – initially demanded a Soviet-style revolution with all of its proletariat trappings. Within this more militant wing, in December 1918, arose the "Work Council for Art," founded by Bruno Taut. This architect had built little prior to the war, but he participated in the Werkbund Exhibition of 1914 with his Glass Pavilion and he sided with Walter Gropius in the showdown against Hermann Muthesius. Also befriending both Gropius and Taut at this time was Adolf Behne, and the friendship of the three men strengthened during the war with their commitment to Marxism. In December 1919 Taut published the "Architectur-Programm" for the Work Council for Art (*Arbeitsrat für Kunst*, the council followed Soviet workers' models). It called for a relocation of people to the countryside and for a massive program of cultural re-education – similar to that which would take place in China at the end of World War II. National elections in January, however, resulted in a ruling coalition of socialist parties and a rejection of more radical politics, while the death of the Spartacist leaders Karl Liebknecht and Rosa Luxemburg in January 1919, in police custody, dramatically changed the political tone of things. Taut immediately resigned his leadership of the Work Council, and its direction passed to Walter Gropius and Adolf Behne, who now sought to tone down the council's polemics while remaining sympathetic to the founding goals. This new and more

Manifesto for Arbeitsrat für Kunst (1919), trans. Michael Bullock and cited from *Programs and manifestoes on 20th-century architecture*, ed. Ulrich Conrads. Cambridge, MA: MIT Press, 1975, pp. 44–5.

modest manifesto appeared in March 1919. Like Taut's original manifesto, it emphasizes the arts and crafts as the socialist touchstone for the new art.

In the conviction that the political revolution must be used to liberate art from decades of regimentation, a group of artists and art-lovers united by a common outlook has been formed in Berlin. It strives for the gathering together of all scattered and divided energies which, over and above the protection of one-sided professional interests, wish to work resolutely together for the rebuilding of our whole artistic life. In close contact with associations with similar objectives in other parts of Germany, the Arbeitsrat für Kunst hopes in the not too distant future to be able to push through its aims, which are outlined in the following programme.

In the forefront stands the guiding principle:

Art and people must form a unity.
Art shall no longer be the enjoyment of the few but the life and happiness of the masses.
The aim is alliance of the arts under the wing of a great architecture.

On this basis six preliminary demands are made:

1. Recognition of the public character of all building activity, both State and private. Removal of all privileges accorded to Civil Servants. Unitary supervision of whole urban districts, streets, and residential estates, without curtailment of freedom over detail. New tasks: people's housing as a means of bringing all the arts to the people. Permanent experimental sites for testing and perfecting new architectural effects.
2. Dissolution of the Academy of Arts, the Academy of Building and the Prussian Provincial Art Commission in their existing form. Replacement of these bodies, accompanied by a redefining of their territories, by others drawn from the ranks of productive artists themselves and free from State interference. The changing of privileged art exhibitions into exhibitions to which entry is free.
3. Freeing of all training in architecture, sculpture, painting, and handicrafts from State supervision. Transformation of all instruction in the arts and handicrafts from top to bottom. State funds to be made available for this purpose and for the training of master craftsmen in training workshops.
4. Enlivenment of the museums as educational establishments for the people. Mounting of constantly changing exhibitions made to serve the interests of the people by means of lectures and conducted tours. Separation of scientific material in specially constructed buildings. Establishment of specially arranged collections for study by workers in the arts and crafts. Just distribution of State funds for the acquisition of old and new works.
5. Destruction of artistically valueless monuments as well as of all buildings whose artistic value is out of proportion to the value of their material which could be put to other uses. Prevention of prematurely planned war memorials and immediate cessation of work on the war museums proposed for Berlin and the Reich.
6. Establishment of a national centre to ensure the fostering of the arts within the framework of future lawmaking.

120 WALTER GROPIUS
from "Program of the Staatliches Bauhaus in Weimar" (1919)

n April 1919, as Walter Gropius was much involved with running the Work Council for Art, he received the directorship of the Weimar School of Art. It would become one of the most important architectural appointments of the twentieth century. Before the war, Weimar had two art schools. In 1902 Henry van de Velde had been invited to the city by the Grand Duke of Saxe-Weimar as an artistic advisor, and he designed a new School of the Applied Arts in 1904–06, for which he served as the director. During this time, adjacent to it, van de Velde also designed a new building for the Weimar Art School (1904–11). With the onset of the war, the Belgian van de Velde was relieved of his position and placed under house arrest. The School of the Applied Arts was transformed into a military hospital, but the Art School continued to function without a director. During the war Gropius (from the war front) was consulted by the Art School and by the state ministry about reforming its curriculum, and on this basis Gropius contacted governmental officials at the end of 1918 and began negotiating for the vacant position. After his appointment in the following spring, Gropius, through a bureaucratic backdoor, changed the name of the Art School to the Staatliche Bauhaus at Weimar, and a new chapter in artistic education was begun.

The program for the new school is notable in several respects. First it was a program and curriculum calling for a return to the crafts, and was therefore a rejection of the technology that had enthused Gropius in the prewar years (the name Bauhaus was a reference to the medieval lodge, built to house the workers of cathedrals). Second it was not a program calling for training in painting or architecture, although the latter was the theoretical underpinning of the program. Third it was initially at least a politically driven program, although here too the polemics were toned down. All of these aspects would lead to friction and factions within and without the school in its early years, and in fact the existing faculty refused Gropius's leadership and a second "fine-arts" school formed unofficially within the Bauhaus, occupying one-half of the building. The success of the Bauhaus, however, was largely due to the highly talented faculty that Gropius attracted to Weimar, which would include such artists as Lyonel Feininger, Johannes Itten, Oskar Schlemmer, and Paul Klee.

The ultimate aim of all visual arts is the complete building! To embellish buildings was once the noblest function of the fine arts; they were the indispensable components of great architecture. Today the arts exist in isolation, from which they can be rescued only through the conscious, cooperative effort of all craftsmen. Architects, painters, and sculptors must recognize anew and learn to grasp the composite character of a building both as an entity and in its separate parts. Only then will their work be imbued with the architectonic spirit which it has lost as "salon art."

The old schools of art were unable to produce this unity; how could they, since art cannot be taught. They must be merged once more with the workshop. The mere drawing and painting world of the pattern designer and the applied artist must become a world that builds again. When young people who take a joy in artistic creation once more begin their life's work by learning a trade, then the unproductive "artist" will no longer be condemned

Walter Gropius, from "Programm des staatlichen Bauhauses in Weimar" (1919), trans. Wolfgang Jabs and Basil Gilbert, in Hans M. Wingler, *The Bauhaus: Weimar, Dessau, Berlin, Chicago*. Cambridge, MA: MIT Press, 1978, pp. 31–2.

to deficient artistry, for their skill will now be preserved for the crafts, in which they will be able to achieve excellence.

Architects, sculptors, painters, we all must return to the crafts! For art is not a "profession." There is no essential difference between the artist and the craftsman. The artist is an exalted craftsman. In rare moments of inspiration, transcending the consciousness of his will, the grace of heaven may cause his work to blossom into art. But proficiency in a craft is essential to every artist. Therein lies the prime source of creative imagination. Let us then create a new guild of craftsmen without the class distinctions that raise an arrogant barrier between craftsman and artist! Together let us desire, conceive, and create the new structure of the future, which will embrace architecture and sculpture and painting in one unity and which will one day rise toward heaven from the hands of a million workers like the crystal symbol of a new faith.

Walter Gropius

Program of the Staatliche Bauhaus in Weimar
The Staatliche Bauhaus resulted from the merger of the former Grand-Ducal Saxon Academy of Art with the former Grand-Ducal Saxon School of Arts and Crafts in conjunction with a newly affiliated department of architecture.

Aims of the Bauhaus
The Bauhaus strives to bring together all creative effort into one whole, to reunify all the disciplines of practical art – sculpture, painting, handicrafts, and the crafts – as inseparable components of a new architecture. The ultimate, if distant, aim of the Bauhaus is the unified work of art – the great structure – in which there is no distinction between monumental and decorative art.

The Bauhaus wants to educate architects, painters, and sculptors of all levels, according to their capabilities, to become competent craftsmen or independent creative artists and to form a working community of leading and future artist-craftsmen. These men, of kindred spirit, will know how to design buildings harmoniously in their entirety – structure, finishing, ornamentation, and furnishing.

Principles of the Bauhaus
Art rises above all methods; in itself it cannot be taught, but the crafts certainly can be. Architects, painters, and sculptors are craftsmen in the true sense of the word; hence, a thorough training in the crafts, acquired in workshops and in experimental and practical sites, is required of all students as the indispensable basis for all artistic production. Our own workshops are to be gradually built up, and apprenticeship agreements with outside workshops will be concluded.

The school is the servant of the workshop, and will one day be absorbed in it. Therefore there will be no teachers or pupils in the Bauhaus but masters, journeymen, and apprentices.

The manner of teaching arises from the character of the workshop:

Organic forms developed from manual skills.

Avoidance of all rigidity; priority of creativity; freedom of individuality, but strict study discipline.

Master and journeyman examinations, according to the Guild Statutes, held before the Council of Masters of the Bauhaus or before outside masters.

Collaboration by the students in the work of the masters.

Securing of commissions, also for students.

Mutual planning of extensive, Utopian structural designs – public buildings and buildings for worship – aimed at the future. Collaboration of all masters and students – architects, painters, sculptors – on these designs with the object of gradually achieving a harmony of all the component elements and parts that make up architecture.

Constant contact with the leaders of the crafts and industries of the country. Contact with public life, with the people, through exhibitions and other activities.

New research into the nature of the exhibitions, to solve the problem of displaying visual work and sculpture within the framework of architecture.

Encouragement of friendly relations between masters and students outside of work; therefore plays, lectures, poetry, music, costume parties. Establishment of a cheerful ceremonial at these gatherings.

121 BRUNO TAUT
letter announcing the "Crystal Chain" (1919)

As Gropius in 1919 was preparing to implement his program at the Bauhaus in Weimar, his friend Bruno Taut remained behind in Berlin and devoted his energies to publishing two books of highly fanciful sketches, *The City Crown* and *Alpine Architecture*. The former dealt with his fascination with crystals and the latter with ending all wars by transforming the Alps into mystical shrines. In the fall he hatched a scheme to turn the Work Council for Art into a secret brotherhood. He (under the pseudonym Glas) asked fourteen artists and architects involved with the organization – among them Max Taut, Wassili Luckhardt, Hermann Finsterlin, and Hans Scharoun (Gropius declined to participate) – to write a series of chain letters under pseudonyms, in which they would secretly record their inspirational ideas and sketches. What is perhaps most apparent here is the depressing atmosphere of this period. Architects were without work, the political revolution (in Taut's view) had taken a false turn, and the one recourse left open for expression was for artists to become "imaginary architects" and speculate on future utopias. This letter, announcing the "crystal chain," also represents Taut at his most expressionistic point. In 1920 he became involved with editing the magazine *Frühlicht*, and in the following year he received an appointment as a municipal architect in Magdeburg.

Dear Friends,

I want to make this proposal to you: Today there is almost nothing to build, and if we can build anywhere, then we do it in order to live. Or are you lucky enough to be working on a nice commission? My daily routine almost makes me ill, and it is basically the same for all of you. As a matter of fact, it is a good thing that nothing is being built today. Things will have

Bruno Taut, letter announcing the "Crystal Chain" (1919), ed. and trans. Iain Boyd Whyte in *The Crystal Chain Letters: Architectural Fantasies by Bruno Taut and His Circle*. Cambridge, MA: MIT Press, 1985, p. 19.

time to ripen, we shall gather our strength, and when building begins again we shall know our objectives and be strong enough to protect our movement against botching and degeneration.

Let us consciously be "imaginary architects"! We believe that only a total revolution can guide us in our task. Our fellow citizens, even our colleagues quite rightly suspect in us the forces of revolution. Break up and undermine all former principles! Dung! And we are the bud in fresh humus.

The individual personality will disappear with commitment to a higher task – if architecture reappears then the master builder will be anonymous.

I can see the beginning of this in our tendency to join and fuse together as a first cell, without asking – who did it? Instead, the idea exists in the realm of endless joy, remote and autonomous. The purpose of my proposal is to strengthen this existing unity. It is as follows:

Quite informally and according to inclination, each of us will draw or write down at regular intervals those of his ideas that he wants to share with our circle, and will then send a copy to each member. In this way an exchange of ideas, questions, answers, and criticism will be established. Above each contribution will be a pseudonym. The mutual sympathy within the circle and the use of terse language will make it difficult for outsiders to understand us. Nevertheless, we must agree not to reveal anything to uncomprehending eyes. Any request to expand the circle or to expel a member of the group should emerge from the contributions themselves. A single vote will suffice for an expulsion, unless all the other members veto it in their next letters.

Let it be a magnet, the snowy core of an avalanche! If nothing comes of the idea, if I am deluding myself, then at least it will be a beautiful memory for each of us.

By the way: Whoever leaves the group before the whole thing comes to an end is obliged to return all the contributions he has accumulated either to me or another member, or to destroy them.

If you agree, could you sign and return this to me as soon as possible, together with the desired pseudonym. I will let you have the result immediately and – the thing will be under way.

With color and glass greetings,

Glas

122   LUDWIG MIES VAN DER ROHE
from "Skyscrapers" (1922)

A native of Aachen, Mies van der Rohe worked in the office of Peter Behrens between 1908 and 1912, and before the war he built several Schinkelesque villas on the outskirts of Berlin. He also served in the German army and in 1919 returned to Berlin to resume his practice. He was, however, at a crossroads. On the one hand he was comfortable with his prewar office practice of designing large suburban houses; on the other hand he

Ludwig Mies van der Rohe, from text published without title in *Frühlicht* 4 (1922), trans. Mark Jarzombek, in Fritz Neumeyer, *The Artless Word: Mies van der Rohe on the Building-Art*. Cambridge, MA: MIT Press, 1991, p. 240.

was becoming active within Dadaist artistic circles. Out of these contacts came his hypothetical designs for a glass skyscraper. The project grew out of a real competition announced in 1921 by a local business society for a glass tower to be situated on Friedrichstrasse. Mies largely ignored the competition guidelines and produced his angular, rather crystallized scheme; in a follow-up version designed in 1922 he turned to a series of curvilinear forms. Mies may have been inspired by some sketches of Taut, and within the context of the postwar economic realities and building codes of Germany, his thinking was entirely utopian. His designs, nevertheless, rather vividly reveal his distance from the handicraft pursuits of so many of his colleagues; they presage as well his later career in the United States.

Only skyscrapers under construction reveal the bold constructive thoughts, and then the impression of the high-reaching steel skeletons is overpowering. With the raising of the walls, this impression is completely destroyed; the constructive thought, the necessary basis for artistic form-giving, is annihilated and frequently smothered by a meaningless and trivial jumble of forms. At very best one remains impressed by the sheer magnitude, and yet these buildings could have been more than just manifestations of our technical skill. This would mean, however, that one would have to give up the attempt to solve a new task with traditional forms; rather one should attempt to give form to the new task out of the nature of this task.

The novel constructive principle of these buildings comes clearly into view if one employs glass for the no longer load-bearing exterior walls. The use of glass, however, necessitates new approaches. In my design for the skyscraper at the Friedrichstrasse railroad station in Berlin, intended for a triangular site, a prismatic form corresponding to the triangle appeared to offer the right solution for this building, and I angled the respective façade fronts slightly toward each other to avoid the danger of an effect of lifelessness that often occurs if one employs large glass panels. My experiments with a glass model helped me along the way and I soon recognized that by employing glass, it is not an effect of light and shadow one wants to achieve but a rich interplay of light reflections. That is what I strove for in the other design published here. At first glance the contour of the ground plan appears arbitrary, but in reality it is the result of many experiments on the glass model. The curves were determined by the need to illuminate the interior, the effect of the building mass in the urban context, and finally the play of the desired light reflection. Ground plan contours in which the curves were calculated from the point of view of light and shadow revealed themselves on the model, if glass was employed, as totally unsuitable. The only fixed points in the ground plan are the stairs and the elevator shafts.

All other subdivisions of the ground plan are to be adapted to the respective needs and executed in glass.

123 LUDWIG MIES VAN DER ROHE
from "Office Building" (1923)

In 1922 Mies joined Novembergruppe, another group of architects and artists committed to modernism, and at the same time he began forming friendships with a group of Berlin artists and intellectuals, among them Hans Richter and Werner Gräff. Another member of this circle was the constructivist El Lissitzy, who had been living in Berlin since 1921. Richter, Gräff, and Lissitzky would join forces to found the journal *G* (short for *Gestaltung* or "design"), and it was through this journal that the principles of the De Stijl and Constructivism first became known in Germany. The anti-expressionist slant of *G* fitted well with Mies's own beliefs, and the architect even assumed some of the editorial work for several issues – the journal itself was sometimes assembled in Mies's office. Among Mies's several conceptual projects published by *G* was his "Office Building," which was a concrete-and-glass structure. This terse statement of his theory is almost symbolic of Mies's minimalist style of design, and the reference to "formalism" is probably directed both to Expressionism and to the evolving teachings of Walter Gropius at the Bauhaus.

Any aesthetic speculation
any doctrine } we reject
and any formalism

Building art is the spatially apprehended will of the epoch.

Alive. Changing. New.

Not the yesterday, not the tomorrow, only the today is formable.

Only this building creates.

Create form out of the nature of the task with the means of our time.

That is our work.

The office building is a building of work, of organization, of clarity, of economy. Bright wide workrooms, uncluttered, undivided, only articulated according to the organism of the firm. The greatest effect with the least expenditure of means.

The materials are concrete, iron, glass.

Ferroconcrete buildings are essentially skeleton structures.

Neither pastry nor tank turrets. Supporting girder construction with a nonsupporting wall. That means skin and bone structures.

The most practical distribution of the work stations determined room depth; it is 16 m. A double-shafted frame of 8 m span-width with 4 m long lateral cantilever brackets on either side was established as the most economical construction principle. The beam distance is 5 m. This post-and-beam system supports the ceiling panel, which, angled vertically upward at the end of the cantilever arms, becomes exterior skin and serves as back wall of the shelving, which was moved to the exterior walls in order to keep the interior uncluttered. Above the 2 m high shelving is a continuous band of fenestration reaching to the ceiling.

Ludwig Mies van der Rohe, from *G* 1 (July 1923), trans. Mark Jarzombek, in Fritz Neumeyer, *The Artless Word: Mies van der Rohe on the Building-Art*. Cambridge, MA: MIT Press, 1991, p. 241.

124 WALTER GROPIUS
from "The Viability of the Bauhaus Idea" (1922)

The first years of the Bauhaus were rocky ones. Gropius was faced with a revolt by the older faculty members and by student protesters, who objected to the fact that they had enrolled for training in the fine arts but were now expected to study the crafts. And officials within the state educational ministry, who had agreed with the new arts-and-crafts orientation of the school, were disappointed with the fact that Gropius hired so many painters. The "Spartacist" orientation of the school's faculty and students infuriated many local residents of Weimar, who were also not impressed with the repeated incidents of political demonstrations and rowdiness among the students. And then Gropius faced yet another rebellion in 1922–3 from his appointed faculty, when the director began to reconsider pedagogical changes for the school.

The forces affecting Gropius's intellectual evolution were myriad. Theo van Doesburg's uninvited stay in Weimar in 1921, where he gave unsanctioned lectures and workshops from his home, produced a strong challenge to his pedagogy. The influence of Constructivism, emanating from the artistic circles in Berlin, provided another. Le Corbusier's writings for *L'Esprit Nouveau* indirectly attacked his beliefs from still a third direction. But perhaps the most important factor was Gropius's own background. In his early years in the office of Peter Behrens he had been a strong champion of technology and mass production – a position that was at odds with his stance in Cologne in 1914. Now in the early 1920s Gropius fell back under the sway of the *Amerikanismus* (Americanism) sweeping across Germany, fostered by the industrial theories of Frederick Winslow Taylor and the great success of Henry Ford. Early in 1922, Gropius decided to begin the process of reforming the curriculum at the Bauhaus by re-orientating its direction away from the crafts and toward technology and mass production. In this circular of 3 February 1922, distributed to the faculty, Gropius first raises the issue of change, which, as he is well aware, will have vehement opposition from several of his own faculty members.

The Bauhaus has made a start in breaking with the usual academic training of artists to be "little Raphaels" and pattern designers, and has sought to bring back to the people those creative talents who have fled the artistic working life, to their own and the people's detriment. It consciously strove to replace the principle of division of labor with that of unified collective work, which conceives the creative process of design as an indivisible whole. To do this, it was necessary to rebuild from the very roots in order to have a chance to be able to give back to the present generation the correct feeling for the interrelation of practical work and problems of form. Genuine crafts also have had to be reborn in order to make intelligible to our youth, through handwork, the nature of creative work. But this by no means implies a rejection of the machine or industry. The only basic contrast lies in the division of labor on the one hand and the unity of labor on the other.... If a creatively talented person had a factory at his disposal with all its machinery, he would be able to create new forms that would differ from those produced by hand crafts.... The Bauhaus could become a haven for eccentrics if it were to lose contact with the work and working methods

Walter Gropius, from circular to Bauhaus Masters, trans. Wolfgang Jabs and Basil Gilbert, cited from Hans M. Wingler, *The Bauhaus: Weimar, Dessau, Berlin, Chicago*. Cambridge, MA: MIT Press, 1978, 51–2.

of the outside world. Its responsibility consists in educating people to recognize the basic nature of the world *in which they live*, and in combining their knowledge with their imagination so to be able to create typical forms that symbolize that world. What is important then, is to combine the creative activity of the individual with the broad practical work of the world! If we were to reject the world around us completely, the only remaining way out would be the "romantic island." I see a danger to our youth in the indications of a wild romanticism that derives from an understandable reaction against the predominating state of mind – numbers and force – and from the breakdown of countries. Some of our Bauhaus members subscribe to a kind of misunderstood "return to nature" doctrine of Rousseau's. It would be consistent if a person who disavowed this whole world were to retreat to an island. But if he remains in this world, the forms of his work will show its rhythms all the more as he strives to understand its challenges. . . .

The entire "architecture" and the "arts and crafts" of the last generation . . . is, with very few exceptions, a lie. In all of these products one recognizes the false and spastic effort "to make Art." They actually stand in the way of the development of pure joy in the art of "building." Today's architect has forfeited his right to exist. . . . The engineer, on the other hand, unhampered by esthetics and historical inhibitions, has arrived at clear and organic forms. He seems to be slowly taking over the heritage of the architect, who evolved from the crafts.

How the broad gulf between the activity we practice in our workshops and the present level of the crafts and industry outside will some day be closed, that is the unknown quantity. . . . Contact with industry and with the practical work of the world can only be established gradually. It is possible that the work in the Bauhaus workshops will lead more and more to the production of single prototypes [which will serve as guides to the craftsman and industry]. Students who have gone through the Bauhaus will be in a position, with the knowledge they have acquired there, to exert a decisive influence on existing craft [enterprises] and industrial works, if they will just decide to join these and exert their influence from within. The big transformation from analytic to synthetic work is proceeding in all areas, and industry will follow suit. It will seek people with the kind of thorough training which we in the Bauhaus try to give, and these people will free the machine from its [lack of creative spirit]! The independent artist, groping his way toward the "useless" machine, is already orienting himself with this compass of the future.

125 OSKAR SCHLEMMER
from "The First Bauhaus Exhibition in Weimar" (1923)

I n 1920 Walter Gropius had been provided with a three-year budget for the Bauhaus from the state of Thurginia. To demonstrate to politicians the progress made at the school, he organized a large exhibition for several locations in Weimar in the summer of 1923. The school had become more unpopular with many in the community, especially for its political orientation. It was still fraught with infighting, as several members of the faculty – Johannes Itten, Lyonel Feininger, and Oskar Schlemmer, among them – had indeed adamantly opposed the new emphasis on technology and its apparent complicity with capitalism. Gropius nevertheless courageously defined the exhibition under the theme "Art and Technology, A New Unity." In the busy days approaching the massive event, Oskar Schlemmer was given the task of preparing the exhibition catalogue and he used the occasion to protest the director's theme by invoking (with a manifesto) the cause of the crafts within this "cathedral of socialism." On the eve of the exhibition's opening, Gropius, who had been unaware of Schlemmer's tactic, worked into the night to remove the overtly political statement from the catalogue, but it was too late; a few advance copies had been sent to the press. Schlemmer's statement provoked the expected outcry and Itten soon left the school after losing his showdown with Gropius over the curriculum. Early in 1924, in Thurginian elections, a right-wing coalition of parties replaced the ruling left-wing coalition, and they soon voted to shut down the school.

The Staatliche Bauhaus, founded after the catastrophe of the war in the chaos of the revolution and in the era of the flowering of an emotion-laden, explosive art, becomes the rallying-point of all those who, with belief in the future and with sky-storming enthusiasm, wish to build the "cathedral of socialism." The triumphs of industry and technology before the war and the orgies in the name of destruction during it called to life that impassioned romanticism that was a flaming protest against materialism and the mechanization of art and life. The misery of the time was also a spiritual anguish. A cult of the unconscious and of the unexplainable, a propensity for mysticism and sectarianism originated in the quest for those highest things which are in danger of being deprived of their meaning in a world full of doubt and disruption. Breaking the limitations of classical esthetics reinforced boundlessness of feeling, which found nourishment and verification in the discovery of the East and the art of the Negro, farmers, children, and the insane. The origin of artistic creation was as much sought as its limits were courageously extended. Passionate use of the means of expression developed in altar paintings. But it is in pictures, and always in pictures, where the decisive values take refuge. As the highest achievement of individual exaggeration, free from bonds and unredeemed, they must all, apart from the unity of the picture itself, remain in debt to the proclaimed synthesis. The honest crafts wallowed in the exotic joy of materials, and architecture piled Utopian schemes on paper.

Reversal of values, changes in point of view, name, and concept result in the other view, the next faith. Dada, court jester in this kingdom, plays ball with paradoxes and makes the atmosphere free and easy. Americanisms transferred to Europe, the new wedged into the old

Oskar Schlemmer, from Manifesto, in "The First Bauhaus Exhibition in Weimar," trans. Wolfgang Jabs and Basil Gilbert, cited from Hans M. Wingler, *The Bauhaus: Weimar, Dessau, Berlin, Chicago.* Cambridge. MA: MIT Press, 1978, 65–6.

world, death to the past, to moonlight, and to the soul, thus the present time strides along with the gestures of a conqueror. Reason and science, "man's greatest powers," are the regents, and the engineer is the sedate executor of unlimited possibilities. Mathematics, structure, and mechanization are the elements, and power and money are the dictators of these modern phenomena of steel, concrete, glass and electricity. Velocity of rigid matter, dematerialization of matter, organization of inorganic matter, all these produce the miracle of abstraction. Based on the laws of nature, these are the achievements of mind in the conquest of nature, based on the power of capital, the work of man against man. The speed and supertension of commercialism make expediency and utility the measure of all effectiveness, and calculation seizes the transcendent world: art becomes a logarithm. It, long bereft of its name, lives a life after death, in the monument of the cube and in the colored square. Religion is the precise process of thinking, and God is dead. Man, self-conscious and perfect being, surpassed in accuracy by every puppet, awaits results from the chemist's retort until the formula for "spirit" is found as well. . . .

Goethe: "If the hopes materialize that men, with all their strength, with heart and mind, with understanding and love, will join together and become conscious of each other, then what no man can yet imagine will occur – Allah will no longer need to create, we will create his world." This is the synthesis, the concentration, intensification, and compression of all that is positive to form the powerful mean. The idea of the mean, far from mediocrity and weakness, taken as scale and balance, becomes the idea of German art.

Germany, country of the middle, and Weimar, the heart of it, is not for the first time the adopted place of intellectual decision. What matters is the recognition of what is pertinent to us, so that we will not aimlessly wander astray. In balancing the polar contrasts – loving the remotest past as well as the remotest future; averting reaction as much as anarchism; advancing from the end-in-itself and from self-directedness to the typical, from the problematical to the valid and secure – thus we become the bearers of responsibility and the conscience of the world. An idealism of activity that embraces, penetrates, and unites art, science, and technology and that influences research, study, and work, will construct the "art-edifice" of Man, which is but an allegory of the cosmic system. Today we can do no more than to ponder the total plan, lay the foundations, and prepare the building stones.

But

We exist! We have the will! We are producing!

126   WALTER GROPIUS
from *International Architecture* (1925)

Despite Oscar Schlemmer's intervention, the Bauhaus Exhibition of 1923 was a great success, in large part because Gropius chose to put on display not only students' work but also the work architects committed to modernism internationally. The event in fact became the first attempt to define what would later go by the name of "Modern Movement." The book that was based on the exhibition appeared in 1925 in Dessau – after

Walter Gropius, from *Internationale Architektur*. Dessau: Passavia Druckerei, 1925, pp. 7–8, trans. Harry Francis Mallgrave.

Gropius had negotiated with the Dessau mayor to move the school's name and faculty to that city, to be housed in a new building designed by Gropius. The genealogy of this new international architecture promoted by Gropius begins with the prewar work of Peter Behrens, Frank Lloyd Wright, Hans Poelzig, and Gropius himself. Gropius then documents the postwar work of Mies van der Rohe, Erich Mendelsohn, J. J. P. Oud, and Le Corbusier, among others. If there was one connecting thread to his selections, it was the factory aesthetic that he himself would display in his new school in Dessau. The short introduction to the images is also interesting in that Gropius now returns to the polemics of cultural determinism and teleological finality that had so enchanted Peter Behrens prior to the war. The one key distinction, following Spengler, is that architects do not create the spirit of the time, they must submit to it. This book would forcefully shape the first histories of modernism that would shortly follow.

Among a multiplicity of harmonious economic possibilities for solutions – there are many for each building task – the creative artist, within the limits, selects that which his time appoints for him, according to his personal sensitivities. The work, as a result, bears the signature of his creativity. But it is false to conclude from this the necessity to emphasize the individual at any price. On the contrary, the will to development recognizes a **unified** global image of our time; it presumes the longing to free spiritual values from their individual limitation and to raise them to **objective validity**. Thus follows the unity of external forms that inevitably leads to culture. In modern architecture the objectivity of the personal and the national are clearly discernible. Yet a unified modern building character, conditioned by world trade and world technology, transcends the natural boundaries that remain bound to nations or individuals; it forges ahead in every cultural land. Architecture is always national, also always individual, but of the three concentric circles – individual, a nation, humanity – the last and the largest also comprises the other two. Therefore the title: ''INTERNATIONAL ARCHITECTURE''!

In considering the illustrations of this book, one should keep this in mind that the concise use of time, space, material, and money in industry and economy are decidedly the factors that determine the image of all modern building organisms. They define precisely impressed form, simplicity in multiplicity, articulation of all architectural elements following the functions of the building fabric, streets, and traffic, the limitation of typical basic forms and their arrangement and repetition. A new will is discernible: to design our surrounding buildings from an inner law without lies and ornamentation, to represent functionally their meaning and purpose through the tension of their building masses, and to reject everything superfluous that masks their absolute form. The architects of this book affirm today's world of machines, vehicles, and tempo; they strive always toward a bolder means of design and to soar above earth-bound torpidity in effects and appearance.

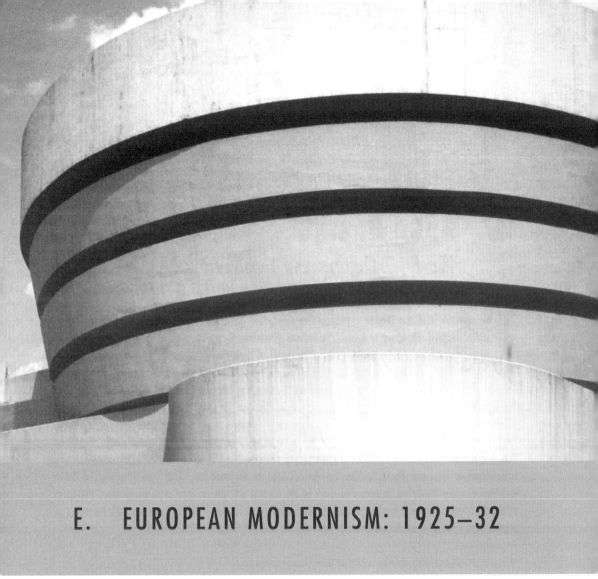

E. EUROPEAN MODERNISM: 1925–32

Introduction

The most evident feature of European architecture in the second half of the 1920s, in relation to the first half, is the fact that building activity resumes. And with the housing shortages created by more than a decade of little or no activity, it was only natural that nearly all building attention was focused on the severe housing problem, to the exclusion of almost all other building types. The architectural issue before European modernists, therefore, was quite simple: how to build the maximum number of living units with the most modest economic outlay possible – and given this reality, former questions such as "style" had simply lost their relevance. Design now came to be defined by such variables as the austerity of means and rapidity of construction. National and international organizations, such as the Congrès Internationaux d'Architecture Moderne (CIAM), at the same time sprang into action, to serve both as political action committees on behalf of modern architects and as vehicles for theoretical research. Concepts such as the controversial "existence minimum" – the minimum square footage established through research for a livable dwelling unit – now worked its way into architectural practice.

Still another attribute of this return to architectural production was its ephemeral nature. No sooner had things to some extent been put back to normal than the global Great Depression of 1929 struck Europe – once again halting building activity while at the same time destabilizing the already fragile political equilibrium. Thus the optimistic words about a new era by European architects in the late 1920s were replaced almost overnight by a deep sense of dread with regard to the future. Not only would architectural commissions soon cease to exist, but Europe as a whole would rush headlong into two of the bloodiest decades in its long and violent history. The face of theory would obviously also be dramatically altered.

127 HUGO HÄRING
from "Paths to Form" (1925)

The assertions of Walter Gropius in *International Architecture* to the contrary, in the mid-1920s there was no unified modern movement in Europe. Modernism throughout Europe was, if anything, represented by its formal diversity, and one example of this is the work of Hugo Häring. A student of Fritz Schumacher and Theodore Fischer, Häring moved to Berlin in 1921, where he shared an office and a friendship with Mies van der Rohe. The association was mutually beneficial. Mies at the time was being initiated into avant-garde circles, and Häring, whose wife was an actress, aided him in this quest. Häring's "organic" theory may also have influenced Mies, as the latter's curvilinear design for the glass tower on Friedrichstrasse is sometimes credited to Häring's sway. And it was Häring's exclusion from the Bauhaus Exhibition of 1923 that stirred the ire of Mies, who complained about the omission in a letter to Gropius. In part owing to this exclusion, Häring and Mies in 1925 – together with Hans Scharoun, Hans and Wassili Luckhardt – banded together to found the "Ring," an association of Berlin architects who saw themselves, in part, as a check on the growing authority of Gropius at the Bauhaus. Häring, in particular, opposed the cubic forms promoted by Gropius and Le Corbusier, which he countered with his notion of organic form-making, which he supported in part with the ideas of Frederick Winslow Taylor.

We want to seek out things and let their own form unfold.

It is wrong to give one form to them, to determine their form from without, to force arbitrary laws on them, to dictate to them. We are wrong when we make them display historical demonstrations; we are likewise wrong when we make them objects of our individual whims.

And we are similarly wrong when we reduce things to geometrical or crystalline figures, because in this way we once again subjugate them (Corbusier). Geometric figures are not original forms, therefore not original designs. Geometric figures are abstractions, contrived lawful restraints. The unity that we achieve on the basis of geometric figures over the form omits many things; it is only a unity of form not a unity of what is living.

We, however, want the unity in living and with the living. A polished metal ball is a fantastic occasion for our spirit, but a flower is an experience.

Geometric figures mean putting something over things; this means uniformity; this means mechanization.

Hugo Häring, from "Wege zur Form" (1925), trans. Harry Francis Mallgrave, in *Hugo Häring: Schriften, Entwürfe, Bauten*, ed. Heinrich Lauterbach and Jürgen Joedicke. Stuttgart: Karl Krämer Verlag, 1956, p. 14.

We, however, do not wish to mechanize things but to mechanize their production.

To mechanize things means to mechanize their life, which is our life; it destroys them. To mechanize production, however, means to win life.

The form of things can be identical with geometric figures, as with a crystal, yet in nature geometric figures never have content or originate as a form. We are therefore against the principle of Corbusier (yet not against Corbusier).

We have to form not our individuality but the individuality of things. Their expression is identical with themselves.

128 ADOLF BEHNE
from *The Modern Functional Building* (1926)

Although Gropius's book *Internationale Architektur* (1925) was the first published book attempting to document the European Modern Movement, Behne's book – written in 1923 – actually provides an earlier and more discerning interpretation of events. The fact that its publication was thwarted in part by Gropius (who was not eager to share his own collection of photographs of recent works) also says something about the competitive personalities of these men. After taking his doctorate in architecture in 1912, Behne moved to Berlin, where he fell into the circle of Gropius and Bruno Taut. The three men formed an alliance at the Werkbund conference in 1914, and their friendship continued during the war years and later at the Working Council for the Arts. This friendship, however, soon cooled. When Gropius took over the directorship of the Bauhaus and pursued the path of the crafts, Behne, who was still in Berlin, was taking note of developments in Russia and Holland and he too was much enthused by the ideas of Frederick Winslow Taylor. His numerous writings were no doubt influencing Gropius at this time, and Behne, in his review of the exhibition in 1923, applauded the fact that Gropius had switched his ideological allegiance to technology. Written in the same year, Behne's book is built around the notion of *Sachlichkeit* – the old term for functional practicality. The idea for Behne unfolds in three stages, beginning with the ideas of Otto Wagner, Hendrik Berlage, Alfred Messel, and Frank Lloyd Wright. In the second stage, outlined in his chapter "No Longer a House but Shaped Space," *Sachlichkeit* now incorporates the theories of Henry Ford and the design innovations of Peter Behrens, Henry van de Velde, and Erich Mendelsohn. Finally, in the third stage, "No Longer Shaped Space but Designed Reality," *Sachlichkeit* achieves its highest mediation in the German melding of constructivist theory with the ideas of Dutch and French architects. Behne, against Gropius, sees the work of Hugo Häring as representative of this highest ideal of *Sachlichkeit*.

The surest guiding principle to absolutely *sachlich*, necessary, extra-aesthetic design seemed to be adaptation to technical and economic functions, which with consistent work must in fact lead to the dissolution of the concept of form. Thus building would unconditionally become a tool.

Strict suitability to functions – what could the building gain by that?

Adolf Behne, from *Die moderne Zweckbau* (1926), trans. Michael Robinson as *The Modern Functional Building*. Santa Monica, CA: Getty Publication Programs, 1996, pp. 119–21.

When the parts of a building are arranged according to a sense of their use, when aesthetic space becomes living space – and this is the kind of order we call dynamic – the building throws off the fetters of the old, fossilized, static order, axes, symmetry, etc., and achieves a new starting point. A cramped, material, stable equilibrium (symmetry) gives way to a new, bolder equilibrium, delicately balanced in broad tensions (polarity) that correspond better to our essence, and with this comes a form that is entirely new and alive, free from constraints and stabilization.

And then, through this suitability to function, a building achieves a much broader and better inner unity: it becomes more organic by abandoning the old conventions and formalisms of representation, which inhibit the materialization of necessary form.

It is therefore no wonder that architects tried to exploit the possibilities of functionalism to the full. Building presumes the optimum functional articulation of the proposed living space; architecture is no more than a fixed and visible structure of the final organization of every movement, every occupation, every purpose and use of the building. It is no small architectural achievement if all the paths through a building relate to each other clearly and coherently, absolutely free and open to every possible combination, and not just in a mechanical sense – "twelve doors in a long corridor" – but with the aim of achieving the finest and most ambitious organization and best possible construction. The architect can only grasp and carry out his truly artistic work, that is, the creative work, when he addresses questions of his client's attitude to life, way of living, business methods – something that of course he can only do with him, not without him or against him. For this reason "being a client" is not just buying a piece of land, some bricks, and an architect. The client must be an activity, whose taking possession of the acquired space is so definite, clear, rich, and organic that it can be transformed into the relationships of masonry walls, indeed relationships governed not by convention or mere custom but by necessity and a living sense.

It is the architect's task to balance spaces freely against each other, simply according to their *sachlich* functions, excluding anything arbitrary; only then is it possible to have the ambition – from floors, circulation, size of interior and exterior space, the best spatial sequence, the disposition to light, to garden, to street, to traffic – of creating the final tectonic order of all factors: the building. In this process all symmetrical axes, all drawing board geometry, all floor plan ornaments must completely disappear; architecture becomes shaped reality.

129 GIUSEPPE TERRAGNI ET AL.
from "The Group 7" (1926)

The polemics and debates that transpired in Russia, Holland, Germany, and France in the postwar years spread rapidly throughout other European countries. Italy was no exception. The country had been home to the Futurist Movement before the war, and this trend was followed in the early 1920s by the Novecento movement, which combined elements of European modernism with a neoclassical concern for order and balance.

From "Il Gruppo 7" (1927), trans. Ellen R. Shapiro, in *Oppositions* 6 (Fall 1976), p. 89.

By the middle of the decade, however, a generation of younger architects – who named themselves "Group 7" – began to align their efforts more specifically with the international movement. The leader of this group was the highly talented architect Giuseppe Terragni, whose design for the Novocomum apartment building in Como (1927–9) would become an icon for Italian modernism. Others originally involved with the group were Ubaldo Castagnoli, Luigi Figini, Guido Frette, Sebastiano Larco, Carlo Enrico Rava, and Gino Pollini. The leading theme of this four-part manifesto, the first part of which appeared in December 1926, was rationalism, inspired in particular by the work of Le Corbusier. The success of this group led to the founding of the "Italian Movement for Rationalist Architecture" (MIAR) in 1928, which became the national organization for the diffusion of modernism in Italy.

A "new spirit" has been born. It exists, we would like to say, in the air, like a thing by itself, independent of single individuals, in all countries, with different appearances and forms, but with the same foundation – a prodigious gift which not all art epochs or historical periods have possessed. We live, therefore, in privileged times since we can witness the birth of a whole new order of ideas. Proof that we are at the beginning of an epoch that will finally have its own well-defined character can be seen in the frequent repetition of the perfect correspondence of the various forms of art, and the influence that the one exercises upon the other – precisely those characteristics of periods in which a style was created.

All over Europe, such a characteristic is now well-known. The exchange of influences among Cocteau, Picasso, and Stravinsky is very evident in the way in which their works complement each other. In addition, the influence Cocteau had on the "Six" is well-known, as is his influence in general on the evolution of French music. What is striking, however, is the correspondence between Le Corbusier, who is without doubt one of the most noteworthy initiators of a rational architecture, and Cocteau. Le Corbusier writes his very clear-cut polemical books, talking about architecture in the style of Cocteau, and constructs his houses according to an identical ideal of rigid, clear, crystalline logic. Cocteau, in his turn, constructs his writings according to a completely architectonic scheme of conciseness and "Corbusian" simplicity. And also, note how a painting, say, by Juan Gris, is perfectly at home in a room by Le Corbusier – only in that kind of ambience can the new spirit appear in all its value.

In their turn, Germany and Austria offer a magnificent example of another type: the example of the refinement of art which a country can attain when the sense of a new architecture is understood by an entire nation, and dominates all decorative forms, so that all objects down to the most modest carry its imprint. From the monumental building to the cover of a book, Germany and Austria possess a *style*. This style, more solid in Germany, more refined and precious in Austria, has an absolute personality: it may please or displease, but *it asserts itself*. What is more, it has a distinct nationalistic character, and this should suffice, where there might not have existed other reasons, to show how wrong were those who believed they were renewing architecture by transplanting German styles, which are very noble ones to be sure, but which are out of place in this country.

In an analogous fashion, in Holland there is a blossoming of architectural forms composed of the most rigorous and constructive rationality, perfectly attuned to the country's climate and landscape. And so, each with its own characteristics, the Nordic countries Sweden and Finland also contribute to the "new spirit."

A group of famous European architects – Behrens, Mies van der Rohe, Mendelsohn, Gropius, Le Corbusier – create architecture tightly connected to the necessities of our time, and from these necessities extract a new aesthetic. Therefore there *exists*, particularly in architecture, a new spirit.

130   WALTER CURT BEHRENDT
from *The Victory of the New Style* (1927)

The years 1927–8 saw the first attempts to consolidate the direction of the Modern Movement and the decisive event for both Germany and Europe was the international housing exposition held in Stuttgart in the summer of 1927: the Weissenhof Siedlung. Altogether, sixteen architects built housing units on the hillside above the city; among the foreign architects represented were Le Corbusier, J. J. P. Oud, Josef Frank, Mart Stam, and Victor Bourgeois. Within Germany, the selection of architects was bitterly contested, as the project coordinator – Mies van der Rohe – limited his selections for the most part to the Berlin architects associated with the Ring. Thus the event in the end turned out to be the first winnowing process of what would become orthodox European modernism. And although the exhibition, collectively and individually, can scarcely be called a success from the viewpoint of design or construction, it was indisputably a victory for modernism in the popular press. Mies organized a massive publicity campaign internationally, and coinciding with the exhibition's opening was the publication of two books that attempted to place the event within the context of an international movement. In *The Victory of the New Style*, Walter Curt Behrendt speaks in glowing terms of the "the mighty drama of a sweeping transformation" now taking place, "the birth of the *form of our time*." History or hyperbole – the view was nonetheless widespread that something truly momentous was occurring.

New Realities

In order to approach the new style's formal problems – to discern them more clearly and grasp them more vividly – we must now inquire into the *new realities of our time* with which the *architect* today has to come to terms in his approach to design.

What are these realities?

The *first reality* is a series of new tools, new machines, and new methods of construction. To deny their existence would be self-delusion; to reject their use would be a waste of energy. Using mechanical means of production for the entire building industry (and not just for civil engineering, where it has long been adopted) is an economic necessity. The industrialization of the building industry will certainly find acceptance on an ever-larger

Walter Curt Behrendt, from *Das Sieg des neuen Baustils* (1927), trans. Harry Francis Mallgrave as *The Victory of the New Building Style*. Los Angeles, CA: Getty Program Publications, 2000, pp. 110, 114–15.

scale and at an accelerating pace, at least within the field of housing, which provides for the needs of the masses. Although trained artisans and specialists are essential to many commissions in the building trades, and especially cultural and luxury buildings, and although future building will remain also in large part a highly skilled and seasoned trade, trained personnel in many fields are nevertheless being replaced more and more by machines and industrial technologies.

Further realities are a number of new building materials, such as iron, concrete, and glass. Previously these materials were either altogether unknown or not used to the same extent or in the same way as today. With their adoption and use, however, they have fundamentally altered traditional building and construction practices.

With these new realities, architecture has been enriched *first of all materially* with a number of new possibilities. To mention just one of these achievements (perhaps not the most important in its nature but the most obvious in its effect), the scale of building today, thanks to the inventiveness of the engineer, far exceeds the limits formerly imposed on it, because of the new methods of iron and reinforced-concrete construction. In fact, every shackle in this regard has been undone. These new construction methods, whose influence has recently also become evident in expanded possibilities for wood construction, make it possible to span the greatest openings and create almost unlimited spaces with no internal supports.

In addition to this material enrichment, however, the adoption of new building materials and construction processes has *also* induced a *spiritual upheaval*. The introduction of these materials and processes has changed completely the basic principles of building – spatial ideas as well as structural concepts. This upheaval is no less far-reaching in its effects than the change of perspectives that took place in medieval building with the invention of the Gothic vault. As with that invention, the upheaval has raised a whole series of formal problems.

131 LUDWIG HILBERSEIMER
from *International New Architecture* (1927)

The second book to coincide with the opening of the Weissenhof exhibition was Ludwig Hilberseimer's *International New Architecture*. Hilberseimer during the 1920s had been active in Berlin circles and he too was a close friend of Mies. Although he was primarily interested in planning, he was selected by Mies to build a project for the event, for which he prepared a modest and relatively undistinguished design. His book differed from that of Behrendt in that it was an illustrative survey of international modernism through 110 photographs. They were prefaced with a short, descriptive manifesto, which succinctly articulates the perception of the time.

Ludwig Hilberseimer, from *Internationale Neue Baukunst*. Stuttgart: Julius Hoffmann, 1927, p. 5, trans. Harry Francis Mallgrave.

The premises and foundations of the new architecture are of the most varied kind. The specific utilitarian demands determine the functional character of the building. Material and construction are the material means of its make-up. In addition, production techniques and management, economic and sociological factors have a considerable influence. Yet above all the creative will of the architect stands preeminent. He determines the dimensions of the individual elements. Out of the contributing elements, he shapes the formal unity of the building.

The type of design process determines the character of the new architecture. It is not directed to superficial decorations, but to the spiritual permeation of all elements. The aesthetic element is therefore no longer superordinate, an end to itself, as with the building organism of previous facade architecture, but is, like all other elements, integrated into the whole. It only receives its value, its meaning, in conjunction with this whole.

A superordination of an element always has a disturbing consequence. Therefore the new architecture strives for a balance of all elements, a harmony. But this harmony is neither superficial nor schematic but something new for each task. No stylistic scheme lies within it; it is the specific expression of the present permeation of all elements under the dominance of a creative will. The new architecture therefore has no style problem, but a building problem.

Thus the surprising accord of the exterior appearance of the international new architecture becomes understandable. It is no fashionable occasion to create forms, as is often assumed, but an elementary expression of a new building sensibility. Although it is much differentiated by local and national particularities and by the personality of the designer, on the whole it is the product of similar premises. Therefore it has unity of appearance. Its spiritual bond transcends all limits.

132   LE CORBUSIER AND PIERRE JEANNERET
from "Five Points for a New Architecture" (1927)

Another legacy of the Weissenhof Siedlung was the publication of "Five Points for a New Architecture," published and signed jointly by Le Corbusier and his brother Pierre Jeanneret. The two partners were just perfecting their villa style in the designs for the Villa Stein-de-Monzie and for the two houses being built in Weissenhof. The points not only neatly summarized the gist of Le Corbusier's particular style, but they provided a succinct outline of the aesthetic implications of the new architecture for the larger European audience.

Le Corbusier and Pierre Jeanneret, from text originally published in *Bau und Wohnen*, Stuttgart: Fr. Wederkind & Co., 1927, pp. 27–8, trans. Michael Bullock, in *Programs and Manifestoes on 20th-Century Architecture*, ed. Elrich Conrads. Cambridge, MA: MIT Press, 1970, 99–100.

The theoretical considerations set out below are based on many years of practical experience on building sites.

Theory demands concise formulation.

The following points in no way relate to aesthetic fantasies or a striving for fashionable effects, but concern architectural facts that imply an entirely new kind of building, from the dwelling house to palatial edifices.

1. The supports. To solve a problem scientifically means in the first place to distinguish between its elements. Hence in the case of a building a distinction can immediately be made between the supporting and the non-supporting elements. The earlier foundations, on which the building rested without a mathematical check, are replaced by individual foundations and the walls by individual supports. Both supports and support foundations are precisely calculated according to the burdens they are called upon to carry. These supports are spaced out at specific, equal intervals, with no thought for the interior arrangement of the building. They rise directly from the floor to 3, 4, 6, etc. metres and elevate the ground floor. The rooms are thereby removed from the dampness of the soil; they have light and air; the building plot is left to the garden, which consequently passes under the house. The same area is also gained on the flat roof.

2. The roof gardens. The flat roof demands in the first place systematic utilization for domestic purposes: roof terrace, roof garden. On the other hand, the reinforced concrete demands protection against changing temperatures. Over-activity on the part of the reinforced concrete is prevented by the maintenance of a constant humidity on the roof concrete. The roof terrace satisfies both demands (a rain-dampened layer of sand covered with concrete slabs with lawns in the interstices; the earth of the flowerbeds in direct contact with the layer of sand). In this way the rain water will flow off extremely slowly. Waste pipes in the interior of the building. Thus a latent humidity will remain continually on the roof skin. The roof gardens will display highly luxuriant vegetation. Shrubs and even small trees up to 3 or 4 metres tall can be planted. In this way the roof garden will become the most favoured place in the building. In general, roof gardens mean to a city the recovery of all the built-up area.

3. The free designing of the ground-plan. The support system carries the intermediate ceilings and rises up to the roof. The interior walls may be placed wherever required, each floor being entirely independent of the rest. There are no longer any supporting walls but only membranes of any thickness required. The result of this is absolute freedom in designing the ground-plan; that is to say, free utilization of the available means, which makes it easy to offset the rather high cost of reinforced concrete construction.

4. The horizontal window. Together with the intermediate ceilings the supports form rectangular openings in the façade through which light and air enter copiously. The window extends from support to support and thus becomes a horizontal window. Stilted vertical windows consequently disappear, as do unpleasant mullions. In this way, rooms are equably lit from wall to wall. Experiments have shown that a room thus lit has an eight times stronger illumination than the same room lit by vertical windows with the same window area.

The whole history of architecture revolves exclusively around the wall apertures. Through use of the horizontal window reinforced concrete suddenly provides the possibility of maximum illumination.

5. Free design of the façade. By projecting the floor beyond the supporting pillars, like a balcony all round the building, the whole façade is extended beyond the supporting construction. It thereby loses its supportive quality and the windows may be extended to any length at will, without any direct relationship to the interior division. A window may just as well be 10 metres long for a dwelling house as 200 metres for a palatial building (our design for the League of Nations building in Geneva). The façade may thus be designed freely.

The five essential points set out above represent a fundamentally new aesthetic. Nothing is left to us of the architecture of past epochs, just as we can no longer derive any benefit from the literary and historical teaching given in schools.

133 CONGRÈS INTERNATIONAUX D'ARCHITECTURE MODERNE (CIAM)
"The Declaration of La Sarraz" (1928)

Still another outgrowth of the Weissenhof exhibition was the founding of the Congrès Internationaux d'Architecture Moderne, better known as CIAM. The exhibition over the course of the spring and summer had attracted many prominent European visitors, among them Hélène de Mandrot. In consulting with officials, she proposed the idea of an international congress of modern architects and put her castle at La Sarraz, Switzerland, at its disposal. Le Corbusier hesitated to accept, fearing a German dominance of the organization, yet when he was given the authority to draw up the program he consented. The first meeting of two dozen architects took place in June 1928. Interestingly, neither Mies van der Rohe nor Gropius attended. The majority of those present were Swiss, led by Mart Stam, Hans Schmidt, and Hannes Meyer – all with ties to Soviet Constructivism. The organization was run by Giedion, who was appointed secretary, and thus the true power initially lay with Le Corbusier himself. Urbanism became the central focus of the organization, and the three urban functions of dwelling, working, and recreation (suggesting a physical separation of the three) became the working program for organization. Also evident in the founding declaration is the demand for eliminating private ownership of land and CIAM's strong preference for multifamily housing.

First Congress/The Declaration of La Sarraz

The undersigned architects, representing national groups of modern architects, declare the unity of their views on the fundamental conceptions of architecture and on their professional obligations.

"The Declaration of La Sarraz" (1928), trans. Anthony Eardley, in *Le Corbusier: The Athens Charter*. New York: Grossman, 1973, pp. 6–8.

They lay particular stress on the fact that "to construct" is an elementary human activity, closely bound up with the evolution of life. The destiny of architecture is to give expression to the spirit of an age.

They declare today the need for a new conception of architecture, which will fulfill the material, sentimental, and spiritual demands of present-day life. Conscious of the profound disturbances brought about by machinism, they recognize that the transformation of the social structure and of the economic order inevitably entails a corresponding transformation of the architectural phenomenon itself.

They have joined together with the intention of seeking to harmonize the elements that confront them in the modern world and of setting architecture back on its true program, which is of an economic and sociological order, dedicated solely to the service of the human being. It is in this way that architecture will escape the sterilizing hold of the Academies.

Armed with this conviction, they declare their association for the realization of their aspirations.

The general economy

The equipping of a country demands a close liaison between architecture and the general economy.

The notion of "output," which has become an axiom of modern life, does not imply maximum commercial profit but a production sufficient to satisfy human needs fully.

Genuine output will be the fruit of rationalization and normalization, as flexibly applied to architectural projects as it is to methods of industrial production.

It is necessary that architecture, instead of calling almost exclusively upon the services of an anemic craftsman class, make equal use of the vast resources afforded by industrial engineering, even though such a resolve would lead to achievements quite different from those that were the glory of ages past.

Urbanism

Urbanism is the disposition of different premises and places to shelter the development of material, sentimental, and spiritual life in all of its individual and collective manifestations. It embraces both urban aggregations and rural groupings.

Urbanism can no longer submit exclusively to the rules of a gratuitous aestheticism. It is functional by its very nature.

The three primary functions that urbanism must fulfill are:

1) dwelling;
2) working;
3) recreation.

Urbanism is concerned with:

a) the occupation of the ground;
b) the organization of traffic;
c) legislation.

The three primary functions indicated above are not favored by the conditions now prevailing in the urban aggregation. The relationships between the different locations assigned to them must be recalculated in order to achieve a just proportion of built volumes and open spaces. Problems of traffic and density must be considered.

The ill-regulated parceling out of the ground into small lots, the result of sub-division, sales, and speculation, must be superseded by an economy that will regroup real-estate holdings.

This regrouping, the basis of any urbanism capable of responding to present needs, will assure both the land holders and the community of the equitable distribution of increased values arising out of works in the common interest.

Architecture and public opinion

It is essential that the architects exert an influence on public opinion and bring the means and the resources of the new architecture to its attention. Academic teaching has perverted public taste and more often than not the authentic problems of habitation are not even raised.

Public opinion is ill-informed, and in the matter of the dwelling the users generally formulate their desires very poorly. Consequently, the dwelling has long been left out of the major preoccupations of the architect.

A handful of elementary truths taught in primary school could establish the core for an education in domestic science. This instruction would have the effect of giving new generations a sane conception of the dwelling. These generations, the future clients of the architect, would be in a position to direct him to the solution of the too-long-neglected problem of housing.

Architecture and the state

The architects here present, having a firm determination to work in the true interests of modern society, believe that, by disregarding the problem of the dwelling in favor of a purely prestigious architecture, the Academies, conservators of the past, impede social progress.

Through their control of teaching, they corrupt the calling of the architect from the outset and, by having nearly exclusive rights to government commissions, they prevent the penetration of the new spirit which alone could enliven and renew the art of building.

La Sarraz, 28 June 1928

134 SIGFRIED GIEDION
from *Building in France, Building in Iron, Building in Ferro-Concrete* (1928)

The apocalyptic tone of the first histories of modern architecture – suggested in the studies of Gropius, Behne, and Behrendt – achieves its first great climax with Sigfried Giedion's classic book. Giedion was born in Prague of Swiss citizens and educated in Vienna (where he studied engineering) and Munich (where he took his doctorate under Heinrich Wölfflin). Although his dissertation was on Baroque architecture, he was soon attracted to modernist literary circles. Upon meeting Walter Gropius at the Bauhaus exhibition of 1923, he shifted his critical interests to architecture and shortly thereafter set out to write a book on the new movement. In 1925 he met Le Corbusier in Paris and he decided to focus solely on this country's contribution to modernism – writing what was essentially a hagiography of Le Corbusier. The book, on every level, is a propagandistic *tour de force*. Built around many of Giedion's own photographs of such works as the Eiffel Tower, and laid out topographically by László Moholy-Nagy, Giedion provides a terse summary analysis of the modern phenomenon for the "hurried reader." The novel theme is that architecture more or less ceased to exist around 1830 and that all of the preparatory work for the new movement was carried out by nineteenth-century French engineers. In such an analysis, traditional historical studies no longer have relevance and they are even to be disdained; the task of the historian is simply "to extract from the vast complexity of the past those elements that will be the point of departure for the future." The new age of the "constructor" (the architect is no more) is thus driven by an imperious *Zeitgeist*, or spirit of the time, that governs all creations. This short passage on the meaning of the new architecture is indicative of Giedion's scriptural tone.

Architecture has been drawn into the current from the isolated position it had shared with painting and sculpture.

We are beginning to transform the surface of the earth. We thrust beneath, above, and over the surface. Architecture is only a part of this process, even if a special one. Hence there is no "style," no proper building style. Collective design. A fluid transition of things.

By their design, all buildings today are as open as possible. They blur their arbitrary boundaries. Seek connection and interpenetration.

In the air-flooded stairs of the Eiffel Tower, better yet, in the steel limbs of a *pont transbordeur*, we confront the basic aesthetic experience of today's building: through the delicate iron net suspended in midair stream things, ships, sea, houses, masts, landscape, and harbor. They lose their delimited form: as one descends, they circle into each other and intermingle simultaneously.

One would not wish to carry over into housing this absolute experience that no previous age has known. Yet it remains embryonic in each design of the new architecture: there

Sigfried Giedion, from *Bauen in Frankreich, Bauen in Eisen, Bauen in Eisenbeton* (1928), trans. J. Duncan Berry as *Building in France, Building in Iron, Building in Ferro-Concrete*. Santa Monica, CA: Getty Publication Programs, 1995, pp. 91, 93.

is only a great, indivisible space in which relations and interpenetrations, rather than boundaries, reign.

The concept of architecture has become too narrow. One can no longer contain, like radium in a bottle, the need to create that which is called art and explain what remains of life devoid of it.

The ponderous movement of human affairs has as its consequence that the new attitude toward life manifests itself much sooner in the objective fields – such as construction, industry – than in those fields that lie close to us.

Only now is the housing form being seized by those hidden forces that a century ago drove man to the constructional and industrial attitude.

Our inner attitude today demands of the house:

Greatest possible overcoming of gravity. Light proportions. Openness, free flow of air: things that were first indicated in an abstract way by the constructional designs of the past century.

Thus, the point is reached where building falls in line with the general life process.

135 ERNST MAY
from "Housing Policy of Frankfort on the Main" (1929)

When the Weissenhof exhibition took place in 1927, the most prominent German architect involved with housing issues – Ernst May – was not invited to participate. May was a student of Theodor Fisher and he had worked on the garden-city concept in London under Raymond Unwin. In 1918 he joined the Silesian building department in Breslau, where he first experimented with methods of prefabrication in multi-family housing, and he brought this experience with him to Frankfurt in 1925, where he became director of planning. May designed several housing estates around Frankfurt and his concepts of standardization and prefabrication revolutionized modern housing. He approached the housing problem with the spirit of Frederick Winslow Taylor by seeking a maximum efficiency of minimal spaces through careful design and the use of built-in elements. For instance, the so-called Frankfurt Kitchen, designed with his colleague Margarete Lihotzky, became famous as a model of efficiency with its built-in cupboards and ironing board. May also favored low-rise townhouses with gardens and communal green spaces, and it was this model of housing that he proposed to CIAM in 1929 at the second CIAM conference in Frankfurt.

Dwellings are articles made in the mass. To supply them in good quality and cheaply one must adopt the methods invariably followed by industry when producing goods for mass consumption. No man would think of ordering a bicycle, a watch or similar things after his own design; everybody is satisfied to choose between the types extant.

Ernst May, from "Housing Policy of Frankfort on the Main" (1928), published trilingually in the *International Housing Association* 2 (1929).

Why should not a similar principle be followed when the problem is how to provide with homes thousands of people having approximately identical wants and incomes and needing two or three rooms, kitchen and appurtenances? Would it not just be wasting the national fortune to act differently, to draw up plans for every small habitation, to make separate calculations for quantities, to buy the material according to the separate estimates and to carry out separate architectural plans for each individual case?

If we look back on the manner in which, since the beginning of the nineteenth century, building has been carried on all the world over, we shall find that in all parts of the globe people used to have certain types of structure for dwellings of a certain kind, types repeated a thousandfold with slight changes i.e. with the variations as to construction and material, due to local usages and custom. Is it not strange that no objection to this was taken in former times and that opposition came forward in our age of rationalization only? The same people who in their workshop or factory are striving after the elimination of the slightest change of idle running, with a view to obtaining a maximum of output with a minimum of effort, think they cannot follow that economic principle in the field of housing, because individuality might be suppressed thereby.

Well, we in Frankfort opine that our age has no longer time for such romantic views and that moreover those apprehensions are not founded: because, just as hundreds of different people are walking about in similar dress, just so the family life in every house, even though it be one of a type, will remain individually different. We hold that the collective element, which is so strong in the life of modern mankind, in work, sport and politics, must logically be reflected also in the houses. Even from an aesthetic point of view however we do not foresee desolation as a result of typification, but rather a quieting down of city architecture, a thing which, after we have passed through a century in which architecture showed strong traits of restlessness, even chaos, must lie at the root of the recovery of architectural art in our cities.

The leading idea guiding the modern town planner when mapping out the General Housing Scheme must also inspire him when shaping the type of dwelling. The ground plan must be made in a manner enabling the inmates to do their work with a minimum of effort, the intention being that they may find the time for things of greater importance: for instance the keeping fit of the body and the spirit and the education of the children.

136 WALTER GROPIUS
from "The Sociological Foundations of the Minimum Dwelling" (1929)

The second CIAM conference held in Frankfurt in the fall of 1929 was organized as a showcase for the work of Ernst May and his team of municipal architects. One hundred and thirty architects from eighteen countries met to study these planning models; only Le Corbusier, who was on his South-American tour, was absent. The conference was notable in two respects: first the proposal of *Existenzminimum* (minimal housing square-footage) for housing; second the debate between May and Walter Gropius over low-rise versus high-rise solutions. Both are addressed in this paper of Gropius, read at the conference by Sigfried Giedion. Gropius's reasoning is fascinating. Citing recent sociological research, he divides human culture into the four stages of tribal law, family law, individual law, and future communal law. He goes on to cite decreasing birth rates in the industrialized West, increasing divorce and illegitimate birth rates, and the general emancipation of women through their entry into the workplace as evidence that society is now passing into the fourth cultural stage – a point at which the idea of a single-family house will become fully outmoded. His solution is the high-rise rental apartment, which allows the modern urban occupant mobility, a minimum of domestic upkeep, and indeed anonymity within the city. May forcefully opposed this high-rise conception and he eventually deleted Gropius's speech from the official congress proceedings. Gropius, however, had the powerful support of Le Corbusier, who had long argued for a similar high-rise solution for the city. The debate, for now at least, was moot. The congress was held at the moment the American stock market had crashed, creating an economic downturn that would soon halt all building activity. Within a year the Marxist May would lead a "red brigade" of sixteen architects to live in Stalin's Soviet Union. Gropius would remain in Germany, but only for another four years.

The problem of the minimum dwelling is that of establishing the elementary minimum of space, air, light and heat required by man in order that he be able to fully develop his life functions without experiencing restrictions due to his dwelling, i.e., a minimum *modus vivendi* in place of a *modus non moriendi*. The actual minimum varies according to local conditions of city and country, landscape and climate; a given quantity of air space in the dwelling has different meanings in a narrow city street and in a sparsely settled suburb. Von Drigalski, Paul Vogler and other hygienists observe that, given good conditions of ventilation and sunlight, man's requirements of living space from the biological viewpoint are very small, particularly if the space is correctly organized for efficiency; a graphic picture of the superiority of a small modern apartment over an obsolete one is provided by the comparison offered by a well-known architect between an ingeniously arranged wardrobe trunk and a crate.

However, if the provision of light, sun, air and warmth is culturally more important and, with normal land prices, more economical than an increase in space, then the rules dictate:

Walter Gropius, from "The Sociological Foundations of the Minimum Dwelling" (1929), in Walter Gropius, *Scope of Total Architecture*. New York: Collier Books, 1962, pp. 98–100.

enlarge the windows, reduce the size of rooms, economize on food rather than heat. Just as it was formerly customary to overestimate the value of food calories in comparison with that of vitamins, many people nowadays erroneously regard larger rooms and larger apartments as the desirable aim in dwelling design.

To allow for the increasing development of more pronounced individuality of life within the society and the individual's justified demand for occasional withdrawal from his surroundings, it is necessary, moreover, to establish the following ideal minimum requirement: *every adult shall have his own room, small though it may be!* The basic dwelling implied by these fundamental requirements would then represent the practical minimum which fulfills its purpose and intentions: the standard dwelling.

The same biological considerations which determine the size of the minimum dwelling are also determinative in regard to its grouping and incorporation into the city plan. *Maximum light, sun and air for all dwellings!* In view of differences in the quality of the air and the intensity of the light, an attempt must be made to establish a numerically defined lower limit, on the basis of which the required amount of light and air can be calculated for given local conditions. General quantitative regulations which fail to allow for differences, as they exist at present, are useless in many cases. To be sure, it is the basic aim of all urban building codes to ensure light and air for dwellings. Every new building code has surpassed its predecessor in striving to decrease the population density and thereby to improve conditions of light and air. However, all means employed thus far for decreasing population density are based on the concept of the permanent, close-knit family. The only ideal solution was thought to be the single detached dwelling, the one-family house with garden, and on the basis of this aim the excessive population density of cities was combatted by limiting building height. However, this aim is no longer adequate today, as sociology shows, because it satisfies only a portion of the public needs, but not the needs of the industrial population, which is the primary object of our investigations. The internal structure of the industrial family makes it turn from the one-family house toward the multistory apartment house, and finally toward the centralized master household. The healthy tendency to progressively decrease the population density in cities is in no way endangered by this new form of dwelling, since the population density of a zone can be controlled without limiting the building height by merely establishing a quantitative ratio of dwelling area or building volume to building lot area. This would pave the way for a vertical development of the multistory apartment building. Whereas the detached one-family house is more suited to the needs of other, wealthier population classes which are not under consideration at present, the large apartment building satisfies more nearly the sociological requirements of present-day industrial populations with their symptomatic liberation of the individual and early separation of the children from the family. In addition, the large high-rise apartment building offers considerable cultural advantages as compared to the walk-up apartment house with a small number of floors.

137   SIGFRIED GIEDION
from *Liberated Living* (1929)

Encouraged by the success of the CIAM congress in Frankfurt, Sigfried Giedion followed up with his primer on housing, *Befreites Wohnen* (Liberated Living). The book's cover displays a modern couple enjoying the fresh air of their sunny terrace, and among the book's fascinating images are those of sanitarium patients on a balcony of a modern hospital, a female tennis player in shorts, and sun-bathers in a Zurich park — all happy signs of modernity. Hence Giedion became one of the first Europeans to sell modernity not as an architectural style, but as a complete change of life style: the ultimate liberation of the industrial age. Only the work of Rudolf Schindler and Richard Neutra in California preceded him in this regard.

Guiding Principles
   Today's View:
1. With regard to **economics:**
The house has a functional value. It should be written off and amortized in a measurable time. A perspicacious Italian architect (Sant'Elia), killed in the World War, already in 1914 advanced the formula: "Every generation its house!"

2. With regard to **production:**
In accord with other ways of production, the house is to be constructed **on an industrial basis**. That is, less expensive and more practical when the industrialist, owner, lender, architect will have completed the transformation. Experience teaches that prices decline and quality rises with more rational, more industrial production, even for complex products (e.g. autos). The advantage goes to the **consumer: reduction of rent**, except that with the transformation the whole national economy would shortly benefit. This is also the only way, without a subsidy, to create housing for everyone with minimum standards for living.

3. With regard to **expression:**
Today we need a house that in its whole structure is in accord with our bodily feeling and way of life, liberated by sports and gymnastics: **light, transparent, flexible**. It is only logical that this o p e n e d house is also a reflection of today's spiritual condition. There are no more isolated concerns. Things interpenetrate.

4. With regard to **economy:**
People dictate the economy. Therefore the conditions of the minimum living space are objectively set and the economy must find the means and ways to keep pace with these demands. Humans are more important than production.

Sigfried Giedion, from *Befreites Wohnen*. Zurich: M. E. Häfeli, 1929, p. 7, trans. Harry Francis Mallgrave.

138 LÁSZLÓ MOHOLY-NAGY
from *From Material to Architecture*
(1929)

A native of Hungary, the painter László Moholy-Nagy moved to Berlin in 1919, where he, together with Raoul Hausmann, Hans Arp, and Ivan Puni, defined an "Elementarist Art" in sympathy with constructivist ideals. He was thus eager to join forces with Theo van Doesburg and El Lissitzky, when the two men arrived in Berlin in 1921. Out of these contacts came the position to teach the Preliminary Course at the Bauhaus, when Johannes Itten departed in 1923 (Gropius wanted someone with constructivist credentials). Moholy-Nagy spelled out the principles of this design course in this book, published by the Bauhaus in 1929. Here, following van Doesburg, is one of the first efforts to speak of architecture as the creation of space – that is, since the work of Germanic theorists of the late-nineteenth century.

In addition to the fulfillment of elementary physical requirements, man should have opportunity in his dwelling to experience the fact of space. The dwelling should not be a retreat from space, but a life in space, in full relationship with it. This means that a dwelling should be decided upon not only on the basis of price and the time it takes to build, not only upon practical considerations of its suitability for use, its material, construction, and economy. The experience of space belongs in the list too, as essential to the physical comfort of the people who are to live in the house.

This requirement is not to be taken as a vague phrase or a mystical approach to the subject; it will not be long before it is generally recognized as a necessary element in the architectonic conception, and one capable of being exactly circumscribed. That is, architecture will be understood, not as a complex of inner spaces, not merely as a shelter from the cold and from danger, nor as a fixed enclosure, as an unalterable arrangement of rooms, but as an organic component in living as a governable creation for mastery of life.

The new architecture on its highest plane will be called upon to remove the old conflict between organic and artificial, between open and closed, between country and city. We are accustomed to neglecting questions of architectonic creation because the emphasis is upon the house as a shelter. The future conception of architecture must consider and realize beyond the single unit the group, the town, the district, the country, in other words, the whole. Individuals who are a part of a rational biological whole should find in their home not only relaxation and recuperation, but also a heightening and harmonious development of their powers. The paths to this end may be of many kinds, but some day we will surely arrive at this elementary requirement of created space. The standard for architects will then no longer be the specific needs in the dwellings of the individual, or of a profession, of a certain economic class, but it will revolve around the general basis, that of the biologically evolved manner of living which man requires. After this general foundation is established, if there are justified individual needs, variations may be introduced.

László Moholy-Nagy, from *Von Material zu Architektur*. Dessau: Bauhaus, 1929, trans. Daphne M. Hoffmann as *The New Vision: From Material to Architecture*. New York: Brewer, Warren & Putnam, 1932, pp. 159–60.

Young people are today conducting investigations of the biological bases and requirements in different fields of life. The revolutionary theses of their researches seem to be generally productive of results which are mutually related.

Efforts toward a new spatial conception and creation should therefore – important as they are – be understood only as a component part in this new orientation. The most primary sources of space experience are even today submerged under technicalities, a state of affairs which prevents the emergence of the future architecture, the creation of a new life space for men.

Architecture will be brought to its fullest realization only when the deepest knowledge of human life as a total phenomenon in the biological whole is available. One of its most important components is the ordering of man in space, making space comprehensible, and taking architecture as arrangement of universal space.

The root of architecture lies in the mastery of the problem of space, the practical development lies in the problem of construction.

139 ERICH MENDELSOHN
from *Russia, Europe, America:*
An Architectural Cross-Section (1929)

From his design for the Einstein Tower in 1918 to his various department stores for the Schocken Company in the 1920s – Erich Mendelsohn was one of the busiest and arguably one of the best designers in Germany. He was also well traveled, well versed in international developments, and highly reflective on the architectural issues of the day. His book *Russland, Europa, Amerika* – an illustrative book with aphoristic reflections interspersed throughout – is a case in point. His curiosity led him to travel to Russia and the United States, and he was especially intrigued by developments abroad when compared with those at home. America he saw as a wild and exploitative nation, but also one "becoming profound" in its search for a future architecture. Russia was mystical and fantastic, but also a social laboratory for a "new order." Among current trends, Mendelsohn was as skeptical of the paper architecture of the Constructivists as he was of the aesthetic formalism of Le Corbusier – positions that found him few allies. But as these few remarks on Europe demonstrate, he was entirely perspicacious in reading the spiritual ennui of Europe, the "dynamite" of its fragile political stability. As a Jew, Mendelsohn was also one of the first German architects to experience the explosion firsthand. Adrift in exile in the 1930s, he lived in England and Palestine before eventually settling in the United States.

But this is Europe!

Her task is to create the balance between the two great continents, the poles of today's world consideration.

This task is of decisive significance for Europe.

Erich Mendelsohn, from *Russia, Europe, America: An Architectural Cross-Section* (1929), cited from the reprint. Basel: Birkhäuser, 1989, p. 170.

Because Europe, poor, sick from the after effects of war, full of economic and political contrasts and consequently full of social fermentation, will gain further world respect only if she rediscovers her own true foundations.

The advantage of America's wealth and power cannot be overridden, nor can Europe match Russia's revolution – her spiritual tension is too lax, her climate too temperate, and a United Europe too far away.

But for ages Europe has been the continent of reason and genius, of science and invention.

Thus she concentrates on herself and on the constitutional foundations of the entire world picture and on every law erected by human beings.

Thus we must decide whether we want to exchange the dynamite of our political quarrels with the conscience of a European solidarity – the spiritlessness of our own selfish emotion, or the all embracing technical spirit of a new world.

But the danger arises out of Europe's own characteristics.

140   KAREL TEIGE
from *Modern Architecture in Czechoslovakia* (1930)

What was often overlooked in twentieth-century histories of modernism was its popularity in such central European countries as Hungary, Poland, and Czechoslovakia. The last country in fact had been a leading center of architectural experimentation, beginning with the work of Jan Kotěra, Josef Gočár, Vlastislav Hofman, and Josef Chochol in the first years of the century. In the 1920s another talented group of designers stepped to the fore, among them Oldřich Tyl, Jamomír Krejcar, Bohuslav Fuchs, Jasoslav Frager, Evžen Linhardt, Josef Hanlček, and Karel Honzik. The housing development for the "International Exhibition of Contemporary Culture," held in Brno in 1928, followed directly on the heels of Weissenhof and in many respects outstripped its predecessor with the quality of its designs. The principal chronicler of these events was Karel Teige – a poet, art historian, and critic. With his political eye turned toward Russia, Teige viewed himself as a Constructivist and he was adamant in his belief that modernism could only thrive in a socialist or Marxist society. Hence Europe (and Czechoslovakia) awaited its final revolution for the transformation to be complete. The irony of his position was that when this country did have its Soviet-style revolution in 1948, Teige found himself persecuted by the communists and died, still young, after several years of unemployment.

Modern creators – that is, those who can be truly considered modern: namely, the constructivists, who support their views and theories with Marxist sociology and a socialist worldview – naturally feel oppressed by the present social and historical situation. Their task is not improvement, but renewal: a revolution. The class struggle forces them to adopt a clear stance. They cannot sacrifice their own creation to the interests and needs of a moribund

Karel Teige, from *Moderní architektura v Československu* (1930), trans. Irena Žantovská Murray and David Britt as *Modern Architecture in Czechoslovakia and Other Writings.* Los Angeles, CA: Getty Publication Programs, 2000, pp. 297–8.

world order. Those who fight to create a new architecture, the liberated architecture of free men, expect as a precondition of creation a new organization of society – a society that does not acknowledge private property, family, or nation. And yet, expectation alone is not a revolutionary strategy. Society has to be readied. It is therefore necessary to *revolutionize architecture* and architectural work, even if only on a theoretical and hypothetical basis; it is necessary to collaborate on a new organization of the world. Architecture is above all an organizational process.

Constructivists cannot be satisfied with commissions limited by existing transient circumstances. They do not want to wait and to guess but to outline and to prepare a new order of life and work. They do not want to wait to present a higher, more evolved style of work or life. If they emphasize integral usefulness as a principle of all creativity, they have no intention of submitting to deteriorating conventions. Most often these are only petrified nonsense, exemplified in today's housing and the patterns of family life. We must remove old, useless conventions, abolish obsolete building codes, preserved habits, and official decrees. What is needed is some respect for logical needs rather than for old fictions and superstitions.

Constructivism does not wish to serve the extant social and cultural state, a state corroded by decadence and anarchy. Through planning and tenacity of purpose constructivism wants to change the status quo. To revolutionize it, not to accept it in resignation.

In one of his programmatic articles, J. J. P. Oud distinguishes "modern architecture" from "new architecture." *Modern* architecture, according to Oud, is that which gradually elaborated the present architectural conception and which slowly freed itself from historicism, formalism, and decorativism; in other words, the architecture of the era inaugurated by Berlage and Wagner and chronologically concluded by the world war. By contrast, *new* architecture is architecture founded on the achievements of the earlier era. It is the international rationalist architecture represented by Le Corbusier, Gropius, Mies van der Rohe, and Oud himself. If we are to follow the sociological aspects of contemporary architecture, it seems appropriate to employ this distinction between "modern architecture" and "new architecture" but in a different way. If we designate the architecture of industrial capitalism from Eiffel or Wagner to Le Corbusier as "modern" then we shall use the term *"new" for that architecture that incorporates a socialist viewpoint and that is engaged in eradicating the old society and in launching the new.*

PART IV   THE POLITICS OF MODERNISM:
1930–45

A. TOTALITARIANISM IN EUROPE

Introduction

The 1930s witnessed the collapse of modernism in Germany, as the unstable government drifted from the Great Depression into World War II. But the dynamics of the picture are nevertheless more complex than they might first appear. Germany, since World War I, had been a country sharply divided along political lines, with a coalition of socialists in control; they were, however, continually challenged and sometimes defeated in local elections by a (numerically) almost equal coalition of conservative parties. Beyond these two blocs lay also two further extremes on the left and right, each awaiting its desired revolution. Compounding this bitter political division was the fact that most architectural jobs were state appointments. Hence, politics had much to say about who achieved positions of power or authority, and this is why German modernism generally came to be associated with the political left. Nearly all architectural appointments went to architects of this political persuasion.

The most evident mixing of architecture and politics in Germany was the Bauhaus. When Walter Gropius was appointed as director of the school in 1919 he was at the height of his political radicalism, and the school in its early years openly came to celebrate its politics as a "Cathedral of Socialism." Gropius, of course, met resistance from the conservative Turginian state in which Weimar was located, and he eventually attempted to play down the connection. Yet his tactfulness came too late, and when Turginian elections in 1924 ushered in a rightist coalition, the school was shut down. Gropius, in turn, moved the school to Dessau at the invitation of the socialist mayor there, and the institution thrived for another four years. Yet when Gropius left his post in 1928 he was replaced by Hannes Meyer, who sought to impose his Soviet-inspired politics on the institution – at a time when political tensions everywhere were heightening. The growing power of the National Socialists (a rightist party) eventually forced the resignation of Meyer and in 1930 Mies van der Rohe was brought in to rid the school of its politics, which he promptly did. The city of Dessau, like Weimar, nevertheless closed the school in 1932, and Mies moved the institution to Berlin, but here again he fought a losing battle against the National Socialists to keep the school alive.

In response to the dire economic situation of the early 1930s, the German national elections of 1933 shifted the lines of political power and the compromise leader to emerge was Adolf Hitler, who effectively carried out a *coup d'état* and achieved supreme power. The gruesome history of his Nazi rule unfolded little by little. His persecution of the Jews began at once, as did his military posturing and war planning. He reoccupied the Rhineland in 1936, assimilated Austria and Czechoslovakia in 1938, attacked Poland in 1939, and France, Great Britain, Denmark, Norway, Belgium, and Holland in 1940. In 1941 he invaded Soviet Russia and followed this disastrous decision by accepting war with the United States. Although he himself at one time wanted to be an architect, Hitler, even before his military campaigns, had succeeded in destroying all remnants of German architectural life. By the end of the 1930s nearly every major German architect had left the country for political exile: some went to the Soviet Union, many more to Britain and the United States.

The situation in other parts of Europe was scarcely better. In the late 1920s Joseph Stalin would take control of communist Russia, and his labor camps would ultimately prove to be at least as destructive in terms of human life as those of Hitler. Stalin also ended the constructivist movement – virtually by proclamation in 1932 – and imposed an anachronistic neoclassicism in its place. By contrast, the architectural situation in the other major Fascist state in Europe – Italy – was more open. Benito Mussolini came to power in 1922 and in his early years his rule was generally benign. Modern architects competed for state commissions, and in such cases as the Fascist Headquarters in Como (1932–6), modernists even produced major monuments. This situation would shortly change with Mussolini's military pact with Germany in 1936, one that would lead this country down the path of destruction.

If there was one architectural bright spot in Europe in the 1930s, it was Great Britain, which embraced modernism belatedly but quite enthusiastically. The new movement was aided by a flood of German refugees, but also by an acceptance of the new style and technologies by British architects. This acceptance would lead to their assumption of the European leadership of modernism in the immediate postwar years.

141 GERMAN BESTELMEYER ET AL.
manifesto for "Der Block" (1928)

Even when politics was not central to architectural decisions in Germany in the 1920s, it was not far below the surface. The Weissenhof Exhibition of 1927 is an excellent case in point. It was conceived in 1925 by Gustaf Stotz, the regional director of the Württemberg branch of the German Werkbund (Württemberg being the state in which Stuttgart is located). Stutz was a progressive and he wanted to host a major event to showcase modern architecture. At the same time he wanted the participation of local architects, as the city of Stuttgart was largely footing the costs of the event. After deliberations within the national Werkbund, Mies van der Rohe was appointed the director of the event, in large part because of his experience with architectural exhibitions. Mies's conception of the exhibition, as it soon unfolded, was quite different from that of Stotz. Mies wanted to display the work of international and German architects, but only those he deemed to be sufficiently pure in their modernism. In short, he wanted to draw his architects almost exclusively from the Ring, a Berlin faction of the German Werkbund – all close friends of Mies. Thus a bitter struggle ensued over the next two years as Mies fought to exclude Württemberg architects from the event and bring in Berlin architects. Two of the ousted Württemberg modernists – Paul Bonatz and Paul Schmitthenner – deeply resented Mies's heavy-handedness. Bonatz, who studied under Theodor Fischer, had designed the Tübingen library (1909–12) and Stuttgart railway station (1913–28), two of the earliest modern buildings in Germany. Schmitthenner, a housing specialist, was principally known for his design of the Staaken housing estate in Berlin, a garden city that was based in part on Hellerau. As a result of their rejections, Bonatz and Schmitthenner joined with Paul Schultze-Naumburg and German Bestelmeyer, among others, in forming the group *Der Block* (The Block). In their quite moderate agenda of 1928, they profess a version of modernism harking back to the realist and *Sachlichkeit* movements of the turn of the century, that is, a regional modernism taking account of inherited traditions, local characteristics, and new building materials. Thus we have here a clear split between the left and right wings of German modernism, a split that would quickly grow more serious.

The Block has brought together a number of German architects who feel united in their cultural understanding and who also seek expression in their works.

They believe that a unique expression must be found for the architectural tasks of our time, one that therefore takes into account both the individual wishes of the people and the characteristics of the landscape. They attentively take note of all of the suggestions and possibilities that are found in the new materials and forms, yet they do not wish to dispense with inherited traditions or what has already been achieved.

They reject all hasty attempts to publicize fashionable results, which must threaten a healthy development of form.

[German] Bestelmeyer, [Erich] Blunck, Bonatz, [Albert] Gessner, Schmitthenner, Schultze-Naumburg, [Franz] Seeck, [Heinz] Stoffregen

German Bestelmeyer et al., manifesto for "Der Block" (1928), trans. Harry Francis Mallgrave, in Anna Teut, *Architektur im Dritten Reich*. Frankfurt, 1967, p. 29.

142   HANNES MEYER

from "An Open Letter to Lord Mayor Hesse of Dessau" (1930)

With the advent of the Great Depression, the political divide in Germany escalated into a fierce internal conflict, and one of the victims of the antagonism would be the Bauhaus. The school, having relocated to Dessau in 1924, thrived for several years. Walter Gropius, now armed with a Bauhaus Press to spread its gospel, became an international celebrity, and in 1927 decided to add an architectural program to the school, choosing the Swiss architect Hannes Meyer to lead it. The latter, influenced by the De Stijl and constructivist movements, had only embraced modernism in the mid-1920s, but he had quickly distinguished himself with futuristic designs for several competitions, including the League of Nations in 1927. And when Gropius decided to step down as the Bauhaus director early in 1928, Meyer assumed the leadership of the school. The appointment promptly became problematic. Several key members of the Bauhaus faculty left with Gropius, and those that remained behind soon united in opposition to Meyer, who insisted that functionalist architecture was simply "pure construction" without aesthetic dimension. Worse still, Meyer allowed the school once again to become politicized with "red brigades" of communist students – just as extremists on the right were gaining the ascendancy. Thus in the summer of 1930 the socialist mayor of Dessau, hoping to save the school, dismissed Meyer, who wrote this angry "open letter" in response. The letter points to the evident hypocrisy among city officials, but it also is not entirely forthcoming on Meyer's part. The Swiss architect soon thereafter led a "red brigade" of seven former Bauhaus students to the Soviet Union to work for Joseph Stalin.

On my return from the opening of the Zurich Bauhaus exhibition which was on tour there, I came to see you on July 29, 1930. There was great excitement in Dessau. The 90 workers' flats of the city housing estate at Dessau-Törten, the first collectively designed commission our architecture department had received, were ready for occupation. Thousands of people visited them. There was unreserved approval in the entire press. A two-and-one-half room flat with kitchen, bathroom, and utilities for RM 37.50 rent a month! At last an achievement in keeping with the role of the new Bauhaus. Although the work was under my guidance, it was independently implemented by a group of young students. I entered your office with a feeling of relief. With a brief reference to the investigation of conditions at the Bauhaus which the government of Anhalt, due to the false report mentioned before, had required of the magistracy, you demanded my immediate resignation. Reason: my alleged introduction of politics into the Institute. A Marxist (you said) could never be Director of the Bauhaus. Cause: my voluntary and private contribution to the relief work of the "International Workers' Relief" to aid the distressed families of striking miners in the Mansfeld area. My repeated assurances that I had never been a member of any political party remained futile. Also futile was my explanation that a "Local Chapter Bauhaus Dessau" of the Communist Party was an absurdity from the party-organization point of

Hannes Meyer, from "An Open Letter to Lord Mayor Hesse of Dessau," trans. Wolfgang Jabs and Basil Gilbert, in Hans M. Wingler, *The Bauhaus: Weimar, Dessau, Berlin, Chicago*. Cambridge. MA: MIT Press, 1986, p. 165.

view, and again futile my assurances that my activities had always been concerned with cultural policies and never with party politics. You cut me short and interpreted my nervous smile as approval.

Thus I was stabbed in the back. Just when the Bauhaus was closed for the vacation and all my Bauhaus intimates were far away. The Bauhaus camarilla rejoiced. The local Dessau press fell into a moral delirium. The Bauhaus vulture Gropius swooped down from the Eiffel Tower and pecked at my directorial corpse, while, at the Adriatic, V. Kandinsky stretched out on the sand with relief: it was all over.

Herr Oberbürgermeister! Zoological gardens, museums, and race courses are expressions of the municipal urge to assert itself. Next to the ''Wörlitz'' and ''Junkers'' plants Dessau has acquired a ''Bauhaus.'' Instead of keeping exotic animals, the city keeps those odd people which the world has come to revere as great artists. It is my deepest conviction that art cannot be taught. The clover-field of young Bauhaus artists, cultivated by the most extraordinary painter individualist, will lie fallow in our period of greatest social transformation and collective need. Moreover, it is a crime to offer young people, who have to be designers in the society of tomorrow, the stale feed of yesterday's art theories as provisions on their way. This is the heart of the matter. You flirt with your ''culturally bolshevistic'' Institute, yet simultaneously you forbid its members to be Marxists. For the camarilla hidden behind you, the Bauhaus is an object of political megalomania and professorial vanity and an esthetic amusement park. For us in the Bauhaus it is a place for creating new forms of life. Local politics require of you to present great Bauhaus achievements, a radiant Bauhaus façade, and a presentable Bauhaus Director. We in the Bauhaus increasingly contend ourselves with the anonymity of our collective work. The advancing proletarianization of the Institute seemed to us to be in accordance with our times, and the Director was a comrade among comrades. Your Bauhaus was outwardly radiant, ours was shining inside. . . .

Herr Oberbürgermeister! You are now attempting to rid the Bauhaus, so heavily infected by me, of the spirit of Marxism. Morality, propriety, manners, and order are now to return once more hand in hand with the Muses. As my successor you have had Mies van der Rohe prescribed for you by Gropius and not – according to the statutes – on the advice of the Masters. My colleague, poor fellow, is no doubt expected to take his pickax and demolish my work in blissful commemoration of the Moholyan past of the Bauhaus. It looks as if this atrocious materialism is to be fought with the sharpest weapons and hence the very life to be beaten out of the innocently white Bauhaus box. . . .

. . . I see through it all. I understand nothing.

143 LUDWIG MIES VAN DER ROHE
"Announcement to the Students of the Dissolution of the Bauhaus" (1933)

The final chapter of the Bauhaus in Germany took place in Berlin. With Hannes Meyer's dismissal from the Dessau school in 1930, Mies van der Rohe, at the urging of Gropius, became the new director and took several unpopular measures to rid the school of its politics. Nevertheless, the Dessau City Council voted to shut down the school in the summer of 1932, and Mies relocated the institution and the faculty to a suburb of Berlin. Hitler assumed power in January 1933, and by March he was well on his way to absolute power. In April he created the Gestapo, the state secret police, who were instructed to rid the country of both Jewish and Bolshevik influence. In this same month the Gestapo raided the offices of the Berlin Bauhaus and temporarily shut down the school. They were seeking information on corruption charges being leveled against Fritz Hesse, the mayor of Dessau, but they were also interested in the students who were members of the (now outlawed) Communist Party. Mies fought to save the school, and at one point even called upon Alfred Rosenberg, in his ministerial office, to convince him of his moderate intentions. In July the Prussian Minister for Science, Art, and Education decided to allow the school to reopen, but, as this letter shows, only with the dismissal of Wassili Kandinsky and Ludwig Hilberseimer. Reluctantly, the Bauhaus faculty voted to shut down the school voluntarily.

Office of the State Secret Police, Berlin
Letter of July 21, 1933 to Mies van der Rohe

Strictly confidential
State Secret Police
Berlin S. W. 11, July 21, 1933
Prinz-Albrecht-Strasse 8
Professor Mies van der Rohe
Berlin, Am Karlsbad 24
Regarding: Bauhaus Berlin-Steglitz
In agreement with the Prussian Minister for Science, Art, and Education, the reopening of the Bauhaus Berlin-Steglitz is made dependent upon the removal of some objections.
1) Ludwig Hilberseimer and Vassily Kandinsky are no longer permitted to teach. Their places have to be taken by individuals who guarantee to support the principles of the National Socialist ideology.
2) The curriculum which has been in force up to now is not sufficient to satisfy the demands of the new State for the purposes of building its inner structure. Therefore, a curriculum accordingly modified is to be submitted to the Prussian Minister of Culture.
3) The members of the faculty have to complete and submit a questionnaire, satisfying the requirements of the civil service law.

Mies van der Rohe, "Announcement to the Students of the Dissolution of the Bauhaus" (1933), trans. Wolfgang Jabs and Basil Gilbert, in Hans M. Wingler, *The Bauhaus: Weimar, Dessau, Berlin, Chicago.* Cambridge, MA: MIT Press, 1986, p. 189.

The decision on the continuing existence and the reopening of the Bauhaus will be made dependent on the immediate removal of the objections and the fulfillment of the stated conditions.

By order: (signed) Dr. Peche

Attested: [illegible]

Chancery staff

Ludwig Mies van der Rohe
Announcement to the Students of the Dissolution of the Bauhaus

To the students of the Bauhaus. August 10, 1933

At its last meeting, the faculty resolved to dissolve the Bauhaus. The reason for this decision was the difficult economic situation of the institute.

The Office of the State Secret Police, the Prussian Ministry for Science, Art, and Education, and the school administration have been informed of this decision.

This announcement has crossed with a notification by the Office of the State Secret Police in which we are told that "in agreement with the Prussian Minister for Science, Art, and Education, the reopening of the Bauhaus is made dependent upon the removal of some objections."

We would have agreed to these conditions, but the economic situation does not allow for a continuation of the Institute.

The members of the faculty are of course available to the students for advice at any time. Grade records for all students will be issued by the secretariat.

From now on please address all letters to Professor Mies van der Rohe, Berlin W 35, Am Karlsbad 24.

(signed) Mies van der Rohe.

144 ALBERT SPEER
from *Inside the Third Reich* (1969)

Architecture was a subject very dear to Adolf Hitler. He was raised in impoverished circumstances in an Austrian village, and in 1907 moved to Vienna and applied to study architecture at the Vienna Academy of Fine Arts, which rejected him. Stunned, Hitler refused to reapply, but he never gave up his interest in architecture. When in prison in 1924–5, he passed his time with sketching building designs, and once in power in 1933 his two closest friends were architects: Paul Ludwig Troost and Albert Speer. Troost, whom Hitler regularly visited in Munich, practiced a spare neoclassicism in the manner of Peter Behrens, while Speer, who had studied under Heinrich Tessenow at the Charlottenburg Technische Hochschule, was also a modern classicist of modest inclination. Both Speer and Hitler, however, had a penchant for megalomania, as seen in their joint plans for rebuilding the city of Berlin in the 1930s. This passage from Speer's memoirs, written during his twenty-one-year prison sentence at Spandau, discusses Hitler's architectural tastes, which can only be described as eclectic and "arrested."

Albert Speer, from *Inside the Third Reich: Memoirs by Albert Speer*, trans. Richard and Clara Winston. New York: Macmillan, 1970, pp. 48–50.

The principal topic during these meals was, regularly, the morning visit to Professor Troost. Hitler would be full of praise for what he had seen; he effortlessly remembered all the details. His relationship to Troost was somewhat that of a pupil to his teacher; it reminded me of my own uncritical admiration of Tessenow.

I found this trait very engaging. I was amazed to see that this man, although worshiped by the people around him, was still capable of a kind of reverence. Hitler, who felt himself to be an architect, respected the superiority of the professional in this field. He would never have done that in politics.

He talked frankly about how the Bruckmanns, a highly cultivated publishing family of Munich, had introduced him to Troost. It was, he said, "as if scales fell from my eyes" when he saw Troost's work. "I could no longer bear the things I had drawn up to then. What a piece of good luck that I met this man!" One could only assent; it is ghastly to think what his architectural taste would have been like without Troost's influence. He once showed me his sketchbook of the early twenties. I saw attempts at public buildings in the neobaroque style of Vienna's Ringstrasse – products of the eighteen-nineties. Curiously enough, such architectural sketches often shared the page with sketches of weapons and warships.

In comparison to that sort of thing, Troost's architecture was actually spare. Consequently, his influence upon Hitler remained marginal. Up to the end Hitler lauded the architects and the buildings which had served him as models for his early sketches. Among these was the Paris Opera (built 1861–74) by Charles Garnier: "The stairwell is the most beautiful in the world. When the ladies stroll down in their costly gowns and uniformed men form lanes – Herr Speer, we must build something like that too!" He raved about the Vienna Opera: "The most magnificent opera house in the world, with marvelous acoustics. When as a young man I sat up there in the fourth gallery. . . ." Hitler had a story to tell about van der Nüll, one of the two architects of this building: "He thought the opera house was a failure. You know, he was in such despair that on the day before the opening he put a bullet through his head. At the dedication it turned out to be his greatest success; everyone praised the architect." Such remarks quite often led him to observations about difficult situations in which he himself had been involved and in which some fortunate turn of events had again and again saved him. The lesson was: You must never give up.

He was especially fond of the numerous theaters built by Hermann Helmer (1849–1919) and Ferdinand Fellner (1847–1916), who had provided both Austria-Hungary and Germany at the end of the nineteenth century with many late-baroque theaters, all in the same pattern. He knew where all their buildings were and later had the neglected theater in Augsburg renovated.

But he also appreciated the stricter architects of the nineteenth century such as Gottfried Semper (1803–79), who built the Opera House and the Picture Gallery in Dresden and the Hofburg and the court museums in Vienna, as well as Theophil Hansen (1803–83), who had designed several impressive classical buildings in Athens and Vienna. As soon as the German troops took Brussels in 1940, I was dispatched there to look at the huge Palace of Justice by Poelaert (1817–79), which Hitler raved about, although he knew it only from its plans (which was also true of the Paris Opera). After my return he had me give him a detailed description of the building.

Such were Hitler's architectural passions. But ultimately he was always drawn back to inflated neobaroque such as Kaiser Wilhelm II had also fostered, through his court architect

Ihne. Fundamentally, it was decadent baroque, comparable to the style that accompanied the decline of the Roman Empire. Thus, in the realm of architecture, as in painting and sculpture, Hitler really remained arrested in the world of his youth: the world of 1880 to 1910, which stamped its imprint on his artistic taste as on his political and ideological conceptions.

145 MARCEL BREUER
from "Where Do We Stand?" (1935)

I t was only in the 1930s that a significant number of British architects first embraced modernism. The most obvious push in this direction came from the flood of German refugees – architects and historians – who began to make their way to England in 1933. Erich Mendelsohn arrived in that year and formed a partnership with the Russian refugee Serge Chermayeff. Walter Gropius came one year later and teamed up with Maxwell Fry. Marcel Breuer, also of Bauhaus fame, arrived in 1935 and formed a (two-year) partnership with Francis Yorke, before joining Walter Gropius at Harvard University. The principal vehicle for the propagation of modernism was *The Architectural Review*, under the editorial lead of P. Morton Shand. This article, published in April 1935, also stands as an early plea for modernism in Britain. It is of interest, in part, in that it – like Hitchcock and Johnson's efforts of a few years earlier – attempts to depoliticize German modernism.

I should like to divorce the 'unbiased' aspect of the New Architecture from association with terms like 'new', 'original', individual', 'imaginative', and 'revolutionary'. We are all susceptible to the persuasion of that word 'new'. Society pays its meed of respect to anything new by granting it a patent. It is common knowledge that international patent law is based on two principles: 'technical improvement' and 'newness'. Thus novelty becomes a powerful commercial weapon. But what is the Modern Movement's real attitude to this business of 'newness'? Are we for what is new, unexpected and a change at any price, in the same way that we are for an unbiased view at any price? I think we can answer this question with an emphatic negative. We are not out to create something new, but something suitable, intrinsically right and as relatively perfect as may be. The 'new' in the Modern Movement must be considered simply a means to an end, not an end in itself as in women's fashions. What we aim at and believe to be possible is that the solutions embodied in the forms of the New Architecture should endure for 10, 20, or 100 years as circumstances may demand – a thing unthinkable in the world of fashion as long as modes are modes. It follows that, though we have no fear of what is new, novelty is not our aim. We seek what is definite and real, whether old or new.

This perhaps invites the retort, 'Be sincere. Look into your motives without trying to make your introspection too moral or positive. Don't all of us get sick of everything after a time? Doesn't everything, even architecture, become tiresome in the end? Isn't our thirst for change greater than we care to admit?'

Marcel Breuer, from "Where Do We Stand?," in *The Rationalists: Theory and Design in the Modern Movement*, ed. Dennis Sharp. New York: Architectural Book Publishing Co., 1979, pp. 87–8.

Here we reach a point where logic ceases to be logical, where consistency loses sense, and anticipation is impossible, because history provides examples for and against. It were easy, but futile, to indulge in prophesy. I would rather interrogate that unwritten law of our own convictions, the spirit of our age. It answers that we have tired of everything in architecture which is a matter of fashion; that we find all intentionally new forms wearisome, and all those based on personal predilections or tendencies equally pointless. To which can be added the simple consideration that we cannot hope to change our buildings or furniture as often as we change, for example, our ties.

If by 'original', 'individual', or 'imaginative' artistic caprice, a happy thought or an isolated flash of genius is meant, then I must answer that the New Architecture aims at being neither original, individual, nor imaginative. Here, too, there has been a transformation in the meaning of terms. According to our ideas, modern architecture is 'original' when it provides a complete solution of the difficulty concerned. By 'individual' we understand the degree of intensity or application with which the most various or directly interconnected problems are disposed of. 'Imagination' is no longer expressed in remote intellectual adventures, but in the tenacity with which formal order is imposed upon the world of realities. The ability to face a problem objectively brings us to the so-called 'revolutionary' side of the Modern Movement. I have considerable hesitation in using the word at all, since it has recently been annexed by various political parties, and in some countries it is actually inculcated into school-children as an elementary civic virtue. In fact, revolution is now in a fair way towards becoming a permanent institution. I believe that what was originally revolutionary in the Movement was simply the principle of putting its own objective views into practice. It should also be said that our revolutionary attitude was neither self-complacency nor propagandist *bravura*, but the inward, and as far as possible outward, echo of the independence of our work. Although, as I have just pointed out, to be revolutionary has since received the sanction of respectability, this causes us considerable heart-searchings: the word inevitably has a political flavour. In this connection it is necessary to state that our investigations into housing and town-planning problems are based primarily on sociological, rather than on formal or representational, principles. In short, that our ideas of what developments were possible were based on the general needs of the community.

146 FRANCIS YORKE
from *The Modern House* (1936)

Francis Yorke had embraced modernism prior to Breuer's arrival in Britain, having helped to form the MARS (Modern Architectural Research) group as a British arm of CIAM. He was one of the first architects to employ reinforced concrete in Britain. He was also one of the first English authors to write about modernism, and the tall housing solution in particular. The Introduction to this second edition of this book opens with an image of Walter Gropius's design for narrow blocks of housing, ten stories high, and it signals a forceful rejection of the individual

Francis Yorke, from *The Modern House*. 2nd ed., London: The Architectural Press, 1936, pp. 1–3.

house in favor of the housing type preferred by Gropius and Le Corbusier. It can thus be seen as the first push in Britain for what would become the style widely accepted by the British government in the postwar creation of new towns.

This book concerns the individual villa type of house; and though the author does not pretend that the building of villas is a good or even a possible solution to the problem of housing the people, he does believe that for some time to come the majority of people will continue to want to live in detached or semi-detached houses, and it is important for the relation of the villa to modern architecture and the modern social system to be appreciated.

Architects and economists and building experts have discussed the fitness of pre-fabrication and mass-production methods for the solution of the housing problem, for housing generally, and particularly for the provision of cheap houses for the poorer of the working classes. No working principle has been agreed, and discussions continue. In the meantime the building of individual houses goes on uncontrolled, though many Continental architects, and some in England, who have studied the problem in its several aspects, are now persuaded that it is impossible to achieve a satisfactory result by providing individual houses for everyone.

At the best such a system can only produce a glorified garden city development, and such development is not in accordance with modern ideas of town-planning. When mass-production methods are applied to the family house, the town continues to spread, even more rapidly than in the past, around the commercial, industrial or governmental city centre, with further complication of electric, gas, water and drainage services, and, especially, lines of communication.

The first principle of modern town planning must be a simplification of all communications, pipes and wires, and so on. The route from the home to the place of work must be as short and quickly covered as possible.

It seems, therefore, that dwellings must be grouped and made higher, but to such an arrangement there is naturally, in the light of present-day practices, a very strong prejudice. Where flats are built in large blocks with dwellings concentrated on several floors, the outline of the building is made to follow the congested plan of the obsolete traditional town: conditions are even worse than they were when the town was first planned, for not only are the buildings increased in height, but land that was once garden is built upon, and the population is segregated from natural scenery. The people, quite reasonably, prefer to go to the suburbs, and there buy mean little individual villas on tiny individual lots, than live under such congested, inhuman conditions.

The solution to the housing problem lies, no doubt, in a reformed type of flat dwelling and controlled land development.

There have been many projects for the lay-out of groups of flat blocks, and for the design of economic and convenient living quarters as standardised units in the scheme, prepared by such men as Gropius and Le Corbusier, but there has been little actual development, partly because it is difficult to find finance for any scheme that makes a great break with normal procedure, but largely owing to difficulties of land-ownership and the high prices of land, which would have to be controlled over a considerable area before such schemes could become really effective.

Modern construction permits higher building, and higher building means economy in land. When a building rises to ten or twelve stories the saving is considerable, and the land that is freed becomes park-land between the building units.

147   NIKOLAUS PEVSNER
from *Pioneers of the Modern Movement* (1936)

Concomitant with the efforts of Francis Yorke were the writings of Nikolaus Pevsner. He arrived in Britain from Germany in 1933, armed with a doctorate on Baroque architecture (written under Heinrich Wölfflin). He also brought with him materials for a book on the history of modern architecture. Yet his project soon takes a new turn, as he now attempts to trace the lineage of modernism to three sources: Art Nouveau (the weakest of his arguments), the work of engineers (for him the industrial process that began in Britain), and the Arts and Crafts movement of William Morris. The fact that two of the three originating points for modernism were British was, of course, a thesis tailored for his new audience, but this historiographic model at the same time stripped German modernism of any theoretical context. Nevertheless, the book would prove enormously successful in the Anglo-Saxon world and even rise to the level of a canon. In his Foreword, Pevsner pronounced it the first history of the modern movement to be published.

It is the principal aim of the following chapters to point out that this new style, a genuine and adequate style of our century, was achieved by 1914. Morris had started the movement by reviving handicraft as an art worthy of the best men's efforts, the pioneers about 1900 had gone farther by discovering the immense, untried possibilities of machine art. The synthesis, in creation as well as in theory, is the work of Walter Gropius (born in 1883). In 1909, Gropius worked out a memorandum on standardisation and mass production of small houses, and on advisable ways of financing such building schemes. At the end of 1914, he began preparing his plans for the reorganisation of the Weimar Art Schools, to which he had been elected principal by the Grand Duke of Saxe-Weimar. The opening of the new school, combining an academy of art and a school of arts and crafts, took place in 1919. Its name was Staatliches Bauhaus, and it was to become, for more than a decade, a paramount centre of creative energy in Europe. It was at the same time a laboratory for handicraft and for standardisation; a school, and a workshop. It comprised, in an admirable community spirit, architects, master craftsmen, abstract painters, all working for a new spirit in building. Building to Gropius is a term of wide import. All art, as long as it is sound and healthy, serves building. Hence all students of the Bauhaus were trained as apprentices, received at the end of their course the freedom of the trade, and were only after that admitted to the building-plot and the studio of experimental design.

Gropius regards himself as a follower of Ruskin and Morris, of van de Velde and of the Werkbund. So our circle is complete. The history of artistic theory between 1890 and the war proves the assertion on which the present work is based, namely that the phase between Morris and Gropius is a historical unit understandable as such. Morris laid the foundation of the modern style; with Gropius its character was ultimately determined. Art historians speak of 'Transitional' preceding the harmonious perfection of 'Early English'. While Romanesque

Nikolaus Pevsner, from *Pioneers of the Modern Movement: From William Morris to Walter Gropius.* London: Faber & Faber, 1936, pp. 41–3.

architecture was still lingering on all over England, William of Sens and the masters of Wells and Lincoln created their immortal works as pioneers of the style to come. What they did for England late in the twelfth and at the beginning of the thirteenth century was done for the whole of Europe late in the nineteenth and at the beginning of this century by Morris and his followers, Voysey, van de Velde, Mackintosh, Wright, Loos, Behrens, Gropius and the other architects and artists, in recognition of whose work the following pages are written.

148   J. M. RICHARDS
from *An Introduction to Modern Architecture* (1940)

The interest in modernism generated in the 1930s culminated in 1940 with this small book by J. M. Richards, written for the "man in the street." The book enjoyed a large following in Britain during the war years. The principal contention is not dissimilar to that of Pevsner: the stylistic unity of the eighteenth century had become displaced in the nineteenth century because of the rise of high industrialism and stylistic pluralism, but the Arts and Crafts movement happily appeared and thwarted these tendencies. It thus allowed the more authentic spirit of the people to shine through. Richards is quick to distinguish true modern architecture from its "modernistic" followers simply seeking effects, and to this end he devotes several chapters to discussing the material and constructional aspects of modernism. He repeatedly stresses that modernism is not a fad or fashion, and that the public will come to embrace it when, in fact, they understand its origin, functionality, and common sense.

THE words "modern architecture" are used here to mean something more particular than contemporary architecture. They are used to mean the new kind of architecture that is growing up with this century as this century's own contribution to the art of architecture; the work of those people, whose number is happily increasing, who understand that architecture is a social art related to the life of the people it serves, not an academic exercise in applied ornament. The question that immediately arises, whether there is in fact enough difference between people's lives as they are lived in this century and as they were lived in previous centuries to justify a truly "modern" architecture being very different from that of the past – and indeed whether "modern" architecture is quite as revolutionary as it is supposed to be – must be discussed later.

But there can be no denying that examples of an architecture entirely different from what we are accustomed to, have appeared on the scene during the last ten years, following their appearance in other countries during the last twenty years. And there can be no denying that the designers of these buildings are extremely sincere. They are not, as their detractors often suggest, "Bolshies" or stunt-mongers. They have thought things out very thoroughly, and they believe that the new architecture that we are calling "modern" (henceforward we will drop the quotation marks) is something that is needed in the world to-day. They believe also that in developing and perfecting it so as to answer this century's problems and to be in tune with its

J. M. Richards, from *An Introduction to Modern Architecture*. Harmondsworth: Penguin, 1940, pp. 9–10.

outlook, they are helping at the revival of architecture as a live art – something that even those who do not wholeheartedly admire the form the new architecture is taking admit that it has not been for many years. For it is a mistake to suppose that, because modern architects are particularly concerned to relate buildings more closely to the needs thay have to serve, they are only interested in the practical side of architecture. They know that they are practising an art, and are therefore concerned with the pursuit of beauty. They feel however that it is time we made clear the difference between beauty itself and the merely conventional forms that habit has made us associate with it. But that also is a question that we must discuss later.

All this, in any case, is what the modern architects themselves think; but the Man in the Street only sees in the new architecture another bewildering addition to the variety of architectural styles he is already offered: a new style which, he feels, must have something to it, because it looks clean and efficient and not too pompous and because he has heard that it is based on an idea called functionalism (or "fitness for purpose") which at least sounds sensible if rather inhuman; but a style that he also rather suspects, simply because he is naturally conservative. He dislikes having something familiar replaced by something unfamiliar without very evident reason, and he has an idea that the people who are responsible for the new architecture are cranks, foreigners, revolutionaries or other kinds of people that he disapproves of.

The purpose of this book therefore is simply to try to describe to people who do not pretend to know anything about architecture, how these new buildings come to look as they do, why they are different for other reasons than for the sake of being different, and why their designers believe them to be the forerunners of a new architecture of the future.

There have been so many misunderstandings about modern architecture that before we begin to discuss what it is, it may be as well to mention a few things that it is not. It is not, for one thing, a fashionable style of jazz ornament; it is not the custom of building in concrete, or with flat roofs and horizontal window-panes; it is not "functionalism." It *is* quite simply, like all good architecture, the honest product of science and art. It aims at once more relating methods of building as closely as possible to real needs. In fact it is nothing more nor less than the exact modern equivalent of the architecture that flourished in previous ages, but fell into decay during the last century through architects having got out of touch with life and having forgotten what architecture was really for.

149   SIGFRIED GIEDION
from *Space, Time and Architecture* (1941)

O f all the books written in the troubled decades of the 1930s and 1940s, the one that would have the most lasting impact was Sigfried Giedion's *Space, Time and Architecture*. Its message would not only enchant the postwar architectural generation, but it would become for many the Holy Book of international modernism – the *sine qua non* of the new architecture and its founding principles. Giedion came to the task by an

Sigfried Giedion, from *Space, Time and Architecture: The Growth of a New Tradition*. Cambridge, MA: Harvard University Press, 1949, pp. 13–14, 424–5.

indirect route. In the late 1930s, when the war in Europe was threatening his native Switzerland, he contacted Walter Gropius at Harvard and asked for help in temporarily moving to the United States. Gropius responded with the Eliot Norton professorship of 1938–9, which required Giedion to give a series of lectures. Giedion began by translating into English several of the chapters of his earlier book on France (see 134), but then he broadened his polemics with his new notion of "space-time" architecture. Many of Giedion's earlier historical premises were also incorporated: the deterministic or teleological necessity of the new architecture, and the momentous nature of the change (appearing every 500 years or so). Added to them was the new psychological theme of the "split personality" of Western consciousness, one militantly underscored by the war but one that also had its architectural roots in the hated eclecticism of the nineteenth century. Fortunately, the new physics of the twentieth century posited an escape route with its theme of space-time, one that was explored visually by painters such as Pablo Picasso and Georges Braque. This new perspective finds its entry into architecture in the 1920s, and with it a new dramatic era begins. In the second of the following passages, Giedion explains the space-time concept by considering Walter Gropius's design for the Bauhaus building at Dessau. Here, too, in a note of gratitude, he famously compares it with a painting by Picasso.

We have behind us a period in which thinking and feeling were separated. This schism produced individuals whose inner development was uneven, who lacked inner equilibrium: split personalities. The split personality as a psychopathic case does not concern us here; we are speaking of the inner disharmony which is found in the structure of the normal personality of this period.

What are the effects of this inner division? Only very rarely do we encounter a master in one field who is capable of recognizing workers of the same stature and tendency in another. Contemporary artists and scientists have lost contact with each other; they speak the language of their time in their own work, but they cannot even understand it as it is expressed in work of a different character. The great physicist may lack all understanding of a painting which presents the artistic equivalent of his own ideas. A great painter may fail entirely to grasp architecture which has developed out of his own principles. Men who produce poetry which is purely an expression of this time are indifferent to the music which is contemporary in the same sense and to the same degree. This is our inheritance from the nineteenth century, during which the different departments of human activity steadily lost touch with one another. The principles of *laissez-faire* and *laissez-aller* were extended to the life of the spirit.

Throughout the nineteenth century the natural sciences went splendidly ahead, impelled by the great tradition which the previous two hundred years had established, and sustained by problems which had a direction and momentum of their own. The real spirit of the age came out in these researches – in the realm of thinking, that is. But these achievements were regarded as emotionally neutral, as having no relation to the realm of feeling. Feeling could not keep up with the swift advances made in science and the techniques. The century's genuine strength and special accomplishments remained largely irrelevant to man's inner life.

This orientation of the vital energies of the period is reflected in the make-up of the man of today. Scarcely anyone can escape the unbalanced development which it encourages. The split personality, the unevenly adjusted man, is symptomatic of our period.
[. . .]

The Bauhaus has a skeleton of reinforced concrete. Because of the German building ordinances, the supporting pillars are much heavier than they would have been in France or

Switzerland. The continuous glass curtain is brought into abrupt juxtaposition with the horizontal ribbons of white curtain wall at the top and bottom of the building. An aerial photograph shows them plainly for what they are: mere ribbons, supporting nothing. In a bird's-eye view the whole cube seems like two immense horizontal planes floating over the ground.

The glass curtain is not the limited and marked-off transparent area which Eiffel had already exploited in the 1878 exhibition: it flows smoothly around the building, the corners showing no vertical supporting or binding members. As in the Fagus works, the pillars from which it hangs are set behind the glass, making the curtain a specimen of pure cantilever construction. The glass curtain is simply folded about the corners of the building; in other words, the glass walls blend into each other at just the point where the human eye expects to encounter guaranteed support for the load of the building.

Two major endeavors of modern architecture are fulfilled here, not as unconscious outgrowths of advances in engineering but as the conscious realization of an artist's intent; there is the hovering, vertical grouping of planes which satisfies our feeling for a relational space, and there is the extensive transparency that permits interior and exterior to be seen simultaneously, *en face* and *en profile*, like Picasso's "L'Arlésienne" of 1911–12: variety of levels of reference, or of points of reference, and simultaneity – the conception of space-time, in short. In this building Gropius goes far beyond anything that might be regarded as an achievement in construction alone.

150 LE CORBUSIER
from *The Athens Charter* (1943)

Le Corbusier's large and successful office of the early 1930s was without commissions by the middle years of the decade, and the Frenchman largely returned to his painting. The rapid German conquest of France created other problems. Le Corbusier fled first to Vézelay, and then to southwest France, near the Spanish border. Here he gained a post with the Vichy government of Marshal Pétain – the wartime government sanctioned by the German occupiers. This position allowed him to make various proposals for rebuilding the country, in which he drew upon his earlier Syndicalist politics (rule by industrial elites) and planning ideas. During the war years he wrote no fewer than seven books articulating these themes, among them *The Athens Charter*. It was intended to inform the Vichy government of the sociological research presented on CIAM's cruise to Athens in 1933, and thus serve as a model for the reorganization of French industry and planning. The book's ninety-five propositions again divide the city into the functional categories of habitation, leisure, work, and traffic, but now with even greater physical separation and certainty. The following is a sampling of four propositions from the total of ninety-five.

Le Corbusier, from *La Charte d'Athènes* (1943), trans. Anthony Eardley as *The Athens Charter*. New York: Grossman, 1973, pp. 53–4, 57, 65, 105.

Observations

9. The population is too dense within the historic nuclei of cities, as it is in certain belts of nineteenth-century industrial expansion – reaching as many as four hundred and even six hundred inhabitants per acre.

Density – the ratio between the size of a population and the land area that it occupies – can be entirely changed by the height of buildings. But, until now, construction techniques have limited the height of buildings to about six stories. The admissible density for structures of this kind is from 100 to 200 inhabitants per acre. When this density increases, as it does in many districts, to 240, 320, or even 400 inhabitants, it then becomes a slum, which is characterized by the following symptoms:

1. An inadequacy of habitable space per person;
2. A mediocrity of openings to the outside;
3. An absence of sunlight (because of northern orientation or as the result of shadow cast across the street or into the courtyard);
4. Decay and a permanent breeding ground for deadly germs (tuberculosis);
5. An absence or inadequacy of sanitary facilities;
6. Promiscuity, arising from the interior layout of the dwelling, from the poor arrangement of the building, and from the presence of troublesome neighborhoods.

Constrained by their defensive enclosures, the nuclei of the old cities were generally filled with close-set structures and deprived of open space. But, in compensation, verdant spaces were directly accessible, just outside the city gates, making air of good quality available nearby. Over the course of the centuries, successive urban rings accumulated, replacing vegetation with stone and destroying the verdant areas – the lungs of the city. Under these conditions, high population densities indicate a permanent state of disease and discomfort. [. . .]

16. Structures built along transportation routes and around their intersections are detrimental to habitation because of noise, dust, and noxious gases.

Once we are willing to take this factor into consideration we will assign habitation and traffic to independent zones. From then on, the house will never again be fused to the street by a sidewalk. It will rise in its own surroundings, in which it will enjoy sunshine, clear air, and silence. Traffic will be separated by means of a network of footpaths for the slow-moving pedestrian and a network of fast roads for automobiles. Together these networks will fulfill their function, coming close to housing only as occasion demands. [. . .]

29. High buildings, set far apart from one another, must free the ground for broad verdant areas.

Indeed, they will have to be situated at sufficiently great distances from one another, or else their height, far from being an improvement of the existing malaise, will actually worsen it;

that is the grave error perpetrated in the cities of the two Americas. The construction of a city cannot be abandoned, without a program, to private initiative. Its population density must be great enough to justify the installation of the communal facilities that will form the extensions of the dwelling. Once this density has been determined, a presumable population figure will be adopted, permitting the calculation of the area to be reserved for the city. To determine the manner in which the ground is to be occupied, to establish the ratio of the built-up area to that left open or planted, to allocate the necessary land to private dwellings and to their various extensions, to fix an area for the city that will not be exceeded for a specified period of time – these constitute that important operation, which lies in the hands of the city authority: the promulgation of a "land ordinance." Thus, the city will henceforth be built in complete security and, within the limits of the rules prescribed by this statute, full scope will be given to private initiative and to the imagination of the artist.

[. . .]

95. Private interest will be subordinated to the collective interest.

Left to himself, a man is soon crushed by difficulties of every kind which he must overcome. If, conversely, he is subjected to too many collective constraints, his personality is stifled by them. Individual rights and collective rights must therefore support and reinforce one another, and all of their infinitely constructive aspects must be joined together. Individual rights have nothing to do with vulgar private interests. Such interests, which heap advantages upon a minority while relegating the rest of the social mass to a mediocre existence, require strict limitations. In every instance, private interests must be subordinated to the collective interest, so that each individual will have access to the fundamental joys, the well-being of the home, and the beauty of the city.

151 SVEN BACKSTRÖM
from "A Swede Looks at Sweden" (1943)

I n this little-known wartime article written in 1943, Sven Backström begins a precocious critique of European modernism that would escalate in the postwar years. As in Great Britain, modernism was relatively late in coming to Scandinavia, but when it did it swept through the Nordic countries in the 1930s, leaving behind more traditional approaches to building. Backström here looks back over the first decade of modern Swedish works, and finds the results somewhat disappointing – in part because the buildings often fail to stand up to the severity of the climate, in part because the designs lack what he deems to be an underlying humanist perspective. This is a serious critique of the rationalist underpinnings of the "new objectivity" movement, and it came, within a few years, to be dubbed "New Empiricism."

Sven Backström, from "A Swede Looks at Sweden," in *The Architectural Review* 94:561 (September 1943), p. 80.

But apart from this development, which has been imposed on us by external factors, our architecture has a line of development to show, as it were, from within. In order to understand this rightly we must go back a matter of some ten years. It was in 1930 that Erik Gunnar Asplund created the Stockholm Exhibition at Djurgårdsbrunnsviken. This meant for us that the new impulses from France and Germany were in a masterly way translated and developed in the Swedish milieu and adapted to the Swedish national temperament. This was the victorious *début* of functionalism in Sweden. The new ideas swept over us like an avalanche and were adopted especially by the younger generation. A clean break was made with the past. There was a determination to clear away all false romanticism and all designing in historical styles. There was a feeling that one was building for new ideal human beings, who were quite different from the older generations. The modern mode of life was considered to be completely new, and consequently the new houses were to be absolutely different from the old ones. Everything connected with tradition was suspect. Architecture was to be objective. The functionalistic principle was the guiding star and everything was to be built in the material of "our time," glass, concrete and iron, and the building had primarily to be right from the point of view of construction. In one word, the architect was to be an engineer.

The years passed, and one "objective" house after the other stood ready for use. It was then that people gradually began to discover that the "new objectivity" was not always so objective, and the houses did not always function so well as had been expected. The big windows, for example, were all too effective as heat-conductors, and people found it difficult to accustom themselves to the heat or cold behind them. They also felt the lack of many of the æsthetic values and the little contributions to cosiness that we human beings are so dependent upon, and that our architectural and domestic tradition had nevertheless developed. It was difficult to settle down in the new houses because the "new" human beings were not so different from the older ones. It was found that one could not with impunity break out of the natural course of development. It was realized that one had to build for human beings as they are, and not as they ought to be. And for a true understanding of our fellows both the feeling and the knowledge of the artist are essential conditions. It is not sufficient for the architect to be an engineer; he must also be an artist.

Architecture began to seek its way on new roads. Architects began to develop an ear for the shifting values and phases of actual life. Man was once more to become the point of departure and the criterion. And it was discovered that man is a highly complicated phenomenon that is not to be satisfied or understood with the help of any new epoch-making formulæ. And one result of this growing insight was a reaction against the all too schematic architecture of the 1930's. To-day we have reached the point where all the elusive psychological factors have again begun to engage our attention. Man and his habits, reactions and needs are the focus of interest as never before. One tries to understand them, and to adapt the building in such a way that it really serves. And there is the desire to enrich it and beautify it in a living way, so that it may be a source of joy. The striving is for the true proportion – the neither too much nor too little. But with the delight in experiment that is part of the Swedish temperament, architecture has already tended to a much too exaggerated differentiation and division. This tendency to lose oneself in petty details of various kinds leads one to forget the whole, and simplicity. People sometimes actually need instructions before they can live in the houses!

The goal must be to reach the essential, the simple and the objective things in architecture. We want, certainly, to retain all the positive aspects of what the nineteen-thirties gave us. A house should of course function properly and be rational in its design. But at the same time we want to re-introduce the valuable and living elements in architecture that existed before 1930, and we want to add to this our own personal contribution. To interpret such a programme as a reaction and a return to something that is past and to pastiches is definitely to misunderstand the development of architecture in this country. Something that to a certain extent leads to a confusion of ideas is perhaps the forced return to building materials and methods of construction that the architecture of the thirties did not need to reckon with, and that for the younger generation of architects are perhaps unknown.

If in our democratic community architecture is allowed to progress without too great interference from without, it should be in a position to develop into a functionalism fulfilling the best and deepest requirements of the term.

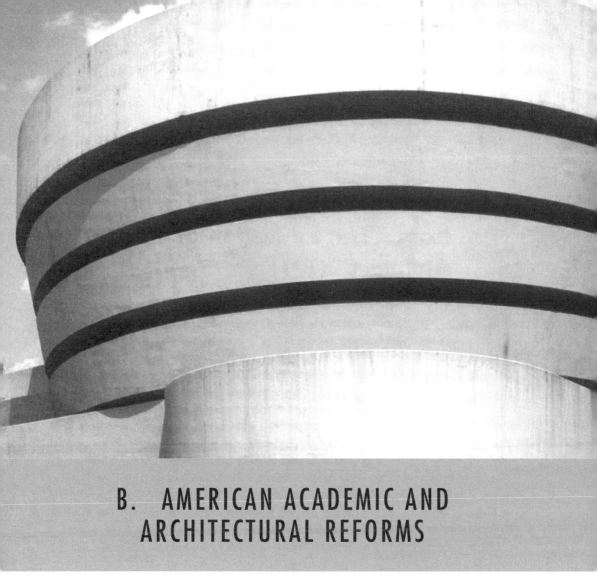

B. AMERICAN ACADEMIC AND ARCHITECTURAL REFORMS

Introduction

I n the 1930s there came about a series of major reforms in the United States: politically, socially, and architecturally. The Great Depression of 1929, whose effects were felt throughout the next decade, ushered in a bevy of legislation, led by the Social Security Act of 1935 and various programs related to federal and state housing. The shutdown of architectural activity during the Depression's worst years at the same time underscored the need to reform architectural education, which, since the teens, had been largely predicated on an antiquated Beaux-Arts system grounded in palatial design. At the same time the flood of European architects and intellectuals to the country in the 1930s not only shifted the center of theoretical activity to North America but also encouraged a dialogue or debate between the competing visions of modernism nurtured simultaneously in Europe and the United States.

World War II left its indelible imprint on the country and its architectural thought. Whereas many of the major urban centers on the continent of Europe suffered major devastation, this was not the case in the United States. Having been forced to organize massive military campaigns on two fronts, America stood alone and intact at the war's end as the leading economic and industrial power. Its full acceptance of modernism was therefore entirely compatible with its technological advancement and high rates of industrial productivity. In the end what emerged from these challenges was a composite vision of modernism very different from what had existed before, either at home or abroad.

152   JOSEPH HUDNUT
from "The Education of an Architect" (1931)

During the Great Depression, architects who had been trained in Beaux-Arts principles of design were drawn into government-funded programs for mass housing and rural development. Rather quickly, schools of architecture came to see their educational premises as outmoded. Thus in the first half of the 1930s, almost every architecture school in the country underwent curricular reform, and leading the way was Joseph Hudnut, a Harvard graduate who received his architectural training at the University of Michigan. Hudnut had maintained an eclectic practice during the 1920s, but sometime around 1930, after having moved to New York City, he converted to modernism. It is essential to note, however, that he did so within the circle of Henry-Russell Hitchcock, Alfred Barr, and Philip Johnson. In this early paper, he addresses the need for curricular reform, which is important because in 1934 he assumed the Deanship at Columbia University and dismantled its Beaux-Arts program. The following year he was hired to make similar changes at Harvard, and his first act there was to hire Walter Gropius as the head of the Graduate School of Design. Hudnut's vision of modernism, however, was not entirely in line with that of the Museum of Modern Art, and he would later clash with Gropius over control of the curriculum. Here his critique of "functionalism" at first glance seems compatible with the views of Hitchcock and Johnson, but his reference to Le Corbusier demonstrates that it is not. In the end Hudnut – like Hitchcock and Johnson – acknowledges that he is principally a formalist.

Two responsibilities of a school of architecture then are plain. First, to teach through processes of instruction and discipline the science of construction, especially in its more abstract and general phases, so that the student may leave the school with that habitual imaginative experience with materials and constructed forms that is the necessary basis for a command of structural design. Second, to explain, so far as these can be explained, the important facts concerning those economic and intellectual currents in which the student lives; to make him so aware of these currents and of their origin, nature and direction, that the need to know them more profoundly will appear urgent and necessary.
[. . .]
The popularity of the doctrine, or doctrines, called *functionalism* has given a new significance to this question. Since Le Corbusier provided the necessary mystifications the dogma of

Joseph Hudnut, from "The Education of an Architect," in *Architectural Record* 69 (May 1931), pp. 412, 413–14.

functionalism has taken on an almost religious character: has it not already its mythology, its saints, its martyrdoms, its rituals, and its pantheon of gods – one of them from Chicago? And now that it is tinctured with romance (quaintly called "City-planning") it seems destined to carry everything before it.

Whatever functionalism may mean to its priests, the public understands it to mean that architectural beauty can be created by a process of logic. Beauty is the satisfaction that we experience when we perceive the fitness of an instrument for its use. Then let an architect merely plan and build intelligently; beauty will dwell unbidden in his organic structure.

Therefore our snooty schools of architecture have no need to concern themselves with beauty. Economics, business, sociology, physics, the cost of materials and the marketing of mortgages ought to be our preoccupation; where these are known, taste and imagination will spring mystically and unconsciously into sudden being. And if they don't spring into sudden being, so much the worse for taste and imagination.

[. . .]

But these processes are relatively unimportant. What is important is the direct and constant search for form. It is most essential that the student throughout his college term should have not merely instruction and exercise in practical planning and building, not merely a growing awareness of the subtle and intimate relation of architecture to society, but, more fundamental than either of these, a sustained experience with esthetic form. It is the urgent business of the school of architecture to organize and direct this experience.

The processes of the school will not be understood unless this intention of the school is kept in mind. The programs in design are written and studied not only with a view to their actual execution but with the hope that they may offer opportunities for the exercise of taste and imagination. Criticism, methods of attack and presentation, judgments and awards are all directed primarily to this end; and although common sense may be commended, the first prizes must always go to those who, proceeding from common sense, arrive at beauty. Good economics, good sociology, good draftsmanship and good telephone service are excellent things; but let's not mistake them for architecture.

153   FRANK LLOYD WRIGHT
from *The Disappearing City* (1932)

Already in the last of his Princeton lectures of 1930, Frank Lloyd Wright had expressed his disdain for the American city, which he felt had become asphyxiated with automobile congestion and skyscrapers. In *The Disappearing City*, he draws upon the traditions of Jefferson, Emerson, and Thoreau, as well as theories of several non-Marxist socialists, in proposing his alternative of "Broadacre City." It is, in essence, a non-urban city. The idea is to guarantee each family a house on one acre of land and to replace money with a system of social credit. People live in proximity to their workplace, but they also cultivate their self-reliance by growing some of their

Frank Lloyd Wright, from *The Disappearing City*, in *Frank Lloyd Wright. Collected Writings: Vol. 3, 1931–1939*, ed. Bruce Brooks Pfeiffer, vol. 3, 1931–9. New York, Rizzoli, 1993, pp. 78–80.

food. The key to this massive rural diffusion is the automobile; roadways are to become inter-county arterial highways and longer travel is to be accommodated by a high-speed rail system. People, Wright argues, no longer have the need to go to a concert hall or a sporting event, as television can now bring all aspects of culture into the home. For the worst of the Depression years — 1932 — it was a fantastic vision of salvation emphasizing individualism, responsibility, and egoism.

We are concerned here in the consideration of the future city as a future for individuality in this organic sense: individuality being a fine integrity of the human race. Without such integrity there can be no real culture whatever what we call civilization may be.

We are going to call this city for the individual the Broadacre City because it is based upon a minimum of an acre to the family.

And, we are concerned for fear systems, schemes, and "styles" have already become so expedient as civilization that they may try to go on in Usonia as imitation culture and so will indefinitely postpone all hope of any great life for a growing people in any such city the United States may yet have.

To date our capitalism as individualism, our eclecticism as personality has, by way of taste, got in the way of integrity as individuality in the popular understanding, and on account of that fundamental misunderstanding we, the prey of our culture-monger, stand in danger of losing our chance at this free life our charter of liberty originally held out to us.

I see that free life in the Broadacre City.

As for freedom; we have prohibition because a few fools can't carry their liquor; Russia has communism because a few fools couldn't carry their power; we have a swollen privatism because a few fools can't carry their "success" and money must go on making money.

If instead of an organic architecture we have a style formula in architecture in America, it will be because too many fools have neither imagination nor the integrity called individuality. And we have our present overgrown cities because the many capitalistic fools are contented to be dangerous fools.

A fool ordinarily lacks significance except as a cipher has it. The fool is neither positive nor negative. But by way of adventitious wealth and mechanical leverage he and his satellites – the neuters – are the overgrown city and the dam across the stream flowing toward freedom.

It is only the individual developing in his own right (consciously or unconsciously) who will go, first, to the Broadacre City because it is the proper sense of the dignity and worth of the individual, as an individual, that is building that city. But after those with this sense the others will come trailing along into the communal-individuality that alone we can call Democracy.

But before anything of significance or consequence can happen in the culture of such a civilization as ours, no matter how that civilization came to be, individuality as a significance and integrity must be a healthy growth or at least growing healthy. And it must be a recognized quality of greatness.

In an organic modern architecture, all will gladly contribute this quality, as they may, in the spirit that built the majestic cathedrals of the Middle Ages. That medieval spirit was nearest the communal, democratic spirit of anything we know. The common-spirit of a people disciplined by means and methods and materials, in common, will have – and with no recognized formula – great unity.

154 LEWIS MUMFORD
from *Technics and Civilization* (1934)

L ewis Mumford also responded to the Great Depression by elevating and intensifying his anti-urban polemics of earlier years, and *Technics and Civilization* has a right to be considered one of the great books of the century. Mumford remained very active in the Regional Planning Association of America (RPAA), and in 1931 he undertook a trip to Europe to view firsthand the European housing experiments of the 1920s. His earlier positions were fortified, but in this book they take on a more general cast. His thesis is that human technology has undergone several stages of evolution and now has entered a "neotechnic" era that allows a complete mechanization of work and therefore a complete break with the capitalist system. As an alternative, Mumford proffers a "basic communism," that is, a non-Marxist planned economy that freely dispenses the basic services of food, shelter, and medical care. Taylorized in theory, anti-consumptive in practice, this society is designed to reduce human labor to a minimum, while at the same time putting an end to liberalism, commercialism, population growth, war, economic downturns, and the destruction of the environment. It is another vision that could only have been conceived at the height of the Great Depression and it reflects the general disenchantment of these gloomy years.

To speak of a "planned economy," without such a basic standard of consumption and without the political means of making it prevail, is to mistake the monopolistic sabotage of large-scale capitalist industry for intelligent social control.

The foundations of this system of distribution already, I repeat, exist. Schools, libraries, hospitals, universities, museums, baths, lodging houses, gymnasia, are supported in every large center at the expense of the community as a whole. The police and the fire services, similarly, are provided on the basis of need instead of on the ability to pay: roads, canals, bridges, parks, playgrounds, and even – in Amsterdam – ferry services are similarly communized. Furthermore, in the most jejune and grudging form, a basic communism is in existence in countries that have unemployment and old-age insurance. But the latter measures are treated as means of salvage, rather than as a salutary positive mechanism for rationalizing the production and normalizing the consumptive standards of the whole community.

A basic communism, which implies the obligation to share in the work of the community up to the amount required to furnish the basis, does not mean the complete enclosure of every process and the complete satisfaction of every want in the system of planned production. Careful engineers have figured that the entire amount of work of the existing community could be carried on with less than twenty hours work per week for every existing worker: with complete rationalization all along the line, and with the elimination of duplications and parasitisms, probably less than twenty hours would suffice to produce a far greater quantity of goods than is produced at present. As it is, some 15 million industrial workers supply the needs of 120 million inhabitants of the United States. Limiting rationed production and communized consumption to basic requirements, the amount of compulsory labor would be even less. Under such provisions, technological unemployment would be a boon.

Lewis Mumford, from *Technics and Civilization*. New York: Harcourt, Brace & Co., 1934, pp. 404–5.

155 CATHERINE BAUER
from *Modern Housing* (1934)

Allied with Mumford and the Regional Planning Association of America was Catherine Bauer. Like Mumford, she had been very active on the issue of housing, and after a visit to Europe in 1930 she too became a strong proponent of European solutions, such as the low-rise housing estates of Ernst May in Frankfurt. Politically, Bauer was also a socialist, highly critical of American capitalism, and she insisted that a more general reform of the current profit system was needed before any real housing reforms could take place. As this passage shows, she allows the single-family house, but only as a row house. Her ideal solution, however, is the self-contained regionally planned new town, a more centralized modification of the Garden City, such as is found in the private experiments at Letchworth and Welwyn in the UK.

The One-Family House

The argument as to the relative merits of low houses and high or medium apartment-buildings has been going on ever since the middle of the last century. However, as very few decent flats were constructed before 1920 or later, the odds were almost always against them. Every housing-reformer believed that the ideal home was a small house with attached garden: anything else could be nothing more than an unfortunate compromise due to uncontrollable circumstances. To a great extent and with fundamental justice this belief still prevails. At least eighty-five per cent of the new English dwellings are small one-family houses or possibly two-story flats. The percentage is just as high in Belgium, and, outside of the central districts of the larger towns, in Holland and the Scandinavian countries as well. In the early years of post-war housing activity a good half of the new German dwellings were two-story one-family houses, and probably even a larger proportion of the French ones. At an exceedingly rough estimate in the eleven localities with which we are most directly concerned, I should say that very nearly half of the four and a half million government-assisted dwellings are of the one-family type.

But the one-family houses of Europe are not like those of America. The individual, free-standing house, except for an occasional open-country farmer or someone of exceptional means, has always been, and still is, practically unknown in most of Europe. The reasons are not merely traditional, and have nothing whatsoever to do with that mythical 'lower standard of living.' They are entirely realistic and thoroughly up-to-date. Why should money be spent for extra outside walls, extra land which always lies useless in the shadow of one house or the other, dead windows (or windows looking directly into other people's rooms), extra feet of pipe-line and street-pavement, and extra interior heat? Such money can be much more efficiently spent on better construction and more and better-lighted space within the house, or it can be saved outright. As Mr. Henry Wright has often pointed out, if

Catherine Bauer, from *Modern Housing*. Boston: Houghton Mifflin, 1934, pp. 188–9.

many of our deep, narrow-fronted individual bungalows were merely turned around so that their short sides adjoined, and if all the windows were then concentrated front and back, a much more economical and very much more livable dwelling-type would result. Not to mention the fact that it would lend itself much better to positive architectural treatment.

The English houses, therefore, even when the general space-standards are very high, are invariably built in attached groups of two, four, six, or more. As a rear entrance is ordinarily considered indispensable (because of the coal fires), there are often through passages between each pair of interior houses. Wherever there is enough money, brick curtain walls connect the various groups, giving privacy to rear yards and enhancing a unified street-front. Small front lawns, usually unfenced, are provided. In Welwyn there is sometimes also a wide trough of grass between the sidewalk and the street-pavement, serving instead of a curb or gutter.

On the Continent one-family houses are usually built in longer rows and at a somewhat higher density. Outside of Holland, they are almost always oriented with care and rarely built solid around the perimeter of the block. The most satisfactory results of the *Zeilenbau* method of layout, from both an economical and a social point of view, according to several German authorities, have been obtained with rows of small one- or two-story houses.

156   FRANK LLOYD WRIGHT
from ''The Jacobs House'' (1938)

Wright's fascination with ''Broadacre City'' continued to expand during the 1930s and out of it came also his concept of a ''Usonian'' house. It was intended to be a solution to the shortage of moderately priced housing – while still retaining his preference (in the face of stern opposition from Catherine Bauer and others) for the individual house. The revolutionary design grew out of an actual commission by Herbert Jacobs for a small house for his family of three. Wright rethought the idea of a house in its entirety and here is the summary of his highly creative design ideas. Wright, it might be argued, was one of the few modern architects to devote much thought and attention to the single-family house for clients of modest means.

Let's see how far the Herbert Jacobs house at Madison, Wisconsin, is a sensible house. This house for a young journalist, his wife, and small daughter, is now under roof: cost $5,500, including architect's fee of $450. Contract let to Bert Groves.

To give the little Jacobs family the benefit of industrial advantages of the era in which they live, something else must be done for them than to plant another little imitation of a mansion. Simplifications must take place. Mr. and Mrs. Jacobs must themselves see life in somewhat simplified terms. What are essentials in their case, a typical case? It is necessary to get rid of all unnecessary materials in construction, necessary to use the mill to good advantage, necessary to eliminate, so far as possible, field labor which is always expensive. It is necessary to consolidate and simplify the three appurtenance systems – heating,

Frank Lloyd Wright, from ''The Jacobs House,'' in *Architectural Forum* 68 (January 1938), pp. 78–9.

lighting, and sanitation. At least this must be done if we are to achieve the sense of spaciousness and vista already necessary.

And it would be ideal to complete the building in one operation as it goes along, inside and outside. One operation and the house is finished inside as it is completed outside. There should be no complicated roofs. Every time a hip or valley or a dormer window is allowed to ruffle a roof the life of the building is threatened. The way windows are used is naturally the most useful resource to achieve the new characteristic sense of space. All of this fenestration can be made ready at the factory and set up as the walls. But there is no longer any sense in speaking of doors and windows. These walls are largely a system of fenestration having its own part in the building scheme – the system being as much a part of the design as eyes are a part of the face.

Now what can be eliminated?

1. Visible roofs are expensive and unnecessary.
2. A garage is no longer necessary as cars are made. A carport will do, with liberal overhead shelter and walls on two sides.
3. The old-fashioned basement, except for a fuel and heater space was always a plague spot. A steam-warmed concrete mat four inches thick laid directly on the ground over gravel filling, the walls set upon that, is better.
4. Interior "trim" is no longer necessary.
5. We need no radiators, no light fixtures. We will heat the house the Roman way – that is to say – in or beneath the floors, and make the wiring system itself be the light fixtures, throwing light upon the ceiling. Light will thus be indirect except for a few outlets for floor lamps.
6. Furniture, pictures and bric-a-brac are unnecessary except as the walls can be made to include them or be them.
7. No painting at all. Wood best preserves itself. Only the floor mat need be waxed.
8. No plastering in the building.
9. No gutters, no down spouts.

Now to assist in general planning, what must or may we use in our new construction? In this case five materials: wood, brick, cement, paper, glass. To simplify fabrication we must use the horizontal unit system in construction. (See lines crossing plans both ways making rectangles 2 × 4 ft.) We must also use a vertical unit system which will be the boards and batten-bands themselves, interlocking with the brick courses.

The walls will be wood board-walls the same inside as outside – three thicknesses of boards with paper placed between them, the boards fastened together with screws. These slab-walls of boards will be high in insulating value, be vermin proof, and practically fireproof. These walls like the fenestration may be prefabricated on the floor and raised up into place, or they may be made at the mill.

157 R. BUCKMINSTER FULLER
from *Nine Chains to the Moon* (1938)

After producing designs for both his Dymaxion house and Dymaxion car, Fuller continued his inventive ways in the 1930s. He devised his Dymaxion Bathroom, an ecologically sound and highly compact, stainless-steel bathroom intended for mass production (the plumber's union vehemently opposed it and production stalled). In 1938 he published his first major book, *Nine Chains to the Moon*, which on its dustjacket carried the subtitle "An Adventure Story of Thought." It is an intellectually challenging, eccentric, and at times humorous revelation of where scientific discoveries are leading the twentieth century, as well as being a primer on such problems as garbage disposal (a plea for recycling) and other issues of ecological import. In his chapter "What is a House?" he presents these requirements for scientific scrutiny and solution, which by their nature diminish any traditional or aesthetic reasoning. Fuller was a generalist in search of universal solutions; he was also the true architect of the house-is-a-machine-for-living-in.

UNIVERSAL REQUIREMENTS OF A DWELLING MACHINE

1. OPPOSITION TO EXTERNAL DESTRUCTIVE FORCES, via spacial control against:

Earthquake	Flood	Gale	Gases
Fire	Pestilence	Tornado	Marauders

   Selfishness (Politics, Business, Materialism)

2. OPPOSITION TO INTERNAL DESTRUCTIVE FORCES, via spacial control for:
   A. Nerve Shock Proofing:
      1. Visual   2. Aural   3. Tactile   4. Olfactoral
   B. Fatigue Proofing (Human Robotism, Drudgery)
   C. Repression Proofing (Don't-proofing, Removal of Fear of Mechanical Inadequacy Developed by Accidents or Arbitrary Cellular Limits of Activity, i.e., Negative Partitioning)

3. PROVISION FOR *UNSELFCONSCIOUS PERFORMANCE* OF *INEVITABLE MECHANICAL ROUTINE* OF THE DWELLING AND ITS OCCUPANTS:
   A. FUELING of House or Occupants (Eating – Metabolism).
   B. REALIGNMENT of House or Occupants (Sleeping – Muscular, Nerve and Cellular Realignment).
   C. REFUSING of House or Occupants (Internal, i.e., Intestinal, etc.; External, i.e., Bathing or Pore Cleansing; Mental, i.e., Elimination by Empirical Dynamics; Circulatory, i.e., Atmospheric Control.

R. Buckminster Fuller, from *Nine Chains to the Moon: An Adventure Story of Thought*. Philadelphia, PA: Lippincott, 1938, p. 35.

4. PROVISION OF ADEQUATE MECHANICAL MEANS FOR ALL DEVELOPMENT REQUIREMENTS OF GROWTH PHENOMENA allowing the Facile, No-time-loss, Scientifically Efficient and Unselfconscious development of:

    A. SELECTIVE AWARENESS OF UNIVERSAL PROGRESSIONS, i.e.:

        Vital data on:

            1. History – News – Forecasts (Library, Radio, Television)

            2. Current Supply and Demand Conditions

            3. Current Dynamic Conditions – Weather – Earthquakes – Latest Scientific Research Findings.

    B. ADEQUATE MECHANICS OF ARTICULATION (Prosaic or Harmonic) through Recording by Typewriter, Drawing Board, Conversation, i.e., Communication, Direct or Indirect, Aural, Visual, or Tactile. (This also includes the necessity of Transportation and bespeaks any and all Means of Objectification or Crystallization of Universal Progress.)

    C. PROCREATION.

    D. RECREATION.

158   KATHERINE MORROW FORD
from "Modern is Regional" (1941)

I n the 1940s the interesting rift that began to appear within American modernism in the 1930s took on a more distinct form. Since 1932, the Museum of Modern Art had been active in promoting its Europeanized vision of the "International Style" based on a somewhat limited and dogmatic reading of European architecture in the 1920s. The museum's lobbying on behalf of such prominent German refugees as Walter Gropius and Mies van der Rohe – its assistance in placing them in important positions within American academe – can be interpreted as a further effort to strengthen the museum's authority in matters of taste. Opposition therefore became inevitable. One of the first challenges to the museum's concept of modernism was a book published in 1940 by James Ford and Katherine Morrow Ford, *The Modern House in America*, which divided examples of modern American domestic architecture into different regions. One year later Katherine Morrow Ford made the point more cogently in a follow-up article "Modern is Regional." Here she politely controverts the "popular impressions" that modernism has but one face and one "precise formula," by arguing that regionalism is not only a fact of modern American design, but a logical and healthy one at that. Thus an interesting counter-movement to the notion of an International Style appears in the United States. It will eventually erupt into a loud debate.

In the work of modern architects on the Atlantic seaboard from Maine to Florida, in the Pacific Coast states, as well as in the Great Lakes Region and the Southwest, regional distinctions are increasingly apparent. Native essentials characteristic of our best regional folk architecture are gradually being fused with the vitality of freed design.

Katherine Morrow Ford, from "Modern is Regional," in *House & Garden* (March 1941), pp. 35, 79.

Contrary to some popular impressions, modern architecture cannot be reduced to a precise formula. Nor is it regimented into the universal placing of a standard mold indiscriminately in the North, the South, the East or the West. Lack of studied uniformity is one of its virtues. Environmental influences are enormously important. Concessions made to climate alone result in modifications in orientation, construction and external forms. Sensitiveness to materials – new and old – and their appropriate use is another of the many facets of the new architecture.

Within a given geographical area, experiencing similar climatic conditions, still further departures from a national "style" are brought about as a result of the variety of available building materials and local craftsmanship in the use of such materials. For example, Massachusetts, with large timber resources, and Pennsylvania, with plentiful stone and ledge formations, enjoy an approximately identical climate of rigorous Winters and hot Summers, but the local building materials and methods differ considerably.

Conversely, dissimilar climates but similar native materials affect the use of identical materials and therefore the ultimate appearance of the structure. Comparison of the external structural forms of more northern sections of the Pacific Coast with those of New England, each region endowed with abundant timber, is evidence of this further regional distinction. Architecture in both these regions is of wood, but the character of each is of an entirely different type.

Many of the elements that have endeared accepted forms of architecture to Americans can be identified as regional traits. Past and present meeting the same conditions may utilize the same expedient to meet a common need. Regional necessity is in each instance the mother of invention and the reason for its continuance.

Social life and habits may of themselves vary by regions and thus dictate house forms. The indoor-outdoor house of the Los Angeles area is expressive of local interests and habits, which in turn respond to climate. Such liberal interpenetration of house and garden is inappropriate for year-round housing in the area of the Great Lakes or New England.

159 ELIEL SAARINEN
from *The City: Its Growth, Its Decay, Its Future* (1943)

The biggest factor supporting the notion of a regional American modernism was the physical size of the United States. Moreover, such regional centers as Chicago, Los Angeles, and San Francisco had by the 1940s long promoted visions of modernism different from those of the Northeast. Yet by this time newer regional centers also began to form, and one of the more interesting of these was Cranbrook Academy, outside of Detroit. The campus of several schools had been founded in the early 1920s by the publisher George Booth, and the recently emigrated architect Eliel Saarinen (of Chicago Tribune fame) began the master planning and design of the campus buildings. One of Booth's dreams was to set up an institution similar to the American Academy in Rome, and to this

Eliel Saarinen, from *The City: Its Growth, Its Decay, Its Future*. New York: Reinhold, 1943, pp. 22–3.

end Saarinen, who would become Cranbrook's director, created what was in effect a paid sabbatical for artists and architects to focus on new ideas. Between 1939 and 1941 Eliel's son Eero, already an accomplished architect, was placed in charge of the architectural program, and during this period he invited to the Academy such talented individuals as Edmund Bacon, Florence Schust Knoll, Charles Eames, Harry Weese, and Ralph Rapson.

Eliel Saarinen was also an important maverick modernist in his own right, as this book demonstrates. Opposing CIAM and such international currents as Le Corbusier's idea of a Radiant City (which favored the massive destruction of older urban fabrics), Saarinen proposed his vision of "organic order" and "organic decentralization" – the surgical repair of deteriorated or blighted areas of failing cities. His image of a successful city was something similar to his native Helsinki, and this somewhat Sittesque vision represents one of the first efforts by an American architect – after the urgings of Lewis Mumford and Henry Wright – to address the problems confronting urban centers.

The most important harvest from this first part of our analysis will be the essential fact that the fundamental reason for success or failure in all town-building depends on **whether or not town formation is based on the architectural principle of organic order. This,** we will find, **is not only an essential fact, but also an imperative one.** Consequently, when we – in the second part of our analysis – come to investigate contemporary and future town-building problems exclusively, we are going to do it with the presupposition that, behold: **any problem must be solved so as to bring the physical formation of the town into accord with this architectural principle of organic order.**

Yet, behold even the following:

While studying contemporary and future town-building problems, we will soon discover that the imperativeness of this architectural principle of organic order **is almost the only lesson that past experiences in town building can teach us. In almost all the other phases of town-building we are confronted with problems so entirely new, so completely reversed, and so utterly absent from the experience of any previous era as to make a thoroughly new orientation most urgent.** Indeed, as radical a change in the means of transportation as we have witnessed during these days of technical progress calls for a correspondingly radical change in the mode of approach to town-planning problems. And this changed mode of approach can be found **"only in and through" present and future conditions of life.**

As for this changed mode of approach, we can already now discern a strong tendency from the present concentration toward a decentralization to come. There is much evidence that the wave of the cities' rapid growth and increased concentration has been met by a counter-wave of decentralization, bringing into existence suburbs, satellite towns, neighbor communities, and all sorts of miscellaneous settlements about the core of the original concentration.

Concentration and decentralization are two opposite poles. Opposite are even their reasons for existence. This means that, once the reasons for concentration are known, it is a matter of simple logic to draw one's conclusions as to the reasons for decentralization. Consequently, our analysis in this second part will deal with the problems of concentration before we undertake to investigate those forces which make decentralization a logical necessity. Through this analysis we will learn that concentration in the overgrown cities has caused compactness and disorder and, through these, deterioration and the spread of slums. Furthermore, we will learn that the only remedy in such circumstances is a decisive surgery which can bring openness into the compact urban situation, and which – if executed gradually according to an organically comprehensive scheme – is the surest road toward decentralization, or rather, toward "organic decentralization."

"Organic decentralization" must be the key-word, and it must be the leading theme throughout our whole analysis of modern problems. So it must be, **for only through an organic solution of the problems of decentralization can organic order be brought into the city and made lastingly effective.**

160 GYÖRGY KEPES
from *Language of Vision* (1944)

Another prominent European modernist making his way to the United States was Lázló Moholy-Nagy, who arrived in Chicago in 1937 to head the New Bauhaus (later renamed the Institute of Design). In attempting to reconstruct the German Bauhaus on American soil, the Hungarian Moholy-Nagy amassed, with a small budget, an extraordinary faculty at the school that included Charles Morris, George Keck, and Ralph Rapson. Also joining the faculty was György Kepes, a countryman of Moholy-Nagy, who was much influenced by Sigfried Giedion's *Space, Time and Architecture* as well as by the research of Gestalt psychologists. Kepes's book, with its remarkable mixture of wartime pessimism and avant-garde theory, argues for an entirely new visual foundation for the new space-time reality of the modern world. It would prove to be an enduring vision and therefore one influential in the immediate postwar years.

Today we experience chaos. The waste of human and material resources and the canalization of almost all creative effort into blind alleys bear witness to the fact that our common life has lost its coherency. In the focus of this eclipse of a healthy human existence is the individual, torn by the shattered fragments of his formless world, incapable of organizing his physical and psychological needs.

This tragic formlessness is the result of a contradiction in our social existence. It indicates our failure in the organization of that new equipment with which we must function if we are to maintain our equilibrium in a dynamic world.

[...]

Technological discoveries have extended and reshaped the physical environment. They have changed our visual surroundings partly by actually rebuilding the physical environment, and partly by presenting visual tools that are of assistance to our discernment of those phases of the visible world which were previously too small, too fast, too large, or too slow for us to comprehend. Vision is primarily a device of orientation; a means to measure and organize spatial events. The mastery of nature is intimately connected with the mastery of space; this is visual orientation. Each new visual environment demands a reorientation, a new way of measuring. Seeing spatial relationships on a flat land is a different experience from seeing them in a mountainous region, where one form intercepts the other. To orient oneself in walking requires a different spatial measurement than is required in riding in a motor-car or in an aeroplane. To grasp spatial relationships and orient oneself in a metropolis of today, among the intricate dimensions of streets, subways, elevated, and skyscrapers,

György Kepes, from *Language of Vision*. Chicago: P. Theobald, 1944, reprint edition New York: Dover, 1995, pp. 12, 13–14.

requires a new way of seeing. Widening horizons, and the new dimensions of the visual environment necessitate new idioms of spatial measurement and communication of space. The visual image of today must come to terms with all this: it must evolve a language of space which is adjusted to the new standards of experience. This new language can and will enable the human sensibility to perceive space-time relationships never recognized before.

Vision is not only orientation in physical spheres but also orientation in human spheres. Man can no more bear chaos in his emotional and intellectual life than he can bear it in his biological existence. In each age of human history man was compelled to search for a temporary equilibrium in his conflicts with nature and in his relations with other men, and thus created, through an organization of visual imagery, a symbolic order of his psychological and intellectual experiences. These forms of his creative imagination directed and inspired him toward materializing the potential order inherent in each stage of history. But until today, the symbolic organization of psychological and intellectual conflicts has been limited in its power because it was fastened to a static system of object concepts. Today, the dynamics of social events, and the new vistas of a mobile, physical world, have compelled us to exchange a static iconography for a dynamic one. Visual language thus must absorb the dynamic idioms of the visual imagery to mobilize the creative imagination for positive social action, and direct it toward positive social goals.

Today, creative artists have three tasks to accomplish if the language of vision is to be made a potent factor in reshaping our lives. They must learn and apply the laws of *plastic organization* needed for the re-establishing of the created image on a healthy basis. They must make terms with contemporary spatial experiences to learn to utilize the *visual representation* of contemporary space-time events. Finally, they must release the reserves of creative imagination and organize them into dynamic idioms, that is, develop a contemporary *dynamic iconography.*

161 KONRAD WACHSMANN
"A Tubular Steel Design" (1944)

Yet another figure to be associated with the Institute of Design was the architect and engineer Konrad Wachsmann. Born in Germany, he trained in Dresden and Berlin before focusing his efforts in the late 1920s on the problem of prefabricated building elements. One of his early commissions was a house for Albert Einstein. His exile from Germany in the 1930s first took him to Rome, where he experimented with reinforced concrete, and then to France, before he settled in the United States in 1941. During the war years he worked with Walter Gropius on the development of a "Packaged House System" (factory-produced houses assembled on site), which went into unsuccessful production in their joint business venture, General Panel Corporation. At the same time, Wachsmann began developing his "Mobilar Structure" – the first of his experiments in devising the "space frame." Wachsmann describes this invention here in retrospect. It would be still further refined in the 1950s with his extraordinary designs for aircraft hangers for the US Air Force.

Konrad Wachsmann, "A Tubular Steel Design," in *The Turning Point of Building: Structure and Design.* New York: Reinhold, 1961, pp. 160–1.

During 1944–45 I developed a wide-span structural system, on which I had already done some preliminary work in France towards the end of the Thirties. This system was subsequently named "Mobilar Structure" and its further development was sponsored by the Atlas Aircraft Corporation.

The problem was to try and utilize the advantageous statical properties of tubular cross sections in steel construction. The chief result of these investigations, which extended over 1½ years and for which I was again able to assemble a team of engineers, designers and technicians, was the development of a new truss joint and a movable wall panel assembly.

The principal link in the joint is formed by a pair of stamped eye plates of different thicknesses, automatically spot-welded at each end of the tube, one on each side of the center-line. The center of the connection is formed by a pin which is passed through the openings in the eye plates at right angles to the axis of the tube. While the inside face of the thicker of the two eye plates coincides with the center-line of the tube, the second, thinner eye plate is mounted in such a way that it counteracts the eccentricity resulting from the reversed orientation of the pair of eye plates with which it mates.

It is a characteristic of this connection that it is light and open precisely at the point where, in conventional construction, an especially large amount of material is used up in gusset plates. The tubes themselves are not in contact, but are held at a proper distance from the center of the joint without interfering with its twin stress-transmitting and separating functions. The tubular-members can thus be combined in any way, though still only in the sense of a two-dimensional structure.

In order to meet increased stresses, particularly those due to cantilevering, since top and bottom chords must be kept parallel for the sake of standardization, and at the same time to avoid changes in the standard connection, the additional forces are taken up by progressively thickening the tube walls.

Thus, a Mobilar structure consists of tubular members of various standard lengths with offset eye plates welded at each end, assembled in any combination of truss, column, purlin, etc. In spite of the fact that eye plates have been used in steel structures for a long time now and were especially prevalent towards the end of the nineteenth century, though restricted mainly to tension joints, the very precise fit which must be achieved between the pin and the various eye plates must be considered a serious weakness in the systems which employ them. Nevertheless, investigations have shown that, in this case too, the precision techniques of industrial production will give a technically effective and economically competitive structure.

The application of this system to a medium-sized aircraft hangar with unrestricted access from all sides is demonstrated in the study illustrated. The basic unit, shown here, consists of two main frames, to which cantilevered secondary trusses are attached. The hangar can be expanded as desired by adding similar units on either side.

The main frames are supported on pairs of columns built up from the same structural elements. Near the supports the structure can be reinforced or stiffened to meet varying conditions of stress by arranging members in clusters. While the use of tubular elements gives the structure sufficient rigidity in the longitudinal direction, it is braced with cables in the transverse direction, as the type of joint selected does not permit members to be connected at right-angles.

It was intended to use prefabricated standard panels for roofing, skylights, etc.

162   JOHN ENTENZA
announcement of "The case study house program" (1945)

O ne of the most innovative experiments in American residential design ever to take place was the Case Study House program. In 1939 John Entenza purchased the magazine *California Arts and Architecture* and promptly dropped the word "California" from the title, in an effort to expand the regional readership of the journal. The magazine, however, continued to be a strong supporter of West-Coast modernism with its distinct regional characteristics. As the war was drawing to a close in 1945, Entenza came up with the scheme for the magazine to commission a number of prominent architects to design (and the magazine to build) a series of low-cost, experimental houses, which would then be open to the public for educational purposes before being sold. The idea again was to provide developers with suggestions on how modernism can be affected with modest means. The venture proved to be a great success, as twenty-three houses were built, often in highly desirable locations. Among the architects participating were William Wilson Wurster, J. R. Davidson, Richard Neutra, Ralph Soriano, Eero Saarinen, Charles Eames, and Pierre Koenig. Several masterpieces of residential design came out of this program.

Because most opinion, both profound and light-headed, in terms of post war housing is nothing but speculation in the form of talk and reams of paper, it occurs to us that it might be a good idea to get down to cases and at least make a beginning in the gathering of that mass of material that must eventually result in what we know as "house – post war".

Agreeing that the whole matter is surrounded by conditions over which few of us have any control, certainly we can develop a point of view and do some organized thinking which might come to a practical end. It is with that in mind that we now announce the project we have called THE "CASE STUDY" HOUSE PROGRAM.

The magazine has undertaken to supply an answer insofar as it is possible to correlate the facts and point them in the direction of an end result. We are, within the limits of uncontrollable factors, proposing to begin immediately the study, planning, actual design and construction of eight houses, each to fulfil the specifications of a special living problem in the Southern California area. Eight nationally known architects, chosen not only for their obvious talents, but for their ability to evaluate realistically housing in terms of need, have been commissioned to take a plot of God's green earth and create "good" living conditions for eight American families. They will be free to choose or reject, on a merit basis, the products of national manufacturers offering either old or new materials considered best for the purpose by each architect in his attempt to create contemporary dwelling units. We are quite aware that the meaning of "contemporary" changes by the minute and it is conceivable that each architect might wish to change his idea or a part of his idea when time for actual building arrives. In that case he will, within reason, be permitted to do so. (Incidentally, the eight men have been chosen for, among other things, reasonableness, which they have consistently maintained at a very high level.)

John Entenza, announcement of "The case study program," in *Arts & Architecture* (January 1945), pp. 37–9.

We will try and arrange the over-all plan so that it will make fairly good sense, despite the fact that building even one house has been known to throw a client off balance for years. Briefly, then, we will begin on the problem as posed to the architect, with the analysis of land in relation to work, schools, neighborhood conditions and individual family need. Each house will be designed within a specified budget, subject, of course, to the dictates of price fluctuation. It will be a natural part of the problem however to work as closely as possible within this budget or give very good reasons for not being able to do so.

Beginning with the February issue of the magazine and for eight months or longer thereafter, each house will make its appearance with the comments of the architect – his reasons for his solution and his choice of specific materials to be used. All this predicated on the basis of a house that he knows can be built when restrictions are lifted or as soon as practicable thereafter.

Architects will be responsible to no one but the magazine, which having put on a long white beard, will pose as "client". It is to be clearly understood that every consideration will be given to new materials and new techniques in house construction. And we must repeat again that these materials will be selected on a purely merit basis by the architects themselves. We have been promised fullest cooperation by manufacturers of products and appliances who have agreed to place in the hands of the architects the full results of research on the products they intend to offer the public. No attempt will be made to use a material merely because it is new or tricky. On the other hand, neither will there be any hesitation in discarding old materials and techniques if their only value is that they have been generally regarded as "safe".

Each architect takes upon himself the responsibility of designing a house which would, under all ordinary conditions be subject to the usual (and sometimes regrettable) building restrictions. The house must be capable of duplication and in no sense be an individual "performance".

All eight houses will be opened to the public for a period of from six to eight weeks and thereafter an attempt will be made to secure and report upon tenancy studies to see how successfully the job has been done. Each house will be completely furnished under a working arrangement between the architect, the designer and the furniture manufacturer, either to the architect's specifications or under his supervision.

This, then, is an attempt to find out on the most practical basis known to us, the facts (and we hope the figures) which will be available to the general public when it is once more possible to build houses.

It is important that the best materials available be used in the best possible way in order to arrive at a "good" solution of each problem, which in the over-all program will be general enough to be of practical assistance to the average American in search of a home in which he can afford to live.

We can only promise our best efforts in the midst of the confusions and contradictions that confront every man who is now thinking about his post war home. We expect to report as honestly and directly as we know how the conclusions which must inevitably be drawn from the mass of material that these very words will loose about our heads. Therefore, while the objective is very firm, the means and the methods must of necessity remain fluid in order that the general plan can be accommodated to changing conditions and conceptions.

We hope to be able to resolve some part of that controversy now raging between those who believe in miracles and those who are dead set against them. For average prospective house owners the choice between the hysterics who hope to solve housing problems by magic alone and those who attempt to ride into the future piggy back on the status quo, the situation is confusing and discouraging. Therefore it occurs to us that the only way in which any of us can find out anything will be to pose specific problems in a specific program on a put-up-or-shut-up basis. We hope that a fairly good answer will be the result of our efforts.

For ourselves, we will remain noncommital until all the facts are in. Of course we have opinions but they remain to be proved. That building, whether immediate or far distant, is likely to begin again where it left off, is something we frankly do not believe. Not only in very practical changes of materials and techniques but in the distribution and financing of those materials lie factors that are likely to expand considerably the definition of what we mean when we now say the word "house". How long it will take for the inevitable social and economic changes brought about by the war years to affect our living standards, no one can say. But, that ideas and attitudes will continue to change drastically in terms of man's need and man's ability to satisfy that need, is inevitable.

Perhaps we will cling longest to the symbol of "house" as we have known it, or perhaps we will realize that in accommodating ourselves to a new world the most important step in avoiding retrogression into the old, is a willingness to understand and to accept contemporary ideas in the creation of environment that is responsible for shaping the largest part of our living and thinking.

A good result of all this then, would, among other things, be a practical point of view based on available facts that can lead to a measurement of the average man's living standards in terms of the house he will be able to build when restrictions are lifted.

We of course assume that the shape and form of post war living is of primary importance to a great many Americans, and that is our reason for attempting to find at least enough of an answer to give some direction to current thinking on the matter. Whether that answer is to be the "miracle" house remains to be seen, but it is our guess that after all of the witches have stirred up the broth, the house that will come out of the vapors will be conceived within the spirit of our time, using as far as is practicable, many war-born techniques and materials best suited to the expression of man's life in the modern world.

What man has learned about himself in the last five years will, we are sure, express itself in the way in which he will want to be housed in the future. Only one thing will stop the realization of that wish and that is the tenacity with which man clings to old forms because he does not yet understand the new.

It becomes the obligation of all those who serve and profit through man's wish to live well, to take the mysteries and the black magic out of the hard facts that go into the building of "house".

This can be and, to the best of our ability, will be an attempt to perform some part of that service. But this program is not being undertaken in the spirit of the "neatest trick of the week." We hope it will be understood and accepted as a sincere attempt not merely to preview, but to assist in giving some direction to the creative thinking on housing being done by good architects and good manufacturers whose joint objective is good housing.
—THE EDITOR.

PART V HIGH MODERNISM IN THE POSTWAR YEARS

A. POSTWAR THEORY IN THE UNITED STATES

Introduction

World War II concluded in Europe with the sack of Berlin in May 1945, one month after the death of Franklin Roosevelt. The tenuous alliance between Great Britain, France, and the United States in the West and the Soviet Union in the East did not survive long thereafter, as Joseph Stalin coolly proceeded to consolidate control of his "spheres of influence" (ceded at Yalta) by erecting the Iron Curtain. Thus the Cold War began almost before the "hot war" ended, leaving Europe fractured in two and many countries in a condition of physical and psychological devastation. Germany, in particular, would take more than a decade to show signs of even a modest recovery. The situation was very different in the United States. Not only had an unprecedented war effort organized on two continental fronts created an economic superpower with unparalleled capacity for technological innovation, but the massive influx of returning GIs, wartime refugees, and relocated intellectuals supplied both the labor and brainpower to take full advantage of the situation.

Thus the postwar years and the decade of the 1950s – notwithstanding the Korean War, McCarthyism, and the Cold War – were largely a period of great optimism and surging economic progress. The veterans returning from the war created a "baby-boom" generation, while the GI Bill allowed unprecedented access to higher education. The European architects who landed in the United States more often than not merged their native sensibilities with those of their new land, just as the demand for construction, especially in the major urban centers, achieved new heights. The earlier competition between European and American traditions of modernism now rises to the level of a healthy debate.

163   PHILIP C. JOHNSON
from *Mies van der Rohe* (1947)

Among the many European architects who came to America, none would achieve greater success and influence than Mies van der Rohe. He decided to leave Germany relatively late, but when he arrived in Chicago in 1938 to head the architecture program at the Armour Institute of Technology (shortly to be renamed the Illinois Institute of Technology), he came with enthusiasm and with the commission to design a new campus for the school on the south side of Chicago. His designs for the brick, steel, and glass buildings began to unfold during the war years, and in 1947 the Museum of Modern Art decided to award its favorite son (favorite since 1932) with an exhibition of his work. As the exhibition's curator Philip Johnson (who himself had just completed his architectural studies at Harvard) noted in the preface to his exhibition catalogue: "Of all the great modern architects Mies van der Rohe is the least known." This situation would not last for long, for by the early 1950s Mies would emerge as one of the world's leading architects. This passage from the catalogue explaining Mies's work on the IIT campus reveals an insight into Mies's approach to design as well as the critical acumen of Johnson, who also would emerge as a prominent American architect in the 1950s.

According to Mies, he would not have designed this building as he has without the example of Berlage. In it he has carried Berlage's theory of structural honesty to a logical extreme. Structural elements are revealed as are those of a Gothic cathedral: the inside and outside of the enclosing walls are identical in appearance, since the same steel columns and brick panels of the exterior are visible on the interior. In other words, he has conceived the design in terms of steel channels and angles, I-beams and H-columns, just as a medieval design is conceived in terms of stone vaults and buttresses. But there is one major difference. He allows no decoration except that formed by the character and juxtaposition of the structural elements. And whereas the medieval architect relied on the collaboration of the sculptor and painter for his ultimate effect, Mies, so to speak, has had to perform the functions of all three professions. He joins steel to steel, or steel to glass or brick, with all the taste and skill that formerly went into the chiseling of a stone capital or the painting of a fresco.

The extraordinary subtleties of his detailing are most easily seen in photographs of two of the completed structures: the Minerals and Metals Research building and the Alumni

Philip C. Johnson, from *Mies van der Rohe*. New York: Museum of Modern Art, 1947, pp. 138–40.

Memorial building. Inside the first, for example, the exposed beams and girders of the roof are arranged as carefully as those of a Renaissance beamed ceiling. In the Memorial building the amount of exposed structure is reduced by fireproofing. For this reason steel columns which would otherwise be visible are necessarily covered with concrete. The columns, in turn, are faced with mullions, but these are not permitted to masquerade as supports; instead they are stopped short just above the ground to reveal their true nature. This is a remarkable subtlety, as is the fact that the mullions, in framing the brick and glass panels, never merge with them, but are clearly separated by shadow-casting indentations, giving to the walls somewhat the quality of a relief. These indentations serve at the same time to minimize the inevitable unevenness of the brick panel edges by removing them from the straight mullions.

The same device is used in the hallway to separate the acoustical ceiling tiles from the walls, thus avoiding the crooked joint that might occur if the two planes met. Other notable refinements here are the rabbeted wooden glass frames and the expertly placed door handles and locks. The cantilevered stairway is of such easy, weightless beauty that it is difficult to imagine the amount of thought behind it. Artistry, a vast accumulation of technical knowledge and many hours of patient experimentation went into the exquisite details: the length and position of the wall railing, the simple joining of the outside railing to the stringer, and the clean articulated sweep of the unsupported flight of steps.

The simplicity of this particular architectural feature is characteristic of every campus building and symptomatic of the philosophy that shaped them. Mies expresses it in the German phrase *beinahe nichts*, "almost nothing." He does not want these buildings to be self-consciously architectural; he desires rather "the absence of architecture" and in its place he practices *Baukunst*, "the art of building." The structures executed so far may strike the untrained eye as unnecessarily barren since they are units of a larger design, the subtle beauty of which will emerge only when the whole is completed.

164 T. H. ROBSJOHN-GIBBINGS
from *Mona Lisa's Mustache* (1947)

T. H. Robsjohn-Gibbings was a Manhattan-based interior designer, whose first book of 1944, *Good-Bye, Mr. Chippendale*, was a jocose upbraiding of the American furniture industry for its obsession with replicating traditional European styles. With *Mona Lisa's Mustache*, Robsjohn-Gibbings continues to track America's sense of cultural inferiority: now by setting his droll sights on the Museum of Modern Art. The book's purposely outrageous theme – "*that the art we call modern art today was actually a revival of the systems used in primitive and ancient magic*" – deserves clarification, because the author's style is to overstate his case. His leading contention is that the avant-garde movements of the teens and 1920s introduced a range of non-artistic and therefore destructive interests into art: primitivism, mysticism, facetiousness, showmanship, and above all politics. His second contention is that the Museum of Modern Art has in effect swallowed this sausage whole, under the naive assumption that avant-garde art had to be serious cuisine because it was European. The exhibition on the International Style of 1932

T. H. Robsjohn-Gibbings, from *Mona Lisa's Mustache: A Dissection of Modern Art.* New York: Alfred A. Knopf, 1947, pp. 211–13.

comes in for some harsh words, as does the Bauhaus and Le Corbusier, as this passage shows. Humor aside, Robsjohn-Gibbings raises serious questions at the beginning of a serious debate.

Certainly there can be no question that in its later phases the Bauhaus was a sort of melting-pot for every brand of magic ism in Europe. Expressionism, futurism, constructivism, suprematism, dadaism, and surrealism, to mention the most obvious ones, could be seen at some time or other as the basis of the Bauhaus productions. It was by no means an exaggeration when one of the American Bauhaus students of 1932 said: "The Bauhaus in Germany was essentially a conglomeration of the principles and methods of various art cliques in Europe.... This æsthetic stew then in its final state became a glorification of that popular fallacy – the Machine God."

Incidentally, the worshippers of the machine god had found that the *machine à habiter* was by no means restricted to the Bauhaus; in fact, the cult of the house as "a machine for living" also centered in a Swiss artist, Charles-Édouard Jeanneret, who went under the pseudonym of Le Corbusier.

Starting as a student of the Art Nouveau movement, Corbusier, inspired by Puccini's *La Bohème*, had studied in Paris in 1908, where he fell in with the futurists and cubists and the primitive magic cults. In 1910 he moved on to Berlin, where he absorbed the grain-elevator and silo mysticism then popular in Germany, and in 1918 he was back in Paris, where he launched his own special ism, purism.

Purism was so close to futurism that it was practically the same thing. It involved an emphasis on "the impersonal elegance of machines"; in fact, the purists insisted that painting should hold its own with machines in precision and workmanship. In 1923 Corbusier began to apply this machine precision to architecture. Echoing Marinetti, he announced that "owing to the machine, our environment is undergoing a comprehensive transformation in its outer aspect as well as in its utilization." He also announced that houses should be thought of as "machines for living" and that architects should become "the elite of society."

Toward the end of the 1920's the neo-futurist machine-precision architecture of Corbusier and the Bauhaus was being labeled by its admirers as "the International Style." In fact, it was even being described as "the only genuine architectural style since the eighteenth century." *It was evidently hoped by the intelligentsia of the machine-approach-to-architecture that a machine "style" could be imposed internationally in the same way Greco-Roman classicism was imposed as a style in feudal times.*

165 LEWIS MUMFORD
from "Status Quo" (1947)

I n the postwar years Lewis Mumford became one of America's best-known intellectuals, and he was hired to write a regular column for *The New Yorker*, which appeared under the banner "The Sky Line." He wrote on a wide range of subjects, but architecture was often not far from his interests. He was a strong critic, for instance, of Le Corbusier's design for the United Nations Building, as he was of the urban redevelopment policies of

Lewis Mumford, from "Status Quo," in *The New Yorker* (October 11, 1947), pp. 106, 109–10.

New York's Robert Moses. In this particular column, which begins by addressing the changing skylines of American cities, Mumford concludes with a brief discussion of what he terms the "Bay Region style" of California. Again, it was an indirect swipe at the Museum of Modern Art and the notion of an "International style," but these words would now draw an immediate response from the museum in "backward old New York." The reference to Hitchcock and Wright refers to their collaboration on *In the Nature of Materials,* a monograph on Wright's work that appeared in 1942.

Meanwhile, new winds are beginning to blow, and presently they may hit even backward old New York. The very critics, such as Mr. Henry-Russell Hitchcock, who twenty years ago were identifying the "modern" in architecture with Cubism in painting and with a general glorification of the mechanical and the impersonal and the aesthetically puritanic have become advocates of the personalism of Frank Lloyd Wright. Certainly Le Corbusier's dictum of the twenties – that the modern house is a machine for living in – has become old hat; the modern accent is on living, not on the machine. (This change must hit hardest those academic American modernists who imitated Le Corbusier and Mies van der Rohe and Gropius, as their fathers imitated the reigning lights of the Ecole des Beaux-Arts.) Mr. Siegfried Giedion, once a leader of the mechanical rigorists, has come out for the monumental and the symbolic, and among the younger people an inclination to play with the "feeling" elements in design – with color, texture, even painting and sculpture – has become insuppressible. "Functionalism," writes a rather pained critic in a recent issue of the *Architectural Review* of London, "the only real aesthetic faith to which the modern architect could lay claim in the inter-war years, is now, if not repudiated, certainly called into question . . . by those who were formerly its most illustrious supporters."

We are bound to hear more of this development during the next decade, but I am not alarmed by the prospect. What was called functionalism was a one-sided interpretation of function, and it was an interpretation that Louis Sullivan, who popularized the slogan "Form follows function," never subscribed to. The rigorists placed the mechanical functions of a building above its human functions; they neglected the feelings, the sentiments, and the interests of the person who was to occupy it. Instead of regarding engineering as a foundation for form, they treated it as an end. This kind of architectural onesidedness was not confined to the more arid practitioners. Frank Lloyd Wright, it is said, once turned upon a client – let's call him John Smith – who had added a few pleasant rugs and comfortable Aalto chairs to Mr. Wright's furnishings, and exclaimed, "You have ruined this place completely, and you have disgraced *me.* This is no longer a Frank Lloyd Wright house. It is a John Smith house now."

Well, it was time that some of our architects remembered the non-mechanical and non-formal elements in architecture, that they remembered what a building says as well as what it does. A house, as the Uruguayan architect Julio Vilamajó has put it, should be as personal as one's clothes and should fit the family life just as well. This is not a new doctrine in the United States. People like Bernhard Maybeck and William Wilson Wurster, in California, always practiced it, and they took good care that their houses did not resemble factories or museums. So I don't propose to join the solemn gentlemen who, aware of this natural reaction against a sterile and abstract modernism, are predicting a return to the graceful stereotypes of the eighteenth century. Rather, I look for the continued spread, to every part of our country, of that native and humane form of modernism which one might call the Bay

Region style, a free yet unobtrusive expression of the terrain, the climate, and the way of life on the Coast. That style took root about fifty years ago in Berkeley, California, in the early work of John Galen Howard and Maybeck, and by now, on the Coast, it is simply taken for granted; no one out there is foolish enough to imagine that there is any other proper way of building in our time. The style is actually a product of the meeting of Oriental and Occidental architectural traditions, and it is far more truly a universal style than the so-called international style of the nineteen-thirties, since it permits regional adaptations and modifications. Some of the best examples of this at once native and universal tradition are being built in New England. The change that is now going on in both Europe and America means only that modern architecture is past its adolescent period, with its quixotic purities, its awkward self-consciousness, its assertive dogmatism. The good young architects today are familiar enough with the machine and its products and processes to take them for granted, and so they are ready to relax and enjoy themselves a little. That will be better for all of us.

166   ALFRED H. BARR, JR.
from "What is Happening to Modern Architecture?" (1948)

Mumford's column obviously ruffled some feathers, for within a year the Museum of Modern Art scheduled a symposium to address the question of just "What is Happening to Modern Architecture?" All of the museum's peacocks attended – Barr, Hitchcock, and Johnson – as well as Walter Gropius, Marcel Breuer, Peter Blake, and Eero Saarinen, among many others. Mumford defended his position of the need for a regional modernism before a generally hostile audience, while Barr harshly condemned the "Bay Region Style" as a form of "*neue Gemutlichkeit*" (new sentimentality). But the condemnation was not altogether uncompromising. Barr, as this passage shows, argued that the principles of the International style were not as rigid and dogmatic as they were generally portrayed, while Gropius even saw the Bay region vernacular as an "enrichment of our architectural idiom." The debate, at least, had now become specific in its intensification.

Another misconception current today is that International Style was conceived as a kind of rigid strait-jacket requiring architects to design cubistic, white stucco boxes on Lally columns, with flat roofs and glass walls. In 1932, Hitchcock and Johnson put the matter differently:

"The idea of style as the frame of potential growth, rather than as a fixed and crushing mould, has developed with the recognition of underlying principles such as archeologists discern in the great styles of the past. The principles are few and broad. They are not mere formulas of proportion such as distinguish the Doric from the Ionic order; they are fundamental, like the organic verticality of the Gothic or the rhythmical symmetry of the Baroque. There is, first, a new conception of architecture as volume rather than as mass. Secondly, regularity rather than axial symmetry serves as the chief means of ordering design.

Alfred H. Barr, from "What is Happening to Modern Architecture?," in *Museum of Modern Art Bulletin* 15 (Spring 1948), pp. 6–8.

These two principles, with a third proscribing arbitrary applied decoration, mark the productions of the International Style.

"This new style is not international in the sense that the production of one country is just like that of another. Nor is it so rigid that the work of various leaders is not clearly distinguishable. The International Style has become evident and definable only gradually as different innovators throughout the world have successfully carried out parallel experiments."

On rereading this book, I find, too, that the authors did not dogmatize about materials. They praised Mies van der Rohe and Le Corbusier for their then recent desertion of flat stucco for fieldstone and marble. About wood, which was generally neglected by the modern architects of the twenties, they wrote: "In many regions, wood, for example, is economically the most satisfactory material. For certain types of building, its relative impermanence is not a disadvantage. Nor is there anything in wooden construction which makes it unsuitable to the esthetic or the functional disciplines of the contemporary style."

Nor did they ignore the human needs of the clients. On the contrary, they made fun of the doctrinaire-functionalists who designed housing for "some proletarian superman of the future," and insisted that "there should be a balance between evolving houses for scientific living and providing comfortable houses for ordinary living." They welcomed the idea of national and personal variants of the style. They paid honor to Frank Lloyd Wright, not only as the most important single source of the style, but also as the magnificent living example of romantic individualism.

They concluded their book with these words:

"The International Style is broad and elastic enough for many varying talents and for many decades of development. We have, as the Egyptians had or the Chinese, as the Greeks and our own ancestors in the Middle Ages before us, a style which orders the visible manifestation of a certain close relationship between structure and function. Regardless of specific types of structure or of function, the style has a definable esthetic. That esthetic, like modern technics, will develop and change; it will hardly cease to exist. It is found in the humblest buildings, as well as in monuments, fully architectural. Those who have buried architecture, whether from a thwarted desire to continue the past or from an overanxiety to modify and hurry on the future, have been premature: We have an architecture still."

What has happened to the International Style since 1932, particularly in this country? That it has been very widely influential, I think no one will deny. One has only to study our architectural magazines, the real estate pages of our newspapers, the work done in our architectural schools to see that the Style has largely transformed architecture in this country. Of course, Frank Lloyd Wright would deny that he has been influenced himself, but I invite you to draw your own conclusions after you have compared his designs made before 1932 with his more recent work.

Of course the Style has developed and changed and mellowed. It has even generated reactions and created new opponents here and abroad. We may mention in passing the bitter hostility of Hitler and his National Socialist architects to the International Style. Fortunately, this is now a matter of history. But parallel to the German reaction has been the Soviet revival of the stylistic chaos and pomposities of the nineteenth century in the name of proletarian taste and socialist realism. In this country at the present moment, I would say that our best architects take the style for granted so far as large buildings are concerned, whether they be office buildings, apartment houses, schools, stores, airports, or, most appropriately, the new buildings for the United Nations.

We have among us, however, some old-line functionalists, some orthodox social realists and, lastly, the designers of houses, in the style which Mr. Mumford has proposed might be called the "Bay Region Style."

That there has developed during the past ten years an informal and ingratiating kind of wooden domestic building cannot be denied, but if one studies British, Swiss, and Scandinavian architectural magazines, it is clear that this style, too, is international. Indeed, I think we might call this kind of building the International Cottage Style, for it appears to be a kind of domestication of the International Style itself, a kind of *neue Gemütlichkeit* with which to supersede the *neue Sachlichkeit* of the 1920's. It would seem to fulfill Hitchcock and Johnson's suggestion made in 1932 that more wood be used in modern architecture. At the same time, it answers their criticism of the doctrinaire functionalists for not providing "comfortable houses for ordinary living."

It is significant, however, that when such a master of the Cottage Style as William Wurster is faced with a problem of designing an office building or a great project for the United Nations, he falls back upon a pretty orthodox version of the International Style.

167 PHILIP C. JOHNSON
from "The Glass House" (1950)

After his early period at the Museum of Modern Art and after some very questionable years in support of Nazi politics, Philip Johnson studied architecture at Harvard Graduate School of Design in the mid-1940s. Upon graduating, this son of considerable financial inheritance curated the show on Mies van der Rohe in 1947, which occasion allowed a friendship to develop between the two men. Out of their architectural discussions came Johnson's "Glass House" in New Canaan, Connecticut. The design of this simple, rectangular glass structure owed everything to Mies's (yet unbuilt) design for the Farnsworth House, as Johnson was not hesitant to note. But when Johnson published photographs of the work in the pages of *Architectural Review* in 1950 he introduced something relatively new into twentieth-century architectural theory. He credited as sources for his design not just Mies but an eclectic array of other influences – effectively reintroducing both eclecticism and historicism into architectural parlance. His article consisted of a number of photographs, under which he placed captions articulating his sources. These first nine captions cited below, even without the accompanying photographs, give a good sense of the curious architectural turn taken by this coauthor of *The International Style*.

1   Le Corbusier: Farm Village Plan – 1933.

The approach to the house through meadow and copse is derived from English Eighteenth Century precedent. The actual model is Count Pückler's estate at Muskau in Silesia. The driveway is straight, however, like the pathways in the plan above. The footpath pattern between the two houses I copied from the spiderweb-like forms of Le Corbusier, who delicately runs his communications without regard for the axis of his buildings or seemingly for any kind of pattern.

Philip C. Johnson, from "The Glass House," in *Architectural Review* 108:645 (September 1950), cited from *Philip Johnson: The Glass House*, ed. David Whitney and Jeffrey Kipnis. New York: Pantheon Books, 1993, pp. 10–12.

2 Mies van der Rohe: Ideal arrangement of Illinois Institute of Technology Buildings, 1939.

The arrangement of the two buildings and the statue group is influenced by Mies' theory of organizing buildings in a group. The arrangement is rectilinear but the shapes tend to overlap and slide by each other in an asymmetric manner.

3 Theo Van Doesburg: The Basso Continuo of Painting. (Published in "G" an *avant garde* magazine by Mies van der Rohe in 1922).

The idea of asymmetric sliding rectangles was furthest developed in the De Stijl aesthetics of war-time Holland. These shapes, best known to posterity through the painting of the late Piet Mondrian, still have an enormous influence on many other architects besides myself.

4 Plan and Perspective of the Acropolis at Athens from Choisy: *L'Histoire de l'Art Grecque.*

Choisy proved that the Greeks restricted the angle of approach to their buildings to the oblique: also that they placed their monuments so that only one major building dominated the field of vision from any given point.

The grouping of my buildings follows Choisy: from the focal point at the beginning of the footpath near the parking lot, the brick house (Propylaea) is passed and forms a wall on the right hand. The statue group (Athene Promachos) is in full view slightly to the right. The glass house comes into view (from an oblique angle) only after the pine tree at the angle of the promontory is circumnavigated.

5 Karl Friedrich Schinkel: Casino in Glienicke Park near Potsdam c. 1830. Entrance façade.

The site relation of my house is pure Neo-Classic Romantic – more specifically, Schinkelesque. Like his Casino my house is approached on dead-level and, like his, faces its principal (rear) façade toward a sharp bluff.

6 Karl Friedrich Schinkel: Casino in Glienicke Park near Potsdam c. 1830. Terrace overlooking the Havel.

The Eighteenth Century preferred more regular sites than this and the Post-Romantic Revivalists preferred hill tops to the cliff edges or shelves of the Romantics (Frank Lloyd Wright, that great Romantic, prefers shelves or hill sides).

7 Claude Nicholas Ledoux: Maison des Gardes Agricoles, at Maupertuis c. 1780.

The cubic, "absolute" from of my glass house, and the separation of functional units into two absolute shapes rather than a major and minor massing of parts comes directly from Ledoux, the Eighteenth Century father of modern architecture. (See Emil Kaufmann's excellent study Von Ledoux bis Le Corbusier.) The cube and the sphere, the pure mathematical shapes, were dear to the hearts of those intellectual revolutionaries from the Baroque, and we are their descendants.

8 Mies van der Rohe: Farnsworth House, 1947. (Now under construction near Chicago).

The idea of a glass house comes from Mies van der Rohe. Mies had mentioned to me as early as 1945 how easy it would be to build a house entirely of large sheets of glass. I was sceptical at the time, and it was not until I had seen the sketches of the Farnsworth House that I started the three-year work of designing my glass house. My debt is therefore clear, in spite of obvious difference in composition and relation to the ground.

9 Philip C. Johnson: Johnson House, New Canaan, 1949. Section at corner.

Many details of the house are adapted from Mies' work, especially the corner treatment and the relation of the column to the window frames. This use of standard steel sections to make a strong and at the same time decorative finish to the façade design is typical of Mies' Chicago work. Perhaps if there is ever to be "decoration" in our architecture it may come from manipulation of stock structural elements such as this (may not Mannerism be next?).

168 MATTHEW NOWICKI
from "Origins and Trends in Modern Architecture" (1951)

The architect Mathew Nowicki was born and trained in Poland and enjoyed success prior to the German invasion of 1939. During the war years he joined the Polish underground, and in 1945 he became the chief municipal architect for Warsaw. Over the next few years he became involved as a planning commissioner for the design of the United Nations Building, and he was in the United States in 1947 when Stalinist communists seized control of the Polish government, forcing him into political exile. Soon thereafter, he joined the faculty at North Carolina State University, where he was charged – by a perspicacious Dean Henry Kamphoefner – with restructuring the curriculum. Contrary to trends elsewhere, Nowicki proposed a curriculum that placed emphasis on the philosophy and psychology of design, and one that also encouraged historical studies. In this essay, published posthumously, Nowicki begins by arguing that modern architecture had indeed become an "international style," which he goes on to criticize in the passage below for its *"functional exactitude"* at the expense of human psychological understanding. Nowicki was a talented designer and an important thinker, but unfortunately he was killed in a plane crash in 1950 on his return from Chandigarh, India.

The recent changes in modern architecture are perhaps as basic as those separating the nineteen twenties from their predecessors. True that we share our vocabulary with this period of yesterday but the same words have for us a different and often a basically opposite meaning. We also speak of functionalism but then it meant the exactitude and now it means the flexibility. Those are two opposite concepts. In our thoughts priority often is given to the psychological and not the physical human function. The concept of a short lived structure removed with the rapid change of technology is replaced by a notion of architecture that will be our contribution to the life of future generations. Le Corbusier introduces a measure on which this contribution can be composed, the "modulor" with its mystery of the golden section. This measure of good proportion is most significant for the change of values. No longer the measure of functional space, no longer the measure of time, but a measure of beauty. Whatever the validity of such a measure may be it is interesting to notice that in the sequence of "time, space and architecture" the emphasis is shifting towards the last word in terms of the mystery of its art. The free plan is replaced by the modular plan. Again these are two opposite notions. A module is the most rigid discipline to which a plan can be subjected. A modular plan in reality is the opposite of a free plan. We are no longer preoccupied with the proximities of related functions but with the nature of space that leads from one function to another. It is no longer "how quickly to get there" but "how to get there," that matters most in our plans. It seems that from a quantitative period we have jumped into a qualitative one.

Matthew Nowicki, from "Origins and Trends in Modern Architecture," in *The Magazine of Art* (November 1951), cited from its revised title "Form and Function," in *Roots of Contemporary American Architecture*, ed. Lewis Mumford. New York: Dover, 1972, pp. 416–18.

These changes are not always conscious nor pronounced to the degree pointed out in my remarks. It is an irresistible temptation to express those changes in the most striking manner. But, in order to be objective one has to realize that a dividing line between periods can never be geometrically defined. This division can better be compared to a wide ribbon which separates and joins at the same time like a gray belt between fields of black and white.

With respect to the main channels of human creation namely the invention and the discovery, one might say that our present period is also different from the yesterday. The discovery of formal symbol of the unchanging laws of the universe seems to replace the invention of the form without a precedent. The eternal story of gravitation is again consciously contemplated. We are aware that the form of the discovery has to change but the object of it remains the same; over and over discovered in many ways.

Along with these elements of philosophy we also react in a different way to the techniques of our craft. Architecture discovered its own medium of creation and the difference between this medium and the others. Picasso writing recently about his "blue period" of 1912 and several later years said that he discovered late the difference between sculpture and painting. Maturity brings a "sense of medium" and mature architecture in the same way discovered the difference between painting and the art of organizing accessible space. As a result we rely in our expression on the potentialities of materials and structures almost picking up the trend of the XIX century. This interest in structure and material may discover within the building medium decorative qualities of ornament much too involved for the purist of yesterday. The symbolic meaning of a support became rediscovered and a steel column is used frankly as a symbol of structure even when it is not part of the structure itself. The period of functional exactitude expressed its mysterious longings for ornament in the decoration of function.

This period of functional flexibility expresses them in the decoration of structure. Art tends not only to discover the truth but to exaggerate and finally to distort it. *And, maybe in this distortion lies the essence of art.*

I have described our stage of the modern design as a style. Will this style repeat the sad story of other styles becoming an addition to the repertoire of a future eclecticism? The life and the decline of cultures follows an organic pattern which seems to be inevitable. But span of life of a culture and its rebirth into another rests in the hands of the people responsible for its creation. Where is the future of modern design?

It seems to me that it depends on the constant effort of approaching every problem with the consciousness that there is no single way of solving it. "Art una-species mille." This battle cry of the Renaissance should be repeated again and again. Art may be one but there are a thousand species. We must face the dangers of the crystallizing style not negating its existence but trying to enrich its scope by opening new roads for investigation and future refinements.

"Form follows function" may no longer satisfy ambitions aroused when form becomes judged for its universal values, but sensitivity to the minute exigencies of life remains the source of creative invention leading through the elimination of "exactitudes" to the more important and more general truth which equals beauty.

169 ELIZABETH GORDON
from "The Threat to the Next America" (1953)

The debate opened at the Museum of Modern Art in 1948 only intensified in the first half of the 1950s. One of the leading and most persistent voices in combating the notion of an International Style was Elizabeth Gordon, the editor of *House Beautiful*. She was a self-proclaimed supporter of Frank Lloyd Wright, whose work, she felt, better represented the individualism of the country, as well as "common sense and reason" in domestic design. She was a harsh critic of such works as Mies's Farnsworth House, because of its lack of basic practical features, such as thermal comfort, privacy, and closet space. The tone of this editorial, which she sent to all of the New York architecture magazines, was judged to be xenophobic by some, but again, the seriousness of her remarks was reflective of the long-standing divisions within American modernism in this decade.

I have decided to speak up.

In this issue, devoted to the wonderful possibilities for the better life in the Next America, I must also point out to you what I consider to be the threat to our achieving the *greater good* which is clearly possible for us, if we do not lose our sense of direction and independence.

What I want to tell you about has never been put into print by us or any other publication, to my knowledge. Your first reactions will be amazement, disbelief, and shock. You will say "It can't happen here!"

But hear me out. You may discover why you strongly dislike some of the so-called modern things you see. You may suddenly understand why you instinctively reject designs that are called "modernistic." For you are right. It's your common sense speaking. For these things are bad – bad in more ways than in their lack of beauty alone.

Here is the story, in its bluntest terms.

There is a well-established movement, in modern architecture, decorating, and furnishings, which is promoting the mystical idea that "less is more." Year after year, this idea has been hammered home by *some* museums, *some* professional magazines for architects and decorators, *some* architectural schools, and *some* designers.

They are all trying to sell the idea that "less is more," both as a criterion for design, and as a basis for judgment of the good life. **They are promoting unlivability, stripped-down emptiness, lack of storage space and therefore lack of possessions.**

They are praising designs that are unscientific, irrational and uneconomical – illogical things like whole walls of unshaded glass on the west, which cause you to fry in the summer, thus misusing one of our finest new materials. Or tricks like putting heavy buildings up on thin, delicate stilts – even though they cost more and instinctively worry the eye. Or cantilevering things that don't need to be cantilevered, making them cost more, too. A strong taint of anti-reason runs through all of their houses and furnishings.

Elizabeth Gordon, from "The Threat to the Next America," in *House Beautiful* (April 1953), pp. 126–7.

No wonder you feel uneasy and repelled!

They are trying to convince you that you can appreciate beauty only if you suffer – because they say beauty and comfort are incompatible.

They are trying to get you to accept their idea of beauty and form as the measure of all things, *regardless* of whether they work, what they do to you, or what they cost.

They are a self-chosen elite who are trying to tell us what we should like and how we should live. And these arbiters have such a narrow, often ignorant, conception of the good life that only non-human, low-performance things get their stamp of approval. **These arbiters make such a consistent attack on comfort, convenience, and functional values that it becomes, in reality, an attack on reason itself.**

"Incredible!" you say. "Nobody could seriously sell such nonsense."

My considered answer is this. Though it *is* incredible, some people *are* taking such nonsense seriously. They take it seriously because this propaganda comes from highly placed individuals and highly respected institutions. Therein lies the danger.

For if we can be sold on accepting dictators in matters of taste and how our homes are to be ordered, our minds are certainly well prepared to accept dictators in other departments of life. The undermining of people's confidence is the beginning of the end.

Break people's confidence in reason and their own common sense and they are on the way to attaching themselves to a leader, a mass movement, or any sort of authority beyond themselves. Nothing better explains periods of mass hysteria or various forms of social idiocy than the collapse of reason, the often deliberate result of an attack on people's self-confidence.

If people don't trust themselves and their own judgment, then they turn helplessly to leaders, good or bad. And they can only recover the good, sensible life when they recover their senses and discover again that, by and large, the ultimate hope for mankind is the application of reason to the world around us. This *re*discovery leads individuals to their own declaration of independence against the frauds, the over-publicized phonies, the bullying tactics of the self-chosen elite who would dictate not only taste but a whole way of life.

So, you see, this well-developed movement has social implications, because it affects the heart of our society – the home. Beyond the nonsense of trying to make us want to give up our technical aids and conveniences for what is *supposed* to be a better and more serene life, there is a social threat of regimentation and total control. **For if the mind of man can be manipulated in one great phase of life to be made willing to accept less, it would be possible to go on and get him to accept less in all phases of life.**

170 HARWELL HAMILTON HARRIS
from "Regionalism and Nationalism" (1954)

Among the more interesting voices to participate in this debate was the West-Coast architect Harwell Hamilton Harris. Originally trained by Richard Neutra on the Lovell Health House in the late 1920s, Harris was exceptionally qualified to respond. After leaving Neutra, Harris opened his practice in 1933 and produced a series of modern designs that moved him to the forefront of California architects. During the war years he moved to New York with his wife Jean Murray Bangs, and there he met most of the European luminaries, including Sigfried Giedion, Walter Gropius, and Marcel Breuer. While in New York he also came into the social circle of T. H. Robsjohn-Gibbings and Elizabeth Gordon, and from this mixture of diverse influences came his notion "Regionalism of Liberation" – his answer to the dilemma of American modernism at that time.

I have gone into so much detail and have recalled half-forgotten names because it is important to recognize the intellectual ferment – the state of mind – that marked the region that was to be distinguished by the architecture of Bernard Maybeck, Greene and Greene, Willis Polk, Myron Hunt, Irving Gill and many other only slightly less gifted designers.

The state of mind that distinguished the region made their work possible. They contributed to that state of mind, but alone they would have been powerless to create it. Architecture, I have no need to tell you, cannot exist without buildings, and buildings cannot exist without clients, and clients cannot be pushed or led very far in advance of the head of the procession – at least not in sufficient numbers to create a movement broad enough to be called a regional expression. And without some degree of general acceptance it is only rarely possible to win the assistance of the builders, the mills, the craftsmen and, perhaps most important of all, the bankers.

I believe there is more than one kind of regionalism. One kind is typified by the Old French Quarter of New Orleans. What is regional there now was once quite general. The small scale of its buildings and its spaces was widespread during the 1840's – "the hungry forties". So was the ironwork, plentifully produced and widely marketed during the hungry decade. These and other features of the Old Quarter have disappeared elsewhere. Because they still remain in New Orleans, they are now regional. This regionalism is the result of standing still while the rest of the world changes. It may be induced by poverty, resulting in meager proportions; by isolation, producing ignorance of developments in more favored localities; by lack of transportation, restricting the choice of building materials to those native to the region; by iron-clad traditions, imposing living patterns rooted in a vanished past. Such regionalism prides itself on its exclusiveness. It cares more for preserving an obscure dialect than for expressing a new idea. It is anti-cosmopolitan and anti-progressive. Such regionalism becomes a cloak for the misplaced pride of the region and serves to build-in ignorance and inferiority. Happily, such regionalism is disappearing as we become more nearly one world. Let's call this type of regionalism the Regionalism of Restriction.

Harwell Hamilton Harris, from remarks made to the Northwest Regional Council of the American Institute of Architects, 1954, cited here from *Harwell Hamilton Harris: A Collection of His Writings*. Student Publication of School of Design, North Carolina State at Raleigh 14:5 (1965), pp. 26–8.

Opposed to the Regionalism of Restriction is another type of regionalism; the Regionalism of Liberation. This is the manifestation of a region that is **especially in tune with the emerging thought of the time.** We call such a manifestation "regional" **only because it has not yet emerged elsewhere.** It is the genius of this region to be more than ordinarily aware and more than ordinarily free. Its virtue is that its manifestation has **significance for the world outside itself.** To express this regionalism architecturally it is necessary that there be building, – preferably a lot of building – at one time. Only so can the expression be sufficiently general, sufficiently varied, sufficiently forceful to capture people's imaginations and provide a friendly climate long enough for a new school of design to develop.

San Francisco was made for Maybeck. Pasadena was made for Greene and Greene. Neither could have accomplished what he did in any other place or time. Each used the materials of the place; but it is not the materials that distinguish the work.

Maybeck used wood, concrete, Transite, steel sash, corrugated iron – all before 1910 – and used them with great distinction. But there is no reason to believe he would not have used marble and bronze equally well and just as cheerfully. He was equally indifferent to where his forms came from. Whether from Imperial Rome, Twelfth Century Italy, a log cabin or a twentieth-century factory, it is only what he made of them that matters. He did not reconstruct the past; he made something altogether new under the sun out of these relics and reminiscences of the past. As a result, any previous incarnation of these forms appears as mere preparation for their present role. Perhaps Maybeck's clients believed him when he told them they had Twelfth Century souls and so he was giving them a Twelfth Century building. But if they did, their leg was being pulled, for the Twelfth Century was never like this!

A region may develop ideas. A region may accept ideas. Imagination and intelligence are necessary for both. In California in the late Twenties and Thirties modern European ideas met a still developing regionalism. What was relevant was accepted and became part of a continuing regionalism. In New England, on the other hand, European Modernism met a rigid and restrictive regionalism that at first resisted and then surrendered. New England accepted European Modernism whole because its own regionalism had been reduced to a collection of restrictions.

171   RICHARD NEUTRA
from *Survival Through Design* (1954)

During the 1930s and 1940s, Richard Neutra built a number of acclaimed luxury homes throughout California. Less known during this period were his numerous designs for medium and low-cost housing, including several experimental models. He also carried out several public-work projects during the war, including a series of open-air schools for Puerto Rico. *Survival Through Design*, largely written during the 1940s, is a landmark in architectural thought. It is a clarion call (arguably the first) to environmentalists, architects, and designers of every type to take heed of the surroundings in which we live, and to plan for a more humane

Richard Neutra, from *Survival Through Design* (1954), cited from the 1969 edition. London: Oxford University Press, pp. 3–4, 91–2.

and rational habitat. Neutra also dwells at length on the most recent research on physiological responses to color, lighting, space, sound, and touch, among other variables. In this regard the book stands at the beginning of the psychological and anthropological concerns of the late 1950s and 1960s. These two passages scarcely encapsulate the breadth of Neutra's argument, but they reveal that Neutra's words are still of importance to today's designers.

Nature has too long been outraged by design of nose rings, corsets, and foul-aired subways. Perhaps our mass-fabricators of today have shown themselves particularly out of touch with nature. But ever since Sodom and Gomorrah, organic normalcy has been raped again and again by man, that super-animal still struggling for its own balance. There have been warners, prophets, great floods, and new beginnings.

What we here may briefly call *nature* comprises all the requirements and characteristics of live organisms. This entire world of organic phenomena is, in the escapades of our still obvious immaturity, often treated against 'the natural grain' and contrary to the 'supreme plan' – that of biological consistency and requirement. In former ages it was a sin to do this and for such failings the deity threatened to liquidate the sinners. We may now have dropped – perhaps too carelessly – the moral accent. Yet to us, too, the issue is still one of survival by virtue of wholesomeness, or damnation and death through our own default.

In human design, we could conceivably see *organic evolution continued*, and extending into a man-shaped future. At any rate, that phenomenally intensive development in the multi-layered cortex of the human upper brain has not yet with certainty been proved a blind alley or a dismal failure. To be sure, this distinctly human brain harbors trouble, but it also may furnish some as yet untried survival aids. We have been laggards in calling upon all our potential powers and resources to arrange for us in a bearable manner an individual and communal living space. The toxic trash piles of our neglects and misdeeds, old and fresh, surround us in our physical environment. The confused wreckage of centuries, unrelated to any current practical purpose, is mixed in a most disturbing manner with our often feeble, often arbitrary, attempts at creating order.

[. . .]

Acceptance of design must turn from a commercial into a physiological issue. Fitness for assimilation by our organic capacity becomes a guiding principle for judging design because such fitness aids the survival of the individual, the community, the race itself. Design must be a barrier against irritation instead of an incitement to it. The everyday insight in this matter is more rudimentary than we would think because of the weight of habit. A diet is not necessarily healthful because it is habitual. The fact that someone is *used* to smoking opium, even craves it, does not make opium a harmless drug. An element of design may be habit-forming and thus attractive but still incompatible with the requirements of our constitutional system. Designers of the future will neither cater to harmful habits nor gratify arbitrary desires. Their decisions will abide by ever-increasing physiological information.

[. . .]

172 LOUIS I. KAHN
"Order and Form" (1955)

Already active as an architect in the late 1920s, Louis Kahn struggled through much of the Great Depression and war years, during which time he focused on city-planning issues and low-income housing. From 1945, however, he began his tenure as a visiting critic at Yale University, while still maintaining his office in Philadelphia. For a few years, at least, he drew close to the international architectural circles of the Northeast, but by the early to mid-1950s he seemingly withdrew, or at least returned to his own path. His personal break with the norms of international modernism would not become fully manifest until his design for the Richards Medical Center, Philadelphia (1957–61), but this short essay published in the Yale student journal *Perspecta* a few years earlier discloses his later direction and some of the issues with which he was struggling. He was influenced at this time by Buckminster Fuller and Pier Luigi Nervi, but his concern with order also resonates with the so-called "empiricist" trends in Scandinavia — that is, his rejection of the abstraction of "space" in favor of a more phenomenological reading of "place."

Order is
Design is form-making in order
Form emerges out of a system of construction
Growth is a construction
In order is creative force
In design is the means – where   with what   when   with how much
The nature of space reflects what it wants to be

       Is the auditorium a Stradavarius
          or is it an ear
       Is the auditorium a creative instrument
           keyed to Bach or Bartok
           played by the conductor
       or is it a convention hall
In the nature of space is the spirit and the will to exist a certain way

       Design must closely follow that will
       Therefore a stripe painted horse is not a zebra.
       Before a railroad station is a building
       it wants to be a street
       it grows out of the needs of street
           out of the order of movement
       A meeting of contours englazed.
Thru the nature – why
Thru the order – what
Thru design – how
A Form emerges from the structural elements inherent in the form.

Louis I. Kahn, "Order and Form," in *Perspecta 3: The Yale Architectural Journal* (1955), p. 57.

A dome is not conceived when questions arise how to build it.

Nervi grows an arch

Fuller grows a dome

Mozart's compositions are designs

They are exercises of **order** – intuitive

Design encourages more designs

Designs derive their imagery from order

Imagery is the memory – the Form

Style is an adopted order

The same **order** created the elephant and created man

They are different designs

Begun from different aspirations

Shaped from different circumstances

Order does not imply Beauty

The same order created the dwarf and Adonis

Design is not making Beauty

Beauty emerges from selection

affinities

integration

love

Art is a form making life in order – psychic

Order is intangible

It is a level of creative consciousness

forever becoming higher in level

The higher the order the more diversity in **design**

Order supports integration

From what the space wants to be the unfamiliar may be revealed to the architect.

From order he will derive creative force and power of self criticism

to give form to this unfamiliar.

Beauty will evolve

B.   POSTWAR THEORY IN EUROPE

Introduction

Europe in the immediate postwar years was a mosaic of conflicting circumstances and directions. Germany, of course, paid the severest price for the war; not only was much of its physical infrastructure destroyed but so was its once unparalleled university system — bringing to a conclusion its importance for architectural theory for several decades. France also faced massive physical destruction in the north, but Le Corbusier would regain his earlier stature as one of the world's most influential architects. In neutral Switzerland, Sigfried Giedion, who had spent much of the war in America, returned to his native Zurich and reclaimed his role as the preeminent historian of modernism as well as secretary of CIAM. Much of central and eastern Europe was enveloped by the Iron Curtain, which severed it culturally from the West.

At the same time there emerged new centers of architectural thought, perhaps foremost of which was Great Britain. This country embraced modernism only in the 1930s, but with the immigration of many European architects and intellectuals to Britain – combined with the need to repair London's wartime damage – at the war's end the country was poised to play a prominent role in theory. Britain now became a crossing point between European and American influences and also found a highly articulate voice of its own. To the east and northeast of Britain lay the Netherlands and Scandinavia, both of which emerged from the war as important centers of thought. The political turn of most of Scandinavia toward socialism directed much of its theoretical emphasis to planning, but at the same time there was cultivated the phenomenon that became known worldwide as "Scandinavian Design," which possessed both a regional and international character of its own. A war-damaged Netherlands, which had been in the forefront of European theory in the 1920s and early 1930s, now reclaimed its former position with a new generation of gifted architects. A fourth European center of theory to rise from the ashes of wartime destruction was Italy. Its rich artistic tradition rapidly reasserted itself, and once again in a way that challenged many of the tenets of modernism.

173   BRUNO ZEVI
from *Towards an Organic Architecture* (1945)

O ne of the leaders in Italy's revival in the postwar years was the architect and historian Bruno Zevi. He began his architectural training in Italy in the mid-1930s, but his opposition to Fascism, combined with his Jewish ancestry, made his life there untenable. He subsequently studied at the Architectural Association in London and at Harvard University, where he took a graduate degree in 1941. Two years later he was back in London assisting the Allies' war effort by day, while – in the midst of the London bombing – writing his first book on architectural theory by night. The leading theme is interesting because it opposes the thrust of Sigfried Giedion's *Space, Time & Architecture*. Against Giedion's thesis that a handful of European pioneers essentially invented a brave new world of space-time architecture, Zevi argues that the European Modern movement stalled in the 1930s owing to its functional abstractions and excessive rationalism. Hence Zevi vehemently rejects the machine analogy of Le Corbusier and – as the second passage shows – favors an organic architecture in a somewhat updated Wrightian sense of the word, which he also sees evident in the new architecture of Scandinavia.

After so many experiments, after the brilliant performances of Le Corbusier, Lurçat, Mallet-Stevens, Roux-Spitz and Beaudouin, modern architecture progressively lost ground, as though from exhaustion. This cannot be dismissed as merely the reflection in architecture of the moral and political decadence of France: to say so would be merely tautology. It is certainly an indication of the artistic sensibility of the French that a genius like Le Corbusier should have been unable to continue at work; but there were other causes, less obvious and more directly connected with architecture, which merit examination. In the free land of France, which had given it fame, modern architecture wearied the public. People reacted psychologically against the functionalism of Le Corbusier even in the intellectual circles which had previously been in favour of it. The corrective applied by neo-classicism has

Bruno Zevi, from *Verso un'architettura organica* (1945), cited from *Towards an Organic Architecture*. London: Faber & Faber, 1950, pp. 47–8, 139.

certainly been a purely negative one, but the criticism directed against the modern was more an expression of feeling than of theoretic belief, and behind that criticism there were real problems which the modern movement had failed to solve. In France it was not the case of a traditionalist reaction with a definite programme winning the day. It was the criticism of the general public that triumphed; and criticism of that kind is certain to have some truth on its side, more especially as modern architecture in France never lacked propaganda.

Among the most obvious causes of the architectural decadence in France is the fact that functionalism no longer had any real basis. Functionalism came into being as a fighting theory with which to combat traditional architecture and it won its decisive victory; but as soon as the modern architects had learned its essential lesson, functionalism was no longer sufficient. It has often been remarked with good reason that Le Corbusier's buildings are very far from being merely functional and merely 'machines à habiter'. This primary formula of the functionalists, which did so much harm to modern architecture, left the architects under a sort of inhibition. They felt it necessary to insist on the functional character of every detail, even of those that were quite evidently the products of fantasy. The worshippers of the 'rational utilitarian' continued to chant the praises of technique and biology when it was clear that modern architecture had freed itself from this first act of its controversial infancy. In other words the new style crystallised before it had explored the whole of its potential range.

[. . .]

The reaction against the town-planning which aped Le Corbusier is almost parallel to the reaction against the inorganic in modern architecture. In town-planning you find the Russian fallacy and the Fascist monumental rhetoric; you find the American organic approach taking the lead in the war-time housing schemes; and, lastly, you have the British trend towards the organic, a triumphal example of this being Abercrombie and Forshaw's L.C.C. plan for London.

In Russia the reaction against the uniform and the rectangular was violent: 'We want a plaza! We want a civic centre for the town!' But this legitimate call for a human approach was exploited by reactionary architects who went back to the classical plaza. In the new Russian towns – in some aspects the best in the world – you often find the monumental plaza with a central building adorned with columns, a marriage of florid vulgarity and dullness.

American architects and their colleagues in Scandinavia are leading the way both in theory and in practice. Many of the war-time housing estates have been designed by modern architects and combine the principles of modern planning with a human approach. If, as the appointment of Richard Neutra to the directorship of the Town-planning Board of California gives reason to hope, the same architects are called in after the war, with their increased experience and especially with more time to give to their work, they will most certainly enrich their country with a new and healthy kind of scenery. The attention given to landscape in almost all the American housing schemes is an important factor in their livableness and compares favourably with corresponding schemes in Sweden.

174   J. M. RICHARDS
from "The New Empiricism" (1947)

O ne of the new directions to emerge in the postwar architectural debate in Europe was the movement of "new empiricism," first identified in this review of contemporary Scandinavian architecture by J. M. Richards. The starting point for the movement, Richards notes, is Sven Backström's critique of modernism in his essay of 1943 (151). Richards goes on to provide photographs of three recent Swedish houses designed by Sven Markelius, Sture Frolen, and Ralph Erskine, and what strikes him as new in all three is the unusual juxtaposition of modern planning ideas and sensibilities and the use of local or traditional building materials. Swedish architects, he decides, were clearly not following the rationalist outlines laid down by the European modernists of France and Germany, but at the same time Richards is not totally unsympathetic to the apostasy. "New Empiricism" would quickly be brought into European parlance and become a recognizable movement within Britain as well.

The mid-nineteenth century rationalism in architectural thought and teaching was a vanguard of theory rather than of practice. Even one of its greatest exponents, Viollet-le-Duc, was unable to realise the full visual implications of his teaching. It needed the creative extrovert – the full-time practising architect – to construct a building in its image. When he did, it was not only a building that he constructed, but also a full-dress æsthetic theory based on the new teaching and called functionalism. This offspring of revolutionary advances in building science married to the new science of sociology inevitably attracted a host of seekers after novelty as well as serious innovators, and it is perhaps true to say that more people in both groups misunderstood its principles than ever understood them. But sufficient time has now passed for the misconceptions to have separated themselves from the real thing and for functionalism to be seen as a distinct phase of the modern movement. In countries like Sweden which were able through the war to go on developing a modern architectural philosophy, new theories are beginning to take shape and new forms are giving them substance. So far no strong reaction is evident against the principles upon which functionalism was founded. Indeed, these principles were never more relevant than now. The tendency is, rather, both to humanise the theory on its æsthetic side and to get back to the earlier rationalism on the technical side. The latter will not provide much opportunity for controversy, for as Viollet said, "Science suffers no eclipses," and the appeal to be more scientific suffers no real danger of repudiation to-day. However, the effort to humanise the æsthetic expression of functionalism is open to many interpretations. The Swedish one, which is illustrated here, may, on the basis of statements made by Swedish architects themselves, be called The New Empiricism. Briefly, they explain it as the attempt to be more objective than the functionalists, and to bring back another science, that of psychology, into the picture. The results have led many true-blue functionalists to wonder whether the principles of objectivity in contemporary architecture they fought so hard to establish are being quietly and skilfully jettisoned by their own team-mates.
[. . .]

J. M. Richards, from "The New Empiricism," in *The Architectural Review* 101:606 (June 1947), pp. 199–200.

That this tendency is not purely a Swedish one is obvious from the concern being expressed in other countries, where other empiricists apparently fear that the enormous post-war opportunities of rebuilding may too easily result in the stereotyping of the functionalism of the thirties under the old argument of establishing it as the international vernacular. For instance, J. J. P. Oud, one of the great early functionalists (in a letter to *The Architectural Record*), answers criticism of his highly ornamented new Shell IBM office building in the Hague, by asking "and why should it be forbidden to give the functional act a spiritual form? Function alone as a first principle – my experience taught me this – results in æsthetical arbitrariness. Don't forget this." Functionalism then, the only real æsthetic faith to which modern architects could lay claim in the inter-war years, is now, if not repudiated, certainly called in question; not by its opponents, but by those who were formerly among its most illustrious supporters. The houses illustrated here are thus particularly significant because they provide the first example published in this country of the new tendencies emerging in Sweden. The first two might appear at first sight to be in local builder's bungalow style; they are, however, the expression of the new outlook of the *avant-garde*. Built in traditional materials they show, on closer examination, a clear resolution of the planning requirements and, particularly in the case of the first, which was largely pre-fabricated, a very thorough attention to structure, equipment and details. The third house, which was built a year or so earlier than the others, is interesting because it shows the more easily recognised expression of the (to us) pre-war phase of functionalism applied to exactly the same kind of problem, and using traditional materials.

175 COLIN ROWE
from "The Mathematics of the Ideal Villa" (1947)

One of the consequences of the architectural inactivity caused by World War II, combined with the flood of German art historians into Britain, was scholarly research on some traditional architectural themes. Among these new interests was the long-dormant issue of architectural proportions. Such interest is found in this classic essay by Colin Rowe, which he penned while pursuing doctoral studies under Rudolf Wittkower at the Warburg Institute in London. Rowe compares floor plans and elevations of several of Palladio's villas with those of Le Corbusier, and points out the mathematical similarity of Palladio's Villa Malcontenta with Le Corbusier's Villa Stein. It is not only the first of various attempts by Rowe and others to endow modern architecture with the aura of "classicism," but it also begins in Britain what amounts to a canonization of this modern master among this particular generation of postwar British critics and architects.

Geometrically, both architects may be said to have approached something of the Platonic archetype of the villa, which the Virgilian dream could be held to represent. The idealisation

Colin Rowe, from "The Mathematics of the Ideal Villa," in *The Architectural Review* 101:603 (March 1947), p. 104.

of the cube house must lend itself very readily to the purposes of Virgilian dreaming. Here is set up the conflict between the contingent and the absolute, the natural and the abstract; the gap between the ideal world and the too human exigencies of realisation receives its most pathetic presentation. The bridging must be as competent and compelling as a well-executed fugue, charged as in these cases with almost religious seriousness, or sophisticated, witty allusion; it is an intellectual feat which reconciles the mind to the fundamental discrepancy of the programme.

Palladio is the convinced classicist with the sixteenth century repertoire of well-humanised forms. He translates this "customary" material with a passion and a high seriousness fitting to the continued validity that he finds it to possess; the reference to the Pantheon in the superimposed porticoes; to the thermæ in the cruciform saloon; the ambiguity, profound, in both idea and form, in the equivocal conjunction of temple front and domestic block. These are charged with meaning, both for what they are and for what they signify; and their impression is poignant. The ancient house is not re-created, but there is in its place a concrete apparition of antique virtue, excellence, Imperial splendour and stoicism: Rome is there by allusion, the ideal world by geometry.

By contrast, Corbusier is in some ways the most ingenious of eclectics. The orders, the Roman allusion, are the apparatus of authority, customary, and in a sense universal forms. The emblematic representations of the moral virtues, the loves of the Gods and the lives of the Saints, the ornamental adjuncts of humanism, have lost their former historical monopoly. Allusion is dissipated at Garches, concentrated at the Malcontenta; within the one cube the performance is mixed, within the other, Roman. Corbusier selects the irrelevant and the particular, the fortuitously picturesque and the incidentally significant forms of mechanics, as the objects of his virtuosity. They retain their original implications of classical landscape, mechanical precision, rococo intimacy; one is able to cease hold of them as known objects, and sometimes as basic shapes; but they become only transiently provocative. Unlike Palladio's forms there is nothing final about their relationship: their rapprochement would seem to be affected by the artificial emptying of the cube, when the senses are confounded by the apparent arbitrariness, and the intellect more than convinced by the intuitive knowledge, that here in spite of all to the contrary, there is order and there are rules.

Corbusier has become the source of fervent pastiches, and witty exhibition techniques: the neo-Palladian villa became the picturesque object in the English park. Content is different in both cases, and a bad portico is usually more convincing than an ill-executed incident. It is the magnificently realisable quality of the originals which one fails to find in the works of neo-Palladians and exponents of "le style Corbu." The difference is that between the universal, and the decorative or merely competent; perhaps in both cases it is the adherence to rules which has lapsed.

176 BRUNO ZEVI
from *Architecture as Space* (1948)

Z evi follows his 1945 book with one of three years later in which he expands his earlier conception and advances arguments on several new fronts. Translated into English under the different title *Architecture as Space*, the book initially returns to the old notion of architecture as "space." His comparison of the spatial interiors of three buildings by Le Corbusier, Mies van der Rohe, and Frank Lloyd Wright is in fact based on his earlier notion of organic architecture, encompassing his critique of rationalism. Zevi wants to reassert humanism into practice. The psychological theme of human "irrationality" in this context resonates with the contemporary philosophical movement of existentialism. But Zevi also later seeks to move beyond the painterly and social limitations of functionalism by boldly recapturing the old notion of "empathy" as a physiological-psychological grounding for the new notion of space. Here, in fact, is the heart of his conception of organic architecture, pieced together from a variety of theoretical sources.

The two most important conceptions of space in modern architecture are those of Functionalism (occasionally called the International Style) and the Organic Movement. Both international by now, the first began in America with the Chicago School of 1880–90, but found its fullest formulation in Europe and its leader in the Swiss-French architect, Le Corbusier. The second has its greatest exponent in the American genius, Frank Lloyd Wright, and only in the last decade has it taken firm hold in Europe. Although these two conceptions have in common the theme of the open plan, they interpret it in different ways; the first strictly rationally, the second organically and with a full sense of humanity.

Among the masterpieces of contemporary residential architecture, the Villa Savoie of Le Corbusier and Falling Water by Wright show clearly the difference in their manner of composition and therefore in their poetic approach. Le Corbusier starts with a reticulated structure, a quadrangle measured regularly by pilasters. Within a rational, geometric formula his space is enclosed by four walls with continuous windows. It is only at this point that we begin to deal with the problem of the open plan. The partitions are not static, but formed by thin movable walls. On the second floor there is a large terrace, and the exterior and interior space meet at a glass wall which can be opened completely. In vertical terms, a continuity between the floors is established by a wide ramp which cuts through the building, rising as far as the terrace of the top floor. All of this is carried out with perfect freedom, but within a precise stereometric scheme.

In Mies van der Rohe's delightful pavilion constructed for the Barcelona Exposition of 1929, the order of the structural elements remains rigidly geometrical, but the architectural volume is broken up. The continuous space is cut by vertical planes which never form closed, geometrically static areas, but create an uninterrupted flow in the succession of visual angles. Here we have a still freer development of the modern theme.

Bruno Zevi, from *Sapere vedere l'architettura* (1948), ed. Joseph A. Barry and trans. Milton Gendel as *Architecture as Space: How to Look at Architecture*. New York: Horizon Press, 1957, pp. 143–4, 157–8, 191.

In the case of Wright, aspiration toward spatial continuity has a far more expansive vitality: his architecture is centered around the living reality of interior space and is therefore in opposition to elementary volumetric forms, to that sense of proud detachment from nature characteristic of Le Corbusier. For Wright the open plan is not a dialectic carried on within an architectural volume, but the final result of a conquest expressed in spatial terms, starting from a central nucleus and projecting voids in all directions. It follows that the resulting drama of volumetrics has an audacity and richness undreamed of by the Functionalists, and its very insistence on decorative elements indicates, quite apart from their sometimes doubtful taste, a desire for freedom from the bare, self-flagellating severity of early European rationalism.

[. . .]

The often-repeated functionalist formula of the "machine for living" echoes a naive, mechanical interpretation of science as fixed, logically demonstrable, mathematically indisputable and invariable truth. This is an old interpretation of science which has been replaced in our time by a more relative, elastic, articulated concept. Today's scientific spirit throws light on the entire field of the irrational in man, uncovering individual and social problems of the unconscious. Architecture, which in the course of twenty years of Functionalism has brought itself up to date with respect to the science and technology of the last century and a half, is now broadening and humanizing itself, not in romantic reaction, but through the natural progress of scientific thought. If problems of town planning for the working masses engage the Functionalists in a heroic struggle for the minimum house, for the standardization and industrialization of building, in other words, if the Functionalists are concentrated on the resolution of *quantitative* problems, then it is organic architecture which recognizes that man has dignity, personality, spiritual meaning, and realizes that the problem of architecture is as much *qualitative* as quantitative.

Organic space is rich with movement, directional invitations and illusions of perspective, lively and brilliant invention. Its movement is original in that it does not aim at dazzling visual effects, but at expressing the action itself of man's life within it. The Organic Movement is not merely a current in taste or an anti-stereometric and anti-prismatic vision of space, but is aimed at creating spaces which are not only beautiful in themselves, but represent the organic life of the people who live in them.

[. . .]

Proceeding from its grammar to its expression, the theory of *Einfuehlung* [empathy] covers an entire building. For its advocates, all architectural criticism consists in the ability to transfer our very spirit into a building, humanizing it, making it talk, vibrating with it in an unconscious symbiosis in which our body tends to repeat the movement of the architecture. Undoubtedly this theory has the great merit of having thawed the cold abstractness of the critic's dictionary of architecture and of having created a familiarity, a sense of interchange, a human relationship between architecture and man.

177 RUDOLF WITTKOWER
from *Architectural Principles in the Age of Humanism* (1949)

The great popularizer of Renaissance and Baroque architecture in Great Britain in the postwar years was Rudolf Wittkower. He obtained his doctorate in art history in Germany in the early 1920s and spent the remainder of this decade in Rome, where he became a leading authority on Renaissance and Baroque architecture. He returned to Germany in 1932, but with the ascension of Hitler to power he moved to England (his father was a British citizen) and became associated with the Warburg Institute. If his earlier studies lacked much of a direct appeal to architects, his *Architectural Principles in the Age of Humanism* became requisite reading for the new generation of postwar architects. The book does not simply concern proportions, but rather draws upon the absolutist belief in the larger cosmic harmony and symbolism governing Renaissance theory. To postwar modern designers, now armed with a minimalist palette, it offered lessons in the higher meaning of visual and intellectual harmony. This concluding passage from the book follows upon Wittkower's summary of the breakdown of proportional systems over the past three centuries, and is, in retrospect, an extraordinary plea for the reinstitution of an absolute aesthetics.

Within the terms of a new conception of the world the whole structure of classical æsthetics was systematically broken up, and in this process man's vision underwent a decisive change. Proportion became a matter of individual sensibility and in this respect the architect acquired complete freedom from the bondage of mathematical ratios. This is the attitude to which most architects as well as the public unconsciously subscribed right down to our own days. It is hardly necessary to support this statement with a great many quotations; but brief reference may be made to two authors who interpreted the general feeling on this point. Ruskin declared that possible proportions are as infinite as possible airs in music and it must be left to the inspiration of the artist to invent beautiful proportions. Julien Guadet, in the *Eléments et théorie de l'architecture*, the often re-printed handbook of the students of the 'Ecole des Beaux-Arts' in Paris, explains that in order to establish a dogma of proportions, authors of the past had invoked science. But 'elle n'a rien à voir ici; on a cherché des combinaisons en quelque sorte cabalistiques, je ne sais quelles propriétés mystérieuses des nombres ou, encore, des rapports comme la musique en trouve entre les nombres de vibrations qui déterminent les accords. Pures chimères . . . Laissons là ces chimères ou ces superstitions. . . . Il m'est impossible, vous le concevez bien, de vous donner des regles à cet égard. Les proportions, c'est l'infini.'

'Les proportions, c'est l'infini' – this terse statement is still indicative of our approach. That is the reason why we view researches into the theory of proportion with suspicion and awe. But the subject is again very much alive in the minds of young architects to-day, and they may well evolve new and unexpected solutions to this ancient problem.

Rudolf Wittkower, from *Architectural Principles in the Age of Humanism* (1949), cited from the 4th edition. London: Academy Editions, 1977, pp. 153–4.

178 LE CORBUSIER
from *The Modulor* (1950)

Le Corbusier's investigation of proportional and modular systems for architecture precedes the war and arguably goes back to his chapter in *Vers une architecture* on regulating lines. But the war changed many things and allowed time for theoretical pursuits. One of his wartime ventures was his organization, in 1942, of younger architects into the research group ASCORAL, which was charged by Le Corbusier with investigating a variety of constructional issues for postwar France, among them the need for a single proportional standard. Utilizing the research of this group as well as drawing inspiration from several books on the golden section, Le Corbusier fashioned what he deemed to be a universal proportional system of progressive measures based on the golden section: two numerical series that he proposed to replace the metric system and serve as dimensional guides. In fact he employed this proposed system in his design for the first of his postwar projects on behalf of the French government – the Unité d'Habitation in Marseilles (1946–52). This passage early in the book speaks to the seemingly timeless issue of architectural proportions.

One thing remains to be explained: the Parthenon, the Indian temples, and the cathedrals were all built according to precise measures which constituted a code, a coherent system: a system which proclaimed an essential unity. Primitive men at all times and in all places, as also the bearers of high civilizations, Egyptian; Chaldean, Greek, all these have built and, by that token, measured. What were the tools they used? They were eternal and enduring, precious because they were linked to the human person. The names of these tools were: elbow (cubit), finger (digit), thumb (inch), foot, pace, and so forth.... Let us say it at once: they formed an integral part of the human body, and for that reason they were fit to serve as measures for the huts, the houses and the temples that had to be built.

More than that: they were infinitely rich and subtle because they formed part of the mathematics of the human body, gracious, elegant and firm, the source of that harmony which moves us: beauty (appreciated, let it be understood, by the human eye in accordance with a well-understood human concept; there cannot and could never be another criterion).

The elbow, the pace, the foot and the thumb were and still are both the prehistoric and the modern tool of man.

The Parthenon, the Indian temples and the cathedrals, the huts and the houses, were all built in certain particular places: Greece, Asia, Europe, and so forth. There was no need for any unification of measures. As the Viking is taller than the Phoenician, so the Nordic foot and inch had no need to be adapted to the build of the Phoenician, or vice versa.

...One day, however, secular thought, in its turn, set out to conquer the world. The French Revolution was a struggle of profoundly human causes. A bid for progress was made, deliverance was at hand – or at least the promise of it: doors were opening upon tomorrow: science and mathematics were entering upon new and limitless paths.

Le Corbusier, from *Le Modulor* (1950), trans. Peter de Francia and Anna Bostoack as *The Modulor: A Harmonious Measure to the Human Scale Universally Applicable to Architecture and Mechanics*. Cambridge, MA: MIT Press, 1977, pp. 18–20.

Do we understand clearly enough what it meant when, one fine day, the zero – key to the decimal system – was created? Calculation is a practical impossibility without the zero. The French Revolution did away with the foot-and-inch system with all its slow and complicated processes. That being done, a new system had to be invented. The *savants* of the Convention adopted a concrete measure so devoid of personality and passion that it became an abstraction, a symbol: the metre, forty-millionth part of the meridian of the earth. The metre was adopted by a society steeped in innovation. One and a half centuries later, when factory-made goods are circulating all over the globe, the world is divided into two halves: the foot-and-inch camp and the metre camp. The foot-and-inch, steadfast in its attachment to the human body, but atrociously difficult to handle: the metre, indifferent to the stature of man, divisible into half metres and quarter metres, decimetres, centimetres, millimetres, any number of measures, but all indifferent to the stature of man, for there is no such thing as a one-metre or a two-metre man.

179   ALISON AND PETER SMITHSON
"House in Soho, London" (1953)

Britsh theory in the immediate postwar years was represented by two main lines. One was defined by the influence of Le Corbusier: the concrete and glass vocabulary that became the favored mode of many of the younger architects working for the London County Council (LCC), the governmental office in charge of rebuilding London. The other, smaller line was opened by the example of New Empiricism, the Scandinavian alternative to international modernism that favored such low-tech materials as brick and wood, and therefore had a natural resonance with the British tradition of arts and crafts. With the publication of this short descriptive essay by Alison and Peter Smithson, a third front begins to open up. The Smithsons formed a partnership in 1950, one year after their marriage. Their first important venture was the commission for Hunstanton Secondary Modern School, Norfolk (1949–54), which was designed in a strict Miesian language. But their interests soon evolved. Through their connection with the Independent Group (IG) and the Institute of Contemporary Art (ICA) – pop artists and critics that included Reyner Banham – the Smithsons became more critical in their outlooks and more "brutal" in their aesthetic sensitivities. This short article on their (unbuilt) design for a London townhouse, which speaks to their new realism, is important because it first invokes the term "new brutalism": originally signifying a rougher and more textural architecture that takes little account of the high aesthetics of modernism. It defines a movement that would become quite prominent in Britain.

The attempt was made to build in Central London, and failed because of difficulty with adjoining owners. It seemed that a series of Trusts held the surrounding land (all bombed) but it turned out to be one man who intended to build kitchens to the left, W.C.'s to the right and restaurants to the rear – this contract was about to be signed after nine months' work.

Alison and Peter Smithson, "House in Soho, London," in *Architectural Design* (December 1953), p. 342.

On the normal city site costing between 15s. and 25s. per sq. ft. one can apparently do little different from the Georgian, but it was considered that a different internal order must be visualised. The air and sunlight of the attics in the daytime suggests that living quarters should be up top, with the bathroom in the cool of the dim basement.

It was decided to have no finishes at all internally – the building being a combination of shelter and environment.

Bare concrete, brickwork and wood. The difficulty of unceiled rooms was satisfactorily overcome by the disposition of rooms which were also placed high up or low down according to light-sunlight desired.

Brickwork may suggest a blue or double burnt or coloured pointing; but the arbitrary use of colour and texture was not conformed with, and common bricks with struck joints were intended. The bars and colour variation have some sort of natural tension when laid by a good bricklayer.

In fact, had this been built it would have been the first exponent of the "new brutalism" in England, as the preamble to the specification shows: *"It is our intention in this building to have the structure exposed entirely, without internal finishes wherever practicable. The Contractor should aim at a high standard of basic construction as in a small warehouse."*

180   SIGFRIED GIEDION
from "The State of Contemporary Architecture" (1954)

Giedion emerged from the war years still as Europe's leading theorist and supporter of international modernism. He remained active in the cause of resurrecting CIAM, but he also became the ablest defender of what many viewed as orthodox modernism. And after witnessing firsthand the controversy in the United States over regional interpretations of modernism, he too shifted his architectural thinking. This essay of 1954 thus becomes important for two reasons. Throughout the first part of his analysis Giedion now opposes the term "International Style" and in fact insists that the term be dropped from general usage. Second, after citing several examples of buildings, Giedion in his concluding pages counters with his conception of regional modernism, which now – not insignificantly – pays homage to the work of Frank Lloyd Wright. This seems to be an act of mediation within a contentious atmosphere, one prepared specifically for an American audience.

Now that we no longer adhere to a creed of production for production's sake, the civilization that is now in the making draws closer to the mental outlook that is shared by primitive man and Eastern man. We in the West are again becoming conscious of something that they never forgot: that the continuity of human experience always exists alongside and in contrast to our day-to-day existence.

Sigfried Giedion, from "The State of Contemporary Architecture," in *Architectural Record* 115:1 (January 1954), p. 135–6, 137.

This may serve to strengthen a realization that the image of this emerging civilization, especially our particular interest – the form of contemporary architecture – cannot be described by so drained and bloodless a term as an "International Style." Moreover the term itself is a complete misnomer, as is the case with many other "styles." It is well known for instance that the term "Gothic Style" when used in the 18th century designated a form of barbarism. It was only after the English had rediscovered the Gothic that it became used as a term of adoration. "Baroque" also was first used to describe something over-extravagant, irregular or undisciplined. But all such labels were only applied by later generations. The architects of the Gothic or Baroque periods gave no stylistic names to their buildings. They just built, as they had to build, in a contemporary manner – and so do we! So let us drop, once and for all, such misleading formalist designations.

[. . .]

I would like to give a name to the method of approach employed by the best contemporary architects when they have to solve a specific regional problem – such as a building for the tropics or the West Coast, for India or for South America – whether it is for a house, a government center or a problem in urbanism. This name is the *New Regional Approach*.

I am thinking of some walk-up apartments built in Morocco by Candilis and Woods for a very poor population who now live, as in Brazil and other tropical climates, in "bidon-villes" or tin shacks made from old gasoline cans. In this case the problem was the erection of several thousand dwellings very rapidly, very cheaply and employing only the simplest techniques. Each dwelling has two bedrooms that open onto a patio living room surrounded by a six ft wall that insures privacy for the family. Great care is taken to see that every corner of the dwelling is at some time penetrated by the bacteria-destroying beams of the sun. Some row houses were built in Cuba by Wiener and Sert for the better paid workers . . . No glass is used but instead a modern version of the lattice-like openings common around the Caribbean. Each dwelling has two bedrooms and a living room that is wide open to a private patio. The neighborhood unit model for 8000 inhabitants shows how these simple units can be variously grouped.

Examples such as these imply that the modern architect should not strive to produce an external appearance in conformity with traditional buildings. Sometimes the new buildings will conform to a certain extent, sometimes they will be basically different. This difference may be due to two reasons: sometimes it will be because of new production methods and the use of new materials; sometimes, more importantly, it will be caused by the new aesthetic, the new emotional expression, that the builder is giving to the habitat of man.

The regional approach that satisfies both cosmic and terrestrial conditions is a developing trend, but there is also another symptom that is emerging, and that hints at the many-sided face of contemporary architecture. In contemporary painting many problems come forward which can also be discerned in the earliest beginnings of art. Architecture is different from painting; it is not so intimately related to man's direct projection of what flows in the subconscious mind. Yet we cannot leave unnoticed a certain symptom which has been appearing in architecture, above all in the recent work of Frank Lloyd Wright (especially since 1940). We can now follow the exciting path that the human mind had to travel before he came to standardize (if we may call it this) upon the rectangular house with its square or rectangular rooms. We are all born with this rectangular house and are so accustomed to live with it that it seems it could never have been otherwise. Yet it is important that an artist like

Frank Lloyd Wright is plunging so deeply into problems that concerned the human spirit at a time when mankind was contemplating the transition from the nomadic herdsman to the settled agriculturalist.

At the very beginning of architecture the paramount type was not the square house, but the curvilinear house – sometimes round, sometimes oval, sometimes freely curving. Now it tries to make a re-appearance. Sometimes this is dictated by mechanistic reasons: such as the mast house of Buckminster Fuller, or the use of a central mechanical core. But Wright follows exclusively the line of his artistic vision, maybe adapted to the site, maybe adapted to the man who is to inhabit the house, maybe under the compulsion of expressing that which slumbers in himself. It is not my intention to discuss the pros and cons of this kind of contemporary architecture, but it seems a duty not to ignore it. What we need more today than anything else is *imagination*, but this subject must wait for a later article.

181   ERNESTO NATHAN ROGERS
inaugural editorial in
Casabella-Continuità (1954)

Almost simultaneous with Giedion's acceptance of regional modernism was this thoughtful editorial in *Casabella*. The Italian journal had been a champion of modernism in the prewar years and its new editor was Ernesto Nathan Rogers, a highly regarded designer and partner in the BBPR studio. Writing under a pseudonym because of his Jewish ancestry, Rogers had contributed several articles to *Casabella* during the 1940s, and in 1944 he had been forced to seek refuge in Switzerland to avoid the concentration camp. Rogers was intent on maintaining *Casabella* as a catalyst for contemporary discussion, and he also took it as his personal task, in the wake of the war's devastation, to reaffirm the importance of history and tradition within Italian practice. On the cover of the first issue of the new journal, which appeared in January 1954, he inserted the word *continuità* (continuity) under the main title. In this editorial he sets out the first of several arguments on behalf of incorporating regional or national traditions into modernism – arguments that would eventually meet with firm resistance.

Casabella might be considered a rather commonplace title for a magazine with our ambitious programme were it not for the vigorous history Casabella has passed through. This history has substantially changed the character of the magazine so that to-day the tension of its subject matter is such as to constitute a symbol: Casabella is the magazine which Giuseppe Pagano and Edoardo Persico guided through the dark period towards the long-postponed goal of discovery, definition, invention, and fantasy.

And we set great store by their legacy.

We love architecture, too; not as an abstract idea, but as an art which perfectly expresses our will to live. Yes, we belong to the few who still believe in the unity of existence, or rather, in the fundamental responsibility of every artist before his work.

Ernesto Nathan Rogers, inaugural editorial in *Casabella-Continuità* 199 (December 1953/January 1954), trans. from p. I (addendum).

We believe in the fruitful cycle of man-architecture-man, and we intend to show its dramatic development, its crises, its few but indispensable certainties, and its many and even more vital doubts.

Accordingly, we believe that being means, above all, accepting the labour of daily rebirth and refusing to harden in fixed positions, means anxiety approaching pain, a perpetual struggle to enlarge the field of human sympathy.

The motto we have chosen to express our way of thinking is "Continuity". We have seen fit to have it printed above the old title as a reminder of the task we have undertaken. It expresses our sense of humility in coming into this legacy and perhaps our presumptuousness in hoping to be worthy of such a responsibility. Continuity, much more than its practical use as a motto for Casabella, means historical awareness, awareness of a deep-running tradition which for Pagano and Persico and for us is expressed in the eternal struggle of the creative spirit against every manifestation of formalism, past and present.

A dynamic carrying on, not a passive imitation is what we seek: not a pose, not a new dogma, but free and unbiased research with an agreed method. We shall consider "ours" only ideas and works which have been thoroughly worked out and, on the other hand, we shall draw attention to works in which we espy even the slightest evidence of a break with hardened preconceptions, of a new freedom, intuition, desire and hope.

We are neither idolaters nor iconoclasts: we love the masters of to-day and yesterday, and we freely recognize the nourishment we have received from the past; but we refuse to give up that most jealously guarded of our possessions, a free and ranging critical mind.

Therefore, Casabella will be following a policy of welcoming the contributions of not only the major exponents of modern architectural thought, but also those of younger, less mature but promising talents whose works are none the less, stirring. To our way of thinking, both these talents, the mature and the promising, represent necessary moments in the progress of architecture, like the systole and diastole of a living organism; they represent continuity.

We have refused every cliché and, on the other hand, every form of agnosticism, our choice falling to whatever work in some degree manifested that passion for freedom the architectural products of which symbolize the sublime effect of the historical process in determining its economic causes. Unity in culture, continuity in time, continuity in space.

No work is truly modern which is not genuinely rooted in tradition, while no ancient work has a modern meaning which is not capable of somehow reflecting our modern temper. Thus, avoiding the extremes of traditionalism and idealism we can examine architecture as it actually is, in its reality.

What are our limits, what our confines? When dead and living coexist in our minds, what issues are irreconcilable between living men?

We are against domination by imposed and poorly assimilated ideologies, against the cosmopolitan drug of the most recent accademic manner, more insidious than a mould; against the chauvinism of the nostalgic, against "reactionary revolutionaries", against demagogic folklorism. We stand for a truly international language sprung of mutual understanding, to which every artist can contribute from his inner freedom and the cultural climate he works in.

Let us remember Bertold Brecht's chorus. Here it is again: "We must be clear, we must be clear! Some say yes but can't agree, Some go unasked, others agree . . . to be wrong; we must be clear, we must be clear!"

After this long period of silence (but for the three issues since the war) we would like to offer our readers something of the polemics raging over vital subjects, because we believe that one can construct with passionate and sincere discussion as well as with bricks and mortar.

The ethical content of our aesthetic might be expressed as the will to test the problems of quantity in the crucible of quality and at the same time strive that quality may progressively become quantity, to bring art and craft back to their original synthesis: techné.

Such a task can only be undertaken by the enlightened efforts of architectural producers (artist, industrialist, artisans) and consumers; we therefore address ourselves to both of these groups: to Italian and to foreign readers, to our old friends and to the new ones we hope to make, to students, to help us give substance to our programme.

182 REYNER BANHAM
from "The New Brutalism" (1955)

In 1953 the Institute of Contemporary Art (ICA) in London held the exhibition "Parallel of Life and Art," which consisted of 169 images of machine parts, found items, biological artifacts, primitive art, and architecture. This realist display of nontraditional artistic forms coalesced into the movement of "New Brutalism," which in 1955 became defined by Reyner Banham. This young historian was at the time working on a dissertation on Italian Futurism under Nikolaus Pevsner, but here he starts his ideological break with his mentor. Banham begins his article by calling New Brutalism "our first native art-movement since the New Art-History arrived here," and the dual objects of its scorn are what he terms the "William Morris Revival" of British communists (the impact of "New Empiricism" on the socialist planning of new British towns) and the "New Humanism" or classicism called into vogue by Rudolf Wittkower. In its architectural guise, Banham finds New Brutalism in the postwar work of Le Corbusier, in the Hunstanton School of Alison and Peter Smithson, and in the Yale Art Gallery of Louis Kahn. In retrospect, this bundling of disparate works seems somewhat odd, yet Banham would soon take an even more dramatic turn with his developing interest in pop art and mass culture.

The history of the phrase itself is revealing. Its form is clearly derived from THE ARCHITECTURAL REVIEW'S post-war *trouvaille* 'The New Empiricism,' a term which was intended to describe visible tendencies in Scandinavian architecture to diverge from another historical concept 'The International Style.' This usage, like any involving the word *new*, opens up an historical perspective. It postulates that an old empiricism can be identified by the historian, and that the new one can be distinguished from it by methods of historical comparison, which will also distinguish it from a mere 'Empirical Revival.' The ability to deal with such fine shades of historical meaning is in itself a measure of our handiness with the historical method today, and the use of phrases of the form 'The New X-ism' – where X equals any adjective root – became commonplace in the early nineteen-fifties in fourth-year studios and other places where architecture is discussed, rather than practised.

Reyner Banham, from "The New Brutalism," in *The Architectural Review* 118:708 (December 1955), pp. 356, 361.

The passion of such discussion has been greatly enhanced by the clarity of its polarization – Communists versus the Rest – and it was somewhere in this vigorous polemic that the term 'The New Brutalism' was first coined. It was, in the beginning, a term of Communist abuse, and it was intended to signify the normal vocabulary of Modern Architecture – flat roofs, glass, exposed structure – considered as morally reprehensible deviations from 'The New Humanism,' a phrase which means something different in Marxist hands to the meaning which might be expected. The New Humanism meant, in architecture at that time, brickwork, segmental arches, pitched roofs, small windows (or small panes at any rate) – picturesque detailing without picturesque planning. It was, in fact, the so-called 'William Morris Revival,' now happily defunct, since Kruschev's reversal of the Party's architectural line, though this reversal has, of course, taken the guts out of subsequent polemics. But it will be observed that The New Humanism was again a quasi-historical concept, oriented, however spuriously, toward that mid-nineteenth century epoch which was Marxism's Golden Age, when you could recognize a capitalist when you met him.

However, London architectural circles are a small field in which to conduct a polemic of any kind, and abuse must be directed at specific persons, rather than classes of persons, since there was rarely enough unanimity (except among Marxists) to allow a class to coalesce. The New Brutalists at whom Marxist spite was directed could be named and recognized – and so could their friends in other arts. The term had no sooner got into public circulation than its meaning began to narrow. Among the non-Marxist grouping there was no particular unity of programme or intention, but there was a certain community of interests, a tendency to look toward Le Corbusier, and to be aware of something called *le beton brut*, to know the quotation which appears at the head of this article and, in the case of the more sophisticated and aesthetically literate, to know of the *Art Brut* of Jean Dubuffet and his connection in Paris. Words and ideas, personalities and discontents chimed together and in a matter of weeks – long before the Third Programme and the monthlies had got hold of the phrase – it had been appropriated as their own, by their own desire and public consent, by two young architects, Alison and Peter Smithson.

The phrase had thus changed both its meaning and its usage. Adopted as something between a slogan and a brick-bat flung in the public's face, The New Brutalism ceased to be a label descriptive of a tendency common to most modern architecture, and became instead a programme, a banner, while retaining some – rather restricted – sense as a descriptive label. It is because it is both kinds of -ism at once that The New Brutalism eludes precise description, while remaining a living force in contemporary British architecture.

[. . .]

The definition of a New Brutalist building derived from Hunstanton and Yale Art Centre must be modified so as to exclude formality as a basic quality if it is to cover future developments and should more properly read: 1, Memorability as an Image; 2, Clear exhibition of Structure; and 3, Valuation of Materials 'as found.' Remembering that an Image is what affects the emotions, that structure, in its fullest sense, is the relationship of parts, and that materials 'as found' are raw materials, we have worked our way back to the quotation which headed this article 'L'Architecture, c'est, avec des Matières Bruts, établir des rapports émouvants,' but we have worked our way to this point through such an awareness of history and its uses that we see that The New Brutalism, if it is architecture in the grand sense of Le Corbusier's definition, is also architecture of our time and not of his, nor of

Lubetkin's, nor of the times of the Masters of the past. Even if it were true that the Brutalists speak only to one another, the fact that they have stopped speaking to Mansart, to Palladio and to Alberti would make The New Brutalism, even in its more private sense, a major contribution to the architecture of today.

183 STEEN EILER RASMUSSEN
from *Experiencing Architecture* (1959)

Whereas the architectural centers of Italy and Britain literally exploded with a burst of theoretical activity in the 1950s, the discourse in Scandinavia remained relatively low-key. What J. M. Richards had dubbed "New Empiricism" continued to develop during this period nevertheless, and much of the best European design work of the 1950s came out of this region. If there was one book that consolidated Nordic theory during these years it was Steen Eiler Rasmussen's *Experiencing Architecture*. Rasmussen had taught at the Royal Academy of Fine Arts in Copenhagen, as well as extensively in the United States, and this book underscores again the interesting parallel between Scandinavian and some American approaches to design. The book treats architecture as a visual, auditory, tactile, and above all psychological art, brought to light through the timeless effects of light, color, rhythm, texture, and materials.

When it had passed historians discovered that a definite style had dominated the period and they gave it a name. But those who lived in that style were not aware of it. Whatever they did, however they dressed, seemed natural to them. We speak of a "Gothic" period or a "Baroque" period, and dealers in antiques and those who make their living manufacturing fake antiques are familiar with all the small details that are characteristic of each style in all its phases. *But details tell nothing essential about architecture, simply because the object of all good architecture is to create integrated wholes.*

Understanding architecture, therefore, is not the same as being able to determine the style of a building by certain external features. It is not enough to *see* architecture; you must experience it. You must observe how it was designed for a special purpose and how it was attuned to the entire concept and rhythm of a specific era. You must dwell in the rooms, feel how they close about you, observe how you are naturally led from one to the other. You must be aware of the textural effects, discover why just those colors were used, how the choice depended on the orientation of the rooms in relation to windows and the sun. Two apartments, one above the other, with rooms of exactly the same dimensions and with the same openings, can be entirely different simply because of curtains, wallpaper and furniture. You must experience the great difference acoustics make in your conception of space: the way sound acts in an enormous cathedral, with its echoes and long-toned reverberations, as compared to a small paneled room well padded with hangings, rugs and cushions.

Man's relation to implements can be broadly described thus: children begin by playing with blocks, balls and other things which they can grasp in their hands. As time goes on they

Steen Eiler Rasmussen, from *Experiencing Architecture*. Cambridge, MA: MIT Press, 1964, pp. 33–4.

demand better and better tools. At a certain stage most children have the desire to build some sort of shelter. It may be a real cave dug into a bank, or a primitive hut of rough boards. But often it is no more than a secret nook hidden among bushes, or a tent made with a rug draped over two chairs. This "cave game" can be varied in a thousand ways but common to them all is the enclosing of space for the child's own use. Many animals are also able to create a shelter for themselves, by digging a hole in the ground or building some sort of habitation above it. But the same species always does it in the same way. Man alone forms dwellings which vary according to requirements, climate and cultural pattern. The child's play is continued in the grown-up's creation, and just as man progresses from simple blocks to the most refined implements, he progresses from the cave game to more and more refined methods of enclosing space. Little by little he strives to give form to his entire surroundings.

And this – to bring order and relation into human surroundings – is the task of the architect.

184 PETER LUIGI NERVI
from "The Foreseeable Future and the Training of Architects" (1962)

I f the statement of one individual can be said to encapsulate the predominant design philosophy of the 1950s and 1960s, it would be these words of Peter Luigi Nervi, the famed Italian engineer. Nervi completed his engineering studies at the University of Bologna in 1913, and, after the interruption of the war, he set up his office in Rome in 1920. Like the Swiss engineer Robert Maillart, Nervi was attracted to the structural possibilities of reinforced concrete, a fascination that evolved over the years with his work on airplane hangars, prefabricated *ferrocemento* techniques, and folded plates. What is so striking about these words, presented in a Charles Eliot Norton Lecture at Harvard in 1962, is their prototypical ring – echoing the near identical sentiments of various modernists from Horatio Greenough to Hermann Muthesius to J. J. P. Oud. Nervi's optimism represents the best of modernism in the period of its greatest flourishing.

Starting from an analogy with the knife, designs for the first steamships, the first dirigibles, the first fast automobiles, tried to achieve increased speed by means of very sharp prows. Only long experience brought about the bulblike prow of today's ships, the rounded form of the front part of the most efficient dirigibles, and the fuselage of subsonic airplanes. To pass from subsonic to supersonic speeds means a considerable change in the most efficient forms, as is seen by the creation of the present-day supersonic military planes.

It is striking that all the work we have seen, although in many different fields, has the common characteristic of adhering as faithfully as possible to natural laws and in addition being aesthetically expressive. No one can deny the beauty of a modern airplane which

Peter Luigi Nervi, from "The Foreseeable Future and the Training of Architects" (1962), in *Aesthetics and Technology in Building: The Charles Eliot Norton Lectures, 1961–1962.* Cambridge, MA: Harvard University Press, 1965, pp. 186–7.

approaches a "form type" – a form that will not change – or of a very large bridge which follows the static requirements to perfection (for instance, a parabolic arch or a continuous beam modeled according to the bending moments), or of the large building which shows a logical structural form for an exceptionally long span or a great height.

It is very difficult to explain the reason for our immediate approval of forms which come to us from a physical world with which we, seemingly, have no direct tie whatsoever. Why do these forms satisfy and move us in the same manner as natural things such as flowers, plants, and landscapes to which we have become accustomed through numberless generations?

It can also be noted that these achievements have in common a structural essence, a necessary absence of all decoration, a purity of line and shape more than sufficient to define an authentic style, a style I have termed the *truthful style*. I realize how difficult it is to find the right words to express this concept.

That this style exists and has entered without our full awareness into the aesthetic tastes of our time is demonstrated by the aerodynamic lines of slow vehicles, such as buses and trucks, of some buildings and bridges, and even more by the rounded forms of objects of common use, such as typewriters, telephones, furniture, even clothing, and particularly the products of industrial design.

It is clear that this style can never again change, but that it will continually become more exact and determining, unless mankind voluntarily or because of some terrible happening renounces technology and industrial progress and goes back to retrace from the beginning the path already traveled through the centuries. How can we help but be struck by the thought that it is precisely our age that has found the direction which mankind will never be able to abandon?

When I make these remarks to friends, I am often told that this view of the near future is terribly sad, that perhaps it would be better to renounce voluntarily the further tightening of the bonds between our creations and the physical laws, if indeed these ties must lead us to a fatal monotony. I do not find this pessimism justified. Binding as technical demands may be there always remains a margin of freedom sufficient to show the personality of the creator of a work and, if he be an artist, to allow that his creation, even in its strict technical obedience, become a real and true work of art.

In every field – literature, music, architecture – the transition from technical correctness to poetry is determined by variations in relationships and in detailing so slight that they will always fall within the margin of freedom allowed to any creative activity, even those most tied down by technical factors, just as in the past works were created within a single style which differed from each other and which revealed the personality of their authors.

How can one deny that the most modern passenger airplanes are considerably different from one another, although they all adhere to the same rigorous aerodynamic style? Why are some more beautiful and harmonious than others? How can one not see that the small difference in the way the jets are attached on the B-707 and on the DC-8 is sufficient to modify the aesthetic aspect of the two airplanes? And how can one deny the architectural value and effectiveness of the chromatic decorations used by the different airlines?

But above all I think that technical correctness, the essential element of a truthful style, will force upon all architecture ethical standards which will lead to ordered and attractive public and private environments, whose silent educational action will be reflected in the lives and feelings of men.

C.   THE RISE AND FALL OF CIAM

Introduction

The one organizational entity attempting to bring together the diverging currents of European planning theory in the postwar years was the reconstituted Congrès Internationaux d'Architecture Moderne, or CIAM. The last significant gathering of this organization, devoted largely to research and issues of urban planning, had been the fourth congress of 1933, where 100 delegates, led by Le Corbusier, sailed on a cruise ship from Marseilles to Athens. Le Corbusier arranged a fifth, largely French conference in Paris in 1937, and in 1943 he published his version of *The Athens Charter*, which presumed to summarize the results of the fourth congress. During the war years, Giedion and the Spanish architect José Luis Sert attempted to draw architects from both England and the United States into CIAM, but only in the former country did their efforts meet with success. Thus it was in Bridgwater, England, that the sixth CIAM conference was held in 1947. Sert was elected president, while

Le Corbusier, Walter Gropius, and the Polish architect Helena Syrkus were named vice-presidents. Giedion continued in his role as the directing secretary.

Based on the principles and demands of the Athens Charter, CIAM thus resumed its operational activities with the greatest enthusiasm. Follow-up conferences were held in Bergamo, Italy (1949), Hoddesdon, England (1951), and Aix-en-Provence, France (1953), and by this last date the organization was seen by some as having become too successful and having grown too large. During the congress of 1953, however, ideological fissures began to appear within CIAM's façade – just as the evidence of some of its planning failures began to become manifest. By the mid-1950s an internal palace revolt was underway and the organization effectively split in two along generational lines. By the end of the decade the once-mighty international organization, founded with the aim to transform the world, would cease to exist.

185   J. H. FORSHAW AND PATRICK ABERCROMBIE
from *County of London Plan* (1944)

As the Allied war campaign against Nazi Germany was taking a decisive turn in 1943, plans were already being prepared in Britain for what would become the extensive rebuilding efforts of the postwar years. The German rocket attacks on London had created not only urban areas with massive damage but also the desire to rebuild the capital with improved infrastructure, traffic control, and housing of sufficient quantity to meet the shortages engendered by the war. The vehicle for the replanning of London was the London County Council (LCC), which in 1944 approved the plan put forth by J. H. Forshaw, the Architect to the LCC, and Patrick Abercrombie, a town planner associated with University College London. The overall plan called for, among other things, a revision of zoning laws, a relocation of industrial areas to outside of the city, new roadways, and a coordinated park system of open spaces. As these two passages show, the plan also considered the forms the new housing should take. Decentralization is the key in this regard, as Forshaw and Abercrombie proposed to relieve overcongested quarters of the city by creating planned neighborhoods – both in selected areas of the county and beyond the county with the creation of eight new towns. For housing types, the plan suggested a mixture of low- and high-rise buildings, the latter modeled on Le Corbusier's concept of towers placed in green settings. The results were controversial, and the stark modernity of the designs (many built in exposed concrete) would in later years also become a target of criticism.

Reconstruction and Decentralisation of the Congested Areas

An American has said: "Social facts are primary and the physical organisation of a city, its industries and its markets, its lines of communications and traffic, must be subservient to its social needs." Industries, in their location, are also a social affair, for one of the most difficult

J. H. Forshaw and Patrick Abercrombie, from *County of London Plan*. London: Macmillan, 1944, pp. 7–8, 34–5.

planning problems to solve is the relation of where people work to where they live. The nearer the worker to his work, whether in Government Department, office, shop, factory or dock, the better, provided proper living conditions are obtained. On the one hand, it is desirable to make the industrial boroughs of London so attractive that people whose work is there will not be forced out to distant suburbs for pleasant houses, gardens, open spaces, schools with playing fields and safe shopping centres: on the other hand, the people whom it is necessary to decentralise, in order to produce these satisfactory conditions, should so far as possible have a choice of work near at hand; the aim should be to avoid their being housed in distant dormitories, yet constrained to rush back to their old work-a-day haunts. The facts of the dilemma are plain, but their consequences are not always grasped. Some have been heard to ask why is it not possible for people to live in nice houses with large gardens, near their central work, and at the same time for the population of the borough to remain at its pre-1938 level? Others, a little more realistic, would cram everyone into lofty close-packed tenements whose high architectural qualities might mask their social deficiencies, and would also keep factories within the town, thus avoiding any further encroachment upon the country-side. Both these points of view ignore two inescapable facts: the first, that to obtain attractive living conditions a much lower density in the industrial boroughs of London must be secured, *i.e.*, a large population must be decentralised, and so far as possible a corresponding amount of industry: the second, that the exodus of people and industry was already taking place before the war. This decentralisation has been happening in an unplanned way; the boroughs see their population dwindling, as their best elements, especially the young married folk, leave the old surroundings, which are not benefited by this reduction except in strictly limited patches of new tenements. What we now propose is to anticipate this loss, to enhance it by means of a bold reduction and to produce a really satisfactory environment by wholesale rebuilding made possible by war damage. In the later sections of this Report and the accompanying drawings we describe large-scale proposals for creating new communities on these lines, in order to show what is meant by wholesale replanning, as compared with piecemeal rebuilding. A notable example of this, for which detailed plans are far advanced, is the proposed redevelopment of some 1,500 acres in Stepney and Poplar. There are many others. It will be realised that the provision of an adequate amount of open space determines the numbers to be decentralised, as much as the reduction of houses to a lower density. The number we estimate it would be necessary to remove from the congested parts of London to secure the conditions postulated in our Plan is between five and six hundred thousand people. [. . .]

The Destination

It is assumed in the Plan which we submit that a large number of people and a considerable amount of industry are to be removed from their present central location and re-situated elsewhere. It is also hoped that these removals will result in a balanced community in which work and home will not be unduly separated – or for which, at any rate, provision is made that diurnal travelling is reduced as much as possible.

The distance of the dispersal will vary between what might be called a re-arrangement within the Greater London area and a removal clean outside the metropolitan influence, *e.g.*, to the north of England. An intermediate between these might be taken on the fifty mile radius from Charing Cross; a development of towns at this distance is probable and a certain amount of it may be attributed to London. But we are chiefly concerned with the redistribution within the Metropolitan Traffic Area.

If an all-round figure of half-a-million persons (and so far as possible a corresponding amount of industry) be taken, it might be advisable to divide this figure equally into a short-term and long-term programme. The short-term includes those for whom accommodation will be wanted at the earliest possible moment, simultaneously with the central rebuilding scheme for the population that remains behind. The long-term figure includes those who may be allowed to continue to live and work in existing (but ultimately to be condemned) premises, and those who may have to be given temporary accommodation in central areas.

The short and long-term policy will be reflected both in the type and location of community to be created. The short-term will in the first place fill in certain gaps and incompleted areas within the County boundary; it will then develop communities somewhat approximating to a pre-war residential scheme of strictly limited size and attached to an existing community for social purposes and for part of its occupation. It will be recognised that at first perhaps a majority of workers will journey inwards for their daily work. But if work places near at hand and trading estate inducements to industrialists are offered, the numbers of people locally employed will tend to increase. It will be the function of the planning authority to see that these decentralised communities become an integral part of the existing local community. They would eventually approximate to true satellites of an inner character, located probably somewhere near the boundary of the Metropolitan Police District.

The long-term community should approximate much closer to the true satellite, planned from the beginning, with its occupational independence and the normal relationship with the Metropolis. By long-term it is not meant to suggest that the short-term should be completed before the long-term is begun; but that there will be more of the single creative effort in the short-term and more of organic growth in the long-term.

The actual location of both short and long-term communities will take place as a part of the London Regional Plan which is being prepared, but it is essential that general ideas as to the destination of people and industry should be studied at this stage, in order to be certain that if they are decentralised they will be found suitable locations, either attached to existing or creating new communities which contain the germ of success.

To summarise, it might be possible to designate five types of units of dispersed industrial population:

   i. Infilling of gaps in incomplete schemes within the County.
   ii. Immediate close-in housing groups, attached to areas where there is already work, and gradually integrating into balanced communities; these might be called metropolitan satellites.
   iii. Satellites located within the Metropolitan Traffic Area.
   iv. Outer satellites, usually developing existing towns on the fifty mile radius.
   v. Dispersal remote from the metropolitan influence.

186 SIGFRIED GIEDION
from "Reaffirmation of the Aims of CIAM: Bridgwater 1947" (1947)

The first postwar meeting of CIAM took place in this English town in 1947, and almost all the major European architects attended. Walter Gropius spoke on architectural education, Le Corbusier on his wartime research activities, and José Luis Sert on human scale within the city. The first matter approved by the congress was this "Reaffirmation of the Aims of CIAM: Bridgwater 1947." Here the reference in section 3 to the stimulation of one's "spiritual growth" raises the issue that would come to the fore in later CIAM discussion, but it was not meant to challenge CIAM's earlier model of four functional categories for planning: housing, work, traffic, and recreation (the last now "cultivation of mind and body").

1. Preamble

We, the CIAM architects from many countries, in Europe, America, Asia and Africa, have met at Bridgwater after an interval of ten years.

These have been years of struggle and separation during which, as a consequence of the threat of Fascist domination, political, economic and social questions have taken on a new significance for everyone. At the same time technical progress has been accelerated by intensive scientific research and the needs of war production. The technique of planning has also moved forward as a result of the experience some countries have gained in social organization.

These factors are together responsible for a new conception of integrated planning which is now emerging. Allied with this is a new contemporary consciousness that finds its definitive expression in the arts.

We are faced with an enormous task in rebuilding the territories devastated by the war, as well as in raising the standard of life in undeveloped countries where great changes are now taking place. We therefore feel that this, our sixth congress, is an occasion when we must review our past activities, examine our present situation and determine our policy for the future.

2. Background

Our earlier declarations – that of La Sarraz in 1928 and the Athens Charter of 1933 – reflected the architect's growing sense of his responsibilities towards society. They were drawn up with reference to a particular time and particular situation, but we consider many of the

Sigfried Giedion, from "Reaffirmation of the Aims of CIAM: Bridgwater 1947," in *A Decade of New Architecture*. Zurich: Editions Girsberger, 1951, pp. 16–17.

statements made in them to be fundamental and we now reaffirm the following points from these declarations.

"We emphasize that to build is a primal activity in man, intimately associated with the evolution and development of human life . . . "

"Our intention . . . is to re-establish the place of architecture in its proper social and economic sphere . . . "

"We affirm today the necessity for a new conception of architecture satisfying the spiritual, intellectual and material needs of present day life. Conscious of the effects on social structure, brought about by industrialisation, we recognise the necessity of a corresponding transformation of architecture itself . . . "

"Planning is the organisation of the functional conditions of community life: it applies equally to town and country, and operates within the divisions: (a) dwelling; (b) places of work and (c) of recreation; (d) circulation, connecting these three . . . "

"The aims of CIAM are:

(a)   to formulate the architectural problem of today;
(b)   to represent the idea of a contemporary architecture;
(c)   to instil this idea into technical, economic and social thought;
(d)   to watch over the contemporary development of architecture.

The Declaration of La Sarraz was primarily an attempt to express some of the realities of the contemporary situation and to recognize the inevitable emergance of new forms from the application of new means to meeting human needs.

Many of the ideas for which we were then working are now widely accepted, and the subsequent Athens Charter has laid a similar foundation in the field of physical and social planning. Among the achievements of recent years are:

A general acceptance of the idea of social planning and, in many countries, the adoption of planning legislation – including legislation for land reform – which will assist the realization of this idea.

A growing recognition of the important part played by scientific method in the development of architecture, which has resulted in the advance of building technique.

A trend towards the reintegration of the plastic arts – architecture, sculpture and painting – and thereby towards a clearer understanding of contemporary forms of artistic expression.

3.   The Aims of CIAM

The progress that has been made in the last ten years and the confidence in the ideals of CIAM expressed by the younger generation convince us that the continuation of the CIAM congresses is fully justified. The sixth congress redefines the aims of CIAM as follows:

"To work for the creation of a physical environment that will satisfy man's emotional and material needs and stimulate his spiritual growth."

To achieve an environment of this quality, we must combine social idealism, scientific planning and the fullest use of available building techniques. In so doing we must enlarge and enrich the aesthetic language of architecture in order to provide a contemporary means whereby people's emotional needs can find expression in the design of their environment. We believe that thus a more balanced life can be produced for the individual and for the community.

187   J. M. RICHARDS
from "Contemporary Architecture and the Common Man" (1947)

The CIAM conference at Bridgwater was hosted by MARS, or the Modern Architectural Research Group, which now also controlled the London County Council and much of the postwar building activity funded by the government. This British arm of CIAM, however, was now splitting apart. The Corbusian preference for housing towers set on lawns was opposed by the "low-tech" approach of those favoring more traditional models of row housing — supporters of the "New Empiricism" of Sweden. The champion of this last movement, as we have seen, was J. M. Richards, who had lost much of his earlier fervor for international modernism. As far back as 1940 he had written an article for *The Architectural Review* that discussed the common man's disdain for much of modern architecture, and it was this sensitivity that he brought to the Bridgwater conference, where he reported the results of his survey of people's views on modern architecture. The comments must have mystified many of those in attendance, including Giedion and Le Corbusier, but they nevertheless represented a harbinger of opposition that would soon form.

The field with which I am concerned is that of architectural expression in relation to the architect's public, a field which does not represent any abrupt break with the line of study that CIAM has pursued hitherto. We have been discussing the contemporary architectural situation with particular emphasis on the realisation of CIAM ideals in various countries, or the reasons why CIAM ideals are not being realised to the full. In doing this we have to face the fact that the CIAM ideals express themselves in an idiom which is by no means accepted or understood by the man in the street. It is natural for the man in the street, however clearly – on an intellectual plane – he may understand the rational basis of modern design, to judge it in practice very largely by what he sees in the street; that is, as a visual art. And if he does not find the visible products of modern architectural thought sympathetic to his own aspirations, then modern architecture as a whole will not obtain his support, and may be in danger of becoming an art of the kind that is appreciated only by connoisseurs.

Need the architect concern himself with the reactions of the man in the street? As long as he has faith in his own integrity as an artist, should he not follow his own inspiration, without worrying about popular appreciation? That is one question modern architects

J. M. Richards, from "Contemporary Architecture and the Common Man," in Sigfried Giedion, *A Decade of New Architecture.* Zurich: Editions Girsberger, 1951, p. 33.

must answer; in particular whether modern architecture has a duty to provide the means of self-expression to the man in the street, and if it has such a duty, what can the architect do consciously to provide the missing link between his own experiments in expression and the public's frustrated wish to participate in them? Perhaps we can go so far as to say that the ordinary man does not so much reject the modern idiom as cling to an earlier idiom because he has no confidence in what the brave new world has to offer him. He has accepted the modern kitchens and bathrooms because, from his own experience, he has found them more efficient and economical, and thence more agreeable and even positively exciting. He may sense occasionally some of the exciting possibilities of modern architecture as a whole, but he will only come to regard them as possibilities to be welcomed into his own life when the scientific progress they stand for is shown to be something that he as an individual will benefit from, not something to be feared and therefore resisted.

The question of the architect's attitude to the man in the street becomes therefore a choice between two alternatives: he can produce what he, for his own reasons, believes to be good architecture and hope that people will come to like it by habit, and by identifying it with the improvement its scientific methods can bring to their environment. This might be a slow progress, in which the architect – in his capacity as architect – can play only a minor part; for an improved environment depends on economics even more than on technics.

Alternatively, the architect can say to himself that he has some direct part to play in preventing a new architecture from being frightening because it commits the public to the unknown. He cannot himself remove economic insecurity, but he is one of the people through whom the abstractions of science are translated to the public in visible form, and the way he translates them is an important link in the process by which modern architecture is enabled to contribute to the better ordering of the modern world.

188 BRUNO ZEVI
from "A Message to the International Congress of Modern Architecture" (1949)

P erhaps the most interesting event surrounding the 1949 CIAM congress in Bergamo was not what took place inside the meeting hall but what transpired on the eve of its opening. Bruno Zevi used the occasion of its Italian setting to publish an article in his journal *Metron*, really the first major criticism on the principles of CIAM by a modernist. Zevi's remarks unfold on two fronts. First he argues that the congress was being run by three aging rationalists – Le Corbusier, Walter Gropius, and Sigfried Giedion – who had essentially lost touch with

Bruno Zevi, "A Message to the International Congress of Modern Architecture" (1949), trans. Andrea Oppenheimer Dean, in *Bruno Zevi on Modern Architecture*. New York: Rizzoli, 1983, pp. 127–8.

contemporary issues and therefore had little to offer postwar theory. Second, the same tight-knit circle had excluded from CIAM's deliberations not only the arguments of "New Empiricism" in Scandinavia, but also the entire wing of modernism represented by Frank Lloyd Wright – essentially the lessons of several decades of American modernism. The words must have shaken Giedion personally, for we have already seen his conciliatory gestures toward Wright in his article of 1954 (192). But Zevi's words also landed a forceful blow to the leadership and soft underbelly of CIAM. From its inception, the organization was run by a small clique of Europeans intent on promulgating a single ideological viewpoint, which indeed dates back to the socialist theory of the 1920s. Thus CIAM could scarcely muster a defense.

The recognition of the practical limits of the CIAM bears with it the necessity of deepening its cultural substance. It is here that we come to the heart of the matter. Can these congresses organized by the CIAM accomplish today achievements of importance equal to those brought about by the first congresses? If these congresses can not have a deep politico-social influence, can they at least attain a worthy cultural level?

These questions may seem abstract. But history teaches that every organization, every movement, is bound to its origins and can evolve out of them only with great difficulty. Every movement has its leading class, its mentality, its tactics. Theoretically all can be changed – and in this case it would not be desirable – in the historical reality not except if one wants it very deeply. The CIAM, in the general feeling of modern architects, is bound to the architectural mentality of Le Corbusier, Walter Gropius, and generally with that period known as the rationalistic one. It is bound to the historical perspectives and interpretations of Sigfried Giedion. These three personalities are most important and determinant figures today, so much so that there is no foreseeable lessening of their influence, which perhaps would facilitate the development of a more appropriate and comprehensive culture. The other branch of modern architecture, that which is no longer rationalistic, the movement which is called organic, or of human architecture, or of the New Empiricism, doesn't have adequate representation in the CIAM and its cultural position has been defended by architects who entered the CIAM as proponents of the rationalist school ten years ago and have since undergone an evolution. An entire generation of young architects who have contributed to the advancement of the modern movement, and all the adherents of the Wright school, have been more or less excluded. Why? The Congress of Bergamo must face this problem. There is no modern architect living who does not recognize the great versatile ability of Le Corbusier and his followers, but many feel that his approach is only one of the aspects in the present order of things. All, and especially this writer who had the good fortune to have been his pupil at Harvard University, recognize in Gropius the most openly human and elastic personality of the modern movement; but Gropius the man and master is one thing, the Bauhaus another. Although a magnificent and fundamental experience is modern history, the Bauhaus has value now largely as an experience of the past. As for the General Secretary of the CIAM, Dr. Giedion, it is enough to say that all of us have always in mind his *Space, Time and Architecture* and that we find in it continually elements and data useful to our research. But to recognize its superior scientific qualities does not mean that we agree with its historical theses. *Space, Time and Architecture* is a splendid book, but a misleading one.

189 ALISON AND PETER SMITHSON, GILLIAN AND WILLIAM HOWELL, AND JOHN VOELCKER

from "Urban Reidentification" Grid, CIAM, Aix-en-Provence (1953)

W hereas the eighth CIAM conference in Hoddesdon in 1951 passed with little fanfare, this was not the case with the ninth, held in Aix-en-Provence in the summer of 1953 and attended by 500 delegates. Now a divide within the organization becomes evident. The theme of the conference was "Human Habitat," a proposed refinement of the Athens Charter for which Le Corbusier had argued for several years. No less than six committees reported on a range of architectural and planning issues, from professional education to urbanism to social programs. Opposition to the planning premises of CIAM, however, appeared along two fronts. One was the perspective gained from the emerging anthropological awareness of third-world countries and the complex physical organization of their social and urban structures. Studies, for instance, were presented by several French teams considering Moroccan and Algerian squatter settlements and the problem of replacing them with "modern" housing. The premises for these solutions – as argued by Michel Ecochard and Georges Candilis – should differ fundamentally from European models, which up to this point were presumed to be universal.

Another challenge to CIAM formed around a contingent of Dutch and British architects who were disputing the fourfold functional zoning of the Athens Charter (dividing the city into areas of housing, work, traffic, and recreation). In the "Urban Reidentification" scheme put forward by the British team, led by Alison and Peter Smithson, several photographs of traditional working-class neighborhoods were mounted on boards (here referred to as a grille), together with text and linear diagrams of future housing complexes. Proposing to replace the fourfold division of the Athens Charter with the organizational notions of house, street, district, and city, this group called for a "hierarchy of human associations," that is, housing schemes that (while still accepting the housing towers on lawns) avoided the physical separation of towers through the use of "streets in the air" and other such devices. In effect, the group called for replacing the isolated residential district with a mixture of functions operating with sufficient layers of complexity.

This Grille is concerned with the problem of identity. It proposes that a community should be built up from a hierarchy of associational elements and tries to express these various levels of association (THE HOUSE, THE STREET, THE DISTRICT, THE CITY) algebraically. It is important to realize that the terms used[,] Street, District, etc.[,] are not to be taken as the reality but as the *idea* and that it is our *task* to find *new* equivalents for these forms of association in our new, non-demonstrative society. The problem of reidentifying man with his environment (contenu et contenant) cannot be achieved by using hierarchical forms of house-groupings, streets, squares, greens, etc., as the social reality they presented no longer exists. In the complex of association that is a community, social cohesion can only be

Alison and Peter Smithson, Gillian and William Howell, and John Voelcker, from "Urban Reidentification" Grid, cited from Eric Mumford, *The CIAM Discourse on Urbanism, 1928–1960*. Cambridge, MA: MIT Press, 2000, p. 234–5.

achieved if ease of movement is possible and this provides us with only second law [sic], that height (density) should increase as the total population increases, and vice versa. In a large city with high buildings, in order to keep ease of movement, we propose a multi-level city with residential "streets-in-the-air." These are linked together in a multi-level continuous complex, connected where necessary to work and to those ground elements that are necessary at each level of association. Our hierarchy of associations is woven into a modulated continuum representing the true complexity of human association. This conception is in direct opposition to the arbitrary isolation of the so-called communities of the "Unité" and the "neighborhood." We are of the opinion that such a hierarchy of human associations should replace the functional hierarchy of the "Charte d'Athenes."

190   JACOB BAKEMA, ALDO VAN EYCK, H. P. DANIEL VAN GINKEL, HANS HOVENS-GREVE, PETER AND ALISON SMITHSON, AND JOHN VOELCKER
"Statement on Habitat" (Doorn Manifesto, 1954)

I n the months following the ninth CIAM conference, the architects offering alternative urban visions came together to present a more unified front. In December 1953 the Smithsons, Howells, and Voelcker met in England to assess their dissatisfaction with CIAM, which they now saw as a large and ineffective organization unwilling to come to grips with more immediate urban problems. Around the same time a group of Dutch architects, led by Jacob Bakema and Aldo van Eyck, assembled and did the same. The two groups then met in January 1954 in Doorn, the Netherlands, where they had arranged a meeting with CIAM's board members Giedion, José Luis Sert, and Cornelis van Eesteren. There the dissidents issued a "Statement on Habitat," also called the Doorn Manifesto, which demanded that if a new "Charter of Habitat" should be enacted, it should be predicated on "vital human associations." The emphasis on the small scale and social complexity of the community – against the functional separation of activities envisaged by the Athens Charter – brought the crisis of CIAM to a head. The dissidents, initially given some leeway by Giedion, would come to call themselves the "Committee for CIAM 10." They operated as a subgroup of CIAM in charge of planning the tenth conference, originally planned for Algeria in 1955. They later became known as "Team 10."

Jacob Bakema, Aldo van Eyck, H. P. Daniel van Ginkel, Hans Hovens-Greve, Peter and Alison Smithson, and John Voelcker, "Statement on Habitat" (1954), cited from *Forum* 7 (1959), p. 231.

Statement on Habitat

1. La Charte d'Athènes proposed a technique which would counteract the chaos of the 19th Century, and restore principles of order within our cities.
2. Through this technique the overwhelming variety of city activities was classified into four distinct functions which were believed to be fundamental.
3. Each function was realized as a totality within itself. Urbanists could comprehend more clearly the potential of the 20th Century.
4. Our statement tries to provide a method which will liberate still further this potential. As a direct result of the 9th Congress at Aix, we have come to the conclusion that if we are to create a Charte de l'Habitat, we must redefine the aims of urbanism, and at the same time create a new tool to make this aim possible.

Urbanism considered and developed in the terms of the Charte d'Athènes tends to produce "towns" in which vital human associations are inadequately expressed.

To comprehend these human associations we must consider every community as a particular total complex.

In order to make this comprehension possible, we propose to study urbanism as communities of varying degrees of complexity.

These can be shown on a Scale of Association:

We suggest that the commissions operate each in a field not a point on the Scale of Association, for example

isolated buildings*)
villages
towns
cities.

This will enable us to study particular functions in their appropriate ecological field. Thus a housing sector or satellite of a city will be considered at the top of the scale, (under City, 4), and can in this way be compared with development in other cities, or contrasted with numerically similar developments in different fields of the Scale of Association. **This method of work will induce a study of human association as a first principle, and of the four functions as aspects of each total problem.**

NOTE

*) These fields are sufficiently finite for general purposes but there may be new forms of association, new patterns of community which replace the traditional hierarchy.

191 ALISON AND PETER SMITHSON
"Open Letter to Sert and Team 10" (1956)

As preparations were made for the CIAM conference in Algeria, Giedion began to back away from his earlier support for the "Committee for CIAM 10." In 1955 Georges Candilis informed his fellow planning members that Giedion, in passing through Paris, had made it known that he was "terribly worried about the spiritual and material organisation of the congress," and was threatening to postpone the event. Later that month Peter Smithson replied that "it was just for that reason – to change *their* organisation – that we took on our task." Le Corbusier also began to feel uneasy about the internal revolt that was taking place. Nevertheless, planning proceeded, although the congress was postponed for a year and had to be shifted from Algeria (whose revolt against French rule had begun) to Dubrovnik. This preparatory statement by Alison and Peter Smithson, responding to an earlier report issued by José Luis Sert, discloses that it was not just the functional divisions of the Athens Charter to which the Committee for CIAM 10 objected, but rather the broader formulation of housing issues. At this point the work of the Smithsons with regard to CIAM was beginning to border on anarchy.

The "relationships" listed in the documents circulated to groups are part of the general field of beliefs which we all hold, but they lack any definite focus on the human associations which it has been Team X's aim to stress.

We believe that our work between now and the Congress and the preliminary work with Sert at the Congress, must be to re-focus on the essentials.

We think it is wrong to accept a list of truisms as "relationships." [...]

"Relationships" must be concerned with realities.

"High and low buildings" are not permanent facts.

"Man's basic needs are unchanging, only his means of satisfying them are changing" is simply not true. In the real situation his needs (aspirations, desires) change all the time, the forces at work are not only physical but ideological – the climate of opinion – the ad-man – the desire for different expressions of the new social set-up (the house as well as the car).

Team X's approach is basically humanistic. Our aim was not to explore every relationship but to find those we could do something with. To put it another way, we should not be concerned at this congress with "relationships between built up volume and the space between buildings" or "between different household types and the architectonic expression," we should be looking for new housing types for the new "you" now, not variations on existing themes.

Alison and Peter Smithson, "Open Letter to Sert and Team 10," in *The Emergence of Team 10 out of C.I.A.M.*, ed. Alison Smithson. London: Architectural Association, pp. 54–5.

192 LE CORBUSIER

"Message of Le Corbusier to the X Congress CIAM at Dubrovnik" (1956)

I n what turned out to be the last CIAM directed by the founding generation of the congress, José Luis Sert opened the proceedings by reading a letter to the audience from Le Corbusier, who was not in attendance. It was, in effect, his letter of resignation from CIAM, in which he contrasted the work of his generation in establishing the tenets of the congress with the work of the younger generation of CIAM members, whose task he now articulates with broad strokes. The letter is written without acrimony, but its leading question – "CRISIS OR EVOLUTION?" – does suggest a certain weariness on his part with the recent disputes within CIAM. Le Corbusier was not alone in his frustration, as at the conclusion of the conference Sert would announce his resignation as president, as well as the breakup of the organization into regional and autonomous groups. The name CIAM would continue for one last conference, but under a whole new organization.

I   CRISIS OR EVOLUTION? Answer: problem of generations.

II   The generation of 1928 (date of Foundation of the CIAM)
- established a programme of international importance (La Sarraz)
- founded the CIAM
- declared the inseperability of architecture and city-planning
- prepared the "Charte d'Athènes"
- obtained world recognition of the principles of the "Charte d'Athènes"
- placed in the foreground of architecture and city planning the urgent need of new building capable of equipping a mechanized civilisation
- considered the notion "to dwell" as the key to this equipment
- in a word, the generation of 1928, in the midst of the confusion of its time, formulated a programme "First CIAM", detailed and put in order its chapters.

III The generation of 1956 will take command. It enters into practical action, using the programme "First CIAM".
- to produce taking into consideration urgent world-wide needs
- to standardise
- to design express, foresee and even predict "the times to come"
- to place on a world plane of architecture and city planning: the dwelling, work, leisure, transportation (of people and things).

Le Corbusier's letter of July 23, 1956 exists as a manuscript copy in various archives. This translated version of a typewritten copy is courtesy of Annie Pedret.

[. . .]

Dear friends of CIAM, here is my way of thinking. Act so that the CIAM continue in their creative passion, in disinterest, reject the opportunists or hot heads.

Good luck

Long live the SECOND–CIAM!

Your friend,

LE CORBUSIER.

193   ERNESTO ROGERS, PETER SMITHSON, AND JACOB BAKEMA

remarks on the design of the Torre Velasca, Milan (1959)

Under new leadership, CIAM held its final conference in Otterlo, Belgium, in September 1959. Team 10, the evolution of Committee for CIAM 10, was now in firm control of the proceedings. The program was livelier and more critical. It was also the last such meeting under the name of CIAM. The atmosphere was contentious during several of the projects presented, but especially so with the office/residential tower in Milan, the Torre Velasca, designed by BBPR. Ernesto Rogers presented the design, whose first eighteen stories of offices rise up as a compact rectangular form above an underground parking garage. The seven stories of housing above the offices, requiring a larger floor area, are extended out from the rectangular prism on all four sides and are supported by concrete piers that rise up from the ground and jut out diagonally to brace the overhung floors. Rogers defended the design on functional grounds, but he was also aware of the formal resemblance of the building to the medieval towers that grace so many Italian towns. This historical allusion to the city's medieval ambiance is what prompts Peter Smithson's furious charge of immorality.

Ernesto Rogers:

[. . .]

The general shape of the building is the result of a very rational design approach. We were required to design a building which was to be occupied partially by offices and partially by dwellings. Our studies of the space distribution requirements for the offices and dwellings led us to conclude that more space was obviously required by the dwellings per floor than by the offices. We therefore increased the floor area of the apartments and expressed this in the façade. We put the apartments above the offices so that they might have better access to the sky, the cleaner air and in particular the splendid view. Putting the offices below was a logical consequence.

Remarks on the the design of the Torre Velasca, Milan (1959), cited from *CIAM '59 in Otterlo*, ed. Oscar Newman. Stuttgart: Karl Krämer Verlag, 1961, pp. 92, 93, 96, 97.

In describing this building, I am mixing the rational and the expressionistic, because they must really be mentioned together. There were people who criticized this building, saying that it was an imitation of the towers of the Middle Ages. I don't mind if it is, but I must say, it is only a casual coincidence resulting from needs which are, for different reasons, similar to those of the Middle Ages.

During the Middle Ages it became necessary to conquer the sky because the space within the fortified walls of the city was limited; of consequence, any new expansion, once all ground was accounted for, had to be upwards. With the increasing population the medieval city found it necessary to widen its streets. In order to maintain suitable large living area, the upper floors of dwellings were cantilevered over the streets below. It can be seen then, that it is only by coincidence that our building is similar to a medieval tower; a similarity which arose from the same needs, but for different things.

[...]

In conclusion I would like to say that when I speak about the past and tradition, and when I speak about the building's life being connected with the past, it is not intended that this be an imitation of the forms of the past. If this building by chance of circumstances has taken the shape that reminds you of the past, that is not the main point of the problem, and I do not care about the form it has taken. Our main purpose was to give this building the intimate value of our culture – the essence of history, we were never given to imitating the shapes and forms of the past, only understanding what has happened before us. This building is a sky-scraper in the very centre of Milan, five hundred metres from the Cathedral. It is at Milan's very historical centre and we found it necessary that our building breathe the atmosphere of the place and even intensify it.

The attitude of the fathers of modern architecture was anti-historical. But this was an attitude which was born of a great revolution and it was necessary that the first premise of our culture be a new attitude to history. But this is now no longer necessary.

[...]

P. Smithson:

Now I would say that we are also concerned with this question of models, but that the model we are after is a model of method. Now for me this building doesn't demonstrate a method of arriving at a building but actually represents a formal plastic vocabulary. This formal plastic vocabulary is so shot through with overtones of a former plastic vocabulary, that it does not represent a model of a moral sort but of an immoral sort.

Now let me try to explain this in simple terms. Your building is significant in three ways. Firstly, its outline, particularly in silhouette, has strong connections with the medieval fortress architecture of Northern Italy, connections which are so explicit that they cannot be fortuitous. Secondly, the means of distinguishing between the dwellings and the offices are expressionistic, and are not functional: that is to say, that the system of stanchions, struts and ties indicates that there are two parts to the building, but does not communicate in any way that the use of the spaces is different; and, thirdly, that the general and highly consistent system of profiling and facetting the structure and wall surfaces does no more than contribute to the visual effect of the building as a whole, seen against the sky. It is, in fact, no more than decoration. In short, it seems that the programme led to the definition of the basic parts of the building, and from then on, the tower was designed within a self-contained formal system.

Any doubts, uncertainties, or inaccuracies in the functional programme were quickly ironed out by the plastic system, and nothing was left open to change. The building has no implications beyond itself, if as an ultimate statement, a solution offered in a closed aesthetic.

In opposition to this closed aesthetic, there is the open aesthetic in which architecture is considered as a strict reciprocation of a situation as it reveals itself, with all its certainties and its doubts. This architecture has no consonants of its own, its links with the past are as casual as are those of the people who will use its buildings, and it has to be used because only then in movement and change can its sequences of form, its implications beyond its physical limits, become apparent. For example, within this open aesthetic, it would not be possible for an architect to make a structural system, such as that used in the Torre Velasca: to represent the fact that there is a difference between offices and city apartment living.

One senses that this "Open Aesthetic" is the living extension of Functionalism whilst, in a closed aesthetic, function is no more than the handmaid of form. In an open aesthetic, one senses that an architect is involved in a changing situation. In a closed aesthetic, an architect provides the solution to a problem which has been arbitrarily limited just for the sake of reaching a formal definition.

Now there is something about the particular use of these forms that reminds one of a closed society. One cannot help associating this particular form of a closed building with the society of 1910. It is from that society which we are now in the most active evolution. I feel that the only model one can accept as being moral is one in which the possibility of a liberation towards an open society finds its expression.

[. . .]

Bakema:

[. . .]

I think that the identity, the form of a building, is a kind of communication about things which are happening in life. Thus when, at the present time, I see a building, I not only see a form, but this form tells me about the life of the time. And when I see a medieval village, it tells me that the people had to defend themselves against an enemy which was outside its walls. When Smithson spoke about an open and a closed society, he was not talking only about an open house or a closed house but about the relationship between man and the totality of which he is a part. Thus the significant thing in the form of the medieval tower is that it was disciplined by a small community which had to defend itself against the attacks of another community. The form of that tower transmits to us an event of a past life. I hope only that we, as architects, working in the present, are able to make building forms and towns which will communicate to the people of some future time what was happening now – in this moment – and that our forms are life-forms.

Now, in your building I do not see where, for example, is the entrance for the cars. Then, too, you said you made a hat for the building and put all the mechanical stuff into it. Well, it may not be necessary to see the machine that reconditions the air or the cars which are going in and out, but I think that you must feel that these things are in it: are going on. No one who looks at your building can say in all sincerity that he feels these things, or the life going on in the building. We have reduced the question to a simple element of life. Let me conclude in this way: I think that form is a communication about life, and I don't recognize in this building a communication about life in our time. You are resisting contemporary life.

194 TEAM 10
"The Aim of Team 10" (1962)

I n 1962 Team 10 produced the first publication of their architectural beliefs in the Team 10 Primer. The founding members of the group were Jacob Bakema, Aldo van Eyck, H. P. Daniel van Ginkel, Hans Hovens-Greve, Rolf Gutman, Georges Candilis, Shadrach Woods, William and Gillian Howell, and Alison and Peter Smithson. The text, while acknowledging the "inadequacies of the processes of architectural thought which they had inherited from the modern movement as a whole," is nevertheless vague or surprisingly generalized, perhaps because of divisions already evident within the small group. Team 10, with a few additions and subtractions, would continue to be active throughout the 1960s, but no longer with the radical sense of confidence of the previous decade.

The Aim of Team 10

Aim of Team 10 has been described as follows:

Team 10 is a group of architects who have sought each other out because each has found the help of the others necessary to the development and understanding of their own individual work. But it is more than that.

They came together in the first place, certainly because of mutual realization of the inadequacies of the processes of architectural thought which they had inherited from the modern movement as a whole, but more important, each sensed that the other had already found some way towards a new beginning.

This new beginning, and the long build-up that followed, has been concerned with inducing, as it were, into the bloodstream of the architect an understanding and feeling for the patterns, the aspirations, the artefacts, the tools, the modes of transportation and communications of present-day society, so that he can as a natural thing build towards that society's realization-of-itself.

In this sense Team 10 is Utopian, but Utopian about the present. Thus their aim is not to theorize but to build, for only through construction can a Utopia of the present be realized.

For them 'to build' has a special meaning in that the architect's responsibility towards the individual or groups he builds for, and towards the cohesion and convenience of the collective structure to which they belong, is taken as being an absolute responsibility. No abstract Master Plan stands between him and what he has to do, only the 'human facts' and the logistics of the situation.

To accept such responsibility where none is trying to direct others to perform acts which his control techniques cannot encompass, requires the invention of a working-together-technique where each pays attention to the other and to the whole insofar as he is able.

"The Aim of Team 10" (1962), cited from *Team 10 Primer*, ed. Alison Smithson. Cambridge, MA: MIT Press, 1968, p. 3.

Team 10 is of the opinion that only in such a way may meaningful groupings of buildings come into being, where each building is a live thing and a natural extension of the others. Together they will make places where a man can realize what he wishes to be.

Team 10 would like to develop their thought processes and language of building to a point where a collective demonstration (perhaps a little self-conscious) could be made at a scale which would be really effective in terms of the modes of life and the structure of a community.

It must be said that this point is still some way off.

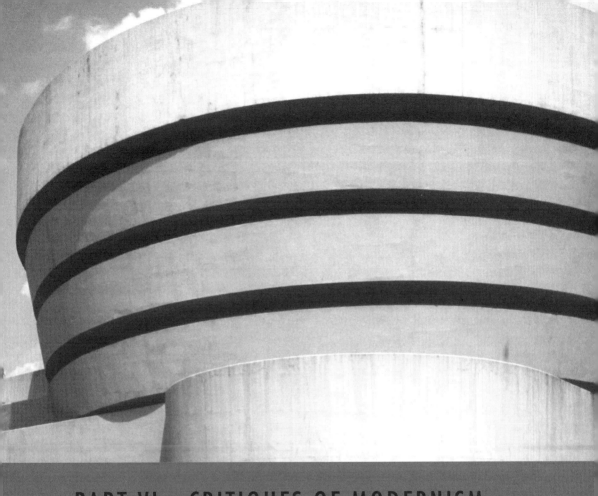

PART VI   CRITIQUES OF MODERNISM: 1959–69

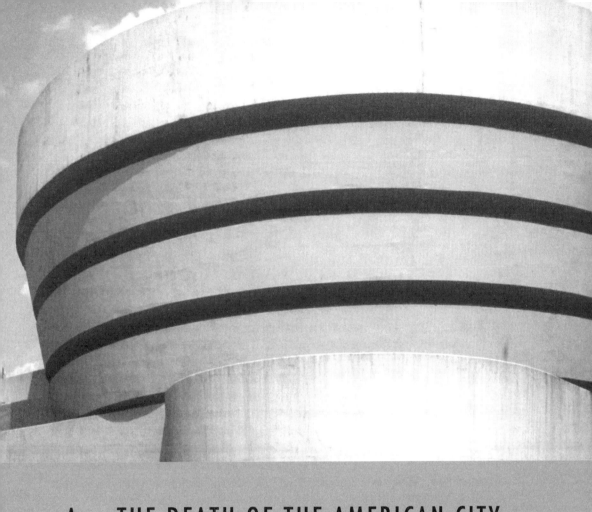

A.   THE DEATH OF THE AMERICAN CITY

Introduction

Whereas the Modern movement in Europe in the late 1950s and 1960s seemingly disassembles from dissenting voices from within, American architecture during this same period finds itself confronted by a series of external pressures, many of which had little to do with architecture. The guarded American optimism of the 1950s in fact stands in vivid contrast to the social anger, cynicism, and violence that simmers in the first half of the 1960s and then volcanically erupts in the middle years of the decade. The focus of this dismay — that is, until the Vietnam conflict trumped all issues — was the declining American city: the rush to the suburbs and the poverty and racial division that was left behind in urban centers. American urban planners, even within academe, had indeed had almost no discussion about urban theory prior to this time. Since the 1920s, Lewis Mumford had proffered his alternative vision to the sprawling metropolis, but he had found few comers to the debate. Specific American realities and values, such as the physical size of the United States, reliance on the automobile, and land statutes, precluded many of the approaches favored in European countries, and the heterogeneity of American society (with its various racial and economic divisions) formed yet another serious barrier. Thus when political power-brokers, with little or no architectural input, proposed massive redevelopment schemes in the 1950s and 1960s, they were for the most part drawn to what seemed modern – that is, the Corbusian solution of multiple high-rise towers removed from the streets. It was a recipe that would soon prove disastrous. If the failed schemes that followed had the saving grace of prompting a serious debate, the debate came much too late to alter many of the social and urban premises built into Lyndon Johnson's "War on Poverty" and "Great Society" agenda of the 1960s. The "solutions" to the urban problem would thus haunt American cities for many decades to come.

195   LEWIS MUMFORD
from ''Prefabricated Blight'' (1948)

With the absence of any significant planning discussion taking place among designers, many of the decisions for urban redevelopment schemes in the 1950s and 1960s passed to politicians and political bureaucrats. And perhaps the most powerful of these individuals was Robert Moses, the long-standing commissioner of parks and coordinator of the Office of City Construction for New York City. Between 1945 and 1958 Moses planned dozens of large-scale housing projects for the city (most put together from federal and private development funds), housing more than half a million people. First and foremost of these was Stuyvesant Town. It was scarcely a town, but – inspired by Le Corbusier's Radiant City – a leveling of sixty-one acres on the West side of Manhattan, and the building of dozens of high-rise housing blocks around a modest green space. Little commercial space was incorporated into these dreary brick blocks, and none of the essential services of schools, libraries, and entertainment. Moses's nemesis from the beginning was Lewis Mumford, who used his regular column in *The New Yorker* to criticize the schemes of Moses. His was one of the few dissenting voices of the time.

There is now, within New York's city limits, a good handful of housing projects in various stages of completion. Since the housing shortage is what it is, any truly critical appraisal of these undertakings will have to come, I am afraid, from a nontenant. Those who are lucky enough to be accepted by the landlords will probably view their new homes through a rosy haze, as a Displaced Person might view Ellis Island. Yet almost all these projects are solemn reminders of how different the postwar world is from what most people hoped it would be.

Perhaps the greatest and grimmest of these housing developments is Stuyvesant Town, the massive palisade of apartments being erected by the Metropolitan Life Insurance Company between Fourteenth and Twentieth Streets, in the area bounded on the east by Avenue C and a small stretch of the Franklin D. Roosevelt Drive, and on the west by First Avenue. By the time this group of buildings is finished, twenty-four thousand people will be living on its sixty-one acres. (The original street and block pattern of New York was planned for a density of from seventy to ninety people an acre; this new development will

Lewis Mumford, from "Prefabricated Blight" (1948), reprinted in *From the Group Up: Observations on Contemporary Architecture, Housing, Highway Building, and Civic Design*. New York: Harcourt Brace Jovanovich, 1956, pp. 108–9.

have a density of three hundred and ninety-three.) That makes this community larger than sixteen thousand other towns in the United States and smaller than only four hundred. Instead of lowering the density in the area, the proprietors of Stuyvesant Town, abetted by the City of New York, have established a pattern of greater congestion. If New York were completely rebuilt in this fashion, even Mr. Robert Moses, who has had a lot to do with setting this pattern in housing, would perhaps cry "Uncle!"

When I first inspected Stuyvesant Town, a year ago, the development seemed to me an unrelieved nightmare. Though the buildings are not a continuous unit, they present to the beholder an unbroken façade of brick, thirteen stories high, absolutely uniform in every detail, mechanically conceived and mechanically executed, with the word "control" implicit in every aspect of the design. This, I said to myself, is the architecture of the Police State, embodying all the vices of regimentation one associates with state control at its unimaginative worst.

196   KEVIN LYNCH
from *The Image of the City* (1960)

O ne of the breakthrough studies of the early 1960s in terms of providing a new direction for urban thinking was *The Image of the City* by Kevin Lynch. The author had been trained at Massachusetts Institute of Technology, and in his earlier urban studies he had followed more traditional approaches to city planning that dealt with such matters as density, zoning, and circulation. In this book, however, he broke fresh ground by going out into the street and interviewing residents of Boston, Jersey City, and Los Angeles. The result of his study was the issue of "imageability," that is, the image or non-image that a resident composes of his everyday urban environment. Lynch argues that the most successful cities are those with a high degree of legibility (memory), which he analyzes through the experiential parameters of paths, edges, districts, nodes, and landmarks.

The contents of the city images so far studied, which are referable to physical forms, can conveniently be classified into five types of elements: paths, edges, districts, nodes, and landmarks. Indeed, these elements may be of more general application, since they seem to reappear in many types of environmental images... These elements may be defined as follows:

1. *Paths*.   Paths are the channels along which the observer customarily, occasionally, or potentially moves. They may be streets, walkways, transit lines, canals, railroads. For many people, these are the predominant elements in their image. People observe the city while moving through it, and along these paths the other environmental elements are arranged and related.

2. *Edges*.   Edges are the linear elements not used or considered as paths by the observer. They are the boundaries between two phases, linear breaks in continuity: shores, railroad cuts, edges of development, walls. They are lateral references rather than coordinate axes.

Kevin Lynch, from *The Image of the City* (1960), cited from the seventh printing. Cambridge, MA: MIT Press, 1971, pp. 46–8.

Such edges may be barriers, more or less penetrable, which close one region off from another; or they may be seams, lines along which two regions are related and joined together. These edge elements, although probably not as dominant as paths, are for many people important organizing features, particularly in the role of holding together generalized areas, as in the outline of a city by water or wall.

3. *Districts.* Districts are the medium-to-large sections of the city, conceived of as having two-dimensional extent, which the observer mentally enters "inside of," and which are recognizable as having some common, identifying character. Always identifiable from the inside, they are also used for exterior reference if visible from the outside. Most people structure their city to some extent in this way, with individual differences as to whether paths or districts are the dominant elements. It seems to depend not only upon the individual but also upon the given city.

4. *Nodes.* Nodes are points, the strategic spots in a city into which an observer can enter, and which are the intensive foci to and from which he is traveling. They may be primarily junctions, places of a break in transportation, a crossing or convergence of paths, moments of shift from one structure to another. Or the nodes may be simply concentrations, which gain their importance from being the condensation of some use or physical character, as a street-corner hangout or an enclosed square. Some of these concentration nodes are the focus and epitome of a district, over which their influence radiates and of which they stand as a symbol. They may be called cores. Many nodes, of course, partake of the nature of both junctions and concentrations. The concept of node is related to the concept of path, since junctions are typically the convergence of paths, events on the journey. It is similarly related to the concept of district, since cores are typically the intensive foci of districts, their polarizing center. In any event, some nodal points are to be found in almost every image, and in certain cases they may be the dominant feature.

5. *Landmarks.* Landmarks are another type of point-reference, but in this case the observer does not enter within them, they are external. They are usually a rather simply defined physical object: building, sign, store, or mountain. Their use involves the singling out of one element from a host of possibilities. Some landmarks are distant ones, typically seen from many angles and distances, over the tops of smaller elements, and used as radial references. They may be within the city or at such a distance that for all practical purposes they symbolize a constant direction. Such are isolated towers, golden domes, great hills. Even a mobile point, like the sun, whose motion is sufficiently slow and regular, may be employed. Other landmarks are primarily local, being visible only in restricted localities and from certain approaches. These are the innumerable signs, store fronts, trees, doorknobs, and other urban detail, which fill in the image of most observers. They are frequently used clues of identity and even of structure, and seem to be increasingly relied upon as a journey becomes more and more familiar.

197   JANE JACOBS
from *The Life and Death of the American City* (1961)

T he first major challenge to Mumford's plea for decentralization came not from an architect or planner, but from an urban sociologist, and with it we have the start of the first American debate regarding the city. Jane Jacobs opens *The Life and Death of the American City* by attacking the three urban conceptions that she feels have dominated much of twentieth-century discussions: the Garden-City idea that had been recently put forward by Mumford, Clarence Stein, and Catherine Bauer (originally by Ebenezer Howard); the Radiant City of Le Corbusier, which also had a large following among American urbanists; and the notion of the City Beautiful, which had become a recognizable movement at the start of the century under the persuasion of Daniel Burnham. She argues that these three trends within the twentieth century have conspired to destroy the livable city and its underlying social fabric. She then counters with a strong defense of traditional, high-density cities with mixed zoning and commensurate rich street life — modeled on her much beloved Greenwich Village. Her efforts opened up entirely new areas for sociological investigation.

To reinforce and dramatize the necessity for the new order of things, the Decentrists hammered away at the bad old city. They were incurious about successes in great cities. They were interested only in failures. All was failure. A book like Mumford's *The Culture of Cities* was largely a morbid and biased catalog of ills. The great city was Megalopolis, Tyrannopolis, Nekropolis, a monstrosity, a tyranny, a living death. It must go. New York's midtown was "solidified chaos" (Mumford). The shape and appearance of cities was nothing but "a chaotic accident . . . the summation of the haphazard, antagonistic whims of many self-centered, ill-advised individuals" (Stein). The centers of cities amounted to "a foreground of noise, dirt, beggars, souvenirs and shrill competitive advertising" (Bauer).

How could anything so bad be worth the attempt to understand it? The Decentrists' analyses, the architectural and housing designs which were companions and offshoots of these analyses, the national housing and home financing legislation so directly influenced by the new vision – none of these had anything to do with understanding cities, or fostering successful large cities, nor were they intended to. They were reasons and means for jettisoning cities, and the Decentrists were frank about this.

But in the schools of planning and architecture, and in Congress, state legislatures and city halls too, the Decentrists' ideas were gradually accepted as basic guides for dealing constructively with big cities themselves. This is the most amazing event in the whole sorry tale: that finally people who sincerely wanted to strengthen great cities should adopt recipes frankly devised for undermining their economies and killing them.

The man with the most dramatic idea of how to get all this anti-city planning right into the citadels of iniquity themselves was the European architect Le Corbusier. He devised in the 1920's a dream city which he called the Radiant City, composed not of the low buildings

Jane Jacobs, from *The Life and Death of the American City*. New York: Random House, 1961, pp. 20–2, 202–3.

beloved of the Decentrists, but instead mainly of skyscrapers within a park. "Suppose we are entering the city by way of the Great Park," Le Corbusier wrote. "Our fast car takes the special elevated motor track between the majestic skyscrapers: as we approach nearer, there is seen the repetition against the sky of the twenty-four skyscrapers; to our left and right on the outskirts of each particular area are the municipal and administrative buildings; and enclosing the space are the museums and university buildings. The whole city is a Park." In Le Corbusier's vertical city the common run of mankind was to be housed at 1,200 inhabitants to the acre, a fantastically high city density indeed, but because of building up so high, 95 percent of the ground could remain open. The skyscrapers would occupy only 5 percent of the ground. The high-income people would be in lower, luxury housing around courts, with 85 percent of their ground left open. Here and there would be restaurants and theaters.

Le Corbusier was planning not only a physical environment. He was planning for a social Utopia too. Le Corbusier's Utopia was a condition of what he called maximum individual liberty, by which he seems to have meant not liberty to do anything much, but liberty from ordinary responsibility. In his Radiant City nobody, presumably, was going to have to be his brother's keeper any more. Nobody was going to have to struggle with plans of his own. Nobody was going to be tied down.

The Decentrists and other loyal advocates of the Garden City were aghast at Le Corbusier's city of towers in the park, and still are. Their reaction to it was, and remains, much like that of progressive nursery school teachers confronting an utterly institutional orphanage. And yet, ironically, the Radiant City comes directly out of the Garden City. Le Corbusier accepted the Garden City's fundamental image, superficially at least, and worked to make it practical for high densities. He described his creation as the Garden City made attainable. "The garden city is a will-o'-the-wisp," he wrote. "Nature melts under the invasion of roads and houses and the promised seclusion becomes a crowded settlement . . . The solution will be found in the 'vertical garden city.' "

[. . .]

Dwelling densities are so important for most city districts, and for their future develop-ment, and are so little considered as factors in vitality, that I shall devote this chapter to that aspect of city concentration.

High dwelling densities have a bad name in orthodox planning and housing theory. They are supposed to lead to every kind of difficulty and failure.

But in our cities, at least, this supposed correlation between high densities and trouble, or high densities and slums, is simply incorrect, as anyone who troubles to look at real cities can see. Here are a few illustrations:

In San Francisco, the district of highest dwelling densities – and highest coverage of residential land with buildings too – is North Beach-Telegraph Hill. This is a popular district that has spontaneously and steadily unslummed itself in the years following the Depression and the Second World War. San Francisco's chief slum problem, on the other hand, is a district called the Western Addition, a place that has steadily declined and is now being extensively cleared. The Western Addition (which at one time, when it was new, was a good address) has a dwelling-unit density considerably lower than North Beach-Telegraph Hill's, and, for that matter, lower than the still fashionable Russian Hill's and Nob Hill's.

In Philadelphia, Rittenhouse Square is the only district that has been spontaneously upgrading and extending its edges, and is the only inner city area that has not been designated for either renewal or clearance. It has the highest dwelling density in Philadelphia. The North Philadelphia slums currently display some of the city's most severe social problems. They have dwelling densities averaging at most half those of Rittenhouse Square. Vast territories of additional decay and social disorder in Philadelphia have dwelling densities less than half those of Rittenhouse Square.

In Brooklyn, New York, the most generally admired, popular and upgrading neighborhood is Brooklyn Heights; it has much the highest density of dwellings in Brooklyn. Tremendous expanses of failed or decaying Brooklyn gray area have densities half those of Brooklyn Heights or less.

In Manhattan, the most fashionable pocket of the midtown East Side, and the most fashionable pocket of Greenwich Village have dwelling densities in the same high range as the heart of Brooklyn Heights. But an interesting difference can be observed. In Manhattan, very popular areas, characterized by high degrees of vitality and diversity, surround these most fashionable pockets. In these surrounding popular areas, dwelling densities go still higher. In Brooklyn Heights, on the other hand, the fashionable pocket is surrounded by neighborhoods where dwelling unit densities drop off; vitality and popularity drop off too.

In Boston, as already mentioned in the introduction to this book, the North End has unslummed itself and is one of the city's healthiest areas. It has much the highest dwelling densities in Boston.

198 LEWIS MUMFORD
from ''Mother Jacobs' Home Remedies'' (1962)

Mumford wasted little time in responding to the attack on his theories, which he addressed in his *New Yorker* column under the sarcastic title of ''Mother Jacobs' Home Remedies.'' He fully agreed with Jacobs's criticism of the high-rise as a solution for regenerating a city, but he forcefully opposed her argument for high densities, pointing out the problems of Brooklyn, Queens, and Harlem – all of which have similarly high densities to Greenwich Village. In the end, however, the problem was really one of aesthetics. Mumford was an urban theorist with little appreciation for the bigness of metropolitan life; finally, as this passage shows, he was much too pessimistic about the American city to expect any kind of a solution to a problem without a major replanning (and rebuilding) of the entire urban infrastructure in the Northeast.

As one who has spent more than fifty years in New York, speaking to a native of Scranton who has not, I must remind Mrs. Jacobs that many parts of the city she denounces because they do not conform to her peculiar standards – and therefore, she reasons, are a prey to violence – were for over the better part of a century both economically quite sound and humanly secure. In the urban range of my boyhood, there were occasional rowdy gangs

Lewis Mumford, from ''Mother Jacobs' Home Remedies'' (1962), cited from *The Urban Prospect*. New York: Harcourt, Brace & World, 1968, pp. 194–5.

even half a century ago – we always ran for cover when the West Ninety-eighth Street gang invaded our street – but their more lethal activities were confined largely to their own little ghettos and nearby territory, like Hell's Kitchen or the Gas House District. With the policeman on his beat, a woman could go home alone at any hour of the night on a purely residential street without apprehension. (She could even, astonishingly, trust the policeman.) As for the great parks that Mrs. Jacobs fears as an invitation to crime, and disparages as a recreation space on the strange ground that no one any longer can safely use them, she treats as a chronic ailment a state that would have seemed incredible as late as 1935. Until the Age of Extermination widened the area of violence, one could walk the eight hundred acres of Central Park at any time of the day without fear of molestation.

Certainly it was not any mistake of Frederick Law Olmsted's in laying out Riverside Drive, Morningside Park, and St. Nicholas Park that has made these large parks unusable shambles today. What is responsible for their present emptiness is something Mrs. Jacobs disregards – the increasing pathology of the whole mode of life in the great metropolis, a pathology that is directly proportionate to its overgrowth, its purposeless materialism, its congestion, and its insensate disorder – the very conditions she vehemently upholds as marks of urban vitality. That sinister state manifests itself not merely in the statistics of crime and mental disorder but in the enormous sums spent on narcotics, sedatives, stimulants, hypnotics, and tranquillizers to keep the population of our "great" cities from coming to terms with the vacuous desperation of their daily lives and with the even more vacuous horrors that their more lunatic rulers and scientific advisers seem to regard as a reasonable terminus for the human race. Lacking any sense of an intelligible purpose or a desirable goal, the inhabitants of our "great American cities" are simply 'Waiting for Godot.'

199   HERBERT J. GANS
from *The Urban Villagers* (1962)

Despite Mumford's protestations, the theories of Jacobs would soon find support in a burgeoning interest in urban sociology within academe. The sociologist Herbert J. Gans, who came out of the University of Chicago, began his career with a well-known study of the suburb of Levittown, New Jersey, in the late 1950s, but for his book *The Urban Villagers* he turned his attention to Boston's West End, a largely Italian immigrant community that between 1958 and 1960 fell victim to the bulldozers of "urban renewal." Gans was fascinated in particular with the internal dynamics of this semi-closed cultural community, whose internal neighborhood dynamics functioned with few problems despite a physical appearance that many outsiders regarded as a ghetto. The book is another landmark in that it underscores the social complexity of a workable community, one that many local and federal policy-makers had scarcely yet to imagine at this date.

Herbert J. Gans, from *The Urban Villagers: Group and Class in the Life of Italian-Americans*. New York: The Free Press, 1962, pp. ix–x.

This book is a report of a participant-observation study of an inner city Boston neighborhood called the West End, and, in particular, of the native-born Americans of Italian parentage who lived there amidst other ethnic groups. The area I studied no longer exists. Declared a slum in 1953, it was torn down under the federal renewal program between 1958 and 1960, and its residents dispersed all over the metropolitan area. At this writing (January, 1962), the first residents of the new West End – a luxury apartment house complex – are just beginning to move in.

I lived in the West End from October, 1957, to May, 1958, just before the onset of redevelopment. My main research interests were two: to study a slum and to study the way of life of a low-income population. Contemporary city planning and professions such as education, social work, public recreation, public health, medicine, and psychiatry, which Erich Lindemann has aptly described as caretakers, use middle-class values to help low-income populations solve their problems and improve their living conditions. As a sociologist and city planner, I wanted to test the validity of this approach. I wanted to know what a slum was like, and how it felt to live in one, because many planners and caretakers believe that it is the source of much of the low-income population's problem. I wanted to study the way of life of a low-income population because planners and caretakers act on the assumption that this way of life is simply a deviant form of the dominant American middle-class one, that it is born partly of deprivation and lack of access to the improved living conditions and other services provided by these professions.

Since I was also interested in other aspects of class and ethnic group behavior, my study developed into an extensive analysis of the Italian-American society and culture. At the end, I concluded that by and large, the planners and caretakers were wrong. The West End was not really a slum, and although many of its inhabitants did have problems, these did not stem from the neighborhood. More important, the West Enders were not frustrated seekers of middle-class values. Their way of life constituted a distinct and independent working-class subculture that bore little resemblance to the middle-class. Consequently, I concluded that the behavior patterns and values of working-class subculture ought to be understood and taken into account by planners and caretakers.

200 PETER BLAKE
from *God's Own Junkyard* (1964)

A more conventional architectural approach to the increasingly discussed problem was given by Peter Blake, the long-time editor of *Architectural Forum*. Blake had connections with the Museum of Modern Art and his earlier book, *The Master Builders: Le Corbusier, Mies van der Rohe, Frank Lloyd Wright* (1960), anointed these three architects as the giants of the twentieth century. On urban issues Blake was a self-styled Jeffersonian, appalled at the increasing squalor of the landscape and townscape. Thus he wrote his book not in anger but in a "fury." The images are what makes Blake's book a polemical masterpiece, as he plays off such idyllic scenes as the

Peter Blake, from *God's Own Junkyard*. New York: Rinehart & Winston, 1964, p. 33.

autumnal lawn of Jefferson's University of Virginia with a busy urban street visually suffocating with automobiles, signs, and overhead wires for streetcars. Blake condemns these chaotic images as byproducts of American commercialism and greed, but Robert Venturi, two years later, would embrace the same images as examples of a Main Street that is "almost all right."

Two American scenes . . . document the decline, fall, and subsequent disintegration of urban civilization in the United States. The two examples are separated by a mere 140 years in time, and by only a few hundred miles in space: Thomas Jefferson's campus for the University of Virginia, in Charlottesville, started in the 1820's [and] Canal Street, the busiest business street in New Orleans, as it appears in the 1960's.

Jefferson's serene, urban space has been called "almost an ideal city – unique in America, if not in the world." Canal Street, one fervently hopes, has not been called anything in particular in recent times. It is difficult to believe that these two examples of what a city might be were suggested by the same species of mammal, let alone by the same nation. Jefferson called his campus "an expression of the American mind"; New Orleans' Canal Street, and all the other dreary Canal Streets that defile America today, have not been called "expressions of the American mind" by any but this nation's mortal enemies.

On the next several pages are further portraits of the American city today – portraits, not caricatures. They need no identification; for these are the places two-thirds of us call "home." We walk or drive through them each day; this is where we work, shop, and are also born, exist, and die. What manner of people is being reared in these infernal wastelands?

One answer is: people who no longer see. Recently, the Honorable Mario Cariello, President of the Borough of Queens, one of the five boroughs of New York City, delivered himself of the considered opinion that his Borough "truly represents the full flowering of advanced, urban living." Oh Mario, son of Rome – and of Florence, Siena, Venice, Pisa, possibly even Orvieto – there was once another son of Italy, a man called Leon Battista Alberti, who asked, "How are we moved by a huge, shapeless, ill-contrived pile of stones?" Alas, he lived and died before there was a fully flowering Borough of Queens; and so you may never know his answer.

201   MARTIN ANDERSON
from *The Federal Bulldozer* (1964)

By the mid-1960s various events were coming together to produce a genuine national crisis. Lyndon Johnson, who assumed office with the assassination of John F. Kennedy in 1963, was steadily escalating the Vietnam conflict into a major war. The landmark Civil Rights legislation of 1964, issued in part to Martin Luther King's nonviolent marches in the South, brought into sharp focus the long-standing racial divide, which would soon spawn a more violent Black Power movement. And the major American urban centers in themselves were collapsing

Martin Anderson, from *The Federal Bulldozer: A Critical Analysis of Urban Renewal, 1949–1962*. Cambridge, MA: MIT Press, 1964, pp. 6–8.

economically owing to "white flight," poverty, crime, drugs, and (soon) urban rioting. In response, Johnson put together a series of programs under the label of "War on Poverty," which included, among other things, major funding increases for urban housing, mass transportation, and the creation of a Department of Housing and Urban Development (HUD). What is clear in retrospect is that while this federal commitment to end poverty may have been well intentioned, the strategy to be employed – the large-scale removal of slum areas and often their replacement with high-rise towers – was ill-conceived from the beginning. At least this was the view of Martin Anderson, a young professor at Columbia University and, from 1961–2, a Research Fellow at the Joint Center for Urban Studies at Massachusetts Institute of Technology.

Perhaps the most widespread belief about the federal urban renewal program is that it has made and is making a significant contribution toward solving the housing problems of low-income and middle-income groups. This belief is false; accepting it gives the program a false rationale for continuing and expanding. In fact, the federal urban renewal program has actually made it *more* difficult for low-income and middle-income groups to obtain housing. It has done this by destroying much more of this kind of housing than it has created. Its net result has been to aggravate the housing shortage for those who have the most trouble finding suitable accommodations.

In line with the belief that urban renewal has alleviated the housing problem is the belief that the federal urban renewal program is essentially another kind of public housing for low-income families. This is not true; only a very small fraction of the total construction in urban renewal areas is devoted to public housing. Most of the new buildings constructed in urban renewal areas are high-rise apartment buildings for high-income families. The public housing program is separate from the urban renewal program, and, if we were to compare these two federal programs, we would see that they have different goals, they have different degrees of power, and they are run by two completely separate government agencies. We shall be concerned primarily with the operations of the federal urban renewal program, and only incidentally with the way in which public housing fits into this program.

The public often takes it for granted that the people who are forced to move from their homes are well taken care of by the government authorities. It is commonly believed that these people move into better housing in better neighborhoods, and, by implication, are glad that they were forced to "better" themselves. On the contrary, a few private authorities have seriously questioned these conclusions, and they suggest that many of the families forcibly evicted drift into housing as bad as or worse than their original homes in neighborhoods that are also as bad as or worse than their original neighborhoods. In addition they often have to pay higher rents. The factual evidence that would answer this question clearly is inconclusive at this time. Government statistics show a more optimistic picture than do private studies. But, although the question cannot be answered definitely, we shall see that there are certain indications which tend to support the gloomier view.

The federal urban renewal program also has some strong racial overtones. Approximately two thirds of the people who are forced out of their homes are Negroes, Puerto Ricans, or members of some other minority group. The problem of finding new homes is complicated for these people because of racial discrimination. The federal urban renewal program is sometimes privately referred to as the "Negro removal" program. The problems of finding new places to live are further complicated by the fact that most of the people who are forced to move have relatively low incomes, which limit them to a small number of homes and apartments in low-rent areas. Most of the people who are seriously affected by the program come from low-income, minority groups that, for various reasons, do not or cannot attempt to correct the injustices to which they are subjected.

By March of 1963 over 609,000 people had been forced to pack their belongings and leave their homes. There were some cases of intensive resistance, which often stopped the urban renewal program in a particular area, but many people appear to have reacted to their eviction notices without much outward indication of their indignation; in fact, many of them have appeared to welcome the program enthusiastically. It is doubtful that this combination of apathy and enthusiasm will long continue in the future. The amount of active resistance seems to be related to the level of ability, education, and income of the people who have to move. People with the knowledge to comprehend the full implications of what is happening and the ability and money to fight it, often resist bitterly.

202   MELVIN M. WEBBER
from "The Urban Place and the Nonplace Urban Realm" (1964)

The commonplace sociological assumption regarding the city in both the United States and Europe in the 1960s was that each city possessed a historic central hub – a downtown – from which all commercial and cultural activities dissipated outward. Yet many American cities over the course of the twentieth century had lost the viability of their downtown areas, and the development of the suburbs did not always follow the model of population dissipation. Planners generally sought to "correct" this problem with lavish plans for "revitalizing" downtown areas and returning the city to its conventional form. One of the first sociologists to challenge this premise was Mel Webber, a professor at the University of California at Berkeley. Webber argued that communication and transportation, not spatial parameters, were the keys to understanding the modern city, and that the traditional model was archaic. In effect, the city was becoming global in its commercial and cultural reaches, and this tendency could not be halted or constrained by traditional assumptions. This model therefore challenged conventional urban-renewal programs in a subtle but profound way.

With quite inadequate data, to be sure, my colleagues and I thus classified the existing centers in the San Francisco Bay Area at the time the Bay Area Regional Plan was being prepared for the 1955 Transit Study. We subsequently prepared a plan proposing an expanded hierarchy of such center places. It was relatively easy to classify the central district of San Francisco as the "regional center," to classify central Oakland as a "subregional center," and in turn to classify a large number of other central districts at a third-order level; we called them "district centers." But it was difficult to understand what this catalogue of centers really meant. We knew full well that not all the people who interact with others

Melvin M. Webber, from "The Urban Place and the Nonplace Urban Realm" (1964), cited from Melvin M. Webber et al., *Explorations into Urban Structure*. Philadelphia: University of Pennsylvania Press, 1965, pp. 139–40, 146–7.

throughout the region are located at San Francisco and that not all activities located there are region serving, but we did not know then how to get around the ambiguity that the title "regional center" carried. It is quite true that a great many of the highly specialized establishments are indeed located at San Francisco, but a very great many that are even more specialized are located in many other places throughout the region: in Berkeley, on the Peninsula, in San Jose, even in Milpitas.

Many of the specialists located in the Bay Area do not participate in the metropolitan realm at all, their linkages being primarily with Washington or New York or Hong Kong or with their local-residence realms. Some of these specialists are located in the Bay Area because of the amenities that the place affords and because they rely upon submetropolitan realms for a complex assortment of services that are available there. These participants in the world realm and the nation realm happen to be placed within the Bay Area, but their primary community is outside. In this sense, to the degree that they function as participants in these highly rarefied realms and interact with others who are spatially removed from their activity places, they are not at all a part of the Bay Area place-community, or even of the so-called Bay Area hinterland – contrary to the Christaller and McKenzie conceptions.
[. . .]

The enlarged freedom to communicate outside one's place-community that the emerging technological and institutional changes promise, coupled with an ever-increasing mobility and ever-greater degrees of specialization, will certainly mean that urbanites will deal with each other over greater and greater distances. The spatial patterns of their interactions with others will undoubtedly be increasingly disparate, less and less tied to the place in which they reside or work, less and less marked by the unifocal patterns that marked cities in an earlier day.

It thus appears to me that the behavioral models, that would explain individual's locational decisions, and the descriptive models, that would portray over-all spatial structures of settlements and regions, would both profit from an orientation to communication patterns. If the previously stated proposition is valid, and settlements exist primarily as a reflection of men's efforts to increase opportunities for interaction, it then follows that both individual locational behavior and over-all spatial structure are mirrors of communications. With the changing patterns of communications that are imminent, then, we can expect that individuals' locations and that over-all spatial structures will also change – possibly in very dramatic ways.

There are large, though latent, opportunities for imaginative metropolitan plans to accommodate to these changes and to foster ease of intercourse. But metropolitan planners are not likely to keep abreast of these changes unless they are able to free themselves from the obsession with placeness and unless they can come to view the urban communities as spatially extensive, processual systems in which urbanites interact with other urbanites wherever they may be. For it is interaction, not place, that is the essence of the city and of city life.

203 CHARLES ABRAMS
from "Housing in the Year 2000" (1967)

Opposing the main contentions of Martin Anderson was Charles Abrams, the chairman of the City Planning Department at Columbia University and one of the founders of the New York Housing Authority. Abrams was a highly influential voice among federal policy-makers and was a strong supporter of federal programs, many of which he helped to craft. In the mid-1960s he also drew sustenance from the fact that major architectural firms, such as I. M. Pei, Mies van der Rohe, and Minoru Yamasaki were now becoming involved with designing model-city projects. In 1967 the American Institute of Planners called a conference in Washington, DC to consider planning policies over the next fifty years. Abrams responded with this plea for the creation of a federal Urban Space Agency (URSA), akin to the space agency NASA, to tackle the problem of urban growth and land use. The plea recalls, in spirit, various proposals put forward by the Regional Planning Association of America in the 1920s and 1930s.

Assuming continuity of present trends, the United States will have some 350 million people a generation hence. To meet their needs, we shall have to build as many structures of all kinds as we have built since our earliest immigrants first moved from their hillside dug-outs. These structures will be consuming at least a million additional metropolitan acres each year and it is this land that must somehow be brought under constructive control if decent homes and environments are to be more than promises. The land to be converted to urban use accounts for only a small fraction of the total cost of the houses and public improvements that will be placed on it – 5 to 15 percent at most. The land currently in urban use represents only about 1 percent of the nation's total space and by the year 2000 should be no more than two or three times that. But how the land is deployed will influence the height, cost, and types of houses and shops; how and whether man will use his feet for negotiating distance; the length of his work journey; the expenditures for roads and throughways; the proximity to friends and recreation; the future appearance of our cities and how people will be functioning in them.

Land regulation with nothing more has proven of limited value. If we are really concerned about the future of the American environment, direct acquisition of the land needed for homes, factories, and services is an imperative. The land could then be planned, the schools, water, drainage, and open spaces provided, and the improved lots for private investment subject to suitable conditions governing its future development. This procedure would be no more than an extension of the urban renewal program to vacant land – it encompasses slum prevention instead of clearance. Unlike the current version of urban renewal, it enforces no mass displacements; it would entail no lesser role for the private builder than he has under existing land development operations; only the sequence of the public and private efforts are reversed. By making the improved land available for private home building, contiguous land

Charles Abrams, from "Housing in the Year 2000," in *The City is the Frontier* (1965), cited from *Environment and Policy: The Next Fifty Years,* ed. William R. Ewald, Jr. Bloomington: Indiana University Press, 1968, pp. 214–15.

would be assembled and planned, waste and shrapnel development avoided, more convenient journeys to work would be assured, and substantial economies in road building would be achieved. Local autonomy would be subordinated at first but be restored thereafter, since upon completion of each development, the public land would be turned over to the existing city or county, to a newly incorporated local government, or to a federally chartered regional agency. Land would be sold for the homes of the rich and the middle class while federal low-interest programs and family subsidies would provide for the lower-paid workers as well. Proper enforcement of the expanded federal nondiscrimination order would bar exclusion because of race or color. What would be built would fulfill the concept of a regional city – a place in which people of all walks of life could work and live with comfort and dignity.

To accomplish this objective, a federal Urban Space Agency (URSA) – comparable in organization to NASA – should be chartered by Congress and funded for the purpose. It would operate through the states where possible, but have superior jurisdiction where regions cross state lines. It would be empowered to buy land to round out the development of existing neighborhoods, to acquire and release land for new neighborhoods, to acquire or finance the acquisition of land in central cities for redevelopment and to facilitate the proper planning of land for housing, commerce, industry, and recreation. Its annual requirements would probably not be greater than its astronomical counterpart.

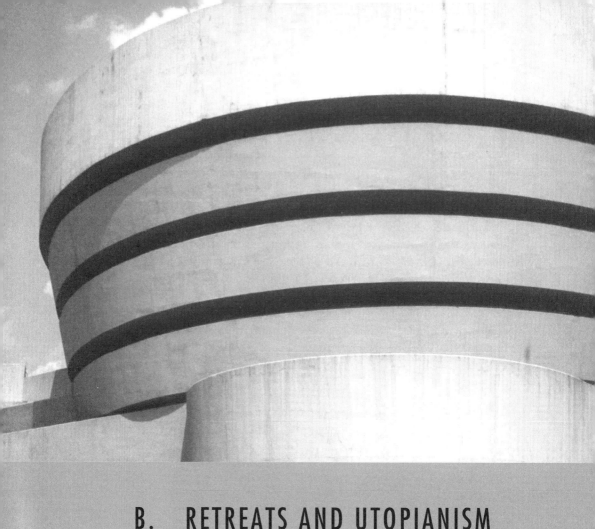

B.   RETREATS AND UTOPIANISM

Introduction

The collapse of CIAM in the late 1950s was but one indication of a more extensive fracturing of modern theory — divisions that would become irreparable over the next decade. Even the members of Team 10 did not hold together for very long, as the Dutch anthropological focus on the city, emanating from Aldo van Eyck and Jacob Bakema, soon clashed with the British interest in New Brutalism and technology. Behind the differences between these two groups, however, were significant social changes and expectations emanating up from below. By the middle of the 1960s a young "counter-culture" (the baby-boom generation) would emerge, a generation that would challenge the status quo in every way. By the end of the decade student unrest would escalate into a full-fledged cultural and political revolution.

From an architectural perspective, technology seems to have been the principal factor driving change throughout much of the decade. The utopian schemes of many young European and Japanese architects around the start of this period signal an early sensitivity toward the global population boom as well as the status quo of architectural production. Technology, led by its guru "Bucky" Fuller, was thus viewed as a saving grace. The creation of the American and Soviet space programs at the same time opened up a new technological frontier of exploration that carried with it a profound implication. Images of the earth from space allowed the human race to see the world not only as a small galactic phenomenon but also as a closed ecological system with fragile biological boundaries. Thus the "environment" was discovered in the 1960s as a significant design issue – a problem that was again brought home by the Israeli/Arab War of 1967, which would culminate in major changes in the world oil market. The contentious planet thus became transformed into "Spaceship Earth."

204   YONA FRIEDMAN
from *Mobile Architecture* (1959)

By the late 1950s the engineering, design, and ecological theories of such thinkers as R. Buckminster Fuller and Konrad Wachsmann were beginning to have a major impact on architectural thinking – just as the world was officially entering the "Space Age." All of these influences can be found in the proposals of Yona Friedman, a Hungarian-born, Israeli-trained architect and engineer who moved his base of operations to Paris in 1957. One year earlier he had formed GEAM (Groupe d'Études d'Architecture Mobile), a study group of engineers devoted to rethinking the entire notion of the fixed urban metropolis rooted to the ground. In his 1959 book Friedman countered with the idea of a "spatial city," a multistory space frame raised off the ground, into which all the components of the city could be plugged on various levels. This proposal was driven not only by environmental concerns but also by the fact that modern living moves increasingly toward the condition of perpetual transformation, requiring the city to respond more urgently to changing conditions. In this particular proposal the inhabitants themselves would have the freedom to locate their lightweight living cells wherever they wish within the spatial infrastructure.

The principle of the spatial city is a multiplication of the surface area of the city through the use of raised horizontal planes. What distinguishes this multiplication from the ordinary city is that instead of the surfaces multiplying only at points or in some isolated zones (as in Manhattan or the Radiant City), the entire urban area is covered with several levels. This *multiplication* of the surface permits city planners to differentiate zones in three dimensions: length, width, and height (for example, it is now possible to place a civic center above an industrial zone, etc.).

The most important application of the principle of the spatial city is that of urbanization by height. The upper levels are reserved for purely human or biological activities (housing, public life, entertainment, pedestrian circulation) and the lower levels for various services (mechanical, circulation, storage, production, air supply, and exhaust).

To visualize the organization of a spatial city, we might say that all services presently underground or peripheral are moved to ground level; by contrast, the greater part of the "real" inhabited city takes place within the layers of a three-dimensional construction raised on supports.

Yona Friedman, from *L'architecture mobile: vers une cité conçue par ses habitants*. Paris: Casterman, 1970, trans. Christina Contandriopoulos and Harry Francis Mallgrave.

Because of the homogeneity of the structure of the upper layers, this system naturally permits the use of any urban design for the inhabited parts of the city. For the same reason, the homogeneity of the ground surface (which remains entirely free) can accommodate any organization or routing of services (circulation, power, exhaust).

The same homogeneity of the two types of surfaces (the raised surfaces within the structure and the free surface of the ground), and their (functional) independence from one another, overcomes any difficult layout, even concentric development. If, for example, the inhabited and raised parts are of the radial/concentric type of plan, the lower parts that serve circulation and other services can be laid out completely differently.

This principle is similar to that of the "free plan" layout proposed by Le Corbusier forty years ago. The different levels of the city (housing, public life, circulation, technical services) remain independent from one another in their functioning and technology. The plan of each level can be organized differently.

Another intrinsic advantage to the spatial-city system is the great efficiency of land use. The utilized surface of the raised structure (at four stories) represents approximately 200–250% of the ground area, the lower structures could go as high as 40%. Adding to these numbers the remaining disposable surface of the ground would give a ratio of 400% of the total area of the city (this number is not less than that of Manhattan and much higher than Le Corbusier's Radiant City).

The spatial city is not an example of the collaboration between the engineer and the architect, but of the engineer and the city planner.

The spatial city is a result of urban indeterminacy; that is to say, the spatial city has no plan to follow, with the exception of the infrastructure (it therefore permits all possible transformations). The volumes that create the spaces of the spatial city are not arranged in advance; they continually change over time. Gardens, housing, public centers, industry, and circulation intertwine. There are residential neighborhoods *above* industrial areas, schools *above* highways and parking areas, offices and housing *in the same place*, without the paths of their users crossing one another. In some places the city looks like the ordinary city, while in other places it resembles a kind of modern Venice. All (functional or formal) possibilities can be had; their realization depends only on the wishes of the inhabitants. Depending on their preference, pedestrians can walk in the air-conditioned "streets" of the lower levels of the infrastructure or wander through the "tourist streets" of the upper level of the infrastructure in order to enjoy the panorama.

All of the unused areas of the infrastructure (the "patios" of the city) are air-conditioned. This solution would be economically impossible in the present city, but not so in the spatial city because of the reduction of surfaces and heat loss.

Moreover (as we have seen) agriculture can also be contained within the spatial city. Air-conditioned greenhouses of several stories could increase the productive agricultural surfaces up to 400%. These greenhouses could provide the whole city with fresh vegetables (whereas presently their transport to the city is the largest component in the price of vegetables) and serve at the same time to regenerate the city's air (green space).

Many systematic studies have been made of the spatial city: for the city of Tunis (Friedman-Aujame), Abidjan (Friedman-Aujame), and spatial Paris (Friedman-Herbé-Preveral).

The spatial city represents a case of utilizing voids within the distribution network. The same formula could provide us with an image of the world of tomorrow.

The distribution systems (transportation) of our world are today continental (from ocean to ocean). The cities (or regions), in relation to these networks, are of two types. They are either *situated on the knots* of this net or they are *in the mesh* of the net. Development tends to increase the importance of the second type. The megalopolis, for example, will be a very densely utilized urban region *in* the mesh of the net because all technically feasible transport necessarily favors this second type.

205 KIYONORI KIKUTAKE, NOBORU KAWAZOE, MASATO OHTAKA, FUMIHIKO MAKI, AND NORIAKI KUROKAWA

from *Metabolism: The Proposals for New Urbanism* (1960)

With the issue of urbanism and its postwar failures now reaching a state of crisis in the West, a series of startlingly original proposals came out of the East from a group of young architects who called themselves the Metabolists. A precursor of what was to come in fact appeared at CIAM's last conference at Otterlo in 1959, when Kenzo Tange discussed his developing interest in the future city, growing out of his grandiose scheme for the expansion of Tokyo into the harbor. Yet a group of younger Japanese architects had by this date long rejected the deliberations of CIAM, and were preparing the agenda for the World Design Conference, to be held in Tokyo in 1960. This meeting turned out to be a major success, as it was well attended by leading architects from around the world, led by the Smithsons, Jean Prouvé, and Louis Kahn. For the conference, the Japanese architects, now rallying around the appellation "Metabolism," published this manifesto along with a series of projects – all stressing the need to view the city as a biological organism perpetually undergoing growth and change. The first passage consists of their manifesto in full, and the second is taken from Kiyonori Kikutake's description of his "Marine City," a series of floating, interconnected disks sprouting circular towers of plug-in units.

"Metabolism" is the name of the group, in which each member proposes future designs of our coming world through his concrete designs and illustrations. We regard human society as a vital process – a continuous development from atom to nebula. The reason why we use such a biological word, the metabolism, is that, we believe, design and technology should be a denotation of human vitality.

We are not going to accept the metabolism as a natural historical process, but we are trying to encourage active metabolic development of our society through our proposals.

Kiyonori Kikutake, Noboru Kawazoe, Masato Ohtaka, Fumihiko Maki, and Noriaki Kurokawa, from *Metabolism: The Proposals for New Urbanism*. Tokyo: Yasuko Kawazoe, 1960, pp. 6, 22–3.

This volume mainly consists of the designs for our future cities proposed only by architects. From the next issue, however, the people in other fields such as designers, artists, engineers, scientists, and politicians, will participate in it, and already some of them are preparing for the next one.

In future, more will come to join "Metabolism" and some will go; that means a metabolic process will also take place in its membership.

[. . .]

Marine City is a proposal to build up the world of tomorrow for man. This proposal is going to confront with the sea which possesses over 70% area of the surface of the globe, have observed the progress of the civilization of continents since, and have refused man's invasion for 5000 years. In other words, as an assembled unit of human community, Marine City is going to challenge the sea to man's new world.

The purpose of Marine City is neither intend to enlarge the land nor to escape from the land. Merely, to escape from the land, the plan of Marine City requests too much prudent studies and discussions, while, to enlarge the land, the plan demands too much excellent combination of synthetic engineering and powerful economy. The existing confusion of land cities should not be brought to Marine City. The sea will refuse such disorder and careless undertaking as she has refused before. The desecration of such fastidious virtue of the sea is the reclamation project of foreshore. It is a clear fact that the excellent condition of human community can not be established on the reclamed ground, if considered the existing relations between man and the land. At present, the engineering would be of no use unless it would assemble and organize the human powers more orderly and synthetically. It could neither be endured nor allowed that the engineering to be utilized in such huge plan might be driven away to the destructive confusion which was being called as "Construction".

The continental shelf down to 200 m. depth of water should be offered to man's use, but man have to reserve enough space for fish and marine plant. The sea is waiting a new discovery of the sea which will promise a true happiness of human being. It is just the time that the civilization of continents must hand over its part to the prospective civilization of sea commenced by Marine City, as well as the coal era had handed over its part to the oil era. It must be studied that Marine City will be a unit of human community, not that of individual life. In case when Marine City became unsatisfactory unit for community, it will be brought to the middle of ocean and be sunken there without the least hesitation. Then, such sunken Marine City will be fish bed at the bottom of sea. Marine City does not be anchored at the definite point. It can cruise to anywhere man wants when necessary. The construction of Marine City will start from the floating manufacturing plants which will be the mother's body of Marine City. From this plant city, new units of Marine City will be delivered out one by one. Marine City will submit stereo-space for human community on the surface, while, it will offer fish bed to preserve and breed fishes by its under water part. As Marine City is the artificial city, it will have each particular function provided by the original scheme. These establishments will be presented to the new human community in the sea, and these will promise man the new world in the coming days.

206 REYNER BANHAM

from *Theory and Design in the First Machine Age* (1960)

B anham's ascension into a position of prominence within the international architectural debate came with the publication of *Theory and Design in the First Machine Age*. The book was based on his doctoral dissertation, but his conclusions were new, at least new within a broader historical context of the time. Conceived as a history of modern theory, the book considers the various avant-garde movements of the twentieth century, as well as the change in living habits and attitudes induced by the technological wonders of the machine, from airplanes to automobiles. Whereas architects paid lip service to the machine, Banham argues, they did not always design in such forward-looking ways; in fact in the 1930s a period of academicism set in, fundamentally at odds with the possibilities that the machine offered. This point almost becomes moot, because in his introduction and final chapter Banham goes on to argue that the Western societies are in fact entering a Second Machine Age, in which machines, now rendered democratic in the form of low-cost or small-scale appliances and electronic devices, are destined to play an even greater role in the transformation of lifestyles. Banham, in his thinking, like many of his generation, is now being influenced by the ideas of Buckminster Fuller, and thus a new direction in architectural thought is being forged here.

Even a man who does not possess an electric razor is likely – in the Westernised world at least – to dispense some previously inconceivable product, such as an aerosol shaving cream, from an equally unprecedented pressurised container, and accept with equanimity the fact that he can afford to throw away, regularly, cutting-edges that previous generations would have nursed for years. Even a housewife who does not possess a washing machine dispenses synthetic detergent from synthetic plastic packs on to synthetic fabrics whose quality and performance makes the jealously-guarded secrets of silk seem trivial. A teen-ager, curled up with a transistorised, printed-circuit radio, or boudoir gramophone, may hear a music that literally did not exist before it was committed to tape, reproduced at a level of quality that riches could not have bought a decade or so ago. The average automobile of today, running on such roads as have been especially contrived for it, provides transport more sumptuous in vehicles more gorgeous than palanquin-borne emperors knew how to desire.

Many technologies have contributed to this domestic revolution, but most of them make their point of impact on us in the form of small machines – shavers, clippers and hair-dryers; radio, telephone, gramophone, tape recorder and television; mixers, grinders, automatic cookers, washing machines, refrigerators, vacuum cleaners, polishers.... A housewife alone, often disposes of more horse-power today than an industrial worker did at the beginning of the century. This is the sense in which we live in a Machine Age. We have lived in an Industrial Age for nearly a century and a half now, and may well be entering a Second Industrial Age with the current revolution in control mechanisms. But we have already entered the Second Machine Age, the age of domestic electronics and synthetic chemistry,

Reyner Banham, from *Theory and Design in the First Machine Age* (1960). New York: Praeger, 1978, pp. 9–10.

and can look back on the First, the age of power from the mains and the reduction of machines to human scale, as a period of the past.

Although the earliest stirrings of that First Machine Age must have appeared with the availability of coal-gas for lighting and heating, the mechanism of light and heat remained a flame, as it had been from the Stone Age onwards. Mains electricity made a decisive alteration here, one of the most decisive in the history of domestic technology. In addition, it brought small, woman-controlled machinery into the home, notably the vacuum cleaner. Electrical techniques brought the telephone as well, and for the first time domestic and sociable communication did not depend on the sending of written or remembered messages. The portable typewriter put a machine under the hands of poets, the first gramophones made music a domestic service rather than a social ceremony.

All these machines are still with us in the Second Machine Age, supplemented and improved by more recent technological advances, but there is a more than quantitative difference between the two ages. In the Second, highly developed mass production methods have distributed electronic devices and synthetic chemicals broadcast over a large part of society – television, the symbolic machine of the Second Machine Age, has become a means of mass-communication dispensing popular entertainment. In the First, however, only cinema was available to a broad public, whose home life was otherwise barely touched and it was in upper middle-class homes that the First Machine Age made its greatest impact, the homes that could afford these new, convenient and expensive aids to gracious living, the homes that tend to breed architects, painters, poets, journalists, the creators of the myths and symbols by which a culture recognises itself.

207 ARCHIGRAM
"Manifesto" (1961)

E manating from the lively British atmosphere of debate in the late 1950s was the group Archigram. Its members – Peter Cook, Warren Chalk, David Greene, Dennis Crompton, Ron Herron, and Michael Webb – were architects working in London offices, and their journal's irreverent, comic-book style of presenting images and ideas (also owing much to Roy Lichtenstein) struck one of the first counter-cultural chords of the new decade. The group's fascination with pop culture, megastructures, and such formerly taboo issues as expendability distinguishes it from more serious-minded urban idealists, but this was precisely one of the reasons for Archigram's founding.

A new generation of architecture must arise with forms and spaces which seem to reject the precepts of 'Modern' yet in fact retain these precepts. WE HAVE CHOSEN TO BY-PASS THE DECAYING BAUHAUS IMAGE WHICH IS AN INSULT TO FUNCTIONALISM.

Archigram, "Manifesto," in Archigram 1 (May 1961).

208 RACHEL CARSON
from *Silent Spring* (1962)

Rachel Carson's *Silent Spring* was not only one of the most popular books to appear in the 1960s (it was published in fifteen countries within a year of its publication), but it was one of the most profound and influential books of the twentieth century. Carson was born in Pennsylvania and received a master's in zoology from Johns Hopkins University in 1932. She joined the US Bureau of Fisheries and rose within the government to become editor of all US Fish and Wildlife publications. Her earlier works were concerned with the ocean, but this emphasis changed in the late 1950s as she became more and more aware of the dangers of chemical pesticides. Her understanding of the ecological balance thus became a crusade, and she is widely lauded for starting the ecological movement. Her holistic thesis can be summarized in these two paragraphs from the second chapter of the book, "The Obligation to Endure."

The history of life on earth has been a history of interaction between living things and their surroundings. To a large extent, the physical form and the habits of the earth's vegetation and its animal life have been molded by the environment. Considering the whole span of earthly time, the opposite effect, in which life actually modifies its surroundings, has been relatively slight. Only within the moment of time represented by the present century has one species – man – acquired significant power to alter the nature of his world.

During the past quarter century this power has not only increased to one of disturbing magnitude but it has changed in character. The most alarming of all man's assaults upon the environment is the contamination of air, earth, rivers, and sea with dangerous and even lethal materials. This pollution is for the most part irrecoverable; the chain of evil it initiates not only in the world that must support life but in living tissues is for the most part irreversible. In this now universal contamination of the environment, chemicals are the sinister and little-recognized partners of radiation in changing the very nature of the world – the very nature of its life. Strontium 90, released through nuclear explosions into the air, comes to earth in rain or drifts down as fallout, lodges in soil, enters into the grass or corn or wheat grown there, and in time takes up its abode in the bones of a human being, there to remain until his death. Similarly, chemicals sprayed on croplands or forests or gardens lie long in soil, entering into living organisms, passing from one to another in a chain of poisoning and death. Or they pass mysteriously by underground streams until they emerge and, through the alchemy of air and sunlight, combine into new forms that kill vegetation, sicken cattle, and work unknown harm on those who drink from once pure wells. As Albert Schweitzer has said, "Man can hardly even recognize the devils of his own creation."

Rachel Carson, from *Silent Spring*. New York: Houghton Mifflin, 1962, pp. 5–6.

209 CONSTANTINOS DOXIADIS ET AL.
"The Declaration of Delos" (1963)

One of the more interesting organizational events of the 1960s was a group of thirty-four intellectuals from various disciplines, assembled by Constantinos Doxiadis for an eight-day cruise around the Greek islands. The purpose of the gathering was to ponder the city of the future. Doxiadis, a Greek architect and town planner, had long been involved with the issue. In 1955 he started the journal *Ekistics* to ponder the problem of growth and housing; in 1958 he founded a research center on this theme to amass global statistics. And in chartering the ship *New Hellas* in Athens in 1963 he hoped to bring together the best minds in the world to consider solutions – among them Buckminster Fuller, Marshall McLuhan, Edmund Bacon, Margaret Meade, and Sigfried Giedion. It was a conscious reenactment of the cruise session of 1932 that produced the "Athens Charter." At the conclusion of the trip on the island of Delos, in quasi-mystical rites, the participants signed the following declaration.

"Meeting in Delos on this, the twelfth day of July, 1963, we the undersigned, drawn from a wide range of different disciplines, nations, political allegiances and cultural groups, affirm and declare that:

1. The city throughout history, has been the cradle of human civilisation and progress. Today, like every other human institution, it is profoundly involved in the deepest and widest revolution ever to overtake mankind.

2. This revolution proceeds under the sign of dynamic change. In the next forty years, the world's population will rise to seven thousand million. Science and technology determine more and more of the processes of human living. As they advance, man's social behaviour is profoundly modified. These changes present themselves in every field as a danger matched by an even greater opportunity. Man can use atomic power to reduce every human settlement to the shambles of Hiroshima. It may give them enough energy to fulfill all human needs. The world's population may far outstrip its food supply. Even to keep pace, to-day's food production must rise threefold by the year 2000. Yet for the first time, we also have the means of securing enough food for everyone.

3. These paradoxes are widely felt. What is not realised is that the failure to adapt human settlements to dynamic change may soon outstrip even disease and starvation as the gravest risk, short of war, facing the human species.

4. A universal feature of the worldwide revolution is the movement of people into urban settlements at an ever faster rate. World population increases by 2 per cent a year, urban population by over 4 per cent. In the next forty years, more urban construction will take place than hitherto in the whole history of man. It is already evident that wrong projections of urban development produce inexcusable waste. The absence of any forecasts leads to chaos in the cities, to the undermining of civic order and the destruction of precious and diverse historical traditions. Thus the need for the rational and dynamic planning of human settlements both now and in the foreseeable-future is inherent in the urban situation to-day.

Constantinos Doxiadis et al., from "The Declaration of Delos," cited from *Ekistics: Reviews on the Problems of Science of Human Settlements* 16:93 (August 1963), n.p.

5. Man can act to meet this new crisis. There are sufficient resources for the task. Modern technology permits the mobilisation of material means on a wholly new scale. Developed nations spend 150,000 million dollars a year on armaments and still their national incomes go up. Billions are spent each year on social services, some of which are made necessary by the inadequacies of urban life. Once a problem is recognised, the resources for meeting it can be found. These resources are not, it is true, uniformly available. Some societies still lack the means for action. But this is not an absolute shortage and while they achieve modernisation, their lack can be made good by sustained assistance from more technologically advanced areas.

6. Guide lines for policy are also clearer than ever before, thanks in part to the great extension of systematic studies in human behaviour. The aim must be to produce settlements which satisfy man not only as parent and worker but as learner and artist and citizen. His active participation is essential in framing his own environment. He must be able to use creatively the still unforeseen possibilities of advancing technology. Planning itself must ensure that such possibilities are not excluded by a static view of human settlements. Above all, the citizen should feel at ease in his own culture and open to the cultures of others.

7. When we turn to the application of these principles to the problems of urbanisation, we feel the need for the most far-reaching reform and reinforcement of existing institutions and procedures. At present, educational systems at every level have not yet taken sufficient action to meet the new problems of human settlements or to explore the possibilities of meeting them through rational planning. In the universities, the application of the basic sciences to human welfare has been fragmented. They have dealt with parts of man – his health, his nutrition, his education – not with the whole man, not with man in community. Thus, we underline with all possible urgency our belief that in every action of ours, in the agencies dealing with these problems at a national or international level, in the institutions of higher learning, whether public or private, our society requires: (a) to establish in its own right a new discipline of human settlements; (b) to initiate basic research of the most far-reaching kind; (c) to bring together specialists from other relevant disciplines to work together on projects in this field; (d) to work out new methods of training the men who can assume leadership and responsibility in the sphere of action; (e) to attract some of the best young minds into this new area of research, development and practice.

8. We come from different nations, from different cultural backgrounds. Our politics differ, our professions are various. But we believe that the problem of human settlements is a general and fundamental problem in our new dynamic world and that it must be viewed and studied in such a way that it will, in common with all great scientific disciplines, transcend our local differences. We agree that the practical implementation of policy – in such vital fields as land use, the location of investment or the planning of cities over time – will be determined by domestic politics and needs, and as citizens we pledge ourselves to attempt to bring these issues into the active political dialogue of our local societies. But we are not divided in what we wish most strongly to affirm – that we are citizens of a worldwide city, threatened by its own torrential expansion and that at this level our concern and commitment is for man himself."

Charles Abrams (U.S.A.). Edmund N. Bacon (U.S.A.). Stewart Bates (Canada). Petro Bidagor Lasarte (Spain). A.K. Brohi (Pakistan). C.S. Chandrasekhara (India). Walter Christaller (Germany). Jacob L. Crane (U.S.A.). Richard Llewellyn Davies (Britain). C.A. Doxiadis (Greece). Leonard Duhl (U.S.A.). O.E. Fischnich (U.N.). Lyle C. Fitch (U.S.A.). R. Buckminster Fuller (U.S.A.). Clifford Furnas (U.S.A.). S. Giedion (Switzerland). J. Gorynski (Poland). Eiichi Isomura (Japan). Barbara Ward Jackson (Britain). Sture Linner (U.N.). M.S. Makiya (Iraq). Edward S. Mason (U.S.A.). Sir Robert Matthew (Britain). Margaret Mead (U.S.A.). Marshall McLuhan (Canada). Waclaw Ostrowski (Poland). Alfred R. Otoo (Ghana). David Owen (U.N.). Charles H. Page (U.S.A.). E. Papanoutsos (Greece). Shafik H. El-Sadr (U.A.R.). Carl Schweyer (Germany). C.H. Waddington (Britain). Sir Robert Watson Watt (Britain).

210 R. BUCKMINSTER FULLER
from "World Design Initiative: Mexico Lecture" (1963)

The year 1963 was a transformational one for this "generalist" thinker. For much of his life, since his first experimental designs for the sustainable "Dymaxion House" in the late 1920s, he had labored in relative obscurity, at least within most architectural circles. This virtual anonymity began to change in the 1950s, as he developed the principles of his geodesic domes and directed built experiments with various architectural schools. This process would culminate with the 250-foot dome he installed at Expo '67 in Montréal. In addition to participating in the Delos discussions in July 1963, Fuller in that year also became a consultant to the Advanced Structures Research Team at NASA, from which he elaborated upon his already keen interest in closed ecological systems. In the same year he coauthored with John McHale the first volume of his *Inventory of World Resources: Human Trends and Needs*. This passage, from a lecture he gave in Mexico in fall 1963, recounts this effort, and thus signals a shift in his focus from geometric experimentation to the idea of the "World Game": an attempt on his part (formalized in 1965 with the aid of hundreds of students) to map the world's resources and consider ways of using the planet's resources more efficiently.

65% of all our steel is now made out of scrap. That is very roughly the ratio of recirculating metal to new mine production metal in all of the metals categories. It is perfectly practical to think about taking the metals out of obsolete automobiles, taking all the two-ton automobiles off the road, melting them up and making twice as many higher performance one-ton automobiles from the same metal. You may say that you don't want more automobiles – that: the parking problems are too great. In speaking of automobiles I have chosen an industrial tool that you are familiar with. I am not advocating more autos. I am simply considering the feasibility of the principles involved through which we can, by design

R. Buckminster Fuller, from "World Design Initiative: Mexico Lecture" (1963), cited from R. Buckminster Fuller, *Your Private Sky: Discourse*, ed Joachim Krausse and Claude Lichtenstein. Zurich: Lars Müller, 2001, p. 278. Originally published in *The Design Initiative: World Design Science Decade, 1965–75*, vol. 2. Carbondale: Southern Illinois University Press, 1964.

science, take care of twice as many people in a given function with a given obsolete scrap resource. I have learned by experience that it is possible and feasible for the world of architectural students to undertake an amplification of the functional effectiveness of the world's resources through design science.

I realized a year ago, from my own experience, and from the frustrated attempt on the part of enthusiastic architectural students in various schools around the world to get going with the world redesign, that it is not going to be a practical matter for the world's architectural students to take a world inventory of resources as well as an inventory of all the trend patternings and needs of men in order to learn how to reorganize the designed use of the total resources to highest advantage. Such economic intelligence harvesting is not within the present training or even the extra-curricula experience of architectural students.

On the other hand I have had extensive experience in making such inventories – in 1936 – for the world copper industry, in 1940 for *Fortune* magazine, and in 1943 for the United States Board of Economic Warfare. Therefore I have undertaken with the help of Southern Illinois University and the assistance of my colleague, John McHale, to prepare for this congress and for the world architectural students, a very complete inventory, not only of the world's resources, but also of the patternings of men's trendings and needs.

This inventory has been completed and printed in book form. I am quite confident that as of this congress, the world architectural students program can go forward for we are distributing the world inventory books to all the delegates of the countries who are attending this Seventh World Congress of the International Union of Architects. There is a world architectural students' organization similar to the senior professional organization of which we are now members. The world architectural students had a meeting in Barcelona this year and asked me to be their speaker, and as a consequence of so speaking and outlining the world resources redesign program I received their affirmation of their enthusiasm for the task. The resource inventories will be dispatched to the world architectural student organization.

211   KENNETH E. BOULDING
from "Earth as a Space Ship"
(1965)

I t is unclear when the idea of "Spaceship Earth" first found its way into general parlance, but, as these lecture notes indicate, it was in use by the middle of the 1960s. Kenneth Boulding was an economist, and it is from this perspective that this future Nobel-Prize-winner begins to consider the implications for life on a planetary spaceship. His prodding of the science of ecology, which "has hardly moved beyond the level of bird-watching," is nothing less than revolutionary. Boulding prepared these remarks for the Committee on Space Sciences, and he delivered them at Washington State University on May 10, 1965.

Kenneth E. Boulding, from "Earth as a Space Ship," Kenneth E. Boulding Papers, Archives (Box 38), University of Colorado at Boulder Libraries.

Let me suggest, then, some of the consequences of earth becoming a space ship. In the first place, it is absolutely necessary for man now to develop a technology that is different from the one on which he now bases his high-level societies. High-level societies are now based on the consumption of fossil fuels and ores, none of which, at present rates of consumption, are likely to last more than a few hundred years. A stable, circular-flow high-level technology is conceivable in which we devote inputs of energy to the concentration of materials into useful form, sufficient to compensate for the diffusion of materials which takes place in their use. At the moment we take fuels and burn them, we take concentrated deposits of iron ore for instance, and phosphates, and we spread these throughout the world in dumps, and we flush them out to the oceans in sewers. The stable high-level technology will have to rely on the oceans and the atmosphere as a basic resource from which materials may be concentrated in sufficient quantity to overcome their diffusion through consumption. Even this, of course, will require constant inputs of energy. There is no way for the closed system to prevent the increase of entropy. Earth, fortunately, has a constant input of energy from the sun, and by the time that goes, man will probably have abandoned earth; and we have also the possibility of almost unlimited energy inputs from nuclear fusion, if we can find means of harnessing it usefully.

Man is finally going to have to face the fact that he is a biological system living in an ecological system, and that his survival power is going to depend on his developing symbiotic relationships of a closed-cycle character with all the other elements and populations of the world of ecological systems. What this means, in effect, is that all the other forms of life will have to be domesticated, even if on wildlife preserves.

The consequences of earth becoming a space ship for the social system are profound and little understood. It is clear that much human behavior and many human institutions in the past, which were appropriate to all infinite earth, are entirely inappropriate to a small closed space ship. We cannot have cowboys and Indians, for instance, in a space ship, or even a cowboy ethic. We cannot afford unrestrained conflict, and we almost certainly cannot afford national sovereignty in an unrestricted sense. On the other hand, we must beware of pushing the analogy too far. In a small ship, there would almost have to be a dictatorial political system with a captain, and a planned economy. A voyaging space ship, like a battleship, almost has to be a centrally planned economy. A large space ship with three billion passengers, however, or perhaps ten billion, may have a very different social structure. Large social organizations are very different from small. It may be able to have much more individual freedom, a price system and a market economy of a limited and controlled kind, and even democratic political institutions. There must be, however, cybernetic or homeostatic mechanisms for preventing the overall variables of the social system from going beyond a certain range. There must, for instance, be machinery for controlling the total numbers of the population; there must be machinery for controlling conflict processes and for preventing perverse social dynamic processes of escalation and inflation. One of the major problems of social science is how to devise institutions which will combine this overall homeostatic control with individual freedom and mobility. I believe this problem to be not insoluble, though not yet solved.

Once we begin to look at earth as a space ship, the appalling extent of our ignorance about it is almost frightening. This is true of the level of every science. We know practically nothing, for instance, about the long-run dynamics even of the physical system of the earth.

We do not understand, for instance, the machinery of ice ages, the real nature of geological stability or disturbance, the incidence of volcanism and earthquakes, and we understand fantastically little about that enormously complex heat engine known as the atmosphere. We do not even know whether the activities of man are going to make the earth warm up or cool off. At the level of the biological sciences, our ignorance is even greater. Ecology as a science has hardly moved beyond the level of bird-watching. It has yet to become quantified, and it has yet to find an adequate theory. Even to an economist, its existing theoretical structures seem fantastically naive, and when it comes to understanding the world social system or the sociosphere, we are not only ignorant but proud of our ignorance. There is no systematic method of data collection and processing, and the theory of social dynamics is still in its first infancy.

The moral of all this is that man must be made to realize that all his major problems are still unsolved, and that a very large and massive intellectual effort is still necessary to solve them. In the meantime we are wasting our intellectual resources on insoluble problems like unilateral national defense and on low-priority achievements like putting a man on the moon. This is no way to run a space ship.

212 IAN McHARG
from *Design with Nature* (1969)

Certainly one of the culminating points in this decade of growing environmental awareness was Ian McHarg's *Design with Nature*. This Scottish landscape designer and planner founded the Department of Landscape Architecture and Regional Planning at the University of Pennsylvania, and the department still bears his impressive mark. And while his book was largely concerned with the preservation of the natural habitat, it was also a sharply worded polemic against the state of Western cities and the policies or lack thereof that led to their creation. What also made the book so popular among architects and landscape architects were the clear and effective graphic techniques that summarized the information in an exceedingly concise way. McHarg set the standard for this newly evolving field.

And what of the cities? Think of the imprisoning gray areas that encircle the center. From here the sad suburb is an unrealizable dream. Call them no-place although they have many names. Race and hate, disease, poverty, rancor and despair, urine and spit live here in the shadows. United in poverty and ugliness, their symbol is the abandoned carcasses of automobiles, broken glass, alleys of rubbish and garbage. Crime consorts with disease, group fights group, the only emancipation is the parked car.

What of the heart of the city, where the gleaming towers rise from the dirty skirts of poverty? Is it like midtown Manhattan where twenty per cent of the population was found to be indistinguishable from the patients in mental hospitals? Both stimulus and stress live here

Ian McHarg, from *Design with Nature* (1969), cited from paperback edition. Garden City, NY: American Museum of Natural History, Doubleday/Natural History, 1971, pp. 20–2.

with the bitch goddess success. As you look at the faceless prisms do you recognize the home of *anomie?*

Can you find the river that first made the city? Look behind the unkempt industry, cross the grassy railroad tracks and you will find the rotting piers and there is the great river, scummy and brown, wastes and sewage bobbing easily up and down with the tide, endlessly renewed.

If you fly to the city by day you will see it first as a smudge of smoke on the horizon. As you approach, the outlines of its towers will be revealed as soft silhouettes in the hazardous haze. Nearer you will perceive conspicuous plumes which, you learn, belong to the proudest names in industry. Our products are household words but it is clear that our industries are not yet housebroken. Drive from the airport through the banks of gas storage tanks and the interminable refineries. Consider how dangerous they are, see their cynical spume, observe their ugliness. Refine they may, but refined they are not.

You will drive on an expressway, a clumsy concrete form, untouched by either humanity or art, testament to the sad illusion that there can be a solution for the unbridled automobile. It is ironic that this greatest public investment in cities has also financed their conquest. See the scars of the battle in the remorseless carving, the dismembered neighborhoods, the despoiled parks. Manufacturers are producing automobiles faster than babies are being born. Think of the depredations yet to be accomplished by myopic highway builders to accommodate these toxic vehicles. You have plenty of time to consider in the long peak hour pauses of spasmodic driving in the blue gas corridors.

You leave the city and turn towards the countryside. But can you find it? To do so you will follow the paths of those who tried before you. Many stayed to build. But those who did so first are now deeply embedded in the fabric of the city. So as you go you transect the rings of the thwarted and disillusioned who are encapsulated in the city as nature endlessly eludes pursuit.

You can tell when you have reached the edge of the countryside for there are many emblems – the cadavers of old trees piled in untidy heaps at the edge of the razed deserts, the magnificent machines for land despoliation, for felling forests, filling marshes, culverting streams, and sterilizing farmland, making thick brown sediments of the creeks.

213   R. BUCKMINSTER FULLER
from *Utopia or Oblivion* (1969)

O n July 20, 1969, Neil Armstrong, the Commander of Apollo 11, successfully touched down the lunar module on the surface of the moon. This extraordinary technological feat came at the end of what had become one of the worst decades in American history – one in which the struggle for Civil Rights, the Vietnam War, and disenchantment among young people nearly tore the nation asunder. It was within this context that Buckminster Fuller penned this vision of a future floating city, one perhaps consciously removed from the world and its unrelenting problems.

R. Buckminster Fuller, from *Utopia or Oblivion: The Prospects for Humanity*. New York: Overlook Press, 1969, pp. 356–7.

A one-hundred-foot-diameter geodesic sphere weighing 3 tons encloses 7 tons of air. The air to structural weight ratio is 2:1. When we double the size so that geodesic sphere is 200 feet in diameter the weight of the structure goes up to 7 tons while the weight of the air goes up to 56 tons – the air to structure ratio changes to 8:1. When we double the size again to a 400-foot geodesic sphere – the size of several geodesic domes now operating – the weight of the air inside goes to about 500 tons while the weight of the structure goes up to 15 tons. The air to structure weight ratio is now 33:1. When we get to a geodesic sphere one-half mile in diameter, the weight of the air enclosed is so great that the weight of the structure itself becomes of relatively negligible magnitude, for the ratio is 1000:1.

When the sun shines on an open-frame aluminum geodesic sphere of one-half-mile diameter the sun penetrating through the frame and reflected from the concave far side bounces back into the sphere and gradually heats the interior atmosphere to a mild degree. When the interior temperature of the sphere rises only 1° Fahrenheit, the weight of air pushed out of the sphere is greater than the weight of the spherical-frame geodesic structure. This means that the total weight of the interior air, plus the weight of the structure, is much less than the surrounding atmosphere. This means that the total assemblage of the geodesic sphere and its contained air will have to float outwardly into the sky, being displaced by the heavy atmosphere around it. When a great bank of mist lies in a valley in the morning and the sun shines upon the mist, the sun heats the air inside the bank of mist. The heated air expands and therefore pushes some of itself outside the mist bank. The total assembly of the mist bank weighs less than the atmosphere surrounding it and the mist bank floats aloft into the sky. Thus are clouds manufactured.

As geodesic spheres get larger than one-half mile in diameter they become floatable cloud structures. If their surfaces were draped with outwardly hung polyethylene curtains to retard the rate at which air would come back in at night, the sphere and its internal atmosphere would continue to be so light as to remain aloft. Such sky-floating geodesic spheres may be designed to float at preferred altitudes of thousands of feet. The weight of human beings added to such prefabricated "cloud nines" would be relatively negligible. Many thousands of passengers could be housed aboard one-mile-diameter and larger cloud structures. The passengers could come and go from cloud to cloud, or cloud to ground, as the clouds float around the earth or are anchored to mountain-tops. While the building of such floating clouds is several decades hence, we may foresee that along with the floating tetrahedronal cities, air-deliverable skyscrapers, submarine islands, subdry-surface dwellings, domed-over cities, flyable dwelling machines, rentable, autonomous-living black boxes, that man may be able to converge and deploy at will around the earth, in great numbers, without further depletion of the productive surface of the earth.

It may be that after we get to the large skyscraper-size airplanes that they may be economically occupiable and economically flyable from here to there with passengers living aboard as on cruise ships.

It may be that human beings will begin to live in completely mobile ways on sky ships and sea ships as they now occupy cruise ships in large numbers, for months, while traveling around the water and sky oceans. As people live completely around the earth, changing from "summer" to "winter" in hours, the old concept of man as a cold-area or warm-area dweller or as a fixed, static dweller anywhere, and all the old concepts of seasons, or even of work as related only to daylight hours, will gradually be eradicated from man's conditioned reflexes.

Man will come to occupy mobile habitats which may at will be anchored habitats and live independently of day and night and season schedules. This will mean a much higher occupancy in use rate of environment-control facilities. Nowadays, at international airport hotels, people with one-to-eight-hour flight-transfer waitovers follow one another in rooms and beds which are made up freshly as one occupant follows the other. The rooms are occupied, not on a noon-to-noon schedule, but on a use schedule which we may call a frequency-modulation schedule. Such frequency-modulated occupancy of rented space in mobile hotels or in dwelling machines will become the fundamental patterning of man's living around the earth.

214 JOHN McCONNELL
from "Earth Day Proclamation" (1970)

The culmination of these growing environmental sensitivities of the 1960s was the creation of "Earth Day," officially proclaimed by U Thant, the Secretary General of the United Nations, in February 1971. The idea for such a day was first put forward by John McConnell, the Chairman of the San Francisco Board of Supervisors, in fall 1969. He actually wrote the proclamation for the city of San Francisco, and it was presented to Mayor Joseph L. Alioto in March 1970. The United Nations received the idea warmly and it was reissued in the following year, and signed by an international group of luminaries led by Buckminster Fuller, Buzz Aldrin, Margaret Mead, René J. Dubos, and Luboš Kohoutek. Earth Day always falls on the Vernal Equinox, March 21, and is celebrated at the United Nations with a Peace Bell Ceremony and a moment of silence.

Earth Day Proclamation

Whereas: A new world view is emerging; through the eyes of our Astronauts and Cosmonauts we now see our beautiful blue planet as a home for all people, and

Whereas: Planet Earth is facing a grave crisis which only the people of Earth Can resolve, and the delicate balances of nature, essential for our survival, can only be saved through a global effort, involving all of us, and

Whereas: In our shortsightedness we have failed to make provisions for the poor, as well as the rich, to inherit the Earth, and our new enlightenment requires that the disinherited be given a just stake in the Earth and its future – their enthusiastic cooperation is essential if we are to succeed in the great task of Earth renewal, and

John McConnell, "Earth Day Proclamation," press release, United Nations.

Whereas: World equality in economics as well as politics would remove a basic cause of war, and neither Socialism, Communism nor Capitalism in their present forms have realized the potentials of Man for a just society, nor educated Man in the ways of peace and creative love, and

Whereas: Through voluntary action individuals can join with one another in building the Earth in harmony with nature, and promote support thereof by private and government agencies, and

Whereas: Individuals and groups may follow different methods and programmes in Earth-keeping and Earthbuilding, nevertheless by constant friendly communication with other groups and daily meditation on the meaning of peace and goodwill they will tend more and more to be creative, sensitive, experimental, and flexible in resolving differences with others, and

Whereas: An international EARTH DAY each year can provide a special time to draw people together in appreciation of their mutual home, Planet Earth, and bring a global feeling of community through realization of our deepening desire for life, freedom and love, and our mutual dependence on each other,

Be it Therefore Resolved: That each signer of this People Proclamation will seek to help change Man's terrible course toward catastrophe by searching for activities and projects which in the best judgment of the individual signer will:

– peacefully end the scourge of war...
– provide an opportunity for the children of the disinherited poor to obtain their rightful inheritance in the Earth...
– redirect the energies of industry and society from progress through products...to progress through harmony with Earth's natural systems for improving the quality of life...

That each signer will (his own conscience being his judge) measure his commitment by how much time and money he gives to these purposes, and realizing the great urgency of the task, he will give freely of his time and money to activities and programmes he believes will best further these Earth renewal purposes. (At least 9 percent of the world's present income is going to activities that support war and spread pollution. Ten percent can tip the balance for healthy peaceful progress.)

Furthermore, each signer will support and observe EARTH DAY on March 21st.... (Vernal Equinox – when night and day are equal throughout the Earth) with reflection and actions that encourage a new respect for Earth with its great potentials for fulfilling Man's highest dreams; and on this day will join at 19:00 Universal Time in a global EARTH HOUR – a silent hour for peace...."

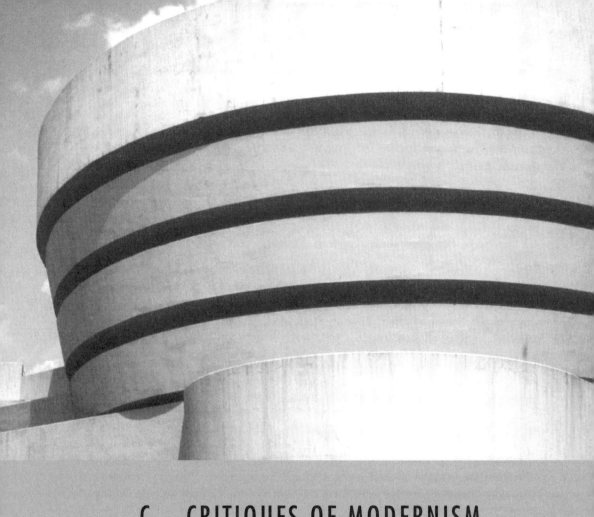

C. CRITIQUES OF MODERNISM

Introduction

As the European and North American continents were experiencing the travails of the 1960s, modern architecture also was experiencing its crisis. This event begins to take place along various fronts. From one direction, the "meaning" of modernism comes under scrutiny, that is, how architectural forms are read and interpreted by their users. This brings into architectural thought several new theoretical structures to approach this problem, such as communications theory, semiotics, phenomenology, and structuralism. Second, there arises a new focus on the methodology of architectural design within an increasingly complex and chaotic world. Third, there appears a new populist approach, one that shifts the basis of architecture from the elitist and idealist aesthetics to a more realist acceptance of existing conditions. Allied with this is a new interest in pre-modern history. Fourth, one sees the basis for a new formalism in design: a tendency that, with a design emphasis simply on form, shields architectural design from the problematic social issues of the world. Fifth, we have the emergence of a highly politicized theory, once again seeking to align the future of architecture within the larger political revolution, which many believed was taking place. However, these competing directions still appeared in a seminal form and their fuller development would take place only over the following decades. But this dynamism, as it were, is also what makes the theory of the 1960s so attractive in retrospect.

215 REYNER BANHAM
from ''The Italian Retreat from Modern Architecture'' (1959)

This purposely provocative essay by the relatively unknown British critic Reyner Banham, which appeared in the journal *The Architectural Review*, made its author an instant international celebrity (if something less positive in Italy). Banham still had his connections with the New Brutalist movement, and he was on the eve of publishing his first book, *Theory and Design in the First Machine Age* (1960). Because the leading topic of this study was the Italian Futurist movement, Banham, in carrying out his research in 1950s Italy, had been a close observer of the Italian scene. Although his phrase ''retreat'' is directed first and foremost at Paolo Portoghesi's recent discussion of the ''Neoliberty'' movement, Banham also has in mind the various attempts within British theory to endow postwar modernism with a ''classical'' aura. For Banham, European modernism defined an unbridgeable break from the past. The machine – from the automobile to the modern-day vacuum cleaner or refrigerator – had changed everything, and thus any attempt to probe pre-modern theory was a rejection of the present reality. Hence the Italian Futurists were correct in hypothesizing the start of a new cultural era, and their machine-age idealism should be the only legacy for modernists to uphold today – albeit in a transformed ''Second Machine Age.'' The severity of this attack is what makes this essay so controversial and historically noteworthy. The ''Liberty'' period refers to Italian architecture at the turn of the twentieth century, and the ''Neoliberty'' to an Italian movement of the 1950s to revisit elements of this style.

The present baffling turn taken by Milanese and Torinese architecture probably appears the more baffling to ourselves, viewing it from the wrong side of the Alps, because of the irrelevant hopes, the non-Italian aspirations of our own, that we have tended to project on Italian architecture since the war. Without realizing what we were doing, we built up a mythical architecture that we would like to see in our own countries, an architecture of social responsibility – stemming, we believed, from such political martyrs as Persico, Banfi, the younger Labo – and of formal architectonic purity – stemming from Lingeri, Figini, Terragni. This architecture, socially and aesthetically acceptable to men of goodwill, we saw embodied in particular in the Milanese *BBPR* partnership, of which the first *B* was the martyred Banfi, the terminal *R* was Ernesto Rogers, the hero-figure of European architecture in the late Forties and early Fifties.

The evidence of the eyes often contradicted the myth; again and again the architectonic qualities that we sought were to be found in work of the Roman school, notably (and

Reyner Banham, from ''The Italian Retreat from Modern Architecture,'' in *Architectural Review* 125 (April 1959), pp. 231–2, 235.

surprisingly) in the work of Moretti, whom the Milanese would brush off as 'not socially serious' while the awkward questions of modern eclecticism raised by the work of Luigi Vagnetti had a way of being unformulable except in terms that put Milan on the spot as well. Nevertheless, our hopes continued to reside in Milan, in the *Triennale*, in *QT8*, in the *Compasso d'Oro*, in *Communità*, in *Domus* and, even more, in *Casabella Continuità*, Persico's famous magazine of the Thirties revived under Rogers's editorship.

But when *Casabella* began to publish, with manifest editorial approval, buildings that went far beyond Vagnetti's in historicist eclecticism, when the BBPR partnership staged for the London Furniture Exhibition of 1958 an Italian section that seemed to be little more than a hymn of praise to Milanese *borghese* taste at its queasiest and most cowardly, and when, finally, the Italian exhibit at the Brussels Exhibition was seen, then confusion followed hard on disillusion. But behind our own private reactions there remain the buildings that produced them, and the attitude that produced the buildings, an attitude that even other Italians, like Bruno Zevi, clearly regard as wrong-headed and misguided. Indeed, these recent works of Gae Aulenti, Gregotti, Meneghotti, Stoppino, Gabetti, their associates and followers, and the polemics advanced in their defence by Aldo Rossi and others – all these call the whole status of the Modern Movement in Italy in question.

[...]

Paolo Portoghesi seems to have been the first to call the style of the Retreat by the apt term 'Neoliberty' as late as the end of 1958, but the Liberty content of the style has been clear from the start, and underlines the fact that this is not just an isolated piece of juvenilia (the Neolibertarians are all young) but something for which the whole body of Italian modernism must share the blame. For more than three years now, leading architectural periodicals in both Milan and Rome have been working over the remaining monuments of Art Nouveau in a degree of detail that bespeaks a more than historical interest. Works of Gaudi, Sullivan, d'Aronco, Horta, and the Viennese school, in particular, have been described and illustrated even to the extent of the original drawings and colour-blocks of their exteriors, supported by texts that were far less expository or explanatory, than they were eulogistic and rhetorical.

Where the oddity of this situation struck the present writer most forcibly was in the way in which Italian writers dealt with Sant'Elia, playing down his Futurism, playing down his influence on later architects, but emphasizing his *origini Liberty*.

[...]

Now a justification of Neoliberty on the basis that Milanese *borghese* life is still what it was in 1900 is indeed implied in the polemics of Aldo Rossi. But it will not wash, because that life is not at all what it was at the beginning of the century, as Marinetti, with his fanatical automobilism, already recognized *in Milan* in 1909, Art Nouveau died of a cultural revolution that seems absolutely irreversible: the domestic revolution that began with electric cookers, vacuum cleaners, the telephone, the gramophone, and all those other mechanized aids to gracious living that are still invading the home, and have permanently altered the nature of domestic life and the meaning of domestic architecture.

[...]

But all such justifications are marginal; the lasting significance of the revolution put in hand in 1907 is that it has given Western architecture the courage to look forward, not back, to stop reviving the forms of any sort of past, middle-class or otherwise. The performance of the revolutionaries may not have matched their promise, but the promise remains and is real. It is the promise of liberty, not *Liberty* or 'Neoliberty,' the promise of freedom from having to wear the discarded clothes of previous cultures, even if those previous cultures have the air of *tempi felici*. To want to put on those old clothes again is to be, in Marinetti's words describing Ruskin, like a man who has attained full physical maturity, yet wants to sleep in his cot again, to be suckled again by his decrepit nurse, in order to regain the nonchalance of his childhood. Even by the purely local standards of Milan and Turin, then, Neoliberty is infantile regression.

216   ERNESTO NATHAN ROGERS
from "The Evolution of Architecture: An Answer to the Caretaker of Frigidaires" (1959)

B anham had published his contentious essay on the "Italian Retreat" in April 1959, and the architect Ernesto Rogers, the editor of the *Casabella-Continuità*, wasted little time in responding to Banham's charges in the June edition of his journal. He begins by acknowledging that the Englishman's article "created quite a fuss in this country," and he goes on to compose a strong rebuttal to Banham's "inconsequential" remarks – in defense of his Italian colleagues. Rogers's point is succinct and explicit. Modernism should be a "continuous revolution" and in its natural transformation it must respond to the specific culture and place of its creation. Moreover, modernism should not and cannot be restricted to some orthodox set of design beliefs; it has its own history, one that must be mediated with the present. Architects must retain the right and indeed the freedom to explore such nuances. Modern architecture in Italy is therefore not in retreat; it is moving ahead.

The Modern Movement is not dead at all for us: our modernity consists in actually carrying on the tradition of the Masters (of course, Wright's tradition as well). But our being sensitive to the beauty (and not only to the documentary values) of a number of manifestations which hitherto had not been sufficiently appreciated, is certainly to our credit. And it is also to our credit to have given a historical framework and a present-day meaning to a number of values which had been neglected in the thick of other battles.

[...]

It is by no chance that Ridolfi, Gardella, B. B. P. R., Albini, Samonà, Michelucci, and Piccinato, among the most ardent defenders of modernity, are no longer doing what they used to and for this very reason are coherent. Hasn't Mr. Banham wondered why? One can hardly believe that these persons and many others have all and at the same time become

Ernesto Nathan Rogers, from "The Evolution of Architecture: An Answer to the Caretakers of Frigidaires," in *Casabella-Continuità* 228 (June 1959), addendum, pp. v, vi.

so irresponsible as to renounce the victories which they had so laboriously achieved. Their strength lies in the very fact that they understood the Modern movement as a "continuous revolution", that is to say, as the continuous development of the principle of adhering to the changing content of life.

Gradually, the thematic material was enriched and as a consequence, the requirements became more subtle; thus, too, the formal results became more difficult, because they tried to include greater and greater numbers of propositions: the enlargement of the range of architectonic problems and the immediate results of critical thought, the historical revision of all movements and styles, especially of those nearer to us in order of time, which, owing to the normal opposition arising from the dialectical clash of generations, had been distorted.

One understood better even (and why not?) the Liberty style, in which there were still energies to rescue and to canalize.

That the Liberty style should not only be considered in its historical framework, as the ancestor of modernism, but in the light of its own values, is moreover so necessary an observation that as a young student I based a thesis on it for my degree.

What is there to be so frightened about?

There is no doubt that we should look at past experiences (all of them), of course without allowing ourselves to be seduced by them, as, unfortunately it happens to someone – and I am the first to admit that.

However slow and elaborate this complex process of review, it has been misunderstood by those less experienced in the field; they have received a shock, but it must be acknowledged that this process may have made even the more experienced overlook a number of cultural components (such as technology) to which they had devoted much more attention at other times. But progress is the result of choice and suspension of judgement, which at any moment may be guilty of incompleteness. Progress is paid for in errors, but I am convinced that the few dangers which Italian architecture risks are quite evident to us even without the arrogant prodding of Mr. Banham, the caretaker of frigidaires, who really believes that "the domestic revolution... began with electric cookers, vacuum cleaners, the telephone, the gramophone, and all those other mechanized aids to gracious living that are still invading the home and have permanently altered the nature of domestic life and the meaning of domestic architecture". We may as well add the mixer which we can use to mix a cocktail of all the other revolutions, the "milestones" of which were, according to him, the "Manifesto of Futurism, the European discovery of Frank Lloyd Wright, Adolf Loos' *Ornament and Crime*, Herman Muthesius's lecture to the Werkbund Congress of 1911, the achievement of fully Cubist painting, and so forth". All this cocktail needs is a pinch of salt.

[...]

No one has stopped; for the masters themselves one might paradoxically paraphrase Nietzsche's aphorism: "He ill repays his own master who remains his disciple".

This applies all the more appropriately to us, for we have no desire to freeze up in any servile dogmatism.

If everything that does not follow in the wake of a scholastic modernism or rashly avoids falling into formalistic bluster were to be considered Neoliberty, then we are in great and good company.

But if Neoliberty is a tendency to follow too closely the steps of Liberty itself, then we should give the right framework to a small picture the figures of which are represented in Italy by a few young architects who are – I hope – sufficiently aware that they do not embody the whole of Italian architecture. And it is also to be hoped that they will soon realize that they have fallen into a needless error.

To conclude, I would suggest that Mr. Banham, who I imagine is much more familiar with English than Italian, read Ruskin directly (*The Poetry of Architecture*), for Ruskin was a great Englishman, without there being any need to adopt the discarded interpretation of Marinetti who was a Fascist "revolutionary" who died with the academic cocked hat: "We shall consider the architecture of Nations as it is influenced by their feelings and manners, as it is connected with the scenary in which it is found, and with the skies under which it was erected".

He will find in it some suggestions as to the evolution of architecture.

217 ALDO VAN EYCK
from ''Is Architecture Going to Reconcile Basic Values?'' (1959)

I f there was a new direction defined by a Team 10 member at Otterlo, it was to be found in this talk given by Aldo van Eyck, during which he presented his recently completed Amsterdam Orphanage. Van Eyck had long stood apart from his British colleagues in Team 10 in several important respects. A native of the Netherlands, he had been trained in Zurich at the Swiss Federal Institute of Technology (ETH), and while there he had befriended Carola Giedion-Welcker, the wife of Sigfried Giedion, and gained an appreciation for avant-garde art. In the early 1950s he made several excursions to the sub-Saharan regions of Algeria and Mali, where he studied in particular the local cultures and unique architecture of Dogon tribes. This strong anthropological bent, sharpened by his appreciation for the structuralist theories of Claude Lévi-Strauss, strongly colored his architectural outlook, and his Amsterdam Orphanage, with its nuanced geometry and small-scale breakdown of spaces, was immediately recognized as an innovative masterpiece of design. In his architecture van Eyck shunned displays of technology in favor of an emphasis on ''place'' and the occasions of human experience they allow.

There was a time not so long ago when the minds of men moved along a deterministic groove; let's call it a Euclidian groove. It coloured their behaviour and vision, what they made and did and what they felt. Then some very keen men, with delicate antennae – painters, poets, philosophers and scientists most of them – jumped out of this groove and rubbed the deterministic patina off the surface of reality. They saw wonderful things and did not fail to tell us about them. Our unbounded gratitude is due to them: to Picasso, Klee, Mondrian and Brancusi; to Joyce, Le Corbusier, Schönberg, Bergson and Einstein, to the whole wonderful

Aldo van Eyck, from ''Is Architecture Going to Reconcile Basic Values?,'' opening passage cited from *CIAM '59 in Otterlo*, ed. Oscar Newman. Stuttgart: Karl Krämer Verlag, 1961, p. 26–7.

gang. They set the great top spinning again and expanded the universe – the outside and the inside universe. It was a wonderful riot – the cage was again opened.

But society still moves along in the old groove, making only sly use of what these men discovered; worse still, applying on a purely technical, mechanical, and decorative level, not the essence but what was gleaned from it in order to give pretense of moving more effectively, but in reality moving securely and profitably along the old circumscribed groove. We know all this. But do we also know that architecture has been doing the same for the last 30 years?

A damnable truth this. When are architects going to stop fondling technique for its own sake – stop stumbling after progress? When are they really going to join the riot and stop gnawing at the edges of a great idea? Surely we cannot permit them to continue selling the diluted essence of what others spent a life-time finding. They have betrayed society in betraying the essence of contemporary thought. Nobody can really live in what they concoct, although they may think so.

Now what is wonderful about this non-Euclidian idea – this other vision – is that it is contemporary; contemporary to all our difficulties social and political, economic and spiritual. What is tragic is that we have failed to see that it alone can solve them. Each period requires a constituent language – an instrument with which to tackle the human problems posed by the period, as well as those which, from period to period, remain the same, i.e. those posed by man – by all of us as a primordial being. The time has come to gather the old into the new; to rediscover the archaic principles of human nature.

To discover anew implies discovering something new. Translate this into architecture and you'll get new architecture – real contemporary architecture. Architecture is a constant rediscovering of constant human proportions translated into space. Man is always and everywhere essentially the same. He has the same mental equipment though he uses it differently according to his cultural or social background, according to the particular life pattern of which he happens to be a part. Modern architecture has been harping continually on what is different in our time to such an extent even that it has lost touch with what is not different, with what is always essentially the same. This grave mistake was not made by the poets, painters and sculptors. On the contrary, they never narrowed down experience. They enlarged and intensified it; tore down not merely the form barriers as did the architects, but the emotional ones as well. In fact the language they evolved coincides with the emotional revolution they brought about. The language architects evolved, however, and this after the pioneering period was over, coincides only with itself and is therefore essentially sterile and academic – literally abstract. We must evolve a richer tool – a more effective way of approach – to solve the environmental problems our period poses today. These problems will not remain the same, but they concern the same man, and that is our cue.

Is architecture going to reconcile basic values? In each culture there are things universally valid which for some reason or other – climate, tradition, taboos – are emphasized whilst others are subdued. Man suffers in many ways from these restrictions; from what is over-emphasized at the cost of what is omitted and often forgotten. Now, surely, what is peculiar in a culture – what gives it the colour – does not necessarily have to depend on what is omitted and what is not. It can depend on how things are combined instead of on what things are omitted or overstressed. Today we can travel to the remotest places and if we can't, we can buy a pocket-book and bring them close. We can meet "ourselves" everywhere – in all places and ages – doing the same things in a different way, feeling the same differently, reacting differently to the same.

218   JOSEPH RYKWERT
from "Meaning and Building" (1960)

A very lucid chime within the sometimes fractious atmosphere of the 1960s is this seminal essay by Joseph Rykwert. A native of Poland, the refugee Rykwert trained in London during the 1940s and developed an early interest in the classical ideas of Rudolf Wittkower as well as those of Sigfried Giedion. During the 1950s, however, he began to spend more of his time in Italy, where he found a harmonious chord in the theoretical discussions taking place there. Drawing upon these varied influences, Rykwert became a sharp critic not only of the overly rationalist approaches of International Style functionalists, but also of the pop-art-inspired, technocratic infatuations of the Brutalist movement in Britain – leaving him to dwell on the meaning of architecture from a rigorously anthropological and quasi-phenomenological perspective. He arrived at these views around 1960 in parallel with the similar soundings of Aldo van Eyck – at this time his closest intellectual accomplice. He would later address the problem of "meaning" from the perspective of symbolism.

The attitude I have just described is familiar enough in Anglo-Saxon countries: it is the attitude of the technocrats and administrators of architecture, of zoners and curtain-wallers. It is very much the majority attitude.

But even technocrats, if they are conscientious are finding it increasingly difficult to give their undivided loyalty to the 'Functional City' and the 'Minimum Dwelling'. Even architects are beginning to realize that the people for whom they build are not physiological automata with brains attached, but complex beings moved by irrational urges. Anyone who claims to be on the side of reason but chooses to ignore this state of affairs, or deny it actively is an idealist. The word 'rationalism' has for too long been associated with such an immoderate ideology, which seemed to rob humanity of all qualities except that of analytical thinking. This of course has now provoked an opposite ideology – based on an appeal to emotion which ignores the claims of reason. As one of Diderot's characters summed up: " . . . we don't really know what we do or want, so that we follow our fancy – which we call reason, or our reason – which is often nothing but a dangerous fancy, that sometimes turns out well, and sometimes badly . . .".

And therefore some of my contemporaries, (and I with them) would argue that the preoccupation of designers and architects with rational criteria has devalued their achievements and cut them off from a mass public, so that now architecture cannot command public support or consent because it has lost the power of touching emotion.

Joseph Rykwert, from "Meaning in Building," in *Zodiac* 6 (1960), pp. 193, 195.

"We do not have the ultimate power yet, because the people is not behind us" Paul Klee said many years ago.

To restate my theme: architects must acknowledge the emotional power of their work; this recognition depends on the methodical investigation of a content, even of a referential content in architecture. I believe this to be the most important and difficult problem which the architects of my generation will have to force next; and so, I can not offer more than a tentative programme.

[. . .]

The designer's responsibility then, whether he knows it or not, is to create order not only in terms of a sensible arrangement of physical function, but also out of the all-but-living objects which we use and inhabit.

Is this abstract discourse not pitching the argument too high? Now that discarding clothes, cars, houses as soon as they have passed from immediate fashion has become a moral duty in some places, is this not demanding too primitive an attitude to inanimate things? Surely – you may ask – we will no longer project in this way onto our environment, now it has become so impermanent?

I think we will. In any case, whether we finally arrive at an economy of total overproduction or not, certain realities will be with us for an indefinite time yet. Let me be quite commonplace. Consider a man returning from work. He should come to his house in the full knowledge that he is returning home. How is he to be assured in this knowledge? By a straight-forward association, some will say. By having inhabited it long enough, bred his children in it, by being physically at ease there. If you have followed my argument, you will agree that all this will not be enough: what a man requires of his house is convinction that he is, in some sense, at the centre af the universe, that his home mediates between him and all the confusing and threatening world outside; that in some definite place the world is summed up for him in a place which is his, all his shelter and his castle.

So each one of the semi-detached houses which make up those wastes of suburbia round British cities will display somewhere a little piece of castellation, and the American equivalent will have odd token survivals from pioneer ranches. No wonder that they are not anonymous apartment, however superior that may be. All the important economic considerations are often ignored – what sways people finally may really be that little piece of castellation or the fretwork on the gable.

[. . .]

Here all the threads I have toyed with: psychology and anthropology, perception study and ergonomics come together at last, to be given a form. What that form shall be can only be worked out in time. But I believe that we have come to the end of a non-figurative architecture, and that we must now look to the scattered material which psychologists and anthropologists have been gathering. Not only myth and poetry, but the fantasies of psychopaths await our investigation. All the elements of our work: pavement, threshold, door, window, wall, roof, house, factory, school – all these have their poetry; and it is a poetry we must learn to draw from the programmes our clients hand us. Not to impose it by a cheap melodramatization, but spell it from the commonplace elements which we fit together.

It would be impardonable bungling and amateurishness to leave a matter of this importance to intuition – like leaving the functioning of the plan to luck. Intuition must be followed where method fails, of course – but the age demands, and demands rightly that we should acknowledge the unconscious element in man through our methods of work and make it a criterion of the workability of our buildings. If anyone objects that such an attitude is impractical. I would beg them to consider American advertising, a highly organized and still growing industry. An increasing proportion of the huge sum – large enough to float most European countries – which is devoted yearly to persuade Americans to spend more than they need, goes on to motivation research and its variants. Which means that it is being spent to harness the findings of psychologists to selling methods; translated into realistic terms, it is the deliberate sharpening of neurotic tendencies: anxiety and inferiority, loneliness fears, auto-eroticism, repression, infantilism – and all the others so that they may be assuaged or averted by some quite superfluous product which the advertiser offers. 'Luxe' – superfluity, gratuitousness – elevated into a moral value, as it is with us, becomes insufferably boring through attrition.

I am not here making a political judgement. We in Europe have not advanced in motivation research as far as the Americans, and I am sure that the psychological pressures in communist countries are equally sharp, perhaps even more inviduous. But American advertising offers a useful instance, because the methods of the 'symbol-manipulators', as American advertising men call themselves, are almost the exact opposite of what I believe the architect's task to be: to make every building an integrating, reconciling and cleansing form.

Through a semantic study of environment we can discover the means of discoursing in our buildings. Only that way will we be able to appeal to the common man again.

219 TOMÁS MALDONADO
from "Notes on Communication"
(1962)

Germany emerged from World War II in a condition of near-complete destruction. Not only were many of its major cities physically destroyed or severely damaged, but its entire infrastructure of industry, agriculture, and education lay in tatters. One new school of design created in this void was the Hochschule für Gestaltung (HfG) in Ulm. Its founding director was the Swiss architect Max Bill, who in the early 1950s built a series of factory-like buildings to house the complex. He then implemented a program based on the curriculum of the Bauhaus. Bill was ousted as the director in a faculty revolt in 1957 and replaced by a triumvirate headed by the Argentine painter Tomás Maldonado. On the surface, Maldonado's pedagogical philosophy of "scientific operationalism" – in its rejection of all aesthetic considerations and in the emphasis placed on economics and technological rationalism – was similar to that of Hannes Meyer in 1928. Nevertheless, his abstract restructuring of the school into programs of industrial design and visual and verbal communication at the same time created a laboratory for

Tomás Maldonado, from "Notes on Communication," in *Uppercase*, 5, ed. Theo Crosby. London: Whitefriars Press, pp. 6, 7.

imaginative ideas, into which a number of prominent thinkers – among them Charles and Ray Eames, Buckminster Fuller, Konrad Wachsmann, Joseph Rykwert, and Christian Norberg-Schulz – brought their design ideas. In 1958 Maldonado, together with Gui Bonsiepe, began to offer courses on communication or semiotics, in which they, in drawing upon the efforts of the Institute of Design in Chicago in the 1940s, resurrected the earlier research of Charles Morris, C. S. Peirce, and Ernst Cassirer. Outside of the studies of Sergio Bettini and Giovanni Klaus Koenig in Italy, this was one of the first efforts to view architecture less as a series of forms responding to abstract functions and more as a complex language of signs or symbols. The publication of "Notes on Communication" in the London journal *Uppercase* by Theo Crosby is important in itself because it introduces such an approach into another architectural culture awaiting a fresh start.

Among many possible ways to understand communication, and therefore to become interested in it, is the technical kind which, directly or indirectly, mostly influences our daily life. The invention, development and improvement of the most effective instrumental resources which we have nowadays at our disposal to transmit messages (telegraphy, telephony, radio, teletype, television and radar) are the result of this strictly technical way to understand communication; i.e. the way to understand communication as a physical system – and only physical, which has to be optimized. This applies to the specialists in telecommunication, and to most of the information theorists principally interested to know 'how' one can transmit, never – or very seldom – 'what' is to be transmitted. Therefore it is concerned with a non-semantic and non-pragmatic interest in communicative phenomena.

There exists, however, also an interest in communicative phenomena which is not purely technical, but semantic and pragmatic; an interest which is not orientated towards the problems of physical optimalization of messages, but towards the problems of individual and collective use (and misuse) of these messages. In this case, it is the human communicative behaviour, both individual and collective, which lies in the centre of interest. The 'meaning', put into brackets by the specialists in telecommunication, and the information theorists, is converted into a factor which must be studied to its most subtle implications. In this semantic and pragmatic interest participate linguists, psychologists, social psychologists and sociologists; and also, of course, the representatives of modern semiotics.
[. . .]
Therefore the immediate task can only be to investigate – always with the above-mentioned methodological rigour – the totality of the communicative processes in our society as well those which we judge normal as those which we call pathological.

It is only a study of this kind which must provide the knowledge and experience about those things which are done today and which will be avoided tomorrow, as well as those things which are not done today and which will be favoured tomorrow.

220 COLIN ROWE AND ROBERT SLUTZKY
from "Transparency: Literal and Phenomenal" (1963 [1955])

Within the context of the mid-1950s – when this essay was written but not published – this analysis of "Transparency" by Colin Rowe and Robert Slutzky must be read in light of Rowe's earlier studies under Rudolf Wittkower and Slutzky's graduate work under Josef Albers. It also owes something to Henry-Russell Hitchcock's *Painting toward Architecture* (1948), which viewed the architecture of the 1920s as conceptually and often visually indistinguishable from the experiments of Cubist, Purist, and De Stijl painters. Rowe and Slutzky were both on the faculty of the University of Texas at Austin in the mid-1950s, and formed a cadre of faculty innovators later branded "The Texas Rangers."

Within the context of its publication date of 1964, this essay had little noticeable impact – except in contributing to the fermentation of ideas that would only come to the fore at the end of the decade. In retrospect, "Transparency" is a landmark essay of architectural thought, the article in which Rowe and Slutzky famously challenge the earlier contentions of Sigfried Giedion with respect to Walter Gropius and offer up their counter-notion of "phenomenal" transparency – "when a painter seeks the articulated presentation of frontally displayed objects in a shallow, abstracted space." Their prime example for this is Le Corbusier's villa at Garches. The essay thus becomes seminal in development of formalism in the 1970s, in which a building can be analyzed simply as an autonomous, complex visual entity without regard to function.

In Picasso's *L'Arlésienne*, the picture that provides the visual support for these inferences, such a transparency of overlapping planes is very obviously to be found. There Picasso offers planes apparently of Celluloid, through which the observer has the sensation of looking; and in doing so, no doubt his sensations are somewhat similar to those of a hypothetical observer of the workshop wing at the Bauhaus. In each case a transparency of materials is discovered. But in the laterally constructed space of his picture, Picasso, through the compilation of larger and smaller forms, offers the limitless possibilities of alternative readings, while the glass wall at the Bauhaus, an unambiguous space, seems to be singularly free of this quality. Thus, for evidence of what we have designated phenomenal transparency, we shall be obliged to look elsewhere.

[. . .]

At Garches the recessed surface of the ground floor is redefined on the roof by the two freestanding walls which terminate the terrace; and the same statement of depth is taken up in the side elevations by the glazed doors which act as conclusions to the fenestration. In these ways Le Corbusier proposes the idea that immediately behind his glazing there lies a narrow slot of space traveling parallel to it; and of course, in consequence of this, he implies a further idea – that bounding this slot of space, and behind it, there lies a plane of which the ground floor, the freestanding walls, and the inner reveals of the doors all form a part; and

Colin Rowe and Robert Slutzky, from "Transparency: Literal and Phenomenal" (1963 [1955]), cited from *Transparency*. Basel: Birkhäuser, 1997, pp. 34–5, 37–8.

although this plane may be dismissed as very obviously a conceptual convenience rather than a physical fact, its obtrusive presence is undeniable. Recognizing the physical plane of glass and concrete and this imaginary (though scarcely less real) plane that lies behind it, we become aware that here a transparency is effected not through the agency of a window but rather through our being made conscious of primary concepts which "interpenetrate without optical destruction of each other".

These two planes are not all; a third and equally distinct parallel surface is both introduced and implied. It defines the rear wall of the terrace and the penthouse, and is further reiterated by other parallel dimensions: the parapets of the garden stairs, the terrace, and the second-floor balcony. Each of these planes is incomplete in itself or perhaps even fragmentary; yet it is with these parallel planes as points of reference that the façade is organized, and the implication of all is of a vertical, layerlike stratification of the interior space of the building, a succession of laterally extended spaces traveling one behind the other.

This system of spatial stratification brings Le Corbusier's façade into the closest relationship with the Léger we have already examined. In *Three Faces* Léger conceives of his canvas as a field modeled in low relief. Of his three major panels (which overlap, dovetail, and alternatively comprise and exclude each other), two are closely implicated in an almost equivalent depth relationship, while the third constitutes a *coulisse* disclosing a location which both advances and recedes. At Garches, Le Corbusier replaces Léger's concern for the picture plane with a most highly developed regard for the frontal viewpoint (the preferred views include only the slightest deviations from parallel perspective); Léger's canvas becomes Le Corbusier's second plane; other planes are either imposed upon, or subtracted from, this basic datum. Deep space is contrived in similar coulisse fashion with the façade cut open and depth inserted in the ensuing slot.

One might infer that at Garches, Le Corbusier had indeed succeeded in alienating architecture from its necessary three-dimensional existence, and in order to qualify this analysis, some discussion of the building's internal space is necessary.

221 CHRISTIAN NORBERG-SCHULZ
from *Intentions in Architecture* (1963)

One of the first individuals to make use of communication theory and semiotics was the Norwegian architect Christian Norberg-Schulz, who had studied under Sigfried Giedion in Zurich and Mies van der Rohe at the Illinois Institute of Technology. Norberg-Schulz also drew upon Gestalt psychology, the educational theories of Jean Piaget, and structuralism in this highly ambitious attempt to define the outlines of "a satisfactory *theory of architecture*." In many respects, this approach resembles many of the German theorists of the 1880s and 1890s in their attempt to view architecture in more scientific terms as a problem of perception or semantics. Then again, Norberg-Schulz, with his disciplined methodological spirit, was responding to the seemingly chaotic situation of

Christian Norberg-Schulz, from *Intentions in Architecture*. Cambridge, MA: MIT Press, 1965, pp. 22–3.

architectural theory in the early 1960s. Norberg-Schulz's approach to the problem would later evolve, but this book nevertheless had a huge impact on architectural thinking in this decade.

In general we may say that architecture is a human *product* which should order and improve our relations with the environment. It is therefore necessary to investigate how human products are brought forth. Hence we should ask: *What purpose has architecture as a human product*? The functional-practical, the milieu-creating and the symbolizing aspects constitute three possible answers to the question, all of which have to be investigated more closely, and which should, if necessary, be supplemented with other factors.

If we return to the layman, we may assert that architecture undoubtedly concerns him in many *different* ways. Our life consists of changing activities which demand changing surroundings. This implies that the environment will 'look' different according to our immediate state or 'role'. To take into consideration this relative and variable relation between man and his environment, it is necessary to stress the question: *How does architecture (the environment) influence us*? It is a truism to say that the environment influences us and determines our 'mood'. That architecture is a part of our environment is just as evident. If we take this point of departure, architecture has not only an instrumental purpose, but also a psychological function. The question could also be put in this way: In what outer circumstances do we have this or that particular experience? And further we shall ask: Do we always have the same experiences in similar outer circumstances? From everyday experience we know that the last question has to be answered in the negative. We do know that we might have very different experiences although the surroundings remain the same. A known object may suddenly appear completely different, and we may say that we have become alive to another of its aspects. Does this relativism mean that architecture only plays a minor role as a background for our daily activities, and at the most, may induce certain 'sentiments'? And if this is the case, does it necessarily have to be like this? Anyway it is evident that the relationship between man and his environment is not as simple as it may seem at first sight. We therefore have to investigate more closely how we really perceive the world around us. A better understanding of this process may also help us to grasp what it means to 'experience architecture' in the changing situations of daily life. It is possible to learn to experience architecture, and the architects need such a training. That the public 'learns to see' is also necessary if we want to increase the respect for architecture and to bridge the gap between the professional man and his client.

To give the questions about the purpose and effects of architecture a basis, it is necessary to inquire whether particular forms ought to be correlated with particular tasks. We thus have to ask: *Why has a building from a particular period a particular form*? This is the central problem in architectural history as well as in architectural theory. We do not intend that the study of history should lead to a new historicism based on a copying of the forms of the past. The information given by history should above all illustrate the relations between problems and solutions, and thus furnish an empirical basis for further work. If we take our way of putting the problem as a point of departure for an investigation of architecture's (changing) role in society, a new and rich field of study is laid open. Today the so-called analytical explanations of works of architecture are usually rather dubious.

To render an account of *why* a building 'looks' as it does, we should first have to *describe* it in an accurate and illuminating way. We here again return to the demand for a well-defined and coherent terminology. This terminology should not only have a logical structure; it should also be empirically founded to enable us to order our subject-matter in a convenient way. We thus have to develop a conceptual scheme which makes it possible to answer the question: *What does 'architectural form' mean?* This is logically related to the preceding question. In both cases we have to study the relations between corresponding structures in different fields. Firstly we should 'translate' a practical-psychological-social-cultural situation into architecture, and subsequently the architecture into descriptive terms. In doing this, we are treating the relation between building task and architectural solution, which is the core of our problem.

222   CHRISTOPHER ALEXANDER
from *Notes on a Synthesis of Form* (1964)

Another highly ambitious attempt to bring a more scientific bearing to architecture was Christopher Alexander's first book *Notes on a Synthesis of Form*. Alexander was born in Austria, educated in England, and received his Ph.D. from Harvard, based upon the doctoral research (both mathematical and architectural) summarized in this book. The premise of this complex study is simple: architectural design has grown too complex and specialized in its variables to be mastered efficiently, and Alexander seeks a methodology of diagrams and set-theory equations to quantify and organize its variables. At first blush this might sound like functionalism in its purest form, but Alexander is more interested in the psychological and anthropological factors to be considered in design. The fact that this methodology is proposed just as the first computers are coming on line is hardly coincidental. Alexander's methodology, like that of Norberg-Schulz, would undergo a transformation, but once again the book was cogent within the changing architectural climate.

The use of logical structures to represent design problems has an important consequence. It brings with it the loss of innocence. A logical picture is easier to criticize than a vague picture since the assumptions it is based on are brought out into the open. Its increased precision gives us the chance to sharpen our conception of what the design process involves. But once what we do intuitively can be described and compared with nonintuitive ways of doing the same things, we cannot go on accepting the intuitive method innocently. Whether we decide to stand for or against pure intuition as a method, we must do so for reasons which can be discussed.

I wish to state my belief in this loss of innocence very clearly, because there are many designers who are apparently not willing to accept the loss. They insist that design must be a purely intuitive process: that it is hopeless to try and understand it sensibly because its problems are too deep.

Christopher Alexander, from *Notes on a Synthesis of Form* (1964), cited from the 1971 edition. Cambridge, MA: Harvard University Press, pp. 8–9.

There has already been one loss of innocence in the recent history of design; the discovery of machine tools to replace hand craftsmen. A century ago William Morris, the first man to see that the machines were being misused, also retreated from the loss of innocence. Instead of accepting the machine and trying to understand its implications for design, he went back to making exquisite handmade goods. It was not until Gropius started his Bauhaus that designers came to terms with the machine and the loss of innocence which it entailed.

Now we are at a second watershed. This time the loss of innocence is intellectual rather than mechanical. But again there are people who are trying to pretend that it has not taken place. Enormous resistance to the idea of systematic processes of design is coming from people who recognize correctly the importance of intuition, but then make a fetish of it which excludes the possibility of asking reasonable questions.

223 STANFORD ANDERSON
from "Architecture and Tradition That Isn't 'Trad, Dad'" (1964)

Yet another voice within the theoretical atmosphere of the 1960s was Stanford Anderson, in this paper first presented to a seminar at the Architectural Association in 1963. The first object of Anderson's critique, as the first passage notes, is Reyner Banham's deterministic regard for technology as the "converse of tradition," but Anderson's argument is actually broader. Drawing upon the philosophy of Karl Popper, Anderson invokes tradition as the necessary context within which any critical debate must be framed, an interpretative context into which the findings of sociology, psychology, and biology can be assimilated. Architecture, therefore, is not and never can be a rigorous science, but it is a continually moving or evolving set of assumptions under critical scrutiny. The paper was re-presented at a seminar held at the Cranbrook Academy in 1964.

Traditionalism, in the sense of seeking to maintain the status quo, has been traditionally, and rightly, combatted by most twentieth-century architects. But, having rejected the authority of tradition, modern architects have then sought a new authority. Most commonly, architects have claimed to find that authority in science or technology. To cite a recent example of such theorising, Dr. Reyner Banham argues that technology "represents the converse of tradition", warns architects to throw themselves wholeheartedly into technology – or else, and summarizes his position as follows: "For the first time in history the world of *what is* is suddenly torn by the discovery that *what could be* is no longer dependent on *what was*."

Between the extremes of traditionalistic "tombstone polishing" and a "compulsive progressivist reflex," the present paper seeks to establish an interpretation of tradition that will recognize our debt to the past without establishing the past as an authority. Furthermore, this paper will encourage a radical adaptation of the methods of scientific

Stanford Anderson, from "Architecture and Tradition That Isn't 'Trad, Dad'" (1964), cited from *The History, Theory and Criticism of Architecture*, ed. Marcus Whiffen. Cambridge, MA: MIT Press, 1965, pp. 71, 78–9.

discovery with neither the implication of a scientific determinism nor the advocacy of leaping on the latest bandwagon.

[. . .]

The Futurists did want to ride the waves of a turbulent and exciting body called "science". As earlier artists derived symbolic and aesthetic stimuli from antique myth or from Christianity, and as certain contemporary artists were stimulated by primitive art and myth, so the Futurists founded their aesthetic on the excitement which they felt for science and technology. In each case, external stimuli are incorporated into certain artistic traditions. The Futurists too retained traditional artistic mediums such as poetry, painting, sculpture, and architecture. Sant'Elia's earlier work evidences formal influences from the contemporary suburban houses of Paris, from the *Sezessionstil* of Vienna, and perhaps also from Mackintosh and Frank Lloyd Wright. Some of his later monumental projects differ decisively from the slightly earlier romantic visions of an architect like Anasagasti only by Sant'Elia's rigorous omission of academic detail and his gradual introduction of cannons as operative architectural features. The project for which Sant'Elia is most justly renowned, his *città nuova*, is an instance in which Sant'Elia very inventively posed a problem which had already begun to trouble the Milan of his day – the drastic impingement of the new means of mass transportation on the old concepts and forms of the city. This is to involve one's self in the problem. Especially in an applied art such as architecture, it would be far more radical – if more arduous and less thrilling than surfboarding – to get in and swim. If we were to take a firm grip on theoretical biology and stay with it whatever the consequences, we might, with talent, become theoretical biologists – an excellent consequence unless we had set ourselves the architect's problem of shaping and re-shaping our physical environment. The radical step would be to formulate problems and hypotheses within our own architectural problem situation, and then to criticize and test them as rigorously as our current information and methods permit. As science and technology have been known to profit from science fiction, so architecture could profit from a form of "architectural fiction." But architects must learn not to take such writings and projects as either predictive history or as established theory. Like science fiction, it would bear fruit only when it had been critically assimilated into the problem situation.

224 ROBERT VENTURI
from *Complexity and Contradiction in Architecture* (1966)

F
ew architectural books have had a more immediate or more lasting impact on the profession than Robert Venturi's *Complexity and Contradiction in Architecture*. Its success may be due to several factors. It differs from other architectural books of its time in the variety of extra-architectural ideas that Venturi brings into his investigation – in this case the (mainly literary) sources of William Empson, Cleanth Brooks, T. S. Eliot, and

Robert Venturi, from *Complexity and Contradiction in Architecture*. New York: Museum of Modern Art, pp. 22–3, 48–9.

August Heckscher. It also differs from other books of this period in the historical images of buildings that Venturi presents: from the baroque historicism of Nicholas Hawksmoor to the regional modernism of Alvar Aalto, both of which support his thesis of a "nonstraightforward" mannerist architecture. At the same time it is a book that focuses squarely on the visual language of architectural design, not on its methodology or sociological underpinnings. Venturi's famous retort "Less is a bore" raised a heretical banner of populism as well as signaling a new direction that would soon meet firm resistance. These brief excerpts convey little of a book rich in ideas, which every architectural student should read in full.

I like complexity and contradiction in architecture. I do not like the incoherence or arbitrariness of incompetent architecture nor the precious intricacies of picturesqueness or expressionism. Instead, I speak of a complex and contradictory architecture based on the richness and ambiguity of modern experience, including that experience which is inherent in art. Everywhere, except in architecture, complexity and contradiction have been acknowledged, from Gödel's proof of ultimate inconsistency in mathematics to T. S. Eliot's analysis of "difficult" poetry and Joseph Albers' definition of the paradoxical quality of painting.

But architecture is necessarily complex and contradictory in its very inclusion of the traditional Vitruvian elements of commodity, firmness, and delight. And today the wants of program, structure, mechanical equipment, and expression, even in single buildings in simple contexts, are diverse and conflicting in ways previously unimaginable. The increasing dimension and scale of architecture in urban and regional planning add to the difficulties. I welcome the problems and exploit the uncertainties. By embracing contradiction as well as complexity, I aim for vitality as well as validity.

Architects can no longer afford to be intimidated by the puritanically moral language of orthodox Modern architecture. I like elements which are hybrid rather than "pure," compromising rather than "clean," distorted rather than "straightforward," ambiguous rather than "articulated," perverse as well as impersonal, boring as well as "interesting," conventional rather than "designed," accommodating rather than excluding, redundant rather than simple, vestigial as well as innovating, inconsistent and equivocal rather than direct and clear. I am for messy vitality over obvious unity. I include the non sequitur and proclaim the duality.

I am for richness of meaning rather than clarity of meaning; for the implicit function as well as the explicit function. I prefer "both-and" to "either-or," black and white, and sometimes gray, to black or white. A valid architecture evokes many levels of meaning and combinations of focus: its space and its elements become readable and workable in several ways at once.

But an architecture of complexity and contradiction has a special obligation toward the whole: its truth must be in its totality or its implications of totality. It must embody the difficult unity of inclusion rather than the easy unity of exclusion. More is not less.
[. . .]

I have been referring to one level of order in architecture – that individual order that is related to the specific building it is part of. But there is convention in architecture, and convention can be another manifestation of an exaggeratedly strong order more general in scope. An architect should use convention and make it vivid. I mean he should use convention unconventionally. By convention I mean both the elements and methods of building. Conventional elements are those which are common in their manufacture, form, and use. I do not refer to the sophisticated products of industrial design, which are usually beautiful, but to the vast accumulation of standard, anonymously designed products connected with architecture and construction, and also to commercial display elements which are positively banal or vulgar in themselves and are seldom associated with architecture.

The main justification for honky-tonk elements in architectural order is their very existence. They are what we have. Architects can bemoan or try to ignore them or even try to abolish them, but they will not go away. Or they will not go away for a long time, because architects do not have the power to replace them (nor do they know what to replace them with), and because these commonplace elements accommodate existing needs for variety and communication. The old clichés involving both banality and mess will still be the context of our new architecture, and our new architecture significantly will be the context for them. I am taking the limited view, I admit, but the limited view, which architects have tended to belittle, is as important as the visionary view, which they have tended to glorify but have not brought about. The short-term plan, which expediently combines the old and the new, must accompany the long-term plan. Architecture is evolutionary as well as revolutionary. As an art it will acknowledge what is and what ought to be, the immediate and the speculative.

Historians have shown how architects in the mid-nineteenth century tended to ignore or reject developments in technology when related to structure and methods as unconnected with architecture and unworthy of it; they substituted in turn Gothic Revivalism, Academic revivalism or the Handicraft Movement. Are we today proclaiming advanced technology, while excluding the immediate, vital if vulgar elements which are common to our architecture and landscape? The architect should accept the methods and the elements he already has.

225 ALDO ROSSI
from *The Architecture of the City* (1966)

I f Venturi's book was destined to lay out one course that would have definite appeal to many in the architectural world, Aldo Rossi's book of the same year charts another alternative strategy. Rossi had been slowly preparing his arguments. A graduate of the Polytechnical School in Milan, he began his critical writings at *Casabella-Continuità* in the mid-1950s under the tutelage of Ernesto Rogers. In 1961 he became one of the journal's two editors; at the same time he began his architectural practice under the formal and theoretical influence of Adolf Loos.

Aldo Rossi, from *L'architettura della città*, trans. Diane Ghirardo and Joan Ockman as *The Architecture of the City*. Cambridge, MA: MIT Press, 1984, pp. 29, 32.

The Architecture of the City is, however, a very different animal. For one thing, it is a work of high scholarship and urban geography, rich in sources. Second, it is a polemical work: an important primer for the reintroduction of the concept of a "type" as well as a critique of "naive functionalism." Rossi counters with a study of "urban artifacts": a city's monuments, routes, neighborhoods, and geographical features that define its particular culture or locus. In essence it is a conservative argument, that is to say, an appeal to the timeless urban values that remain the same notwithstanding the changing functions over centuries. It is also a strict reduction of architecture to the syntax of its most essential forms, now nearly emptied of their earlier meaning. The passage is from the first chapter and his discussion of the Palazzo della Ragione in Padua.

Our description of the city will be concerned primarily with its form. This form depends on real facts, which in turn refer to real experiences: Athens, Rome, Paris. The architecture of the city summarizes the city's form, and from this form we can consider the city's problems.

By architecture of the city we mean two different things: first, the city seen as a gigantic man-made object, a work of engineering and architecture that is large and complex and growing over time; second, certain more limited but still crucial aspects of the city, namely urban artifacts, which like the city itself are characterized by their own history and thus by their own form. In both cases architecture clearly represents only one aspect of a more complex reality, of a larger structure; but at the same time, as the ultimate verifiable fact of this reality, it constitutes the most concrete possible position from which to address the problem.

We can understand this more readily by looking at specific urban artifacts, for immediately a series of obvious problems opens up for us. We are also able to perceive certain problems that are less obvious: these involve the quality and the uniqueness of each urban artifact.

In almost all European cities there are large palaces, building complexes, or conglomerations that constitute whole pieces of the city and whose function now is no longer the original one. When one visits a monument of this type, for example the Palazzo della Ragione in Padua, one is always surprised by a series of questions intimately associated with it. In particular, one is struck by the multiplicity of functions that a building of this type can contain over time and how these functions are entirely independent of the form. At the same time, it is precisely the form that impresses us; we live it and experience it, and in turn it structures the city.

Where does the individuality of such a building begin and on what does it depend? Clearly it depends more on its form than on its material, even if the latter plays a substantial role; but it also depends on being a complicated entity which has developed in both space and time. We realize, for example, that if the architectural construction we are examining had been built recently, it would not have the same value. In that case the architecture in itself would be subject to judgment, and we could discuss its style and its form; but it would not yet present us with that richness of its own history which is characteristic of an urban artifact.

In an urban artifact, certain original values and functions remain, others are totally altered; about some stylistic aspects of the form we are certain, others are less obvious. We contemplate the values that remain – I am also referring to spiritual values – and try to ascertain whether they have some connection with the building's materiality, and whether they constitute the only empirical facts that pertain to the problem. At this point, we might discuss what our idea of the building is, our most general memory of it as a product of the collective, and what relationship it affords us with this collective.

It also happens that when we visit a palazzo like the one in Padua or travel through a particular city, we are subjected to different experiences, different impressions. There are people who do not like a place because it is associated with some ominous moment in their lives; others attribute an auspicious character to a place. All these experiences, their sum, constitute the city. It is in this sense that we must judge the *quality* of a space – a notion that may be extremely difficult for our modern sensibility. This was the sense in which the ancients consecrated a place, and it presupposes a type of analysis far more profound than the simplistic sort offered by certain psychological interpretations that rely only on the legibility of form.

We need, as I have said, only consider one specific urban artifact for a whole string of questions to present themselves; for it is a general characteristic of urban artifacts that they return us to certain major themes: individuality, *locus*, design, memory. A particular type of knowledge is delineated along with each artifact, a knowledge that is more complete and different from that with which we are familiar. It remains for us to investigate how much is real in this complex of knowledge.

I repeat that the reality I am concerned with here is that of the architecture of the city – that is, its form, which seems to summarize the total character of urban artifacts, including their origins. Moreover, a description of form takes into account all of the empirical facts we have already alluded to and can be quantified through rigorous observation. This is in part what we mean by urban morphology: a description of the forms of an urban artifact. On the other hand, this description is nothing but one moment, one instrument. It draws us closer to a knowledge of structure, but it is not identical with it.

Although all of the students of the city have stopped short of a consideration of the structure of urban artifacts, many have recognized that beyond the elements they had enumerated there remained the *âme de la cité*, in other words, the *quality* of urban artifacts. French geographers, for example, concentrated on the development of an important descriptive system, but they failed to exploit it to conquer this ultimate stronghold; thus, after indicating that the city is constituted as a totality and that this totality is its raison d'être, they left the significance of the structure they had glimpsed unexamined. Nor could they do otherwise with the premises from which they had set out: all of these studies failed to make an analysis of the actual quality of specific urban artifacts.

226 CHARLES MOORE

from "Plug It in Rameses, and See if It Lights up, Because We Aren't Going to Keep It Unless It Works" (1967)

Very much swept up into the energy and politics of the second half of the 1960s was the architect Charles Moore. The Michigan native had attended Princeton, where he learned an appreciation of history from Enrico Peressutti (of BBPR) and Louis Kahn, the second of whom regularly sat in on his juries. In 1959 he joined the faculty at Berkeley under the deanship of William Wilson Wurster, another strong influence on his development. And when he moved to Yale in 1965 he was also ascending to "star" status, with his work on Sea Ranch, Kresge College, and the Santa Barbara Faculty Club, all in California. Moore was an iconoclast of sorts, as this essay shows. He begins his argument by rejecting such well-known examples of place as the Piazza San Marco (unsuited to the unhierarchical nature of American cities), as well as the architecture of "exclusion" as practiced by Frank Lloyd Wright and Mies van der Rohe. In this passage, Moore instead prefers the scenography of the Santa Barbara County Courthouse and the eclecticism of the Madonna Inn, near San Luis Obispo — where, respectively, historical symbolism and the joyous enthusiasm of unschooled taste are keynotes of the architecture of inclusion.

That the idiom does not matter all that much to an architecture of inclusion is demonstrated by the Santa Barbara County Court House, of 1929, one of the century's great monuments of the architecture of inclusion. The Courthouse, after decades of critical abuse, still attracts streams of tourists who come to see it as architecture, to revel not only in its Hollywooden extrapolation of certain vaguely Spanish themes (in what Osbert Lancaster calls Spanish Supercolonial) but also in its syncopated orchestration of window openings, door shapes, and arcade in the white walls which respond as much to the Chicago jazz of the year it was built as to any far away clicking of castanets. People and activities are included here from horseback riders re-enacting an almost nonexistent Spanish past to passersby for whom the building opens up the grandeur of the site and the thrill of the place, whose history may be ephemeral, but whose presence is nonetheless real.

Santa Barbara's inclusion into its fabric after an earthquake in 1925 of an almost mythical Spanish history has been as clear a source of vitality for that particular place as the hopped-up forms of the commercial strip. Our Faculty Club for the University of California at Santa Barbara seeks to include this special vitality as Lyndon's Fashion Fabrics building sought to pick up the vitality of Monterey Peninsula's commercial strip, not to borrow a set of forms, but rather to take for our own a dizzily vigorous way of flinging up simple (but lofty) white walls whose crashing incongruities of scale will, we hope, seem eerily comforting in the soft white sunlight, without letting go for a moment of the place's crazy made-up past, but

Charles Moore, from "Plug It in Rameses, and See if It Lights up, Because We Aren't Going to Keep It Unless It Works," in *Perspecta* 11 (1967), pp. 42–3.

rather collecting the memory of it, even as Le Corbusier's Carpenter Center of Visual Arts is, I think, meant not to be built around a pokey little pedestrian ramp but rather around a form made to collect the image of motion on a freeway, which simply had to be reduced and symbolized in order to get it onto the lot.

That's a sly device, juxtaposing one's own yet unbuilt work with a Corbusier masterwork. It is, however, even more of a pleasure to give notice to a new building with no architect of record which is a moving example of this architecture of inclusion. The Madonna Inn, on the highway south of San Luis Obispo. California, would never get a passing grade in a school of architecture where tastefulness was prized. It was built (and keeps being built) by a family of highway contractors whose involvement with bulldozers and enormous pieces of earth-moving equipment puts them in close touch with huge boulders, which they have, with enormous feeling, piled together to make a gas station and a motel. Entry into this motel, past a rock and down a stair into a dining room upholstered in purple velvet, is one of the most surprising and surprisingly full experiences to be found along an American highway. It may be beside the point, but I don't think so, that in the men's room, next to a giant shell with gold faucets, the approach to a great rock grotto, which serves as a urinal, interrupts the beam of an electric eye and sets going a waterfall down over that grotto. It is disquieting in another way to note that armies of Italian craftsmen are even today meticulously carving grapes into wooden column capitals and beating sheets of copper into shape over tables in the coffee shop. It is not at all disquieting, but rather exhilarating to note that here there is everything instead of nothing. A kind of immediate involvement with the site, with the user and his movements, indeed with everything all at once, with the vitality and the vulgarity of real commerce, quivers at a pitch of excitement which presages, more clearly than any tidy sparse geometry, an architecture for the electric present.

227 DENISE SCOTT BROWN AND ROBERT VENTURI
from "On Ducks and Decoration" (1968)

In the 1960s Robert Venturi had a close intellectual ally in the person of Denise Scott Brown. The two had met at the University of Pennsylvania in 1960, after Scott Brown had finished her architectural studies at the Architectural Association in London. She had come to Penn to study under Louis Kahn, but she ended up in the Urban Planning Program, and later taught a course on theory with Venturi. Informed by the theories of Melvin Webber, Scott Brown's first important essay, "The Meaningful City" (1965), dealt with the urban environment and how messages are conveyed. In 1968 Venturi and Scott Brown, now married, pursued this theme by offering a joint design studio at Yale University, "Learning from Las Vegas, or Form Analysis as Design Research." The result of this

Denise Scott Brown and Robert Venturi, from "On Ducks and Decoration," in *Architecture Canada* 45:10 (October 1968), p. 48.

activity was an evolution in Venturi's thesis of "complexity and contradiction," as the honky-tonk elements earlier alluded to in the book now come decidedly to the fore in their collaborative analysis of the Strip. All of this would eventually to be published in their bestselling book, *Learning from Las Vegas: The Forgotten Symbolism of Architectural Form* (1972, written with Steven Izenour). In this essay of 1968, the two authors first lay out the theme of the "decorated shed."

We believe a new interest in the architecture of communication involving symbolism and mixed media will lead us to reevaluate the eclectic and picturesque styles of the last century, to reappraise our own commercial architecture – Pop architecture, if you wish – and finally to face the question of decoration. We have distinguished in a previous article between two types of heraldry in the commercial environment: the sign which *is* the building (for example, the road side duck, first brought to fame in Peter Blake's book) and the sign which *fronts* the building. The first distorts the less important inside function, eating, for the more important outside function of drawing you in. The second, applied to the building or separated from it with the parking lot between, allows the modest eating function to take place without distortion in a modest building, right for it, and permits the symbolic function its own leeway as well – they need not coincide and it is probably cheaper and easier if they don't.

Our thesis is that most architects' buildings today are ducks: buildings where an expressive aim has distorted the whole beyond the limits of economy and convenience; and that this, although an unadmitted one, is a kind of decoration, and a wrong and costly one at that. We'd rather see the need admitted and the decoration applied where needed, not in the way the Victorians did it but to suit our time, as easily as the billboard is pasted on its superstructure; with the building it is applied to allowed to go its own conventional way, no more distorted than are the functional windbracing and catwalks of the superstructure. This is an easier, cheaper, more direct and basically more honest approach to the question of decoration; it permits us to get on with the task of making conventional buildings conventionally and to deal with their symbolic needs with a lighter, defter touch. It may lead us to reevaluate Ruskin's horrifying statement, "architecture is the decoration of structure." But add to it Pugin's warning: it is all right to decorate construction, but never construct decoration.

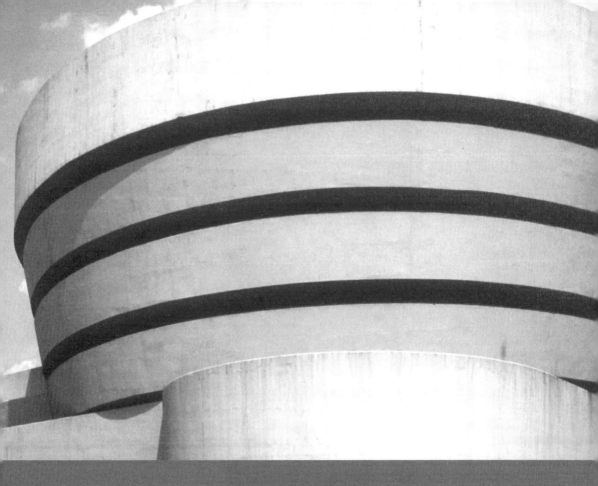

PART VII   THE PROSPECT OF
A POSTMODERN THEORY: 1969–79

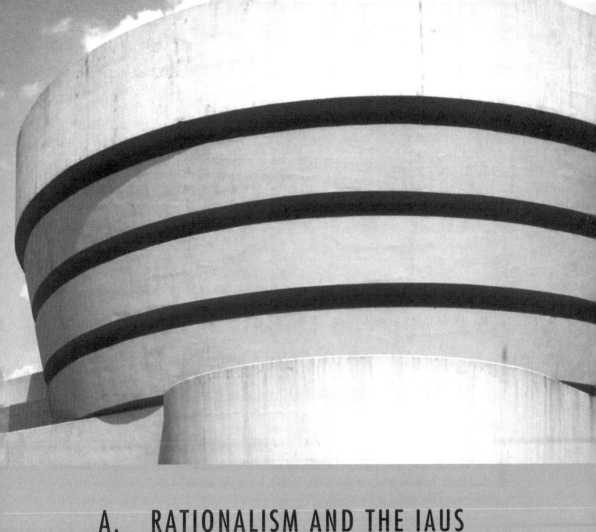

A.   RATIONALISM AND THE IAUS

Introduction

Spurred on by the social and cultural upheavals of the previous decade, several of the key tenets of modernism began to collapse in the early 1970s. Instrumental in the overturning of the status quo were the arguments of those associated with the European Rationalist movement and of the individuals and activities composing the Institute of Architecture and Urban Studies (IAUS) in New York.

The former front, as we have seen, had its beginnings in the urban typologies put forth by Aldo Rossi in the mid-1960s, sentiments that would be echoed and expanded by the Marxist criticisms of Manfredo Tafuri later in the decade. Rationalism was formally christened as a movement at the 15th Triennale of Milan in 1973, but these architects did not, as their chosen name suggests, seek to emulate the principles of the Italian rationalist movement of the 1920s. Rather, they attempted to draft a politically charged rationalism or political realism into service with the aim of carrying out a rigorous purification of what they deemed to be bourgeois architectural forms. Their counter-thesis was a return to traditional urban types: that is, pre-modern types of space, pre-modern types of urban elements, pre-modern types of building forms, pre-modern types of construction. The gabled roofs and simple geometries that characterized much of the new rationalist architecture therefore can be seen as both a metaphysical reduction of sorts and as an overt and consciously abstract return to historical solutions.

The architects involved with the IAUS, by contrast, seized in particular on the forms of the so-called avant-garde architects of the 1920s. Some viewed this strategy as a way to explore the undeveloped motifs of this iconic language, while others practiced what can only be described as a revival of a (largely Corbusian) style. One of the ostensible aims of this neo-modernism was to provide contemporary architects with the shelter of autonomy or withdrawal from the pressing social problems associated with a failed modernism. Thus in turning to formal exercise, these architects at the same time revived the idea of architecture as a high visual art akin to painting. In retrospect, such an affected stance can be interpreted in a more generous way as little more than a temporary stopping point for the architects involved — an attempt to break out of the theoretical impasse at which architecture found itself in the late 1960s.

228   MANFREDO TAFURI
from "Toward a Critique of Architectural Ideology" (1969)

The one Italian theorist to be most affected by the political turmoil and rise of the radical left in the late 1960s was Manfred Tafuri. He received his architectural degree in 1960 and worked as a teaching assistant under Saul Greco, Adalberto Libera, and Ludovico Quaroni. During this decade he also cultivated his interest in history and theory with studies on the Renaissance, the Baroque, and the city — to which he appended his growing interest in the Marxist theories of Walter Benjamin, Georg Lukács, and Theodor Adorno. His first book, *Theory and History of Architecture* (1968), addressed not only the perceived "crisis" of modern theory but also the question of whether modernism could in fact be interpreted as a unified body of ideas. His critical fervor intensified in the spring of 1968 when he arrived as a new professor at the University of Venice in the midst of political anarchy. His essay "Toward a Critique of Architectural Ideology" was penned for the Marxist journal *Contropiano* in the summer and fall of this year, and in it he makes the first of his several assertions regarding the death of architecture — at least the death of architecture's avant-garde or utopian ideals in the face of its usurpation by late capitalist forces. A reading of Tafuri's theory demands an elaborate preparation, and his overall contention is both nihilistic and liberating, both seen in the fact that he deprives architects of their former meliorist obligation to create a better world within a capitalist culture.

There is no denying that we are faced with two concurrent phenomena. On the one hand, the fact that building production remains confined to broad, comprehensive plans continues to reduce the functionality of architecture's ideological role. On the other, the economic and social conflicts exploding with ever greater frequency within urban and outlying areas seem

Manfredo Tafuri, from "Per una critica dell'ideologia architettonica" (1969), trans. Stephen Sartarelli, in *Architecture Theory since 1968*, ed. K. Michael Hays. Cambridge, MA: MIT Press, 2000, pp. 31–3.

to be imposing a pause on capitalism's Plan. Faced with the notion of the rationalization of the urban milieu – a central, determinant theme – capital seems, for the moment, unable to find within itself the strength and means necessary to fulfill the tasks rightly pointed out by the ideologies of the modern movement.

This has forced a return to activism – to strategies of stimulus, critique, and struggle – on the part of the intellectual opposition, and even of class organizations, which to this day have assumed the task of fighting to resolve such problems and conflicts. The harshness of the struggle over urban-planning laws (in Italy as well as the US), over the reorganization of the building industry, over urban renewal, may have given many the illusion that the fight for planning could actually constitute a moment in the class struggle.

Architects now work in a climate of anxiety, owing to the discovery of their decline as active ideologues, the realization of the vast potential of technology in the rationalization of the city and outlying areas together with the daily awareness of its waste, and the obsolescence of specific planning methods even before they have had a chance to be tested. All this points to a concrete development on the horizon, feared as the worst of all evils: the proletarianization of the architect, and his insertion – with no more neo-humanistic delays – within the planning programs of production.

When this new professional situation – already realized in advanced capitalist countries like the US or in countries of socialized capital such as the USSR – is feared by architects and avoided with the most neurotic sorts of formal and ideological contortions, it shows only the political backwardness of that particular intellectual group.

Having ideologically anticipated the iron law of the Plan, architects, unable to interpret historically the distance traveled, are now rebelling against the extreme consequences of processes that they themselves helped to set in motion. What's worse, they are attempting pathetically to relaunch modern architecture "ethically," assigning it political tasks suitable only for temporarily calming abstract, unjustified frenzies.

We must realize one thing: that the entire course of modern architecture and the new systems of visual communication was born, developed and brought into crisis in a grandiose attempt – the last of bourgeois culture – to resolve, on the level of an ideology all the more insidious because it lies entirely within concrete activities and real production cycles, the imbalances, contradictions and delays typical of the capitalistic reorganization of the world market.

Order and disorder, in this light, cease to be in opposition to each other. If we interpret them according to their true historical significance, it becomes clear that there is no contradiction between constructivism and "protest art," between the rationalism of building production and informal subjectivism or Pop irony, between the capitalist plan and the urban chaos, between the ideology of planning and the poetics of the object.

The *destiny* of capitalist society, in this interpretation, is not at all extraneous to the *project*. The ideology of the project is as essential to the integration of modern capitalism, with all its structures and superstructures, into human existence, as is the illusion of being able to oppose that *project* with the tools of a *different* project or with those of a radical "anti-project."

It may even be that many marginal and rearguard roles exist for architecture and planning. Of primary interest to us, however, is the question of why, until now, Marxist-oriented culture has very carefully, and with an obstinacy worthy of better causes, denied or concealed the simple truth that, just as there can be no such thing as a political economics of class, but only a class critique of political economics, likewise there can never be an aesthetics, art or architecture of class, but only a class critique of aesthetics, art, architecture and the city.

A coherent Marxist critique of architectural and urbanistic ideology can only demystify the contingent, historical – and in no way objective or universal – realities that lie hidden behind the unifying categories of the terms "art," "architecture," and "city."

In assuming its historic, objective role as class critique, architectural criticism must become a critique of urban ideology, and avoid in every way the danger of entering into "progressive" dialogue with the techniques for rationalizing the contradictions of capital.

And first among the intellectual illusions to be dispelled is that which strives to anticipate, through mere imagery, the conditions of an architecture "for a liberated society." Anyone who proffers such a slogan avoids the question of whether, even leaving aside its manifest utopianism, such an objective could ever be sought without a linguistic, methodological and structural revolution reaching well beyond the simple subjective will or the simple updating of a syntax.

Modern architecture has marked the paths of its own destiny by becoming the bearer of ideals of progress and rationalization to which the working class is extraneous, or in which it is included only in a social democratic perspective. One might well recognize the historical inevitability of this phenomenon; yet having done so, one may no longer hide the ultimate reality that makes the choices of "leftist" architects so uselessly anguished.

Uselessly anguished because it is useless to struggle when one is trapped inside a capsule with no exit. The crisis of modern architecture does not issue from "weariness" or "dissipation." Rather, it is a crisis of the ideological function of architecture. The "fall" of modern art is the ultimate testimony of bourgeois ambiguity, poised as it is between "positive" goals – the reconciliation of contradictions – and the merciless exploration of its own objective commodification. There is no more "salvation" to be found within it: neither by wandering restlessly through "labyrinths" of images so polyvalent that they remain mute, nor by shutting oneself up in the sullen silence of geometries content with their own perfection.

This is why there can be no proposals of architectural "anti-spaces":[1] any search for an alternative within the structures determining the mystification of planning is an obvious contradiction in terms.

Reflection on architecture, as a critique of the concrete ideology "realized" by architecture itself, can only push further, and strive for a specifically concrete dimension in which the systematic destruction of the mythologies sustaining its development is only one of the objectives. But only the future conditions of the class struggle will tell us whether the task we are setting ourselves is that of an avant-garde or a rearguard.

NOTE

1   The Italian word here is *controspazi* – in the original, an obvious polemical reference to the polemical contemporary architectural journal, *Controspazio*. [Translator's note.]

229 PETER EISENMAN

from "Notes on Conceptual Architecture: Towards a Definition" (1970)

In addition to CASE, Peter Eisenman's other major organizational activity of the 1960s was the founding of the Institute for Architecture and Urban Studies (IAUS) in 1967. Initially the research component of the IAUS closely resembled that of CASE, but organizationally it was a very different entity. Eisenman received the start-up funds for the IAUS with the help of Arthur Drexler at the Museum of Modern Art, and thus the old alliance between architecture and this institution that had been formed in the 1930s was renewed. Eisenman initially brought Colin Rowe, Robert Gutman, Emilio Ambasz, and Robert Slutzsky into the Institute as faculty, and they were soon joined by Kenneth Frampton and Stanford Anderson. A critical journal of history and theory was also proposed, and did appear in 1973 under the title *Oppositions*.

This particular essay precedes the journal. As Eisenman was setting out the program of the IAUS, he was asked to put together a special issue of *Casabella* on the theme "The City as Artifact." These passages of Eisenman's article actually derive to some extent from his doctoral dissertation of 1963, but they are also written very much in response to Venturi's *Complexity and Contradiction in Architecture*. Effectively, they are the first mature statement of Eisenman's lifelong quest to desemanticize architecture.

An art object as opposed to any object, possesses an aesthetic intention. An aesthetic intention in art does not always depend on the object or the aesthetic qualities of the object. For example, in the case of a Duchamp where by taking an object and changing its context, the object can be classified as an art object. While all objects, whether designed or not, will have an inherent aesthetic, the object in Duchamp's case receives its art appellation not from the aesthetic in the object or its objects qualities, but from something external to the object – in the case of Duchamp's urinal a change in context. Thus, it can be said that an aesthetic intention, without necessarily including the idea of the object of the qualities of the object, qualifies something as art.

In architecture this is not the case. First, because architecture in a literal sense is the context. Second, the idea of an architecture as distinguished from a painting will always contain in the idea, ideas of functional and semantically weighted objects such as walls, bathrooms, closets, doors, ceilings. There is no conceptual aspect in architecture which can be thought of without the concept of pragmatic and functional objects, otherwise it is not an architectural conception. To make these conceptual and still remain architecture is quite another matter. Even if it were possible to disregard all of the semantic impositions on form in architecture, lines which are columns, planes which are walls, must always, because of the fact of gravity, hold something up; thus a physical presence would exist even as an idea. Equally, in architecture, the ground plane will always be semantically different than the roof

Peter D. Eisenman, "Notes on Conceptual Architecture: Towards a Definition" (1970), cited from the version in *Casabella* 359–360 (1971), pp. 51, 53.

plane, and the entry plane acknowledges the difference from exterior to interior. But the idea of wall as plane, or column as line is not enough to qualify the idea as conceptual architecture. Conversely, merely because architecture both in the idea and in the built state has objects does not exclude it from being conceptual. To make something conceptual in architecture would require taking the pragmatic and functional aspects and place them in a conceptual matrix, where their primary existence is no longer interpreted from the physical fact of being a bathroom or closet, but rather the functional aspect bathroom or closet becomes secondary to some primary reading as a notation in a conceptual context. Again, what makes architecture conceptual is that unlike art, it demands not only the primacy of intention to take something from the sensual to the intellectual realm, but also that this intention be present in the conceptual structure; again, whether it is built or not, is not at issue. [. . .]

A comparison between Le Corbusier and Giuseppe Terragni illustrates an example of what is meant by the difference between perceptual and conceptual within the syntactic aspect. While the work of both is structured by a syntax, the primary intention in each is slightly different. By virtue of their similarity, a subtle distinction helps to explain a difference between perceptual and conceptual.

Le Corbusier essentially took the forms of known objects – from machines, ships and aircraft, – the intention of this imagery was to force a shift in meaning through its appearance in a new context. As has been seen above, with a change in context, the intention is primarily a semantic one. In Terragni, there are obvious semantic implications as in his reference to historical buildings. For example, there is a similarity which can be seen in a comparison of the plans of the Casa del Fascio, and the Palazzo Farnese, and the Palazzo Thiene. But, while the semantic reference is to the high culture of the Italian Renaissance, the ultimate intent in Terragni's use of such a plan would seem to divest such type forms of their traditional meaning, and instead use the formal type as a deep level syntactic referent to which his specific forms correspond.

230   COLIN ROWE
from Introduction to *Five Architects* (1972)

Growing out of the CASE conference and exhibition of 1969 was a publication that would, almost instantly, give international standing to Peter Eisenman and the circle of architects that would soon become known as the "New York Five." With a preface by Arthur Drexler, an introduction by Colin Rowe, an analytical essay by Kenneth Frampton, and the comments of architects and others on the illustrated projects – the book is much more than an exhibition catalog. It is in part a publicity brochure, but also in part a manifesto, a controversial one

Colin Rowe, from "Introduction," in *Five Architects: Eisenman, Graves, Gwathmey, Hejduk, Meier.* New York: Wittenborn, 1972, pp. 4, 7.

indeed in the face of the Marxist rhetoric emanating from a politically charged Europe. Rowe apologetically yet lucidly captures the book's unrevolutionary premise: an open withdrawal from the tenets of modernism, which the architects carry out by instituting a new historicist revival, and by eliding from architecture all outside interests, political or otherwise. More succinctly, the book is a decree on aesthetic formalism. Eisenman, for his part, revives the abstract compositional principles and forms of Giuseppe Terragni. Richard Meier, Michael Graves, and Charles Gwathmey follow by borrowing freely from the formal vocabulary of Le Corbusier. John Hejduk builds his compositions upon Frank Lloyd Wright, De Stijl, and Soviet Constructivism. Rowe's introductory essay is a masterpiece of ironic understatement.

These, had they been conceived c. 1930 and built in France, Germany, Switzerland or Italy, had then they been illustrated by Alberto Sartoris or even F. R. S. Yorke, would today very likely be approached as ancient monuments; and as exemplary of the heroic periods of modern architecture, they would be visited and recorded. Indeed one can imagine the tourists and almost concoct the historical evaluations. But these buildings were not conceived c. 1930. They are of comparatively recent origin; they are built in, or proposed for, the vicinity of New York City; and therefore, whatever their merits and demerits, such is the present constellation of critical ideas, they can only be regarded as constituting a problem.

For we are here in the presence of what, in terms of the orthodox theory of modern architecture, is heresy. We are in the presence of anachronism, nostalgia, and, probably, frivolity. If modern architecture looked like this c. 1930 then it should not look like this today; and, if the real political issue of the present is not the provision of the rich with cake but of the starving with bread, then not only formally but also programmatically these buildings are irrelevant. Evidently they propound no obvious revolution; and, just as they may be envisaged as dubiously European to some American tastes, so they will seem the painful evidence of American retardation to certain European and, particularly, English judgments.

Now these evaluations will not be made to go away. A grass roots Neo-Populist Americanism will approve of these buildings no more than a Pop-inspired and supercilious European, or English, neo-Marxism; and, given the situation in which opposite but sympathetic extremes will, alike, both smell abomination, it might be best to address arguments to neither of these two states of mind but, instead to withdraw attention to that body of theory, alleged or otherwise, of which these buildings, like so many of their predecessors of the Nineteen-Twenties and Thirties, may be construed as violation.

[. . .]

To repeat: this choice became visible once it became almost too evident to bear that the central and socialist mission of modern architecture had failed – or, alternatively, that this mission had become dissolved in the sentimentalities and bureaucracies of the welfare state. The simple fusion of art and technology, of symbolical gesture and functional requirement was now not to be made; and, in default of this fusion, a variety of alternatives have offered themselves.

These have included what has already been listed: Miesian neo-classicism (with some kind of dependent theory of Platonic form); the New Brutalism (with the inference that self-flagellation may elicit the better world); the Futurist Revival (with the very popular supposition that science fiction might provide the ultimate hope); and the neo-*art nouveau* (which, both in its Shingle Style and Italian ramifications, insists that if we only retreat to the Eighteen-Nineties – and also simulate a naivete – then health will inevitably ensue.

And, to this catalogue, there must also be added the notion that we ignore the situation altogether: that, in default of that convenient anti-'art' entity of the Twenties called 'the machine,' we substitute the equally useful entities designated 'the computer' and 'the people' and that, if these two abstractions are absolutely at variance with each other, we will not indulge ourselves in too many scruples about this problem. It is a problem which exists only in the minds of the far too sensitive; and if research and data-collection are the wave of the future – if the public wisdom so indicates – then it is certainly to the future we belong.

It is in this context of choices (none of them very agreeable) that we should place what is here published; and, having recognized this context, we should not then be too ready to impute charges of irresponsibility. It is difficult to generalize the work of these five architects. Eisenman seems to have received a revelation in Como; Hejduk seems to wish affiliation both to Synthetic Cubist Paris and Constructivist Moscow. Nor will the more obviously Corbusian orientation of Graves, Gwathmey and Meier so readily succumb to all encompassing observations. But, for all this, there is a point of view shared which is quite simply this: that, rather than constantly to endorse the revolutionary myth, it might be more reasonable and more modest to recognize that, in the opening years of this century, great revolutions in thought occurred and that then profound visual discoveries resulted, that these are still unexplained, and that rather than assume intrinsic change to be the prerogative of every generation, it might be more useful to recognize that certain changes are so enormous as to impose a directive which cannot be resolved in any individual life span.

231   ROBERT A. M. STERN AND JAQUELIN ROBERTSON
from "Five on Five" (1973)

In 1973 Robert A. M. Stern organized for *Architectural Forum* a rebuttal to the book *Five Architects*. Entitled "Five on Five," it consisted of a critique by five architects – Stern, Jaquelin Robertson, Charles Moore, Allan Greenberg, and Romaldo Guigola – of the projects displayed in *Five Architects*. Whereas the responses were respectful of the design efforts of the newly christened "New York Five" – soon to be more descriptively known as the "Whites" – they were at the same time highly critical of Five's theoretical underpinnings. Stern, in choosing to compare *Five Architects* with the recent release of *Learning from Las Vegas*, opens his essay "Stompin' at the Savoye" by taking Colin Rowe to task for his long-standing infatuation with the Corbusian vernacular of the 1920s, which Stern opposes by countering with the ideas of Venturi. Robertson, in his article "Machines in the Garden," follows with a more extended analysis of the New York Five's shortcomings, and the summary of his points is presented here. This coordinated attack on the "Whites" launched the contrary movement of the "Grays," who would soon define their ideological position.

Robert A. M. Stern and Jaquelin Robertson, from "Five on Five," in *Architectural Forum* 138:4 (May 1973), pp. 46–7, 52–3.

The almost simultaneous publication of *Five Architects* and the Venturis' *Learning from Las Vegas* marks, one hopes, an opportunity to step back and consider what it is that our architecture stands for at this time; it gives us a chance to evaluate opposing points of view that have been described as European/idealist on the one hand, American/pragmatic on the other, exclusive and inclusive, conceptual and perceptual, invulnerable and vulnerable. Although the two books, and for that matter the positions they embody, are pretty much opposite to each other, they are not of equal importance.

Las Vegas builds upon the most important architectural text of the 1960's, *Complexity and Contradiction in Architecture*, by Robert Venturi. Whereas *Five Architects* is a perhaps premature effort at polemical assertion by architects who really have no claims as a group, *Las Vegas* is a cohesive record of six productive years of work by Venturi and his partners. Together with the writings of Herbert Gans, Jane Jacobs and some others, *Las Vegas* is helping us at least to break from the hot-house aesthetics of the 1920's, to see familiar things in fresh contexts, and to assimilate diverse experiences into our work.

Five Architects, and particularly its introductory essay by Colin Rowe, the intellectual guru of the group whose work is presented therein, contains an implicit reply to the Venturis' work and especially to Vincent Scully's introduction to *Complexity and Contradiction*. In that introduction, Scully made claims not only for the book in relationship to Le Corbusier's *Towards a New Architecture* but also, by implication, for Venturi's position as logical complement to that of Le Corbusier as form-giver. Such a claim sticks in Rowe's craw. After all, for the last fifteen years or so, as design critic and theorist, he has initiated architectural students into a systematized version of 1920's Corbusian form. The irony of his faithfulness to the most questionable aspects of Le Corbusier's philosophy is nowhere clearer than in his 1966 Museum of Modern Art project for Harlem, where despite previous efforts to develop Corbusier's ideas about town planning on that part of Shad Woods and others, and in the face of major reassessments by other participants in the exhibition, he and his team projected the most sweeping and absolute "ville radieuse" scheme ever.

Rowe states in *Five Architects* that "rather than constantly to endorse the revolutionary myth, it might be more reasonable, and more modest to recognize that, in the opening years of this century, great revolutions in thought occurred and that then profound visual discoveries resulted, that these are still unexplained, and that rather than assume intrinsic changes to be the prerogative of every generation, it might be more useful to recognize that certain changes are so enormous as to impose a directive which cannot be resolved in any individual life span." Thus, as Rowe sees it, the revolution of the twenties is so fundamental to our architecture as to preclude its own evolution. I think it is not. Indeed, there seems to be a certain inconsistency of position on Rowe's part as manifest by his sudden affection for Aldo van Eyck, under whose slogan his essay is written, and even more clearly by his suggestion that we place the work of the "five architects" in a "context of choices" that include "Miesian neo-classicism ...; the New Brutalism ...; the Futurist Revival ...; and the *neo-art nouveau*" which I guess means Yale/Philadelphia architects with "Shingle Style and Italian ramifications ..." This concept of choice (stylistic choice to boot), reveals more about Rowe's misgivings (not to mention his predilections) than

I would have imagined possible, and finally, casts doubt on the firmness of his convictions in the five architects as logical successors to Le Corbusier, even on his own terms.

[. . .]

[*Robertson*]

The cult of modern art has badly maimed much of modern architecture by making it unduly conscious of and responsive to requirements of painting and display and, without realizing it almost, by divorcing it from day-to-day life. Graves and Hejduk and many others are victims of this, though Hedjuk seems more content at making architectural art per se.

Where does this leave us? Let me try to sum up my essential dissatisfaction with neo-Corbusianism and its practitioners by going back to that long list of rhetorical questions asked earlier. This is not a conclusive list of dissatisfactions nor a consistent one (we all know about consistency). I do believe it is relevant to the work shown in *Five Architects*.

1) Serge Chermayeff's comment. "Environments are still conceived of largely either as receptacles for machinery, or as sculpture or scenery," is true of modern architects in general and of this group particularly. "Nature," the surroundings (context), they see as a separate, neutral stage or backdrop for the artistic placement of the unrelated pieces or groups of sculpture, often neo-machinery; buildings conceived as objects, final in themselves, requiring only our appreciation of the "magnificent play of light" upon their forms. They neither carry with them instructions about such a larger order when and if this is required nor do they, when aggregated, create one.

Our culture offers many "well-designed" buildings and almost no architecturally integrated communities or even streets. (Corb's architect must do it all from scratch; "everything must be wrought afresh"; architecture is "a human operation directed *against* nature.")

Yet, as we are finding out, everything cannot be built anew; the need is not so much for the ability to lay out an entire new order (whether as a single house or a new community) as to incrementally build one within or next to what exists. The fact that the requirements of "within" and "next to" are different from those of isolation and the difference is crucial to the "ecology of ideas" inherent in the architectural (or any creative) act. It is probably both improper and impossible to separate ideas of form from those of substance which was Eisenman's effort.

Precisely what is new in architectural thinking is not abstract "revolution" but the issue of "incrementalism:" A change of view that attempts to encompass the notion, to paraphrase Bateson that all change can be understood as the effort to maintain some constancy and all constancy as maintained through change.

The "solution" to the Gwathmey's Beach House for example does not contain within it a structure applicable to the Beach Colony. Such direction towards a larger cohesion is usually attained in architecture not only through a common albeit variable vocabulary of materials, details, scales, shapes, and hierarchies, but by an agreement as to the "social" placement of the next unit (part of the deep structure) on the next piece of ground by *someone else*. This agreement as to siting and landscaping, the architectural "social contract," is the essential "glue" bonding the whole. It allows and dissolves great variety and even dissimilarity among the parts within a readily discernible matrix of the whole.

2) The imagery of much of neo-Corbusianism – the sculpture in the garden, which invokes the ship, the airport, farm equipment, gun emplacements, etc – is not only misleading but intellectually wrong-headed and psychologically damaging.

3) Similarly, the propositions and logics of cubism – or any other school of painting – are neither appropriately nor safely transferred to architecture and this continuous and synthetic transformation of sometimes mutually exclusive logics clouds rather than clears the very real differences between the processes needed for two-dimensional rendering and usable buildings (it's all too easy to confuse drawings with buildings without having the confusion canonized).

4) Because of this fault it follows that the requirements of the museum world as it is now conceived are particularly crippling to the production of a healthy, variable, and living architecture; and that the museum "scoring system" demoralizes both those who judge and those who practice architecture.

5) Since the strain of recent architecture labelled "modern" threw almost everything learned from the past away (and was usually most successful when it didn't, i.e., Corb's honoring of classical proportioning devices) it soon became increasingly synthetic and unsatisfactory to architects and public alike. It was short-lived.

Much of the weakness of neo-Corbusianism with its polemical deification of technology and the neo-machine image lies precisely in its inability to provide a vocabulary of details – the framing around openings, cornices, base-boards, chair rails, choice of boarding – that solve real and commonplace technical problems in the process of enrichment. This kind of refinement of the details posed by the original style did not for the most part, occur in its evolution.

6) Since decoration of the surface was doctrinally unacceptable and yet its total absence unsupportable (no one could live for long in a squash court) the disposition of shapes and rooms in plan took the place, so to speak, of ornamentation of the wall and ceiling planes. The occupant was being asked in much of this modern architecture to live in the ornament instead of just look at it. (Of course, wall/ceiling ornamentation did come back but not so much in terms of an articulation of details of the surface plane as the attempt to make certain architectural features – stairs, balconies, openings, etc. – become a kind of wall-mounted sculptural furniture. Interior walls and ceilings become continually and increasingly more violent and aggressive; to be followed by a calmer period of applied ornamentation, "cut-outs" and supergraphics.)

7) A part of this neo-Corbusian "ornamentation of the plan" was a particularization of the spaces, a proliferation of oddly shaped areas, increasingly in contradiction to the initial stated purpose of the "open plan." This particularization, justified partially as a response to so-called "functional" needs, has depended in many cases for its aesthetic success on the careful placement of freestanding furniture (more as works of art than accommodation) and resulted either in a kind of frozen territory immune to the vicissitudes and irregularities of life or to a maze of shapely but ultimately tiresome enclosures. Indeed, as we have found out there is nothing more impractical, inflexible, and in some cases uncomfortable than the so-called free-flowing space of the open plan unless it's the wedged, diagonal, rooted plan. Both are rigid, hard-programmed; and in comparison to, say, the Regency House's ordered arrangement of discrete, simply arranged and regular spaces neither is as amendable, as reusable. Tailor-making the house to the particular requirements and eccentricities of a given client or program destroyed its general usefulness.

Architecture has to be able to survive many tests including not smudging under a variety of tenant's uses and/or decorating styles. Neo-Corbusianism doesn't meet this test very well.

8) The emphasis on space *per se* and on spatial variety, on movement and violent shifts in orientation inside and out all but killed any ability of a space or an occupant to be at rest. All spaces circulate; the style is a continual trauma of movement and dislocation; a style obsessed with creating "exciting" spaces which too rarely produces any places pleasing to remain in.

9) As a replicable, usable, consumer environment most modern houses in this mold are not as satisfactory as your Williamsburg replica – and a neighborhood of them (much) less satisfactory. Modern architecture, in not yet producing attractive modern suburbs, compares badly with some of the styles of the past; and even to the "unmodern" but contemporary suburbs of say, a Beverly Hills.

10) As a result of all of the above, the style, unpopular from the outset, is not now in good health, and is only being maintained precariously in a special isolation wing through the donated intravenous feeding of the "art world."

Having said all this let me counter it all by saying how much I admire so much of what is shown here (much of it is beautiful) simply because doing good architecture is so hard – and there is no easy or proper way.

All routes are legitimate...and many of the criticisms I level here also apply to too much of the architecture of the past which I love.

The real test will come when and if these architects take on larger projects – wholes rather than parts. Our architectural culture will be affected by that outcome.

232   PETER EISENMAN, KENNETH FRAMPTON, AND MARIO GANDELSONAS
inaugural editorial in *Oppositions* 1 (1973)

With the launching of the journal *Oppositions*, Peter Eisenman brought the IAUS to the forefront of the international architectural debate. The idea for such a journal goes back to CASE discussions in 1965, but its appearance in 1973, under the initial editorial control of Eisenman, Frampton, and Gandelsonas, places it and its focus within an entirely different theoretical context. With such important predecessors as *Shelter* and *Arts and Architecture*–*Oppositions*, with the subtitle "A Journal for Ideas and Criticism in Architecture," may not claim to be the first journal to be launched on American soil, but it would soon become one of the most informative and widely read. With its related book series and exhibition program, the IAUS would new dominate American theory for the next decade and more.

OPPOSITIONS is an attempt to establish a new arena for architectural discourse in which a consistent effort will be made to discuss and develop specific notions about the nature of

Inaugural editorial in *Oppositions* 1 (September 1973), n.p.

architecture and design in relation to the man-made world. It is our joint belief that truly creative work depends upon such an extension of consciousness. To this end, OPPOSITIONS will orient itself towards the process of critical assessment and re-assessment. It will regularly feature a number of articles which critically examine either a building, a book, or a theoretical position with a view to interpreting and evaluating the general complex of ideas involved. It is hoped that a series of dialogues will result which will occasion an exchange of views not only among the editors, but also between the reader and other outside contributors. To this end we will extend some of this discourse into a series of forums to permit an open discussion of the issues raised by OPPOSITIONS. These forums will be held at The Institute for Architecture and Urban Studies. A record of the discussion will be edited for publication in an issue of OPPOSITIONS.

In all this, no attempt will be made to establish a single editorial line. The Institute will maintain its independence while we, as editors, will simply attempt to maintain the discourse at a high level and to concentrate on issues which in one way or another must necessarily affect the future status of architecture and design. Naturally our respective concerns as individuals for formal, socio-cultural and political discourse will make themselves felt in our joint editing of OPPOSITIONS. The opposition alluded to in the title will first and foremost begin at home.

OPPOSITIONS will address itself to the evolution of new models for a theory of architecture. It will attempt to relate such models to specific buildings and theories which, in our opinion, either directly state or implicitly evoke the existence of such models. We will not, in all this, restrict our discourse to the very latest work. On the contrary, we will attempt to link the present to the past to assess the overall contribution of major individuals and movements which still have relevance today. Our editorial position will be to attempt to create a climate of opinion where ideas and action are seen as being necessarily complementary to any vital architectural culture.

Peter Eisenman
Kenneth Frampton
Mario Gandelsonas

233 MASSIMO SCOLARI
from "Avant Garde and the New Architecture" (1973)

In the wake of Rossi's focus on architecture's urban typology of forms, and Tafuri's radical denial to architecture of any future with traditional avant-garde formulae, Italian theory was due for a reconstitution, which took place at the 15th Triennale of Milan in 1973. The international event displayed the work of Rossi, Carlo Aymonino, Leon Krier, Adolfo Natalini, Nino Dardi, and Ludwig Leo, together with projects of the New York Five.

Massimo Scolari, from "Avanguardia e nuova architettura" (1973), trans. Stephen Sartarelli, in *Architecture Theory since 1968*, ed. K. Michael Hays. Cambridge, MA: MIT Press, 2000, p. 140.

Whereas Rossi's return to classicism and monumentality, encapsulated in his earlier words – "to focus on a rigid world with few objects" – had found an appreciative audience by this date, it was left to the architect Massimo Scolari to identify the movement as the *Tendenza*, better known internationally under the exhibition publication title of "Rational Architecture." The characteristics of the *Tendenza*, according to Scolari, were myriad. One was to endow architecture with its own autonomy, that is, as an internal and logical discipline or repertoire of "types" and forms, devoid of extraneous design methods, economic or social contamination. This rationale, as it were, was necessary not only to limit avant-garde expression (against which the "New Architecture" was juxtaposed in the essay's title) but also to recapture a relationship with history and (on an urban level) with monumentality, which had been largely shunned by the dogmatic functionalism of modern design. In the Platonic world of Rossi, monumentality came to constitute what was a near-reduction of architectural elements to the essential forms of Laugier's Neoclassicism, yet one also accepting of A. C. Quatremère de Quincy's notion of "type" as a rule for the model and not as something to imitate. It was a bold experiment in traditionalism that would have a significant following over the next decade in both Europe and North America.

Monumentality is based above all on a need that emerges from a more than superficial examination of the *urban phenomenon*. Indeed, the destiny of the community seems to express itself "with characteristics of permanence" at those physically and psychologically pivotal points that are urban monuments. One of the most important contributions of the "scuola di Rossi" to the foundation of an urban science is having individuated within the *city as product* the dialectic between primary elements (monuments) and residential areas. In particular, says Rossi, "monuments, signs of the collective will expressed through the principles of architecture, seem to present themselves as primary elements, fixed points of the urban dynamic."

This conception of the *city as work of art* has specific reference points in the work of Lévi-Strauss and even more in the thought of Maurice Halbwachs, who finds the typical nature of urban reality to lie in the characteristics of imagination and *collective memory*.

In this conception of the city, the monumental highlights above all the outgrowths (dimensional and qualitative) around which the urban topography revolves. For the Tendenza, however, its role, which might be seen only to concern the results of historical and formal analysis, lies also and above all in planning as an *indication of simplicity and formal rarefaction*.

The choice of monumentalism thus comes to convey a new vision of the city. It critiques the undifferentiated expansion and misery of quantity deceptively guided by the tools of *zoning*, in a city in which one might instead recognize and design the *parts* organically related to its structure: *city parts* within which the *relationship between urban morphology and building typology* would isolate and foreground those collective fixed points around which the private city builds and transforms itself.

What the city today is in danger of losing forever is its own consciousness, its individuality, its character of civilization. It is on the verge of losing (like Milan) its historic center, devastated by the service-industry invasion, which has destroyed those precious signs that once culturally anchored the city's transformations and development to an awareness of its own history.

The *new monumentality* thus implies a demand for *unity* and *simplicity*. It is a response that is supposed to counter the disorder of the modern city with the clarity of *few but decisive rules*. It expresses a wish to recuperate definitively a *character* of the city, by starting with *simplicity* of the needs of the collective spirit and with the feeling of *unity* in the means used to satisfy them.

The concept of monumentality also aims to recuperate a new dignity for art, whether it is the art identifiable in the city plan, in the city's texture as product [*manufatto*], or in the single building. Moreover, "the monument" foregrounds the collectivity dominant in the very structure of the city and controls it, so to speak, "democratically." On a more broadly social level, the choice of monumentalism opposes the consumerism of the private city, the artificial demand for the new – since, with the growth of the needs of capitalist society, private interests tend to search for *minute combinations* unable to satisfy real needs but efficient in continually creating new ones, both on the physical and psychological levels. And satisfying the *desire for novelty* seems in the end to be one of those circumstances shaped by the few to the detriment of the many.

234 JOSEPH RYKWERT
from "15ª Triennale" (1974)

Perhaps the most interesting of the reviews of the 15th Triennale was that written for the Italian journal *Domus* by Joseph Rykwert. His remarks concerning "this generally deplorable show" was anything but flattering, as the England-based professor – still very much concerned with the rituals and meanings of architecture – revolted at Rossi's and Tafuri's suggestion that architecture could somehow be made mute. There is a serious political divide here, but also a larger breach between Italian and Anglo-American theory underlying these remarks. Rykwert, as the passage shows, also found fault with the inclusion of the work of the New York Five in the show.

Aldo Rossi's competition scheme for the cemetery at Modena was another focus: a rigid arrangement of elementary geometries, which still dominates the panorama (literally) in this exhibition. The conjunction is not accidental. Rossi, who heads the team which has organized the most important part of this exhibition, that concerned with "rational" architecture and the building and the city, has often and loudly proclaimed the independence, the abstraction of architecture from all ideology, and from any "redemptive" role, to use his word. His is a "pure" architecture, form without utopia; at best it achieves a sublime uselessness; these are Tafuri's words, his apologia for Rossi: "We will always prefer, to any mystifying attempt at decking architecture in ideological dress, the sincerity of him who has the courage to speak of its silent and irrelevant purity".

So that's it, then. Architecture may stay alive as long as she stays dumb. Dumb and beautiful maybe, but dumb. Those of us who refuse this condition are sternly set aside. Tafuri is right in a way, of course. Architecture is pretty dead.

[. . .]

Going round the exhibition, so deliberately tendentious, it is curious to see what is absorbed into the show: the *sventramenti* of Krier fit well enough; Costantino Dardi and Adolfo Natalini (when at his most apocalyptic) are also clearly of the company. But what is James Stirling doing in it? Or even Vittorio Gregotti? Even odder, what are the five New York

Joseph Rykwert, from "15ª Triennale," in *Domus* 530 (January 1974), pp. 2–3.

architects up to in this *galère*, with their cabbalistic reinterpretation of the next historical phase due for revival (I mean the Persico-Albini-Terragni phase) or even more remote, their studied absorption of a cubist plasticity into the shingle style?

This is a little unfair to the five architects who are not a homogeneous group. Certainly Michael Graves would not share the theoretical position of the *Tendenza*, and I suspect would want to contradict it; the same is true, to a lesser degree, of Richard Meier and even Peter Eisenmann. Hejduk was perhaps nearest to them at one point. But even he is changing. Their almost decorative, small-scale use of the Cubist idiom and sometimes of the Stijl techniques (in Hejduk's case particularly) is a deliberate attempt to achieve the sort of variation which Rossi and his followers equally deliberately eschew. This is perhaps clearest in the matter of proportion. The *Tendenza's* almost exclusive devotion to three most elementary shapes: square, circle, equilateral triangle, gives their buildings a look of a willed rigidity.

235 MANFREDO TAFURI
from ''L'Architecture dans le Boudoir: The Language of Criticism and the Criticism of Language'' (1974)

I n 1973 Tafuri published his book *Progetto e Utopia* (translated into English in 1976 as *Architecture and Utopia*), which expanded upon the pessimistic theme of his essay on ideology of 1969. The following year Tafuri received an invitation to address students at Princeton University, at a conference arranged by Diana Agrest. Out of the event came the first critical essay by Tafuri to appear in English. Tafuri's subsequent visit to New York and the publication of this lecture also initiated an interesting cultural interchange between the architectural powers of New York and Venice; more specifically, between the IAUS and the history department of the University of Venice chaired by Tafuri.

Such an alliance, even in its day, must have seemed somewhat odd, as aspects of this essay make clear. Tafuri's pessimistic and critical outlook had not substantially changed since its radicalization in 1968–9 (it later would evolve), but the context had shifted in a near-dramatic fashion. Tafuri takes the occasion of the Princeton lecture to consider the ''New Trends'' of Aldo Rossi and James Sterling, alongside the work of the New York Five, and the judgments are none too happy. Invoking the title of a book by the libertine Marquis de Sade, who in turn had recently been made fashionable by Michel Foucault, Tafuri sees the mute intellectualizations (signs) of these new ''knights of purity'' (Sterling, Rossi, Scolari, the Kiers, and Eisenman, among others) as a retreat from praxis, as a sadistic display of the seductive power of feigned avant-gardism, one that in the end would transform itself into an ''architecture of cruelty'' – an architecture to be banished to the mirrored walls of the boudoir.

Manfredo Tafuri, from ''L'Architecture dans le Boudoir: The Language of Criticism and the Criticism of Language,'' in *Oppositions* 3 (May 1974), pp. 48, 52–3.

To what point then is this attitude comparable to that of the "Five Architects" who, in the panorama of international architecture, appear closest to conceiving of architecture as a reflection upon itself and upon its internal articulations? Is it indeed possible to speak of their work as "mannerism among the ruins"?[1] Mario Gandelsonas has correctly singled out the specific areas of interest in the work of Michael Graves – the interest in the classicist code, cubist painting, the traditions of the Modern movement, and nature.[2] Yet we should be wary. We are again dealing with "closed systems," within which the themes of polysemy and pluralism are formed and controlled, and within which the *possession* of the aleatory is resolved in an institutional, or at best "monumental," format. (The only source which appears to defy such an interpretation is that which refers to the Modern movement; nevertheless, this is read by Graves as only signifying "metaphysical" and "twentieth century," thus permitting our schema to remain valid.) Having established a system of limitations and exclusions, Graves is able to manipulate his materials in a finite series of operations; at the same time this system allows him to show how a clarification or an explication of linguistic processes permits an indirect control over the design, *always within the predetermined system of exclusions*. In other words, Michael Graves, Peter Eisenman and Richard Meier give new life to a method which springs from the classification of the syntactic processes. It is the sort of formalism, in its original guise, which is perpetuated through their work. "Semantic distortion," the pivotal point of the Russian formalists, is thus brought to life again in an obvious manner at the Benacerraf House by Graves. Within this work, as well as in the more hieratic and timeless syntactic decompositions of Eisenman, we may see a sort of analytic laboratory devoted to experimentation upon highly select forms, rather than just a mere penchant for Terragni or a taste for the abstract.

It is of little interest to us to ask how such works may appear as a heresy within the American culture. However, their objective role is without doubt to provide a selected catalogue of design approaches applicable to predetermined situations. It is then useless to ask if their "neo-purist" tendencies are or are not effective.[3] As examples of linguistic structures, we can only ask that they be rigorous in their absolute ahistoricism. Only in this fashion can their nostalgic abandon be neutralized, and thereby acknowledge their need to remain in isolation (an acknowledgement, by the way, which would never be apparent from the self-satisfied stylistic gestures of Philip Johnson).

Let us attempt to reconstruct the analysis to date. It requires a specific reading of the languages employed as well as the use of different modes of approach to their analysis. To understand Stirling's work it is necessary to refer to the technological aesthetic and the theory of information. Only by so doing will it be possible to become completely aware of the rationale behind his semantic distortions. But the theory of information reveals little to us about Rossi's study of typological constraints. Indeed, Rossi's formalism appears to want to challenge even the original formulation of the linguistic formalism of Viktor Sklovsky or of Vsevolod M. Eichenbaum. We do not wish to put forward a theory of critical empiricism. We rather intend to point out that every critical action is seen, in fact, as a composite of itself and the object being analyzed. Today then, a highly specialized analysis of an architecture, strongly characterized by linguistic sense, can have only one result – a tautology.

To dissect and rebuild the geometric metaphors of the "compositional rigorists" may prove to be an endless game which may eventually become useless when, as in Eisenman's work, the process of assemblage is altogether explicit and presented in a highly didactic manner. In the face of such products, the task of criticism is to begin from within the work only to escape from it as soon as possible so as not to be caught in the vicious circle of a language that speaks only of itself. Obviously the problems of criticism lie elsewhere. We do not believe in the artificial "New Trends" within contemporary architecture.[4] Yet there is little doubt that there exists a widespread attitude that is intent on repossessing the unique character of the object by removing it from its economic and functional contexts and highlighting it as an exceptional event – and hence a surrealistic one – by placing it in parentheses with the flux of objects generated by the production system. It is possible to speak of these acts as an *"architecture dans le boudoir."* And not only because we find ourselves faced with an "architecture of cruelty," as the works of Stirling and Rossi have demonstrated with their cruelty of language-as-a-system-of-exclusions, but also because the magic circle drawn around linguistic experimentation reveals a pregnant affinity with the structural rigor of the literature of the Marquis de Sade. "There, where the stake is sex, everything must speak of sex." That is, the utopia of Eros in Sade – resolved within the discovery that maximum freedom springs forth from maximum terror – where the whole is inscribed within the supreme constraint of a geometric structure in the narrative. To regain an "order of discourse" may today prove to be a safeguard for certain subjective liberties – particularly after its destruction by the avant-garde through questioning the techniques of mass information and with the disappearance of the work of art into the assembly line. There are two contradictions, however. On the one hand, as with the Enlightenment utopia, such attempts are destined to reveal that liberty serves only to make a silence speak; that is, one cannot bring voluntary action to oppose a structure. On the other hand, the "orders of discourse" are an attempt to go beyond this impasse and propose a foundation for a new statute of architecture. Such contradictions are actually theorized in the work of Kahn since the mid-fifties. Yet we have not escaped the hermetic play of language.

NOTES

1   Cf. Bruno Zevi, "Manieristi fra le macerie," *L'Espresso*, n. 15., 1973. Concerning the work of the "Five," see also essays by Colin Rowe and Kenneth Frampton, *Five Architects* (New York; George Wittenborn, Inc., 1972); Mario Gandelsonas, "On reading architecture," *Progressive Architecture*, n. 3., 1972, pp. 68–87; Robert Stern, "Stompin' at the Savoye," Jaquelin Robertson, "Machines in the Garden," Charles Moore, "In similar states of undress," Alan Greenberg, "The Lurking American Legacy," Romaldo Giurgola, "The Discreet Charm of the Bourgeoisie," *Architectural Forum*, vol. 138, n. 4, 1973, p. 46.

2   Gandelsonas, "On reading architecture," pp. 78–9. We may note that what Argan has seen fit to recognize in the work of Louis Kahn is perhaps better suited to the work of the "Five": "The most profound currents today, those which are most aware of the crisis move towards a methodic analysis, almost scientific and always critical, of the structural components of the artistic phenomenon: to thereby establish whether it is possible for art to still become phenomenalized, critically questioning why a surface is a surface, a volume a volume, a building a building, a painting a painting. By so doing they recognize that art cannot be defined by its placement or position, and from its role in the system they then try to see if it can be defined as a closed system, an autonomous structure." Giulio Carlo Argan, "I due stadi della critica," *Ulisse: Dove va l'arte*, vol. XII, n. 76, Nov. 1973.

3   Cf. Walter Segal, "The Neo-Purist School of Architecture," *Architectural Design*, vol. XLII, n. 6, 1972.

4   We are referring here to the "Nuova Architettura" (with a capital N and A) in Nino Dardi, *Il gioco sapiente* (Padua: Marsilio, 1971) and to the "Nuova Tendenza" (note the persistence of capital letters) of Massimo Scolari, "A vanguardia e nuova architettura," ibid. If the objective is to define a continuity with the abstract movements of the twenties and thirties, rather than defining what is "new," one ought to have the courage to speak of revival or of survival. If the intention is to establish the importance of linguistic consideration greater care should be exercised in the selection or exclusion of examples.

236   MARIO GANDELSONAS
from "Neo-Functionalism" (1976)

When the first issue of *Oppositions* appeared in 1973, it supported no identifiable theoretical position. Yet as each of its editors — Kenneth Frampton (see 244), Mario Gandelsonas, Peter Eisenman (see 237), and Anthony Vidler (see 238) — came to pen lead editorial statements in separate issues, a complement of competing positions began to emerge. Mario Gandelsonas, an Argentinean architect schooled in Paris in the late 1960s, crafted his position with this essay, "Neo-Functionalism." The editorial begins with his distinction between the "neo-rationalist" school of Aldo Rossi, Peter Eisenman, and John Hejduk, and the "neo-realist" school of Robert Venturi. Both schools, he argues, are "anti-functionalist," in that both regard the functionalism of modernism (form follows functionalism) as regressive and destructive within today's architectural context. Both schools again, as their appellations describe, developed only fragments of modernism, that is, rationalism and realism. Gandelsonas counters with his vision of "neo-functionalism" — now extending the formerly limited meaning of "function" into a broader symbolic dimension.

The fundamental doctrine of functionalism was synthesized in the dictum "form follows function." Since function is itself one of the meanings that could be articulated by form, we see, in fact, that functionalism was essentially based on a simple and embryonic *idea of meaning*. Functionalists in general (and Le Corbusier in particular) did not use or develop in depth this dimension of architecture; firstly, because their work was an attack on the symbolic architecture of the Academy and secondly, because there existed no rigorous theoretical context that would allow such a development.

Now, however, the dimension of meaning, present but underdeveloped in the first phase of functionalism, can be confronted. The polemical conditions facing architecture in the beginning of this century no longer exist, while the historical perspective and theoretical means to conceptualize the role of meaning in architecture, have been created. That is, it is now possible to reintegrate the tendencies of the 1960s and early 1920s into a more comprehensive ideology which fundamentally emphasizes the development of the symbolic dimension – the introduction of the problem of meaning within the process of design in a systematic and conscious way. Such an approach might be seen as a "neo-functionalism."

Mario Gandelsonas, from "Neo-Functionalism," in *Oppositions* 5 (Summer 1976), pp. 7–8.

The idea of such a neo-functionalism is opposed to the respective neo-rationalist and neo-realist positions in the sense that they have developed isolated fragments of the original doctrine and, in this way, have eliminated the complex contradictions inherent in function-alism. A neo-functionalist position would neither eliminate nor solve these dialectical contradictions but rather would assume them as one of the main forces which keep alive the development of ideas in architecture. Thus the concept of neo-functionalism would exclude neither the neo-realist nor the neo-rationalist notions, but rather add and develop the fundamental dimension of *meaning*, thereby reconstituting all dimensions of the original doctrine.

This should not be seen, however, as a mere revival or development of functionalism as originally conceived, nor as a reconsideration of functionalism in order to realize its dated and, for us, timid propositions and basically reformist aims.

A neo-functionalist position abandons the pendular movement (which is not real change) that has characterized the passage from one ideology to the next, now represented by functionalism, now by neo-rationalism and neo-realism. Such an association tends, through the underlying idealism inherent not only in functionalism but in most archi-tectural ideologies, to eliminate or neutralize contradiction. Rather, such a position proposes the development of the progressive aspects of functionalism, an action which implies the effective transformation of its idealistic nature, building a dialectical basis for architecture.

237   PETER EISENMAN
from "Post-Functionalism" (1976)

Peter Eisenman, in the following issue of *Oppositions*, wrote his editorial "Post-Functionalism" as a response to that of Mario Gandelsonas, and he did so in a way to knock the philosophical underpinnings (form and function) out from under the latter's model. In Eisenman's view, we are standing on the threshold of an entirely new architectural world, one transcending the oppositional dialectic of form and function, and one characterized largely by the "absence" of the subject or "originating agent." Hence this passage to the post-humanist and post-functionalist world is more significant, more momentous. This editorial represents one of the first instances of French poststructuralist ideas making their way into the architectural discourse (they would find a broader footing in the 1980s), but, almost nostalgically, there is also something of the spirit and ghost of Sigfried Giedion appearing behind these words. Giedion's book *Space, Time and Architecture*, incidentally, had appeared thirty-five years earlier, or roughly the span of a single generation.

The critical establishment within architecture has told us that we have entered the era of "post-modernism." The tone with which this news is delivered is invariably one of relief, similar to that which accompanies the advice that one is no longer an adolescent. Two indices of this supposed change are the quite different manifestations of the "Architettura

Peter Eisenman, "Post-Functionalism," in *Oppositions* 6 (Fall 1976), n.p.

Razionale" exhibition at the Milan Triennale of 1973, and the "Ecole Des Beaux Arts" exhibition at The Museum of Modern Art in 1975. The former, going on the assumption that modern architecture was an outmoded functionalism, declared that architecture can be generated only through a return to itself as an autonomous or pure discipline. The latter, seeing modern architecture as an obsessional formalism, made itself into an implicit statement that the future lies paradoxically in the past, within the peculiar response to function that characterized the nineteenth century's eclectic command of historical styles.

[. . .]

Both the Triennale and the Beaux Arts exhibitions suggest, however, that the problem is thought to be somewhere else – not so much with functionalism *per se*, as with the nature of this so-called modernist sensibility. Hence, the implied revival of neo-classicism and Beaux Arts academicism as replacements for a continuing, if poorly understood, modernism. It is true that sometime in the nineteenth century, there was indeed a crucial shift within Western consciousness: one which can be characterized as a shift from humanism to modernism. But, for the most part, architecture, in its dogged adherence to the principles of function, did not participate in or understand the fundamental aspects of that change. It is the potential difference in the nature of modernist and humanist theory that seems to have gone unnoticed by those people who today speak of eclecticism, post-modernism, or neo-functionalism. And they have failed to notice it precisely because they conceive of modernism as merely a stylistic manifestation of functionalism, and functionalism itself as a basic theoretical proposition in architecture. In fact, the idea of modernism has driven a wedge into these attitudes. It has revealed that the dialectic form and function is culturally based.

In brief, the modernist sensibility has to do with a changed mental attitude toward the artifacts of the physical world. This change has not only been manifested aesthetically, but also socially, philosophically, and technologically – in sum, it has been manifested in a new cultural attitude. This shift away from the dominant attitudes of humanism, that were pervasive in Western societies for some four hundred years, took place at various times in the nineteenth century in such disparate disciplines as mathematics, music, painting, literature, film, and photography. It is displayed in the non-objective abstract painting of Malevich and Mondrian; in the non-narrative, atemporal writing of Joyce and Apollinaire; the atonal and polytonal compositions of Schönberg and Webern; in the non-narrative films of Richter and Eggeling.

Abstraction, atonality, and atemporality, however, are merely stylistic manifestations of modernism, not its essential nature. Although this is not the place to elaborate a theory of modernism, or indeed to represent those aspects of such a theory which have already found their way into the literature of the other humanist disciplines, it can simply be said that the symptoms to which one has just pointed suggest a displacement of man away from the center of his world. He is no longer viewed as an *originating agent*. Objects are seen as ideas independent of man. In this context, man is a discursive function among complex and already-formed systems of language, which he witnesses but does not constitute. As Levi-Strauss has said, "Language, an unreflecting totalization, is human reason which has its reason and of which man knows nothing." It is this condition of displacement which gives rise to design in which authorship can no longer either account for a linear development which has a 'beginning' and an 'end' – hence the rise of the atemporal – or account for the invention of form – hence the abstract as a mediation between pre-existent sign systems.

Modernism, as a sensibility based on the fundamental displacement of man, represents what Michel Foucault would specify as a new *épistème*. Deriving from a non-humanistic attitude toward the relationship of an individual to his physical environment, it breaks with the historical past, both with the ways of viewing man as subject and, as we have said, with the ethical positivism of form and function. Thus, it cannot be related to functionalism. It is probably for this reason that modernism has not up to now been elaborated in architecture.

But there is clearly a present need for a theoretical investigation of the basic implications of modernism (as opposed to modern style) in architecture. In his editorial "Neo-Functionalism," in *Oppositions* 5, Mario Gandelsonas acknowledges such a need. However, he says merely that the "complex contradictions" inherent in functionalism – such as neo-realism and neo-rationalism – make a form of neo-functionalism necessary to any new theoretical dialectic. This proposition continues to refuse to recognize that the form/function opposition is not necessarily inherent to any architectural theory and so fails to recognize the crucial difference between modernism and humanism. In contrast, what is being called post-functionalism begins as an attitude which recognizes modernism as a new and distinct sensibility. It can best be understood in architecture in terms of a theoretical base that is concerned with what might be called a modernist *dialectic*, as opposed to the old humanist (i.e., functionalist) opposition of form and function.

This new theoretical base changes the humanist balance of form/function to a dialectical relationship within the evolution of form itself. The dialectic can best be described as the potential co-existence within any form of two non-corroborating and non-sequential tendencies. One tendency is to presume architectural form to be a recognizable transformation from some pre-existent geometric or platonic solid. In this case, from is usually understood through a series of registrations designed to recall a more simple geometric condition. This tendency is certainly a relic of humanist theory. However, to this is added a second tendency that sees architectural form in an atemporal, decompositional mode, as something simplified from some pre-existent set of non-specific spatial entities. Here, form is understood as a series of fragments – signs without meaning dependent upon, and without reference to, a more basic condition. The former tendency, when taken by itself, is a reductivist attitude and assumes some primary unity as both an ethical and an aesthetic basis for all creation. The latter, by itself, assumes a basic condition of fragmentation and multiplicity from which the resultant form is a state of simplification. Both tendencies, however, when taken together, constitute the essence of this new, modern dialectic. They begin to define the inherent nature of the object in and of itself and its capacity to be represented. They begin to suggest that the theoretical assumptions of functionalism are in fact cultural rather than universal.

Post-functionalism, thus, is a term of absence. In its negation of functionalism it suggests certain positive theoretical alternatives – existing fragments of thought which, when examined, might serve as a framework for the development of a larger theoretical structure – but it does not, in and of itself, propose to supply a label for such a new consciousness in architecture which I believe is potentially upon us.

238 ANTHONY VIDLER
from "The Third Typology" (1976)

In what amounted to the fourth straight manifesto to appear in the journal *Oppositions*, Anthony Vidler, having now joined the editorial staff, appends his efforts to those of Frampton, Gandelsonas, and Eisenman. Vidler, up to this point, was preeminently a historian specializing in French theory of the late eighteenth century, but with this essay he crosses over into the contemporary debate. His argument is succinct: architecture over the last two centuries had operated from the ontological underpinning of two typologies or formal systems. The first type employed in design was the "primitive hut" of Marc-Antoine Laugier, subsequently modified by A. C. Quatremère de Quincy, which was predicated on both nature and reason. The second type was the "machine," as chiefly articulated by Le Corbusier's famous comment regarding the house as a machine for living in. It was in effect a typology of mass production, one engendering not only machine forms but also the meliorist vision that architecture improves the lot of humanity through its technological development. With the work of the "new Rationalists," Vidler argues, a new typology is emerging: one founded on history ("the clarity of the eighteenth-century city") and the autonomy of the architectural language itself, a tradition of forms now stripped of its utopian premises.

This new typology is explicitly critical of the Modern Movement; it utilizes the clarity of the eighteenth-century city to rebuke the fragmentation, de-centralization, and formal disintegration introduced into contemporary urban life by the zoning techniques and technological advances of the twenties. While the Modern Movement found its hell in cities, and its Eden in the uninterrupted sea of sunlit space filled with greenery – a city become a garden – the new typology as a critique of modern urbanism raises the continuous fabric, the clear distinction between public and private marked by the walls of street and square, to the level of principle. Its nightmare is the isolated building set in an undifferentiated park. The heroes of this new typology are therefore to be found not among the nostalgic, anti-city utopians of the nineteenth century nor among the critics of industrial and technical progress of the twentieth, but rather among those who, as the professional servants of urban life, direct their design skills to solving the questions of avenue, arcade, street and square, park and house, institution and equipment in a continuous typology of elements that together coheres with past fabric and present intervention to make one comprehensible experience of the city.

For this typology, there is no clear set of rules for the transformations and their objects, nor any polemically defined set of historical precedents. Nor should there be; the continued vitality of this architectural practice rests in its essential engagement with the precise demands of the present and not in any holistic mythicization of the past. It refuses any "nostalgia" in its evocations of history, except to give its restorations sharper focus; it refuses all unitary descriptions of the social meaning of form, recognizing the specious quality of any single ascription of social order to an architectural order; it finally refuses all eclecticism, resolutely filtering its "quotations" through the lens of a modernist aesthetic. In this sense, it is an entirely modern movement, and one that places its faith in the essentially public

Anthony Vidler, from "The Third Typology," in *Oppositions* 7 (Winter 1976), pp. 2–4.

nature of all architecture, as against the increasingly private visions of romantic individualists in the last decade. In it, the city and typology are reasserted as the only possible bases for the restoration of a critical role to an architecture otherwise assassinated by the apparently endless cycle of production and consumption.

239 MAURICE CULOT AND LEON KRIER
from ''The Only Path for Architecture'' (1978)

I n 1978 Anthony Vidler's essay "The Third Typology" was drafted into the service of another book entitled *Rational Architecture*, and became, as it were, one of the working manifestos of this movement in northern Europe, as supported by the Luxembourg architects Leon and Rob Krier, and Maurice Culot, a professor at the École Nationale Supérieure de La Cambre in Brussels. Leon Krier, who exhibited in Milan in 1973, helped to organize an exhibition in London in 1975 under the same name of "Rational Architecture." In its publication, he argued that typology (the types of historical spaces, buildings, and streets) was the natural corrective to the anti-historicism of modernism, and the medicament for moving past the urban debilitation of the present. In this essay written in the same year, composed with Maurice Culot, their polemics have sharpened noticeably – as seen in this essay's early reference to the antihero Robert Venturi ("there is thus nothing to be 'learned from Las Vegas' ") and later to disquieting remarks on the American city in general. It points to a political divide opening between European and American thought in the 1970s, one that would pit the rhetoric of European Marxists against what they perceived to be the frivolity of American pop culture. With all of its overtly "savage" Europhilia, the demand for "A Copernican Revolution" is a powerfully worded manifesto capturing the high spirit and passion of the day.

A Copernican Revolution

When we allude to the necessity for a global project, we do not intend by any means to say that we wish to cover the territory with plans, but rather that basic models which take man as their measure must be studied as a first priority – man as he is normally constituted, not man stricken with elephantiasis as he wanders through the projects of Speer, or that deaf and dumb man who surveys from his automobile the empty and discontinuous spaces of modern urbanism.

In Bologna, the ancient parishes have finally become an authentic model for democratic administration; in Brussels, the inhabitants of the most popular district have obliged a reactionary municipal administration to reconstruct their quarter in terms of real streets and real squares.

For the concept of streets and squares does not derive from fashion, but rather constitutes a historic concept inscribed within the European tradition, and it is not a matter of imitating them as style but as precise types.

Maurice Culot and Leon Krier, from "The Only Path for Architecture," trans. Christian Hubert, in *Oppositions* 14 (Fall 1978), pp. 41–3.

A street is a street, and one lives there in a certain way not because architects have imagined streets in certain ways. As opposed to television and the automobile, which have already succeeded in changing the physical qualities of American man, the terrorism of modern architecture has fortunately not yet succeeded in changing the character of European man. (Scenario for a horror film: crabman from Barbicane meets oblique-man from the city of Claude Parent.)

We must forcefully reject the American city and become savagely European; our objective is not a sort of supernationalism incompatible with the very notion of culture, but aims at the development of an intense social life, at the development of the highest and most differentiated levels of communication, in complete opposition to the industrialized media. *Against the agglomeration of buildings and of individuals we posit the city and its communities.* The inevitable results for a society which refuses the pleasure in work are suicide or collective fascism, toward which the most industrialized countries are inevitably drawn. The only means of avoiding this fate lie in the rejection of the social and industrial division of labor as well as in the espousal and even reinforcement of the professional division of labor, and at the same time the rejection of the social stratification between manual and intellectual work. Our project for architecture works in this direction: it tends to reduce the differentiation of social divisions. This is precisely where the essence of its political nature lies.

To "augment our well-being without reducing our pleasure" or at the limit to insure our survival, we must immediately take part in the recognition and reconstruction of artisanry, of manual work. The latter, which has always been the basis for human creativity and personal realization, has become an exercise in degradation through the division of labor. And it is the schools themselves that have proceeded to destroy the culture and intelligence of the people.

Yesterday this willful destruction was still dictated by a "bourgeois coldness"; today this illegitimate rationality is weighed down further by stupidity and cynicism. More than ever before, the Modern Movement, in all its expressions – written, built, and pedagogical – presents the European city as a natural field for the experiments of the 'creators'. Those who are experiencing the destruction of the cities directly through the urban struggles know that administrative and artistic neutrality is a delusion and that technicians (engineers and architects) have played a determining role in the contagion and generalization of the destructuring models of the Athens Charter. This is why we insist upon participating in the urban struggles while at the same time developing new architectural models that anticipate a decentralized and self-governed society, as opposed to the Athens Charter, which stands on an argument based on a principle of outrageous levels of industrialization, of unbridled mobility, of zoning, of political and cultural centralization, etc. The freedom sold daily by the media through every possible trick is none other than the slavery of mobility, which has become today the cause and means of social fragmentation – a fragmentation necessary for the destruction of any resistance, of all intelligence awakening against the industrial system, the suicidal alienation of those with no other project but consumption.

Within the framework of an anti-industrial resistance carried out at the European scale, we are engaged in theoretical exercises and their practical applications (to the architectural project), with the reconstruction of the cities in mind. These stimulating exercises have no innocent character; they permit us to verify hypotheses, to stimulate questions, debates, and works that are all situated along the only path of architecture.

B.   SEMIOTICS AND PHENOMENOLOGY

Introduction

Within the unsettled atmosphere of this decade, architectural theory in the 1970s also came under the strong influence of three theoretical models from outside of the profession. All three were employed in opposition to behaviorist models drafted into the service of architecture in the 1960s.

The intellectual roots of structuralism and semiotics are virtually indistinguishable. Both approaches arose out of linguistics, and in particular were given definition by Ferdinand de Saussure's *Course of General Linguistics* (1916), which first articulated the paradigm of *langue* (the relatively stable structure or rules of "language") from *parole* ("speaking" or the variable expression given by the speaker). In the 1950s Claude Lévi-Strauss imported structuralism into anthropological theory when he, in his research into the mythological narratives of remote tribal societies, came to argue that there were universal and unconscious mental structures (mathematically accessible to analysis) underlying the activity of human thought. Kenzo Tange and other Japanese Metabolists introduced the term structure into architecture in the 1960s, and in the 1970s the term also came to be employed in Dutch architecture to characterize (retroactively) the ideas of Aldo van Eyck, who himself was much influenced by Lévi-Strauss but who never in fact used the term structuralism.

The science of semiotics, or semiology (the term sometimes preferred by French and British theorists), has similar roots in the linguistics of de Saussure, but also in the linguistic investigations of the Americans Charles Sander Peirce and Charles W. Morris. Semiotics is the study of signs or meaning, and in the system of Morris it is divided into pragmatic, syntactic, and semantic realms. The last two, in the late 1960s and 1970s, now find extensive architectural application. Syntactics treats the relationships of signs to one another without regard to meaning. If in linguistics syntactics concerns the rules of grammar, in architecture it often relates to the constructional language, for instance, the relation of a column to an intersecting beam. Semantics, by contrast, deals exclusively with the meaning of things, and the theories of Peirce and Morris further divide signs into the categories of indexes, icons, and symbols. When the Argentinean Tomás Maldonado first introduced semiotics into the architecture curriculum at Ulm's Technical Hochschule (HfG) in the late 1950s, he argued that architecture operates at multiple levels of communication that can be measured. Several authors took up this suggestion in the 1960s, particularly in Italy, where there appeared several studies by Sergio Bettini, Giovanni Klaus Koenig, Ronato De Fusco, Maria Luisa Scalvini, and Umberto Eco, among others. Analyses of architectural meaning exploded in the 1970s, as semiotics now became a tool to critique the (presumably exhausted) language of modernism and to suggest ways to support alternative formal systems.

The philosophical approach of phenomenology was also imported into architecture as a critical tool. First proposed by Edmund Husserl at the start of the twentieth century, phenomenology concerned itself with discerning the workings (inner and outer horizons) of human consciousness. Husserl's student, Martin Heidegger, initially employed the discipline in a hermeneutic investigation of being, but in the 1930s he began to shift his focus to such issues as art and technology. His essay "Building, Dwelling, Thinking" (a lecture initially given in 1951) contained strong architectural overtones that would eventually be seized upon by architects. In parallel with this lead, Maurice Merleau-Ponty's *Phenomenology of Perception* (1945) opened up another field ripe for architectural interpretation.

240   CHARLES JENCKS
from "Semiology and Architecture" (1969)

I n 1969 Charles Jencks and George Baird assembled a group of essays by various contributors under the title *Meaning in Architecture*. This book brought to light the high level of theoretical speculation – centered at the Architectural Association in London in the late 1960s – about the application of structuralist and semiological ideas to architecture. It also set the stage for the considerable architectural research to be devoted to these two areas in the 1970s. Both Jencks and Baird penned influential essays, and both derived their analysis from the semiological models of Ferdinand de Saussure and Roland Barthes. Although Jencks's main point (following Barthes) – that "semantization is inevitable" if not also ephemeral and sometimes aleatory – draws close to conventional linguistic theory, the semantic process is vastly different. Jencks shares, for instance, Reyner Banham's iconographic appreciation for and juxtaposition of high and pop art. *Meaning in Architecture* also had the interesting editorial device of inserting a side column to allow the other contributors to critique each essay.

Charles Jencks, from "Semiology and Architecture," in *Meaning in Architecture*. New York: George Braziller, 1969, pp. 11–13.

This is perhaps the most fundamental idea of semiology and meaning in architecture: the idea that any form in the environment, or sign in language, is motivated, or capable of being motivated. It helps to explain why all of a sudden forms come alive or fall into bits. For it contends that, although a form may be initially arbitrary or non-motivated as Saussure points out,[1] its subsequent use is motivated or based on some determinants. Or we can take a slightly different point of view and say

BAIRD: It need not even be 'invented'; all it has to do is ▶ that the minute a new form is invented it will acquire, *inevitably*, a meaning. 'This semantization is inevitable; as soon as there is a society, every usage is converted into a sign of itself; the use of a raincoat is to give protection from the rain, but this cannot be dissociated from the very signs of an atmospheric situation'.[2] Or to be more exact, the use of a raincoat can be dissociated from its shared meanings if we avoid its social

BAIRD: I don't agree about the efficacy of these 'explicit decisions'. Meanings are not 'voted down', or controlled by elites (Barthes is ▶ use or explicitly decide to deny it further meaning.

wrong about that, I feel, even for the elite world of haute couture). The only way meanings dissolve is through atrophy, across a whole social totality.

It is this conscious denial of connotations which has had an interesting history with the avant-garde. Annoyed either by the glib reduction of their work to its social meanings or the contamination of the strange by an old language, they have insisted on the intractability of the new and confusing. 'Our League of Nations symbolizes nothing' said the architect Hannes Meyer, all too weary of the creation of buildings around past metaphors. 'My poem means nothing; it just is. My painting is meaningless. Against Interpretation: The

BROADBENT: See also ▶ Literature of Silence. Entirely radical.' Most of these statements are objecting to the 'inevitable semantization' which is

Stravinsky: '...I consider that music is, by its very nature, powerless to *express* anything at all, whether a feeling, an attitude of mind, a psychological mood, a phenomenon of nature, etc....' An Autobiography, 1936.

trite, which is coarse, which is too anthropomorphic or old. Some are simply nihilistic and based on the belief that any meaning which may be applied is spurious; it denies the fundamental absurdity of human existence. In any case, on one level, all these statements are paradoxical. In their denial of meaning, they create it. This may account for the relative popularity among the avant-garde of the Cretan Liar Paradox, the Cretan who says 'All Cretans are liars'. It seems as if the statement is true, then it is false; if false then true. A very enjoyable situation, to some the essence of life. Yet by expanding the statement and avoiding its self reference the paradox can be avoided. Thus Hannes Meyer's statement might read: 'Our League of Nations symbolizes something, and that something is nothing'. I say might read, because it is quite apparent from the context in which he made the remark that he meant that his building symbolized not all the previous ideas of government, but new ones based on utility. In any case, two points are relevant to my purpose:(1) that every act, object and statement that man perceives is meaningful (even 'nothing') and (2) that the frontiers of meaning are always, momentarily, in a state of collapse and paradox.

The first point is the justification for semiology, the theory of signs. It contends that since everything is meaningful, we are in a literal sense condemned to meaning, and thus we can either become aware of how meaning works in a technical sense (semiology), or we can remain content with our intuition. This dichotomy is probably a false antithesis since, *ex hypothesi,* semiology holds that we cannot be aware of, or responsible for, everything at once. Yet the goal of semiology, even if ultimately vain, is to bring the intuitive up to the conscious level, in order to increase our area of responsible choice.

The second point seems at variance with the first, for it appears to deny the existence of ultimate meanings (in its nihilistic stance) and it certainly undercuts the responsibility toward past, social meanings (except to upset them). To give an example, the position of Reyner Banham is relevant. In one book he starts a sentence 'The Dymaxion concept (of Fuller) was entirely radical . . .' in another, he says 'Given a genuinely functional approach such as this, no cultural preconceptions . . .' Now these three avant-garde ideas, from a semiological (and factual) viewpoint, are demonstrably false. There simply cannot be anything created which is *entirely* radical, *genuinely* functional and with *no* cultural preconceptions (see below). Yet if re-qualified these statements would be semiologically acceptable and, more important, highly relevant. Because they point to that underlying experience where new meanings are actively generated and it seems as if one were totally free from preconceptions. Since there is a real sense in which this is true, one can agree with the emphasis on the radical and undomesticated. Except that, if taken as absolutely true, this tends to discourage a more radical creativity; because it limits the area of criticism and active re-use of the past. It is one of the basic assumptions of semiology that creation is dependent on tradition and memory in a very real sense and that if one tries to jettison either one or the other, one is actually limiting one's area of free choice.

NOTES

1   *Course in General Linguistics,* Saussure, McGraw-Hill, 1966, pp. 67–9.
2   *Elements of Semiology,* Roland Barthes, Cape, 1967, p. 41.

241 GEORGE BAIRD

from " 'La Dimension Amoureuse' in Architecture" (1969)

I f one were to summarize Baird's complex argument in this essay with a few words, one might say that he makes the case for allowing "rhetoric" back into design. The argument, however, is what is interesting. He begins by considering two polar projects: Eero Saarinen's recently completed CBS Building in New York City and Cedric Price's "Potteries Thinkbelt" project for a technical university in the English Midlands. The first is an exercise in high design, a controlled *Gesamtkunstwerk* (synthesis of the design arts) in the spirit of the modern masters; the second is an exercise in the virtual abstraction of advocacy planning, a non-impositional approach to design that is characterized as "life conditioning." Both fail, Bair argues: the first because it is paternalistic toward the building occupants, the second because it is scientistic or objectifying of those occupants. Drawing next upon de Saussure's distinction between *langue* (the collective and unconscious aspect of language) and *parole* (the individual and conscious reflections of speech), Baird argues that both projects again fail because both shift the design emphasis away from the rhetorical level of *parole* and concern themselves with the *langue* of design. Baird – invoking Claude Perrault's distinction between absolute and relative beauty – insists on a mediation of the existing architectural language with the rhetorical flourish of individual speech, which in turn is essentially grounded in changing customs.

The part of semiological theory which bears most directly on the problem of modern designers' attempts to assume privileged positions, is the part Saussure described by means of the *langue/parole* distinction. For semiology, any social phenomenon is made up of both a *langue* and a *parole*. In the first of three senses, the *langue* is the collective aspect of the phenomenon, and the *parole* the individual aspect. Thus, semiology incorporates the fundamental sociological insight that human experience, in so far as it is social, is simultaneously collective and individual.

In the second of the three senses, semiology sees the *langue* as the unconscious aspect of a social phenomenon, and the *parole* as the conscious aspect. In this way, it incorporates one of the most obvious insights of post-19th century psychology, and posits that any conscious gesture in a social context always involves an unconscious component. With respect to these two senses of the *langue/parole* distinction in language, Barthes has said: 'The *langue* is both a social institution and a system of values. As a social institution, it is never an act; it utterly eludes premeditation; it is the social part of language; the individual can, by himself, neither create it, nor modify it; it is essentially a collective contract, which, if one wishes to communicate, one must accept in its entirety. What is more, this social product is autonomous, like a game which has rules one must know before one can play it . . . As opposed to the *langue*, institution and system, the *parole* is essentially an individual act of selection and actualization . . .'

In the most modern sense of the distinction, the *langue* of a social phenomenon is considered to be its 'code', and the *parole* its 'message'. In some respects, this new sense of the distinction is the most interesting, because it introduces into semiology a number of

George Baird, from " 'La Dimension Amoureuse' in Architecture," in *Meaning in Architecture*. New York: George Braziller, 1970, pp. 81–2.

precise mathematical techniques of analysis, commonly grouped under the name 'information theory'. In terms parallel to the collective/individual and unconscious/conscious senses of the distinction, we may say that the particular 'message' which any gesture in a social context constitutes, necessarily involves the use of the 'code' which that context entails.

Of course, information theory goes even further than that nowadays, viewing communication systems as dynamic. While the *relation holding between* the *langue* and the *parole* is necessarily constant, the system as a whole is in a continuous process of development. More specifically, 'information' occurs as a function of 'surprise' within a matrix of 'expectancy'. In order to register, a message must be somewhat surprising, yet not utterly unexpected. If it is too predictable, the message won't register at all. It is in this sense that 'background noise' tends to slip below the threshold of awareness, and that we speak of clichés as not having enough 'information value'. Conversely, if the message is too unpredictable, the result is the same. As Paul McCartney has said, ' . . . if music . . . is just going to jump about five miles ahead, then everyone's going to be left standing with this gap of five miles that they've got to all cross before they can even see what scene these people are on . . .'

We can now, I think, begin to see how the *Gesamtkünstler* and the life-conditioner become involved in their attempts to assume privileged positions. If, for example, we examine their stances in the light of the collective/individual sense of the *langue*/*parole* distinction, the following becomes apparent. In undertaking 'total design', the *Gesamtkünstler* presumes *ipso facto*, either individually, or as part of a small élite, to take over comprehensive responsibility for the *langue* of architecture, and to do so, moreover, in a fashion which leaves the *langue*'s collective validity unimpaired. In other words, 'total design' amounts to an attempt to shift the impact of the individual design act from the level of *parole* to that of *langue*. On the other hand, in making his individual design gesture, the life-conditioner pretends to act altogether independently of the *langue* of architecture. But of course, since he, like the *Gesamtkünstler*, is only an individual acting in a social context, his pretence really amounts to a single-handed attempt at a radical modification *of* the *langue*. And that is just another way of saying that he too attempts to shift the impact of the individual design act from the level of *parole* to that of *langue*.

242 CHRISTIAN NORBERG-SCHULZ
from *Existence, Space &*
Architecture (1971)

The idea of space as a focal point of design had, of course, become a fixture of modern theory since the efforts of Sigfried Giedion and Bruno Zevi. By the early 1970s, however, the idea was receiving less currency owing to the new emphasis placed on dissecting architectural form and its various meanings. In this sense, Christian Norberg-Schulz's book *Existence, Space & Architecture* represents a rearguard attempt to salvage the

Christian Norberg-Schulz, from *Existence, Space & Architecture*. New York: Praeger, 1971, pp. 11–12.

notion of space as an important architectural concept — now by updating its meaning and endowing it with a phenomenological cast. His sources were twofold: first, the path-breaking investigations of Jean Piaget on the perceptual and conceptual development of human consciousness; second, a score of phenomenological writers and architectural thinkers from Martin Heidegger to Maurice Merleau-Ponty and Rudolf Schwarz. The result, similar to the efforts of Aldo van Eyck before him, is a serious attempt to make concrete the formerly abstract notion of "space" by exalting the idea of "place." Within the writings of Norberg-Schulz this book represents a transitional stage, but it is an important pivotal point around which his later writings turn.

We thus see that the synthetic space of primitive man has been split into several specialized constructs which serve us in our orientation and adaptation to different aspects of the environment. In addition to the cognitive spaces, we have within the psychological dimension to distinguish between immediate *perceptual space* and the more stable *space schemata*. The latter are composed of elements which have a certain invariance, such as universal elementary structures (archetypes) and socially or culturally conditioned structures, and, of course, some personal idiosyncrasies. Together these make up man's 'image' of his environment, that is, a stable system of three-dimensional relations between meaningful objects. We will therefore unify the schemata in the concept *existential space*. Perceptual space, on the contrary, is egocentric and varies continuously, although the variations are linked to form meaningful totalities (experiences) because they are assimilated to the subjects' schemata, which are in turn somewhat modified by the new experience. We have so far distinguished between five space concepts: the pragmatic space of physical action, the perceptual space of immediate orientation, the existential space which forms man's stable image of his environment, the cognitive space of the physical world and the abstract space of pure logical relations. Pragmatic space integrates man with his natural, 'organic' environment, perceptual space is essential to his identity as a person, existential space makes him belong to a social and cultural totality,[1] cognitive space means that he is able to think about space, and logical space, finally, offers the tool to describe the others. The series shows a growing abstraction from pragmatic space at the 'lowest' level to logical space at the top, that is, a growing content of 'information'. Cybernetically, thus, the series is controlled from the top, while its vital energy rises up from the bottom.[2]

One basic aspect, however, has still been omitted. From remote times man has not only acted in space, perceived space, existed in space and thought about space, but he has also created space to express the structure of his world as a real *imago mundi*. We may call this creation *expressive* or *artistic space*, and it finds its place in the hierarchy next to the top, together with cognitive space. Like cognitive space, expressive space needs a more abstract construct for its description, a space concept which systematizes the possible properties of expressive spaces. We may call this 'aesthetic space'. The creation of expressive space has always been the task of specialized persons, that is, builders, architects and planners, while aesthetic space has been studied by architectural theorists and philosophers. In the present book, therefore, we will talk about *architectural space* rather than expressive space, and aesthetic space as the theory of architectural space. In a certain sense, any man who chooses a place in his environment to settle and live, is a creator of expressive space. He makes his environment meaningful by assimilating it to his purposes at the same time as he accommodates to the conditions it offers.

What then are the relations between architectural space and the other members of the system? Architectural space certainly has to adapt itself to the needs of organic action as well as facilitating orientation through perception. It could also 'illustrate' certain cognitive theories of space, as when building a Cartesian co-ordinate system with concrete materials. But above all it is related to the space schemata of man's individual and public world. Obviously man's schemata are created through interaction with existing architectural spaces, and when these do not satisfy him, that is, when his image becomes confused or too unstable, he will have to change architectural space. Architectural space, therefore, can be defined as a concretization of man's existential space.[3]

NOTES

1   The social basis of schemata is discussed by Piaget in *The Psychology of Intelligence* 1950, p. 156ff., where he stresses that the social environment in part determines the interactions from which the schemata stem. He says: 'Without interchange of thought and co-operation with others the individual would never come to group his operations into a coherent whole: in this sense, therefore, operational grouping presupposes social life' (p. 163), and further: 'The grouping consists essentially in a freeing of the individuals perceptions and spontaneous intuitions from the egocentric viewpoint . . .' (p. 164).

2   The proposed model is related to Talcott Parsons' 'System of Action' (*Societies* 1966, p. 28). His system is divided into four sub-systems which form 'environments' to each other: the behavioural organism, the personality system, the social system and the cultural system.

3   For a discussion of the concept of 'concretization' see C. Norberg-Schulz *Intentions in Architecture* 1963, pp. 61ff.

243   ALAN COLQUHOUN
from "Historicism and the Limits of Semiology" (1972)

Someone who also contributed an essay to *Meaning in Architecture*, but who was less optimistic about the forthcoming role semiology might play in architectural theory, was Alan Colquhoun. This essay, written three years after the appearance of the book, follows upon his earlier campaign to oppose the abstract drift architectural theory was taking with respect to practice. Colquhoun's position is nevertheless ambivalent. At the beginning of this article he acknowledges that semiology can play an important role as a "critical tool" for theory, but at the same time he warns against its acceptance as "explanatory science" or as a "prescriptive tool." Behind this warning lies his high regard for the freedom of the designer, and for rejecting any "scientific" discipline (in the 1960s it was positivism or behaviorism) that seeks to limit this freedom. In this way his position is actually quite similar to that of Baird, in that the field of rhetoric is always or should always be open-ended.

Alan Colquhoun, from "Historicism and the Limits of Semiology" (1972), in *Essays in Architectural Criticism: Modern Architecture and Historical Change*. Cambridge, MA: MIT Press, 1985, pp. 130–1.

It is possible to show that aesthetic systems have properties which do not belong to language as defined by de Saussure. I will give a few examples:

1. In language, change only occurs in one part of the system at a time. In aesthetic systems, change often occurs in the whole system, e.g., the change from Gothic to classical architecture, or from eclecticism to modern.
2. In language, change is always unintentional. In aesthetic systems, change is always intentional (though the intention may not be rationalized).
3. In language, the existence of precise perceptual degrees of difference in the phonic object is relatively unimportant, since it is sufficient for one word to be different from another for differences in meaning to adhere to those two words, or for analogies to exist between words to bring to mind associative meanings. In aesthetic systems, however, precise degrees of difference are important – the difference between the interval of a third and a fifth in music, for example. In music, the ability to distinguish degrees of difference is used to make a structure which is interesting in itself and to create meaning. In language, the ability to distinguish between different degrees of phonetic change is not used in this way, since in language the phonic object is absorbed by its meaning. What are interesting in language are the meanings that are attached to phonic objects, not those objects themselves.
4. De Saussure discusses language as being analogous to economic exchange: "It is not the metal of a piece of money that fixes its value." But in an aesthetic system using metal, it is precisely the intrinsic quality of the metal that is important (though, of course, the semantic properties attributed to this quality will vary from one culture to another).

By aesthetic systems, therefore, I mean systems whose sensible form is interesting in itself. In language, the indissoluble relationship between the signifier and the signified is a function of the arbitrary value of the signifier.

In aesthetic systems, on the other hand, the meaning that can be attached to the sign is due to the fact that the sign is itself motivated and the signifier is invested with potential significance. This motivation may take the form of physiognomic properties, or of analogies between the form and the meaning (de Saussure quotes the example of the symbol of Justice carrying a pair of scales). Aesthetic systems in this sense include all the systems traditionally grouped under the fine arts and the applied arts – even though their only, or even their main, purpose may not be a signifying one.

These fundamental differences between language and art mean that in aesthetic systems the study of the diachronic dimension takes on a peculiar importance. Because the changes which occur in aesthetic systems are revolutionary and intentional, these changes are directly related to ideology, and ideology can only be understood in a historical context.

244 KENNETH FRAMPTON
from "On Reading Heidegger"
(1974)

[The German word] *Raum* means a place cleared or freed for settlement and lodging. A space is something that has been made room for, something that is cleared and free, namely within a boundary, Greek *peras*. A boundary is not that at which something stops but, as the Greeks recognized, the boundary is that from which something *begins its presencing*. This is why the concept is that of *horismos*, that is, the horizon, the boundary. Space is in essence that for which room has been made, that which is let into its bounds. That for which room is made is always granted and hence is joined, that is, gathered, by virtue of a location, that is, by such a thing as a bridge. *Accordingly, spaces receive their being from locations and not from "space."*

Martin Heidegger, "Building Dwelling Thinking" (trans. Albert Hofstadter)

Frampton's commentary on Heidegger's essay "Building Dwelling Thinking" (a lecture given in 1951) was the first of the four editorial statements penned by the editors of *Oppositions*, and it stands apart from its successors. Frampton's earlier opinion of the American city has not changed, although here it takes on a new cast. His bane in this instance remains the urban populism of Robert Venturi and Denise Scott Brown, which he attacks through the theories of their presumed ideological source, Melvin Webber. But Heidegger's emphasis on the meaning of place and location soon takes on a life of its own, for the German essay quickly becomes required reading for architects in the 1970s. Frampton invokes the German philosopher as an act of resistance against sprawling urban tendencies, and in this way phenomenological thinking enters the arena of architectural theory.

It becomes increasingly clear, as the utopian hallucinations of the Enlightenment fade, that we have long been in the habit of using too many synonyms; not only in our everyday speech but also in our more specialized languages. We still fail, for example, to make any satisfactory distinction between architecture and building, despite the fact that we are, at the same time, inconscionably aware that such a distinction should be made. We know, for instance, that Mies van der Rohe was at pains throughout his life to recognize this distinction and that in his own work he asserted the mediatory realm of *Baukunst* (the "art of building"), a Teutonic term for which there is no satisfactory English equivalent. All of this would be mere etymological speculation were we not constantly being reminded of the issue by those cultural and operational discrepancies that invariably arise between the generation of built form and its reception by society. This *lapsus* is sufficient to suggest that these everyday disjunctions must have at least some of their origins in our persistent failure to make such a distinction in building practice. There, in the physical realm of the built world, we seem to be presented with dramatic proof of the paradoxical Heideggerian thesis that language, far from being the servant of man, is all too often his master. We would, for instance, invariably prefer to posit the ideal of architecture – the monument in every circumstance be it public or private, the major opus – for situations that simply demand "building" and we are commonly led to realize the irreducibility of this fact, fatally after the event.

Kenneth Frampton, from "On Reading Heidegger," in *Oppositions* 4 (October 1974), n.p.

As with that which we would fain idealize in the projection, so with that which we would rationalize after the misconception and here we find that the ironic mystifications of Candide have much in common with the deception of our own more recent ideologies. Surely this was never more evident than in, say, Daniel Bell's presumptuous announcement of the end of ideology or in Melvin Webber's ingenious celebration of the "non-place urban realm"; that apotheosis of late liberal capitalism posited, not to say "deposited," as the existing paradise of Los Angeles. In this last context, we are supposed (according to the received program of the idealogues) not only to recognize but further even to welcome with enthusiasm the utopian advent of this "community without propinquity," to quote yet another appealing phrase of more than a decade ago.

The intervening lapse of time has done little to neutralize such rationalizations. The actual phrases may have passed from our lips but the mental sets largely remain and it is these that unavoidably condition us as we go about our work. Should we choose, through some inner inadequacy or protracted sense of responsibility, to eschew autonomous art or the liberating promise of the poetic intellect, then all too often, we will find ourselves conflating in the name of populism the objects of elitist culture with elaborate rationalizations of the environment as found. In such a vein, we will seek to sublimate the frustrations of utopia with the sadness of suburbia or with the enervations of the strip; and while we will self-consciously appeal, by way of justification, to an illusory vernacular, the true nature of our Western predicament will continue to escape us. Between the Charybdis of elitism and the Scylla of populism, the full dimension of our historical dilemma will remain hidden.

Nowhere are the turns of this labyrinth more evident, as Heidegger tries to make clear, than in our language, than in our persistent use of, say, the Latin term "space" or *"spatium"* instead of "place" or the Germanic word *"Raum"* – the latter carrying with it, as it does, the explicit connotations of a clearing in which *to be*, a place in which to come into being. We have only to compare the respective Oxford English Dictionary definitions to appreciate the abstract connotations of "space" as opposed to the socially experienced nature of "place"; to confront construction *in extensio* with the act of significant containment.

This, again, would be empty speculation could we not point directly to our present all but total incapacity to create places; an incapacity that is as prevalent in our architectural schools and in the monuments of the elite, as it is in "motopia" at large. Place now appears as inimical to our received mental set, not only as architects but also as a society. In our ubiquitous "non-place" we congratulate ourselves regularly on our pathological capacity for abstraction; on our commitment to the norms of statistical coordination; on our bondage to the transactional processes of objectification that will admit to neither the luxury nor the necessity of place. We exonerate the strip, ever fearful to admit that we might have eliminated, once and for all, the possibility of ever being anywhere. We vaunt our much prized mobility, our "rush city," to coin Neutra's innocent phrase, our consumption of frenetic traction, only to realize that should we stop, there are few places within which any of us might significantly choose to be. Blithely, we exchange our already tenuous hold on the public sphere for the electronic distractions of the private future. Despite this, outside the "mass" engineered somnambulism of television, we still indulge in the proliferation of roadside kitsch – in the fabricated mirage of "somewhere" made out of billboard facades and token theatrical paraphenalia – the fantasmagoria of an escape clause from the landscape of alienation. In all this, the degeneration of the language speaks for itself. Terms such as "defoliation" and "pedestrianization" enter everyday speech as categories drawn from the same processes of technological rationalization. With "newspeak" overtones, they testify to a fundamental break in our rapport with nature (including our own), they speak of a laying waste that can only find its ultimate end in ourselves.

Against this, it would seem that the apparent universal triumph of the "non-place urban realm" may only be modified through a profound consciousness of history and through a rigorous socio-political analysis of the present, seen as a continuing fulfillment of the past. We have no choice but to reformulate the dialectical constituents of the world, to determine more consciously the necessary links obtaining between *place* and *production*, between the "what" and the "how." This reciprocation of ends and means binds us to an historical reality wherein the *tabula rasa* fantasies of the Enlightenment lose a deal of their authority. With the manifest exhaustion of non-renewable resources the technotopic myth of unlimited progress becomes somewhat discredited and, at this juncture, the *production of place* returns us by way of economic limit not to architecture but to *Baukunst* and to that which Aldo Van Eyck has already called the "timelessness of man."

245 CHARLES JENCKS
from *The Language of Post-Modern Architecture* (1977)

The growing emphasis on semiotics in the 1970s came to a somewhat dramatic head in 1977 with this bestselling book by Charles Jencks. It was a spirited and wide-ranging study of the expressive content (intentional or unintentional) of architectural forms, which – after a brief excoriation of the high modernism of Le Corbusier and Mies van der Rohe – goes on to consider the symbolic meaning of hotel lobbies, hot-dog stands, movie sets, and yes, even a few buildings. Jencks was not only convinced that modernism had been overtaken by a postmodernist sensitivity to language, but he, as the following excerpt shows, was even able to pin down the precise minute of modernism's demise. These opening paragraphs of the book, published with a photograph of the now infamous Pruit-Igoe housing project in St. Louis collapsing under a dynamite charge, were perhaps the most read paragraphs of the 1970s. The question for many was no longer whether modernism was giving way to changing approaches, but just how radical this change would become.

Happily, we can date the death of modern architecture to a precise moment in time. Unlike the legal death of a person, which is becoming a complex affair of brain waves versus heartbeats, modern architecture went out with a bang. That many people didn't notice, and no one was seen to mourn, does not make the sudden extinction any less of a fact, and that many designers are still trying to administer the kiss of life does not mean that it has been miraculously resurrected. No, it expired finally and completely in 1972, after having been flogged to death remorselessly for ten years by critics such as Jane Jacobs; and the

Charles A. Jencks, from *The Language of Post-Modern Architecture*. New York: Rizzoli, 1977, pp. 9–10.

fact that many so-called modern architects still go around practising a trade as if it were alive can be taken as one of the great curiosities of our age (like the British Monarchy giving life-prolonging drugs to 'The Royal Company of Archers' or 'The Extra Women of the Bedchamber').

Modern Architecture died in St Louis, Missouri on July 15, 1972 at 3.32 p.m. (or thereabouts) when the infamous Pruitt-Igoe scheme, or rather several of its slab blocks, were given the final *coup de grâce* by dynamite. Previously it had been vandalised, mutilated and defaced by its black inhabitants, and although millions of dollars were pumped back, trying to keep it alive (fixing the broken elevators, repairing smashed windows, repainting), it was finally put out of its misery. Boom, boom, boom.

Without doubt, the ruins should be kept, the remains should have a preservation order slapped on them, so that we keep a live memory of this failure in planning and architecture. Like the folly or artificial ruin – constructed on the estate of an eighteenth-century English eccentric to provide him with instructive reminders of former vanities and glories – we should learn to value and protect our former disasters. As Oscar Wilde said, 'experience is the name we give to our mistakes', and there is a certain health in leaving them judiciously scattered around the landscape as continual lessons.

Pruitt-Igoe was constructed according to the most progressive ideals of CIAM (the Congress of International Modern Architects) and it won an award from the American Institute of Architects when it was designed in 1951. It consisted of elegant slab blocks fourteen storeys high with rational 'streets in the air' (which were safe from cars, but as it turned out, not safe from crime); 'sun, space and greenery', which Le Corbusier called the 'three essential joys of urbanism' (instead of conventional streets, gardens and semi-private space, which he banished). It had a separation of pedestrian and vehicular traffic, the provision of play space, and local amenities such as laundries, crèches and gossip centres – all rational substitutes for traditional patterns. Moreover, its Purist style, its clean, salubrious hospital metaphor, was meant to instil, by good example, corresponding virtues in the inhabitants. Good form was to lead to good content, or at least good conduct; the intelligent planning of abstract space was to promote healthy behaviour.

Alas, such simplistic ideas, taken over from philosophic doctrines of Rationalism, Behaviourism and Pragmatism, proved as irrational as the philosophies themselves. Modern Architecture, as the son of the Enlightenment, was an heir to its congenital naivities, naivities too great and awe-inspiring to warrant refutation in a book on mere building. I will concentrate here, in this first part, on the demise of a very small branch of a big bad tree; but to be fair it should be pointed out that modern architecture is the offshoot of modern painting, the modern movements in all the arts. Like rational schooling, rational health and rational design of women's bloomers, it has the faults of an age trying to reinvent itself totally on rational grounds. These shortcomings are now well known, thanks to the writings of Ivan Illich, Jacques Ellul, E. F. Schumacher, Michael Oakshott and Hannah Arendt, and the overall misconceptions of Rationalism will not be dwelt upon. They are assumed for my purposes. Rather than a deep extended attack on modern architecture, showing how its ills relate very closely to the prevailing philosophies of the modern age, I will attempt a caricature, a polemic. The virtue of this genre (as well as its vice) is its license to cut through the large generalities with a certain abandon and enjoyment, overlooking all the exceptions and subtleties of the argument. Caricature is of course not the whole truth.

Daumier's drawings didn't really show what nineteenth-century poverty was about, but rather gave a highly selective view of *some* truths. Let us then romp through the desolation of modern architecture, and the destruction of our cities, like some Martian tourist out on an earthbound excursion, visiting the archaeological sites with a superior disinterest, bemused by the sad but instructive mistakes of a former architectural civilisation. After all, since it is fairly dead, we might as well enjoy picking over the corpse.

246   JUAN PABLO BONTA
from *Architecture and its interpretation* (1977)

What Jencks had achieved largely through images, Juan Pablo Bonta carried out through stricter semiotic reasoning. Bonta's study was important for at least two reasons. First, his fourfold semiotic model of indicators – consisting of signals (deliberately produced and rightly interpreted communication), indexes (indications), pseudo-signals (unintended signals), and intentional indexes (intended but unrecognized indexes) – presented a clear and succinct way to consider how architecture functions or fails to function in a semiotic regard. Second, his emphasis on the inherent instability of any linguistic (stylistic) convention in design, centered on the perceived shortcomings of the modernist language, pointed to the fact that architectural form is in a continual state of re-semantification (socialization), whether architects like it or not. In his study Bonta went on to consider but three options for architecture: a redeployment of the modernist language (formerly indexical) as aesthetic signals (the New York Five), employing some other non-modern vernacular (Venturi), or a mannerist dissolution of the modernist language altogether.

Epochs of architectural history can be characterized by their predominant attitudes with regard to semiotic issues – for example, by people's acceptance or rejection of signals or indexes as legitimate components of their expressive system. The semiotic characterization is no less significant than the description of a period or a style in terms of the predominant building materials, construction methods or building types. Furthermore, semiotic analysis can help explain historical developments that elude other explanations. For example, it can help explain why the International Style was condemned to be short-lived. With its radical assault on architectural communication and its emphasis on indication, the International Style could only withstand socialization for a very short time. Gropius saw the danger sooner than anyone else, and expressed his alarm at seeing the style he had helped to initiate being so widely accepted. He realized that this would lead ultimately to sacrificing the very driving force which led to the creation of the style – the search for new indexes as opposed to outworn signals. The indexes, if socialized, would inevitably become signals. Their forms would become increasingly more schematic, simplified, and distorted, and the philosophy of

Juan Pablo Bonta, from *Architecture and its interpretation: a study of expressive systems in architecture*. New York: Rizzoli, 1979, pp. 46–9.

the movement would be betrayed. Gropius thought in the late thirties that this process had, indeed, already taken place. He wrote in 1937:

> Worst of all, 'modern' architecture became fashionable in several countries; with the result that formalistic imitation and snobbery distorted the fundamental truth and simplicity on which this renascence was based.

The ultimate crisis of the ideals of the Modern Movement could have been forecast from its very outset. It was not the result of an unpredictable mishap, but the necessary consequence of a crippling self-imposed limitation. There were times in architectural history in which the attack against the established architectural language proved to be culturally useful. The decade of the International Style may well have been one such time. But linguistic revolution is only one side of cultural creation. For culture to survive, there is also a need for stability and continuity. Life would be impossible if the shape of the seat had to be rediscovered from the basic principles each time we sat down to eat.

Designers may consider nothing but indexes when they design their forms. But as soon as their products begin to be used, they are socialized. Indexes *will* become signals, and these *will* become out-worn and then be re-semanticized. Any architectural movement which tries to violate this principle is condemned to be short-lived. A movement cannot subsist if its apostles denounce their followers as being formalistic imitators and snobs who have distorted their fundamental truths. Every movement needs its prophets; but if their good news is to be shared at any socially significant scale, there is also a need for priests who can institutionalize the message.

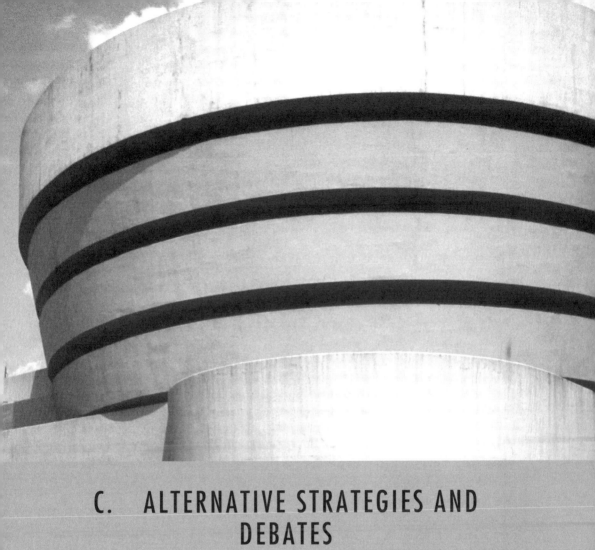

C. ALTERNATIVE STRATEGIES AND DEBATES

Introduction

With the resurgence of theoretical activity in the 1970s came also a grouping of architects along differing ideological lines, which became in fact more fractured as the decade advanced. If the "New York Five" and the European Rationalists were the first to stake out their own theoretical terrain, they were by no means alone in this pursuit. The "Main-Street" populism of Robert Venturi and Charles Moore gained increasing favor in the 1970s, and by the middle of the decade it came to be identified with the larger movement of the "Grays," now set up in opposition to the "Whites." As defined by Robert A. M. Stern, the Grays traced their roots back to the writings of Vincent Scully at Yale and to the architectural ideas of Louis Kahn at Penn, and perhaps its one characterizing feature — beyond the populism of Venturi and Moore — was a willingness to revisit pre-modern history. The exhibition held at the Museum of Modern Art in 1975–6, which displayed the architectural drawings of the École des Beaux Arts, became a moment of crystallization for this group. This new "historicism" in fact would continue to be one of the most visible architectural trends of the 1980s.

There were, however, a number of other ideas being interwoven into this intellectual fabric, which led to the unraveling of modern theory. A Dutch school of "structuralism" emerged from the lead earlier taken by Aldo van Eyck. A small book by the Egyptian architect Hassan Fathy, supporting traditional and non-industrial building techniques, contained explosive criticism of modernism and its failures. And in the late 1970s we meet the inspired surrealism of Rem Koolhaas and the political nihilism of Bernard Tschumi. If the former's hypothetical projects drew upon sources as far-reaching as the Dutch artist Constant, Archigram, superstudio, and the surrealists of the 1920s, Tschumi, in relocating to London and then New York, brought with him an awareness of French poststructural theory, which would later be gathered under the heading of "deconstruction." Hence the threads holding together the garment "history," which lies behind this spirited eclecticism, were being insidiously loosened by disparate forces.

247 DENISE SCOTT BROWN
from "Learning from Pop" (1971)

I n 1972 Robert Venturi and Denise Scott Brown (together with Steven Izenour) published the book *Learning from Las Vegas*. The book, as we have noted, was based on their design-studio research of 1968. Thus the substance of their arguments on behalf of Las Vegas was discussed for several years before the book's actual publication. The critical response to their ideas actually reached its first climax in 1971 when the Italian journal *Casabella*, in a special issue organized by the Institute for Architecture and Urban Studies, considered the theme "City as Artifact." Here references to Venturi's and Scott Brown's ideas on urbanism were numerous, but it was capped off by a debate between Scott Brown and Kenneth Frampton in the form of two commentaries. In a third piece, Scott Brown was given the opportunity to rebut Frampton's rebuttal in one of the more memorable architectural exchanges of the 1970s. The principal message of Scott Brown – that architects can and should learn from Las Vegas – is the same as her earlier argument, but the context has now shifted in light of the failures of the American urban-renewal policies of the 1960s and the ensuing social and political upheavals of the late 1960s.

Las Vegas, Los Angeles, Levittown, the swinging singles on the Westheimer Strip, golf resorts, boating communities, Co-op City, the residential back-grounds to soap operas, TV commercials and mass mag ads, billboards and Route 66 are sources for a changing architectural sensibility. New sources are sought when the old forms go stale and the way out is not clear; then a classical heritage, an art movement, or industrial engineers' and primitives' "architecture without architects" may help to sweep out the flowery remains of the old revolution as practiced by its originators' conservative descendants.

In America in the 1960's an extra ingredient was added to this recipe for artistic change: social revolution. Urban renewal, supplier of work for architects for two decades and a major locus of the soft remains of the Modern movement, was not merely artistically stale, it was socially harmful. The urgency of the social situation, the social critique of urban renewal and of the architect as server of a rich narrow spectrum of the population – in

Denise Scott Brown, from "Learning from Pop," in *Casabella* 359–360 (1971), pp. 15–17.

particular the criticism of Herbert Gans – have been as important as the Pop artists in steering us toward the existing American city and its builders. If high-style architects are not producing what people want or need, who is, and what can we learn from them?

Needs, Plural

Sensitivity to needs is a first reason for going to the existing city. Once there, the first lesson for architects is the pluralism of need. No builder-developer in his right mind would announce: I am building for Man. He is building for a market, for a group of people defined by income range, age, family composition and life style. Levittowns, Leisureworlds, Georgian-styled town houses grow from someone's estimation of the needs of the groups who will be their markets. The city can be seen as the built artifacts of a set of sub-cultures. At the moment, those sub-cultures which willingly resort to architects are few.

Of course learning from what's there is subject to the caveats and limitations of all behavioristic analysis – one is surveying behavior which is constrained, it is not what people might do in other conditions. The poor do not willingly live in tenements and maybe the middle classes don't willingly live in Levittowns; perhaps the Georgian-styling is less pertinent to the townhouse resident than is the rent. In times of housing shortage this is a particularly forceful argument against architectural behaviorism since people can't vote against a particular offering by staying away if there is no alternative. To counteract this danger one must search out for comparison environments where for some reason the constraints do not hold. There are environments which suggest what economically con-strained groups' tastes might be if they were less constrained. They are the nouveau riche environments; Hollywood for a former era, Las Vegas for today, and the homes of film stars, sportsmen and other groups where upward mobility may resemble vertical takeoff yet where maintenance of previous value systems is encouraged.

Another source is physical backgrounds in the mass media, movies, soap operas, pickle and furniture-polish ads. Here the aim is not to sell houses but something else, and the background represents someone's (Madison Avenue's?) idea of what pickle buyers or soap opera watchers want in a house. Now the Madison Avenue observer's view may be as biased as the architect's, and it should be studied in the light of what it is trying to sell – must pickle architecture look homey like my house or elegant like yours if it is to sell me pickles? But at least it's another bias, an alternative to the architectural navel contem-plation we so often do for research; i.e., ask: What did Le Corbusier do? Both Madison Avenue and the builder, although they can tell us little of the needs of the very poor, cover a broader range of the population and pass a stiffer market test than does the architect in urban renewal or public housing, and if we learn no more from these sources than that architecture must differ for different groups, that is a great deal. But an alternative to both is to examine what people do to buildings, in Levittowns, Society Hills, grey areas and slums, once they are in them. Here, costs and availability are less constraining forces since the enterprise is smaller. Also, changes tend often to be symbolic rather than structural and aspirations can perhaps be more easily inferred from symbols than from structures.

Attention to built sources for information on need does not imply that asking people what they want is not extremely necessary as well. This is an important topic, as is the relation between the two types of survey, asking and looking; but it is not the subject of this enquiry, which is on what can be learned from the artifacts of pop culture.

Formal Analysis as Design Research

A second reason for looking to pop culture is to find formal vocabularies for today which are more relevant to peoples' diverse needs and more tolerant of the untidinesses of urban life than the "rationalist", Cartesian formal orders of latter day Modern architecture. How much low-income housing and 19th century architecture has been cleared so some tidy purist, architect or planner could start with a clean slate?

Modern architects can now admit that whatever forces, processes, and technologies determine architectural form, ideas about form determine it as well; that a formal vocabulary is as much a part of architecture as are bricks and mortar (plastics and systems, for futurists); that form does not, cannot, arise from function alone, new born and innocent as Venus from her shell, but rather that form follows, "inter alia", function, forces, and form. Formal biases, if they are consciously recognized, need not tyrannize as they have done in urban renewal; and formal vocabularies, given their place in architecture, can be studied and improved to suit functional requirements, rather than accepted unconsciously and unsuitably – some old hand-me-down from some irrelevant master. The forms of the pop landscape are as relevant to us now as were the forms of antique Rome to the Beaux Arts, Cubism and machine architecture to the early Moderns, and the industrial midlands and the Dogon to Team 10, which is to say extremely relevant, and more so than the latest bathysphere, launch pad, or systems hospital (or even, "pace" Banham, the Santa Monica pier).

248 KENNETH FRAMPTON
from "America 1960–70: Notes on Urban Images and Theory" (1971)

Frampton rejoined Scott Brown's shorter commentary with a more extended review of the decade of the 1960s in America – a response that echoed the harsh criticisms of American culture earlier voiced by Thomas W. Adorno. The visual imagery selected by Frampton in itself was powerful; beginning with the juxtaposition of the Vesnin brothers' project for the Pravda Building (1923) with an aerial view of the Las Vegas strip, and continuing with Andy Warhol's grim photographic productions of *Saturday Disaster* (a fatal car accident, 1964)

Kenneth Frampton, from "America 1960–70: Notes on Urban Images and Theory," in *Casabella* 359–360 (1971), p. 31.

and *Electric Chair* (1965). Frampton censures the erosion of American cities by laissez-faire urban and suburban growth, and therefore ever greater reliance on the automobile and its roadways. The urban ideas of Scott Brown and Venturi, while admittedly analytical, are rudely dismissed, essentially as an exercise in pop-inspired picturesqueness. The South African Scott Brown, in her counter-rebuttal, would chide Frampton for his disingenuous European political cant, while "sitting in a plush American university" and "taking superior armchair-revolutionary pot shots at the capitalists that support you there." The passage below follows immediately upon Frampton's censure of Donald Appleyard and John R. Myer's recent book of time-framed images, *A View from the Road*.

In "Learning from Pop", Denise Scott Brown advocates a very similar cinematic use of sophisticated technology. She writes: "New analytical techniques must use film and video tape to convey the dynamism of sign architecture and the sequential experience of vast landscapes; and computers are needed to aggregate mass repeated data into comprehensible patterns". Is this because they are incomprehensible otherwise, or is it that like Trajan's Column, the Star-dust Sign is imperially destined to be codified and then disseminated throughout the world?

There is no doubt that such research, properly programmed, would yield useful operational and aesthetic data, in respect of kino-graphic communication vis-a-vis visibility, reaction time, etc; yet once informational/commutational processes are emphasized, as they are now, above places of arrival and departure, the very notion of place itself tends to become threatened, to the potential detriment of "human" experience. As Hannah Arendt has put it, "The "in order to" (becomes) the content of the "for sake of" (and) utility established as meaning generates meaninglessness".[1] It is ironic that Denise Scott Brown should attempt to bestow upon such reservoirs of process and pseudo points of arrival, as parking lots, those very attributes which previous cultures reserved for "space of human appearance";[2] such as those churches, so clearly revealed as "res publica" in Nolli's maps of Rome. Of the latter she writes: "Nolli's late 18th Century mapping technique which he applied to Rome, when it is adapted to parking lots, throws considerable light on Las Vegas". Rather less light, one would have thought, than that already thrown by Eduard Ruscha who has exhaustively demonstrated, to arcane ends, that parking lots, unlike swimming pools and gasoline stations, are at their best when seen from the air; that is when alienated from the normal field of human vision.[3] Pop clearly has little feel for a "camp" historicism such as would see A & P parking lots as corresponding to the "tapis verts" of Versailles.

What then are we to learn from two phenomena so superficially similar yet so different in ultimate intent as Motopia (i.e., Las Vegas, Los Angeles, Levittown, etc.) and Pop Art, for surely Pop Art is not quite synonymous with consumer folk culture, as now industrially mass-produced and marketed? Do designers really need elaborate sociological ratification à la Gans, to tell them that what the people want is what they already have?[4] No doubt Levittown could be brought to yield an equally affirmative consensus in regard to current American repressive policies, both domestic and foreign. Should designers like politicians wait upon the dictates of a silent majority, and if so, how are they to interpret them? Is it really the task of under-employed design talent to suggest to the constrained masses of Levittown – or elsewhere – that they might prefer the extravagant confines of the West Coast nouveau-riche; a by now superfluous function which has already been performed more than adequately for years by Madison Avenue? In this respect there is now surely little left of our much vaunted pluralism that has not already been overlaid with the engineered fantasies of mass taste.

NOTES

1   Arendt, H., "The Human Condition", Doubleday Anchor Books Edition, 1959, page 135. See also Venturi, R., "Complexity and Contradiction in Architecture", MOMA Papers, No. 1, Museum of Modern Art, New York, 1966, page 133; wherein the "space of human appearance is to be seen as having "unpatriotic" connotations". Venturi writes: "The piazza, in fact, is "un-American". Americans feel uncomfortable sitting in a square: they should be working at the office or home with the family looking at television". There are only two possibilities presumably. This argument is twisted with nice sophistry in the last sentences of Venturi's book which read: "We are in the habit of thinking that open space is precious in the city. It is not. Except in Manhattan perhaps, our cities have too much open space in the ubiquitous parking lots, in the not-so-temporary deserts created by Urban Renewal and in the amorphous suburbs around".
2   Arendt, H., "The Human Condition", op. cit., p. 45.
3   Ruscha, E., "Thirty Four Parking Lots", Los Angeles, 1967. See also other books by Ruscha: "Twenty Six Gasoline Stations", 1963; "Every Building on the Sunset Strip", 1966; "Nine Swimming Pools", 1968.
4   Gans, H. J., "The Levittowners: Ways of Life and Politics in a New Suburban Community", New York, 1967.

249   HERMAN HERTZBERGER
from "Homework for More Hospitable Form" (1973)

I n an act of homage to his mentor Aldo van Eyck, Herman Hertzberger built this special issue of the Dutch journal *Forum* around the notion of "hospitable form." He does so to counter what he sees as the coldness and rudeness of modern building forms, as well as the animosity and sense of alienation that architecture evokes in many people. His solution is to propose forms with the richer capacity to absorb, carry, and convey meanings. He argues for forms that people can take possession of through their mental associations, forms that are archetypical with respect to human imagination. In practice, this translates to breaking down large building volumes, to designing spaces that can be changed or be modified over time, and to creating forms that are incomplete and therefore allow people the freedom to fill them in, as it were – to take command of or expropriate their living and working environments. Hertzberger constructs his argument as a series of numbered propositions, and in these passages from the concluding pages he discusses his notion of a "musée imaginaire," which forms the central thesis of his phenomenology.

Herman Hertzberger, from "Homework for More Hospitable Form," in *Forum* 24:3 (1973), n.p., trans. (appearing with the original text) Angela Blom van Assendelft and Anne van Bladeren.

9.2 The only available escape from the fundamental limitations of our imaginative faculty lies in directing our attention more to the experiences we all have in common, the collective memory, some of it innate (!) some of it transmitted and acquired, which in one way or another must be at the base of our common experiential world.

We don't have knowledge of everybody's personal images and associations with forms, but we assume that they can be seen as individual interpretations of a collective pattern. This relationship between collective pattern and individual interpretations can perhaps be likened with the relationship between language and speech.

(We each use language in our own way; both individuals and groups can express themselves with it, and as long as they keep more or less within the framework of recognised declensions and rules, and use recognisable words then the message comes across.) Indeed we assume an underlying "objective" structure of forms – which we will call arch-forms – a derivative of which is what we get to see in a given situation.

The whole "musée imaginaire" of forms in situations whatever their time and place can then be conceived of as an infinite variety out of which people help themselves, in constantly changing variety, to forms which in the end refer back to the fundamentally unchangeable and underlying reservoir of arch-forms.

9.3 In designing, apart from the usual information, by association we can try to dig up from our memory as many images as possible of situations relating to our problem, and gather these around us. The farther the images are separated from each other in time and place, and the more characteristic they are for the situation at hand, the more our collection of images will gain in depth.

By referring each one back to its fundamentally unchangeable ingredients, we then try to discover what the images have in common, and find thus the "cross section of the collection", the unchangeable, underlying element of all the examples, which in its plurality can be an evocative form-starting-point.

The richer our collection of images, the more precise we can be in indicating the most plural and most evocative solution, and the more objective our solution becomes, in the sense that it will hold a meaning for, and be given a meaning by, a greater variety of people.

9.4 We cannot make anything new, but only reevaluate already existing images, in order to make them more suitable for our circumstances. What we need to draw on is the great 'Musée Imaginaire' of images wherein the process of change of signification is displayed as an effort of human imagination, always finding a way to break through the established order, so as to find a more appropriate solution for his situation.

It is only when we view things from the perspective of this enormous collage, that, with the aid of analogies, we can resolve the unknown and, by a process of extrapolation arrive at solutions which can improve our circumstances.

Design cannot do other than converting the underlying and the idea of ever being able to start off with a clean slate is absurd, and moreover, disastrous when, under the pretext of its being necessary to start completely from the beginning, what already exists is destroyed so that the naked space can be filled up with impracticable and sterile constructions.

When we do away with what has gone before us, and pay no attention to what more stable groups of people next door to us, elsewhere, still possess, and thus make no use of the accumulation of images at our disposal, we nip the possibility of renewal in the bud.

The various significations of everything that has taken place, and is still taking place now, are like old layers of paint lying one on top of another, and they form for us, in their entirety, the undercoat on which a new layer may be placed; a new signification which will slightly alter the whole thing.

This transformation process, whereby the outmoded significations fade into the background, and new ones are added, must be ever-present in our working methods. Only by such a dialectical process, will there be a continual thread between past and future, and the maintenance of historical continuity.

10.1 Whatever goal architecture may have set for itself, it can only be meaningful today if it is making a demonstrable contribution towards the improvement of living conditions and circumstances.

Form must improve conditions, or rather, must lend a helping hand to people, inciting them to make their own improvements.

250 HASSAN FATHY
from *Architecture For the Poor* (1973)

The idea of a "global village," so much bandied about in the 1960s, began to lose some of its force in the following decade, and perhaps no one was more responsible for this than Hassan Fathy. Trained as an architect in Cairo in the 1920s, Fathy's early projects were largely based on classical European models, but by the late 1930s he had come to reject such foreign impositions in favor of a design approach modeled on traditional forms and building materials. Inspired by Nubian mud-brick vaulting, shading, and ventilation techniques, his designs for the village of New Gourna in the 1940s not only returned vaults and courtyards to its occupants, but engaged residents to participate both in the planning and construction of the town – clearly a vernacular alternative to international modernism. This passage on character reads as a manifesto of his traditional beliefs.

Architectural Character

Every people that has produced architecture has evolved its own favorite forms, as peculiar to that people as its language, its dress, or its folklore. Until the collapse of cultural frontiers in the last century, there were all over the world distinctive local shapes and details in architecture, and the buildings of any locality were the beautiful children of a happy marriage between the imagination of the people and the demands of their countryside. I do not propose to speculate upon the real springs of national idiosyncrasy, nor could I with any authority. I like to suppose simply that certain shapes take a people's fancy, and that they make use of them in a great variety of contexts, perhaps rejecting the unsuitable

Hassan Fathy, from *Architecture For the Poor: An Experiment in Rural Egypt*. Chicago: University of Chicago Press, 1973, pp. 19–21. His book first appeared in a limited edition in Cairo under the title *Gourna: A Tale of Two Villages* (1969).

applications, but evolving a colorful and emphatic visual language of their own that suits perfectly their character and their homeland. No one could mistake the curve of a Persian dome and arch for the curve of a Syrian one, or a Moorish one, or an Egyptian one. No one can fail to recognize the same curve, the same signature, in dome and jar and turban from the same district. It follows, too, that no one can look with complacency upon buildings transplanted to an alien environment.

Yet in modern Egypt there is no indigenous style. The signature is missing; the houses of rich and poor alike are without character, without an Egyptian accent. The tradition is lost, and we have been cut off from our past ever since Mohammed Ali cut the throat of the last Mameluke. This gap in the continuity of Egyptian tradition has been felt by many people, and all sorts of remedies have been proposed. There was, in fact, a kind of jealousy between those who regarded the Copts as the true lineal descendants of the Ancient Egyptians, and those who believed that the Arab style should provide the pattern for a new Egyptian architecture. Indeed, there was one statesmanlike attempt to reconcile these two factions, when Osman Moharam Pasha, the Minister of Public Works, suggested that Egypt be divided into two, rather as Solomon suggested dividing the baby, and that Upper Egypt be delivered to the Copts, where a traditional Pharaonic style could be developed, while Lower Egypt should go to the Moslems, who would make its architecture truly Arab!

This story goes to show two things. One is the encouraging fact that people do recognize and wish to remedy the cultural confusion in our architecture. The other – not so encouraging – is that this confusion is seen as a problem of style, and style is looked upon as some sort of surface finish that can be applied to any building and even scraped off and changed if necessary. The modern Egyptian architect believes that Ancient Egyptian architecture is represented by the temple with its pylons and cavetto cornice, and Arab by clustered stalactites, whereas Ancient Egyptian domestic architecture was quite unlike temple architecture, and Arab domestic architecture quite different from mosque architecture. Ancient Egyptian secular buildings like houses were light constructions, simple, with the clean lines of the best modern houses. But in the architectural schools they make no study of the history of domestic buildings, and learn architectural periods by the accidents of style, the obvious features like the pylon and the stalactite. Thus the graduate architect believes this to be all there is in "style," and imagines a building can change its style as a man changes clothes. It was thinking like this that led some architect to ruin the entrance to the classrooms at Gourna school by transforming the original archway into an Ancient Egyptian-style temple doorway complete with cavetto cornice. It is not yet understood that real architecture cannot exist except in a living tradition, and that architectural tradition is all but dead in Egypt today.

As a direct result of this lack of tradition our cities and villages are becoming more and more ugly. Every single new building manages to increase this ugliness, and every attempt to remedy the situation only underlines the ugliness more heavily.

Particularly on the outskirts of provincial towns where the most recent building has been taking place the ugly design of the houses is emphasized by the shoddy execution of the work, and cramped square boxes of assorted sizes, in a style copied from the poorer quarters in the metropolis, half finished yet already decaying, set at all angles to one another, are stuck up all over a shabby wilderness of unmade roads, wire and lines of washing hanging dustily over chicken runs. In these nightmarish neighborhoods a craving for show and modernity causes the house owner to lavish his money on the tawdry fittings and decorations of urban houses, while being miserly with living space and denying himself absolutely the benefits of real craftsmanship. This attitude makes the houses compact and outward-facing, so that the family has to air bedding over the public street, and air itself exposed to the neighborhood upon its barren balconies; whereas if the owners were less cheap-minded they could take advantage of the only house type that can make life tolerable in these places, the courtyard house, and enjoy both space and privacy. Unfortunately this suburban architecture is the type that is taken by the peasants as a model of modernity and is gaining ground in our villages; on the outskirts of Cairo or Benha we can read the approaching fate of Gharb Aswan.

To flatter his clients and persuade them that they are sophisticated and urban, the village mason starts to experiment with styles that he has seen only at second or third hand, and with materials that he cannot really handle with understanding. He abandons the safe guide of tradition, and without the science and experience of an architect tries to produce "architects' architecture." The result is a building with all the defects and none of the advantages of the architect's work.

Thus the work of an architect who designs, say, an apartment house in the poor quarters of Cairo for some stingy speculator, in which he incorporates various features of modern design copied from fashionable European work, will filter down, over a period of years, through the cheap suburbs and into the village, where it will slowly poison the genuine tradition.

So serious is this situation that a thorough and scientific investigation of it becomes quite imperative if ever we are to reverse the trend toward bad, ugly, vulgar, and inefficient housing in our villages.

Sometimes I have despaired at the size of the problem, and given it up as insoluble, the malign and irreversible operation of fate. I have succumbed to a feeling of helplessness, sadness, and pain for what was becoming of my people and my land. But when I found myself having to deal with the actual case of Gourna, I pulled myself together and began to think more practically about the problem.

251   COLIN ROWE AND FRED KOETTER
from "Collage City" (1975)

Against the idea of a universal urban typology proposed by the European Rationalists, Colin Rowe and Koetter in the 1970s developed their idea of a "Collage City." The essay, which was expanded and published as a book in 1979, begins with a spirited critique of modernism's utopian premises of a New Jerusalem, an eschatological vision or mythology fittingly exploded with the infamous "urban renewal" towers of Pruit-Igoe in

Colin Rowe and Fred Koetter, from "Collage City," in *Architectural Review* 158:942 (August 1975), pp. 83–4.

1973. Drawing upon Isaiah Berlin's distinction between the hedgehog (he who knows one big thing) and the fox (he who cunningly knows many things), Rowe and Koetter go on to compare the contrary approaches of Versailles (absolute and total control of the environment, one big idea) and the Roman Villa Adriana at Tivoli (a collage or iconography of complex and orchestrated pieces). It is the latter that supplies the model for their theory. The governing concept is the French word *bricoleur*: someone who composes with odd or left-over pieces and who combines them in an ingenious way. The urban *bricoleur* is, in effect, the antipode to Le Corbusier's modernist hero, the engineer, who controls every detail of the design from the initial conception to the completion.

For, if we can divest ourselves of the deceptions of professional *amour propre* and accepted academic theory, the description of the *bricoleur* is far more a 'real-life' specification of what the architect-urbanist is and does than any fantasy deriving from 'methodology' and 'systemics'. Indeed the predicament of architecture which, because it is always, in some way or another, concerned with amelioration, with by some standard, however dimly perceived, making things better, with how things ought to be, is always hopelessly involved with value judgements and can never be scientifically resolved – least of all in terms of any simple empirical theory of 'facts'. And, if this is the case with reference to architecture, then, in relation to urbanism (which is not even concerned in making things stand up) the question of any scientific resolution of its problems can only become more acute. For, if the notion of a 'final' solution through a definitive accumulation of all data is, evidently, an epistemological chimera, if certain aspects of information will invariably remain undiscriminated or undisclosed, and if the inventory of 'facts' can never be complete because of the rates of change and obsolescence, then, here and now, it surely might be possible to assert that *the prospects of scientific city planning should, in reality, be regarded as equivalent to the prospects of scientific politics.*

For, if planning can barely be more scientific than the political society of which it forms an agency, in the case of neither politics nor planning can there be sufficient information acquired before action becomes necessary. In neither case can performance await an ideal future formulation of the problem as it may, at last, be resolved; and, if this is because the very possibility of that future where such formulation might be made depends on imperfect action now, then this is only once more to intimate the role of *bricolage* which politics so much resembles and city planning surely should.

But are the alternatives of 'progressivist' total design (propelled by hedgehogs?) and 'culturalist' *bricolage* (propelled by foxes?) genuinely, at the last analysis all that we have available? We believe that they are; and we suppose that the political implications of total design are nothing short of devastating. No ongoing condition of compromise and expediency, of wilfulness and arbitrariness, but a supremely irresistible combination of 'science' and 'destiny', such is the unacknowledged myth of the activist or historicist Utopia; and, in this complete sense, total design was, and is, make believe. For, on a mundane level, total design can only mean total control, and control not by abstractions relating to the absolute value of science or history but by governments of man; and, if the point scarcely requires emphasis, it can, still, not be too strongly asserted that total design (however much it may be loved) assumes for its implementation a level of centralised political and economic control which, given the presumption of political power as it now exists anywhere in the world, can only be considered thoroughly unacceptable.

'*The most tyrannical government of all, the government of nobody, the totalitarianism of technique.*' Hannah Ahrendt's image of a horror may also now come to mind; and, in this context, what then of 'culturalist' *bricolage*? One may anticipate its dangers; but, as a deliberate recognition of the deviousness of history and change, of the certainty of future sharp temporal caesuras, of the full tonality of societal gesture, a conception of the city as intrinsically, and even ideally, a work of *bricolage* begins to deserve serious attention. For, if total design may represent the surrender of logical empiricism to a most unempirical myth and if it may seem to envisage the future (when all will be known) as a sort of dialectic of non-debate, it is because the *bricoleur* (like the fox) can entertain no such prospects of conclusive synthesis, because, rather than with one world – infinitely extended though subjected to the same generalisations – his very activity implies a willingness and an ability to deal with a plurality of closed finite systems (*the collection of oddments left over from human endeavour*) that, for the time being at least, his behaviour may offer an important model.

252   ARTHUR DREXLER
preface to the exhibition catalogue
The Architecture of the Ecole des Beaux-Arts (1975)

I n the fall of 1975 the Museum of Modern Art again inserted itself into the contemporary architectural debate with a large exhibition of student drawings from the École des Beaux-Arts. The exhibition, curated by Philip Johnson's successor Arthur Drexler, would soon prove to be controversial – but not for the reasons that one might have expected. If the École des Beaux-Arts for many modernists (and Le Corbusier in particular) had been a scapegoat of everything wrong with the nineteenth century (the architecture of "styles"), such criticism was noticeably muted in the changing atmosphere of the 1970s. Those architects and critics who opposed the exhibition generally did so not for a lack of appreciation of the drawings or the exhibition's content, but rather – and seemingly – out of fear of how this content might be interpreted by other practitioners. In other words, many feared it signified modernism's imminent demise and that a historicist revival might be in the offing. Neither of these fears proved to be unfounded and thus the exhibition, in retrospect, represents a rather significant tectonic shift within American architectural theory and practice, one that would be fully manifested in the 1980s.

"The battle of modern architecture," Philip Johnson declared in 1952, "has long been won." His observation prefaced *Built in USA: Post-war Architecture*, a Museum of Modern Art catalog devoted to "the great post-war flowering of architecture in this country – which is so obvious around us." "With the mid-century," he concluded, "modern architecture has come of age."

Arthur Drexler, preface to the exhibition catalogue *The Architecture of the Ecole des Beaux-Arts*. New York: Museum of Modern Art, 1975, pp. 3–4.

By the end of the third quarter of the century, the theoretical basis of modern architecture is as much a collection of received opinions as were the doctrines it overthrew. We think we know what modern architecture is – although it is notoriously difficult to define – and how it differs from what preceded it; but we are no longer so certain as to what it should become and how it should be taught. And since history is written by the victors, the literature of the modern movement has helped to perpetuate confusion as to what was lost, let alone what the battle was about.

The triumph of modern architecture is inseparable from ideas given their clearest embodiment in the teaching and practice of the German Bauhaus, which replaced a French educational system that had evolved for over two hundred years. Ecole des Beaux-Arts practice before the First World War could not keep pace with Ecole theories, and that the theories themselves were preventing a reintegration is a historical judgment not likely to be reversed. The Ecole des Beaux-Arts seemed intent on solving what were no longer perceived as "real" problems. Defining – and solving – what seemed to be the right problems was the great achievement of the Bauhaus. Founded in 1919 and disrupted only fourteen years later by the upheaval of Nazism, the Bauhaus disappeared as an institution but flourished as a doctrine. It dominated architecture in America by effecting pervasive changes in education, and then, within the lifetimes of its protagonists, subsided without having generated its own succession.

Although Bauhaus ideas were as varied as the personalities of its faculty and its best students, our generalizations about what they thought they were doing are likely to be as partial as were those pronouncements made in the 1920s about the Ecole des Beaux-Arts. Nevertheless, we may observe that the Bauhaus began as a craft school, regarding crafts-manship as a necessary step toward the higher task of designing for machine production. Prompted in part by the supposed moral integrity of the craftsman as distinguished from the factory-hand, social concern was reinforced by a preference for treating form as simple geometric elements of unchanging value, at last enabling man's artifacts to be free of the shifting fashions of historical styles. The immutable nature of pure geometry was supposed to make it peculiarly well-suited to the demands of machine production, although there is nothing about machinery that inherently limits it to the replication of simple geometric forms. The result of this conjunction of ideas was, of course, the creation of a brilliant historic style, lucid in its reductionist simplicity but not necessarily simple in fact; reasonably responsive to the requirements of practical use (function); and most successful in the design of small-scale objects, particularly furniture. In architecture, its moralizing fixation on utility and industrial technique led to an anti-historical bias the consequences of which have yet to be fully understood, although they are all too painfully obvious wherever modern architecture has dealt with the urban environment. The modern movement has prided itself on its "urbanism," but to be anti-historical is to be anti-urban. The old architecture defined itself as the design of public buildings which, *pro bono publico*, quite naturally must be grand. The new architecture defined itself as the design of everything in the built environment – "total architecture," in Walter Gropius's alarming phrase – but perceived grandeur only as an instrument of oppression.

Fifty years ago redemption through design – *good* design – was the mystic hope hidden within the humane reordering of earthly things. Today, in architecture as in everything else, messianic fervor seems naïve when it is not actually destructive. But architecture has yet to benefit from the sense of new possibilities generated by a relaxation of dogma. The kind of freedom achieved by Italian design in the '60s replaced moral imperatives with irony and humor, but not with new convictions, and it is scarcely surprising that once again architects agree about very little concerning the nature of their art. Indeed, if there is one thing about which they do agree, at least enough to sign manifestos and march on picket lines, it is the necessity of preserving what is left of Beaux-Arts architecture wherever it may be found. Reviled during the first quarter of the century, and forgotten until the '60s (when Louis Kahn's buildings and Kahn himself reminded us of the origin of some interesting ideas), the architecture taught and practiced by the Ecole des Beaux-Arts again rewards thoughtful study. We have rediscovered some of its problems.

Throughout the twentieth century, the planning concepts of the Ecole des Beaux-Arts have been the most readily accessible of all its productions. This was not only because of the formal interest of Beaux-Arts plans but because the majority of architects who reached professional maturity in the 1940s had received at least an American version of Beaux-Arts training. What remained incomprehensible to the modern movement – and for good reason – was the apparent unrelatedness, or independence, of elevation and section from the nature of the plan, despite the fact that a favorite Beaux-Arts theme was the correspondence of a building's exterior to its internal organization. Particularly disturbing was the eclectic use of historic styles, which during the last decade of the nineteenth century exploded in a frenzy of ornament and megalomania. And yet the Beaux-Arts was of course no more monolithic in its ideas and objectives than was the Bauhaus. Today, the variety of those ideas tends to clarify and enhance the underlying continuities. Some Beaux-Arts problems, among them the question of how to use the past, may perhaps be seen now as possibilities that are liberating rather than constraining. A more detached view of architecture as it was understood in the nineteenth century might also provoke a more rigorous critique of philosophical assumptions underlying the architecture of our own time. Now that modern experience so often contradicts modern faith, we would be well advised to reexamine our architectural pieties.

253 BERNARD TSCHUMI
from "Architecture and Transgression" (1975)

S ince 1970 the Swiss-born architect Bernard Tschumi had been teaching at the Architectural Association in London. In 1976 he became a visiting lecturer at Princeton University and the Institute for Architecture and Urban Studies. This change of venue coincided with important changes in his theoretical development, as he was becoming fascinated both with the theme of space and with the work of Roland Barthes, Dennis Hollier, and

Bernard Tschumi, from "Architecture and Transgression," in *Oppositions* 7 (Winter 1976), pp. 58–9.

Georges Bataille, among others. In effect, his earlier affinity with the strategies of the Situationists melded with the formation of poststructural ideas, resulting in several studies on the uneasy theme of paradoxes: the paradox of real and ideal space, the paradox of modernism and ornament, the paradox of architectural pleasure ("where architectural language breaks into a thousand pieces, where the elements of architecture are dismantled and its rules transgressed"). These impiously sensual musings on the meaning of modernism, concluding with his "postcard" on the derelict Villa Savoye, thus segues into both *The Manhattan Transcripts* (1976–81) and his competition-winning design for the Parc de la Villette (1982–3).

Part Two: eROTicism

It appears that there is a certain point in the mind wherefrom life and death, reality and imaginary, past and future, the communicable and the incommunicable cease to be perceived in a contradictory way.
André Breton, The Second Manifesto

Paradoxes equivocate. They lie, and they don't, they tell the truth, and they don't. Each meaning has always to be taken with the others. The experience of the liar paradox is like standing between two mirrors, its meanings infinitely reflected. The paradox is literally speculative.[1] To explore it, it is useful to consider two correspondences without which much remains obscure.[2]

First correspondence

The first correspondence is obvious and immediate. It is the correspondence of eroticism. Not to be confused with sensuality, eroticism does not simply mean the pleasure of the senses. Sensuality is as different from eroticism as a simple spatial perception is different from architecture. "Eroticism is not the excess of pleasure, but the pleasure of excess": this popular definition mirrors our argument. Just as the sensual experience of space does not make architecture, the pure pleasure of the senses does not constitute eroticism. On the contrary, "the pleasure of excess" requires consciousness as well as voluptuousness. Just as eroticism means a double pleasure that involves both mental constructs and sensuality, the resolution of the architectural paradox calls for architectural concepts and at the same instant the immediate experience of space. Architecture has the same status, the same function, and the same meaning as eroticism. At the possible/impossible junction of concepts and experience, architecture appears as the image of two worlds: personal and universal. Eroticism is no different; for one whose concept leads to pleasure (excess), eroticism is "personal" by nature. And by nature it is also "universal." Thus, on the one hand, there is sensual pleasure, the other and the I; on the other hand, historical inquiry and ultimate rationality. Architecture is the ultimate erotic "object," because an architectural act, brought to the level of excess, is the only way to reveal both the traces of history and its own immediate experiential truth.[3]

Second correspondence

The junction between ideal space and real space is seen differently in the second correspondence. This second correspondence is immensely general and inevitably contains the present argument as it would contain many others. It is nothing less than the analogy of life-and-death, applied here to one celebrated architectural example.

Each society expects architecture to reflect its ideals and domesticate its deeper fears. And architecture and its theorists rarely negate the form that the society expects of it. Loos' celebrated attack on the intrinsic criminality of ornament was echoed by the Modern Movement's admiration for engineering "purity," and its admiration was translated into architectural terms by an unconscious consensus. "The engineers fabricate the tools of their time – everything except moth-eaten boudoirs and moldy houses...."[4] This consistent repudiation of the so-called "obscene scrawl"[5] (as opposed to the puritan sense of hygiene) is not unlike mankind's horror for decaying and putrefied bodies. Death is tolerated only when the bones are white: if architects cannot succeed in their quest for "healthy and virile, active and useful, ethical and happy"[6] people and houses, they can at least be comfortable in front of the white ruins of the Parthenon. Young life and decent death, such was the architectural order.

Calling itself "modern" as well as independent of the "bourgeois" rules of the time, the heroic tradition of the thirties nevertheless reflected the deep and unconscious fears of society. Life was seen as a negation of death – it condemned death and even excluded it – a negation which went beyond the idea of death itself and extended to the rot of the putrefying flesh. The anguish about death, however, only related to the phase of decomposition, for white bones did not possess the intolerable aspect of corrupted flesh. Architecture reflected these deep feelings: putrefying buildings were seen as unacceptable, but dry white ruins afforded decency and respectability. From being respectful to seeking respectability, there is only one step. Are the rationalists or the New York "Five" today unconsciously striving for respect through the white and timeless skeletons they propose?

Moreover, the fear of decaying organisms – as opposed to the nostalgic search for the "outmoded purity of architecture" – appears in conservationist enterprises as much as in utopian projects. Those who in 1965 visited the then derelict Villa Savoye certainly remember the squalid walls of the small service rooms on the ground floor, stinking of urine, smeared with excrement, and covered with obscene graffiti. Not surprisingly, the long campaign to save the threatened "purity" of the Villa Savoye doubled in intensity in the months that followed, and finally succeeded.

NOTES

1   This infinite tension between the two mirrors constitutes a void. As Oscar Wilde once pointed out, in order to defend any paradox, the wit depends on *memory.* By absorbing and reflecting all information, the mirrors – and the mind – become a wheel, a sort of circular retrieval system. In architecture, between the mirrors of ideal space and real space, the same thing happens. Long proscribed in an amnesic world where only progress and technological advance count, architectural memory returns. Cf. Antoine Grumbach, "L'Architecture et l'Evidente Nécessité de la Mémoire," *L'Art Vivant,* no. 56, January 1975.

2 I only discuss here the resolution of the paradox in terms of a space *outside* the "subject." The argument could indeed be extended to the unqualifiable pleasure of drawing and to what could be called the "experience of concepts." Tracing Chinese ideograms, for example, means a double pleasure: for the experience of drawing reveals itself as a praxis of the sign, as a sensitive materiality with meaning. While with the paradox, it is tempting to try to uncover the mode of inscription of architectural concepts upon the unconscious. Especially if we admit that there is libido in all human activities, we may also consider that some architectural concepts are the expression of a sublimated model. See Sibony's article in *Psychanalyse et Sémiotique*, 10/18 (Paris: Collection Tel Quel, 1975).

3 Too little research has been done on the relationship between architectonic concepts and the sensory experience of space: "Those who negate sensations, who negate direct experience, who negate personal participation in a praxis which is aimed at transforming reality, are not materialists" (Mao Tse Tung, *Four Philosophical Essays* [Peking: 1967]).

4 Le Corbusier, *Vers Une Architecture* (Paris: L'Esprit Nouveau, 1928). One chapter is entitled "Architecture et Transgression." Not surprisingly, Le Corbusier's interpretation considerably differs from Bataille's and from the one discussed in my text.

5 Ibid.

6 Ibid.

254 CHRISTOPHER ALEXANDER
from *A Pattern Language* (1977)

After his early attempts to define a quantifiable design methodology in *Notes on the Synthesis of Form* (1964), Alexander began to develop the idea of a "pattern language," which he first put forward in *A Pattern Language which Generates Multi-Service Use Centers* (1968) and *Houses Generated by Patterns* (1969). Both were published by the Center for Environmental Structure he founded at the University of California at Berkeley in 1967. A pattern, notes Alexander, "describes a problem which occurs over and over again in our environment, and then describes the core of the solution to that problem, in such a way that you can use this solution a million times over, without ever doing it the same way twice." Patterns collectively generate a design language based on empirical study and anthropological investigation, and, as the title of this book shows, they can be applied to any level of design. By the late 1970s, Alexander, from his West-Coach perch at Berkeley, was amassing a cadre of collaborators, and this large book (253 patterns) is the first definitive explication of his design theory. It forms a trilogy with *The Timeless Way of Building* (1979) and *The Oregon Experiment* (1975). This selection of pattern 61, "Small Public Squares," is indicative of his overall approach.

A town needs public squares; they are the largest, most public rooms, that the town has. But when they are too large, they look and feel deserted.

It is natural that every public street will swell out at those important nodes where there is the most activity. And it is only these widened, swollen, public squares which can

Christopher Alexander, from *A Pattern Language: Towns, Buildings, Construction*. New York: Oxford University Press, 1977, pp. 311–13.

accommodate the public gatherings, small crowds, festivities, bonfires, carnivals, speeches, dancing, shouting, mourning, which must have their place in the life of the town.

But for some reason there is a temptation to make these public squares too large. Time and again in modern cities, architects and planners build plazas that are too large. They look good on drawings; but in real life they end up desolate and dead.

Our observations suggest strongly that open places intended as public squares should be very small. As a general rule, we have found that they work best when they have a diameter of about 60 feet – at this diameter people often go to them, they become favorite places, and people feel comfortable there. When the diameter gets above 70 feet, the squares begin to seem deserted and unpleasant. The only exceptions we know are places like the Piazza San Marco and Trafalgar Square, which are great town centers, teeming with people.

What possible functional basis is there for these observations? First, we know from the pattern, PEDESTRIAN DENSITY (123), that a place begins to seem deserted when it has more than about 300 square feet per person.

On this basis a square with a diameter of 100 feet will begin to seem deserted if there are less than 33 people in it. There are few places in a city where you can be sure there will always be 33 people. On the other hand, it only takes 4 people to give life to a square with a diameter of 35 feet, and only 12 to give life to a square with a diameter of 60 feet. Since there are far far better chances of 4 or 12 people being in a certain place than 33, the smaller squares will feel comfortable for a far greater percentage of the time.

The second possible basis for our observations depends on the diameter. A person's face is just recognizable at about 70 feet; and under typical urban noise conditions, a loud voice can just barely be heard across 70 feet. This may mean that people feel half-consciously tied together in plazas that have diameters of 70 feet or less – where they can make out the faces and half-hear the talk of the people around them; and this feeling of being at one with a loosely knit square is lost in the larger spaces. Roughly similar things have been said by Philip Thiel ("An Architectural and Urban Space Sequence Notation." unpublished ms., University of California, Department of Architecture, August 1960, p. 5) and by Hans Blumenfeld ("Scale in Civic Design," *Town Planning Review*, April 1953, pp. 35–46). For example, Blumenfeld gives the following figures: a person's face can be recognized at up to 70 or 80 feet; a person's face can be recognized as "a portrait," in rich detail, at up to about 48 feet.

Our own informal experiments show the following results. Two people with normal vision can communicate comfortably up to 75 feet. They can talk with raised voice, and they can see the general outlines of the expression on one another's faces. This 75 foot maximum is extremely reliable. Repeated experiments gave the same distance again and again, ± 10 per cent. At 100 feet it is uncomfortable to talk, and facial expression is no longer clear. Anything above 100 feet is hopeless.

Therefore:

Make a public square much smaller than you would at first imagine; usually no more than 45 to 60 feet across, never more than 70 feet across. This applies only to its width in the short direction. In the long direction it can certainly be longer.

255 ROBERT A. M. STERN
from "New Directions in Modern American Architecture" (1977)

As the debate between members of the "Whites" and "Grays" intensified in the mid-1970s, Robert A. M. Stern took the occasion of this article to announce that from their "inclusivist Post-Modernist position," the Grays' had now proclaimed their break from modernism. This was not true of the Whites; they were the "third generation" of modernists who were engaging in a neo-modern revival. Thus their differences with the Grays had been raised to a "battle of styles." Such a proclamation was only the first of many similar ones to be made over the next several years, and Stern's attempt to categorize the elements of gray architecture should be read as provisional. Nevertheless, the essay escalated the terms of the debate and it defined a polemical crusade that would only grow louder in the 1980s.

I began my book *New Directions in American Architecture* in 1969 by posing a debate between the group of architects whom I described as 'exclusivist' and a new 'inclusivist' group, a debate that continues to be the central focus of my concern in writing this postscript.[1] In 1969 I saw the inclusivists – since 1974 often referred to as the 'grey' architects – as third generation modernists. At the present time, however, I see their position rather differently: they are the first post-modern generation of architects, establishing a position that marks a significant break with the three generations of the Modern Movement and its so-called International Style, that is with the first generation of Le Corbusier and Mies; the second generation of Johnson, Roche and Rudolph; and the third represented by Richard Meier, Charles Gwathmey and Peter Eisenman.

Although the idea of 'modernism' has long been intertwined with a belief that art is shipwrecked in a commercial society, the second generation of the Modern Movement continues to ride the crest of the enormous prosperity that engulfed American architecture in the wake of World War II.[2] While the heroic ambitions of some and the technological bravura of others among this group no longer embodies for many Americans the same mystique of power and progress they once did, a market for this work still exists, particularly in those so-called 'developing' countries whose vision of America remains rooted to the values that most of us rejected the night Lyndon Johnson told the nation that we could have guns and butter, war in Vietnam, peace and progress at home.[3]

The third generation of the Modern Movement – the so-called 'white' architects – has emerged as much in reaction to the permissive inclusivism of the 'grey' architects as to the dilution of the fundamental values and forms of modernism that has characterised the largely commercial work of the second generation. This third generation seeks to revitalise the Modern Movement by a process of purification based on a return to the philosophical idealism that motivated European Modernism in the 1920s and 1930s and to the most abstract aspects of its form-making: the mechanomorphological cubism of Le Corbusier, and the rigorous, highly cerebral constructs of such architects as Hannes Meyer and Giuseppi Terragni.[4]

Robert A. M. Stern, from "New Directions in Modern American Architecture: Postscript: At the Edge of Modernism," in *Architectural Association Quarterly* 9:2–3 (1977), p. 66.

To some degree, the debate between 'white' exclusivism and 'grey' inclusivism can be seen as a battle of styles not unlike the one that took place in America during the last great economic depression, when International Style modernism struggled for acceptance against the prevailing progressive traditionalist modes.[5] But the battle of the 1970s is not without irony: the brave-new-world modernism of 50 years ago is now seen by the insurgent post-modernists as orthodox, stifling, and not a little irrelevant, while the third generation modernists seek to return to the forms and values of the pioneer Modernism of the 1920s, even though their built work often comes closer to the provincial, pragmatic and derivative American International Style of the 1930s, than to the purer and more rigorously abstract European prototypes.[6]

NOTES

1 My use of these terms derived from Charles Moore who had in turn picked them up from Robert Venturi *Complexity and Contradiction in Architecture* pp. 22–3.

2 See Vincent Scully 'Introduction' to Robert Venturi *Complexity and Contradiction in Architecture* pp. 15–16; Henry-Russell Hitchcock 'Introduction' to Yukio Futagawa *Kevin Roche/John Dinkeloo Associates 1962–75* ADA Edita, Tokyo 1975; Paul Goldberger 'High Design at a Profit' *New York Times Magazine* 14 November 1976, pp. 77–9; William Marlin 'Penzoil Place' *Architecture Record* CLX number 7, November 1976, pp. 101–10.

   The 'silver' architecture of such West Coast architects as Cesar Pelli and Anthony Lumsden seems at this writing not much more than an extension of second-generation modernism. The work of Eugene Kupper, another member of that loose affiliation, seems very closely related in intention to the architecture of the 'whites', while Thomas R. Vreeland's work not unexpectedly connects up with that of the 'greys'. See 'Images from a Silver Screen' *Progressive Architecture* LVII number 10, October 1976, pp. 70–7, and Thomas R. Vreeland Jr. 'The New Tradition' *LA Architect* October/November 1976.

3 On the architecture of 'developing' countries see John Morris Dixon '1001 Paradoxes' *Progressive Architecture* LVII number 10, October 1976, p. 6; Sharon Lee Ryder 'A Place in Progress' ibid, pp. 49–55; Suzanne Stephens 'The Adventures of Harry Barber in OPEC Land' ibid, pp. 56–65.

4 Arthur Drexler 'Preface' to Peter Eisenman et al *Five Architects* Wittenborn, New York 1972, p. 1; See also Colin Rowe 'Introduction' ibid, pp. 3–7; Kenneth Frampton 'Criticism' ibid, pp. 9–17; Robert A. M. Stern, Jaqeulin Robertson, Charles Moore, Allen Greenberg, Romaldo Giurgola 'Five on Five' *Architectural Forum* CXXXVIII, May 1973, pp. 46–57; David Morton 'Richard Meier' *Global Architecture* number 22, 1973, pp. 2–7; Eisenman 'From Object to Relationship II: Guiseppe Terragni – Casa Giuliani Frigerio; Casa del Fascio' *Perspecta* 13/14, 1971, pp. 36–65; Richard Meier 'Les Heures Claires' *Global Architecture* number 13, pp. 2–7.

5 See Peter Eisenman and Robert A. M. Stern 'White and Grey' *Architecture and Urbanism* number 52, April 1975, pp. 3–4, 25–180; Robert A. M. Stern, George Howe *Towards a Modern American Architecture* Yale, New Haven 1975, chapter 6.

6 I first made this point in my *40 Under 40, Young Talent in Architecture* American Federation of Arts, New York 1966. See also Manfredo Tafuri 'European Graffiti: Five × Five = Twenty Five' *Oppositions* 5, Summer 1976, pp. 35–73; Robert Venturi, Denise Scott Brown and Steven Izenour *Learning from Las Vegas* MIT, Cambridge 1972, p. 47; Vincent Scully *The Shingle Style Today or the Historian's Revenge* Braziller, New York 1974, pp. 38–40; Arthur Drexler 'Preface' to *The Architecture of the École des Beaux-Arts* Museum of Modern Art, New York 1975.

256 REM KOOLHAAS
from *Delirious New York* (1978)

With this tongue-in-cheek "Retroactive Manifesto" for the "Capital of Perpetual Crisis," Rem Koolhaas formally enters the architectural discourse. A native of Rotterdam, Koolhaas trained at the Architectural Association in London and at Cornell University under Oswald Mathias Ungers. In 1975 – together with Madelon Vriesendorp and Zoe and Elia Zenghelis – he opened the Office for Metropolitan Architecture (OMA) in London and embarked initially on a series of hypothetical and ironical projects for New York, among them the Hotel Sphinx (a stepped hotel on Times Square whose sphinx head atop the tower can be turned to "stare" at any event in the city), New Welfare Island, and the Welfare Palace Hotel. All were published as an appendix to *Delirious New York*, a book that expanded upon an article earlier published in *Architectural Design*. Koolhaas ponders on the spectacle of the Big Apple with indelicacy and wit, but his conceptual musings (here and later) carry more the imprint of studious gravity than ingenuous frivolity. With Koolhaas, the unraveling of theoretical certainty that characterizes much of the architectural debate of the 1970s takes a new and interesting turn, one not uncritical in its implied anti-criticality.

Manifesto

How to write a manifesto – on a form of urbanism for what remains of the 20th century – in an age disgusted with them? The fatal weakness of manifestos is their inherent lack of evidence.

Manhattan's problem is the opposite: it is a mountain range of evidence without manifesto.

This book was conceived at the intersection of these two observations: it is a *retroactive manifesto* for Manhattan.

Manhattan is the 20th century's Rosetta Stone.

Not only are large parts of its surface occupied by architectural mutations (Central Park, the Skyscraper), utopian fragments (Rockefeller Center, the UN Building) and irrational phenomena (Radio City Music Hall), but in addition each block is covered with several layers of phantom architecture in the form of past occupancies, aborted projects and popular fantasies that provide alternative images to the New York that exists.

Especially between 1890 and 1940 a new culture (the Machine Age?) selected Manhattan as laboratory: a mythical island where the invention and testing of a metropolitan lifestyle and its attendant architecture could be pursued as a collective experiment in which the entire city became a factory of man-made experience, where the real and the natural ceased to exist.

This book is an interpretation of that Manhattan which gives its seemingly discontinuous – even irreconcilable – episodes a degree of consistency and coherence, an interpretation that intends to establish Manhattan as the product of an unformulated theory, *Manhattanism*, whose program – to exist in a world totally fabricated by man, i.e., to live *inside* fantasy – was so ambitious that to be realized, it could never be openly stated.

Rem Koolhaas, from *Delirious New York: A Retroactive Manifesto for Manhattan*. New York: Oxford University Press, 1978, pp. 9–10.

Ecstasy

If Manhattan is still in search of a theory, then this theory, once identified, should yield a formula for an architecture that is at once ambitious *and* popular.

Manhattan has generated a shameless architecture that has been loved in direct proportion to its defiant lack of self-hatred, respected exactly to the degree that it went too far.

Manhattan has consistently inspired in its beholders *ecstasy about architecture*.

In spite – or perhaps because – of this, its performance and implications have been consistently ignored and even suppressed by the architectural profession.

Density

Manhattanism is the one urbanistic ideology that has fed, from its conception, on the splendors and miseries of the metropolitan condition – hyper density – without once losing faith in it as the basis for a desirable modern culture. *Manhattan's architecture is a paradigm for the exploitation of congestion.*

The retroactive formulation of Manhattan's program is a polemical operation.

It reveals a number of strategies, theorems and breakthroughs that not only give logic and pattern to the city's past performance, but whose continuing validity is itself an argument for a second coming of Manhattanism, this time as an explicit doctrine that can transcend the island of its origins to claim its place among contemporary urbanisms. With Manhattan as example, this book is a blueprint for a "Culture of Congestion."

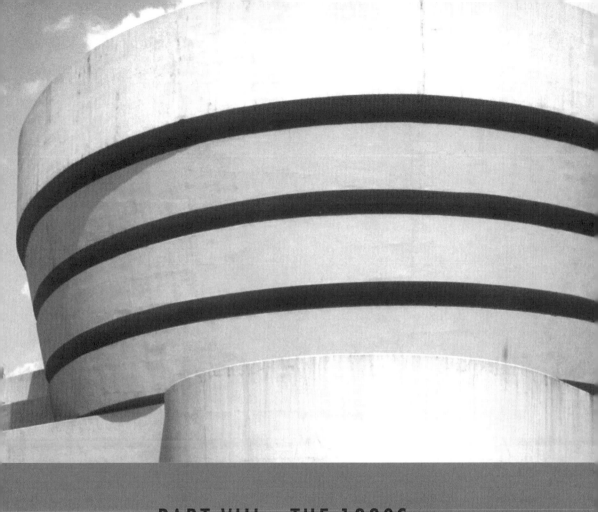

PART VIII   THE 1980S

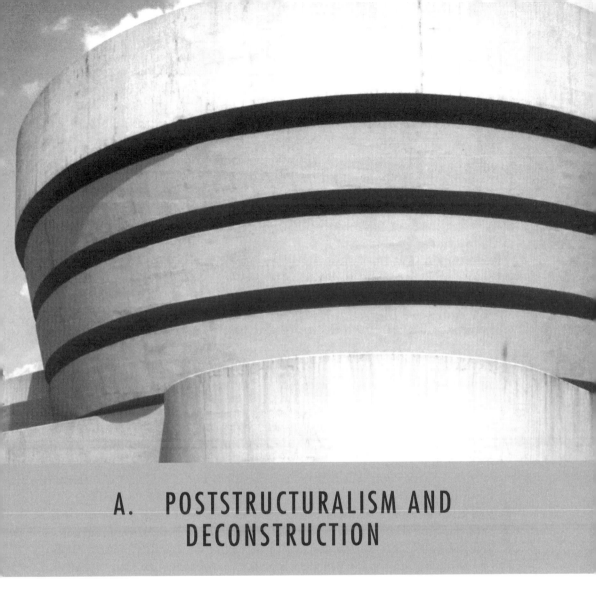

A. POSTSTRUCTURALISM AND DECONSTRUCTION

Introduction

I f the 1970s put forward a host of competing directions for architects, the 1980s brought forth an abundance of additional players and competing notions. Much of this energy and terminological innovation had much to do with the perceived shift within the larger philosophical terrain, and the general belief that Western civilization had indeed entered a new intellectual era. Two words often used to describe this change were poststructuralism and Deconstruction.

The former relates to the scientific methodology of structuralism (especially prominent between 1950 and 1970), such as is found in the theories of Jean Piaget and Claude Lévi-Strauss. In general, structuralism postulates universal patterns or structures within human thought and therefore a unitary basis for eventually understanding the human mind and the world. Poststructuralism, hailed by the writings of Michel Foucault and François Lyotard (among others), rejects any such notion of a supreme "metanarrative" or unitary knowledge. Hence all knowledge is fragmentary and localized at best. Translated into architecture, poststructuralism not only rejects such unified models as an "International Style," but also modernism's "metanarrative" of leading humanity on a progressive march toward a new and better world.

Deconstruction cannot be divorced from poststructuralist thinking, but it was initially bound more closely with the philosophical views of Jacques Derrida. Through Derrida's "close-reading" of various texts, he came to argue that there are always conflicting conceptions or representations of meaning inherent in any text, and thus it is never possible to support one meaning in a definitive way over another. It is not that texts (also read buildings) are meaningless, but rather that they are always contaminated, as it were, with linguistic and rhetorical forces that are at heart psychological. Thus Derridean Deconstruction reinforces the fragmentary and localized view of poststructuralism, at the same time intrinsically suggesting a critique of such unitary constructs as Marxism, to name but one example.

Deconstruction also has the distinction (some might call it unfortunate) that it is a natural architectural metaphor. Hence it has sometimes been literally drafted into this field as a way to describe non-unitary or fragmented designs inherently opposed to the balanced and unified compositional principles of high modernism. Strikingly, architects inspired by deconstructionalist thought often turned to such early modernist strategies as Soviet Constructivism for paradigms or images, which too lacked compositional unity and stressed the diagonal as an empathetic force.

257   JEAN-FRANÇOIS LYOTARD
from *The Postmodern Condition*
(1979)

In the late 1970s the French philosopher François Lyotard was asked by the Quebec government to write a report on the state of knowledge, science, and technology within the rapidly developing informational society. He responded with his book, *The Postmodern Condition*, which opened with the working hypothesis "that the status of knowledge is altered as societies enter what is known as the postindustrial age and cultures enter what is known as the postmodern age." His argument was actually more radical in that he insisted that the new condition of postmodernity was, in essence, the rejection of the two great metanarratives (legitimizing constructs for science and society as a whole) of modernism: (1) that knowledge and science seek the successive liberation of humanity, and (2) that there is a speculative unity to all knowledge. What is left, he concluded, is the new reality of smaller working narratives regarding knowledge: provisional, contingent, and relative. Lyotard's book not only challenged the epistemological foundations of structuralism and semiotics (now limiting their field merely to the pragmatic realm), but also the Marxist suppositions of nearly all European theory in the 1960s and 1970s (Marxism was now seen as just another totalizing construct projecting its utopian end). The role of postmodernism is to question and critique (deconstruct) these metanarratives in whatever form they appear – from broad educational principles to architectural aesthetics. Thus the term postmodernism, which had already found currency in architectural literature, finds a philosophical mantle to dress itself.

François Lyotard, from *The Postmodern Condition: A Report on Knowledge*, trans. Geoff Bennington and Brian Massumi. Minneapolis: University of Minnesota Press, 1984, pp. xxiii–xxiv.

The object of this study is the condition of knowledge in the most highly developed societies. I have decided to use the word *postmodern* to describe that condition. The word is in current use on the American continent among sociologists and critics; it designates the state of our culture following the transformations which, since the end of the nineteenth century, have altered the game rules for science, literature, and the arts. The present study will place these transformations in the context of the crisis of narratives.

Science has always been in conflict with narratives. Judged by the yardstick of science, the majority of them prove to be fables. But to the extent that science does not restrict itself to stating useful regularities and seeks the truth, it is obliged to legitimate the rules of its own game. It then produces a discourse of legitimation with respect to its own status, a discourse called philosophy. I will use the term *modern* to designate any science that legitimates itself with reference to a metadiscourse of this kind making an explicit appeal to some grand narrative, such as the dialectics of Spirit, the hermeneutics of meaning, the emancipation of the rational or working subject, or the creation of wealth. For example, the rule of consensus between the sender and addressee of a statement with truth-value is deemed acceptable if it is cast in terms of a possible unanimity between rational minds: this is the Enlightenment narrative, in which the hero of knowledge works toward a good ethico-political end – universal peace. As can be seen from this example, if a metanarrative implying a philosophy of history is used to legitimate knowledge, questions are raised concerning the validity of the institutions governing the social bond: these must be legitimated as well. Thus justice is consigned to the grand narrative in the same way as truth.

Simplifying to the extreme, I define *postmodern* as incredulity toward metanarratives. This incredulity is undoubtedly a product of progress in the sciences: but that progress in turn presupposes it. To the obsolescence of the metanarrative apparatus of legitimation corresponds, most notably, the crisis of metaphysical philosophy and of the university institution which in the past relied on it. The narrative function is losing its functors, its great hero, its great dangers, its great voyages, its great goal. It is being dispersed in clouds of narrative language elements – narrative, but also denotative, prescriptive, descriptive, and so on. Conveyed within each cloud are pragmatic valencies specific to its kind. Each of us lives at the intersection of many of these. However, we do not necessarily establish stable language combinations, and the properties of the ones we do establish are not necessarily communicable.

Thus the society of the future falls less within the province of a Newtonian anthropology (such as stucturalism or systems theory) than a pragmatics of language particles. There are many different language games – a heterogeneity of elements. They only give rise to institutions in patches – local determinism.

258 COOP HIMMELBLAU
"Architecture Must Blaze"
(1980)

I f one wanted to make a case for new architectural attitudes of the 1980s, one could point to the Austrian architectural office of Coop Himmelblau, founded in 1968 by Wolf D. Prix, Helmut Swiczinsky, and Rainer Michael Holzer (who left in 1971). In 1968 this avant-garde studio, initially engaged in hypothetical projects, professed to want no more than to strike an atonal note within the architectural chorus and inject a little fun into the street. By 1980, as this essay demonstrates, their attitude had become more aggressive – just at the moment when they were getting their first actual building commissions. Indeed this poetic manifesto perhaps has its basis in a project for a fifteen-story apartment building of 1978 called "Hot Flat," through which a large truss is diagonally rammed and cantilevered at both ends. At night, the architects proposed that this truss, fed with gas pipes, would literally blaze in a hot rejoinder to the cold alienation of the modern life. The spirit of Archigram is now infused with postmodern sensitivities.

Architecture must Blaze (1980)

You can judge just how bad the 70's were when you look at its super tense architecture.

Opinion polls and a complacent democracy live behind Biedermeier-facades.

But we don't want to build Biedermeier. Not now and at no other time.

We are tired of seeing Palladio and other historical masks. Because we don't want architecture to exclude everything that is disquieting.

We want architecture to have more. Architecture that bleeds, that exhausts, that whirls and even breaks. Architecture that lights up, that stings, that rips, and under stress tears. Architecture should be cavernous, fiery, smooth, hard, angular, brutal, round, delicate, colorful, obscene, voluptuous, dreamy, alluring, repelling, wet, dry and throbbing. Alive or dead. Cold – then cold as a block of ice. Hot – then hot as a blazing wing.

Architecture must blaze.

Coop Himmelblau, "Architecture Must Blaze," in *Architecture is Now: Projects, (Un)Buildings, Actions, Statements, Sketches, Commentaries, 1968–1983*, trans. Jo Steinbauer and Roswitha Prix. New York: Rizzoli, 1983, p. 90.

259 BERNARD TSCHUMI
from "The Violence of Architecture" (1981)

The theoretical path that Tschumi had been pursuing since the mid-1970s (see 253) culminated in 1981 with the exhibition *The Manhattan Transcripts*, a visual, programmed extravaganza (in retrospect) that was first shown to a few visitors in a small Manhattan gallery. In the same year he published this essay on violence, which concluded a sequence of near-blasphemous études on the themes of pleasure, limits, geometry, and lust. Tschumi put forward his own precise definitions for these terms, but the text and the accompanying images certainly convey the high level of intensity with which he was now viewing spatial events. His "deeply Dionysian" urges regarding architecture can no longer be quelled, and in the following year the architect began work on his competition-winning project for the Parc de la Villette – the event that would transform him overnight from an unknown artist/theorist into a major architect of international prominence.

There is no architecture without action, no architecture without events, no architecture without program. By extension, there is no architecture without violence.

The first of these statements runs against the mainstream of contemporary architectural thought, whether "modernist" or "post-modernist," by refusing to favor space at the expense of action. The second statement argues that although the logic of objects and the logic of man are independent in their relations to the world, they inevitably face one another in an intense confrontation. Any relationship between a building and its users is one of violence, for any use means the intrusion of a human body into a given space, the intrusion of one order into another. This intrusion is inherent in the idea of architecture: any reduction of architecture to its spaces at the expense of its events is as simplistic as the reduction of architecture to its facades.

By "violence." I do not mean the brutality that destroys physical or emotional integrity, but a metaphor for the intensity of a relationship between individuals and their surrounding spaces. The argument is not a matter of style: "modern" architecture is neither more nor less violent than classical architecture, or than Fascist, Socialist or vernacular variations. Architecture's violence is fundamental and unavoidable, for architecture is linked to events in the same way that the guard is linked to his prisoner, the police to the criminal, the doctor to the patient, order to chaos. This also suggests that actions qualify spaces as much as spaces qualify actions; that space and action are inseparable and that no proper interpretation of architecture, drawing or notation can refuse to consider this fact.

[. . .]

If violence is the key metaphor for the intensity of a relationship, then the very physicality of architecture transcends the metaphor. There is a deep sensuality, an unremittent eroticism in architecture. Its underlying violence varies according to the forces that are put into play – rational forces, irrational forces. They can be deficient or excessive. Little

Bernard Tschumi, from "The Violence of Architecture," in *Artforum* 20:1 (September 1981), pp. 44, 46–7.

activity – hypoactivity – in a house can be as disturbing as hyperactivity. Asceticism and orgiastic excesses are closer than architectural theorists have admitted, and the asceticism of Gerrit Rietveld's or Ludwig Wittgenstein's house inevitably implies the most extreme bacchanals. (Cultural expectations merely affect the perception of violence, but do not alter its nature; slapping your lover's face is perceived differently from culture to culture.)

Architecture and events constantly transgress each other's rules, whether explicitly or implicitly. These rules, these organized compositions, may be questioned, but they always remain points of reference. A building is a point of reference for the activities set to negate it. A theory of architecture is a theory of order threatened by the very use it permits. And vice versa.

The integration of the concept of violence into the architectural mechanism – the purpose of my argument – is ultimately aimed at a new pleasure of architecture. Like any form of violence, the violence of architecture also contains the possibility of change, of renewal. Like any violence, the violence of architecture is deeply Dionysian. It should be understood, and its contradictions maintained in a dynamic manner, with their conflicts and complementarity.

260 DANIEL LIBESKIND
from "Symbol and Interpretation" (1981)

Another new voice to sound in the early 1980s was that of Daniel Libeskind. Born in Poland in 1946, Libeskind immigrated to the United States in 1959. After taking advanced musical training in Israel, he shifted his interest to architecture and enrolled at Cooper Union in New York City (under John Hejduk). He later completed graduate studies in history and theory at Essex University (under Dalibor Vesely and Joseph Rykwert). After several years of teaching and practice in both London and Toronto, Libeskind moved to Michigan in 1978 to head the architecture department at the Cranbrook Academy of Art. Thus began a period of abstract reflection and artistic exploration that would culminate in 1983 with his celebrated exhibition *Chamber Works: Architectural Meditations on Themes from Heraclitus*. Thus his particular essay, published in 1981 within a larger book documenting his work at Cranbrook, represents a relatively early but nevertheless informative display of his philosophical outlook and creative powers. His phenomenological inclinations are evident, but so is his impassioned desire to break free from the trends of the 1970s.

To simplify, we have today a conflict between two differing tendencies. One claims that the 'natural' development of Architecture depends on the appropriation and ultimate domination of technique, inevitably leading to the objectification and quantification – the consumption of the space of encounters. The other tendency sees Architecture as an autonomous and self-referential discipline, inventing its own tradition through mute monuments. However,

Daniel Libeskind, from "Symbol and Interpretation," in *Between Zero and Infinity: Selected Projects in Architecture*. New York: Rizzoli, 1981, p. 29.

there is an approach which is not as simple or clear to define as the above, but which attempts nevertheless to deal with the poetic complexity of Architecture in time. It seeks to explore the deeper order rooted not only in visible forms, but in the invisible and hidden sources which nourish culture itself, in its thought, art, literature, song and movement. It considers history and tradition as a body whose memories and dreams cannot be simply reconstructed. Such an approach does not wish to reduce the visible to a thought, and architecture to a mere construction. An orientation such as this admits in its methods and testifies in its intentions to the intensity of experience, to its 'opaque transparency', and by its deferred expectations continually calls its own presuppositions into question.

The work in the studio at Cranbrook attempts to deal with architecture in an analytic, interpretive, symbolic, non-representational manner. We believe that nothing is ever fully figurative because a certain density clings to all our symbolic encounters, be they expressed in words or figures; cyphers or codes. Significance never fully exhausts its resources because there is always a residue left over which points to the correspondence or analogy which mediates the density of things and the ambiguity of meaning. Our point of departure therefore is never the abstract programming of an object but rather the search for valid objectives.

The ways of systematically objectifying architectural values, a conversion of objects into objects, is an effort to project experience as a process devoid of depth and concealment. But in whatever manner we represent architecture, be it as idea, matter, energy or the eternal recurrence of the same types, we must remember that objects appearing to us have already been revealed on a primordial and non-figurative level. There can be nothing fully figurative in the sense that meaning remains occluded in the symbols which convey it. If we understand architecture as having a symbolic nature, then we have already entered into a domain both more fundamental and original; a realm where the decisions and interpretations of meaning are already historically underway.

The necessity of rigorous imagination and the project of discovering possible means of emancipation in architecture must be recognized as crucial, as the concrete sources of inspiration in progressively more advanced societies expire in institutionalized habits of thought and action. The poverty of the so-called 'real world' must be unmasked as a form of a ruling ideology whose interests and ambitions do not necessarily coincide with our full existence and its aspirations. It has been pointed out more than once that good taste is only a form of acquired censorship. The awareness that pleasing, flattery and 'service to society' are often so many codes for techniques of deception, compels us to rethink the widely held belief that there is a predestined and correct expression assigned a priori to each form by the 'language of Architecture' itself, as if this 'language' belonged to the ceremonies and rituals themselves.

In order to release creative architectural interpretation from the grip of and the fidelity to the petty and circumstantial preoccupations of rhetoric (form-for-form's-sake), and especially from the representational narration of the past (historicism-ecclecticism), we are pursuing a projective poetics of architecture. We see in this phenomenology of space the polymorphic, shifting oneiric substance of Architecture – the interrogation which is the fragile and precise kernel of understanding and invention.

In the end, we are brought back to questioning the relation between signs and symbols. Can we say that the plastic meaning of architecture consists in an internal self-sustaining structure, and that this autonomy forms the hidden secret of space, so that finally it is in the splendour of the visible that its truth is revealed and exhausted? Or does the significance of architectural works and its affirming power lie in a movement of the truth-of-time as a whole, rising from the plastic-sensible as does lightning from thunder, abandoning the visible to the inertia and contingency of its own obscurity? Can visible form still carry the destiny of Architecture? In any case, forms are not yet dead and it is finally in the transfiguration of the concrete that we have access to that mystery of which forms and meanings give us only a provisional and portentous outline.

261 JÜRGEN HABERMAS
from "Modern and Postmodern Architecture" (1981)

Upon receiving the Adorno Prize in Frankfurt in 1980, the German philosopher and Marxist Jürgen Habermas delivered an address entitled "Modernity – An Incomplete Project," in which he responded forcefully to the assertions made on various fronts that a postmodern era had begun. Habermas's defense of the modern aesthetics of Theodore Adorno and what he termed the "Project of Enlightenment" (the development of science, morality, and art according to their inner logic) concluded with his characterizing opponents to modernism as young conservatives (the French deconstructionists), old conservatives, and neoconservatives. This same hostility toward postmodern viewpoints is also found in this essay, devoted to architecture, of the following year, in which those rejecting the socialist/political underpinnings of the avant-garde movements of the 1920s (now filtered of their earlier nihilistic and anarchical undercurrents) are labeled "escapists." Architecture was not a strong suit within Habermas's philosophical deliberations, and he admits contemporary tendencies were already growing quite complex. Nevertheless his defense of modernism echoes the anxiety that many Marxists felt about postmodern tendencies at the start of the 1980s – and not just those theorists associated with the Frankfurt School.

It is not easy to sort out the fronts in this battle. For all agree in their critique of a soulless container architecture, of the absence of relationship to the environment and the solitary arrogance of blocklike office buildings; of monstrous department stores and monumental university buildings and conference centers; of the lack of urbanity and the misanthropy of commuter towns; of housing developments, the brutal posterity of bunker architecture, the mass production of A-frame doghouses; of the destruction of city centers for the sake of the automobile, and so forth – so many catchwords, and no dissent to be found anywhere. From Sigfried Giedion, a passionate advocate of modern architecture for more than a generation, there are critical statements dating from the year 1964 that could have been written today by Oswald Matthias Ungers or Charles Moore. Of course, what one group presents as immanent critique is *opposition to modernity* in the other group; the same grounds on which the one side is encouraged to continue an irreplaceable tradition from a critical

Jürgen Habermas, from "Modern and Postmodern Architecture" (1981), in *The New Conservatism: Cultural Criticism and the Historians' Debate*, trans. Shierry Weber Nicholsen. Cambridge, MA: MIT Press, 1989, pp. 6–8.

perspective are sufficient for the other side to proclaim the postmodern era. And these opposing groups, furthermore, draw opposite conclusions depending on whether they approach the problem as a cosmetic one or in terms of criticism of the system. The *conservatively minded* are content to cover up stylistically what will go on in any case – whether they do so as traditionalists, like Branca, or, like the contemporary Robert Venturi, as a pop artist who turns the spirit of the Modern Movement into a quotation and mixes it ironically with other quotations to form garish texts that glow like neon lights. The radical antimodernists, in contrast, attack the problem at a more fundamental level, wanting to undermine economic and administrative constraints on industrial construction with the aim of dedifferentiating architecture. What one group sees as problems of style the other understands as problems of the decolonization of devastated lifeworlds. Thus those who want to continue the uncompleted project of a modernity that is on the skids see themselves confronted with a variety of opponents who are in accord only in their determination to bid farewell to modernity.

The modern architecture whose origins in Frank Lloyd Wright and Adolf Loos were both organic and rationalist, and which flowered in the most successful works of a Gropius and a Mies van der Rohe, a Le Corbusier and an Alvar Aalto – this architecture remains the first and only binding style, the first and only style to have shaped even everyday life, since the days of classicism. It is the only architectural movement to have sprung from the spirit of the avant-garde, the only one equal in stature to the avant-garde painting, music, and literature of our century. It continued the line of tradition of Western rationalism and was powerful enough to create models, that is, to become classical itself and to establish a tradition that from the beginning transcended national boundaries. How are we to reconcile these indisputable facts with the fact that those monstrosities we unanimously condemn arose after World War II as the successors to, even in the name of, this International Style? Is the true face of modernity revealed in them – or are they falsifications of its true spirit? I will move toward a provsional answer by listing the problems that faced architecture in the nineteenth century, describing the New Architecture's programmatic responses to them, and showing the kinds of problems that could *not* be solved with this program. These considerations, finally, should permit a judgment on the recommendation that this exhibition, if I understand its intentions correctly, is making. How sound is the advice that we steadfastly appropriate the tradition of modernity and continue it critically, instead of pursuing the escapist movements dominant today – whether the escape be to a tradition-conscious neohistoricism, to the ultramodern "stageset" architecture presented at the Venice Biennale in 1980, or into the vitalism of the simple life in an anonymous, deprofessionalized vernacular architecture?

262 ANDREAS HUYSSEN
from "Modernity and Postmodernity" (1984)

Virtually unique in the 1980s was the philosophical stance staked out by Andreas Huyssen. A defender of the proposition that indeed a new postmodern era was dawning, this professor of German and Comparative Literature at Columbia University nevertheless rejected Fredric Jameson's thesis of a wholesale paradigm shift within the cultural order, as well as the idea of a perfect synchronicity between French poststructuralist theory and the postmodern phenomenon. If Huyssen, through both training and philosophical inclination, was sympathetic toward the teachings of the Frankfurt School, he nevertheless rejected Habermas's defense of modernism as futile and unproductive. He thus saw poststructuralism, in essence, as a "modernist" critique of modernity at the stage of its inevitable exhaustion, and conversely – postmodernism (of resistance) as an attempt to raise the legitimate relational issues of tradition and innovation, conservation and renewal, mass and high culture.

Architecture gives us the most palpable example of the issues at stake. The modernist utopia embodied in the building programs of the Bauhaus, of Mies, Gropius and Le Corbusier, was part of a heroic attempt after the Great War and the Russian Revolution to rebuild a war-ravaged Europe in the image of the new, and to make building a vital part of the envisioned renewal of society. A new Enlightenment demanded rational design for a rational society, but the new rationality was overlayed with a utopian fervor which ultimately made it veer back into myth – the myth of modernization. Ruthless denial of the past was as much an essential component of the modern movement as its call for modernization through standardization and rationalization. It is well-known how the modernist utopia shipwrecked on its own internal contradictions and, more importantly, on politics and history. Gropius, Mies and others were forced into exile, Albert Speer took their place in Germany. After 1945, modernist architecture was largely deprived of its social vision and became increasingly an architecture of power and representation. Rather than standing as harbingers and promises of the new life, modernist housing projects became symbols of alienation and dehumanization, a fate they shared with the assembly line, that other agent of the new which had been greeted with exuberant enthusiasm in the 1920s by Leninists and Fordists alike.

Charles Jencks, one of the most well-known popularizing chroniclers of the agony of the modern movement and spokesman for a postmodern architecture, dates modern architecture's symbolic demise July 15, 1972, at 3:32 p.m. At that time several slab blocks of St. Louis' Pruitt-Igoe Housing (built by Minoru Yamasaki in the 1950s) were dynamited, and the collapse was dramatically displayed on the evening news. The modern machine for living, as Le Corbusier had called it with the technological euphoria so typical of the 1920s, had become unlivable, the modernist experiment, so it seemed, obsolete. Jencks takes pains to distinguish the initial vision of the modern movement from the sins committed in its name later on. And yet, on balance he agrees with those who, since the 1960s, have argued against

Andreas Huyssen, from "Modernity and Postmodernity," in *New German Critique* 33 (Autumn 1984), pp. 13–16.

modernism's hidden dependence on the machine metaphor and the production paradigm, and against its taking the factory as the primary model for all buildings. It has become commonplace in postmodernist circles to favor a reintroduction of multivalent symbolic dimensions into architecture, a mixing of codes, an appropriation of local vernaculars and regional traditions. Thus Jencks suggests that architects look two ways simultaneously, "towards the traditional slow-changing codes and particular ethnic meanings of a neighborhood, and towards the fast-changing codes of architectural fashion and professionalism." Such schizophrenia, Jencks holds, is symptomatic of the postmodern moment in architecture; and one might well ask whether it does not apply to contemporary culture at large, which increasingly seems to privilege what Bloch called *Ungleichzeitigkeiten* (non-synchronisms), rather than favoring only what Adorno, the theorist of modernism par excellence, described as *der fortgeschrittenste Materialstand der Kunst* (the most advanced state of artistic material). Where such postmodern schizophrenia is creative tension resulting in ambitious and successful buildings, and where, conversely, it veers off into an incoherent and arbitrary shuffling of styles, will remain a matter of debate. We should also not forget that the mixing of codes, the appropriation of regional traditions and the uses of symbolic dimensions other than the machine were never entirely unknown to the architects of the International Style. In order to arrive at his postmodernism, Jencks ironically had to exacerbate the very view of modernist architecture which he persistently attacks.

One of the most telling documents of the break of postmodernism with the modernist dogma is a book coauthored by Robert Venturi, Denise Scott-Brown and Steven Izenour and entitled *Learning from Las Vegas*. Rereading this book and earlier writings by Venturi from the 1960s today, one is struck by the proximity of Venturi's strategies and solutions to the pop sensibility of those years. Time and again the authors use pop art's break with the austere canon of high modernist painting and pop's uncritical espousal of the commercial vernacular of consumer culture as an inspiration for their work. What Madison Avenue was for Andy Warhol, what the comics and the Western were for Leslie Fiedler, the landscape of Las Vegas was for Venturi and his group. The rhetoric of *Learning from Las Vegas* is predicated on the glorification of the billboard strip and of the ruthless shlock of casino culture. In Kenneth Frampton's ironic words, it offers a reading of Las Vegas as "an authentic outburst of popular phantasy." I think it would be gratuitous to ridicule such odd notions of cultural populism today. While there is something patently absurd about such propositions, we have to acknowledge the power they mustered to explode the reified dogmas of modernism and to reopen a set of questions which the modernism gospel of the 1940s and 1950s had largely blocked from view: questions of ornament and metaphor in architecture, of figuration and realism in painting, of story and representation in literature, of the body in music and theater. Pop in the broadest sense was the context in which a notion of the postmodern first took shape, and from the beginning until today, the most significant trends within postmodernism have challenged modernism's relentless hostility to mass culture.

K. MICHAEL HAYS
from "Critical Architecture: Between Culture and Form" (1984)

n the opening lines of this essay, K. Michael Hays notes that he wishes to examine a "critical architecture," that is, "one resistant to the self-confirming, conciliatory operations of a dominant culture and yet irreducible to a purely formal structure disengaged from the contingencies of place and time." The theoretical space between this dichotomy of reading buildings as instruments or carriers of cultural values, and buildings as autonomous forms largely devoid of historical concerns, is where he wishes to locate his historical operation of criticality, a notion that also carries within it the adjectives of "resistant" and "oppositional." In short, Hays views architecture as inevitably a resistant response to the prevailing cultural and political order, effectively as a valiant act of individual negation. As with the theory of Manfredo Tafuri, Hays's notion of criticality is both politically informed and psychoanalytical in its range of historical maneuverings.

[...]

The rather startling image of the 1922 skyscraper project, published in the second issue of G, comprises two architectural propositions. One, a result of experiments already begun in Mies's Friedrichstrasse project, is a building surface qualified no longer by patterns of shadow on an opaque material but by the reflections and refractions of light by glass. The other, a radical departure from even the earlier skyscraper studies, is a building form conceived not in terms of separate, articulated masses related to one another by a geometrically derived core, but as a complex unitary volume that does not permit itself to be read in terms of an internal formal logic. With these two related propositions Mies confronted the problem of physically and conceptually relating the architectural object to the city. The glass curtain wall – alternately transparent, reflective, or refractive depending on light conditions and viewing positions – absorbs, mirrors, or distorts the immediate images of city life. The convex, faceted surfaces are perceptually contorted by the invasion of circumstantial images, while the reflection each concavity receives on its surface is that of its own shadow, creating gaps which exacerbate the disarray.

These surface distortions accompany and accentuate the formal inscrutability of the volumetric configuration. In classically derived form, the viewer can grasp an antecedent logic of the object, deciphering the relationships between its parts and connecting every part to a coherent formal theme; the alternative posited by Mies is an object intractable to decoding by formal analysis. It is impossible, for example, to reduce the whole to a number of constituent parts related by some internal armature or transformed through some formal operation; indeed, no such compositional relationships exist. Neither is it possible to explicate the object as a deflection from some type; Mies has rejected the meanings that such

K. Michael Hays, from "Critical Architecture: Between Culture and Form," in *Perspecta 21: The Yale Architectural Journal* (1984), pp. 47–9.

classical design methods tend to promote. Instead he has invested meaning in the sense of surface and volume that the building assumes in a particular time and place, in a contextually qualified moment.

Mies insists that an order is immanent in the surface itself and that the order is continuous with and dependent upon the world in which the viewer actually moves. This sense of surface and volume, severed from the knowledge of an internal order or a unifying logic, is enough to wrench the building from the atemporal, idealized realm of autonomous form and install it in a specific situation in the real world of experienced time, open to the chance and uncertainty of life in the metropolis.[1] Mies here shares with Dada an antagonism against a priori and reasoned order; he plunges into the chaos of the new city and seeks another order within it through a systematic use of the unexpected, the aleatory, the inexplicable.[2]

This solicitation of experience is intrinsic to the meaning of the work; it serves to identify and individuate the work itself as an event having sensuous particularity and temporal duration, both of which are infrangible to its capacity for producing and conveying meaning. Nevertheless, Mies's skyscraper project is not conciliatory to the circumstances of its context. It is a critical interpretation of its worldly situation.

[. . .]

NOTES

1 Rosalind Krauss makes a distinction between what she calls analytic or narrative time – in which the viewer can grasp the a priori transcendent structure of the object – and real time – in which the viewer encounters form open to change and circumstance. The development of each in modern sculpture is discussed in "Passages in Modern Sculpture" New York, Viking Press 1977.
2 Mies's well-known friendship with the Dadaists Kurt Schwitters and Hans Richter and his collaboration with the editors of "G" support this reading of the 1922 skyscraper. The implications of Mies's affiliation with the Dadaists have yet to be fully explored.

264 PETER EISENMAN
from "The End of the Classical: The End of the Beginning, the End of the End" (1984)

C losely allied with Peter Eisenman's 1970 essay, "Notes on Conceptual Architecture: Toward a Definition," is this classic restatement of his position from the new vantage point of the mid-1980s. The difference (to use a dangerously loaded word) now is that his earlier desire to rid architecture of all semantic content has been filtered through the poststructuralist strategies of Michel Foucault, Jacques Derrida, and Jean Baudrillard. Eisenman's

Peter D. Eisenman, "The End of the Classical: The End of the Beginning, the End of the End," in *Perspecta 21: The Yale Architectural Journal* (1984), cited here from *Architectural Theory since 1968*, ed. K. Michael Hays. Cambridge, MA: MIT Press, 2002, pp. 529–31.

opening contention is that architecture since the Renaissance has been conceived under the influence of three "fictions:" the fiction of "representation" or the simulation of meaning, the fiction of "reason" or the simulation of truth, and the fiction of "history" or the simulation of the timeless. All three fictions, he further argues, are paradigms of the "classic," which holds true even in the periods of high and late modernism. Eisenman now proposes that architectural creation becomes a purposeless "dissimulation" in a Baudrillardian sense, that is, a "not-classical" architecture "other" than its predecessor. Herein, for Eisenman, lies the authentic postmodern condition.

The Not-classical: Architecture as Fiction

The necessity of the quotation marks around the term "fiction" is now obvious. The three fictions just discussed can be seen not as fictions but rather as simulations. As has been said, fiction becomes simulation when it does not recognize its condition as fiction, when it tries to simulate a condition of reality, truth, or non-fiction. The simulation of representation in architecture has led, first of all, to an excessive concentration of inventive energies in the representational object. When columns are seen as surrogates of trees and windows resemble the portholes of ships, architectural elements become representational figures carrying an inordinate burden of meaning. In other disciplines representation is not the only purpose of figuration. In literature, for example, metaphors and similes have a wider range of application – poetic, ironic, and the like – and are not limited to allegorical or referential functions. Conversely, in architecture only one aspect of the figure is traditionally at work: object representation. The architectural figure always alludes to – aims at the representation of – some *other* object, whether architectural, anthropomorphic, natural, or technological.

Second, the simulation of reason in architecture has been based on a classical value given to the idea of truth. But Heidegger has noted that error has a trajectory parallel to truth, that error can be the unfolding of truth. Thus to proceed from "error" or fiction is to counter consciously the tradition of "mis-reading" on which the classical unwittingly depended – not a presumably logical transformation of something a priori, but a deliberate "error" stated as such, one which presupposes only its own internal truth. Error in this case does not assume the same value as truth; it is *not* simply its dialectical opposite. It is more like a *dissimulation*, a "not-containing" of the value of truth.

Finally, the simulated fiction of modern movement history, unwittingly inherited from the classical, was that any present-day architecture must be a reflection of its zeitgeist: that is, architecture can simultaneously be about presentness and universality. But if architecture is inevitably about the invention of fictions, it should also be possible to propose an architecture that embodies an *other* fiction, one that is not sustained by the values of presentness or universality and, more importantly, that does not consider its purpose to reflect these values. This *other* fiction/object, then, clearly should eschew the fictions of the classical (representation, reason, and history), which are attempts to "solve" the problem of architecture rationally; for strategies and solutions are vestiges of a goal-oriented view of the world. If this is the case, the question becomes: What can be the model for architecture when the essence of what was effective in the classical model – the presumed rational value of structures, representations, methodologies of origins and ends, and deductive processes – has been shown to be a simulation?

It is not possible to answer such a question with an alternative model. But a series of characteristics can be proposed that typify this aporia, this loss in our capacity to conceptualize a new model for architecture. These characteristics, outlined below, arise from that which can *not* be; they form a structure of *absences*. The purpose in proposing them is not to reconstitute what has just been dismissed, a model for a theory of architecture – for all such models are ultimately futile. Rather what is being proposed is an expansion beyond the limitations presented by the classical model to the realization of *architecture as an independent discourse*, free of external values – classical or any other; that is, the intersection of the *meaning-free*, the *arbitrary* and the *timeless* in the artificial.

The meaning-free, arbitrary, and timeless creation of artificiality in this sense must be distinguished from what Baudrillard has called "simulation:" it is not an attempt to erase the classical distinction between reality and representation – thus again making architecture a set of conventions simulating the real; it is, rather, more like a *dis*simulation. Whereas simulation attempts to obliterate the difference between real and imaginary, dissimulation leaves untouched the difference between reality and illusion. The relationship between dissimulation and reality is similar to the signification embodied in the mask: the sign of pretending to be *not* what one is – that is, a sign which seems not to signify anything besides itself (the sign of a sign, or the negation of what is behind it). Such a dissimulation in architecture can be given the provisional title of the *not-classical*. As dissimulation is not the inverse, negative, or opposite of simulation, a "not-classical" architecture is not the inverse, negative, or opposite of classical architecture; it is merely different from or other than. A "not-classical" architecture is no longer a certification of experience or a simulation of history, reason, or reality in the present. Instead, it may more appropriately be described as an *other* manifestation, an architecture *as is*, now as a fiction. It is a representation of itself, of its own values and internal experience.

The claim that a "not-classical" architecture is necessary, that it is proposed by the new epoch or the rupture in the continuity of history, would be another zeitgeist argument. The "not-classical" merely proposes an end to the dominance of classical values in order to reveal other values. It proposes, not a new value or a new zeitgeist, but merely another condition – one of reading architecture as a text. There is nevertheless no question that this idea of the reading of architecture is initiated by a zeitgeist argument: that today the classical signs are no longer significant and have become no more than replications. A not-classical architecture is, therefore, not unresponsive to the realization of the closure inherent in the world: rather, it is unresponsive to representing it.

265 SANFORD KWINTER
from "La Città Nuova: Modernity and Continuity" (1986)

I n one of the most original analyses of the 1980s, Sanford Kwinter attempts to sever the idea of modernity
from the now disparaged notion of modernism. The innovation is not in this particular disassociation, but rather
in the ground he traverses in advancing his argument. His topic is Italian Futurism, and in particular the "new
city" of Antonio Sant'Elia. Before considering it, however, he reviews the scientific context of the late nineteenth and
early twentieth centuries – the parallel development of field theory in physics. When he brings this notion to
the work of Sant'Elia, he attempts to demonstrate that this particular "myth of the machine" followed neither the
mecanolatria of Marinetti nor the efficiency-producing machines of Frederick Winslow Taylor, but rather an open-
ended "mechanic" allowing "social, political and erotic flows." Whether one accepts this conclusion or not is almost
immaterial, for what is new here is the notion of "field theory," which will soon be seized as an innovative strategy
for design. Kwinter's essay appeared in the first volume of the highly acclaimed "Zone" series.

Until the introduction of dynamics the Greek system was adequate for all geometric needs
(e.g., Brunelleschi, Desargues, Mercator, etc.), but the new Cartesian system would be
absolutely indispensable for Newtonian physics, in which equations of motion and acceleration play a dominant role. This is because acceleration cannot be expressed or defined as a
relation between points alone but only in relation to an abstract ground of space as a whole.
Events could now be conceived of as taking place against a fixed backdrop which also served
as their unaffected carrier.

Not until the 19th century did this concept of space and the relations between movements
and bodies begin to change. First thermodynamics (problems of heat conduction in solid
bodies), then the discovery of the electromagnetic interaction and the wave-theory of light
provided both the first treatment of matter as a continuum and the first evidence of states
in free or empty space which are propagated in waves. In the former case matter is treated as
a *system* of states, characterized by independent quantitative variables – thermal differences,
volume, pressure – expressible as a *function* of space coordinates and, most importantly, of
time. In the latter it was a simple transposition of these same mathematics (partial
differential equations) to the propagation of magnetic and light phenomena. Passing from
a field theory of masses (thermodynamics) to a field theory or empty space (electrodynamics)
meant that classical mechanics had to be superseded. Maxwell's breakthrough in the theory
of electromagnetic processes went far in this direction, but unable to make the final
conceptual break he was obliged to posit a material vehicle or medium for this electromagnetic field: the luminiferous ether. The ether functioned in a purely mechanical sense as the
material seat and carrier of all forces acting across space – though it was imperceptible and
only logically derivable, based as it was on the presupposition that every state is capable of

Sanford Kwinter, from "La Città Nuova: Modernity and Continuity," in *Zone 1/2*, ed. Jonathan Crary, Michel Feher, Hal Foster, and Sanford Kwinter.
New York: Urzone, 1986, pp. 87–9.

mechanical interpretation and therefore implies the presence of matter. The famous Michelson-Morley experiment of 1888 failed to yield any evidence of the material existence of such an ether. Between this event and the Special Theory of Relativity of 1905 came Lorentz's important work, which, while accounting for the Michelson-Morley results, established, according to Einstein, that ether and physical space "were only different terms for the same thing."[1] It was a momentous conceptual leap if only a short mathematical step that Einstein took to emancipate the field concept entirely from any association with a substratum. For the Special Theory of Relativity Einstein employed the Riemannian conception of space,[2] whose plastic structure is susceptible both to partaking in physical events and to being influenced by them. The Einsteinian field, and its corresponding notion of space-time, dispensed entirely with the need to posit a material substratum as a carrier for forces and events by identifying the electromagnetic field – and ultimately gravitational fields as well – with the new metrical one. This notion of "the field" expresses the complete immanence of forces and events while supplanting the old concept of space identified with the Cartesian substratum and ether theory. The field emerges as "an irreducible element of physical description, irreducible in the same sense as the concept of matter in the theory of Newton."[3]

The field describes a space of propagation, of effects. It contains no matter or material points, rather functions, vectors and speeds. It describes local relations of difference within fields of celerity, transmission or of careering points, in a word, what Minkowski called the *world*. Einstein offered as an example of a field phenomenon the description of the motion of a liquid:

> At every point there exists at any time a velocity, which is quantitatively described by its three "components" with respects to the axes of a coordinate system (vector). The components of a velocity at a point (field components) [fulfill the conditions of the field for they, like the temperature in a system of thermal propagation] are functions of the coordinates (x, y, z) and time (t).

This hydrodynamic model, of course, deserves no particular priority in Einstein's system for it was still only a rudimentary mechanical model describing a state of matter, whereas Einstein's physics was an attempt to think the pure event, independent of a material medium or substratum. Yet the field theory it typified was emerging in other areas of endeavor, often finding expression through similar or related models of dynamics in fluids. Its mysterious charm was none other than the partial differential function through which alone it was possible to express the principles of immanence, dynamism and continuity.

NOTES

1 Albert Einstein, *Ideas and Opinions*, New York, Three Rivers Press, 1995, p. 281.
2 Einstein asserts this, however, only retrospectively. Cf. "The Problem of Space, Ether and the Field of Physics," in *The World as I See It*, New York, Covici, 1934, p. 281.
3 Albert Einstein, *Relativity: The Special and General Theory*, New York, Bonanza Books, 1961, p. 150.

266 IGNASI DE SOLÀ-MORALES
from "Weak Architecture" (1987)

Building directly on Gianni Vattimo's idea of "weak thought" is Ignasi de Solà-Morales's notion of "weak architecture." Also informing his analyses are his readings of Friedrich Nietzsche and Martin Heidegger. The result is a predictably nihilistic understanding of the contemporary situation in which the grounding for all judgments has been lost and architecture has been stripped of any referential framework. Thus he argues against the "fundamentalist" positions of both the Italian Rationalists and the New York Five, as architecture is now forever marginalized or decentered from the experience of reality. The salvation of the "event" as the preferred contemporary response, however, curiously recalls not only Tschumi embrace of this concept but also Baudelaire's modernist emphasis on the transitory and the fleeting. Such is the paradox of the 1980s.

Certain theoretical discourses, sustained by leading academics at the influential Istituto Universitario di Architettura in Venice, as well as certain positions adopted by the New York Five group in the late 1960s, put forth the claim that only by going back to what was essential, germinal, and initial in the modern experience – Le Corbusier's *purisme*, in effect – was it possible to find the true path, picking up once again the thread of authentic experience. These voices called for an established line of orthodoxy and correctness to counter the diversion and diversification of the time. This was, in my opinion, a fundamentalist expression of the modern tradition. While it was understood by some as the recovery of the most pristine language of the avant-garde movements of the twenties, for others this experience served to take them further: they sought the lost tradition of the modern in still more primal origins, tracing the founding moments of modernity back to the primary forms of the Enlightenment.

The architecture of the Tendenza in Italy amounted to nothing less than a call to fundamentalism: an attempt at rereading the hardest, most programmatic, most radical architecture of the strictest exponents of rationalism of the interwar years, as well as of the architects of the Enlightenment. It was no accident that this situation saw the popularizing of the most laudatory images of the work of the most intensely Enlightened architects, in an effort to proclaim origins and a return to original purity. Certainly figures such as Aldo Rossi have taken it on themselves to deny the possibility of this undertaking. Rossi's work increasingly asks to be seen as a process that is above all self-critical. More and more, he demonstrates a progressive loss of confidence in that fundamentalism that was so decisive in his book *The Architecture of the City*, and that has nevertheless metamorphosed in his recent work into an intimate, private game.

Whether it be through such an enlightened fundamentalism or the fundamentalism of a Richard Meier, repeating over and over the linguistic tropes of twenties purism, these responses, for all their good intentions, amount to nothing more than pure historicism. With their fine words and noble aims, they constitute merely nostalgic attempts to return to

Ignasi de Solà-Morales, from "Weak Architecture," in *Differences: Topographies of Contemporary Architecture*, trans. Graham Thompson and ed. Sarah Whiting. Cambridge, MA: MIT Press, 1995, pp. 60–2, 67–8.

supposedly authentic roots, whether in Le Corbusier's Villa Savoye, in Ludwig Hilberseimer's desolate apartment blocks, in Claude-Nicolas Ledoux's drawings, or in any other source of iconography taken for the wellsprings of the true tradition.

[. . .]

This diversity of times becomes absolutely central in what I have chosen to call weak architecture. In sympathy with the visions of Joyce and others, and in contrast to the idealist narrative sustained by Giedion, these architectures transform the aesthetic experience of the artwork, and specifically of architecture, into *event*. Temporality does not present itself as a system but as an aleatory instant that, responding above all to chance, is produced in an unforeseeable place and moment. In certain works of contemporary art, in dance, in music, in installation, the experience of the temporal as event, occurring once and then gone forever, ably explicates a notion of temporality that finds in the event its fullest form of expression.

If the notion of event allows us to approximate more closely one of the characteristics of weak architecture, the Deleuzean notion of the *pli*, or fold, is no less definitive. Gilles Deleuze published a book that, under the apparently innocuous guise of a summary of Foucault's thought, set out to develop a whole project constitutive of a contemporary vision of reality. The seductive appeal of this text lies, among other things, in its grasp of the fact that in contemporary thought the objective and the subjective are not different and opposing fields but constitute what he calls "folds of a single reality." For architecture, this notion of the fold proves exceptionally illuminating. Reality emerges as a continuum in which the time of the subject and the time of external objects go round together on the same looped tape, with the encounter of objective and subjective only occurring when this continuous reality folds over in a disruption of its own continuity.

267 MARK WIGLEY
from "Deconstructivist Architecture" (1988)

On the heels of a London symposium on the same theme, the exhibition "Deconstructivist Architecture" opened in June 1988 at the Museum of Modern Art in New York. The continuity of this event with such earlier architectural exhibitions at this institution – such as "Mies van der Rohe" (1947) and "The International Style" (1932) – is cogent, if only because Philip Johnson was one of the inspirational forces behind all three spectacles. Here the indefatigable Johnson is joined by Mark Wigley, who also co-edited the exhibition catalogue. The exhibition featured projects by Frank O. Gehry, Daniel Libeskind, Rem Koolhaas, Peter Eisenman, Zaha M. Hadid, Coop Himmelblau, and Bernard Tschumi. Wigley's distinction between "deconstruction" and "deconstructivism" departs from the premise of the London symposium, and the Freudian undertones to this

Mark Wigley, from "Deconstructivist Architecture," in Philip Johnson and Mark Wigley, *Deconstructivist Architecture*. New York: Museum of Modern Art, 1988, pp. 10–11.

"kind of nightmare" of a movement signals yet another influential force now making its repressed way into architectural theory.

Architecture has always been a central cultural institution valued above all for its provision of stability and order. These qualities are seen to arise from the geometric purity of its formal composition.

The architect has always dreamed of pure form, of producing objects from which all instability and disorder have been excluded. Buildings are constructed by taking simple geometric forms – cubes, cylinders, spheres, cones, pyramids, and so on – and combining them into stable ensembles, following compositional rules which prevent any one form from conflicting with another. No form is permitted to distort another; all potential conflict is resolved. The forms contribute harmoniously to a unified whole. This consonant geometric structure becomes the physical structure of the building: its formal purity is seen as guaranteeing structural stability.

Having produced this basic structure, the architect then elaborates it into a final design in a way that preserves its purity. Any deviation from the structural order, any impurity, is seen as threatening the formal values of harmony, unity, and stability, and is therefore insulated from the structure by being treated as mere ornament. Architecture is a conservative discipline that produces pure form and protects it from contamination.

The projects in this exhibition mark a different sensibility, one in which the dream of pure form has been disturbed. Form has become contaminated. The dream has become a kind of nightmare.

It is the ability to disturb our thinking about form that makes these projects deconstructive. It is not that they derive from the mode of contemporary philosophy known as "deconstruction." They are not an application of deconstructive theory. Rather, they emerge from within the architectural tradition and happen to exhibit some deconstructive qualities.

Deconstruction itself, however, is often misunderstood as the taking apart of constructions. Consequently, any provocative architectural design which appears to take structure apart – whether it be the simple breaking of an object or the complex dissimulation of an object into a collage of traces – has been hailed as deconstructive. These strategies have produced some of the most formidable projects of recent years, but remain simulations of deconstructive work in other disciplines, because they do not exploit the unique condition of the architectural object. Deconstruction is not demolition, or dissimulation. While it diagnoses certain structural problems within apparently stable structures, these flaws do not lead to the structures' collapse. On the contrary, deconstruction gains all its force by challenging the very values of harmony, unity, and stability, and proposing instead a different view of structure: the view that the flaws are intrinsic to the structure. They cannot be removed without destroying it; they are, indeed, structural.

A deconstructive architect is therefore not one who dismantles buildings, but one who locates the inherent dilemmas within buildings. The deconstructive architect puts the pure forms of the architectural tradition on the couch and identifies the symptoms of a repressed impurity. The impurity is drawn to the surface by a combination of gentle coaxing and violent torture: the form is interrogated.

To do so, each project employs formal strategies developed by the Russian avant-garde early in the twentieth century. Russian Constructivism constituted a critical turning point where the architectural tradition was bent so radically that a fissure opened up through which certain disturbing architectural possibilities first became visible. Traditional thinking about the nature of the architectural object was placed in doubt. But the radical possibility was not then taken up. The wound in the tradition soon closed, leaving but a faint scar. These projects reopen the wound.

268   CATHERINE INGRAHAM
from "Milking Deconstruction, *or* Cow Was the Show?" (1988)

The "Deconstructivist" exhibition of 1988 at MoMA, like many of its predecessors, provoked both positive and negative responses. Joseph Giovannini, the architectural critic for *The New York Times*, lauded the opening of the event, and he also claimed credit for inventing the word "deconstructivism" by conflating the terms "deconstruction" and "constructivism." Against Giovannini's claim, Catherine Ingraham took another position in a review published in the Chicago journal *Inland Architect*. Ingraham was not opposed to the projects shown at the event, which she felt represented "the most interesting work being done in architecture right now." But at the same time she was highly disapproving of the descriptive terminology being used by Giovannini and Wigley. She likewise objected to the role the Museum of Modern Art was attempting to play in usurping the new "movement" as one of its own, that is, for applauding a formalist position similar to the "International Style" exhibition of fifty-six years earlier.

The "invention" of the so-called "deconstructivist movement" in architecture is a trivialization/stylization of the far more amorphous, complex, powerful, and radical – the far more brilliant – critical movement called "deconstruction" (or, more appropriately, poststructuralism). Both Wigley and Giovannini claim that deconstructivism is "sort of related" to deconstruction. The relationship, from my point of view, is a parasitic and predatory one – in orthographic (deconstruct-) as well as ideological ways. Deconstruct*ivism* evokes all the power of the "deconstructing consciousness" – the challenge to harmony, unity, stability – at the same moment that it decides (with perplexing nicety) that it is more "architectural," more related to "form," more "buildable." As Wigley writes in the exhibition catalogue, this movement (deconstructivism) is meant to "disturb our thinking about form" very much in the same way as deconstruction disturbs our thinking about structure, but that apparently doesn't mean that it is *derived* from deconstruction. Wigley's tacit division between form and theory (and form and structure) is only one problematic assumption among many. If I were reviewing this exhibition for an audience as obsessed as I am with the relationship between language and architectural form, I would spend the rest of this essay trying to expose more precisely what the architectural *vism-ing* of deconstruction means – although it would be a gruesome account. However, I should go on.

Catherine Ingraham, from "Milking Deconstruction, or Cow Was the Show?," in *Inland Architect* 32:5 (September/October 1988), pp. 62–3.

I know that Mark Wigley is interested, as am I, in the specifically architectural implications of deconstruction and, along with this, in the challenge that architecture offers to the philosophical movement of deconstruction/poststructuralism. But the exhibition catalogue, as well as the exhibition itself, seems explicitly to avoid articulating contemporary critical questions facing architecture – questions having to do with formalist repression, historical reformulation, nostalgia, architectural meaning, intentionality, and so on. Because these critical questions are left unposed, the so-called challenge of architecture to critical theory is also left unposed. Instead, the style of the catalogue and exhibition wanders aimlessly between a loose form of constructivism and a loose form of poststructural theory as if it were trying to conceal the tensions between these two positions. Indeed, the catalogue as a whole feels like a barely concealed argument between people (Johnson and Wigley?) who hold radically different views but are afraid, for political reasons, to present a picture of disunity. For example, in the preface Johnson takes care to deny that the exhibition has any aims toward summing up contemporary architecture. But in almost the same breath he reminds us that he, Henry-Russell Hitchcock, and Alfred Barr were the ones who summed up the architecture of the 1920s – this, I assume, so that we know with whom we are dealing. In the final four paragraphs Johnson thanks the people from whom he essentially stole the idea for the deconstructivist show – which Michael Sorkin documented last December in The *Village Voice* as a scandal of appropriation – and then, in an equally disarming manner, he thanks Giovannini as a "valuable source of preliminary information." There is clearly someone – an editor, a voice – speaking in this preface who is neither Johnson nor Giovannini, but an editorial voice that knows that neither Philip Johnson nor Joseph Giovannini knows what he is talking about. The telling phrase, of course, came up in Sorkin's review of the exhibition in which he cites Johnson as requesting from MOMA, for the exhibit, any Constructivist paintings that had "diagonals in them." Deconstructivism for Giovannini and Johnson is essentially a matter of form and style – the thinnest kind of formal architectural description.

It is odd, but not surprising, that writers (or architects, or anyone) always betray themselves when they are building an argument, or a building, out of political convenience rather than political passion (intellectual or artistic obsessions, for example). Discourse/art cannot betray its intentions but it does seem to betray an "aura of production." For the deconstructivist exhibition the aura of production was a melange of pretty distasteful political desires – none of which qualify as radical or even interesting. This aura swallowed up the opportunity for commenting on the more remarkable moments of play and intelligence in some of the architectural projects – such as Hadid's free-floating geological/architectural beams, or Tschumi's explosions. The few very penetrating observations – such as Wigley's discussion of architectural ornament as a kind of *pharmakon*, that is, both a cure for and a poisoning of architecture's love of geometric purity – were also subordinated to displays of Johnson's and Giovannini's desires to be "founders of a movement"; the Museum of Modern Art's desire to update its image in the contemporary art/architecture world; New York's desire to be the place where the "new" is perpetually named and performed first; the architects' desires to be legitimized and so on.

B.   POSTMODERNISM AND HISTORICISM

Introduction

Distinct and often at odds with the conceptually charged sallies of Deconstruction in the 1980s were various manifestations of "postmodernism" that very directly sought to draw upon historical traditions. If most were unrelated in their philosophical underpinnings, all were united in rejecting what they saw as the semantically mute or machine-inspired values of high modernism, and in their insistence that architecture must respond more coherently to the given local fabric and historical traditions.

Historicism – once the scourge of the early modernists – is a difficult term to define beyond an acceptance of historical motifs. The figurative or allusional use of history by Michael Graves, Charles Jencks, and Robert Venturi, for instance, play on the perimeter of history, as it were, sometimes with semantic irony, sometimes with serious intention, but always consciously as strategies. The politicized historicism of Maurice Culot and Rob Krier, by contrast, takes historical design one stage further by insisting on a return to genuine historical forms and on a readaptation of historical craft techniques – as a kind of typological language understood by all and one exhibiting long-proven value. Somewhere in between lies the historical sensitivity of architects like Josef-Paul Kleihues and Robert A. M. Stern, who respond openly to historical types, but at the same time update these conventional forms with a postmodern aesthetic.

269 *HARVARD ARCHITECTURE REVIEW*
from the inaugural editorial
"Beyond the Modern Movement"
(1980)

I n 1980 a group of students at the Harvard Graduate School of Design launched the first issue of the *Harvard Architecture Review*. The issue's theme derived from a conference held at Harvard in 1977, but the delayed timing of the new journal, given the great enthusiasm of the later moment, could scarcely have been more propitious. Perhaps the most interesting statement among the entries was the lead editorial prepared by the staff, which addressed the issue of modernism and its still-contested passing. The staff's analysis was ambivalent. On the one hand, the editors argued that "Post-Modernism" was by nature a "reactionary phenomenon," that is, simply the latest in a long line of critical engagements with modernism, and, moreover, no comprehensive postmodern theory had yet to emerge. On the other hand, they proceeded to isolate a series of themes around which postmodern architects seemed to be rallying. That history – once struck from the Harvard curriculum by no less a modern hero than Walter Gropius himself – should head this list of postmodern concerns, is in itself indicative of changing times and this new spirit coalescing around the theme of historicism.

History

While the Modern Movement attempted to sever its ties with its immediate and distant forbears, recent trends have emphasized the continued relevance of history. Dissatisfied with an ascetic visual language and restrictive design methodology, architects are looking to the past once again for figurative and organizational resources. On the one hand, a search for a more communicative architectural language has provoked an interest in forms which make direct reference to previous architectural modes; on the other hand, a concern for a more intellectually disciplined approach has promoted the study of principles of architectural organization, means of planimetric and spatial ordering which although transformed by present circumstance maintain their organizational integrity and relationship to their original source.

From the inaugural editorial, in *Harvard Architecture Review 1* (Spring 1980). Cambridge, MA: MIT Press, pp. 5–7.

Both concerns embody a particularly Post-Modern dilemma: if the radical break with the past posited by the Moderns is no longer acceptable, how is one to incorporate history once again as a legitimate source of inspiration? The trends mentioned here are but two answers to this question, one perhaps more literal, the other more abstract, both seeking a practicable *modus operandi*; but emulating, copying, or learning from history has always been a difficult business and it is likely to remain so despite its new-found popularity.

Cultural Allusionism

Akin to the renewed interest in architectural history is the fascination with cultural phenomena outside the realm of architecture proper. The motivation behind both is similar: to expand the figurative and organizational palette of the architect, and to develop a visual language which might communicate more directly to a public confused and alienated by current architectural practice. Modern Movement architects, too, looked beyond their accepted contemporary architectural language for inspiration; indeed they had to, for a new architectural vocabulary was not to be found in the prevalent affections for Beaux Arts Classicism and the other revival styles. Yet the models *they* chose – mills, factories, ships and automobiles – were designed to shock their audiences into a recognition of a new beginning. The alienation which resulted was perhaps inevitable, given the crusader-like zeal of the Modern Movement avant garde, seeking as it was to establish a radical new language of architecture.

Post-Modern cultural allusionism, by contrast, is more accommodating than alienating in intention. It attempts to bring existing symbols and expressive forms, understood and accepted by broad segments of the population, into the realm of architecture. Post-Modernism recognizes that the abstract play of masses in light may not be enough to retain the involvement of the observer, that private dialogues directed at a professional audience may not alone satisfy the requirements of a civic art. Reference to widespread cultural phenomena is seen as one means of creating a more meaningful architectural expression. Like historical allusion, this approach does present problems of translation and application, yet the distance travelled from the point of reference to final use is not so great, as it involves boundaries of taste, not time.

Anti-Utopianism

Modernist theory was Utopian and positivist in orientation: it pledged a better world environmentally and socially, through rational thinking and the new-found tools of its technologically advanced age. This attitude filtered down into virtually every aspect of Modernist practice: the perfect chair could be designed, the correct planning relationships established, the ideal city laid out. Man was conceived of as an abstract, universalized entity, for whom a universal pan-cultural language of forms could be developed. The particular, the eccentric, the unique was to be excluded from architectural expression in pursuit of more urgent needs and goals.

The last few decades have seen a gradual erosion of such Utopian and positivist convictions. The design of housing, for instance, has become less generalized and more attuned to the problems of specific locations and particular users. The social, economic, and physical (i.e. building) conventions of the local population may now form an integral part of the design and programming process, producing more idiosyncratic and contextually responsive solutions. Underlying this approach is the conviction that architecture can profit more by working with what 'is' rather than what 'should be,' on dealing with the messiness and imperfectability of the present rather than the clarity and order of an ideal world. It reflects a growing awareness of the limited impact architecture may have on the tastes and preferences of its users, and that to make a more meaningful environment may not suggest that it be more revolutionary, but more a product of shared sensibilities.

Urban Design and Contextualism

Much Post-Modernist criticism in the area of urban design is a recapitulation, on a larger scale, of the anti-Utopian outlook described above. Yet the image of the new city was so important to the ideology of the Modern Movement, and its application often so devastating that it has provoked a reaction strong and extensive enough to warrant a particular focus here. From a policy-making point of view, this reaction has promoted more limited planning horizons, localized community participation, and small-scale decision making – accepting what is found, socially, economically, and physically, rather than calling for extensive revisions of existing patterns. The meteoric rise in architectural preservation and restoration may be attributed, at least in part, to this more accommodating urban outlook.

On a formal level, the Modernist penchant for the city in the park – the object-building surrounded by open green space – has provoked a new interest in traditional urban space, scale, and organization. The conceptualization of the city as 'fabric,' with dense areas of building (the '*poché*') interrupted by carefully designed and defined public spaces, has again come to the fore, with the requisite respect for existing structures, street frontages, views, axes, and patterns of movement. Indeed, the traditional city has become the starting point for entire theories of architecture, which, by identifying the nature of historic urban forms – their inherent order and flexibility – may then posit similar approaches for architecture at a more general level. Here the notion of the architectural *type* has been most persuasive, where the principle of order, or spatial organization, or construction, is rooted in precedent, yet may be re-applied, in principle, to present circumstance. Thus, the traditional city may become not only the source of *ideas*, but also the source of a *method* – of reference, accommodation, and change, stabilized by the order of continuing urban morphologies.

Formal Concerns

If traditional languages of form were rejected by the Modern Movement in its quest for a new architecture, then similarly rejected were traditional notions of organization, composition, and design process. Yet the methods and aesthetic guidelines which were developed to replace them are now being questioned and re-considered. The idea of program, for instance, once the basis of architectural organization and expression, is losing that pre-eminence to a conception of design which values means of organization more general than those provoked by the specifics of each project. Asymmetrical composition, once considered the hallmark of 'contemporary' design, is slowly giving way to a preference for, or at least a tolerance of, symmetry and balance, in both plan and elevation. Free-flowing, universal, open-ended space, once the accepted convention of three-dimensional composition, is being challenged by a conception of space as a closed, static, and well-defined entity. Ornament, once considered 'criminal' in the standard Modern Movement dogma, is gradually re-appearing in diverse architectural projects. The landscape, once merely the 'ground' for the pristine architectural object may now be wedded to the architectural product, not in the literal sense of interior-exterior spatial flow, but in the more profound sense of creating outside rooms and sequences of spaces which integrate the formal arrangement of the interior into a larger environmental design. And architectural drawing, once tied to the fine-line and color-coded conventions of CIAM, is now being explored for all its inherent creative potential, and as a beautiful product in itself.

All these facets reinforce the architect's traditional role as the willful creator of form, in direct contrast to the notion of the architect as the mere translator of economic, social, and technical forces into an appropriate architectural expression. Consequently, the subjectivity and idiosyncrasy which the Modernists hoped to exclude from the process are now returning, as the formal restrictions of the Modern Movement are being recognized and rejected.

270   ROBERT A. M. STERN
from "The Doubles of Post-Modern" (1980)

Also contained within the inaugural issue of the *Harvard Architecture Review* was this essay by Robert A. M. Stern that summarizes his ideas of the preceding three years. Like Venturi before him, Stern by this date drew upon literary sources as well as a number of historians and social commentators (such as Daniel Bell). While arguing forcefully on behalf of the postmodern epoch, he in fact divides postmodernists into "schismatic" and "traditional" camps. The former, in his view, see postmodernism as a complete break with the values of modernism, and with the entire tradition of Western humanism (read Peter Eisenman). By contrast traditional postmodernists, like Stern himself, acknowledge a cultural continuity with modernism, but also seek to break down the rigid constraints of modernism (its anti-historical bias, for instance) and reject its nihilistic aspects (Dadaism, for instance). Effectively, then, traditional postmodernism reaches around modernism and connects with the larger historical past.

Traditional post-modernism is simultaneously inside contemporary society and critically detached from it; it uses art to comment on everyday life; it is at once 'satiric' and accepting in its view of culture; in this sense it seeks to make telling interpretations of everyday life.

Robert A. M. Stern, from "The Doubles of Post-Modern," in *Harvard Architectural Review* 1 (Spring 1980). Cambridge, MA: MIT Press, pp. 84, 85–6.

Such a post-modernism begins to 'restore that state of balance between unchecked fabulation and objective social realism' necessary to prevent artistic production from degenerating into trivial self-indulgence.[1]

In painting and in architecture, traditional post-modernism relies increasingly on representational as opposed to abstract or conceptual modes. [...]

Nonetheless, traditional post-modernism does not advocate stylistic revival, though it does support the concept of emulation. Traditional post-modernism looks back to history to see how things were done and to remind itself that many good ways of doing things which were cast aside for ideological reasons can be usefully rediscovered. Thus, for example, inclusive post-modernism can employ recognizable imagery in an abstract way – it can be at once pre-modernist and modernist.[2]

Traditional post-modernism opens up artistic production to a public role which modernism, by virtue of its self-referential formal strategies, had denied itself. In painting, as William Rubin has observed, 'one characteristic of the modern period *seems* to be ending. That is the tradition of the private picture – private in its character and subject matter as well as in its destination – that is, for the small circle of collectors and friends of artists, who sympathize with vanguard art.'[3] In this sense, the current interest in photography should be seen as a last-gasp modernist stance.

Architecture, of course, is by definition a public art. Yet in its modernist phase, it often spoke the private language of painting – one need only recall the arguments advanced in Henry-Russell Hitchcock's book *Painting Toward Architecture*.[4] More importantly, as Suzannah Lessard points out:

> between the abstract beauty of technological principles and the underpinning of intricate solutions to innumerable minute problems, there is a kind of middle ground which was overlooked in the exuberant rush to modernity. Between man's desire to expand his ego and the needs of man as ant – I can think of no better way to express the dual preoccupation of the age of technology – the question of what human life would be in the new world floated unasked, unnoticed.[5]

It is this aspect of social and cultural responsibility – not in the narrowly simplistic sense of architectural do-goodism but in a broader and more profound sense of a genuine and unsentimental humanism – that characterized traditional post-modernism's distinction from the abstract, self-referential schismatic post-modernism which we have already discussed.

Traditional post-modernism rejects the anti-historical biases of modernism; influences from history are no longer seen as constraints on either personal growth or artistic excellence. History, no longer viewed as the dead hand of the past, now seems at the very least a standard of excellence in a continuing struggle to deal effectively with the present. Modernism looked toward the future as an escape from the past; traditional post-modernism struggles with the legacy of that attitude, a world filled with objects whose principal artistic impetus often came from a belief that in order to be 'Modern' they must look and function as little as possible like anything that had been seen in the world before. The traditional post-modernist struggle then, is not to free itself from the past, but to relax what has been characterized as 'the stubborn grip of the values created by the rebellion against the past.'[6]

Traditional post-modernism rejects what Charles Moore has described as the 'obsessive normalization of the recent past, where we have drawn our expressive elegance out of poverty...(and) our process out of crisis.'[7] It argues that it is proper and sufficient to struggle with the problems of the present viewed in relation to the values continuing from the past while leaving the future to those who will inherit it.

Traditional post-modernism recognizes that the public has lost confidence in architects (though it still believes in the symbolic power of architecture). Modernist architecture offered very little in the way of joy or visual pleasure, its conceptual basis was limited and disconcertingly materialistic. By once again recognizing the common assumptions a culture inherits from its past, traditional post-modernism is not only an announcement that Modern architecture has emerged from its puritan revolution, its catharsis at last behind it, but it is also an avowal of self-confidence in contemporary architecture's ability and willingness to re-establish itself on a basis which cannot only deal with the past but also match it, value for value, building for building.

Traditional post-modernism seeks to look backward in order to go forward. It should not be regarded as a jettisoning of Modern architecture itself, but as an attempt to pick up the threads of theory and style which were cut by the pioneers of the Modern Movement, especially the concerns for architectural history and for visually comprehensible relation-ships between old and new buildings. In its inclusiveness, traditional post-modernism does not propose an independent style; it is a sensibility dependent on forms and strategies drawn from the modernist and the pre-modernist work that preceded it, though it declares the obsolescence of both. It is *a* Modern style but not *the* Modern style. In its recognition of the transience and multiplicity of styles within the historical epoch we call Modern, it rejects the emphasis on unity of expression that was so central to modernism itself. Traditional post-modernism recognizes both the discursive and expressive meaning of formal language. It recognizes the language of form as communicating sign as well as infra-referential symbol: that is to say, it deals with both physical and associational experience, with the work of art as an act of 'presentation' and 'representation.' It rejects the idea of a single style in favor of a view that acknowledges the existence of many styles (and the likely emergence of even more) each with its own meanings, sometimes permanently established, but more often shifting in relation to other events in the culture.

NOTES

1   Gerald Graff, 'Babbitt at the Abyss: The Social Context of Postmodern American Fiction,' *Tri Quarterly* #33 (Spring 1976) 307–37.
2   Traditional post-modernism should not be confused with the neo-traditionalism of Henry Hope Reed, John Barrington Bayley, Conrad Jameson. For Bayley and Reed, see Henry Hope Reed, *The Garden City* (New York: Doubleday, 1959) passim.
3   Rubin is quoted by Douglas Davis' 'Post-Modern for Stories Real and Imagined/Toward a Theory,' in his *Art Culture – Essays on the Postmodern* (New York: Harper & Row, 1977). See also the 'Post-Modernist Dilemma,' a dialogue between Davis and Suzi Gablik, *Village Voice*, March 24, April 3 and April 10, 1978.
4   Henry-Russell Hitchcock, *Painting Toward Architecture* (New York: Duell, Sloan and Pearce, 1948) passim.
5   Suzannah Lessard, 'The Towers of Light,' *The New Yorker*, 54 (July 10, 1978) 32–6, 41–4, 49, 52, 58.

6   Lessard, *op. cit.*; James D. Kornwolf makes the interesting observation that 'Le Corbusier's generation was misguided not to recognize that the nineteenth century's struggle with the past was also its struggle, and that a new understanding of the past, not a denial of it, was what was needed.' *M. H. Baillie Scott and the Arts and Crafts Movement: Pioneers of Modern Design*, (Baltimore: Johns Hopkins University Press, 1972) 519.

   Peter Collins observes that "the idea of an 'International Style' was a product of the Renaissance. In fact, the so-called 'battle of the styles' might be more reasonably and meaningfully interpreted as an attempt to refute the concept of an 'International Style,' rather than as a conflict between 'Gothicists' and 'Classicists.' This was certainly the essence of the position taken by Viollet-le-Duc and Ferguson." *Architectural Judgement* (Montreal: McGill-Queen's University Press, 1971) 171–2 n. 2.

7   Charles Moore, 'Foreword,' in Sam Davis, editor, *The Form of Housing* (New York: Van Nostrand Reinhold, 1977) 6.

271   MAURICE CULOT
"Nostalgia, Soul of the Revolution" (1980)

Maurice Culot's harsh anti-industrialism of two years earlier, voiced in collaboration with Leon Krier, takes on an even more strident tone with this manifesto. Disdaining postmodern's strategy of simply engaging formally with the past, Culot insists on turning back the architectural clock to the pre-industrial past and imitating its best creations. For him this return is a strategy of reconstruction in the wake of the urban and ecological devastation wrought by architects and urban planners over the preceding century or so. It is not just the building forms of the past that are to be imitated, but also the urban scale, materials, and craft modes of production – a political view with echoes of William Morris. Only in this way will Europe be saved.

'But come now, Mr. Krier, we can't go backwards!' exclaimed Albert Speer, during a recent interview with the London architect.

But we can! At the risk of disappointing the former Armaments Minister and numerous other architects, engineers and municipalists, we should think seriously about going backwards.

For anyone who sees things like a normally-constituted human being and not in terms of photo frames, 'superb views' and other 'escapes from your daily life', the situation is clear and irrevocable: the advanced industrial societies – with Germany, Japan and Belgium leading the rest of the field by a short head – will use up or destroy everything: centuries-old towns and villages, the country-side, forests and oceans.

If you have any doubts, then do the following test: add up the 1980 European budgets for public works, motorways, power stations, massive housing zones, elevated and underground carparks, the infrastructure for public transport, etc and then project this budget for

Maurice Culot, "Nostalgia, Soul of the Revolution," in *Architectural Design* 11/12 (1980), p. 44.

the next 10 years. For anyone who is not a hypocrite the answer is obvious: the massacre of the Costa Brava, the folly of Créteil and Ivry, etc, the dismantling of Brussels, will be the common lot of the whole of Europe. No disconnected impulses will be able to oppose the steamrollers of industry. In the face of this destruction process, which also waters down responsibilities, all we can propose is an overall plan and strategy for the reconstruction of Europe's cities.

And this strategy, which, for an architect, will also serve to rebuild the philosophy of architecture, can find a solid foundation only in the past, in imitation – and I mean imitation and not interpretation – of pre-industrial architectural and urban culture. Not only because such culture is a reality and not an abstraction, but also because to fight for architecture and traditional urban forms and all the historic concepts behind them constitutes a direct confrontation with the structure of industrial production: it is to unite with the workers in their struggle. For the financial monopolies and economic power take possession of the city and destroy it, thus ensuring their hegemony to the detriment of all political and cultural activity.

It things are to change – and who is not in favour of that? – we have to counteract the watering down of political and cultural responsibilities with ideas that give simple expression to the complexity of an overall plan for the city, for without this any participation in an anti-industrial resistance movement would savour of the charge of the Light Brigade.

Architects will therefore be the intellectuals, not the technicians, of this resistance movement and will have avowed theoretical responsibilities. This position will mean that, as architects, we shall be concerned with the historic and theoretical meaning of our actions as the basic element of our disciplinary and teaching activities.

Typological, technical and construction problems must consequently receive simple solutions that are not in useless contradiction with the theoretical statements; as Léon Krier has pointed out, we are not interested in planning or building techniques that will be superseded tomorrow by innovations in industrial production and market fluctuations. We are not interested in ideas for consumers of industrial gadgets.

Our plans will be of direct use to the population and, what is more, constitute manifestoes for specific techniques for rebuilding the city and the architectual language and hierarchy thus implied. These plans and what we learn from their confrontation in urban struggles have led us to formulate extremely simple theses, which will provide the bases for this work of reconstruction. It is the frequency of this two-way action between the theory and its extensions in our daily struggles that will determine and define the content of the popular consensus, failing a community system of symbols.

But going backwards is neither painless nor easy, even if we are not suggesting rewriting the history of architecture from the time of the mud hut but merely that we take it up at that point where frantic industrialization censored it.

The stronger the associations of ideas, the more harrowing the revisions will be. And we shall need strategies that have been carefully developed far from the noise of the building site if we are to adhere vigilantly to our political course and at the same time get accepted ideas on the profoundly alienating nature of the concept of mobility, on the demand for a city organized into neighbourhoods where one can live and work, on the necessity for building techniques that give priority to the use of natural materials, on the multiplication of small building projects and the limitation of large-scale operations, etc.

Our weakness is that we believe that the most successful creations of the past are still within our grasp, can still be imitated, and, in terms of strategy, can still be mobilised, at least in Europe.

Let me say it again: it is a question of imitation, not of stylistic variations, of free forms, of taking liberties with classic proportions, sizes and measurements...

To prevent the full settlement of the exorbitant ransom of progress, not to mention the experiments for the improvement of the human race, the sap of nostalgia can today be prescribed with some chance of success, even if some diehard optimists consider that life in Sarcelles 'is getting organized'. In one hand old postcards and engravings, in the other the alternative project and the overall plan for the city, and we have a homeopathic cure for sadness, despair, waking dreams, nervous disorders, diarrhoea and a gradual wasting away that could lead to death.

272 ALDO VAN EYCK
from "Rats, Posts and Pests"
(1981)

The avalanche of writings in the late 1970s and early 1980s on the postmodern phenomenon brought with it at least one unexpected consequence – what the *RIBA Journal*, in a moment of extreme adjectival moderation, referred to as a "withering attack on Post Modernism and all the architectural fashions that are attempting to supersede functionalism." The withering (scathing, cutting, stinging may have been more appropriate qualifications) attack must have appeared all the more daunting to those in the audience that March evening of 1981, because it was delivered by the Dutch architect Aldo van Eyck, the one-time Team 10 member and notorious CIAM rebel in his own right. The occasion was the annual address delivered to the Royal Institute of British Architects in London. But behind the hyperbole of van Eyck's rhetorical style (honed over the previous two years in lectures given in Philadelphia and elsewhere) lay a serious message. It is not the "Great Gang" of modernists he is defending, but the idea that architecture should indeed possess a humanistic pulse in its function and art. The lecture opens with a tirade against Leon Krier, and, as these two passages show, the blame is soon enough spread around to others within the profession. RPP is van Eyck's shorthand for "Rats, Posts and other Pests."

There is no way of knowing how many RPPs there really are – nor how many of them are here now – who are given to bending over backwards trying to twist architecture into what it simply is not: *not even in the sense that an apple is not a pear but still a fruit.*

Architecture does not mean, nor has it ever meant, and it has meant many things, nor will it ever come to pass that it will someday mean, what people (to sweep them into a single heap) like Tafuri, that *italic* Rasputin, or Hero-Rossi, that other Aldo, or the Krier pirates crossing the channel, or Robert contradicting Denise and more recently Robert himself, wish you to think it means. People like Eisenman – Tigerman – Superman – Simpleman – or

Aldo van Eyck, from "Rats, Posts and Pests," in *RIBA Journal* 88:4 (April 1981), pp. 48, 49.

the Cooper Union Circuit, which at first I thought was the name of a racing car, or Charles Semio-Something of London who, given to sign-spotting, will soon be Post-Post if he isn't already, or delirious OMAMA mix, turned surrealist 50 years too late and all sorts of other naughty boys like Robert S (in Holland offenders' surnames are abbreviated in the Press), Michael G, Arata I, Hans H, Ricardo B, and – though too good not to change his mind – big Jim Silver, and finally, although there are many more – old Philip J whose buildings I have from the very beginning disliked most of all.

Notions about notions about . . . that's what's so nasty . . . often good ones originally, but seldom about anything as substantial and down to earth as a *building* – its *use and usefulness*. Instead they just gobble up the forbidden fruits that were never really forbidden – the Puritans!

I find the RPPs' most extravagant fantasies as stale as pornography and certainly as uninventive. And, what is far worse: perversion – even perversion – is rendered distasteful in their hands. But what really excites my anger more than their little flirtations with absurdity, irony, banality, incoherence, contradictions and ugliness is the wilful inclusion of elements that are intended to be disconcerting, intended to aggravate, to pester. Who could ever have thought that one day, buildings, counter to any conceivable kind of logic, would, instead of assisting people's homecoming by helping to ease inner stress, wilfully provoke it.

[. . .]

Let me return to Venturi's book for a while, which I still regard as a good one, but how badly it has been digested! Even by Venturi himself! Particularly the misuse/abuse of Mannerism. One thing is certain, *one should and cannot derive one's own little mannerisms from true Mannerism which had profound sources.*

Contradiction and Complexity in architecture, regarded as formal qualities that are thought to be opposed to Coherence and Consistency on the one hand, Simplicity and Clarity on the other, are not effective medicines against the shallowness of mainstream Modern. True Mannerism, for example that of Michelangelo, Julio Romano and Rafael, although born of inner conflict, mitigated the stress by coaxing harassing paradoxes into significant architectural form with astounding artistry. Emotional extremes were brought together – contained (not *reconciled*) by introducing contrary forms and qualities simultaneously. The audacity of it! Herein lies the lasting *humanity* – that rejected word – of their work, which spans the full scope of our emotional reality: reflecting it, it is also open to it. The RPPs' scorning humanism as they do, should keep their soiled hands off Mannerism. Take the Laurentian Library. It is, among many things, the highly controlled outcome of inner conflict – Michelangelo's sonnets can tell us more about that – but *it does not transmit distress*. The anguish is kept within the architecture through the language invented to hold it. That is where it was persuaded to settle – where it *rests*. Yes, *rests*, thus easing instead of causing anxiety in others. Its greatness and beauty lies in its generosity.

But let me descend from these heights to the bottom of the pit where there is no light at all.

Parading stolen feathers and feigning inner stress the RPP not only play the fool instead of the game, but they also play foul. Ladies and Gentlemen, I beg you, *hound them down – and let the foxes go.*

It is interesting, is it not, the way all those historicists, eclectics and pastichists are producing hardly more than a single standard mono-mix? The taste is perhaps not always

the same, but one does recognise the brand. It is also interesting to note that the best Post
Modern is as stale and stereotyped as the worst Modern. *So never mind the Minnesota Six.*
What is really required is functionalism – functionalism on more levels – of a broader
inclusive kind. RPP makes that abundantly clear. *For there is no such thing as a solid teapot*
that also pours tea. Such an object might be a penetrating statement about something and thus
perhaps still a work of art, but it is simply not a teapot – not one that can pour tea. Nor is there
such a thing as a building which is wilfully absurd, banal, ugly, incoherent, contradictory or
disconcerting and still a building or architecture.

273 GEOFFREY BROADBENT
from ''The Pests Strike Back!''
(1981)

One of the replies to Aldo van Eyck's remarks to the RIBA came in the form of this essay, published in the November issue of the *RIBA Journal.* Broadbent constructs his argument (not all of which is opposed to van Eyck) around the premise that van Eyck, with his reference to the ''Great Gang'' of modernists, is defending the abstraction of the building forms, while the buildings of the machine-aesthetic of Le Corbusier and others in fact had numerous functional and constructional flaws. Broadbent's earlier interest in symbolism and semiotics has not abated, whereas the ''Post-Machine Age'' is his preferred appellation for postmodernism.

How strange that the more honest decoration of Post-Machine Age is still called "kitsch" by
some. Indeed some of Van Eyck's "Rats" see it that way, especially the Krier Brothers who
are looking for something more solid in *craftsmanship* again. They look to architects such as
Quinlan Terry, and his revered master Raymond Erith, who continued to demand – and to
get – craftsmanship right through the heroic days of the Machine Age.

They also used Neo-classical forms, which worries Van Eyck because Albert Speer also
did. But when I go to Bath I say to myself "As a matter of principle, I oughtn't to like this
(Stall Street) because here Classical forms of 200 years ago were built next to the real thing
from 2,000". But I do like it. So should it worry me if they were 20 years old or even two
instead of 200. In all conscience my answer has to be "Not if they function well in all the
ways I have mentioned".

I don't see how Van Eyck can dismiss so lightly the "Rats" with their evident joy in
craftsmanship, not to mention their concern for urban space. Designed space got lost,
literally, in those bleak open areas of tarmac between the towers and the slabs of the Modern
Movement but the Kriers, in their projects and books, have shown us again its importance.
I don't much like the rigid geometries they draw; I'd rather have more responsive spaces,
responsive that is to the site, like Spoerri's Port Grimaud or Moore's Kresge College, but that

Geoffrey Broadbent, from ''The Pests Strike Back!,'' in *RIBA Journal* 88:11 (November 1981), pp. 33–4.

isn't quite the point. The point is that in this and many other ways Post-Machine Age design *functions* better than Machine Age ever could. Take the fit of spaces to activities. I know of no more efficient planner than Venturi; see, for instance, his Humanities Building for the State University of New York at Purchase. Stern too, in his houses, plans the most marvellous sequences from the most public to the most private spaces while Moore plans for a sense of human movement through space, indeed he plans directly for the human senses. In his *House for a Blind Man* for instance, the sightless client can ''sense'' his way around through the soles of his feet (floor textures), through the smells of the varied planting, the sounds of his own and other voices reflected off the walls of the varied rooms. You can't do that in Machine Age abstract boxes.

This care for the senses extends with Moore, Stern and Venturi to the overall forms themselves. Such things as window size, shape and position, the use of screens, pierced planes and other shading devices mean that each facade can take the form it should according to view, sunpath and so on for good environmental control. As for costs, their buildings are miracles of economy which sometimes shows – it must be said – in the quality of their construction. Yet the most unlikely buildings, such as Moore's *Piazza d'Italia* show the most amazing economic performance. This Neo-classical fountain was intended to ''seed'' a derelict area of New Orleans, just as Beaubourg has ''seeded'' the Marais in Paris.

It should be obvious by now that such Post-Modern architecture (or, as I prefer to call it, Post-Machine Age) has a potential for making comfortable, humane, economic and truly functioning architecture of the kind which Abstraction and the Machine Aesthetic never could. The architects of the latter fought battles and crusades against an unwilling public, but the ''Rats, Posts and Pests'' above all *want* to be liked. They want to do things that ordinary people will love, so we need far better reasons than those of *architects* such as Van Eyck for rejecting it in favour of that architecture of the 1920s which, while it was called ''Functional*ism*'' actually functioned very badly.

274 ROB KRIER
''10 Theses on Architecture''
(1982)

I n Rob Krier's first book of 1975, *Urban Space*, he made known his interest in typology as a vehicle for urban composition. The following year he accepted a teaching position in Vienna, and it was during the late 1970s that he refined his notions of block formation, streets, and squares as the basis for his vision of ''New Urbanism,'' which bears some similarities with this movement's later development in the United States. The ''10 Theses on Architecture'' consolidate his urban-design thinking into a few concise points, but they also reveal much more of his thinking. Krier, in his urban thinking, seeks to restore the historical spatial experience rather than the imposition of historical forms for their own sake.

Rob Krier, ''10 Theses on Architecture,'' in *On Architecture*. London: Academy Editions, 1982, p. 5.

These principles have applied since man began to plan his buildings rationally and see architecture as an aesthetic product, that is, give his building form beyond its useful purpose.

1
FUNCTION, CONSTRUCTION AND FORM

are of equal value and together determine the architecture. None should have priority over the others.

2
FUNCTION AND CONSTRUCTION

are elements of a useful nature whose fulfilment should be a matter of course in building. Only when they are raised to an aesthetic level does a building become architecture.

3
THE MEANS OF AESTHETIC SUBLIMATION ARE:

– Proportion
– Structure
– The handling of materials and colour and the artistic interpretation of these.

4
THE AESTHETIC DIMENSION

The deeper significance of beauty in architecture lies in man's need to give his useful objects a poetic dimension which will communicate the 'spirit' of his age to future generations. (". . . it is useful because it is beautiful . . ." Antoine de Saint-Exupéry)

5
GEOMETRY

is the basis of all architectural articulation. As organised geometry, architecture derives its force from the contrast with living nature, not from a formal adjustment to it. Architecture is the creation of man.

6
SCALE

in architecture should be adjusted to the size of the human body and its patterns of behaviour, perception and sensitivity. It should not be orientated to technical or structural principles or to economic considerations only.

7
URBAN ARCHITECTURE

Any new planning in a city should be such that it fits into the general order and offers a formal response to existing spatial patterns.

8
THE CITY AS A WHOLE

has been forgotten in 20th-century urban planning. Our new cities consist of collections of individual buildings. Five thousand years of urban history show that the complex structures of streets and squares are necessary as communication zones and centres of identity. The modern city needs the traditional concepts of urban planning as well.

HISTORY

The proper appreciation of our historical heritage will filter the experience of the past to the advantage of planning for the future.

THE RESPONSIBILITY OF THE ARCHITECT

The architect alone is responsible for the product which emerges from his drawing board and bears his signature. No politician or financier will take the cultural blame from the architect's shoulders for a mis-planned environment. It is the responsibility of our universities to prepare future generations of architects for this overwhelming ethical and moral task.

275 MICHAEL GRAVES
from "A Case for Figurative Architecture" (1982)

A longside Robert Venturi, Michael Graves emerged as one of the two best-known American practitioners of postmodernism in the 1980s. A recent dissenter from the white Corbusian language of the New York Five, Graves gained increasing prominence during the 1970s with projects such as those for the Fargo-Moorhead Cultural Center Bridge (drawing its inspiration from Claude-Nicholas Ledoux), the Plocek House (classicism recomposed), the Portland Building (Art Deco revisited), and the San Juan Capistrano Library (California Mission). In making "A Case for Figurative Architecture" he reveals his design intentions to explore — admittedly in an eclectic manner — the mytho-poetic realm of architectural meaning, a sharp departure from the Corbusian symbolism and abstraction of his earlier style. For better or for worse, Graves and Venturi now became the face of American postmodernism, as well as targets at whom many opponents would take aim.

A standard form and a poetic form exist in any language or in any art. Although analogies drawn between one cultural form and another prove somewhat difficult, they nevertheless allow associations that would otherwise be impossible. Literature is the cultural form which most obviously takes advantage of standard and poetic usages, and so may stand as a model for architectural dialogue. In literature, the standard, accessible, simple ranges of daily use are expressed in conversational or prose forms, while the poetic attitudes of language are used to test, deny, and at times, to further support standard language. It seems that standard language and poetic language have a reciprocal responsibility to stand as separate and equal strands of the greater literary form and to reinforce each other by their similarity and diversity. Through this relationship of tension, each form is held in check and plays on the other for its strength.

Michael Graves, from "A Case for Figurative Architecture," in *Michael Graves: Buildings and Projects 1966–1981*, ed. Karen Vogel Wheeler, Peter Arnell, and Ted Bickford. New York: Rizzoli, 1982, p. 11.

When applying this distinction of language to architecture, it could be said that the standard form of building is its common or internal language. The term internal language does not imply in this case that it is non-accessible, but rather that it is intrinsic to building in its most basic form – determined by pragmatic, constructional, and technical requirements. In contrast, the poetic form of architecture is responsive to issues external to the building, and incorporates the three-dimensional expression of the myths and rituals of society. Poetic forms in architecture are sensitive to the figurative, associative, and anthropomorphic attitudes of a culture. If one's goal is to build with only utility in mind, then it is enough to be conscious of technical criteria alone. However, once aware of and responsive to the possible cultural influences on building, it is important that society's patterns of ritual be registered in the architecture. Could these two attitudes, one technical and utilitarian and the other cultural and symbolic, be thought of as architecture's standard and poetic languages?

Without doubt, the inevitable overlap of these two systems of thought can cause this argument to become somewhat equivocal. However, the salient tendencies of each attitude may be distinguished and reasonably discussed. This is said with some critical knowledge of the recent past. It could be maintained that dominant aspects of modern architecture were formulated without this debate about standard and poetic language, or internal and external manifestations of architectural culture. The Modern Movement based itself largely on technical expression – internal language – and the metaphor of the machine dominated its building form. In its rejection of the human or anthropomorphic representation of previous architecture, the Modern Movement undermined the poetic form in favor of nonfigural, abstract geometries. These abstract geometrics might in part have been derived from the simple internal forms of machines themselves. Coincident with machine metaphors in buildings, architecture in the first half of this century also embraced aesthetic abstraction in general. This has contributed to our interest in purposeful ambiguity, the possibility of double readings within compositions.

While any architectural language, to be built, will always exist within the technical realm, it is important to keep the technical expression parallel to an equal and complementary expression of ritual and symbol. It could be argued that the Modern Movement did this, that as well as its internal language, it expressed the symbol of the machine, and therefore practiced cultural symbolism. But in this case, the machine is retroactive, for the machine itself is a utility. So this symbol is not an external allusion, but rather a second, internalized reading. A significant architecture must incorporate both internal and external expressions. The external language, which engages inventions of culture at large, is rooted in a figurative, associational and anthropomorphic attitude.

276 JOSEF-PAUL KLEIHUES

from "1984: The Berlin Exhibition, Architectural Dream or Reality?" (1982)

By the late 1970s German architectural theory was beginning to emerge once again as a force. And its new prominence had much to do with the organizational work of Josef-Paul Kleihues, an architect trained in the 1950s under Peter Poelzig and Hans Scharoun. In 1977 Kleinhues was appointed as the Director for New Building for the Internationale Bauaustellung (IBA), or International Architectural Exhibition in Berlin. With the collaboration of the journalist Wolf Jobst Siedler, Kleihues succeeded in turning the publicly and privately funded IBA into a triple-edged sword of theory and practice, education, and design experimentation. Exhibitions composed one tactic of the IBA's overall strategy. Another was a series of symposia and advisory consultations with a number of the leading international theorists and historians – from Vittorio Gregotti to Kenneth Frampton and Kurt W. Forster. Yet a third arm of the IBA's strategy was the most ambitious: the reconstruction of a number of the bombed-out areas of Berlin, a city still divided by the Wall. In responding to the idea of an international building exhibition in 1984 (with obvious overtones to Weissenhof in 1927), Kleinhues successfully argued against building a series of isolated showpieces on one site, and on behalf of a series of architectural competitions for projects to be integrated into the existing historical fabric of Berlin, drawing upon the specific historical traditions of the city. A large number of projects were thus undertaken in the 1980s in Tegel, around Prager Platz, and in the Friedrichstadt and Tiergarten districts, and by such well-known architects as Aldo Rossi, Carlo Aymonino, James Sterling, Charles Moore, and Rob Krier. Kleihues's own strategy of "critical reconstruction" embodied both rationalism and a poetic emphasis on the "memory" of place. By the time that he left the IBA in 1987 to return to practice, Berlin had almost overnight become a new Mecca for architectural innovation.

Let us be honest: this criticism is pervasive. It is directed at the avant-garde generally. In the twenties it was directed against the Weissenhof estate in Stuttgart and against the Waldsiedlung at Onkel Toms Hütte in Berlin. *'For people differ intellectually'*, as Scharoun said, *'and no-one can (or will) see anything which goes beyond him.'*

The aesthetic, the moral verdict, are easier to achieve than a readiness for critical assessment. But verdicts of this kind are largely general:

They apply to Aldo Rossi's stereometry, his return to the archaic and the archetype in architecture even where these are made of wood, the incarnation of the proverbial imagination of the transient, a swimming architecture.

They apply to the open cube by Mario Botta in the Swiss landscape and to the 'Homo ludens' fantasies by Rem Koolhaas for New York.

They apply to the intellectual claims of Robert Venturi in spite of the critical reflection of everyday architecture. For a long time they have applied in Germany to O. M. Ungers, whose works have always aroused reaction but for a long time were seldom built and tried out.

Josef-Paul Kleihues, from "1984: The Berlin Exhibition, Architectural Dream or Reality?," in *Architectural Association Quarterly* 13:2/3 (January–June 1982), p. 42.

There are many more examples which could be quoted. But we need the impetus of the 'outsiders'. They provide necessary criticism of routine and of the still prevailing instrumental rationality. We need provocative theories and artistic stimulus. We need these as a critical impulse for our competitions, for our seminars, for our exhibitions, for the International Building Exhibition as a whole.

For we cannot be concerned with creating easier terms for architects.

We must make the effort to reflect on historical experience, and this includes the tradition of forms of expression: historical documents of enlightenment, hope and artistic intention as an orientation for our own work.

We must make the effort to study measurements and numbers and geometry, not as means in themselves but as the grammatical and formal basis of communication through architecture.

We must make the effort to grasp the meaning, the significance, the symbolism of architecture, that is, architecture as a language on the basis and with the use of this grammar, a grammar which, itself dead, neither good nor evil, needs to be translated into life by architects, engineers and urban planners.

We must make the effort to fight for an independent architecture, an autonomy of architecture not against but for people: an autonomy which has to prove itself not in the abstract but in the concrete. Not only in great things, but in small things too. Not only in expensive projects but in modest ones as well. An independent architecture, not worn down by routines, which can only exist with the recognition that it cannot give way to trends towards determinism, even if this is hypocritically or expectantly clothed in the metaphors of happiness and hope, nor indeed to political, artistic, philosophical or epistemological determinants either.

We must make the effort to see architecture not only as something reserved for the out-of-the-ordinary, but as part of our everyday lives, an artistic obligation.

No criticism must discourage us from this.

Nor must we be discouraged if we have to live with the experience that some critics have resigned themselves to accepting the asphalting of our land-scapes as an unavoidable evil, concentrating on the opposite pole as a surrogate, so to speak, for their critical obligations.

Criticism of what is artistic is often that criticism which is purely negative; for years it has helped so many architects either to forget, or to suppress, with music, gaiety, with literature, engagement, with philosophy, questioning, with mathematics, clarity of thought and with painting, their dreams.

Do not let us be discouraged! On the contrary, let us call out with Hölderlin:

> 'That it is better to die, because one has lived,
> Than to survive because one has never lived.
> Do not envy those who are free from suffering,
> Blocks of wood who lack nothing
> Because their souls are so poor;
> Who do not ask after the rain and
> The sun,
> Because they have nothing
> Which needs care.'

Architecture, that is what I wanted to say, needs all our care for the sake of the future.

277   CHARLES JENCKS
from *What is Post-Modernism?*
(1986)

The architect who first proclaimed the death of modern architecture in 1977 had by this date emerged as the most enthusiastic champion of the movement. With his numerous contributions to *Architectural Design*, he was also perhaps the most prolific writer on architecture of the decade. As his definition of postmodernism shows, his views had not changed since the mid-1970s, but this amusing polemical defense of postmodernism against those attacking it at the same time shows just how intense the debate had become over the preceding few years.

I   The Protestant Inquisition

In October 1981 *Le Monde* announced to its morning readers, under the section of its newspaper ominously headed 'Décadence', that a spectre was haunting Europe, the spectre of Post-Modernism.[1] What Frenchmen made of this warning as they bit into their croissants is anybody's guess, especially as it came with the familiar Marxist image of a ghost looming over their civilisation (and their coffee) – but they probably soon forgot the phantom and looked forward to next morning's 'Décadence' column, for in our culture one ghost grows boring and must be quickly replaced by the next. The problem, however, has been that critics – especially hostile, Modernist critics – won't let this one dissolve. They keep attacking the phantom with ever-increasing hysteria, making it grow into quite a substantial force that upsets not only *le petit déjeuner* but also international conferences and price quotations on the international art market. If they aren't careful, there will be a panic and crash at the Museum of Modern Art as certain reputations dissolve like dead stock.

Clement Greenberg, long acknowledged as the theorist of American Modernism, defined Post-Modernism in 1979 as the antithesis of all he loved: that is, as the lowering of aesthetic standards caused by 'the democratization of culture under industrialism.'[2] Like our 'Décadence' columnist he saw the danger as a lack of hierarchy in artistic judgement, although he didn't go so far as the Frenchman in calling it simply 'nihilism'. Another art critic, Walter Darby Bannard, writing in the same prestigious *Arts Magazine* five years later, continued Greenberg's crusade against the heathens and re-stated the same (non) definition, except with more brutal elaboration: 'Postmodernism is aimless, anarchic, amorphous, self-indulgent, inclusive, horizontally structured, and aims for the popular.'[3] Why did he leave out 'ruthless kitsch' or the standard comparison with Nazi populism that the architectural critic Ken Frampton always adds to the list of horrors? Ever since Clement Greenberg made his famous opposition between 'Avant-Garde and Kitsch' in a 1939 article, certain puritanical intellectuals have been arguing that it has to be one thing or the other, and it's clear where they classify Post-Modernism, although of course if it's really 'horizontally structured' and

Charles Jencks, from *What is Post-Modernism?* London: Academy Editions, 1986, pp. 12–14.

'democratic' it can't be at the same time Neo-Nazi and authoritarian. But consistency has never been a virtue of those out to malign a movement.

Quite recently the Royal Institute of British Architects (RIBA) has been hosting a series of revivalist meetings which are noteworthy for their vicious attacks on Post-Modernism. In 1981 the Dutch architect Aldo van Eyck delivered the Annual Discourse titled 'Rats, Posts and Other Pests', and one can guess from this appellation how hard he attempted to be fair-minded. He advised his cheering audience of Modernists in a capital-lettered harangue. 'Ladies and Gentlemen, I beg you, HOUND THEM DOWN AND LET THE FOXES GO' – tactics not unlike the Nazi ones he was deploring, although the hounds and foxes give this pogrom an Oscar Wilde twist. If Van Eyck advised letting the dogs loose on Post-Modernists, the older Modern architect Berthold Lubetkin limited himself, on receiving his Gold Medal at the RIBA, to classing them with homosexuals, Hitler and Stalin: 'This is a transvestite architecture, Heppelwhite and Chippendale in drag.' And he continued to compare Post-Modernism with Nazi kitsch in subsequent revivalist *soirées* in Paris and at the RIBA, even equating Prince Charles with Stalin for his attack on Modernism. One could quote similar abuse from old-hat Modernists in America, Germany, Italy, France, indeed most of the world. For instance the noted Italian critic Bruno Zevi sees Post-Modernism as a 'pastiche . . . trying to copy Classicism' and 'repressive' like fascism.

We can see in all these howls of protest something like a negative definition emerging, a paranoic definition made by Modernists in retreat trying to hold the High Church together, issuing daily edicts denouncing heresy, keeping the faith among ever-dwindling numbers. It is true they still control most of the academies, sit on most of the aesthetic review boards, and repress as many Post-Modern artists and architects as they can, but the mass of young professionals have fled from the old Protestant orthodoxy and are themselves bored and fed up with the taboos and suppressions. In any international competition now more than half the entries will be Post-Modern, and that generality applies as much to sculpture and painting as it does to architecture. The door is wide open, as it was in the 1920s when Modernism had knocked down the previous academic barriers; the irony is that today's old-time Modernists are determined to be just as paranoic, reactionary and repressive as their Beaux-Arts persecutors were before them. Indeed the slurs against Post-Modernists occasionally sound like the Nazi and academic vitriol poured on Le Corbusier and Walter Gropius in the 1920s. Is history repeating itself in reverse? I'm not sure, but I do believe that these characterisations have not done what they were supposed to do – stem the tide of Post-Modernism – but rather have helped blow it up into a media event. My nightmare is that suddenly the reactionaries will become nice and civil. Everyone, but particularly the press, loves an abusive argument carried on by professors and the otherwise intelligent: it's always entertaining even if it obscures as much as it explains. And what it has hidden are the root causes of the movement.

II   Post-Modernism Defined

Post-Modernism, like Modernism, varies for each art both in its motives and time-frame, and here I shall define it just in the field with which I am most involved – architecture. The responsibility for introducing it into the architectural subconscious lies with

Joseph Hudnut who, at Harvard with Walter Gropius, may have wished to give this pioneer of the Modern Movement a few sleepless nights. At any rate, he used the term in the title of an article published in 1945 called 'the post-modern house' (all lower case, as was Bauhaus practice), but didn't mention it in the body of the text or define it polemically. Except for an occasional slip here and there, by Philip Johnson or Nikolaus Pevsner, it wasn't used until my own writing on the subject which started in 1975.[4] In that first year of lecturing and polemicising in Europe and America, I used it as a temporising label, as a definition to describe where we had left rather than where we were going. The observable fact was that architects as various as Ralph Erskine, Robert Venturi, Lucien Kroll, the Krier brothers and Team Ten had all departed from Modernism and set off in different directions which *kept a trace of their common departure*. To this day I would define Post-Modernism as I did in 1978 as *double coding: the combination of Modern techniques with something else (usually traditional building) in order for architecture to communicate with the public and a concerned minority, usually other architects.*

NOTES

1 Gérard-Georges Lemaire, 'Le Spectre du post-modernisme', 'Décadence', *Le Monde Dimanche*, 18 October 1981, p. XIV.

2 Clement Greenberg, 'Modern and Post-Modern' – presented at the fourth Sir William Dobell Memorial Lecture in Sydney, Australia, on 31 October 1979 and published the following year in *Arts Magazine*.

3 Walter Darby Bannard, 'On Postmodernism', an essay originally presented at a panel on Post-Modernism at the Modern Languages Association's annual meeting in New York, 28 December 1983, published later in *Arts Magazine*.

4 My own writing and lecturing on Post-Modernism in architecture started in 1975 and 'The Rise of Post-Modern Architecture' was published in a Dutch book and a British magazine, *Architecture – Inner Town Government*, Eindhoven, July 1975, and *Architecture Association Quarterly*, No. 4, 1975. Subsequently Eisenman and Stern started using the term and by 1977 it had caught on. For a brief history see the 'Footnote on the Term' in *The Language of Post-Modern Architecture*, fourth edition, Academy Editions, London/Rizzoli, New York 1984, p. 8.

278 HEINRICH KLOTZ
from "Postscript: Since 1980" (1987)

The German professor and art historian Heinrich Klotz published the first definitive history of postmodern architecture – *Moderne und Postmoderne: Architektur der Gegenwart* – in 1984. For the English translation published by Roger Conover at MIT Press in 1988, Klotz added a postscript in which he attempted to bring the history of this movement up to date, that is, by reflecting on the events that transpired between 1980 and 1987.

Heinrich Klotz, from "Postscript: Since 1980," in *The History of Postmodern Architecture*, trans. Radka Donnell. Cambridge, MA: MIT Press, 1988, pp. 433–4.

The result is an interesting snapshot of a moment: displaying evident excitement at the architectural activity of the decade, mixed with the interesting foreboding that the "end of postmodernism" might indeed be at hand. The double conundrum is whether the use of historical irony by early postmodernists might have evolved into a fully-fledged historicism, and whether those who stand aloof from historicizing forms, such as the deconstructionists, hold a viable alternate strategy.

At present, the American architectural scene is certainly the most interesting in the Western world. With its great variety of schools and trends, there is nothing that it does not include. The attention to Rossi and Ungers has given European Rationalism a foothold in the United States, and the work of Leon Krier has had an impact even on the independent and inventive Michael Graves.

There are two increasingly sharply defined opposing tendencies in the American architectural discussion that, although they do not exactly dominate it, certainly shed light on its practical and theoretical aspects. One of these tendencies is embraced by the historicists Allan Greenberg, Robert Stern, and Thomas Gordon Smith; the other by the Californian Frank Gehry.

The New York historicists have drawn from postmodernism the impetus to revive the historical architecture of their own country. Leaving the British architect Quinlan Terry out of account, only in the United States can we observe that historicist architecture has become the avowed goal of several gifted architects. Greenberg has come the closest to an imitative architecture; his interiors for government buildings in Washington seem to stem from the early nineteenth century; they recall both Robert Adam and William Strickland. Stern, like Greenberg, uses his historicist vocabulary not ironically but literally, as if he actually aims to erect a historical building; however, Stern likes to introduce some ingenious alienating feature into the overall conception of a building as a contrast to the historicizing details. Smith, in a theoretical treatise, has gone so far as to reintroduce the Vitruvian canon of orders and to use the Renaissance concepts of *regula* and *inventione* to determine the degree of deviation from the former rule. His goal is to approximate historical architecture as closely as he can without succumbing to it. In all these attempts it becomes evident that historicism, which at first seemed to be a transitional phase, has turned into a persistant attitude in American architecture. Where once the New York historicists leaned toward reinterpretation in consciously ambivalent and modern forms, now they identify themselves with the historical models – even, in Greenberg's case, to the point of tasteful imitation. Ironic reinterpretation was their starting point and their alibi. The alibi, they believe, is no longer needed.

The other position is championed in the United States by Frank Gehry, whose works continue to be ruled by the intention to make them vocal and articulate while renouncing all historicizing forms. Remaining within the tradition of modernism, Gehry breaks the muteness to which its aesthetic was reduced and strives for a narrative manner of representation whose theme is the fracturing of the building as a perfect whole. He has been joined in this undertaking by many European architects, among them the members of the Viennese group Coop-Himmelblau and also Zaha Hadid, who has worked in the studio of Rem Koolhaas. Hadid's architectural fantasies – splintered and fissured visions of space – derive their narrative quality of uncertainty from their lack of a unified perspective. These and many other attempts articulate the striving to hold onto the tradition of modernism and to keep alive the modernist insistence on a self-referential justification independent of history. By manifesting this insistence, architectural expression becomes more imaginative. The form becomes articulate of its own accord, even if only to represent the blowing up of the building. The expressionist intensification defends modernism as much as it submits to the new need for representation and the urgency of a narrative fiction.

However, a question arises: How much of an effort does it take to maintain ahistorical modernism? Rem Koolhaas has concluded that "a building cannot dissolve like Zaha Hadid wants it to but has to remain a built structure."

While Frank Gehry performs poetic balancing acts for the preservation of the building as a whole, Rem Koolhaas has already returned to Mies. But, as Koolhaas says, his Mies is "twisted," and the buildings he has conceived lately are impure and contradictory. What the post-modernists did with the historicizing forms, Koolhaas now does to the modern ones: He ironizes them.

This highly charged relation to architecture, this dialectical ambiguity, is an essential feature of present-day building. Yet many of the architects who introduced the ironizing dialectic of historicism into architecture as a response to modernism's loss of articulation were among the first to give it up. They demanded a new absolute unequivocalness, and they became historicists.

The result of such daring adventures – trying to reach identity with the historical styles and still stay in the present – necessarily leads to the announcement of the "end of postmodernism." The final stage seems to have been reached, yet there is still much to come.

279 COLIN DAVIES
from *High Tech Architecture* (1987)

Although few would characterize Davies's high-tech approach to architecture as representative of postmodernism, the logic is nearly identical. Davies argues that just as modernists imitated airplanes, ships, and automobiles in the 1920s, so the architects of today (presumably of a postmodern era) should imitate contemporary values and technologies. The argument is also similar in that Davies insists that because strict functionalism and mass-production technologies are not always economically viable, architects are often left with the task of symbolizing or representing technology. In another act of neo-rationalist logic, Davies also resurrects Giedion's old *Zeitgeist* premises.

Function and Representation – Technique or Style?

The exponents of High Tech, like the pioneer Modernists of the 1920s, believe that there is such a thing as the "spirit of the age" and that architecture has a moral duty to express that spirit. The spirit of our age, according to High Tech architects, resides in advanced

Colin Davies, from *High Tech Architecture*. New York: Rizzoli, 1987, p. 6.

technology. Architecture must therefore participate in and make use of that technology – the technology of industry, transport, communication, flight, and space travel. Why, they ask, should buildings be any different from the other artifacts of industrial culture? Why do we continue to make buildings out of cumbersome, messy, imprecise materials such as bricks, mortar, concrete, and timber when we could be making them out of light, precision components of metal and glass, fabricated in factories and quickly bolted together on site?

The High Tech architect sees architecture as a branch of industrial technology. He claims no social or artistic privileges. He wishes his buildings to be judged by the same criteria of performance as any of the other tools of everyday life. He wants them to be functional and efficient, not artistic or symbolic.

But there is an ambiguity here. Architecture, it seems, can never be purely functional, no matter how hard it tries. The typical High Tech building symbolizes and represents technology rather than simply using it in the most efficient way possible. It may be cheaper and quicker to build a load-bearing brick wall, but the High Tech architect will always prefer the steel frame and the lightweight metal panel because this is a technique more in tune with the spirit of the age. He is committed to the idea that building must eventually catch up with the rest of technology, and he is determined to "drag building into the twentieth century". In this endeavour, symbolism and representation have an important part to play. The motifs of High Tech – exposed steel structure, visible air conditioning ducts, plug-in service pods, and so on – are almost never the most economical solutions. There is nearly always a cheaper, more practical alternative. But this is architecture, not engineering.

High Tech architecture, then, is not purely functional. But neither is it purely representational. It is an article of the High Tech faith that there must be a functional justification for every design decision. Take, for example, the tension structure of Nicholas Grimshaw's Ice Rink in Oxford. It converts a straightforward, shed-like building into a dynamic, self-advertising, instantly identifiable piece of architecture that irresistibly brings to mind the romantic image of a sailing ship. A similar effect might have been achieved by the application of a couple of fake masts to an ordinary portal frame structure. But the true High Tech architect would never resort to such deception. The structure has to be real and there has to be a functional justification for it. In this case, the justification is the low bearing capacity of the subsoil. Of all the possible ways to overcome this problem, the tension structure was chosen, however, not for its economy but for its symbolic power.

Le Corbusier described the house as a machine for living in, but he built houses that were technologically primitive and looked nothing like machines. High Tech buildings do look like machines. The machine is more than a metaphor; it is a source of technology and of imagery. Machines are usually mass-produced, either mobile or portable, and made of synthetic materials such as metal, glass, and plastic. These characteristics have become the reference points of High Tech architecture. The buildings may not be mass-produced, or even assembled from mass-produced components, but they look mass-produced, or at least capable of repetition. They may not be mobile, like cars, or portable, like television sets, but they will usually be made of distinct components and will often appear to hover a few inches above the site as if, one day they might be dismantled or moved.

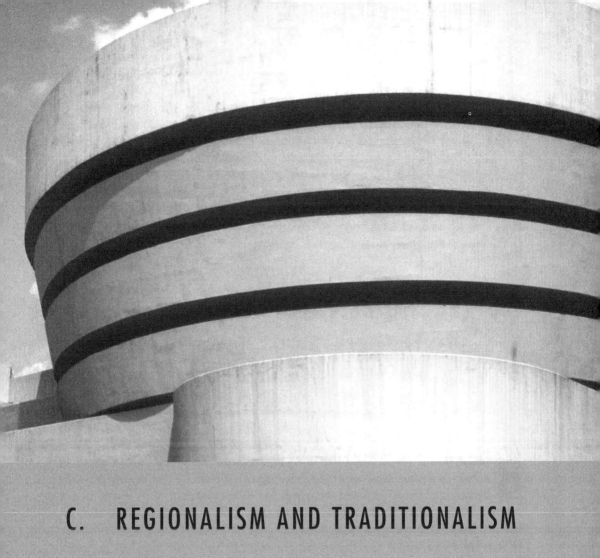

C.   REGIONALISM AND TRADITIONALISM

Introduction

I f the twin (and often competing) phenomena of Deconstruction and Postmodernism captivated the architectural media during the 1980s, there were nevertheless other important viewpoints expressed in the discourse. They arose in part to counter the cultural nihilism implicit in the poststructural world and in part to offer an alternative to historical eclecticism. They also arose from the positive desire to develop design strategies that drew upon certain historical traditions, while adapting them to the new realities of the postmodern world.

Regionalism, for instance, was a concept explored in German theory in the 1890s, in American theory in the 1920s, in the years surrounding World War II, and again in Italy in the late 1950s. What distinguishes the regionalist debate of the 1980s is both an awareness of these earlier discussions and a more confident sense that modernism had indeed exhausted its formal possibilities without having achieved its promised objectives. Some architects, for instance, in pointing to the failure of modernism in many less-developed cultures, advocated regionalism as a way to draw in more local characters and building traditions. Others touted a "critical regionalism" as a strategy to stave off or thwart the perceived commodification of culture in late capitalist societies.

Traditionalism also has its diverse sources. Many architects who viewed postmodern eclecticism as a degenerate practice bordering on kitsch embraced the classical tradition, for instance, as a true station for a displaced architecture. Aligned with this perception was often the view that modernism had indeed rudely intruded upon the landscape of European culture – an intuition for preservation and conservation often overlaid with nineteenth-century sensibilities. Still other movements, such as "New Urbanism" in the United States, embraced historical planning models as a way to escape from the suburbanized society trapped in such ecologically damning technologies as the automobile. The parallelisms of their formal proposals with those of the European Marxists demonstrate how the conscious return to themes of the past can indeed transcend seemingly major cultural and political boundaries. All things considered, the theoretical strength of the 1980s lay just in these diverging worldviews.

280 BRUNO REICHLIN

from "Reflections: Interrelations between Concept, Representation and Built Architecture" (1981)

Between 1972 and 1974 the Swiss partnership of Bruno Reichlin and Fabio Reinhart created a sensation by erecting – in plan and overall form – the Palladian-inspired Casa Tonini. The harmonic proportions of the idealized form, however, contrasted sharply with the "modern" materiality of the exposed concrete skeleton and timber roof-structure. Reichlin follows a similar track in this essay by playing off the abstraction inherent in so much of the axonometric "paper architecture" of the 1970s against the notion of built architecture. His words here are not critical of Peter Eisenman and John Hejduk, the two architects whose work he considers in detail. If the material world remains the devoutly-to-be-wished-for consummation of architectural production, the paper world nevertheless represents "the mental viewpoint of the architect-demiurge" at its inspired moment of gestation.

Architecture has let itself be seduced by its own image, it would seem, judging by the current pageantry of graphic architecture in the great circus of architectural journalism. The art of the spraygun, of watercolour and tea-soaked paper, and the glorious recipes of the "grands prix de Rome", are like rouge on the promises of a new urban landscape, garnished with happy flaneurs, reinstated craftsmen and prestige knick-knacks – classical torsos, cippuses and towers – scattered in meditated disorder. Indeed colleagues hardly glance at the refined architectural inventions, but want to know instead how the devil this or that dotted line or shading was done.

Bruno Reichlin, from "Reflections: Interrelations between Concept, Representation and Built Architecture," in *Daidalos: Berlin Architectural Journal* 1 (1981), pp. 60, 67, 69, 72.

Does this betrayal of building in favour of drawing mean anything? Is there some impediment? Have we entered a period of deferment where weapons are being sharpened for a future laden with promise? Does the new architecture not find a response in practice or more clearly, does it still not find a client? Or did Narcissus already give Echo the cold shoulder? The fact is, that constructed architecture often stummer the latest incomprehensible letters of new tendencies and – by remaining in the picture and the cliché – it continues to build well-known concrete deserts.

There may be some truth in these suppositions, which are like balm to a certain latent pessimism. Architects are feeding on dreams, and "when they wake up, the world of hard facts will see to it that the ruthless wall is erected between the image of estrangement and the reality of its own laws", decrees Tafuri. Tafuri's warning was addressed expressly to the researches conducted by the New York's "Five", who have in fact made a decisive contribution to architectural representation, not so much in its culinary aspects as in its epistemological ones. It is not therefore altogether fortuitous that the lucid determination of P. Eisenman must take credit for having produced perhaps the first architectural object in which the reflection of architecture in its own image is the actual theme of the project. The house El Even Odd (1980) is conformed and deformed so that its roof and oblique corners describe a reticulum of lines which cause the observer to perceive the familiar image of the axonometric reproduction of a cube. By reversing "the natural order of things", the real object – the referent – produces the perceptive conditions of what ought, by convention, to be its image. "House El Even Odd is an axonometric object", says P. Eisenman, pointing out that "it explores the conditions of representation reading in architecture. As such it is concerned with the limits of the discipline of architecture".
[. . .]

Acquisition number one: axonometry is not so much a means of representation as a tool for work and for objectified work. It can be as perspicuous as you like (and it is not always so, since it is a fact that the public very often can't decipher it). Nonetheless it first of all reveals a poetic viewpoint and calls for specialized knowledge. To put it schematically: if perspective "realism" has to do with "consumption" and represents a service to the client, as Alberto Sartoris maintained, and who for that reason allowed Terragni to embellish with "greenery" his lean perspective for a housing estate at Reggio, axonometry on the other hand has to do with the architectural workshop.
[. . .]

Acquisition number two: complementary to the first: although architects had never hitherto insisted so strongly on the social ends of architecture, the new architectural conformation does not however aim to signify socializing or symbolic contents in accordance with a centuries-old custom that immediately made them understandable to common sense. The "subject" – or "argument" – of the work are rather the processes and the system of rules which an increasingly skilled craft – and art – impose upon the architectural object: on the one hand the distributive and constructional organization, the preparations, etc., and on the other, the application of autonomously artistic codes relating to volumetric, proportional and spatial conformation, etc., all within a system of interdependences the appreciation of which requires a specialist ability to recognize the necessary character but also the play of rules that governs it. As for axonometry, the "magic moment" – the beauty – of the housing estate Dessau-Törten is all, or almost all, in its axonometric constructional diagram.

[. . .]

Acquisition number three: in the particular use noticed in the examples mentioned, axonometry also favours a methodological innovation. So much more explicit and concrete than an enunciation, yet sufficiently abstract not to be identified as a model to be copied, those axonometric drawings synthetically substantiate – at a level that might be defined as "meta-design" – the intersection between the needs (functional, constructional, process and expressive) that the object has to satisfy and the diagram of the physical structure that satisfies them. From this viewpoint those drawings may be likened to what Christopher Alexander has called a "constructional diagram": "The constructional diagram is the bridge between requirements and form. But its great beauty is that it goes much deeper. The very duality between the requirement and the form which the constructional diagram is capable of expressing and unifying, is revealed at a second level: the duality is itself characteristic of our knowledge of form."

Exaggerating a little, for the sake of strong images, let us say that axonometric representation manifests, in the two-dimensionality of the drawing sheet, the mental viewpoint of the architect-demiurge. In the measure in which it favours the moment of architectural gestation, it is also the symbol of the steady falling back by architectural culture – by the Modern Movement but by a conspicuous part of contemporary trends too – on to the more technical aspects of the craft and – this is the specific of positions like that of the "Five" – on to the autonomous artistic demands of architecture.

It is on this road that architecture has estranged itself much more from the common understanding. Van Doesburg had realised: "The audience has its own inner life and environment, the artist has another one. Both are so different that it is impossible to bring the inner life and environment of the former to the latter." This deduction has no critical intentions; it merely records an effect of the progressive division of work. For those who want order at home: one of the possible merits of "House El Even Odd" might be to remind us of these facts – as is proper to a genuine catharsis – and to rid ourselves of them.

281   ALEXANDER TZONIS AND LIANE LEFAIVRE
from "The Grid and the Pathway" (1981)

With this brief yet discerning essay, Alexander Tzonis and Liane Lefaivre revisit the issue of regionalism and project it into the 1980s. The subject of the article is presented in its first subtitle, "An Introduction to the Work of Dimitris and Susana Antonakakis," two Greek architects whose work was being reviewed. But the broader purpose of the analysis is found in the essay's second subtitle, "With Prolegomena to a History of the

Alexander Tzonis and Liane Lefaivre, from "The Grid and the Pathway," in *Architecture in Greece* 15 (1981), pp. 176–8.

Culture of Modern Greek Architecture." Tzonis and Lefaivre begin by identifying two earlier stages of regionalism in Greek architecture: the first more or less coinciding with the picturesque movement of the eighteenth century; the second found in the nineteenth-century nationalist strands of historicism (classicism) growing out of Greek political independence from Ottoman rule. The third stage of "critical regionalism" is a more complex phenomenon with its artistic roots spread across Greek culture, including the earlier architectural work of Dimitris Pikionis. It is critical because it has roots internationally in earlier criticisms of modernism, in sources as diverse as Lewis Mumford and Team 10.

The development of critical regionalism in Greece was full of difficulties and contradictions. There was always the danger of abandoning the more difficult critical approach for a sentimental utopianism, making architecture an easy escape to the rural Arcadia, poor but honest.

There was also a strong resistance to development by these groups who saw that their interests would be curtailed by an advancement of the Welfare State. Critical regionalism could very easily succumb to such an opposition and be absorbed by it. These difficulties and contradictions we find expressed most visibly in the work of D. Pikionis.

Pikionis has been a true pioneer of the critique of modernism. Aldo van Eyck evidently once mentioned that he ought to have been considered as the first member of Team X and Mumford[1] unhesitatingly includes his work as one of the best examples of regionalism.

If his work very often slips into soft reconstructions of the *fermes ornées*, next to such examples, however, there is an explosion of tragic and critical spirit.

The dissenting spirit of Pikionis finds its best expression in the design of the path around the hill of Philopappus. Pikionis puts into action here the program of the epigones of the modern movement who, in reaction to the dehumanising effects of the modernist escapades, embodied in the formalism of International Style, asked for the rehumanisation of architecture, for "a place made for an occasion" instead of one made as abstract space.[2] Pikionis proceeds to make a work of architecture free of technological exhibitionism and compositional conceit – so typical of the main stream of architecture of the 1950's – a stark naked object almost dematerialised, an ordering of "places made for the occasion" unfolding around the hill for solitary contemplation, for intimate discussion, for a small gathering, for a vast assembly.

To weave this extraordinary braid of niches and passages and situations, Pikionis identifies appropriate components from the lived-in spaces of folk architecture, but in this project the link with the regional is not made out of tender emotion. In a completely different attitude, these envelopes of concrete events are studied with a cold empirical method as if documented by an archeologist. Neither is their selection and their positioning carried out to stir easy superficial emotion. They are platforms to be used in an everyday sense but to supply that which, in the context of contemporary architecture, everyday life does not. The investigation of the local is the condition for reaching the concrete and the real, and for rehumanising architecture.

But the path is not only a facility. As in the work of A. Constantinidis, it is a cultural object; it carries with it a commentary about contemporary architecture, life, society. It is a moral statement that this petrified stream of passages and places, these "vessels of life" carry; even when empty, they have a voice. It is a protest against the destruction of community, the splitting of human associations, the dissolution of human contact.

The pathway pattern emerges in the work of the Antonakakis, as a shorthand version of the vast stream of the Philopappus hill, as a miniature which preserves the ideals and organising principles in an individual building, a house, an apartment, even a room. Thus it brings to mind the saying of Alberti – once more quoted by a Team X member – that a house and a city have an equivalent structure.

Indeed, the pattern comes very close to the search by the members of Team X[3] for an architecture that grows out of movement and meeting, a search which leads to the development of the elements of "stem" and "infrastructure", and to Chermayeff's conception of the building as a set of hierarchies, of separation and mixing, target points and exchange knots.[4] It also recalls the preoccupation with process and stasis across a line of circulation, preoccupation that characterised the Japanese architects[5] and American "action architecture"[6] during the 1960's. These were all critical efforts directed against ailing modernism, in an attempt to sustain the humanistic spirit of modern architecture.

The pathway, in the case of the Antonakakis, is never an abstract principle of organisation, a network through which people only flow. As in the work of Pikionis, the components come out of the concrete lived-in places for meeting that we find in local, popular architecture: doorsteps, passages, courts. They have a memorable shape and notable position in human associations; they have a history and belong to a social life.

The pathway is the backbone from which each place grows and to which each place leads. As in the case of the grid, it may control also aspects of microclimate, the flow of air, the view or the course of service lines; but its primary role is to be a catalyst of social life. Every time its circuit is layed down and every time one passes through it, it can be seen as the reenactment of a ritual, the confirmation of the human community and a criticism of the alienating effects of contemporary life. Together with the grid, the pathway is a commitment to architecture as a cultural object in a social context.

The designs of the Antonakakis are deeply rooted in the developments of modern Greek architecture. They are in fact mainly the product of the marriage between patterns derived, as we have seen, from the work of two other Greek architects, of two other regionalist efforts. But as in the case of the painting of Tsarouchis, merging the tradition of Parthenis with Kontoglou, and as in the poetry of Seferis, bringing together Solomos and Cavafy, more than an imitation, this debt places the work of the Antonakakis inside the dialectic of Greek culture and makes it the next step forward. The regionalism of the Antonakakis differs from the efforts of A. Constantinidis and Pikionis in moving further away from an attachment to a nostalgic utopian attitude and in avoiding regressions to an escapist historicism. The regionalism of the Antonakakis is much the same as Mumford's. From the patterns of the Antonakakis a new building typology emerges which is neither arbitrary nor positivist or "documentary". It is far from the recent contentless formalistic typology whose lofty claims to objective, rationalist and universal value only serve to cover up a yearning for the security of a forlorn, law-and-order paternalistic past.[7]

To some degree, the Antonakakis typology might bring to mind the pattern languages of Christopher Alexander.[8] But the identification does not rely exclusively on empirical observation; nor is the pattern perpetuated in a non-commital manner. Both grid and pathway come close to reflecting the particular historical condition through which they have passed and they are clearly engaged in a critical framework. The typology at hand, therefore, has not rejected a historical and social context; it approaches to some extent what may be called a "realistic" typology.

Certainly, critical regionalism has its limitations. The upheaval of the populist movement – a more developed form of regionalism – has already brought to light these weak points. No new architecture can emerge without a new kind of relations between designer and user, without new kinds of programs. There is a serious retardation in relation to both these aspects, not only in most projects of critical regionalism and in the work examined here, but in the current situation of Greek architecture.

Despite these limitations, critical regionalism is a bridge over which any humanistic architecture of the future must pass, even if the path may lead to a completely different direction. We should be grateful that the work of the Antonakakis has contributed considerably in constructing this bridge. It is of a unique significance not only to Greek architecture but also to contemporary architecture in general.

NOTES

1 Lewis Mumford, *The City in History,* New York 1961, εἰκ. 10 καί σ. 79.

2 Aldo van Eyck, στό Oscar Newman (ἐπιμ.), *Documents of Modern Architecture,* New York 1961, σ. 28.

3 A. Smithson (ἐπιμ.), *Team Ten Primer,* Λονδίνο 1965.

4 S. Chermayeff καί C. Alexander, *Community and Privacy,* Νέα Ύόρκη 1965. S. Chermayeff καί A. Tzonis, *Shape of Community,* Λονδίνο 1971.

5 N. Kurokawa, "Architecture of the Road", *Kenchiku Bunka,* Ἰαν. 1963.

6 G. Kallman, *Architectural Forum,* Ὀκτ. 1959, σ. 132–7.

7 Ἀναφερόμαστε στήν τυπολογία ὅπως τή χρησιμοποιεῖ κυρίως ὁ Aldo Rossi. Βλ. A. Vidler, "The Idea of Type", *Oppositions* 8, Νέα Ύόρκη, ἄνοιξη 1977. G. Argan, "Sull concetto di tipologia architettonica", *Progetto e destino,* Μιλάνο 1965. A. Rossi, *L'architettura della città,* Πάντοβα 1966.

8 C. Alexander, *A Pattern Language,* Νέα Ύόρκη 1979.

282 DEMETRI PORPHYRIOS
from "Classicism Is Not a Style" (1982)

C ertainly one of the most widely read journals of the 1980s was *Architectural Design,* published in London by Andreas C. Papadakis. Each issue was guest-edited and centered on a theme (either historical or topical), and thus over a few years it gave substance to a number of clearly defined debates. One of the more important early essays to appear in the journal was this article by Demetri Porphyrios, whose title was also the theme of the issue. Porphyrios had just received his graduate degree from Princeton University and thus was familiar with trends in the United States; as a native of Greece, he also possessed sensitivity toward architecture and the architectural use of history that was not entirely in line with postmodern historicism. Thus in his essay, infused with the politics of Adorno's Frankfurt School, he harshly condemns the frivolity of what he terms "Modern Eclecticism." His alternative

Demetri Porphyrios, from "Classicism Is Not a Style," in *Architectural Design* 52:5/6 (1982), pp. 52–6.

is classicism, which for Porphyrios is not a style but rather a philosophy of life and a respect for tradition (finely adjusted to regional and cultural conditions) that one brings to design. He even concludes his essay with photographs of vernacular classical houses on various Greek islands.

Contemporary architecture bathes in the pantheistic limbo of eclecticism. Torn between the dilemma for a frenetic search for novelty and an inherited social mission for a popular language, architecture leafs through history caricaturing remembrances. Who influenced this trend? Virtually everybody: the American shingle style revival, the Arabic tracery of the Middle-East corporate capital, the lyrical neo-Corbusianism, neo-Constructivism, the Queen Anne revival, or the recent Hollywood 'neon'-classicism. The incomprehensibility of designed and non-designed kitsch is reified into culture by the literati of post-Modernism. Lack of common conviction and the ethos of indiscriminate toleration are mistaken for democratic freedom. Collective myth is systematically fractured into countless individualistic trivia, into fastidious and uncompassionate evasions of the human situation.

The tactics of Modern Eclecticism have been explicitly clear. In an effort to recapture culture – for it is only in culture that man can recognise authenticity and freedom – Modern Eclecticism has plunged into history. Utilising the techniques of metaphor and quotation, Modern Eclecticism has undertaken to construct culture overnight. And yet, the 'culture' it inaugurated has been a kind of shorthand, whereby through abbreviation, one caresses the confused multiplicity of stylistic genres, esteeming all, but none in particular, creating, in this way, the illusion of authenticity cherished by the collector of reproductions. Modern Eclecticism started as a quest for the lost 'aura' and has grown into the exemplar of industrial kitsch.

Suffusing the entire sense of Modern Eclecticism has been a readiness to believe that to aestheticise industrial kitsch was to invite its annihilation and to clear the way for a healthy moral growth of ideals. In their attempts to endow industrial kitsch with moral and aesthetic value, the literati of pluralism resorted mainly to two operative techniques: first, that of aestheticising the real; second, that of aestheticising the process of communication. The technique of aestheticising the real was, of course, well known to the Dadaists and Surrealists. For Dada and Surrealism, however, the aesthetisation of reality was fundamentally subversive and infused with a deep moral concern to regain a lost purity. Instead, for Modern Eclecticism the aesthetisation of the real has been an attempt to reify the strategies of an economy which, by its own nature and for its own priorities of profit, has been founded exclusively on the 'production of waste'. In that sense, Modern Eclecticism has attempted to aestheticise the real by moralising infatuation. For *'it is only infatuation . . . that does justice to what exists . . . Something that must be thought beautiful because it exists, is for that very reason ugly.'*[1]

The second strategy, that of aestheticising the process of communication, is fundamentally linked to the experience of kitsch. For kitsch demands of its users the violent jerkiness of advertisement. We know only too well the source of violence in advertisement: its rhetorical figures of speech are used not in order to please, or to incite us to reflect and thereby gain knowledge of our situation, (as is invariably the case with art) but rather in order to abbreviate a message and send it home by tapping our image of the world. Advertisement is by nature aggressive for when it shocks or tactfully seduces us, we are left with a pervasive feeling of having been cheated; while when due to its boldness or irrelevance it fails to touch us, we are left idiotically embarrassed since we, the interlocutors, have been trivialised.

In a manner similar to advertisement, Modern Eclecticism, by aestheticising the process of communication, links experience to mere anagnosis, reading or decodement. Such an architecture tolerates no aesthetic surplus that would resist consumption and thereby survive as the core of experience. Instead, figurative and syntactic sensuality takes on the quality of nightmare: weightless pediments, 'neon'-classical cornices, emasculated orders, metopes enfeebled by the arrogance of architects in search of fame, engrossed voussoirs, drooping garlands, frenzied volumetric articulations and androgynously historicist plans, in short all sorts of upholstered coteries degenerate into a mere 'style-heap'; without essential meaning other than the cult of 'irony' and the illusion of a make-believe culture. This is an architecture with no discourse; simply quotations, parentheses, brackets, and a kind of disjointed, insidious whisper that spells: advertisement.

It is exactly that quality of advertisement which accounts for Modern Eclecticism's ability to capture the illusion of culture cheaply. The word 'cheaply' should be understood here in its most literal sense. By focusing exclusively on the techniques of communication at the expense of tectonic *Logos*, Modern Eclecticism did not have to address the fundamental problem that all architecture had to face when confronted with industrial production: namely, that of reconciling *construction* with *style*.

Instead, the theoretical and enacted formalisation of the 'decorated shed' has functioned exactly as a strategy for discriminating between shelter and symbolism; that is, between need and myth. The principle of the 'decorated shed' provided for a system of thought which could isolate the budgets to be allocated to shelter and symbolism, exactly at a time when the excesses of Brutalism were stirring a certain disquietude amidst the circles of capital investment. One should be reminded here that Brutalism was an attempt to reinstate an 'aura' to the mute reality of industrial production by aestheticising the latter's abstract emotive possibilities. In that sense Brutalism was doubly suspect: both because of its abstract, non-communicative idiom (as the Eclectics maintained) and because of its dangerous – to the building industry – commitment to individualise the standard unit of industrial production.

The principle of the 'decorated shed', however, while encouraging a figurative enrichment of modernist construction, safeguarded against the reorganisation of the building industry that any ontological fusion of construction with style would have necessitated. A reorganisation that would have upset all three levels of the building industry: capital expenditure, skilled labour, and profit distribution. By means of an intuitively resourceful twist, the 'decorated shed' took the modernist precept of 'flexibility' and displaced it from the realm of spatial distribution to that of symbolic attribution. 'Pragmatics, Technics and Semantics' were to be defined by Modern Eclecticism as three independent layers of the architectural experience; as three independent budgets to be shifted around in a game which aimed at delectable fantasy at minimum cost.

The predicament of contemporary architecture, therefore, is our twofold inheritance: a) the semantically mute elements of industrial production – inherited from Modernism, and b) the semantically expendable historicist signs of industrial kitsch – inherited from Modern Eclecticism.

This raises, in my opinion, the crucial problem we face today: if there is a polar opposition between the economic priorities institutionalised by mass industrial society and the yearning for an authentic culture that would sustain individual freedom in public life, under what qualifications is it possible to practise architecture at all? Paradoxically, the only possible critical stance that architecture could assume today is to construct slowly an ontology of building that would contain a mythical representation of itself. To construct, that is, a *tectonic* discourse which, while addressing the pragmatics of shelter, could at the same time represent its very tectonics as myth.

It is from such a perspective that classicism should be re-evaluated today: not as a borrowed stylistic finery but as an ontology of building. Renouncing novelty, ephemeral pleasurability, consumable iconographic individualism, and unmediated industrial production, we make an urgent plea for closing architectural discourse towards the constructional logic of vernacular and its mimetic elaboration: classicism.

NOTE

1 Theodor Adorno, *Minima Moralia*, translated by EFN Jephcott (London: New Left Review Editions, 1974) pp. 76–7.

283 VITTORIO GREGOTTI
from "The Obsession with History" (1982)

Vittorio Gregotti first honed his critical talents on the staff of *Casabella* in the late 1950s under the editorial leadership of Ernesto Rogers. History and regionalism were thus prominent themes in his early formation, but — unlike the efforts of such early colleagues as Aldo Rossi and Giorgio Grassi — Gregotti resisted the reductivist aspects of Italian Rationalism and sought out a more modest tectonic grounding for his designs, which shifted into high gear in 1974 with the founding of Gregotti Associati. In building this multidisciplinary design firm into one of the largest in Europe, Gregotti also found the time, between 1982 and 1995, to serve as the directing editor of *Casabella*, which allowed him to become an active critic of contemporary developments. This essay on history speaks not to the necessary historical tradition within which good architecture must develop, but rather to the superficial way history in the early 1980s was now being begged, borrowed, and stolen in the rush to overturn modernism. It was one of the few cautious statements amid the polemical bravado of the time, and it set the basis for his more sustained criticisms of the coming years of an architectural discipline divorced from its environmental and social needs.

Nowadays an architectural magazine is an instrument unconnected with the times. I am referring here neither to the mere existence of other means of mass communication which can be managed in simpler or more articulate ways nor to the deliberate bias which

Vittorio Gregotti, from "The Obsession with History," in *Casabella* 478 (March 1982), p. 41.

accompanied the "raison d'être" of the classical avant-garde movements, but, rather, to the considerable influence of these magazines in falsifying what is at stake in the field of architecture itself. The attribution of this factor simply to the production processes of these magazines or to demands of mass market culture, would not be the whole truth.

The architects who, even if as "amateurs", used to be directly involved in the problems of their tradition up to the 1950s (and here, perhaps, my generation provides the clearest example), have handed over this task to specialized historians. Now, with very few exceptions, it is only specialists who deal with architectural press, who manage the magazines and see to their publication. It should also be noted that there has never been such a wealth of historical studies on architecture as in this period. Never have so many important specialists been trained at schools concentrating on the history of architecture, so that historians seem to consider the preoccupation with contemporary fact almost a minor concern.

These specialists have come to form a separate group from architects with a separate culture but simultaneously a new class of clients for the architects themselves; a class of clients with highly peculiar features and special requirements as far as the nature of the publishing material is concerned. This class of special clients has been thriving increasingly and beyond all expectations and, in recent years, has gained considerable power, which architects must virtually always acknowledge in order to have access to authority, notoriety, success and so on.

This phenomenon introduces the most conspicuous obsession dominating architectural design of latter years and reflected, and magnified by the distorting mirror of the specialized magazines: the obsession with history. This idea is somehow symmetrical to another idea which has been haunting contemporary culture for more than half a century: the obsession with novelty. The awareness of history's complexity, hence a critical awareness of architecture, was one of my generation's more difficult and important achievements. However, its value has gradually shifted and eventually reached a point where its meaning has been completely upset.

Never, as in these years, architects (and I specially mean those architects who consider their activity as a true liberal profession, i.e. as an activity involving responsibility both of a creative and intellectual kind) have been obsessed by the question of history. Or, more correctly, never has the obsession with history been as apparent as in latter years: it may be defined the shadow over contemporary design.

Of course, reflection would indicate that the shadow of history is also behind the polemical statements of the more inflamed of the classical avant-garde movements. However, the main concern then was to direct one's work against – i.e. vis-à-vis history: namely beyond its shadow, in the light of its reason and dialectics, rather than in the enchantment of its depth.

How could anyone forget that "angel of history" running forth while turning its eyes to the past, carried away by the wind of time, in the poetic and tragic image drawn by Klee and described by Benjamin in his famous passage? This image of history has now been replaced by a far more conciliatory one: history as the mother's womb, as a continuous flux, hence as the locus of replacement, of one's legitimation, of reconcilement with the past. The problem of the relationship with the past is no longer one of comparison, but one of consensus. Thus, even the preoccupation with symbolism, characterizing contemporary research carried on in the field of design, is discarded as sheer nostalgia.

Historical material is increasingly being used in design: it has shifted from an ideological to a stylistic, evocative, demonstrative instance of a rejection of contemporaneity rather than of novelty. The tradition itself of the "Modern Movement" is often adopted only stylistically and, therefore, neutralized as an ideal standpoint. The idea of a "design method" – resulting from Husserl's development of the notion of "essence" – is opposed to composition, imitation, analogy or quotation as a principle.

The uncertainty of the present is so marked, the opportunities for identification so few, the authentic is buried so deeply that the primacy of pure collective behaviour (whose acceptance has become another widespread design ideology) seems to be challenged only by the authority of history, as crystallized in its more conventional moments, as the only ones which should govern the access to truth. Here, too, any attempt to attribute this phenomenon to the underemployment of architects, especially of the younger ones, for whom drawing has become the only possible means of expression, would amount to a half-truth.

I believe that this period's obsession with history is, somehow, the answer to the loss of integrity of architecture. The integrity of architecture requires the existence of real relationships. The breakdown of these relationships with the world of needs, production, urban growth, collective meaning, tradition itself and professional practice correspond to their projection onto an imaginary plane of historical conjecture.

I can easily imagine the readers' smiles. What does the "reality" of today's society mean exactly? Can anybody know or judge it as a whole? Of course not: the contradictory signals resulting from the complexity of society prevent us doing so. Yet a confused, muddled trend does exist, which no intellectual can escape, to which he must respond through interpretations, never mind how partial and allusive, often conjuring up that which does not exist. Instead, a wide gap has formed between reality on the one hand and the construction of architecture on the other. This gap is presently unfittingly filled by the various parties engaged in political and economic plunder, which have turned it into a ground for their raids and for oppression.

So, what is the answer? There is no answer except reverting to the uncertainty of reality, maintaining "a total lack of illusions about one's age, yet supporting it relentlessly". How to revert to "enduring reality" is, undoubtedly, a very complex theoretical and ideal matter; this becomes apparent as soon as one goes beyond reality's empirical, tangible surface and defines it in terms of deliberate choices and projects, as a "concrete utopia", a "principle of hope", to borrow Ernst Bloch's beautiful expression (today such terms are so much out of fashion as to appear either naïve or self-interested). But it is also a constructive effort, a problem concerning the choice of tools and methods.

In the course of thirty years – during which the obsession with history emerged and developed – the belief has taken root that architecture cannot be a means for changing social relationships; but I maintain that it is architecture itself that needs, for its very production, the material represented by social relations. Architecture cannot live by simply mirroring its own problems, exploiting its own tradition, even though the professional tools required for architecture as a discipline can be found only within that tradition.

284 ALBERTO PÉREZ-GÓMEZ
from *Architecture and the Crisis of Modern Science* (1983)

Also conceived in a contrary way to the architectural atmosphere of the early 1980s was *Architecture and the Crisis of Modern Science* by the Mexican-born Alberto Pérez-Gómez. The phenomenological theme of the book – the rationalization of the design process through the instrumental approaches of such theorists as Claude Perrault and Jacques-Nicholas-Louis Durand – seemingly would have little import for contemporary issues, but, as this excerpt from his introduction shows, the ramifications of scientific rationalism still intrude on architectural design. Pérez-Gómez is concerned above all with meaning, the mytho-poetic meaning that resides within our existential understanding of the world. Hence all attempts to recapture meaning through a quick reading of history or excessive conceptualization must always ring hollow in the end. Meaning rather springs from a living mythology.

The Rational Horizon

The present work argues that modern architecture, and the crisis it faces, has its roots in a historical process touched off by the Galilean revolution, a process whose development is marked by two great transformations, the first of which occurred toward the end of the seventeenth century, and the second, toward the end of the eighteenth.

In the first transformation, the assumption, which had been inherited from medieval and Renaissance cosmology, that number and geometry were a *scientia univeralis*, the link between the human and the divine, was finally brought into question by philosophy and science. At the same time, technique and the crafts were freed from their traditional magical associations. In architecture, this laid the basis for a new approach. Architects began to consider their discipline a technical challenge, whose problems could be solved with the aid of two conceptual tools, number and geometry.

But in the eighteenth century, the transcendental dimension of human thought and action was sustained through the myth of Divine Nature. This myth lay at the root of Newtonian natural philosophy. The eighteenth century rejected as fiction the closed geometrical systems of seventeenth-century philosophers, but accepted Newton's empirical methods as universally valid. The influence of Newton paved the way for the systematization and mathematization of knowledge, a knowledge that held that immutable, mathematical laws could be derived from the observation of natural phenomena, and that would eventually take on the form of nineteenth-century positivism. Implicit in eighteenth-century Newtonianism, though to the modern mind it may seem thoroughly empiricist, was a Platonic cosmology, usually complemented by some form of deism, in which geometry and number had transcendental value and power in and of themselves. Architectural theory

Alberto Pérez-Gómez, from *Architecture and the Crisis of Modern Science*. Cambridge, MA: MIT Press, 1983, pp. 10–12.

absorbed the fundamental intentions of Newtonian science, and in doing so, it sidetracked earlier developments.

Around 1800 a second great transformation took place. Faith and reason were truly divorced. Scientific thought came to be seen as the only serious and legitimate interpretation of reality, denying any need for metaphysics. Euclidean geometry was functionalized. Infinitesimal calculus was purged of its residual symbolic content. Geometry and mathematics were now purely formal disciplines, devoid of meaning, value, or power except as instruments, as tools of technological intentionality.

It is around this time that the great obsessions of contemporary architecture were first clearly expressed. Practice was supposed to follow theory since theory now assumed that one day, through the fruits of mathematical reason, it would thoroughly control design and building. Eventually, the split between thinking and doing became a critical problem. The belief in the symbolic richness of the external world, in a Divine Nature that ultimately revealed its meaning through observation, was replaced by the notion, by now familiar, of the material world as a mere collection of inanimate objects. In such a framework, architecture could no longer be an art of imitation. Once it adopted the ideals of a positivistic science, architecture was forced to reject its traditional role as one of the fine arts. Deprived of a legitimate poetic content, architecture was reduced to either a prosaic technological process or mere decoration.

It was now that style, that is, the articulation and coherence of architectural "language," became a theoretical problem. The obsession to find immutable laws also invaded the field of aesthetics. But once architecture was reduced to the status of material structure, even the best architects concerned with the problem of meaning could not avoid insurmountable contradictions. History of architecture itself came to be regarded during the nineteenth century as the evolution of rational structure, and style, or *mélange*, was judged on purely rational terms. The problem "In which style should we build?" was not a problem of traditional architecture; an invisible *mathemata* had guaranteed the value of its work, and a symbolic intention had generated both structure and ornament. Only after 1800 do we find a distinction between "necessary" structure, that is, prosaic construction, and "contingent" ornament; the *École des Beaux Arts* did not merely continue a traditional "academic" practice in France. The transformation after Durand was profound, and the illusion of stylistic continuity between the eighteenth and nineteenth centuries has created much confusion in our understanding of modern architecture.

Even today, architects who recognize an affinity between their profession and art usually play formal games, but fail to understand the transcendental dimension of meaning in architecture. The lively discussions over the possibility of applying typological or morphological strategies in design also betray the same illusion. Before 1800 the architect was never concerned with type or integrity of a formal language as a source of meaning. Form was the embodiment of a style of life, immediately expressive of culture and perhaps more analogous to a system of gestures than to articulated language. Today architects often work under the absurd assumption that meaning and symbol are merely products of the mind, that they can be manufactured a priori and that they possess somehow the certainty of number.

285 KENNETH FRAMPTON
from "Towards a Critical Regionalism: Six Points for an Architecture of Resistance" (1983)

B y the early 1980s Kenneth Frampton's theory was turning a new page. His earlier, Adorno-inspired critiques of late capitalism and consumer culture were not abating, nor was his respect for the ideas of Hannah Arendt, Paul Ricoeur, and Martin Heidegger. But the essay of Alexander Tzonis and Liane Lefaivre on regionalism, as well as the earlier arguments of Hamilton Harwell Harris, now combined to move his theory toward the idea of critical regionalism – for him doubly defined through the notion of place and architectural tectonics. If Frampton did not coin the term "critical regionalism," he at least gave the idea a new twist as a strategy of resistance: resistance to what he perceived to be the increasingly technocratic dehumanization of late twentieth-century society. Here was also his response to the figurative postmodernism of the early 1980s, which Frampton counters by exalting the work of Alvar Aalto and Jørn Utzon, among others.

Architecture can only be sustained today as a critical practice if it assumes an *arrière-garde* position, that is to say, one which distances itself equally from the Enlightenment myth of progress and from a reactionary, unrealistic impulse to return to the architectonic forms of the preindustrial past. A critical arrière-garde has to remove itself from both the optimization of advanced technology and the ever-present tendency to regress into nostalgic historicism or the glibly decorative. It is my contention that only an arrière-garde has the capacity to cultivate a resistant, identity-giving culture while at the same time having discreet recourse to universal technique.

It is necessary to qualify the term arrière-garde so as to diminish its critical scope from such conservative policies as Populism or sentimental Regionalism with which it has often been associated. In order to ground arrière-gardism in a rooted yet critical strategy, it is helpful to appropriate the term Critical Regionalism as coined by Alex Tzonis and Liliane Lefaivre in "The Grid and the Pathway" (1981); in this essay they caution against the ambiguity of regional reformism, as this has become occasionally manifest since the last quarter of the 19th century:

> Regionalism has dominated architecture in almost all countries at some time during the past two centuries and a half. By way of general definition we can say that it upholds the individual and local architectonic features against more universal and abstract ones. In addition, however, regionalism bears the hallmark of ambiguity. On the one hand, it has been associated with movements of reform and liberation; ... on the other, it has proved a powerful tool of repression and chauvinism. ... Certainly, critical regionalism has its limitations. The upheaval of the populist movement – a more developed form of regionalism – has brought to light these

Kenneth Frampton, from "Towards a Critical Regionalism: Six Points for an Architecture of Resistance," in *The Anti-Aesthetic: Essays on Postmodern Culture*, ed. Hal Foster. Seattle, WA: Bay Press, 1983, pp. 20–1.

weak points. No new architecture can emerge without a new kind of relations between designer and user, without new kinds of programs. . . . Despite these limitations critical regionalism is a bridge over which any humanistic architecture of the future must pass.

The fundamental strategy of Critical Regionalism is to mediate the impact of universal civilization with elements derived *indirectly* from the peculiarities of a particular place. It is clear from the above that Critical Regionalism depends upon maintaining a high level of critical self-consciousness. It may find its governing inspiration in such things as the range and quality of the local light, or in a *tectonic* derived from a peculiar structural mode, or in the topography of a given site.

But it is necessary, as I have already suggested, to distinguish between Critical Regionalism and simple-minded attempts to revive the hypothetical forms of a lost vernacular. In contradistinction to Critical Regionalism, the primary vehicle of Populism is the *communicative* or *instrumental* sign. Such a sign seeks to evoke not a critical perception of reality, but rather the sublimation of a desire for direct experience through the provision of information. Its tactical aim is to attain, as economically as possible, a preconceived level of gratification in behavioristic terms. In this respect, the strong affinity of Populism for the rhetorical techniques and imagery of advertising is hardly accidental. Unless one guards against such a convergence, one will confuse the resistant capacity of a critical practice with the demagogic tendencies of Populism.

The case can be made that Critical Regionalism as a cultural strategy is as much a bearer of *world culture* as it is a vehicle of *universal civilization*. And while it is obviously misleading to conceive of our inheriting world culture to the same degree as we are all heirs to universal civilization, it is nonetheless evident that since we are, in principle, subject to the impact of both, we have no choice but to take cognizance today of their interaction. In this regard the practice of Critical Regionalism is contingent upon a process of double mediation. In the first place, it has to "deconstruct" the overall spectrum of world culture which it inevitably inherits; in the second place, it has to achieve, through synthetic contradiction, a manifest critique of universal civilization. To deconstruct world culture is to remove oneself from that eclecticism of the *fin de siècle* which appropriated alien, exotic forms in order to revitalize the expressivity of an enervated society.

286 MARCO FRASCARI
from "The Tell-the-Tale Detail" (1984)

T he currents of architectural thought can be affected by many things, but only rarely are they influenced by the "discovery" of the labor of a single, recently deceased architect, whose work had spanned a half-century. Yet this was the case with the newfound interest in the early 1980s in the work of the Venetian Carlo Scarpa, who revealed a way of conceiving and construing a regional architecture altogether alien from the postmodern

Marco Frascari, from "The Tell-the-Tale Detail," in *VIA 7: The Building of Architecture*. Philadelphia: Graduate School of Fine Arts, University of Pennsylvania and MIT Press, 1984, pp. 30–1.

culture of the times. Scarpa was a "modernist" with design roots going back to the 1920s, but he was sufficiently removed from media centers, and sufficiently arcane in his highly symbolic vocabulary to have eluded notice for many decades. Thus when his powerful tectonic language became newly revealed in the 1980s, a few years after his death in 1978, it underscored among other things the imaginative power of detailing as a tectonic device in its own right, as Marco Frascari shrewdly relates in this essay. Frascari, after graduating from the University of Venice in 1969, worked in Scarpa's office and later became a teaching assistant.

Scarpa's architecture can be generically classified as the merging of the principles of the organic architecture as expressed by Frank Lloyd Wright with a learned distilling of Veneto craftsmanship with a blend modern and ancient technologies. However, the definition is inadequate; whereas Scarpa's understanding of Wright's architecture was passive, based on an appreciation of photographs and drawings, his understanding of Veneto craftsmanship was active, based on his daily working and dealing with the stonecutters, masons, carpenters, glassmakers, and smiths of Venice. The result is a modern architecture that is more than rational structures and functional spaces. The teaching of functionalism is present in Scarpa's work, but the functionality is mediated by the search for representation and expression through the making. Scarpa's architecture stands against the bare structure of logic; it stands for the union of *res* and *verba*, that is, for the union of representation and function. This concept rules Scarpa's architecture from structure to expression. In his architectural objects the *technè* of the *logos*, the construing, becomes the manner of production of signs that are the details. The *logos* of the *technè*, the constructing, which results from the expression of Veneto craftsmanship, becomes the dialectical counterpart in the generation of the details as signs. Scarpa's buildings show indeed a constant search set between the actual form (the built one), and the virtual form (the perceived one). The constant manipulation of the discrepancies between virtual and actual forms is the method used for achieving expression. "In architecture," Scarpa once said, "there is no such thing as a good idea. There is only expression."[1]

The analysis of Scarpa's detail can be satisfactorily managed visually only by a continuous comparison between drawings and built objects, on the one hand, and the historical, practical, and formal reference that generated any single detail, on the other. It is also necessary to see Scarpa's details from two different sides. On one side, his detailing is the result of interfacing of design and craftsmanship on the site and of the constant "sensorial verification" of details during the assembly of the building. Scarpa made a practice of visiting the building site during the night for verification with a flashlight, thereby controlling the execution and the expression of the details. In the normal daylight it would indeed be impossible to focus on details in such a selective manner. It is also a procedure by which the phenomenon of the indirect vision becomes an element in the process of decision in the design. The flashlight is a tool by which is achieved an analog of both the process of vision and the eye's movement in its perception field (with only one spot in focus and the eye darting around). Another Veneto architect, Piranesi, used the same technique in visiting the sites of the buildings he was going to survey and represent in his etchings of the *Antichita Romane*. To single out the "expression of the fragments," that is, the details, he used the light of a candle.[2]

On the other side, Scarpa's details are the result of an intellectual game performed on the "working drawings" that are the result of the interfacing of design and draftsmanship. That game is the matching of the construction of a representation with a construction of an edifice. The relationship between architectural drawings and buildings is generally thought of as a Cartesian representation based on visual matching of lines. However, Scarpa's drawings show the real nature of architectural drawings, that is, the fact that they are representations that are the results of constructions. They are a construing of perceptual judgments interfaced with the real process of physical construction of an architectural object. The lines, the marks on the paper, are a transformation from one system of representation to another. They are a transformation of appropriate signs with a view to the predicting of certain architectural events, that is, on the one hand the phenomena of construction and the transformation by the builders, and on the other hand, the phenomena of construing and the transformation by the possible users. Consequently, on the same drawing there are present several layers of thought.

A design is developed by the same technique in which the drawing is made. The continuous inference process on which the design process is based is transformed in a sequence of marks on paper that are an analog for the processes of construction and construing. The piece of drawing paper selected for supporting the slow process of the construction of a design presents concurrently vertical and horizontal sections, as well as elevations of the designed piece. These drawings are surrounded by unframed vignettes that analyze tridimensionally any joint of the object, as in a prediction of the role of each detail in generating the whole text and in the perception of them in the "indirect vision." Scarpa's drawings do not define future architectural pieces as a simple sum of lines, surfaces, and volumes. Rather they present the process of transformation of the details from one system of representation to another, from drawing to building.

NOTES

1   Carlo Scarpa, "Frammenti, 1926–78," *Rassegna* 7 (1981), p. 82.
2   H. Focillon, *Piranesi* (Bologna, 1962), p. 166.

287   RAFAEL MONEO
from "The Idea of Lasting" (1988)

R afael Moneo raised still another dissenting voice within the postmodern din of the 1980s. The architect had formed the first wave of the great resurgence of Spanish architecture that had begun in the late 1960s, and at the time of this interview with the editors of *Perspecta* he had just completed his widely acclaimed National Museum of Roman Art in Médina, Spain – built directly over the historical Roman site. The city had been the most important in Spain toward the end of the Roman Empire, and the artifacts that had been unearthed over

Rafael Moneo, from "The Idea of Lasting," in *Perspecta 24: The Yale Architectural Journal* (1988), pp. 154–5.

the years required a suitable place for display. Moneo responded with a spectacular series of brick walls axially penetrated with arches, in which the chaste materiality of the Roman forms was complemented with a soft ambiance of natural light. The "eternal" nature of this Roman-inspired design serves as a thematic backdrop to his comments of creating an architecture that is "lasting."

Editors

Do you think that the problem of materiality is different in recent architecture than it has been in the past?

Moneo

Yes, I believe so. I am very concerned about that. Not in the sense that it makes me sad, but rather in the sense that I am ready to accept that architecture can become something different from what it has been in history. I have the impression that buildings are going to last less well than they have in the past. This is not simply a matter of lack of solidity. There is a widespread yet largely unarticulated belief that buildings are going to disappear, and I share this sensation as well. Architecture is now prepared for being an ephemeral art. That is very evident in this world – particularly the United States, where the society is so sensitive to changes and advancements in building technology. That is one of the reasons why architecture today so frequently appeals to the superficial image of its predecessors; today's society does not believe in the lasting condition of its own creations. The initial impact of the building is what counts, not its long life. My point of view, however, is that this durability – this condition of being built to last – is very powerful. One must still fight for that. Of course, I understand that I am going against the mainstream in this, but I believe that from many points of view, it would be favorable to have more stable cities, more stable architecture, more durable and less ephemeral constructions. I realize that being against ephemerality is a very difficult issue, but that is the position which I have taken, with the awareness that I could be mistaken.

Editors

Could you explain what you mean by "ephemeral"? A literal definition might suggest that it refers simply to a condition of "not lasting." Since very few architects would advocate such a position, we assume you mean something different. Are you speaking of the ephemerality that concerns the world of ideas – the notion that architecture should somehow transcend the physical, or refer to an idea that is ostensibly more critical or of a higher order than the lasting quality of the building itself?

Moneo

I would say that in other times, ideas were realized through the building itself. Now it seems that these ideas don't exist except in a description of the process, and that once the building has been completed, it doesn't deserve to last. For those architects who believe that the most important issues at hand concern their own ideas, the problem of ephemerality is of no importance; you simply keep records of those ideas in other media. Others would argue, however, that by defining a project, you are providing life to a building, creating this new being that is going to be itself. Then the idea of lasting – the idea that this being must support itself – means that you are connecting the idea of permanence with the idea of architecture. If you believe that you are providing life to something that did not exist before, you are naturally trying to provide the longest life. From this point of view, I would say that I am trying to provide a long life to the buildings I have conceived. The idea of permanence has for me a value. Architecture is not simply the brilliant expression of an idea. After the architect has finished his work, the idea which motivated it is somehow dead, and at the same time, kept alive by the reality of the building. I believe that this reality of the building idea transcends into a new thing that should be sustained by itself.

It should be remembered that when we are speaking of buildings and ideas, we are exaggerating relationships. I would be in absolute agreement with the notion that buildings are charged with theoretical content, but I don't know exactly what kinds of ideas a building conveys. It is certainly true that buildings are done with ideological commitments, but I don't think buildings are mere translations of ideas. Sometimes you will find a particularly clear solution to the problems posed by a given building, but there are few that do not at least approach this condition. This is the contradiction we face: the more our buildings are about specifics, the more they can be submitted to ideas. However, people who speak about ideas in building do not want to consider their specificity in the contention that architecture conveys ideas.

When I speak of lasting and permanence – of an architecture that is not ephemeral – I mean only to emphasize the *actuality* of the building as its lasting domain. As one comes to understand that a building conveys its reality through the support of material, it becomes increasingly possible to will the long life of the building. There is no doubt that the work of the architect should be an expression of personal commitment, but once this commitment has been clearly expressed, one should not worry too much if it disappears from the reading of the work itself.

We are speaking of very slippery issues, concepts that each generation has considered, and continues to think about. From this point of view, I see architecture as always addressing the same questions throughout history. Each generation will try to answer this question of meaning in the work of architecture – what we are calling the reality of the building – in its own way. For some, this reality will be found in the fulfillment of perceived functional concerns, for others in the interpretation of program or in the investigation of typology. For others still, the reality of the building will be sought in its lasting tangible presence, which speaks about the architectural principles behind its construction. That is where I would like to be.

288 JUHANI PALLASMAA
from "Tradition & Modernity: The Feasibility of Regional Architecture in Post-Modern Society" (1988)

The Finnish artist Juhani Pallasmaa began his architectural practice in 1963 and his teaching career at the Helsinki University of Technology in 1965. Much of his time between 1974 and 1983 was taken up with his duties as the Curator and Acting Director at the Museum of Finnish Architecture. As a result he brought together a breadth of experience in nurturing an architectural philosophy, anthropologically augmented – like his spiritual mentor Aldo van Eyck – with travels to remote regions of the world. In Pallasmaa there is a strong resonance with the first wave of Finnish national pride that erupted around the start of the twentieth century, but there is also a quiet international sophistication. Pallasmaa's interpretation of regionalism (he prefers the terms "situational" and "culture-specific") holds nothing but disdain for the "quasi-intellectualisation" of "today's neurotic architectural climate." He rather insists upon restraint, asceticism, and what he terms traditional Nordic morality. This essay is not his first to consider the themes of tradition and modernity, but the distinction of two modernisms rather succinctly encapsulates his essential ideas. His pantheon of successful regional architects includes Luis Barragán, Alvaro Siza, Imre Makovecz, and of course Alvar Aalto.

The Two Modernisms

The First Modernism was a utopian, idealistic, purist and demagogic movement, which drew its artistic strength from an innocent faith in a future brought about by new architecture and art. It was a fighting movement with impetus and polemic. It believed in the possibility of cultural expansion and radical change, which could quickly lead to a humane, healthy and sane world.

The Second Modernism is a realistic view of culture unblinded by illusions. It has lost its innocent faith in an immediate victory of humanism and it sees its potential merely as a strategy of cultural resistance in slowing down undesirable anti-human development.

Stylistic change has been equally multi-faceted. The First Modernism aspired to immaterial and weightless movement, whereas the Second frequently expresses gravity and stability and a sense of materiality and earth. The return of earth and gravity as expressive means of architecture has more than metaphoric meaning; after its arrogant and utopian journey, architecture has returned to the safety of Mother Earth, back to the source of rebirth and creativity.

Juhani Pallasmaa, from "Tradition & Modernity: The Feasibility of Regional Architecture in Post-Modern Society," in *Architectural Review* 188:1095 (May 1988), pp. 32–3.

In its aspiration for pure plastic expression the First Modernism avoided symbolism, allusion and metaphor, which have become an essential part of the expression of the Second. As the first phase aimed at an impression of timelessness, new Modernism seeks an experience of time through material, memory and metaphor. The First Modernism admired perfection and finiteness, while unfinishedness, process and imperfection, are part of the new expression. The First Modernism aimed at perpetual innovation, the Second consciously uses stylistic borrowings. I want to stress, however, that the contemporary use of quotation takes place in two directions in history and it gives the past a new meaning as opposed to the one-directional appropriation of eclecticism. There is always an air of necrophilia in eclectic art because of its inability to resurrect the dead.

Motifs of Change

The motive forces behind the change are alterations in consciousness that have taken place during the past two decades and which are more radical than most of us are willing to accept. The Third World, the energy crisis, the university revolution, the development of mass-communication and data-processing are all part of the mosaic of change as well as the whole Post-Modern debate. But also an awareness of the dangers implied by the technical development and a disappointment with the achievements of Western democracy lie behind the Second Modernity.

The transformation of Modernity did not happen at once. Even in the early phases of Modernism, expressionist, organic and regionalist tendencies existed within the Movement. The momentum of the First Modernism began to run out in the '50s and the emerging change was revealed in the discussions of CIAM. Louis Kahn and Aldo van Eyck appeared as the most outspoken heralds of change. Kahn brought back the archaic and metaphysical dimensions and Van Eyck introduced an anthropological and structuralist view.

My view of continuous Modernity is based on a view of the dialectics of evolution which is more explanatory and hopeful than the popular thought of a bankruptcy of Modernity. Fundamentally I see Modernity as a dialectic view of culture that perpetually challenges and resurrects the past.

The New Tradition

The touching and optimistic vitality of early Modernism arises from its origins at the confrontation of tradition and reform. Modernity lost its spiritual depth through the generations, which accepted the style as a ready-made aesthetic without its cultural background and the continuity of tradition implied by Modernism.

The interdependence of architecture and culture has not been sufficiently recognised. The international, consumerist architectural journalism of today violently detaches buildings from their cultural context and presents them in an arena of individual architectural showmanship.

The Second Modernity has to relearn a way of seeing architecture as part of cultural tradition as well as analysing the timeless essence of architecture. It is also significant that the creators of First Modernism were themselves artists or collaborated closely with artists. The spiritual withering of Modernism is associated with the post-war generations that alienated themselves from the fine arts both through prevailing educational practice and shallow professionalism. The New Modernism of today seeks again inspiration from the soil of the arts.

289 CHARLES, PRINCE OF WALES
from "The Ten Commandments for Architecture" (1989)

Prince Charles, the heir to the British throne, became a phenomenon within British architectural circles in the 1980s with two addresses given in 1984 and 1987. In the first (a speech presented to the RIBA (Royal Institute of British Architects) on the occasion of its 150th anniversary), he voiced disdain for the course of British modernism since the conclusion of World War II and famously likened the proposed extension of the National Gallery on Trafalgar Square to a "monstrous carbuncle" on the face of a dear friend. In a second address given three years later, he harshly condemned the various competition schemes for the Paternoster area just north of St. Paul's Cathedral — once again for defacing the character of this historic area. He initially opposed both modern and postmodern tendencies with his ad hoc strategy of "Community Architecture" (taking the needs of ordinary people into account), but within a few years his opposition grew into a popular crusade to reclaim more rigorously the building traditions of Britain's historic past. These "Ten Commandments" grew out of his polemics for a popular BBC film, an exhibition, and a book entitled "A Vision of Britain." Many architects resented his intrusion into the architectural debate, but the vast majority of the British public, it seems, strongly supported his intervention.

At the opening of *A Vision of Britain*, the latest episode in the current architectural debate and the subject of a recent issue of AD 5/6 89, Prince Charles finally revealed his Ten Commandments (the ten principles on which we can build). Forming the centrepiece of the show, each commandment, reproduced here without comment, was accompanied by an evocative watercolour together with examples of the good and the bad.

THE PLACE
We must respect the land. It is our birthright and almost every inch of it is densely layered with our island history.

HIERARCHY
There are two kinds of hierarchy which need concern us here. One is the size of buildings in relation to their public importance. The other is the relative significance of the different elements which make up a building – so that we know, for instance, where the front door is.

Charles, Prince of Wales, from "The Ten Commandments for Architecture," in *Architectural Design* 59: 11–12 (1989), p. XIV. An expanded version appears in *A Vision of Britain: A Personal View of Architecture*. London: Doubleday, 1989.

SCALE

Man is the measure of all things. Buildings must relate first of all to human proportions and then respect the scale of the buildings around them. Each place has a characteristic scale and proportion: farmhouses in Nottinghamshire may be tall and thin and in Northumberland they may be low and squat. It is high, and out-of-scale buildings that are damaging.

HARMONY

Harmony is the playing together of the parts. Each building that goes beside another has to be in tune with its neighbour. A straggling village street or a wide city avenue which may consist of buildings belonging to different periods can look harmonious.

ENCLOSURE

One of the great pleasures of Architecture is the feeling of well designed enclosure. It is an elementary idea with a thousand variants and can be appreciated at every level of building from the individual room to the interior of St. Paul's Cathedral, or from the grand paved public square to the walled garden.

MATERIALS

Britain is one of the most geologically complicated countries in the world, and as a result it is one of the most beautiful. Our rich variety of building materials is a source of constant pleasure and surprise, for our villages and towns were built from what came closest to hand: stone in Northamptonshire, timber in Herefordshire, cob in Devon, flint in the Sussex downs, brick in Nottinghamshire. Each town and each village has a different feel, and fosters a fierce loyalty in those who belong there. We must retain this feeling; we must ensure that the local character is not permanently ended.

DECORATION

There seems to be a growing feeling that the modern functionalist buildings with no hint of decoration give neither pleasure nor delight. The training of the modern architect rarely encompasses the rules of ornament or the study of past examples of applied decoration. There is no longer a universal language of symbolism, and the gropings of some critics towards the imposition of meaning on what they call post modern architecture has been fairly unfruitful.

ART

While decoration is concerned with repetition and pattern, a work of art is unique. Why is it that contemporary artists play such a small part in the creation of our surroundings? Architects and artists used to work together naturally; today they are worlds apart. Look at so many of the great buildings of the past, where the architect needed the contribution of the artist to complete the splendor of his total vision.

SIGNS AND LIGHTS

Far too many of the marks of 20th-century progress take the form of ugly advertising and inappropriate street lighting, apparently designed only for the motor car. The car and commerce are both vital to the wellbeing of the country, but it is the junk they trail with them that we have to tackle.

People should be involved willingly from the beginning in the improvements of their own surroundings. You cannot force anyone to take part in the planning process. Legislation tries to make it possible for people to share some of the complex processes of planning, but participation cannot be imposed: it has to start from the bottom up.

290 ANDRES DUANY, ELIZABETH PLATER-ZYBERK, AND CHESTER E. CHELLMAN
"New Town Ordinances and Codes" (1989)

I n the late 1970s the architectural and planning firm of Duany Plater Zyberk & Co. (DPZ), based in Miami, began to design the new resort town of Seaside, Florida. The idea was to revive local Southern traditions of town planning by taking into account not only the humid climate of Florida but also the South's cultural values based on centuries of small-town life. After several years of study, the 80-acre master plan was incorporated in 1982 and by the late 1980s the first rave reviews of the new community – with designs by Steven Holl, Victoria Casasco, and Leon Krier, among others – were appearing in the media. Duany and Plater-Zyberk, in writing a new zoning ordinance for this community, had in fact transcended their immediate task and defined a design philosophy for pedestrian-scaled, tightly grained urban/suburban planning that would soon be christened "New Urbanism." The Seaside ordinance, in turn, became the basis for the generic TND (Traditional Neighborhood Development) Ordinance. Related to but still distinct from the efforts of Prince Charles in Britain, New Urbanism would have an enormous (and in many ways quite positive) impact on planning theory in the coming years.

The congested, fragmented, unsatisfying suburbs and the disintegrating urban centres of today are not the products of *laissez-faire*, nor are they the inevitable results of mindless greed. They are thoroughly planned to be as they are: the direct result of zoning and subdivision ordinances zealously administered by thousands of planning departments.

America since the war is the result of these ordinances – 'conventional' lot subdivisions in the 40s and 50s and Planned Unit Developments (PUDs) since. If the results are dismaying, it is because the current model of the city being projected is dismal. Today's ordinances dictate only four criteria for urbanism: the free and rapid flow of traffic; parking in quantity; the rigorous separation of uses; and a relatively low density of building. The latter two demand an amorphic waste of land, and car traffic has become the central, unavoidable experience of the public realm.

Andres Duany, Elizabeth Plater-Zyberk, and Chester E. Chellman, from "New Town Ordinances and Codes," in *Architectural Design* 59:11–12 (1989), pp. 71–2.

The traditional pattern of walkable, mixed-use neighbourhoods is not encouraged and, more often than not, inadvertently proscribed by some provisions of these ordinances. Designers find themselves in the ironic situation of being forbidden from building in the manner of our most admired historic places. One cannot propose a new Charleston or New Orleans without seeking substantial variances from current codes.

There are over 38,000 municipalities in the United States. Most of them are projecting their growth on the basis of ordinances which are virtual recipes for urban disintegration. There are not the means, nor is there time, to educate the hundreds of thousands of planners and administrators who are now active, of the needed changes. There is, however, a mechanism in place to effect the change efficiently; that is to change the ordinances themselves. Planners are not prepared to be re-educated, but they are accustomed to following the law. It is thus possible, by modifying these codes, to prescribe a more workable and rational urbanism. The Traditional Neighbourhood Development Ordinance (TND) is such an ordinance.

The TND Ordinance is a declaration for new neighbourhood planning to be guided by the sensible and desirable attributes of traditional neighbourhoods. The TND Ordinance promotes independence from the automobile by bringing the needs of daily living within walking distance of the residence. By reducing the number of automobile trips and the length of those trips, certain social objectives are achieved; increased personal time, reduced traffic congestion, and conservation of land and fuel. The TND Ordinance promotes security through neighbourliness. By walking instead of driving, citizens come to know each other and the bonds of an authentic community are established. The TND Ordinance promotes social integration of age and economic classes by providing a full range of housing types and commercial opportunities. Finally, the TND Ordinance promotes the democratic initiatives of education, recreation, health maintenance, child care, and public assembly by providing incentives for civic facilities.

1.   Intent

This ordinance is designed to ensure the development of open land along the lines of traditional neighborhoods. Its provisions adopt the urban conventions which were normal in the United States from colonial times until the 1940's.

Traditional neighborhoods share the following conventions:

- Dwellings, shops and workplaces, all limited in size, are located in close proximity to each other.
- A variety of streets serve equitably the needs of the pedestrian and the automobile.
- Well-defined squares and parks provide places for informal social activity and recreation.
- Well-placed civic buildings provide places of purposeful assembly for social, cultural and religious activities, becoming symbols of community identity.
- Private buildings are located along streets and squares forming a disciplined edge unbroken by parking lots.

Traditional neighborhoods achieve certain social objectives:

- By reducing the number and length of necessary automobile trips, traffic congestion is minimized and commuters are granted increased personal time.
- By bringing most of the needs of daily living within walking distance, the elderly and the young gain independence of movement.
- By walking in defined public spaces, citizens come to know each other and to watch over their collective security.
- By providing a full range of housing types and workplaces, age and economic class are integrated and the bonds of an authentic community are formed.
- By promoting suitable civic buildings, democratic initiatives are encouraged and the organic evolution of the society is secured.

Until the advent of postwar zoning ordinances, traditional neighborhoods were commonplace in the United States. Many survive as examples of communities which continue to be practical and desirable today.

PART IX   MILLENNIAL TENSIONS

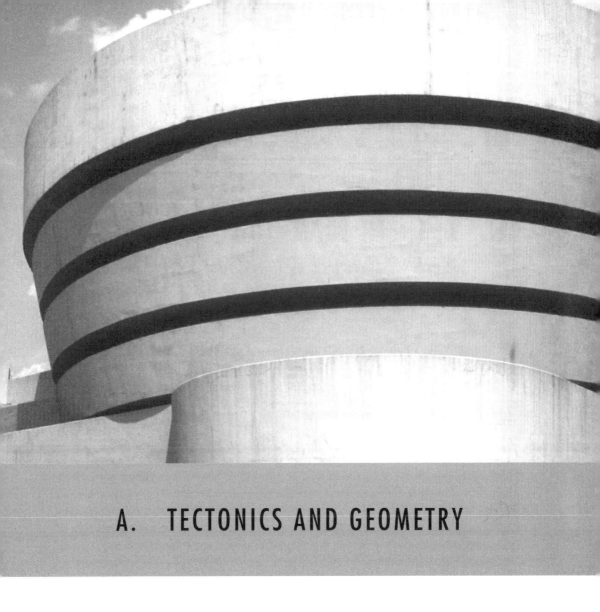

A. TECTONICS AND GEOMETRY

Introduction

The deconstructivist exhibition of 1988 and the broader movement of postmodernism achieved something of a critical mass by the end of the 1980s, such much so that much of the literary activity of the first years of the next decade was drafted in large part in response to these tendencies. Reactions came from older and newer sources. One clarion call was sounded by Kenneth Frampton's Rappel à l'ordre (call to order), which invoked this phrase used by those in the Purist movement earlier in the century in response to the perceived excesses of Cubism. By the time that Frampton had completed his tectonic theory with *Studies in Tectonic Culture* (1995), however, both Deconstruction and postmodernism had already lost much of their earlier appeal.

The causes for their decline are both manifold and interesting. As we shall see, a new environmental and ecological awareness strongly contested architecture's recent preoccupation with purely aesthetic issues. Yet from another direction came intellectual stimulation on a purely theoretical level. Thus a single new book by the French philosopher Gilles Deleuze vividly affected architectural thinking, as almost overnight the "disjunctions" and "dislocations" of Deconstruction came to be replaced by the new curvilinear surfaces of the "fold." New paradigms within the biological and physical sciences, such as theories of complexity and chaos, also intervened, raising the concepts of the "field" and "nonlinearity" as architectural possibilities. Behind this new wave of exploration lay, of course, the new digital softwares and technologies. The question now became how to ground these boundless spatial and structural possibilities within the realities of practice.

291 KENNETH FRAMPTON
from "*Rappel à l'ordre*: The Case for the Tectonic" (1990)

Frampton's *Rappel à l'ordre* was in many respects a homecoming for this influential Columbia professor – a return to the theme of construction and detailing that had been so prominent during his university years in the 1950s. Hannah Arendt, Martin Heidegger, and critical regionalism had been important stops along the way, as was his continuing allegiance to the ideological premises of the Frankfurt School. But a new awareness of nineteenth-century German tectonic theory now helped to clarify a position that had been evolving for several years. Frampton's immediate target here remains postmodern historicism.

I have elected to address the issue of tectonic form for a number of reasons, not least of which is the current tendency to reduce architecture to scenography. This reaction arises in response to the universal triumph of Robert Venturi's decorated shed; that all too prevalent syndrome in which shelter is packaged like a giant commodity. Among the advantages of the scenographic approach is the fact that the results are eminently amortisable with all the consequences that this entails for the future of the environment. We have in mind, of course, not the pleasing decay of 19th-century Romanticism but the total destitution of commodity culture. Along with this sobering prospect goes the general dissolution of stable references in the late-modern world; the fact that the precepts governing almost every discourse, save for the seemingly autonomous realm of techno-science, have now become extremely tenuous. Much of this was already foreseen half a century ago by Hans Sedlmayr, when he wrote, in 1941:

> The shift of man's spiritual centre of gravity towards the inorganic, his feeling of his way into the inorganic world may indeed legitimately be called a cosmic disturbance in the microcosm of man, who now begins to show a one-sided development of his faculties. At the other extreme there is a disturbance of macrocosmic relationships, a result of the especial favour and protection which the inorganic now enjoys – almost always at the expense, not to say ruin, of the inorganic. The raping and destruction of the earth, the nourisher of man, is an obvious

Kenneth Frampton, from "*Rappel à l'ordre*: The Case for the Tectonic," in *Architectural Design* 60 (1990), pp. 19, 20–1.

example and one which in its turn reflects the distortion of the human microcosm for the spiritual.[1]

Against this prospect of cultural degeneration, we may turn to certain rearguard positions, in order to recover a basis from which to resist. Today we find ourselves in a similar position to that of the critic Clement Greenberg who, in his 1965 essay 'Modernist Painting', attempted to reformulate a ground for painting in the following terms:

> Having been denied by the Enlightenment of all tasks they could take seriously, they (the arts) looked as though they were going to be assimilated to entertainment pure and simple, and entertainment itself looked as though it were going to be assimilated, like religion, to therapy. The arts could save themselves from this levelling down only by demonstrating that the kind of experience they provided was valuable in its own right, and not to be obtained from any other kind of activity.[2]

If one poses the question as to what might be a comparable ground for architecture, then one must turn to a similar material base, namely that architecture must of necessity be embodied in structural and constructional form. My present stress on the latter rather than the prerequisite of spatial enclosure stems from an attempt to evaluate 20th-century architecture in terms of continuity and inflection rather than in terms of originality as an end in itself.

In his 1980 essay, 'Avant Garde and Continuity', the Italian architect Giorgio Grassi had the following comment to make about the impact of avant-gardist art on architecture:

> ...as far as the vanguards of the Modern Movement are concerned, they invariably follow in the wake of the figurative arts...Cubism, Suprematism, Neoplasticism, etc, are all forms of investigation born and developed in the realm of the figurative arts, and only as a second thought carried over into architecture as well. It is actually pathetic to see the architects of that 'heroic' period and the best among them, trying with difficulty to accommodate themselves to these 'isms'; experimenting in a perplexed manner because of their fascination with the new doctrines, measuring them, only later to realise their ineffectuality...[3]

While it is disconcerting to have to recognise that there may well be a fundamental break between the figurative origins of abstract art and the constructional basis of tectonic form, it is, at the same time, liberating to the extent that it affords a point from which to challenge spatial invention as an end in itself: a pressure to which modern architecture has been unduly subject. Rather than join in a recapitulation of avant-gardist tropes or enter into historicist pastiche or into the superfluous proliferation of sculptural gestures all of which have an arbitrary dimension to the degree that they are based in neither structure nor in construction, we may return instead to the structural unit as the irreducible essence of architectural form.

Needless to say, we are not alluding here to mechanical revelation of construction but rather to a potentially poetic manifestation of structure in the original Greek sense of *poesis* as an act of making and revealing.

[...]

The dictionary definition of the term 'tectonic' to mean 'pertaining to building or construction in general; constructional, constructive used especially in reference to architecture and the kindred arts,' is a little reductive to the extent that we intend not only the structural component *in se* but also the formal amplification of its presence in relation to the assembly of which it is a part. From its conscious emergence in the middle of the 19th century with the writings of Karl Bötticher and Gottfried Semper the term not only indicates a structural and material probity but also a poetics of construction, as this may be practised in architecture and the related arts.

The beginnings of the Modern, dating back at least two centuries, and the much more recent advent of the Post-Modern are inextricably bound up with the ambiguities introduced into Western architecture by the primacy given to the scenographic in the evolution of the bourgeois world. However, building remains essentially *tectonic* rather than scenographic in character and it may be argued that it is an act of construction first, rather than a discourse predicated on the surface, volume and plan, to cite the 'Three Reminders to Architects', of Le Corbusier. Thus one may assert that building is *ontological* rather than *representational* in character and that built form is a presence rather than something standing for an absence. In Martin Heidegger's terminology we may think of it as a 'thing' rather than a 'sign'.

I have chosen to engage this theme because I believe it is necessary for architects to re-position themselves given that the predominant tendency today is to reduce all architectural expression to the status of commodity culture. In as much as such resistance has little chance of being widely accepted, a 'rearguard' posture would seem to be an appropriate stance to adopt rather than the dubious assumption that it is possible to continue with the perpetuation of avant gardism. Despite its concern for structure, an emphasis on tectonic form does not necessarily favour either Constructivism or Deconstructivism. In this sense it is astylistic. Moreover it does not seek its legitimacy in science, literature or art.

NOTES

1   Hans Sedlmayr, *Art in Crisis: The Lost Centre*, Hollis and Carter Spottiswoode, Ballantyne & Co., Ltd., New York and London, 1957, p. 164.
2   Clement Greenberg, 'Modernist Painting', 1965. Republished in *The New Art* edited by Gregory Battcock, Dalton Paperback, New York, 1966. pp. 101–2.
3   Giorgio Grassi, 'Avant-Garde and Continuity', *Oppositions* No: 21, Summer, 1980 IAUS & MIT Press, pp. 26–7.

292 TOYO ITO

"Vortex and Current: On Architecture as Phenomenalism" (1992)

After several years of working in relative obscurity, the architect Toyo Ito achieved acclaim in 1986 with his gleaming design for the "Tower of Winds" in Tokyo. Placed over an underground shopping center, the tower appears to be a solid aluminum cylinder by day, but by evening it transforms itself into an efflorescent and colorfully transparent sound and light chamber. Although Ito refers to this ephemeral character as phenomenalism in this essay, his futuristic architecture is often characterized by a sophisticated tectonic framework of glass, steel, and aluminum. The tent-like structure suggested here consists of a fabric stretched across a conic geodesic structural frame of exceedingly thin proportions.

The scene of a cherry-blossom viewing party, where people drink sake with friends on a red carpet under the trees and paper lanterns, or inside open tents, represents the fundamental character of Japanese architecture.

First of all, people come together to see the cherry blossoms in full bloom, and then primitive architecture (i.e., the carpet and the tent) is built for the event. It is not that the architecture is there at the beginning; on the contrary, it is the human act of getting together that exists first. It is only afterwards that architecture comes into being to envelope this action.

Such architecture does not confront, but assimilates nature completely. This is because the presence of cherry trees alone is capable of creating a unique space; with petals dancing in the wind, the beauty of the scene is visually enhanced. As carpets are spread on suitable ground, and tents are stretched, taking into account the favourable wind and sunshine conditions, architecture is installed as a minimal filter to visualise natural phenomena rather than disregard or suppress them. Cherry trees stretch their branches above the tents, petals incessantly fall on people who fully enjoy the pleasant scene within nature.

The party reaches its peak when at sunset dusk deepens and the scene is veiled in increasing darkness. Some start singing while others dance to the music. As the night wears on, the people, getting tired of pleasure, take down the tents and go home, leaving the cherry blossom floating in the dark like white clouds. The end of the event means the simultaneous end of the architecture as well.

It may be said that the architecture here is evoked by something extremely transient; like a piece of film wrapping the human body, it does not have much substance nor does it imply significant weight.

Designing architecture is an act of generating vortexes in the currents of air, wind, light, and sound; it is not constructing a dam against the flow nor resigning itself to the current. For instance, if a pole is erected in the river, changes are caused in the current around the

Toyo Ito, "Vortex and Current: On Architecture as Phenomenalism," in *Architectural Design* 62:9/10 (September-October 1992), pp. 22–3.

pole. If two poles are placed at a short distance from each other, the movement of water changes complicatedly due to their synergetic effect.

In nature, the place where people choose to gather is determined by the terrain, the location of the trees, or the direction of the wind. If the gathering place is in an urban setting, it is also selected by other considerations: the relationship among buildings, the flow of transportation and communication and the information exchange among all the constituents. In both natural and urban settings, however, when architectural elements such as posts and screens are placed within space, the natural currents – the flow of wind, sound, information, transportation, etc. – change, instantly causing small eddies around the installations. A vortex like this could be regarded as a minimal device to create a place for the gathering of people. In order to turn such a gesture into an architectural act, it is necessary to organise these architectural elements into an entity. The organisation may be a kind of structure or style in an abstract sense. When given a certain form, the place for an event becomes architecture. This is done so that the flow of phenomena will not end as merely a passing one, but is to be perpetuated while incorporated into a more stable and orderly system.

When architecture is defined according to the concept outlined above, people can remain within the surrounding currents of nature and/or the city, while at the same time situated in a framework of architectural form; they are enveloped simultaneously in two contradictory spaces: in an unstable, ephemeral phenomenon, as well as in a system which constantly seeks stability and continuity. Architecture today is bound to have a precarious existence; it has to keep a delicate balance in an ambiguous and unstable space, insofar as there is no longer a solid foundation on which architecture can stand firmly. Architecture seeking a passing phenomenon alone and resigning itself to the present with no resistance, will be immediately and completely consumed. Conversely, a piece of architecture which is anachronistically monumental, relying on a style that is no more than a cliché, would not attain empathy in our contemporary dynamic world.

A more appropriate act of architecture may be analogous to the linguistic art which extracts words as symbols from the fleeting feeling of an individual, gives them a style, and organises them. Vivid verbal expressions can be created only from the confrontation of a style with a direction while deviating from it to voice individual emotion. The same is applicable to architecture.

To give life today to architecture and let it breathe, it is vital to constantly generate vortexes of events and currents connecting these vortexes against the movement of formalisation which always seeks a rigidly fixed and stable order. It is critical to aim at spaces of unstable states which may be conducive to a movement or flow. Such spaces are also analogous to the physical movement of humans. In *Noh*, one of the traditional stage arts of Japan, comparable to *Kabuki*, the posture of the actor reveals a certain anxiety as his sight is extremely limited by his mask. His torso is inclined forwards and then lifted upwards throwing out his chest. Only when the actor assumes this posture can he attain a counter-force against the anxiety. Noh-dance is not a mere walk on the stage but a movement induced by the force drawn from inside the body. As Keiichiro Tsuchiya described, Noh-dance becomes a dynamic fluid and, as the actor undergoes a passive experience by wearing his mask, restructures the whole space of the stage.

According to a master of *kendo*, the basic technique of this martial art lies in the use of instability. More precisely, in kendo an unstable posture of standing on two feet is seen as an advantage rather than as a deficiency. Therefore, students are trained to move both feet simultaneously to remove the fulcrum of the body.

Just as the human body, supported by a stable structure, can generate force or movement only when in an unstable state, architecture also needs to create a flow of space against stability while constantly seeking stable forms.

The act of creating, or rather, choreographing a piece of architecture in a city like Tokyo is akin to playing chess. It is a completely unpredictable game. Buildings all around a particular construction site differ in volume, form, height, material and structure. Moreover, there is no way of knowing when these buildings will be demolished and replaced by something else. And this is also an endless game. What then is the context we can consider or hope for against such a fleeting urban scene as background?

In a chessboard-like urban space such as ours, what we can achieve with any of our next moves is merely to create a temporary, tense relationship. In other words, what we can do is simply to throw in a new vortex to stir or stimulate the space and to induce a new flow.

A new vortex is like a tent for the improvised theatre on a vacant lot. We don't need any other forms of architecture apart from those which, like video images, appear for an event and disappear when the event ends. Tokyo no longer requires the lasting stability of formalistic expressions, let alone the permanence of monuments.

293 GILLES DELEUZE
from *The Fold: Leibniz and the Baroque* (1993)

I n *A Thousand Plateaus* (1979), the French philosopher Gilles Deleuze first explored his distinction between smooth and striated space, presaging his concept of the "fold." In this later book, which first appeared in France in 1988, Deleuze considers this new spatial realm by exploring Gottfried Leibniz's notion of a monad (irreducible ontological entities lacking spatial parts but with perceptions and appetites) through the concept of folding. This idea of Leibniz, Deleuze argues, informs not just his philosophical thought but the entire baroque era in which he wrote – that is, Leibniz's concepts cannot be understood outside of the curvilinear or involuted shapes of baroque architecture, to take but one example among the sciences and arts. And whereas the fold for Leibniz possessed a metaphysical dimension (joining the soul to the mind), the idea also possessed the material dimension of a pleat or crease, a joining but also a division of matter. Such thinking finds a parallel with something that several architects found very appealing in the early 1990s: the exploration of warped or complex curvatures in virtual space.

Wölfflin noted that the Baroque is marked by a certain number of material traits: horizontal widening of the lower floor, flattening of the pediment, low and curved stairs that push into space; matter handled in masses or aggregates, with the rounding of angles and avoidance of

Gilles Deleuze, from *Le Pli: Leibniz et le baroque* (1988), trans. Tom Conley as *The Fold: Leibniz and the Baroque*. Minneapolis: University of Minnesota Press, pp. 4–6.

perpendiculars; the circular acanthus replacing the jagged acanthus, use of limestone to produce spongy, cavernous shapes, or to constitute a vortical form always put in motion by renewed turbulence, which ends only in the manner of a horse's mane or the foam of a wave; matter tends to spill over in space, to be reconciled with fluidity at the same time fluids themselves are divided into masses.[1]

Huygens develops a Baroque mathematical physics whose goal is curvilinearity. With Leibniz the curvature of the universe is prolonged according to three other fundamental notions: the fluidity of matter, the elasticity of bodies, and motivating spirit as a mechanism. First, matter would clearly not be extended following a twisting line. Rather, it would follow a tangent.[2] But the universe appears compressed by an active force that endows matter with a curvilinear or spinning movement, following an arc that ultimately has no tangent. And the infinite division of matter causes compressive force to return all portions of matter to the surrounding areas, to the neighboring parts that bathe and penetrate the given body, and that determine its curvature. Dividing endlessly, the parts of matter form little vortices in a maelstrom, and in these are found even more vortices, even smaller, and even more are spinning in the concave intervals of the whirls that touch one another.

Matter thus offers an infinitely porous, spongy, or cavernous texture without emptiness, caverns endlessly contained in other caverns: no matter how small, each body contains a world pierced with irregular passages, surrounded and penetrated by an increasingly vaporous fluid, the totality of the universe resembling a "pond of matter in which there exist different flows and waves."[3] From this, however, we would not conclude, in the second place, that even the most refined matter is perfectly fluid and thus loses its texture (according to a thesis that Leibniz imputes to Descartes). Descartes's error probably concerns what is to be found in different areas. He believed that the real distinction between parts entailed separability. What specifically defines an absolute fluid is the absence of coherence or cohesion; that is, the separability of parts, which in fact applies only to a passive and abstract matter.[4] According to Leibniz, two parts of really distinct matter can be inseparable, as shown not only by the action of surrounding forces that determine the curvilinear movement of a body but also by the pressure of surrounding forces that determine its hardness (coherence, cohesion) or the inseparability of its parts. Thus it must be stated that a body has a degree of hardness as well as a degree of fluidity, or that it is essentially elastic, the elastic force of bodies being the expression of the active compressive force exerted on matter.

NOTES

1   See Heinrich Wölfflin, *Renaissance et Baroque*, trans. Guy Ballangé (Paris: Poche, 196).

2   *Nouveaux essais*, preface (*New Essays in Human Understanding*, ed. and trans. Peter Remnant and Jonathan Bennett [Cambridge: Cambridge University Press, 1981], 59).

3   Letter to Des Billettes, December 1696 (*Die Philosophischen Schriften von Gottfried Wilhelm Leibniz*, ed. C. I. Gerhardt [Berlin: Weidman, 1875–90].)

4   Table de définitions (*Opuscules et fragments inédits de Leibniz*, ed. Louis Couturat [Paris: Félix Alcan, 1903]). And *Nouveaux essais*, II, chap. 23, § 23.

294   GREG LYNN

from "Architectural Curvilinearity: The Folded, the Pliant and the Supple" (1993)

In 1993 Greg Lynn edited a special issue of *Architectural Design*, in which he presented a lengthy excerpt from Deleuze's recently published book and to which he wrote an introduction. In many ways it represents the start of his architectural practice and theoretical influence. In his early writings Lynn staunchly opposed the rectangularity of modernist compositions and – with the aid of sophisticated computer modeling – he began exploring non-rectilinear geometries and biomorphic forms. His notion of a "blob" (a large, binary object, originally a computer program in which spheres could be joined and mutated with other spheres) became important to his topological thinking, but so did folds, pleats, creases, and other pliant forms produced by morphing or warping surfaces. Lynn opens this essay by contrasting his approach to Robert Venturi's argument for complexity and contraction, as well as to the fragmented and conflicting complexities of deconstruction. His suggestion that the idea of the fold was alien to the discontinuities of Deconstruction was also a challenge to the logic of such designs.

In response to architecture's discovery of complex, disparate, differentiated and heterogeneous cultural and formal contexts, two options have been dominant; either conflict and contradiction or unity and reconstruction. Presently, an alternative smoothness is being formulated that may escape these dialectically opposed strategies. Common to the diverse sources of this post-contradictory work – topological geometry, morphology, morphogenesis, Catastrophe Theory or the computer technology of both the defence and Hollywood film industry – are characteristics of smooth transformation involving the intensive integration of differences within a continuous yet heterogeneous system. Smooth mixtures are made up of disparate elements which maintain their integrity while being blended within a continuous field of other free elements.

Smoothing does not eradicate differences but incorporates free intensities through fluid tactics of mixing and blending. Smooth mixtures are not homogeneous and therefore cannot be reduced. Deleuze describes smoothness as 'the continuous variation' and the 'continuous development of form'. Wigley's critique of pure form and static geometry is inscribed within geometric conflicts and discontinuities. For Wigley, smoothness is equated with hierarchical organisation: 'the volumes have been purified – they have become smooth, classical – and the wires all converge in a single, hierarchical, vertical movement.' Rather than investing in arrested conflicts, Wigley's 'slipperiness' might be better exploited by the alternative smoothness of heterogeneous mixture. For the first time perhaps, complexity might be aligned with neither unity nor contradiction but with smooth, pliant mixture.

Both pliancy and smoothness provide an escape from the two camps which would either have architecture break under the stress of difference or stand firm. Pliancy allows architecture

Greg Lynn, "Architectural Curvilinearity: The Folded, the Pliant and the Supple," in *Architectural Design* 102 (March/April 1993), pp. 8–9.

to become involved in complexity through flexibility. It may be possible to neither repress the complex relations of differences with fixed points of resolution nor arrest them in contradictions, but sustain them through flexible, unpredicted, local connections. To arrest differences in conflicting forms often precludes many of the more complex possible connections of the forms of architecture to larger cultural fields. A more pliant architectural sensibility values alliances, rather than conflicts, between elements. Pliancy implies first an internal flexibility and second a dependence on external forces for self-definition.

If there is a single effect produced in architecture by folding, it will be the ability to integrate unrelated elements within a new continuous mixture. Culinary theory has developed both a practical and precise definition for at least three types of mixtures. The first involves the manipulation of homogeneous elements; beating, whisking and whipping change the volume but not the nature of a liquid through agitation. The second method of incorporation mixes two or more disparate elements; chopping, dicing, grinding, grating, slicing, shredding and mincing eviscerate elements into fragments. The first method agitates a single uniform ingredient, the second eviscerates disparate ingredients. Folding, creaming and blending mix smoothly multiple ingredients 'through repeated gentle overturnings without stirring or beating' in such a way that their individual characteristics are maintained. For instance, an egg and chocolate are folded together so that each is a distinct layer within a continuous mixture.

Folding employs neither agitation nor evisceration but a supple layering. Likewise, folding in geology involves the sedimentation of mineral elements or deposits which become slowly bent and compacted into plateaus of strata. These strata are compressed, by external forces, into more or less continuous layers within which heterogeneous deposits are still intact in varying degrees of intensity.

A folded mixture is neither homogeneous, like whipped cream, nor fragmented, like chopped nuts, but smooth and heterogeneous. In both cooking and geology, there is no preliminary organisation which becomes folded but rather there are unrelated elements or pure intensities that are intricated through a joint manipulation.

[...]

Along with a group of younger architects, the projects that best represent pliancy, not coincidentally, are being produced by many of the same architects previously involved in the valorisation of contradictions. Deconstructivism theorised the world as a site of differences in order that architecture could represent these contradictions in form. This contradictory logic is beginning to soften in order to exploit more fully the particularities of urban and cultural contexts. This is a reasonable transition, as the Deconstructivists originated their projects with the internal discontinuities they uncovered within buildings and sites. These same architects are beginning to employ urban strategies which exploit discontinuities, not by representing them in formal collisions, but by affiliating them with one another though continuous flexible systems.

Just as many of these architects have already been inscribed within a Deconstructivist style of diagonal forms, there will surely be those who would enclose their present work within a Neo-Baroque or even Expressionist style of curved forms.

295 PETER EISENMAN
from "Folding in Time: The Singularity of Rebstock" (1993)

I n the 1990s Eisenman and his approach to architectural design had also undergone further evolution. Here he seems to bow to his former student Lynn by following the excerpt by Deleuze with a presentation of the spatial idea behind his master plan for Rebstock Park, a housing estate in Frankfurt. His claim that this "new conception of space and time" will replace "static, figural space" is a bold one, curiously reminiscent of Sigfried Giedion's similar claim of a half-century earlier.

For Gilles Deleuze, the fold opens up a new conception of space and time. He argues in *Le Pli* that, 'Leibniz turned his back on Cartesian rationalism, on the notion of effective space and argued that in the labyrinth of the continuous the smallest element is not the point but the fold.' If this idea is taken into architecture it produces the following argument. Traditionally, architecture is conceptualised as Cartesian space, as a series of point grids. Planning envelopes are volumes of Cartesian space which seem to be neutral. Of course these volumes of Cartesian space, these platonic solids that contain the stylisms and images of not only classical but also modern and post-modern space, are really nothing more than a condition of ideology taken for neutral or natural. Thus, it may be possible to take the notion of the fold – the crossing or an extension from a point – as an *other* kind of neutrality. Deleuze goes on to argue that Leibniz's notion of this extension is the notion of the event: 'Extension is the philosophical movement outward along a plane rather than downward in depth.' He argues that in mathematical studies of variation, the notion of object is change. This new object for Deleuze is no longer concerned with the framing of space, but rather a temporal modulation that implies a continual variation of matter. The continual variation is characterised through the agency of the fold: 'No longer is an object defined by an essential form.' He calls this idea of an object, an 'object event.'

[. . .]

Place and time when no longer defined by the grid but rather by the fold, will still exist, but not as place and time in its former context, that is, as static, figural space. This other definition of time and place will involve both the simulacrum of time and place as well as the former reality of time and place. Narrative time is consequently altered. From here to there in space involves real time; only in mediated time, that is, the time of film or video, can time be speeded up or collapsed. Today the architecture of the event must deal with both times: its former time and future time of before and after and the media time, the time of the present which must contain the before and the after.

Peter D. Eisenman, from "Folding in Time: The Singularity of Rebstock," in *Architectural Design* 102 (March/April 1993), pp. 24–5.

JEFFREY KIPNIS
from "Towards a New
Architecture" (1993)

S
till another important article to appear in this issue of *Architectural Design* was that by Jeffrey Kipnis, who
goes so far as to raise the possibility of a "New Architecture." Kipnis argues that the two criteria for any new
architecture – new principles and new forms – are indeed in the early stages of being devised, and that they
coincide with the interest in non-Cartesian geometries, folded topologies, and the catastrophe theories of science.
Kipnis argues further that these new strategies are arising in response to two things: a general fatigue with
postmodernism, and the exhaustion of collage (a technique of Deconstruction) as a design paradigm. With that, he
divides the new design strategies into the groups of "InFormation" and "DeFormation." If the first strategy works
with traditional monolith boxes of modernism and informs their internal spaces with programmatic innovation, the
latter idea of DeFormation is more closely allied with non-Cartesian geometries and folded topologies.

At the beginning of this essay, I noted that a handful of recent projects offer specific terms
and conditions for a New Architecture. While, in general, these projects show a shift away
from a concern for semiotics towards a concern for geometry, topology, space and events, in
my view, they subdivide broadly into two camps, which I term DeFormation and InFormation. DeFormation, the subject of this volume, seeks to engender shifting affiliations that
nevertheless resist entering into stable alignments. It does so by grafting abstract topologies
that cannot be decomposed into simple, planar components nor analysed by the received
language of architectural formalism.

The strategy of InFormation, of which Koolhaas' Karlsruhe and Tschumi's Le Fresnoy are
exemplary cases, is to form a collecting graft, usually by encasing disparate formal and
programmatic elements within a neutral, modernist monolith. The resultant incongruous,
residual spaces are then activated with visual layering, programmatic innovation, technological effects and events.

Although both evolve from the same problem, the architectures of DeFormation and
InFormation are by no means simply collaborative. In general, both agree on certain
architectural tactics that can be understood in terms of Unger's criteria (as modified).
Both, for example, rely on such devices as box-within-box sections with an emphasis on
interstitial and residual spaces (vast, incongruous); also, both deploy monolithic forms and
avoid any obvious applied ornament or figurative reference (blank, intensive cohesion).

Yet the tensions between them are pronounced. While DeFormation emphasises the role
of new aesthetic form and therefore the visual in the engenderment of new spaces,
InFormation de-emphasises the role of aesthetic form in favour of new institutional form,
and therefore of programme and events. The event-spaces of new geometries tend to drive
the former, while the event-spaces of new technologies occupy the latter.

Jeffrey Kipnis, from "Towards a New Architecture," in *Architectural Design* 102 (March/April 1993), p. 43.

One of the pervasive characteristics of InFormation is its unapologetic use of the orthogonal language of Modernism. When post-modernist architecture first emerged, the formal language of Modernism was simply condemned as oppressive and monotonous – recall Venturi's 'Less is a bore'. Subsequently, that critique was deepened as architects and theorists demonstrated that, far from being essentialist, the language of Modernism constituted a sign-system. Once the demonstration that architecture was irreducibly semiotic was complete, the essentialist justification for the austere language of Modernism dissolved and the door opened to the use of any and all architectural signs in any and every arrangement.

InFormation posits that the exhaustion of collage is tantamount to a rendering that is irrelevant of all aesthetic gestures.[1] The architectural contribution to the production of new forms and the inflection of political space therefore can no longer be accomplished by transformations of style. Furthermore, InFormation argues that the collective architectural effect of the orthogonal forms of Modernism is such that it persists in being Blank; often stressing that blankness by using the forms as screens for projected images. Pointing is accomplished by transformations of institutional programmes and events. For, DeForm-ation, on the other hand, architecture's most important contribution to the production of new forms and to the inflection of political space continues to be aesthetic. Far from being Blank, DeFormation perceives the modernist language of InFormation as nothing less than historical reference and the use of projected images no more than applied ornament. Instead, DeFormation searches for Blankness by extending Modernism's exploration of monolithic form, while rejecting essentialist appeal to Platonic/Euclidean/Cartesian geo-metries. Pointing is accomplished in the aesthetics; the forms transform their context by entering into undisciplined and incongruous formal relationships. InFormation sees the gestured geometries of DeFormation as predominantly a matter of ornament style.

NOTE

1   Rem Koolhaas stresses this point in his short programme for the recent Shinkenchiku Housing competition, entitled, 'No Style', cf. JA 7.

297   MARK C. TAYLOR
from "Seaming" (1993)

I n this counterpoint to the Deluzean concept of the "fold," the theologian and philosopher Mark C. Taylor presents the concept of "seaming," in a lecture given at Columbia University in 1993. Taylor's principal argument is ethical: architecture, through its conceptual abstractions and populist attention to decoration, has lost its way and thus no longer supports any ethical and political mission. He counters with the Semperian notion of

Mark C. Taylor, from "Seaming," in Newsline: Columbia Architecture, Planning, Preservation 6:1 (September/October), p. 5.

the seam, which he feels draws emphasis away from form and surface, while at the same time serving as a metaphor for our anxious times.

The notion of the seam makes it possible to rethink the problem of surface and thereby to reassess important aspects of both modernism and postmodernism. In the absence of depth, there is nothing other than surface. Surface, however, is not necessarily superficial but can be infinitely complex. The complications of surfaces are a function of convolutions created by creases that cannot be explicated. The site of the crease is the seam. Appearances to the contrary notwithstanding, surfaces are neither seamless nor seemly but are always seamy. Stitching together what seems to drift apart, "seam" derives from the stem *s(i)u*, which means bind or sew and gives rise, inter alia, to the Sanskrit *sutra*, as well as the Greek *hymen*. As a noun, "seam" means, "a line or junction formed by sewing together two pieces of material along their margins; any line across a surface, as a crack, fissure, [fault], or wrinkle." "Seam" can also designate a "suture, scar or wound" – perhaps even a tear or tear. In its verbal form "seam" means either to join, "put together with;" or "to crack open, become fissured or furrowed."...

The seam cannot be placed, for it displaces everything, including itself. Since the displacement of the seam always entails contrasting rhythms, it locates as much as dislocates, and unsettles as much as settles. To mark the edge of the seam is to trace the evasive site where differences can be negotiated without being either repressed or synthesized. In the context of current debate, it is important to stress that though the seam is unavoidably complex, it is not simply a fold. The current fascination with folding in architecture represents a recognition of some of the same problems I am attempting to probe in these remarks. For example, the fold is presented as a possible alternative to the homologic of formalism and structuralism and the heterologic of decorative collage and post-structuralism. If, however, one reads the *texts* of theoreticians of the fold – the buildings *might* imply something altogether different – it is clear that a certain privileging of a certain homogeneity lingers. Most importantly, the fold always seems to be *smooth*. There are, to be sure, eddies of difference but these pockets do not disfigure the smoothness of the fold. A seam, by contrast, articulates the wound of difference whose scar can never be erased....

There is nothing to cover – always nothing to cover. Thus, there is only surface – surface upon surface, endless, infinite surface, which can be interrupted neither from the heights nor the depths. Nothing – nothing but surface. But, as I have insisted, surface is not superficial. The seaming of surface complicates the seamlessness of seeming. While never leaving the surface, seams disturb, disrupt and dislocate by faulting façades that once seemed pure and secure. The furrows of the seam creates pockets of resistance where difference need not become hostile opposition. To cultivate this furrow, it is necessary to realize that neither the politics of identity nor the politics of difference is acceptable. Both hegemony that represses difference and heterogeneity that rejects unity are irresponsible. The mean toward which I am pointing is not a dialectical third that holds out the promise of synthesis, reconciliation and harmony. To the contrary, the mean of the seam entails a nondialecticizable altarity that opens the space for the negotiation of differences that can never be reconciled. To live a life of seaming is to struggle to find ways to hold together what drifts apart and hold apart what drifts together....

Perhaps architects can rediscover their ethico-political mission by developing something like a *seamy architecture*. Such an architecture would be preoccupied with neither seamless forms and folds nor seemly ornaments but with the countless seams that articulate the surfaces on which we live. For the past several decades the radical move has been associated with the assertion of difference. While reclaiming difference has been critical, it is now precisely our differences that threaten to tear us apart. In this situation, it seems to me, the radical move shifts; we must once again ask how we can find areas of communality. The answer to this question is far from easy, for, as recent analyses of difference and others have demonstrated, the models of unity that have dominated Western – but not only Western – thought and practice tend to be either exclusive or totalizing. In both cases the inevitable result is exploitation and repression. The difficulty of the task of rediscovering a nontotalizing and nonrepressive commonality must not deter us from undertaking it. It is not too much to insist that our very survival hangs in the balance. Never has the need for ethically responsible and politically effective architecture been greater. From questions of rebuilding cities in which community is not impossible to intervening in the design of the electronet to insure that the virtual environment is not uninhabitable, architecture – and not only architecture – must think in ways and on a scale never before imagined.

298   GEVORK HARTOONIAN
from *Ontology of Construction* (1994)

The idea of the fold nevertheless retains a certain metaphysical resonance with aspects of poststructuralist theory. In this ambitious study, Hartoonian draws much of the historical material for his investigation from the tectonic theories of Karl Bötticher, Gottfried Semper, Adolf Loos, and Mies van der Rohe, but his reasoning is also imbued with the nihilistic "weak thought" of Gianni Vattimo, with the fabric analogies of Gilles Deleuze and Félix Guattari, and above all with Walter Benjamin's notion of "montage." The result is a conceptualization of the "tectonic" that strips it of any allegiance to place, while also focusing ever more intently on the detailing of construction. Hartoonian, in fact, views the idea of montage as "radicalizing the process of demythification of construction" – another indication for him that we have long crossed that unbridgeable postmodern divide.

The idea of montage parallels the art of construction; but montage also has to do with the secularization of cultural production. Developed out of cinematography and shared by different industries, the making of a montage is a process that permeates a structural-spatial experience far beyond that of nineteenth-century architects.

Montage also empties the natural content of an organic understanding of the concept of construction, or to put it in Benjamin's words, the aura of *techne* and the tectonic. To this end it is important to mention the similarities between montage and sewing; both modes of

Gevork Hartoonian, from *Ontology of Construction: On Nihilism of Technology in Theories of Modern Architecture*. New York: Cambridge University Press, 1994, pp. 26–7.

making bring together fragmented pieces, leaving the seam for ornamental purposes. This anology is interesting when one also notices the material differences between cotton felt and woven fabric within the textile industry. The latter follows the most conspicuous characteristics of a Cartesian vision of making: hierarchy, which is a sense of directionality from the lowest to the highest level, and symmetry. The former, however, made of diverse fabrics and without following any preconceived plan, can be spread in different directions and forms. Yet the spatial differences between felt and fabric discussed by Gilles Deleuze and Félix Guattari convincingly suggest the import of montage and its spatial constructs for the demythification of the classical discourse on construction.[1] For example, montage dispenses with the analogies that classicism draws between the human body and architecture, or the concept of the hearth as discussed by Semper, and restores the art of construction according to its contemporary perceptual and technical experience.

The historical progression of secularization should also figure in the discussion. It undermines filiative relations (and even the very concept of dwelling, which connects one to a place) in favor of affiliative or transpersonal relationships. We can therefore trace the transformation of relationships from organic to cultural,[2] and the same metamorphosis relates montage to the tectonic. Montage disconnects the relation of the whole to the part that is essential to the classical discourse on construction. Its concept of the whole is neither representational nor the logical result of a hierarchical composition of its parts, whether it is discussed in terms of the Vitruvian triad or the principle of three-part composition shared by some modern architects. Instead, the whole arises out of the juxtaposition of fragments and by the act of montage itself, and therein lies the dialectic between intention and construction, or as Semper would say, in the structural-symbolic. In this understanding of the whole, the coherent totality of architectural form is weakened, and montage plays a significant role in generating a tectonic form.

Montage reveals its tectonic form in the "dis-joint" (seam?), a weak form that distances sign from signifier. Traditionally, the function of the joint was to cover the anomalies of construction and to create the illusion of an aesthetic unity. The "dis-joint," in contrast, integrates material and detailing in such a way that the final form, somewhat like a well-crafted movie, does not completely hide the fragmented process of its production.

NOTES

1   Deleuze and Guattari, *A Thousand Plateaus*, (Minneapolis: University of Minnesota Press, 1987).
2   According to Edward Said, "If a filial relationship was held together by natural blood and natural forms of authority, the new affiliative relationship changes these bonds into what seems to be transpersonal forms – such as guild consciousness, consensus, collegiality, professional respect, class, and hegemony of a dominant culture. The filliative scheme belongs to the realm of nature and of "life," whereas affiliation belongs exclusively to culture and society." See Said, *The Words, the Text, and the Critic* (Cambridge, Mass.: Harvard University Press, 1983), p. 20.

299 MITCHELL SCHWARZER
from "Tectonics of the Unforeseen" (1996)

I n response to the appearance of Kenneth Frampton's *Studies of Tectonic Culture* in 1995, the critical journal *ANY (Architecture New York)* devoted a whole number to the theme of tectonics. The issue was organized and guest-edited by Mitchell Schwarzer, a professor at California College of Arts and Crafts and a specialist on nineteenth-century German tectonic theory. Whereas Schwarzer was quite critical of what he perceived to be the positivism inherent in Frampton's "neomodern" aesthetic, he goes on to argue — drawing support from the theories of Gianni Vattimo and Massimo Cacciari — that the strategies of "postmodern tectonics" (avant-garde in character) do not differ substantially from the *"arrière-garde"* principles of Frampton. Schwarzer, in this essay, is ultimately opposed to layering any theory of tectonics with either a spirit of authenticity or any guise of "essentialist metaphysics." Hence, postmodern tectonics, in his conceptualization, seems to assume a necessary aura of muteness.

Ephemeral and Durable

Especially in architectural circles that stress theory and extradisciplinary relations, the appeal of postmodern tectonics is great. Nonetheless, it would be a mistake to believe that postmodern sensibilities have neatly succeeded their modern predecessors. Aspects of modernist idealism and objectivity still underwrite much contemporary architectural criticism and design, especially projects that invoke the name *tectonics*. Rafael Moneo's Museum of Roman Art in Mérida, Spain is a good example of neomodern tectonics. The building's up-to-date structural system is concrete while its veneer counteracts presentness through an ancient brick régime. Continuities and differences over time are evoked through manipulations of new material relations (dry-jointed brick) and old material memories (Roman arches and barrel vaults). Moneo's philosophy of design is minimalist, overtly concerned with stark materiality and very much in favor of sending a message of architectural durability as opposed to ephemerality.

For neomodern architects and theorists, postmodernity, post-structuralism, and theories of representation have become the dark blots on the map of neomodern tectonics. Their economies are roundly criticized as those of surface rather than depth, artifice rather than authenticity, instability rather than stability. Epistemological complexity and perplexity are seen as a form of defeat.

Not so apparent at first glance, however, is the fact that postmodern tectonics is narrated through many of the same oppositions as neomodernism. Both neomodern and postmodern tectonics, today's so-called *arrière*- and avant-gardes, share a common foreboding. Tectonic theorists of a neomodern bent, their hopes for enduring aesthetic ideals, definable regional

Mitchell Schwarzer, from "Tectonics of the Unforeseen," in *ANY* 14 (1994), p. 65.

expressions, and crafted technological assembly notwithstanding, are apprehensive of the master narratives that defined the modern epoch. They simply do not share the hysteria at the loss of essence that resulted in earlier authoritarian modern projects. Frampton's theory of tectonics, for example, recognizes that constructional authenticity or regional vitality cannot be proven in terms of truth values or recourse to an eternal condition but must be supported by a resistant agenda that depends upon contestable, rhetorical powers. Quite distinct from earlier modern tectonics, Frampton places no faith in teleological destiny. Likewise, the earlier humanist distinction between high and low style has also been widely abrogated, neomodern tectonics generally does not discriminate between the noble and the humble, those actions relating to a divine spiritual world and those of a common human world.

For these reasons, postmodern tectonics is not as much of an anathema to neomodern tectonics as one might first think. After all, postmodern tectonics participates with neomodern tectonics in a rejection of any ideology of blind progress or global homogenization. Both camps share a view of the world as characterized by fragmentation, conflict, and otherness. Differences boil down to a choice between resolving (and often reviving historical associations) or dramatizing (and frequently experimenting with outmoded aspects of) architecture's ephemeral existences – not denying and overriding them as the moderns would have. What is more, resistance to commodity profit curves or corporate standardization is by no means a monopoly of neomodern tectonics. As we have seen, postmodern tectonics spreads in resistant directions from architecture's predicament within its socioeconomic employments like consumerism and family values.

Postmodern tectonics takes the critical stance that architecture can neither retreat from nor solve the problems of the world. An activity inflected by art and intellect as well as by technology and business, architectural construction must be immersed in the greater culture wars of its age. As was the case in the modern era, tectonics today must engage its own time, the unfamiliar forms, technical operations, and opinions of the turn of the millennium. Tectonics has always been a discourse on architecture through the terms of displacement, at earlier moments catapulted away from the unique everyday encounter by historical master narratives, now immersed in presentness through the penetration of consciousness by nonrational, nontranscendent figuration.

A postmodern tectonics of hybridized aesthetics and electrified structure is a much-needed critique of the values of authenticity, universality, and positivism that have underlaid architectural schemes of essentialism for much of the past two centuries. It displays the irreducible tension of human interaction and production in a world without divine God and human gods.

Consequently, the negative challenge facing all tectonic approaches is to resist the urge to fill in the antinomies of contemporary architectural existence with an essentialist metaphysics. The positive challenge is to enter into the gestures of these antinomies, to engage the representational zones of tension that are isotropic to the culture of construction. Tectonics is neither lasting authenticity nor thoughtless fragmentation. Rather, between these poles of argument, tectonics is accomplice to the sober and tipsy plots of construction, to virtuous craft and indecent exposure, to architecture's monuments to its unassimilable identity.

300 LINDY ROY
from "Geometry as a Nervous System" (1997)

T he fact that the journal *ANY* in the 1990s also devoted a special issue to a retrospective review of the theories of Buckminster Fuller underscores very well the "scientific" turn taken in architectural theory in this decade. Reinhold Martin, in his opening editorial remarks, spoke of Fuller's conception of architecture as "a kind of organism," while Lindy Roy, the South African architect based in New York, followed with this essay. Roy begins her piece by considering the neurobiological understanding of a "stimulus," but the dynamics of this complex function turn within a few pages to the interdisciplinary project of testing Swarm, a computer simulations project under development at the Santa Fe Institute. A better understanding of Fuller's notion of synergy, she argues, will lead us away from conceiving form as a static entity, and – similar to the symbiosis and cooperation recently being demonstrated in atomic and cellular life – to the understanding that form might be better seen as a set of organic relationships within a condition of dynamic equilibrium.

Swarm

"...*neither a thing nor a concept, but a continual flux or process.*" – William Morton Wheeler, "Ant Colony as an Organism," 1911.

Swarm, as a formalizable, mathematical entity owes its being to the synergy concept. A swarm is a network of distributed decision making: a real-time generator, processor, *and* integrator of stimulus-response patterns. A swarm takes form by integrating a multitude of individual performances. These performances are translated into patterned signals that permeate the swarm's entire field of operation. The signaling media and its means of transmission vary between one swarm aggregate and another. In economic markets, for instance, where endless data streams are instantaneously processed, prices transmitted via electronic networks are a form of feedbacksignaling that cues the activities of thousands of competitive agents. In insect colonies, on the other hand, all forms of cooperative interactive behavior (from foraging to nest building) are triggered by pheromones, hormonelike chemicals regulated by airborne gradients – not unlike the *Tonustäler* in von Uexküll's landscapes.

The idea of swarms as "super-organisms" or "collective brains" is hardly new, but the allusion misses the more interesting aspect of spontaneously organized apparatuses; from a matrix saturated with signal, interference, modulation, and cross talk – all of the stuff of communication – a single, albeit malleable form emerges, the one most likely to succeed in producing a particular global effect. If, as has been suggested by researchers, a swarm is in fact a model of a kind of brain, it is a brain whose cells are mixed in with the problem at

Lindy Roy, from "Geometry as a Nervous System," in *ANY* 17 (1997), p. 27.

hand. No single agent has a comprehensive overview of the entire field of activity – each depends on a continuous exchange of localized information. It is a form that persists because it constantly learns.

What now can be said about form? Since Fuller's so-called comprehensive design science, form can no longer, even in design disciplines, be said to be a thing but at the very least *a set of variable relations held in dynamic equilibrium*. Anticipatory design science consciously used nature as a model of successfully applied principles. It held that natural form was the physical record of *interrelated patterns of activity* occurring in time and space.

While design science certainly created the possibility for an entirely new framework for design, it could not but fail to reach its full potential within Fuller's rigid system where form was no more than the transparent demonstration of a static state of equilibrium. Once hyped as "the discovery of the coordinates of the universe," synergetics remained just that: another model of a coordinate system (the 90-degree Cartesian axis simply replaced by the 60-degree tetrahedron) not the transformative coordinating apparatus that Fuller sought.

The full force of Fuller's project can be understood as the attempt to develop an *integrative apparatus* possessing the capacity to establish *temporal* rather than mere physical stability. It is the rhythmic tiling of events in time that produces coherent form (witness von Holst's neural oscillators). Superseding the reactive neural system of the early 20th century, it is instead a complex *predictive nervous apparatus* capable of anticipating the physical and sensory consequences of a course of action that successfully integrates multiple processes in pursuit of a form for action.

301 STAN ALLEN
from "From Object to Field" (1997)

Deriving in part from Sanford Kwinter's discussion of "field theory," this essay by Stan Allen now brings together his design experiments of the 1990s under the same term. These are not determinate or overarching – the operations he suggests here are built on a series of spatial strategies and oppositions, often generated through computer modeling. The key is that the designer does not initially seek to impose any overall order, including a preconceived compositional arrangement of parts. Rather, the spaces between the objects subjected to these local forces (rather than to objects themselves) become the defining criteria. The seemingly random delineation of fields is never arbitrary, and local field conditions may in themselves suggest formal patterns. Field strategies thus seek to create a fluid architecture accessible to accident and improvisation, one opposed to semiotic or scenographic design, and one not necessarily hostile to the tectonic variables of this process.

The term 'field conditions' is at once a reassertion of architecture's contextual assignment and at the same time a proposal to comply with such obligations. Field conditions moves

Stan Allen, from "From Object to Field," in *Architectural Design*, 67:5/6 (May–June 1997), p. 24.

from the one toward the many: from individuals to collectives, from objects to fields. The term itself plays on a double meaning. Architects work not only in the office or studio (in the laboratory) but in the field: on site, in contact with the fabric of architecture. 'Field survey', 'field office', 'verify in field': 'field conditions' here implies acceptance of the real in all its messiness and unpredictability. It opens architecture to material improvisation on site. Field conditions treats constraints as opportunity and moves away from a Modernist ethic – and aesthetics – of transgression. Working with and not against the site, something new is produced by registering the complexity of the given.

A distinct but related set of meanings begins with an intuition of a shift from *object* to *field* in recent theoretical and visual practices. In its most complex manifestation, this concept refers to mathematical field theory, to non-linear dynamics and computer simulations of evolutionary change. It parallels a shift in recent technologies from analogue object to digital field. It pays close attention to precedents in visual art, from the abstract painting of Piet Mondrian in the 1920s to Minimalist and Post-Minimalist sculpture of the 60s. Post-war composers, as they moved away from the strictures of Serialism, employed concepts such as the 'clouds' of sound, or in the case of Yannis Xenakis, 'statistical' music where complex acoustical events cannot be broken down into their constituent elements. The infrastructural elements of the modern city, by their nature linked together in open-ended networks, offer another example of field conditions in the urban context. Finally, a complete examination of the implications of field conditions in architecture would necessarily reflect the complex and dynamic behaviours of architecture's users and speculate on new methodologies to model programme and space.

To generalise from these examples, we might suggest that a field condition would be any formal or spatial matrix capable of unifying diverse elements while respecting the identity of each. Field configurations are loosely bounded aggregates characterised by porosity and local interconnectivity. The internal regulations of the parts are decisive: overall shape and extent are highly fluid. Field conditions are bottom-up phenomena: defined not by over-arching geometrical schemas but by intricate local connections. Form matters, but not so much the forms of things as the forms between things.

Field conditions cannot claim (nor does it intend to claim) to produce a systematic theory of architectural form or composition. The theoretical model proposed here anticipates its own irrelevance in the face of the realities of practice. These are working concepts, derived from experimentation in contact with the real. Field conditions intentionally mixes high theory with low practices. The assumption here is that architectural theory does not arise in a vacuum, but always in a complex dialogue with practical work.

302 CECIL BALMOND
from "New Structure and the Informal" (1998)

The first part of Cecil Balmond's career (in relation to the 1990s) appears simply successful, if not exceptional. He was a structural engineer at the highly respected London engineering firm Arup, working in the same technological vein as his famous colleague Peter Rice. Sometime in the late 1980s, however, the Sri Lankan began to undergo an intellectual reinvention, from which he emerged in the late 1990s as one of the leading structural thinkers in the world – the inspirational force behind a number of renowned structural designs. If the sources of his transformation are as varied as Pythagoras, genetic research, and notions of chaos, his philosophy of design is as simple as the two terms "new structure" and "informal." Both definitions are found in this article prepared for the Italian journal *Lotus* in 1998, in which he also succinctly presents his notion of "subversion" – that is, the breaking down of traditional "cages" either by mutating or even seemingly eliminating structural forms. The "informal," for Balmond, is the nonlinear process of seeking out the creative solution, and the answer for this mystically inclined mind often lies in an emergent rather than a fixed patterning, where Newtonian absolutes are replaced by nonlinear translations of force through a dynamic field of local conditions and interiorly driven algorithmic rules. Here the application of organic principles without the emulation of organic forms creates a field of potentials in which asymmetrical ordering systems emerge and are then translated into novel structural and spatial solutions.

We make cages out of our structures. We want our buildings to have frameworks but out of a Cartesian compulsion we compartmentalize space into strict horizontals and verticals.

Our designs reinvent the topographies of rigid skeletons.

Locked in right angles, the assumption is of order as a rigorous delineation and within that the building as object. So the external boundary is set, and by grid and sub-grid a method of exact subdivisions begins; a diminution into regular, repetitive fixings of space. Within the rigidity nothing moves. Like soldiers on the parade ground everything is at arm's length, the formation of regiment being taken as more important than the individual impulse. The formal is taken as read and a regimental concept of order accepted as the status quo. The imagination is immobilized. We trap movement.

In the static perfection of the modernist cube, with its minimalist palette of glass and transparency, we see right into the emptiness of the container. Structure seems to have no response but to stand mute. In high-tech elaborations we see only the extension of a mechanistic tradition; steel mast and cable, structure as machine. In terms of space and configuration, inspiration seems to have given way to an overpowering technology. But is geometry this artificial wasteland or does it have some kind of animation, allowing the outcome of an intervention in its potential to be guesswork rather than a predestined plot? If there is life to this geometry perhaps we should go forward more cautiously, trading more on intuition, more on instinct than on the assumption of space being neutered, capable only of containerization.

Cecil Balmond, from "New Structure and the Informal," in *Lotus International* 98 (1998), pp. 76–9, 83.

In the irregular rhythms and diversity we see all around us, the real is highly complex; it is rich in entanglements. So why not look for characteristics that "seed" the complex and give starting points to an inner logic which could lead outwards to the idea of ensemble and coherence? Traditionally, A relates to B and then B to C in hierarchical connections of formal logic. But could the idea of A into B back into A back into B build on some kind of feedback loop? Why not structure as trace, as episode, as staccato or punctuation? Then as catalyst, the idea of *local* would arise; *juxtaposition* becomes rhythm; *hybrid* entities are taken as natural and positive and not as odd, freaky, or the exception. We enter a general domain of overlap where what is site specific, at a particular instant or viewpoint, may become order. Ambiguities arise, interpretation is the only way forward. There is no single reading of such a building.

The Informal

The informal is not random or arbitrary; it relies on overlap to bring forward a series of shifting certainties – its logic is contingent upon initial conditions. Chaos is seen as a succession of several orders, quite different to the idea we have of trapping the arbitrary and calling it order. The twisting in and out of a Moebius strip is informal. A roof that turns to wall and floor, a floor that is skin, where boundary does not mean border, is also part of it. Two columns out of step, side by side, of different shapes and material are part of it. Instead of regular formally-controlled measures, varying rhythms and wayward impulses take root. Opportunity is seen to give chance, a chance!

The classical determinism of Newton pictured force as an arrow, straight and true. It bridged the void in unwavering linearity – the fixed link of a rigid chain of logic. Now we see force differently, as a minimum path through a field of potential. Dependent on local conditions, that path may vary but the trajectory is based on moments of mutual cooperation, a simultaneous juxtaposition that charts a minimum path.

In the informal there are no distinct rules, no fixed patterns to be copied blindly. If there is a rhythm it is in the hidden connections that are inferred and implied but not noticed as obvious. The answers lie in the relationship between events. Hybrid situations are taken as valid starting points and not unfortunate accidents.

Two events close together are not seen as exceptional but as a dynamic that sends out particular vibrations.

Structural solutions that arise from the informal impart hidden energies to a building. The connectivity is improvising; the equilibrium put together in ad hoc instants. *The informal acts as an agent of release* and architecture is free from the traditional notions of fixed grid and locked in cage – the topography of such buildings is different.

What is new is the intuitive rational and a new kind of structure.

[. . .]

New Structure

New structure is a dynamic. Enquiring into form and configuration from first principles it admits into the solution the complex as *a priori*. New structure takes overlap and ambiguity as a basis for design and the stringent notion of order along Cartesian tramlines is discounted – a methodology that is taken as fixed, reductionist, and ultimately limiting in scope.

New structure animates geometry. It reawakens an original inspiration of form, enquiring of space itself as to its nature and interpretation. In this scenario buildings become rhythm and sequence and clash and confrontation; if symmetry is there it is in the active coming together of separate tendencies, in balance for only one moment. The traditional pursuit of external object cut by dissecting and unthinking subdividing grid is rejected. Instead, a holistic approach is taken of inner logic informing the whole. The imperative is in-to-out.

In the name of modernism, a final stripping down and denuding of form has taken place and "structure" relegated to mute submission. The result is a giving up of thought to blankness and transparency, glass and steel – evaporating substance and leftover cage; there is nowhere else left to go. Reductionism has reached its dead end. Design has deconstructed, and minimalism has become a reward label.

Twisted shameless multiplications of surface or texture of form are nowhere to be found. The desire is to conform and offer up constructions in orthodox containers, without the fun of elaborations – no syncopated rhythms, and none of the "irrational" and spontaneous. Why not a new multiplicity, the idea of a new gothic or romantic?

New Science

Surprisingly, new science offers a fresh start.

Rejecting the linear and hand-me-down logic of a top-down hierarchical thinking, new science openly embraces the complex. The nonlinear is adopted. What is new is the admittance of feedback as motive. There is overlap, and the simultaneous is empowered. Incredibly, such starting points of the chaotic are seen to lead towards stabilities and coherence, driven by internal self-organizing wills. The paradigm is one of emergence, a gathering together of disparate tendencies that move towards one expression of separate wills. Flying in the face of conventional ideas of pre-arrangement, new science proposes the plan instead as the starting point, and the resulting boundary as surprise. Order is only a transient part of the picture, on the edge of turbulence. Somehow able to come together by internal improvisations, order in the sense of organization and coherence is seen as a safe bet – arising out of the chaotic and unpredictable. Such ideas fly in the face of entropy and the permanent run down holy-grailed into us by the second law of thermodynamics. But then creativity has always been a surprise!

The world is complex and it shifts gear and jumps. We shy away from this difficulty because the mind has to bend around corners and the mathematics is difficult. But the power of modern computing is unleashing what was never before thought possible; we do not have to think anymore along tramlines or be contained to derived notions of linearity. There is a richness out there – we should delight in it. We should explore it.

The fallacy of a reductionist science has been to make us think that the whole can be cut into bits and then reduced down to one final bit – but something always gets lost on the surface of that cutting or splitting knife. Physics has taken us into this atomic and monadic world and now we find that reality blurs, and certainty, chameleon like, transforms into doubt. Is a particle a wave or is it the other way around? Is matter itself a particular vibration of overlapping multidimensional "strings" or a quantum jump out of the virtual?

The shadowy and the fantastic seem to be the new realities; virtual and nascent, rather than fixed and concrete. We want to understand, make linear relays and logical chains out of the complex, but in trying to remove uncertainty we remove the invisible glue that holds things together. Inevitably something gets lost.

Mathematics is racing forward with nonlinear dynamics high on the agenda. Given a starting point or initial sequence, improvisation and internal rhythms are calculated to lead to coherence. Economic crashes and heart attacks are explained. Research into quasi-crystals and amorphous forms question our hard fixed notions of boundary and structure. Biology is in the vanguard of the new science; chemistry and the other disciplines follow. Where is architecture?

New Science = New Architecture?

The current investigations and research of the new sciences are based on dynamic living systems. How then does it relate to architecture, built out of fixed forms and static structures?

One to one translation of the new science to a new architecture does not seem to be realistic – it only leads to mimicry. Copying nature or chaos ends up looking forced. What is more interesting is to look into the basis of the paradigm that embraces "risk," and the building up of internal processes that throw up conflict and clash. Ambiguities will arise, such a building will give separate readings due to overlap. One has to interpret as opposed to assume a preconcept.

Does it matter? Why not go on planning containers and repeating equalities and subscribing to static, fixed, ideals of symmetry?

I propose that more than the eye sees the body senses. In response to new structure we may find in the configuration of such network a deeper resonance than the superficial visual. Out of chaos we came; within us is a derived sense of order, not linear and logical, but odd and complex. Responding with one's instinct to raise ancient spells is important – sharpening one's intuition to investigate the runes of form a necessary act. Gaining an insight is important.

Conclusion

There are no fixed rules for new structure, the informal takes care of that. If there is a set rhythm it is in the hidden connections that are implied and felt but not seen, leading to the skewed and oblique or towards the regular and symmetric – it all depends on where one starts.

There is no one reading of such designs – ambiguity forces interpretation. Juxtaposition and hybrid situations are valid and not unfortunate accidents; on a small and intimate scale local actions are trusted to spread outwards and inform the whole. At some point coherence is reached and an "object" defined. Order, in this sense, is a travelling transient. The method is informal, the framework is new structure. The inspiration is new science.

303 BERNARD CACHE
from "Digital Semper" (1999)

Bernard Cache first took his degree in architecture at the École Polytechnique Fédérale de Lausanne, and later participated in Gilles Deleuze's philosophy seminars at the University of Paris. Since then he has explored the issue of design in various ways, from CAD systems to furniture design to architecture – now marshaled within the Paris design firm Objectile. Cache also possesses a keen fascination with the ideas of Gottfried Semper, which is a curious place to find someone who is perched on the leading edge of computer design and material technologies. But as the introductory paragraphs to this essay demonstrate, seemingly new ideas sometimes possess a lengthy pedigree worth considering. Cache weaves Semper's conceptual principles into contemporary practice with remarkable clarity and subtlety.

"Digital Semper." To put these two words together seems like a contradiction in terms. Starting with an analysis of the first word, however, I will try and dismantle the apparent contradiction.

L'atelier Objectile, which I created with Patrick Beaucé, experiments with technologies in architecture by focusing primarily on software development in order to digitally design and manufacture building components. Beginning with a period dedicated to building research, furniture design, and sculpture, we worked for more than ten years with the French company TOPCAD in designing complex surfaces in order to debug our developing software. Three years ago we created Objectile and started to focus our work on flat and supposedly simpler components like panels or doors in order to tackle the problems generated by the industrial production of varying elements.

Industrial production forces us to confront many basic problems like zero-error procedures and stress-free MDF panels. A key element in digital manufacturing is to avoid bending a panel

Bernard Cache, from "Digital Semper," in *Anymore*, ed. Cynthia C. Davidson. New York: Anyone Corporation, 2000, p. 191.

when machining one of its faces. Our experience now enables us to think of a fully digital architecture like our museum project and the pavilion we recently built on the occasion of the Archilab conference in Orléans. The four elements of this pavilion are the result of previous experiments with screens, panels, and tabletops. In that process, we noticed that our approach had a clear affinity to Gottfried Semper's theory as he articulated it in *Der Stil* (1863) not only because we come to architecture through the technical arts, or because we came to invent new materials in order to create new designs, but because our interest in decorative wooden panels is consistent with Semper's *Bekleidung Prinzip* (cladding principle). Even our investigations into the generation of software to map key elements of modern topology, like knots and interlacing, consist of a contemporary transposition of Semper's *Urmotive* or primitive pattern.

What does it mean today to refer to Gottfried Semper? Why, in 1999, should we look back to the 19th century just as everybody claims the 21st will be digital? And why focus on Semper, whose architecture seems to reveal nothing but the Renaissance historicism rejected by the Moderns? Are we not in a very different period? We live in an age not of iron but silicon. Why would we need to reconnect the end of our iron, concrete, and glass century to the history of wood, stone, clay, and textiles? Do we not run the risk of a new technological determinism, by which the information age, the so-called "third wave," would create a second break with the past, definitively negating any historical experience, leaving us with no alternative other than a choice between the dinosaurs and the space shuttle? Or should we not instead be reminded that information technologies themselves are deeply rooted in the past? The computer is not an Unidentified Flying Object that landed one day in a California garage.

B.   THE END OF THEORY?

Introduction

Since the 1960s, we have followed architectural theory pursuing an increasingly independent and often diverging path from architectural practice, one in which theory tended to draw many of its ideas from outside of architecture proper. Thus it was very predictable that a kickback was inevitable, that challenges would be put forward to theory's supposed philosophical autonomy. These challenges took several forms. One was the interest in tectonics, which, as we have seen, was proffered as a way to ground architecture in its constructional basis. Another was the continuing use of phenomenology as a way to refocus concern on the concrete experiences of architecture itself. Still a third way was suggested by the very dramatic changes overtaking the practice of architecture. Not only was the scale and pace of practice (its global reach) now exerting a profound pressure on designers, but so too was the level of technical sophistication required to market and manage these increasingly larger projects across the globe. Thus the 1990s was also characterized by a remarkable theoretical fallback to the true and trusted notion of pragmatism. None of this of course is to suggest that theory entirely collapsed — only that its supporters were now forced to restate its reason-for-being.

The new "Dutch School" of architects was prominent in this regard. The founding of the Berlage Institute in 1990 was predicated on bringing new substance and grounding to the debate, and thereby bringing to an end the hegemony of abstract critical reasoning. Several of the Netherlands' highly successful firms, such as OMA, MVRDV, and UN Studio, defined themselves as spontaneous, innovative, and multidisciplinary planning organizations with a major emphasis on research — specifically in opposition to earlier over-conceptualizations. This sea change, however, was not limited to the Netherlands, as within the United States an allied front began to form around similar concerns. Whereas this debate was scarcely concluded by the century's end, it nevertheless became very evident that theory was in the process of reconstituting its very premises. Such is the nature of the beast.

304 MOSHEN MOSTAFAVI AND DAVID LEATHERBARROW
from *On Weathering* (1993)

The startlingly simple thesis of this study — that "weathering inheres in all construction" — might seem self-evident. But when it is placed within the context of this particular period, with its large focus on the visual medium of architectural representation, the phenomenological thesis appears almost strikingly novel. Here the building is considered as a body endowed with a physical age and signs of memory. Mostafavi and Leatherbarrow underscore two other points as well. Not only do bad design and bad detailing have their fateful and unintended consequences, but the "soiling" patina of time can also be anticipated and exploited as a powerful design element in itself.

Weathering marks the passage of time. This time is not the moment of a pre-occupancy photograph; time's passage in architecture includes a building's inception, construction, and inhabitation. The project, too, endures *through* these phases. In construing an architectural project the introduction and consideration of the time of weathering brings the project closer to a condition of actuality based on its potential transformations through time. This condition of actuality and potential for staining and fault complements the ideality of the project, making it both independent of the passage of time and caught up within it. Thought of in this way, weathering brings the virtual future of a building into dialogue with its actual present, as both are entangled in its past.

This temporal structure of building can be compared to a person's experience of time. At every moment in one's life earlier times of infancy, childhood, youth, and all other stages up to now are still present, increasing in number yet unchanged and familiar, and subject to redefinition and appropriation. Never is one's past not present, nor is the individual's past ever cut off from the tradition of one's culture and the time of the natural world. Duration invokes recollection in each of its advancing moments. The differentiation of the present

Moshen Mostafavi and David Leatherbarrow, from *On Weathering: The Life of Buildings in Time.* Cambridge, MA: MIT Press, 1993, pp. 112–14.

(as something in itself) presumes the reality of the past as the context from which it has emerged. Every act preserves the coherence of temporal continuity against its theoretical disintegration into separate parts: past, present, and future. Yet one's sense of the past or of the future involves a reach out of the present into some time when it (one's present) was not yet, or some time when it will be no longer. Events in the past – at least our feelings, thoughts, tastes, and so on about them – "mark" the memory, like a signet on a "good thick slab of wax" said Socrates in *Theaetetus*. What remains from the past is a trace or impression of an event, not the thing itself as it existed when present. Likewise, mnemic experience in architecture is not of the present but of the past. The past in this sense is not a specific and limited period or time over and done with, rather it can be seen as "what has come to be."[1]

The fact of weathering inheres in all construction. No architect can avoid this fact; it was never escaped in the past, nor can it be in the present. Weathering reminds one that the surface of a building is ever-changing. While a potential nuisance, the transformation of a building's surface can also be positive in that it can allow one to recognize the necessity of change, and to resist the desire to overcome fate – an aspiration that dominated much of modernist architectural thought through its resistance to time. The preoccupation with the image or appearance of the building in current practice is in part symptomatic of this desire. Images are media of representation that communicate a building's style, character, and identity and are often thought to do so without change, like the printed word. This ironically vindicates Hugo: buildings have become like books because their images have attained the status of text, whether the text-image simulates historical buildings or not. What makes this ironic is that books themselves are "artifacts" that sustain multiple readings – as buildings always do.

The ideas of a project, hypothesized in sketches, drawings, and models, are its past, which will be soiled by the marks of weathering after construction. The effects of these marks can be retarded through inventive solutions. These solutions could be elements that direct or prevent the flow of water, or they could respond to the effects of the weather by creating situations that both recognize and utilize the ever-changing characteristics of materials as a way of renewing beginnings by allowing refinishing.

NOTE

1   David Farell Krell, *Of Memory, Reminiscence and Writing* (Bloomington, 1990), p. 14. Plato's account of memory is summarized fully and clearly in Jacob Klein, *A Commentary on Plato's Meno* (Chicago, 1989). The problem is cast in a historical perspective in Peter Munz, *The Shapes of Time* (Middletown, Conn., 1977); as well as George Kubler, *The Shape of Time: Remarks on the History of Things* (New Haven, 1962). Also useful is Edward Said, *Beginnings* (New York, 1985).

   Much recent reflection on memory elaborates phenomenological philosophy; see Erwin Straus, "Memory Traces," in *Phenomenological Psychology* (New York, 1966), pp. 75–100; Edward Casey, *Remembering: A Phenomenological Study* (Bloomington, 1987); David Michael Levin, *The Body's Recollection of Being: Phenomenological Psychology and the Deconstruction of Nihilism* (Boston, 1985); David Carr, *Time, Narrative, and History* (Bloomington, 1986); and most important perhaps, Paul Ricoeur, *Time and Narrative*, 3 vols. (Chicago, 1984–8).

305 JUHANI PALLASMAA
from "An Architecture of the Seven Senses" (1994)

Pallasmaa follows up his earlier support for regionalism and traditionalism with this essay, which explores the theme of perception and phenomenology in architecture. The seven named senses in the title are those of acoustics, tranquility, scents, touch, muscle and bone, bodily identification, and visual taste. The text, with its Heideggerian undertones, reads as if it could have been written several decades earlier, which can be interpreted as a sign of its timelessness as well as a timely return from what Pallasmaa perceives as the overabundance of attention in recent times given to the visual image or appearance of a building.

The architecture of our time is turning into the retinal art of the eye. Architecture at large has become an art of the printed image fixed by the hurried eye of the camera. The gaze itself tends to flatten into a picture and lose its plasticity; instead of experiencing our being in the world, we behold it from outside as spectators of images projected on the surface of the retina.

As buildings lose their plasticity and their connection with the language and wisdom of the body, they become isolated in the cool and distant realm of vision. With the loss of tactility and the scale and details crafted for the human body and hand, our structures become repulsively flat, sharp-edged, immaterial, and unreal. The detachment of construction from the realities of matter and craft turns architecture into stage sets for the eye, devoid of the authenticity of material and tectonic logic.

Natural materials – stone, brick and wood – allow the gaze to penetrate their surfaces and they enable us to become convinced of the veracity of matter. Natural material expresses its age and history as well as the tale of its birth and human use. The patina of wear adds the enriching experience of time; matter exists in the continuum of time. But the materials of today – sheets of glass, enameled metal and synthetic materials – present their unyielding surfaces to the eye without conveying anything of their material essence or age.

Beyond architecture, our culture at large seems to drift towards a distancing, a kind of chilling, de-sensualization and de-eroticization of the human relation to reality. Painting and sculpture have also lost their sensuality, and instead of inviting sensory intimacy, contemporary works of art frequently signal a distancing rejection of sensuous curiosity.

The current over-emphasis on the intellectual and conceptual dimensions of architecture further contributes to a disappearance of the physical, sensual and embodied essence of architecture.

[...]

Architecture, more fully than other art forms, engages the immediacy of our sensory perceptions. The passage of time; light, shadow and transparency; color phenomena, texture, material and detail all participate in the complete experience of architecture. The limits of two-dimensional representation [in photography, painting or the graphic arts], or

Juhani Pallasmaa, from "An Architecture of the Seven Senses," in *a + u* (July 1994), pp. 29, 41.

the limits of aural space in music only partially engage the moving sensations evoked by architecture. While the emotional power of cinema is indisputable, only architecture can simultaneously awaken all the senses – all the complexities of perception.

Architecture, by unifying foreground, middle ground, and distant views, ties perspective to detail and material to space. While a cinematic experience of a stone cathedral might draw the observer through and above it, even moving photographically back in time, only the actual building allows the eye to roam freely among inventive details; only the architecture itself offers the tactile sensations of textured stone surfaces and polished wooden pews, the experience of light changing with movement, the smell and resonant sounds of space, the bodily relations of scale and proportion. All these sensations combine within one complex experience, which becomes articulate and specific, though wordless. The building speaks through the silence of perceptual phenomena.

While sensations and impressions quietly engage us in the physical phenomena of architecture, the generative force lies in the intentions behind it. Goethe's remark that "one should not seek anything behind the phenomena; they are lessons themselves..." stops short of a more modern philosophical approach, which originated with Brentano and Husserl and was later developed by Maurice Merleau-Ponty.

Questions of architectural perception underlie questions of intention. This "intentionality" sets architecture apart from a pure phenomenology that is manifest for the natural sciences. Whatever the perception of a built work – whether it be troubling, intriguing, or banal – the mental energy which produced it is ultimately deficient unless intent is articulated. The relationship between the experiential qualities of architecture and the generative concepts is analogous to the tension between the empirical and the rational. Here the logic of pre-existing concepts meets the contingency and particularity of experience.

306 OMA, REM KOOLHAAS, AND BRUCE MAU
from "Bigness, or the problem of Large" (1994)

After the appearance of *Delirious New York* in 1977, the office (OMA) and career of Rem Koolhaas catapulted him into the limelight. Projects such as the Netherlands Dance Theater (1987), the Kunsthal, Rotterdam (1992), and the Lille Grand Palais (1994) were widely lauded, and in 1995 he was honored with an exhibition at the Museum of Modern Art in New York. In the same year, in collaboration with the graphic designer Bruce Mau, Koolhaas produced his version of a "new realism" under the title *S, M, L, XL*. It is a somewhat chaotic (consciously so), retrospective collection of his designs, writings, and images – proposing to disclose to the public "the conditions under which architecture is now produced." Among the more controversial of his essays was that on

OMA, Rem Koolhaas, and Bruce Mau, from "Bigness, or the problem of Large," in *S, M, L, XL*. New York: Monacelli Press, 1995, pp. 509–11, 513–15.

"Bigness, or the Problem of the Large," which derives from the increasing scale of his projects and, indeed, from the recent phenomenon of mega-projects in general. Interestingly, Koolhaas argues that here, where a multitude of disciplines collaborate, is where theory effectively hits the wall, alongside the notion of architectural autonomy.

The absence of a theory of Bigness – what is the maximum architecture can do? – is architecture's most debilitating weakness. Without a theory of Bigness, architects are in the position of Frankenstein's creators: instigators of a partly successful experiment whose results are running amok and are therefore discredited.

Because there is no theory of Bigness, we don't know what to do with it, we don't know where to put it, we don't know when to use it, we don't know how to plan it. Big mistakes are our only connection to Bigness.

But in spite of its dumb name, Bigness is a theoretical domain at this *fin de siècle*: in a landscape of disarray, disassembly, dissociation, disclamation, the attraction of Bigness is its potential to reconstruct the Whole, resurrect the Real, reinvent the collective, reclaim maximum possibility.

Only through Bigness can architecture dissociate itself from the exhausted artistic/ ideological movements of modernism and formalism to regain its instrumentality as vehicle of modernization.

Bigness recognizes that architecture as we know it is in difficulty, but it does not over-compensate through regurgitations of even more architecture. It proposes a new economy in which no longer "all is architecture," but in which a strategic position is regained through retreat and concentration, yielding the rest of a contested territory to enemy forces.

[. . .]

Team

Bigness is where architecture becomes both most and least architectural: most because of the enormity of the object; least through the loss of autonomy – it becomes instrument of other forces, it *depends*.

Bigness is impersonal: the architect is no longer condemned to stardom.

Even as Bigness enters the stratosphere of architectural ambition – the pure chill of megalomania – it can be achieved only at the price of giving up control, of transmogrification. It implies a web of umbilical cords to other disciplines whose performance is as critical as the architect's: like mountain climbers tied together by life-saving ropes, the makers of Bigness are a *team* (a word not mentioned in the last 40 years of architectural polemic).

Beyond signature, Bigness means surrender to technologies; to engineers, contractors, manufacturers; to politics; to others. It promises architecture a kind of post-heroic status – a realignment with neutrality.

Bastion

If Bigness transforms architecture, its accumulation generates a new kind of city. The exterior of the city is no longer a collective theater where "it" happens; there's no collective "it" left. The street has become residue, organizational device, mere segment of the continuous metropolitan plane where the remnants of the past face the equipments of the new in an uneasy standoff. Bigness can exist *anywhere* on that plane. Not only is Bigness incapable of establishing relationships with the classical city – *at most, it coexists* – but in the quantity and complexity of the facilities it offers, it is itself urban.

Bigness no longer needs the city: it competes with the city; it represents the city; it preempts the city; or better still, it *is* the city. If urbanism generates potential and architecture exploits it, Bigness enlists the generosity of urbanism against the meanness of architecture.

Bigness = urbanism vs. architecture.

307 WINY MAAS
from "Datascape" (1996)

If the creation of the Berlage Institute and the success of OMA combined to lead a resurgence of Dutch architecture in the 1990s, one firm to take full advantage of these changing conditions was MVRDV – an acronym for the partners Winy Maas, Jacob van Rijs, and Nathalie de Vries. Both Maas and van Rijs began in Koolhaas's office, and thus it is not unexpected that MVRDV (formed in 1991) continued many of the design strategies of OMA, including a propensity for methodical research and a willingness to think outside of the traditional box. Central to their design methodology is the notion of "datascapes," which is not unrelated to some of the concerns voiced in the preceding essay. This short manifesto defines it succinctly, as well as drawing out both its pragmatic and ethical dimensions. In the latter regard this empirical notion reveals a fundamental aversion to abstract theoretical speculation often found in the Dutch school.

How to deal with the moral in an era where architecture has been overoccupied by chaos theories that function as rhetorical hide-aways and mythical retreats? Should architecture still aspire to expressing 'chaos' even when it is already surounded by it?

Everything can be made, every object is imaginable, nothing seems strange or extravagant anymore.

What should we make under these circumstances? Do we still aspire to the ultimate extravaganza? Are we suffering from 'object fatigue', a consequence of the multitude of objects competing for our attention, all these buildings clamouring to tell us something?

In our search for the 'one-off' in a veritable slew of the 'unique', the expression of the individual object has become ridiculous: in a massive 'sea of uniqueness' the individual object simply ceases to exist. In this massiveness, architecture bifurcates: on one side it introverts, which leads to a stronger emphasis on the role of the interior. On the other side architecture becomes synonymous with urbanism.

The lion's share of the building production is concerned with the banal and the normal. In our desire to be avant-garde, this signifies an all-absorbing massiveness, a prescribed

Winy Mass, from "Datascape," in *Farmax: Excursions on density*, ed. Winy Maas and Jacob van Rijs with Richard Koek. Rotterdam: 010 Publishers, 1998, pp. 100–3.

experience, a pasteurized reality. Why are we still not interested in it? Are we afraid of the banal in ourselves?

It has become the emblem of something that is past its peak, a vivid illustration of the twentieth century dilemma: in our search for the unique we all make or find the same things; desiring en masse the authentic and exceptional, it all turns out banal. ·

If we regard this phenomenon ironically, we are denying all its humanity. The way we look down on it, must be the same as the way the Victorian bourgeoisie looked down on the working classes, with contempt, mixed with shame. Now as then, a Dickensian type is needed to give back to banality that human face.

When architecture becomes urbanism, it enters the realms of quantities and infrastructure, of time and relativism.

Things come, things go. Events take place in apparently unorganized patterns, the very chaos of which possesses hidden logics, allowing 'gravities' to emerge from within this endless tapestry of objects.

These gravities reveal themselves when sublimated beneath certain assumed maximized circumstances or within certain maximized constraints.

Because of tax differences the borders between Belgium and the Netherlands are occupied with vast numbers of villas generating a linear town along the frontier. Market demands have precipitated a 'slick' of houses-with-a-small-garden in Holland. Political constraints in Hong Kong generate 'piles' of dwellings around its boundaries. The popularity of white brick in Friesland causes a 'white cancer' of housing estates alongside all the villages. In its desire for a cosmetic nineteenth-century identity, Berlin forces its new buildings into tight envelopes. This pushes larger programmes underground, turning the streets into mere components in the midst of vast programmes.

Monumental regulations in Amsterdam limit the demand for modern programmes, generating 'mountains of programme' invisible from the street behind the medieval facades. Throughout the Ruhr, accessibility demands create virtually enclosed types of infrastructure precipitating a string of linear towns. In La Defense in Paris, to avoid the high-rise rules massive programmes manifest themselves as ziggurats with 18 metre high accessible 'steps' so that all offices can be entered by the maximum length of the fire ladders. Psychological issues, anti-disaster patterns, lighting regulations, acoustic treatments.

All these manifestations can be seen as 'scapes' of the data behind it.

If 'progress' remains the main reason for 'research', the hypothesis remains the most effective way to deal with it. In order to understand the behaviour of massiveness, we have to push it to the limits and adopt this 'extremizing' as a technique of architectural research. Assuming a possible maximization (the word 'maximum' already implies rules), society will be confronted with the laws and by-laws that it has set up and that are extrapolated with an iron logic. It will begin questioning these regulations.

The protection of certain areas push programmes to the left-over corners of our countries. Do we want that? More comfort raises the issue that we are becoming dependent on it. Do we want that?

More massiveness and higher densities leads to the question of whether we still should use our light and air regulations. Or if we should cope with noise in another way. And so on.

Under maximized circumstances, every demand, rule or logic is manifested in pure and unexpected forms that go beyond artistic intuition or known geometry and replace it with 'research'. Form becomes the result of such an extrapolation or assumption as a 'datascape' of the demands behind it. It shows the demands and norms, balancing between ridicule and critique, sublimizing pragmatics.

It connects the moral with the normal. Having found the opportunity to criticize the norm and the moral behind it, it constructs a possible 'argument'. Artistic intuition is replaced by 'research': hypotheses that observe, extrapolate, analyse and criticize our behaviour.

308 MICHAEL SPEAKS
from "It's Out There... the Formal Limits of the American Avant-Garde" (1997)

After taking his doctorate under the prominent Marxist critic Fredric Jameson earlier in the decade, Michael Speaks would seem to be an unlikely candidate to lead an assault on the avant-garde underpinnings of American theory in the 1990s. The example of the young Dutch firms — their practical revision of the limits and process of architectural design — had clearly presented an increasingly popular alternative (and therefore a problem) to the abstraction of American theorists. And it is the example of these Dutch practitioners with which Speaks opens this essay: their de-emphasis on form and their "just there" attitude. Much of this essay is devoted to a discussion of the contrary approaches of Greg Lynn and Peter Eisenman, both of whom, Speaks argues, never succeed in moving beyond the issue of "form." Over the next few years, Speaks would sharpen his polemics on these issues and become a persistent critic of the critical avant-garde in the United States. The essay was first presented — fittingly — as a lecture at the Berlage Institute in October 1997.

The real question not only for Lynn, but for this form-driven American avant-garde, is whether they will be able to discover a dislocative architecture that, rather than dislocating form or type, dislocates the form of architectural practice itself; that, in other words, calls into question the interiority of architecture as a practice of form production, opening it to the kind of expansion that has occurred in the Dutch context where the freshest practices focus on animate forms of practice, not on animate forms. Such a dislocation would necessarily take leave of the discourse of architectural interiority altogether and focus on architecture as a practice of fixity that manipulates or exploits movement in order to induce the production of new urban life. Architecture would then be able to become both a stabilising *and* an animating force in the metropolis without feeling compelled to make its forms move.

As Rem Koolhaas has observed in his distinction between Mies and Rietveld, there are practices which fix in order to open up avenues of freedom, and those that seem to offer an infinity of choice but which give no choice or freedom. Forms that 'look like' they are fluid

Michael Speaks, from "It's out There... the Formal Limits of the American Avant-Garde," in *Architectural Design* 68:5/6 (May–June 1998), pp. 30–1.

with their urban contexts may in fact interdict, and forms which 'look like' they are interdictive may in fact be fluid with their urban contexts. If this were to be recognised, the question would no longer be 'what is the essence of architecture?', (form, light, image, etc) but 'what can architecture do' when it looks to its exterior, to the globalised metropolis?

This is a question that Eisenman, Lynn, Kipnis, *Assemblage*, and indeed the entire American avant-garde seem never to ask, and that is because they are always stopped at the border, stopped by form. Only such a dislocation can guarantee architecture continuous life in a world in which it seems to have lost its object, its mission and its way. Indeed, this is precisely what is at stake in Koolhaas' 'Bigness', in which the art of architecture must give way to a reduced, and interconnected set of practices that 'depend', as he says: on technologies, engineers, contractors, manufactures and currency markets. This is also what is at stake in the new practice of urbanism implied in 'What Ever Happened to Urbanism?', an approach and not a professional practice which takes up the problem of shaping the conditions under which new urban life can emerge and proliferate. Of course this is also what is at stake in Sanford Kwinter's 'new pastoralism', and Bernard Cache's insistence that architecture is the art of the frame, that it is the framing of the conditions under which life emerges.

Ultimately, architecture will have to develop a dynamism that matches that of the globalised metropolis. In order to do so, it must become, among other things, an animate form of form shaping, a practice of creating forms which themselves may not be animate, but which induce or create the conditions under which new urban life will emerge.

309   JOHN RAJCHMAN
from "A New Pragmatism?"
(1997)

One of the featured centers for critical theory in the 1990s was an annual series of international conferences held by the Anyone Corporation, each of which spawned a book. The nonprofit corporation's director was Peter Eisenman, and the editor in charge of the publications (as well as the journal *ANY*) was Cynthia C. Davidson. The empirical turn taken by Dutch firms was an issue raised at the "Anyhow" conference, which took place in Rotterdam in 1997, hosted by John Rajchman and Rem Koolhaas. The philosopher Rajchman noted the changing climate of recent years and declared that we were witnessing the birth of a "new pragmatism," one taking its lineage back to William James. Yet Rajchman, in his remarks, also goes on to draw heavily upon the ideas of Michel Foucault, Gilles Deleuze, and Félix Guattari, and therefore reveals that he was by no means retreating from his former viewpoint (as a student of Foucault), as much as assimilating pragmatism into his interpretation of the critical process as a way to bring a certain vagueness or complexity of process to avant-garde abstractions. Pragmatism, in Rajchman's view, thus assumes a mediatory ground between practice and theory within the ongoing debate.

John Rajchman, from "A New Pragmatism?," in *Anyhow*, ed. Cynthia C. Davidson, Cambridge, MA: MIT Press, 1998, p. 217.

What then does the "new pragmatism" – the pragmatism of diagram and diagnosis that I have been trying to imagine – involve? What does it do? In the first place, the diagrammatic supposes a pragmatic relation to a future that is not futuristic, not imagistic. It is concerned in the present with those multiple unknown futures of which we have no image just because we are in the process of becoming or inventing them. It follows that the diagrammatic requires and excites different kinds of solidarity or "movement" among us than those of the traditional avant-garde group, the organization of a political party, or even a nice progressive social-democratic public sphere, inasmuch as those forms rest on the presumption of a future we are able to know and master. The diagrammatic "mobilizes and connects" us in other, indirect ways that work more through linkages, complicities, and alliances that grow up around new questions or in response to new conditions or forces than through adherences to the prior supervenient generalities of a theory, a project, or a program. Perhaps in this way the pragmatism of diagram and diagnosis might help transform the sense of what is "critical" in our thought and our work. It might help move beyond the impasses of older images of negative theology, transgression, or abstract purity and introduce a new problem: that of resingularizing environments, of living an indefinite "complexity," prior to set determinations, which questions the simplicities and generalities of our modes of being and suggests other possibilities. Such a pragmatism would differ from the "communicational" or "informational" pragmatics promoted by globalization discourse – it ties creation and resistance to the present.

310 CYNTHIA C. DAVIDSON
from "Architecture between theory and ideology" (1998)

John Rajchman's lecture at the "Anyhow" conference suggested one way to integrate the Dutch example into critical theory, and it also prompted this response from Cynthia Davidson, the long-standing editor of *ANY*. Davidson draws upon Rajchman's mediating interpretation of pragmatism, but what makes this analysis interesting is how she extends this notion of pragmatism to encompass the work of Alejandro Zaera-Polo, Ben van Berkel, Greg Lynn, and Rem Koolhaas. Her mention of Richard Rorty in this passage is a reference to his book *Achieving Our Country: Leftist Thought in Twentieth-Century America* (1988), in which Rorty criticized the political Left for its embrace of philosophical speculation at the expense of revolutionary activity. Thus Davidson's interpretation of pragmatism places it in a mediating position between theory and ideology – thus retaining a political component.

Rajchman's new pragmatism suggests an alternative for architecture, a theory of the speculative that continually responds to a changing present. In Rajchman's terms there is no need or should. His is a more theoretical view of the pragmatic as opposed to its

Cynthia C. Davidson, from "Architecture between theory and ideology," in *archis* 7 (1998), pp. 10–11.

continued use as an ideology that sustains architecture. This new idea of pragmatism seems to be operative in the work of several younger architects today, including Alejandro Zaera-Polo, Ben van Berkel and Greg Lynn. Each has attempted to lay out a kind of architectural practice that in various ways deals with information as material and technique and, most especially, with motion, what Lynn calls 'motion techniques [to] be added to the architects' toolbox' and van Berkel sees as 'mobile forces'. These forces, whether they be the weighted magnetic fields that Lynn has used or the movement of crowds that van Berkel has tracked, are considered by them to be the very material of architecture. The primary understanding and interpretation of this material is gained through techniques of animated diagramming available on the computer.

The resulting work places them very close to a new vitalism, but it is their dependency on a new technology that, in the Heideggerian sense, gives this work an ideological bent, in which engineering, technology, science and research are combined in a 'powerful system ... of labor and needs'.[1] This reading of the work raises the question of whether this is more akin to Rorty's ideological pragmatism than Rajchman's new pragmatism. It certainly distinguishes their work on information from the more textually based theoretical strategies of Peter Eisenman and Bernard Tschumi.

There is another line of investigation, one which differs in many respects from each of the above. This is the pragmatism that might apply to Rem Koolhaas's research in China's Pearl River Delta. Working with students, his Harvard Project on the City compiles cultural, social and economic data and then represents it as sheer information in the form of ordinary bar graphs and pie charts that allow him to question the validity of current form-producing practice, if not the entire question of form production. (How an architectural practice as opposed to a purely theoretical practice can be non-form producing is a question that Koolhaas often avoids.) Koolhaas acknowledges and names conditions in the Pearl River Delta, copyrighting familiar terms such as tabula rasa and infrastructure, but takes no action on that condition other than to bring it to light. This research-based work may be cloaked in pragmatism, but in fact it is a critical attitude about architecture and urbanism that is clearly theoretical. Koolhaas could be said to be operating a Deleuzian 'abstract machine' that is neither physical, corporeal or semiotic but is 'diagrammatic (it knows nothing of the distinction between the artificial and the natural either) ... operates by matter, not by substance; by function, not by form.'[2]

Much of the antagonism shown toward theory in architecture has been an antagonism against deconstruction and the 1988 Museum of Modern Art exhibition that propagated it. Theory in architecture is not just a product of current French thought, which has been popular in architecture since the students took to the streets of Paris in 1968 – the same year that Rorty claims the American Left took a wrong turn. Thirty years after those tumultuous times, another idea of architectural theory, one different from a theory of the new, of an ever-changing future, is being promulgated by those who have left both theory and ideology for a history of theory and ideology. Powered by Heidegger's idea of 'a historicity of being', critics as diverse as Beatriz Colomina and Colin Rowe ask why buildings need to look new, why old models embodied with the values of architecture's tradition can't just be repeated. A history of theory is like any history, but it is very different from Heidegger's idea of historicity. Historicity is a way of theorizing being, not a retreat from being. These historical strategies appear to be a far more virile attack on both Rajchman's new pragmatism and

Lynn's technological blobs than the well-worn social critique supported by, for example, **Archis**. The retreat to history consigns theory to the bookshelves of academia and removes the idea of a historicized theoretical practice from the realm of the present, of building the present. A new pragmatism, however, both historicizes and theorizes a possible practice for architecture today.

NOTES

1 Zie ook/see also Rüdiger Safranski, Martin Heidegger, **Between Good and Evil**, trans. Ewald Osers, Cambridge, Mass./London (Harvard University Press) 1998, p. 294.
2 Gilles Deleuze, Félix Guattari, '587 B.C.–A.D. 70: On Several Regimes of Sign' in **A Thousand Plateaus**, vert./trans. Brian Massumi, Minneapolis (University of Minnesota Press) 1987, p. 141.

311 K. MICHAEL HAYS
from Introduction to *Architecture Theory since 1968* (1998)

K. Michael Hays also responds to the pragmatic currents in his Introduction to *Architecture Theory since 1968*. Architectural theory, Hays argues, has a critical role, but also a mediatory one: at times transposing or mediating other intellectual codes ("from Marxism and semiotics to psychoanalysis and rhizomatics"), while at other times attending to architecture's practical realities. Critical theory, for Hays, remains at heart an act of political resistance.

From Marxism and semiotics to psychoanalysis and rhizomatics, architecture theory has freely and contentiously set about opening up architecture to what is thinkable and sayable in other codes, and, in turn, rewriting systems of thought assumed to be properly extrinsic or irrelevant into architecture's own idiolect. And while it is correct to point out that today there still remain vestiges of older, "philosophical" criticisms that simply apply various philosophical systems to architecture in occasional and opportunistic ways, architecture theory has been, in part, a displacement of traditional problems of philosophy ("truth," "quality," and the like) in favor of attention to distinctly and irreducibly *architectural* ideas, and an attempt to dismantle the whole machinery of master texts, methods, and applications, putting in its place concepts and codes that interpret, disrupt, and transform one another.

Thus, for example, Manfredo Tafuri's work on modernism and contemporary architectural production, which I take as initiating one important trajectory of architecture theory, enfolds the old Marxian terms of base and superstructure and makes architecture *when it is*

K. Michael Hays, from "Introduction," in *Architecture Theory since 1968*. Cambridge, MA: MIT Press, 1998, pp. xi–xii.

most itself – most pure, most rational, most attendent to its own techniques – the most efficient ideological agent of capitalist planification and unwitting victim of capitalism's historical closure. In a certain sense, this is just the maximization of the classical mediating term of critical theory, *reification* (or *Verdinglichung*, as used from Georg Luckács to Theodor Adorno to Fredric Jameson), but now with the twist that architecture's utopian work ends up laying the tracks for a general movement to a totally administered world.

Or semiology, another dominant paradigm of architecture theory, links architecture and the social city (often including popular culture and consumerism) through the fraction of the sign (signifier/signified), setting off a fission that leads to the theorization of postmodernism itself, whose dust lingers on almost all subsequent discourse. But it should be clear that, while architecture theory preserves the fundamental structuralist apparatus of the sign, and language as the predominant model of that apparatus, it also, early on, mobilized its mediatory techniques in order to query of semiological systems how, by what agents and institutions, and to what ends they have been produced. Theory's situating of architecture in history and production – or, to use different terminology, its interrogation of the structurality of semiological structures – ensures that any simple distinction between structuralism and poststructuralism in architecture theory cannot easily be maintained. One should note, too, that, while the logics of communication and type were the first products of theorizing the architectural sign, the concept of media – understood as including specific technologies and institutions as well as forms – would by the 1980s become the logical elaboration of that of the sign.

Architecture theory's mediatory function releases unnoticed complicities and common-alities between different realities that were thought to remain singular, divergent, and differently constituted. Mediating among different discourses has sponsored a rich literature that addresses itself to a whole range of practical issues – the role of the unconscious, the socially constructed body, ecology, the politics of spatial relations – which connoisseurs of unmediated form nevertheless regard as an occultation of architecture's original object and seekers of certainty find maddeningly frustrating. But a primary lesson of architecture theory is that what used to be called the sociohistorical contexts of architectural production, as well as the object produced, are both themselves *texts* in the sense that we cannot approach them separately and directly, as distinct, unrelated things-in-themselves, but only through their prior differentiation and transmutation, which is shot through with ideological motivation. The world is a totality; it is an essential and essentially *practical* problem of theory to rearticulate that totality, to produce the concepts that relate the architectural fact with the social, historical, and ideological subtexts from which it was never really separate to begin with.

312 SANFORD KWINTER

from "FFE: Le Trahison des Clercs (and other Travesties of the Modern)" (1999)

The responses of Rajchman and Hays with regard to the Dutch challenge were not the same as that of Sanford Kwinter, also a long-standing board member of *ANY*. Kwinter enters the intellectual fray with the promise to take no prisoners. His words are directed at the Dutch firm MVRDV and the Dutch school in general, as well as the economic irrational exuberance of the late 1990s which, in his view, is not unrelated to this "breach of trust." Nevertheless, the ferocity of his counter-attack at the same time suggests that the defenders of poststructural criticality, of which Kwinter had long been a prominent member, were now fully aware of the seriousness of the challenge. In a curious way (and not just with the bracketed subtitle of the essay), Kwinter's charge recalls that of Reyner Banham of forty years earlier with regard to the "Italian Retreat from Modern Architecture."

Ours is an extraordinary moment. Rarely has architectural production been so well and richly served by theory, nor theory so well-legitimated by, and so happily submissive to, production. It is not rare today for the theorist to design nor for designers to contribute lucidly to the culture with concepts, arguments, and texts. The two sectors, often separate, are today so busily serving one another that they seem unaware of the deeper deprivations to which they are giving place. For today's lovefest hides a sad, possibly ugly side that has become a matter of aggressive indifference to everyone, simply because we are nearly all party to its interests. Just as certain economists today, with clear reason, warn that current rates of growth are unsustainable, that public assets are overvalued, and that gravity continues to guide ballistic trajectories in markets and spreadsheets, yet are scorned and ignored with apparent impunity, so too has the architectural discipline all but abandoned the external and long-range viewpoints to which both its future and its soul, as well as its deepest ideas, belong. Everyone is reveling at the party but there are no designated drivers to be found.

These are not, of course, sober times given to sober claims, and as a writer I have been no exception. I have served as an apologist for flawed architectures and as a less than temperate rehabilitator of others' homeless and inchoate concepts. Never, though, have I been an apologist for that particular type of neoconservative fundamentalism that, over the last decade, has swept corporate, cultural, and academic milieus, and which is now settling into our own field like a dry rot out of control. The current intoxication with the magical flame of neocapitalism – expressed primarily through the exaltation of market forces and their legendary, but not proven efficacy and intelligence – has so subsumed contemporary culture, society, and media that even our intellectuals, if one can still call them that, can no longer muster the awareness that something troubling has happened. And yet, the discipline of architecture, once a poor relation to the humanities and the social-scientific disciplines, has

Sanford Kwinter, from "FFE: Le Trahison des Clercs (and other Travesties of the Modern)," in *ANY* 24 (1999), pp. 61, 62.

today reached a level of popular sophistication exceeded only by business management theory and software research and development. But all this really means is that these fields have come to resemble one another in both substance and expression to a disturbingly high degree.

It is well known that architects have rarely bothered to hide their status as whores to patronage (perhaps shamelessness is the best way to conceal the humiliations of subservience, precisely because it routinizes them), but today a new (but not different) ethos is attempting to generalize this posture into a radical and, for the first time, systematic program. Rising up like an improbable tidal wave from the dry side of the Lowlands' dikes, a new movement – Dutch this time, like the Italian, Japanese, Spanish, and Swiss ones that preceded it – is poised to seduce and submerge us with a quirky juxtaposition of toy forms and unsentimental bureaucrat logic. To date, the evidence submitted is that of a deliciously inventive body of work, one brimming with wit and charm and especially paradox while remaining disciplined and – how should one phrase it – *conspicuously* intelligent (though this depends considerably on what one means by intelligent). What makes the work topical, necessary, and immediate, according to the compelling promotional arguments that have risen up to meet it,[1] is the immensely refined and up-to-date "pragmatism" it demonstrates, a feature that makes of it, along with that of such "masters" as Herzog and de Meuron, perhaps the first really "new" architecture of the neomodern period. Disencumbered however of all social or physiological intensity – that is, of anything with the historical, existential thickness of ideals, dreams, or "transvaluing" values – the work actually aspires to nothing beyond pure "megamachine" architecture (to use the once ominous but now fully denatured phrase of Lewis Mumford created to denote the vast technical knowledge systems and devices that make up modern rationalized society). Clever and playful, and never less – nor more – than briefly endearing (a function no doubt of the work's pointed renunciation of any claim to importance), this work nevertheless represents an architecture of resignation and disorientation masquerading as enlightenment, an architecture of spiritual exhaustion presenting itself as scientific activity, as hip unsentimentality and even as a "coolness" in the technical sense of possessing an apparent poise or collectedness that reigns over a fast play of relationships. There is simply no cool, however, without magically woven *restraint*, that is, no cool without a hot substrate held in tense equilibrium. The central thesis of this new school is supposed to consist in the embrace of (global) infrastructure as a shaping force, but the host of Koolhaasian concepts of which this new work is assembled is being considerably watered down and one-dimensionalized (albeit often elegantly distilled into slogans such as MVRDV's term *datascapes*) so that it no longer represents anything thicker than the rote numeric sequencing of market behaviors and demographic pressures. A naive determinism is inevitably allowed to intervene here, one that neglects the panoply of real, unstable social processes and their own infinitely dense, and ever-shifting, psychic, political, erotic, and anthropological infrastructures. The "pragmatism" that the new Dutch work represents, as rich in possibility as it is poor in its present expression, is a pragmatism of the worse kind: it remains little more than ill-digested and reductionist Koolhaasianism, to which is added the petty bureaucrat's compulsion to justify impotence ("planning is impossible, the market rules!") by inflating his/her ineffectuality into an historical and aesthetic ideal. In the hands of the new Dutch architects, the dramatically new perception of embedded (abstract, invisible) expert systems – that is, human and social engineering – as the constitutive shaping forces of our time becomes a glib and often merely touristic drive through an all-too-familiar media landscape of thinfrastructure.

Were this group of architects but a second-rate bunch, it would mean no harm done and no attention in need of being paid. But the new Dutch work is nothing if not compelling and cogent and, were it not so unabashedly derivative and middlebrow, it might almost credibly stand as the "new" platform that it is touted to be. Yet because emulation plays such an enormous role in the dissemination of architectural ideas, and because so little intelligence or understanding is required simply to emulate, this work, and the attenuated ideas that drive it, are not only gaining wide attention but in some cases are already earning a vigorous following. That the material our colleagues and students are now perusing is not the real or even living thing but rather a more or less earnest and denatured copy of a richer, more demanding, more ambiguous and complex original is becoming especially important now that critical unanimity has begun to join the herd in embracing facility and accessibility to the complete exclusion of difficulty and of historical density and singularity. It is not just the crushing dominance of the OMA office on the Dutch intellectual scene that diminishes much of the new work, it is the imitative poverty of these practices – partially occluded by their own savage brilliance – that threatens to diminish everyone's capacity to read and to think the more raw and resistant, the more ambiguous and unstable becomings that make up historical process and material life.

The avowed task of the new B-movie architectures is to reflect existing conditions and existing knowledge (gleaned from financial pages, official briefs, and "research") and they do this well enough, but unlike the model from which they were spawned, they lack the complexity of vision and imagination and the existential gravity to project latent, or emissary, structures *forward* into a truly unknown future that may well be entirely *different* from the present. More than anything, what these new, lite, hyperstylists represent is the gradual replacement of *qualitative* – the delirious in New York, by *quantitative* – Maastricht bean-counting. How the cloying *Heimlichkeit* of the MVRDV universe, for example, ever made it past the critical gate-keepers in Germany and America (indeed, how it even graduated from the local Dutch joke mill) is a mystery beyond the powers of this writer to explain. There seems to be a willingness, first on the part of the Dutch, then on that of the rest of the world, when faced with the fearful OMA sublime (I use this word only with irony and to note the irrational fear that their activities seem to inspire in their colleagues) to take neurotic refuge in masochism and burlesque.[2]

[. . .]

The social imagination has all but vanished from advanced internationalist design today, and this has had the temporary effect of rendering its occasional appearances as dismissably quaint, regionalist, or nostalgic, at any rate, as lacking the hardheadedness necessary to fraternize in the esperanto world of e-commerce and globalism. The fierce inventiveness and productivity that we are experiencing in so many of our social and cultural economies today is obscuring the emergence and spread of a new poverty, the poverty of *liberal* pragmatism.

We designers are the inventors of images of freedom. Yet what has become corrupt of late are the means by which the last term is defined: no longer the freedom to transform absolutely the very possibility of what might come, but the freedom merely to harvest, in relative fashion, temporary advantage from the world that already exists. This does not mean our world and our culture are any more fixed or stagnant than before, only that their course or development is no longer even theoretically subject to design intervention. This is the failure of *our* practice and theory and no one else's. The new ideas we believe to be celebrating in the new European work, and in stylistic neomodernism in general, are but half-ideas, recycled clichés and fiscal propaganda (consider, for example, how powerfully and smoothly they have been integrated into the British shopping scene and retail culture by *Wallpaper* magazine). As long as markets continue to soar, the neoliberal logic that is being used to excuse (though not explain) them will continue to inspire insipid, soulless, and complacent "superstructural" works because the measure of what permits emancipation from mediocrity in this and all other times does not belong to the world of the balance-sheet, but to that river of indeterminism and desire that characterizes the world of invention and *will*. Intelligence can only optimize what it has been commanded to do, but design is far more basic an affair of creative will; it gives place to what did not previously exist. Should not design today learn again to command the intelligence, not merely make public parade of its subservience to more prosaic forces?

NOTES

1 See Stan Allen and Bart Lootsma in El Croquis, no. 86; Winy Maas in FARMAX (Rotterdam: 010 Publishers, 1998); Michael Speaks in the "Big Soft Orange" catalogue; and ARCH+, "Die Moderne der Moderne: Entwurfe zur Zwelten Moderne," no. 143, October 1998.
2 Van Berkel and Bos are the notable exception that proves the rule.

313 WILLIAM J. MITCHELL
from *e-topia: "Urban Life, Jim – But Not As We Know It"* (1999)

Perhaps one of the better arguments on behalf of the new pragmatism in design was put forth not by a participant in the debate, but rather by someone who was exploring the implications of the new technologies and environmental awareness. Throughout the 1990s this Dean of Architecture and Planning at MIT produced a bevy of books on architectural cognition, visual perception, CAD systems, computer technologies, and the transformation of human life in the digital age. Here, in echoing the earlier investigations of Melvin M. Webber, he considers the city of the twenty-first century and its architectural implications. These "lean, green" cities should be planned according to five design principles: Dematerialization, Demobilization, Mass customization, Intelligent operation, and Soft transformation, of which the first point is cited here.

William J. Mitchell, from *e-topia: "Urban Life, Jim – But Not As We Know It."* Cambridge, MA: MIT Press, 1999, pp. 148–9.

Dematerialization

When a virtual facility like an electronic home banking system substitutes for a physical one like a branch bank, there is a net dematerialization effect; we no longer need so much physical construction, and we no longer have to heat and cool it. Replacement of big, physical things by miniaturized equivalents – as when silicon chips begin to do the job of vacuum tubes, and hair-thin fiber optics substitutes for heavy copper cables – accomplishes much the same result. And there are analogous benefits when we separate information from its traditional material substrates; an email message, read on the screen, does not consume paper.

Furthermore, we can win coming and going. If we never produce a material artifact, and make use of a dematerialized equivalent instead, it never turns into waste that has to be managed. A used bit is not a pollutant!

All this is becoming so obvious that the term "weightless economy" has gained increasing currency among economists and business commentators. (Before long, of course, "weightless" will seem as quaintly anachronistic as "horseless," "wireless," and "zipless.") And we can no longer take the architectural implications lightly. Now, less really can be more.

Until recently, so-called green architecture has typically been pursued under the assumption that physical construction is unavoidable and the task is therefore to carry it out it as efficiently as possible. Consequently, it has rarely amounted to much more than well-intentioned tinkering with building massing and orientation, material choices, and energy systems, and it has not had the large-scale impacts that its proponents have sought. Today, though, the new economy of presence affords us the possibility of repeatedly asking the more radical questions, "Is this building really necessary? Can we wholly or partially substitute electronic systems instead?"

The overall effect of electronic dematerialization does depend, to be sure, on the levels of resource consumption required in the manufacture and operation of computational devices. These are not insignificant. Semiconductor manufacture consumes energy, photochemicals, acids, hydrocarbon-based solvents, and other materials. IBM estimated that junked computers were taking up a couple of million tons of U.S. landfill at the turn of the century. It was also estimated that computers were consuming ten percent of the total U.S. electric power supply. But these levels are certainly modest enough to promise very substantial savings of resources through substitution of electronics for construction. And the trend is toward smaller devices, greener manufacture, and lower power consumption.

314 BEN VAN BERKEL AND CAROLINE BOS
"The new concept of the architect" (1999)

Another of the talented young Dutch firms to emerge during the 1990s was UN Studio, founded in 1988 by Ben van Berkel and Caroline Bos. Like Koolhaas at OMA, they too quickly produced an outpouring of theoretical designs and literary collage, in addition to several significant built works. The firm's philosophy of design is expounded in a three-volume study, *Move*, which – in addition to the following short polemic – concerns the themes of imagination, techniques, and effects. Van Beckel and Bos refer to their design process as one of "deep planning," an approach that draws heavily on digital analytical procedures as well as on traditional research into the larger economic, traffic, urban, and programmatic issues that often are, by nature, in a state of social reinterpretation and flux. The opening sentence of this polemic might be viewed as a salvo proclaiming the new millennium.

The architect is going to be the fashion designer of the future. Learning from Calvin Klein, the architect will be concerned with dressing the future, speculating, anticipating coming events and holding up a mirror to the world. The architect's practice will be organised as a limitless virtual studio, like Andy Warhol's Factory scattered; a network of superstars. Network practice extends existing forms of co-operation with clients, investors, users and technical consultants to include design engineers, finance people, management gurus, process specialists, designers and stylists. The new architectural network studio is a hybrid mixture of club, atelier, laboratory and car plant, encouraging plug-in professionalism. As in contemporary manufacturing, efficiency and diversity, continuity and differentiation are inseparable, with customised Audis and Volkswagens rolling off the same production line. Making use of new technologies, the network architect benefits from the increased transferability of knowledge. The will to invent is fundamental, ensuring that the basic values of the discipline, ranging from geometry to materialisation, are always evolving. Because all experiments require proof of evidence, the experimental practice continually oscillates between the abstract world of ideas and the physical world. New procedures and new techniques are tested out in site-specific, project-based experiments.

The actual design process of architecture will be like making a film: invisible research and business culminating into a short time of intense action, when mixed teams decide how to fit out a new city, a new airport. Time is on the architect's side. The correlative approach to plan development makes use of the mapping of time to reveal relations in informational data and logistics. Developing specific visualising techniques, re-thinking virtual and material organisational structures, engaging public space, public forces and the public imagination, puts the architect once more at the centre of his own world. New concepts of control transform the untenable position of master builder into a public scientist. As an expert on everyday public information, the architect collects information that is potentially structuring, co-ordinates it, transforms it and offers ideas and images for the organisation of public life in an endless, seamless system.

Ben van Berkel and Caroline Bos, "The new concept of the architect," in *Move: Imagination*, vol. 1. Amsterdam: UN Studio and Goose Press, 1999, pp. 27–8.

C. BEYOND THE NEW MILLENNIUM

Introduction

If the computer and all of the ramifications of globalization were not enough to transform architectural theory in the 1990s, a startling re-found awareness of the fragility of the world's ecological system – Spaceship Earth – would also bring into question all of the intellectual pursuits of the previous three decades, if not much of the twentieth century. There is of course a certain irony in this return. The 1960s, as we have seen, was imbued with an environmental and ecological sensitivity, which in many ways grew out of the technological euphoria that also characterized the decade. Fuller, Otto, McHale, and McHarg, in the 1960s, were for a large number of young architects the intellectual gurus who promised to lead the world to a more balanced and sustainable existence. But this optimism and energy, so promising at the time, would all be dissipated by the end of the 1970s, coincident but hardly coincidental with the rise of postmodern thought. When viewed from this perspective, the broad spectrum of theoretical fronts that appeared in the 1970s can be unified specifically in its aesthetic rejection of technology. In the 1990s, as the wheel turns, the situation reverses itself and ecological considerations and their (often) technological solutions are reinvoked to cast aesthetics from architecture, that is, at least to subordinate it to the more pressing issues at hand.

Of course no one will argue that the wheel will stop here, but then again no one will dispute that taking these environmental concerns into account will not only empower architects to come up with innovative and creative solutions but also profoundly alter the course of practice. Quite naturally, this will be the challenge for the next generation of architects entering the profession.

315 JAMES WINES
from ''Green Dreams'' (1991)

James Wines's thinking over the previous twenty years had clearly undergone a major shift. In 1970, together with Allison Sky, he had founded the firm SITE (acronym for Sculpture in the Environment). The firm became renowned for its sometimes whimsical designs – crumbling walls and buckling parking lots – which were seen as early examples of postmodern irony. His tone by the start of the 1990s, however, had turned seriously ''green,'' as his firm began to emphasize both artistic creativity and sensitivity to nature. This passage presages a much broader change that would take place in this decade, and this new appreciation of the work of Frank Lloyd Wright discloses just how the course of architectural history never ceases to evolve.

With the exception of the ''organic architecture'' of Frank Lloyd Wright, 20th-century dwellings have offered few persuasive, theoretically and philosophically based approaches to the fusion of nature and architecture. It was a conceit of early Modernism that if the house were cleansed of its residual symbols of domesticity, a new vision of living space would emerge. Unhampered by historical baggage and conceived in the image of the machine, this revolutionary, almost abstract house would liberate humanity from the past by programming domestic life as smoothly as the running of an engine. More recently, in the 1970s and '80s, architects reacted against the sterility of abstraction and minimalism by resurrecting the 19th-century imagery of the house. Mostly, though, these Postmodernists merely superimposed a pastiche of historical references over Modernist underpinnings. The result was a kind of cardboard classicism that quickly degenerated into fashion and style. Postmodernism has been followed in the past few years by ''Deconstruction,'' an appropriation from literary criticism that uses theoretical tactics to sidestep conventional Modernism and to reject the decorative excesses of the past decade. But again, the Deconstruction movement in general has simply cribbed from an earlier source (this time a 20th-century one, specifically Russian Constructivism), exaggerating its formal devices – rotated axes, tilted walls, fragmented grids – rather than infusing it with a concern for the typology of the house, the psychology of situation, or the ecology issue.

What is consistently apparent is the overwhelming tendency of 20th-century architecture to treat a building's environment as something apart from or adjacent to it. Connections between a structure and its surroundings through attention to topography, vegetation, regional history,

James Wines, from ''Green Dreams,'' in *Artforum* (October 1991), pp. 83–4.

and community character have been regarded as peripheral or subservient to the design process. Le Corbusier's Villa Savoye of 1929–30, in Poissy-sur-Seine, outside Paris, must be considered an influential precedent for this pervasive attitude – a dwelling raised on pilotis and dropped onto a pastoral French hillside like a space station. The site is merely the "setting" for the house. This imperious attitude toward landscape has become more prevalent as the century has evolved, ultimately resulting in the arid but ubiquitous potted trees and gridded landscapes that characterize most urban and suburban environments.

Wright was the major pioneer of the environmental and contextual theory and practice of architecture in this century. But his proposals somehow got buried under the deluge of less substantive movements and theoretical positions that succeeded him. The Wright exhibition planned by the Museum of Modern Art, New York, in two or three years will surely bring on a flood of revisionist thinking and nimble fence-leaping by marginal neo-Modernists and Deconstructivists trying to jump on the bandwagon of ecological advocacy. When this onslaught begins, it will be important to keep in view Wright's profound observations on the environment as one of architecture's intrinsic raw materials.

316 WILLIAM McDONOUGH
"The Hannover Principles" (1992)

I n the early 1990s the city of Hanover, Germany, was chosen as the site for EXPO 2000, an international exposition that would focus on the themes of "Humanity, Nature, and Technology." In order to begin preparations, the city commissioned a series of principles that would inform the international design competitions for the event and serve as a broader manifesto on behalf of sustainability for the design community. William McDonough, of William McDonough Architects, drafted the principles in consultation with various other representatives of the design and environmental communities. They could very well stand as a manifesto for this decade as a whole.

In this spirit the **Hannover Principles** have been assembled, after extensive consultation with representatives from the design, environmental, and philosophical communities. It is hoped that, if accepted, they will evolve to adapt to the concerns of different cultures and countries across the globe, so that all may find a way to endure and build into the future without compromising the future's ability to meet its own challenges.

The Hannover Principles

1. **Insist on rights of humanity and nature to co-exist** in a healthy, supportive, diverse and sustainable condition.
2. **Recognize interdependence.** The elements of human design interact with and depend upon the natural world, with broad and diverse implications at every scale. Expand design considerations to recognizing even distant effects.

William McDonough, "The Hannover Principles," from *The Hannover Principles: Design for Sustainability* (1992), pp. 5–6.

3. **Respect relationships between spirit and matter.** Consider all aspects of human settlement including community, dwelling, industry and trade in terms of existing and evolving connections between spiritual and material consciousness.

4. **Accept responsibility for the consequences of design** decisions upon human well-being, the viability of natural systems and their right to co-exist.

5. **Create safe objects of long-term value.** Do not burden future generations with requirements for maintenance or vigilant administration of potential danger due to the careless creation of products, processes or standards.

6. **Eliminate the concept of waste.** Evaluate and optimize the full life-cycle of products and processes, to approach the state of natural systems, in which there is no waste.

7. **Rely on natural energy flows.** Human designs should, like the living world, derive their creative forces from perpetual solar income. Incorporate this energy efficiently and safely for responsible use.

8. **Understand the limitations of design.** No human creation lasts forever and design does not solve all problems. Those who create and plan should practice humility in the face of nature. Treat nature as a model and mentor, not as an inconvenience to be evaded or controlled.

9. **Seek constant improvement by the sharing of knowledge.** Encourage direct and open communication between colleagues, patrons, manufacturers and users to link long term sustainable considerations with ethical responsibility, and re-establish the integral relationship between natural processes and human activity.

The **Hannover Principles** should be seen as a living document committed to the transformation and growth in the understanding of our interdependence with nature, so that they may adapt as our knowledge of the world evolves.

317 BERNARD CACHE
from *Earth Moves* (1995)

The original French edition of this book, *Terre Meuble*, first appeared in 1983, and several of the concepts voiced here influenced Gilles Deleuze and his concept of the "fold." But Cache's early study remained little known and without influence until its English translation in 1995, at which time its ideas fell in line with the new architectural experiments with curvilinearity and pliant forms. Yet this chapter of his book, entitled "Territorial Image," addresses itself to the image of landscape. The object of his deliberations here is the Swiss city of Lausanne, which, as he shows, has a complex historical foundation, in large part due to the unique interface of geological features formed by glacial moraines, which divide a Swiss plateau from the lake below. Cache describes the geological entities that compose the city as four geometric elements: the conical perch of the Cité (where the cathedral stands), the inclined prism of the Bourg crest below, the intervening river valley or dihedral of the Flon,

Bernard Cache, from *Terre Meuble* (1983), trans. Anne Boyman as *Earth Moves*, a project of the Anyone Corporation. Cambridge, MA: MIT Press, 1995, pp. 13–15.

and the nineteenth-century construction of the Pichard plane, in part mediating the Bourg crest with the city center. Cache's analysis leads him to question the gravitational notion of grounding an architectural object within a Cartesian field, as well as the idea that a specific *genius loci* (nature of the place) allows the architect to respond to a stable and fixed identity. Instead, Cache argues for a more open and dynamic layering of landscape and framing of images, one that considers these given geological and historical vectors in a way that induces new images or more dynamic forms of life.

Throughout the ages, the identity of Lausanne has not so much changed, or repeated itself, as it has lived with itself under the determination of these four sorts of vectors. It would still be possible for us today to relate each of these urban identities to the diverse communities that make up the city as well as to the individual consciousness of its inhabitants. The problem is not so much that of the collective or individual memory that sustains these identities as that of the coexistence of these four apparently incompatible urban figures that are the cone, the prism, the dihedral, and the plane. The real question is then to find a solution of contiguity between these four geometrical figures; it is a question of deploying a space of transistance from one identity to another.

It is also a question of craft. In the exercise of their profession, architects can choose to ground their practice in the concept of site. The work of architecture then becomes the expression of the specificity of the site that is to be built upon. This has in fact been the option of a number of architects, of whom Vittorio Gregotti is probably the best contemporary example. But this position runs the danger of falling into a mistaken notion of site, equating all too easily the notion of specificity with that of identity. The case of Lausanne demonstrates clearly enough that the identity of a place is not given, and that if the expression "genius loci" has a meaning, it lies in the capacity of this "genius" to be smart enough to allow for the transformation or transit from one identity to another. These four figures of Lausanne are virtualities that each architect can decide to ignore or to actualize as he or she formulates his or her project for the city. Lining up cornices for the Pichard plan, or paving the boulevard along the bottom of the valley, are gestures through which an architect can position him or herself with respect to a site. But in no case does the identity of a site preexist, for it is always the outcome of a construction.

Generally, today, it no longer seems possible to think in terms of identity. Whether it refers to the identity of a place or of a self, a substantialist way of thinking seems to lead to a dead end. For as soon as one attributes a particular identity to a particular place, the only possible modes of intervention then become imitation, dissimulation, or minimalism. A false notion of the past prevents the present from happening. A difficult position must then be maintained: between, on one hand, the desire to make use of the specificity of the place, and on the other, the danger of "identifying" local differences. Opting for difference only becomes tenable when one learns how to distinguish specificity and identity.

This task of working beneath the surface of identities has been a focus of recent philosophy. For the most part, however, this sort of work has only served to renew the practices of negative theology. According to this way of thinking, language belongs to the "identical," and thus any discourse that is held "beneath" it can only proceed through negation or reduction. In architectural theory, this gives rise to statements such as "reinforce the identity of a place," which implicitly means that identity is not given and must be constructed; but in fact identity is already there, and has only to be emphasized.

318 KEN YEANG
from *Designing with Nature* (1995)

One of the most talented and environmentally sensitive architects to emerge in the 1990s was the Malaysian Ken Yeang. After studies at Cheltenham College, the Architectural Association, and the University of Pennsylvania (under Ian McHarg), Yeang took his doctorate in ecological design at the University of Cambridge. This architect has a very unique and personable style of design, one that emphasizes opening up the interiors of a building to light and natural ventilation and incorporating into the design abundant greenery on a multitude of levels. In this important early book of his – whose title itself is a homage to McHarg – Yeang spells out what separates the ecological approach to design from the more traditional one.

The traditional view of architecture will have to be revised in an ecological approach to design. The ecologist is concerned more specifically with the systemic aspects of architecture than with its aesthetic or social aspects (even though these aspects may indirectly have ecological implications in the sense that they affect the behavior of people in the ecosystem). The ecologist is more concerned with the ecological implications of the built environment's use of energy and materials and their flow. For the ecologist, the creation of architecture is no more than the management of energy and material resources assembled and concentrated in a transient stage in the context of the processes in the biosphere. Ecologically, the built environment may be said to be a potential waste product whose reuse requires further design effort. A work of design may be regarded as more than just a traditional statement of the designer's aesthetic aspirations and user functions; it is a physical and symbolic statement of the environmental impact of the proposed design.

The traditional professional responsibilities of the designer also need to be reconsidered. For instance, if the designer is aware of the ecosystem implications of the forms of energy and materials used in the built environment and the ways in which they are used, then he or she is obliged to be responsible for the total ecosystem impact of the design. This implies that the designer is responsible not only for the built system's creation and construction but also for the choice of materials and technical systems prior to its construction and the way that they are used, reused, or disposed of after its construction at the end of their physical life. Accompanying this is that considerably more research needs to be done on the ecosystem impact of the energy and material resources used in the built environment.

A system of monitoring needs to be developed so that the designer can check the ecosystem impacts of a designed system throughout its life cycle. This is a cyclical concept of architecture in which architecture cannot be regarded as completed once it is erected on site. In the ecological approach, it must be considered in the context of its entire life cycle *from source to sink*.

Ken Yeang, from *Designing with Nature: The Ecological Basis for Architectural Design*. New York: McGraw-Hill, 1995, pp. 190–1.

319 VICTOR PAPANEK
from *The Green Imperative* (1995)

T he manifesto-like tone that the Austrian-born Victor Papanek adopts in these pages did not arise without considerable experience. His first book, *Design for the Real World: Human Ecology and Social Change* (1971) was one of the great design books of the decade, and Papanek was soon internationally recognized as a thoughtful expert in product design and safety. He was, however, initially trained as an architect, first under Frank Lloyd Wright and later at Cooper Union and MIT. In the 1980s he did extensive work with UNESCO and the World Health Organization on the problem of third-world poverty. His interest in ecologically sound design was thus but a part of a larger philosophical outlook.

Throughout this book, many ideas and approaches to architecture and design have been explored. If we now attempt to weave them together, we realize that inevitably a new aesthetic must emerge out of the web of necessities, solutions and concepts.

1. The sustainability of life on this planet – not only for humankind but for all our fellow species – is paramount.
2. Sustainability can be helped or hindered by design. The impact of petrol-powered automobiles on the environment, wars, foreign policy, economics, morals and jobs is profound enough to serve as a chilling example.
3. Ethical design must also be environmentally sound and ecologically benign. It needs to be human in scale, humane and embedded in social responsibility.
4. Such design requires the help of governments, industry, entrepreneurs and laws, and the support of ordinary people through local user groups and individual decisions to shop intelligently and invest ethically.
5. Designers and architects all seem to be waiting for some fresh style or direction that will provide new meaning and new forms for the objects we create, based more on real requirements than on an arbitrarily invented style.
6. All objects, tools, graphics and dwellings must work towards the needs of the end-user on a more basic level than mere appearance, flamboyant 'gesture', or semiotic 'statements'. Nevertheless, the lack of any spiritual basis for design will make ethical and environmental considerations mere well-intentioned afterthoughts.
7. Design, when nourished by a deep spiritual concern for planet, environment, and people, results in a moral and ethical viewpoint. Starting from this point of departure will provide the new forms and expressions – the new aesthetic – we are all desperately trying to find.

Anyone with even a speck of sensitivity will agree that in the 1990s most dwellings, public buildings, means of transport are disturbingly ugly. Everyday objects look shoddy, mean and self-assertive. They need to look assertive; at the point of purchase every item on display

Victor Papanek, from *The Green Imperative: Natural Design for the Real World.* New York: Thames & Hudson, 1995, pp. 235–6.

must, visually speaking, screech for attention. This visual dominance is needed to distinguish it from its near-identical neighbours. Allowance is seldom made for the fact that this design assault will continue when the appliance is installed in one's home.

This dismaying visual pollution signals the imminent emergence of a new aesthetic, and most designers and architects will readily agree that, after Modernism, Memphis, Post-Modernism, Deconstructivism, Neo-Classicism, Object-Semiotics, and Post-Deconstructivism, a new direction – transcending fad, trend or fashionable styling – is long overdue. New directions in design and architecture don't occur accidentally, but always arise out of real changes in society, cultures and concepts.

320   JAMES CORNER
from "Eidetic Operations and New Landscapes" (1999)

James Corner, the founder of the landscape and planning firm Field Operations, begins this influential essay by defining "eidetic" as "a mental conception that may be picturable but may equally be acoustic, tactile, cognitive, or intuitive." With this broader definition in hand he rejects the traditional view of landscape design as a "scenic" or scenographic art bound to idealized images of the collective past. He poses instead a more active design alternative. Drawing in part on the "datascapes" of Dutch firms and other diagrammatic techniques, Corner views the "new landscape" and its design process as more dynamic, pragmatic, anticipatory, ecologically friendly, and conceptual at the same time. His firm has led the way in what has become a veritable renaissance of landscape theory and design predicated on ecological modeling.

The preceding paragraphs simplify the case greatly, but it is not my purpose here to outline a further critique of scenography. I am more interested in drawing a distinction between *landskip* (landscape as contrivance, primarily visual and sometimes also iconic or significant) and *landschaft* (landscape as an occupied milieu, the effects and significance of which accrue through tactility, use, and engagement over time). Both terms connote images, but the latter comprises a fuller, more synaesthetic, and less picturable range than the former. Furthermore, the working landscape, forged collectively and according to more utilitarian demands than anything artistic or formal, has been more the traditional domain of descriptive analysis by historians and geographers than of speculation by landscape architects.

And yet, given the obvious limits of landscape as representation, not to mention the pathetic failing of most of what passes as landscaping today, is it possible to realign the landscape architectural project toward the productive and participatory phenomena of the everyday, working landscape? By this I mean to suggest a return neither to agrarian existence nor to functionalist practices but rather to emphasize the experiential intimacies of

James Corner, from "Eidetic Operations and New Landscapes," in *Recovering Landscape: Essays in Contemporary Landscape Architecture*, ed. James Corner. New York: Princeton Architectural Press, 1999, pp. 158–60.

engagement, participation, and use over time, and to place geometrical and formal concerns in the service of human economy. In this sense, the city is as much a participatory landscape as are the highly technological energy and agricultural fields of the Southwest, the worked plots of private gardens, and the activities circulating across vast urban surfaces. Similarly, we might say that gardens are defined less by formal appearances than through the *activities* of gardening, just as agricultural fields derive their form from the logistics of farming, and cities from the flows, processes, and forces of urbanization. In the working *landschaft*, performance and event assumes conceptual precedence over appearance and sign.

The emphasis here shifts from object appearances to processes of formation, dynamics of occupancy, and the poetics of becoming. While these processes may be imaged, they are not necessarily susceptible to picturing. As with reading a book or listening to music, the shaping of images occurs mentally. Thus, if the role of the landscape architect is less to picture or represent these activities than it is to facilitate, instigate, and diversify their effects in time, then the development of more performative forms of imaging (as devising, enabling, unfolding techniques) is fundamental to this task.

A move away from ameliorative and scenographic *designs* toward more productive, engendering *strategies* necessitates a parallel shift from appearances and meanings to more prosaic concerns for how things work, what they do, how they interact, and what agency or effects they might exercise over time. A return to complex and instrumental landscape issues involves more organizational and strategic skills than those of formal composition per se, more programmatic and metrical practices than solely representational. Under such an operational rubric, issues such as program, event space, utility, economy, logistics, production, constraints, and desires become foregrounded, each turned through design toward newly productive and significant ends.

321   KENNETH FRAMPTON
from "Seven points for the millennium: an untimely manifesto" (1999)

Kenneth Frampton's writings on critical regionalism and tectonics over the previous two decades were never unsympathetic to environmental issues, but this address — the keynote address given to the UIA (Union Internationale des Architectes) conference in Beijing in 1999 — signals how pervasively environmental concerns have insinuated themselves into the architectural discourse in just a few years. All seven points articulated here (four explicitly and three implicitly) deal with the environment and the architect's power, or lack of power, in dealing with land and building issues in a rational manner. Against the "overly aestheticized discourse" of recent years, Frampton, in his fourth and fifth points, makes his case for sustainable design.

Kenneth Frampton, from "Seven points for the millennium: an untimely manifesto" (1999), in *Journal of Architecture* 5 (Spring 2000), pp. 26–9.

Landscape Form as a Redemptive Strategy

Since megalopolitan development now takes place at a global scale, it is obvious that few options are available that are capable of improving in any significant way the socio-cultural and ecological character of the average urbanised region. Other than the insertion of new systems of public transport only one possible strategy seems to be universally available, namely the blanket application of landscape interventions, in one form or another, as a way of ameliorating the environmental harshness of large tracts of our urbanised regions. The ubiquitous black-top parking lots of the North American continent are a case in point for clearly all such lots could be transformed into shaded parking areas through the subsidised application of tree planting as a co-ordinated public programme. Given the present escalation of global warming, the ecological low-term benefit accruing from such a provision would be considerable. The related enclosure of such spaces by planted berms would lead to further benefits of a more cultural nature, together with the enactment of legislation prohibiting the use of asphalt for the surfacing of parking areas, in order to reduce the destructive distribution of water run-off produced by the automotive system. It is well known that one may easily construct parking bays out of perforated, pre-fabricated concrete paving elements. These may be filled with earth and seeded with grass, so that the entire parking network throughout a megalopolis could be transformed into a landscape. The ecological and cultural benefits of such provisions ought to be self-evident.

This general 'greening' strategy possesses other pastoral benefits that we have so far not addressed; *first* that the current tendency to reduce the built environment to an endless proliferation of free-standing objects (of a more or less aesthetic quality depending on the circumstances) would be overcome by a landscape provision which would integrate all such objects into the surface of the ground and *second*, landscape would have the advantage of being much more culturally accessible to 'the average' person, than the contemporary built environment with all the seemingly unavoidable harshness of its instrumentality. This may also go some way towards explaining why landscape architects may be more readily allowed to treat the reorganisation of large tracts of land where planners and urban designers run into different forms of obstruction and resistance.

It is for these reasons among others that I am convinced that architectural and planning schools throughout the world should give much greater emphasis to the cultivation of landscape as an overarching system rather than concentrating exclusively, as they have tended to do up to now, on the design of buildings as free-standing objects.

Product-form versus Place-form

The terms *product-form* and *place-form* are, I believe, my own coinage and as such they need to be defined before proceeding further. I have in fact borrowed the term *product-form* from Max Bill for his usage referring to the way in which industrial design items are invariably determined as much through the constraints imposed by the modes of production as by ergonomic function. It is fairly obvious that the so-called hi-tech architects who have reinterpreted the craft of building in terms of modern productive methods have in effect been engaged in creating buildings, the forms of which are largely determined by the production methods employed in their constitution. It is clear that this deployment of sophisticated technology constitutes a fundamental challenge to traditional building methods where these are either too expensive or for other reasons unattainable today in terms of traditional craft production. Against this we may set the *place-form* or we may say, the foundational, topographic element that in one way or another is cast into the ground as a heavyweight site component that offers a literal form of resistance to the lightweight, productional superstructure poised on top of it. This is exactly the point that Renzo Piano made, in his contribution to the Jerusalem Seminar in Architecture of 1996, when he insisted that:

> the primary structure itself constitutes the place; it is sculpted in position, as it were, like a bas relief. This part is normally massive, opaque and heavy. Then you craft a light, transparent, and even temporary piece of architecture, which is poised on top of it. In such a combination, the heavy is permanent and the light is temporary. I believe that it is possible to create a tension between these two aspects, the place and the building, or rather the place and the crafted fabric. They are of two different worlds, but they may certainly coexist.[1]

Whether the superstructure need be light or temporary may no doubt be debated but clearly this perception of the dialogical relationship between the 'earthwork' and the 'roofwork' is a productive way of regarding the interaction between the 'wet' *landscaped place-form* and the 'dry,' *rationally assembled product-form*.

The capacity of the *place-form* to resist the homogenising tendency of universal technology may not be exclusively restricted to the 'earthwork,' particularly if we turn our attention to the roof and the membrane, both of which are potentially susceptible to the specific location of the work. In this respect, the case can be made and indeed is being made with increasing frequency in advanced contemporary practice that both cladding and fenestration are directly expressive of implicit and explicit values as these may be incorporated into a work of architecture in a given location at a specific moment in time. Some obvious examples may be cited which illustrate the way such values come to be expressed. For instance under the current building legislation obtaining in the Netherlands it is normally not possible to construct office buildings without operable windows, whereas in the United States it has long been standard practice to fully air-condition office structures and hence hermetically seal the fenestration throughout the building. This last has two maximising results, first, that it becomes impossible to ventilate the building naturally when the climate happens to be temperate according to the season and second, there is a corresponding maximisation of the amount of energy consumed by the building. As many experts have argued in the past, technological maximisation invariably entails negative side effects in whatever field it occurs, whether this be the maximised use of antibiotics in the field of allopathic medicine or the over-dependence on nitrates and insecticides in modern agricultural practice. In the first instance the invariable consequence is negative side effects and the generation of drug-resistant bacteria, in the second, we are confronted with the progressive pollution of non-renewable water sources. One may also cite innumerable examples of similar negative consequences in building culture, from the bulldozing of a gently undulating site completely flat in order to achieve an optimum economy in terms of the site work to the designing of museums in which no natural light is admitted in order to exclude even the slightest trace of ultra-violet light; in other words to maximise the conservation of the art object as opposed to the sensuous pleasure of the perceiving subject.

Against such practices we may set the recent efforts of certain hi-tech architects, such as Ken Yeang from Malaysia and Thomas Herzog from Germany, who have attempted to design buildings which are ecologically responsive and which are conceived of as operating climatically in a hybrid fashion, that is to say they are designed as louvered, sun-screened and filtered structures that are partly air-conditioned and partly ventilated by natural means.[2] It ought to be self-evident from an examination of traditional building culture that such structures possess the potential of giving specific expression to the cultural and physical values of the regions in which they happen to be situated and that these climatically responsive features may appear as a *répétition différente* of local cultural patterns.

A rather unusual example of such an instance are the so-called timber 'cases' that Renzo Piano incorporated into his cultural centre for the Kanak people in Noumea, New Caledonia. Aside from the multiple means provided for ventilating such structures, we enter here into the symbolic significance of the materials used and the way in which these may or may not allude to an idea of the place in an overt way. In this instance, the basket-like timber structures refer rather directly to the traditional dwellings of the Kanak people without literally mimicking them. We will find a parallel cultural reference, but perhaps to an entirely different culture, in the dense urban housing that the Renzo Piano Building Workshop realised in the Rue de Meaux, Paris in 1992. Here what we might call a high-tech/low-tech finish, namely terracotta tiles, is clearly intended to invoke the atmosphere and pattern of traditional building form. In as much as terracotta is commonly read as a traditional 'low-tech' material, this also opens the door to a reciprocity between the 'place-form' and the 'product-form' that need not necessarily solely involve the use of light-weight systems. It entails a 'hi-tech' expression that is as much heavy as it is light and dematerialised.

NOTES

1   R. Piano, in K. Frampton, *Technology, Place and Architecture* (New York, Rizzoli, 1998), p. 133.
2   See Yang's *Menara Mesiniaga Tower* (Selanger, Malaysia, 1982) and Herzog's *Halle 26* (Hanover, Germany, 1996).

322 JOHN BEARDSLEY
from "A Word for Landscape Architecture" (2000)

T he influence of the new complexity theories in the sciences, which inform so much of architectural and structural thinking in the 1990s, can also be found in this essay by John Beardsley, whose earlier career had focused largely on the aesthetics of landscape design. In this essay Beardsley considers several recent landscape projects that are concerned principally with preserving or creating ecological balance, such as the recently completed Xochimilco Ecological Park in Mexico City, designed by the Grupo de Diseño. They underscore for him the very dramatic changes that have very recently overtaken landscape practice and how they will direct all landscape planning in the future.

Of course, entropy is only one of many forces at work in the world. Current scientific studies of complexity propose that there may be some counterforce to the Second Law of Thermo-dynamics, exemplified in the tendency of matter and biological life toward ever-greater levels of organization. Many natural systems are aptly described as chaotic – the weather, the flow of turbulent fluids, the orbit of particles – and in such systems, small changes in initial circumstances can produce big differences in subsequent conditions. But complex systems seem to change within predictable limits and to exhibit tendencies toward self-similar patterns, or fractals. Thus the temperatures at a given place on the globe will vary, but within predictable limits; clouds and waves will resemble each other but will not be exactly the same.

Complexity science attempts to describe such patterns. It depicts a world that is dynamic and mutable but self-organizing at ever finer levels, for instance in the emergence of life from inert matter, in the evolution of more elaborate life forms from simpler ones, and in the increasingly intricate interdependencies within complex ecosystems like coral reefs and rain forests. Complexity theory might serve as a useful metaphor for contemporary cultural practice.

Complexity isn't necessarily *better*; but it increasingly characterizes our environmental and social circumstances. An appreciation of complexity might make cultural responses more discriminating, more robust. Landscape architecture is today exhibiting, in its own way, the tendency toward greater organization and complexity described by theorists and scientists, and in so doing it is endeavoring to keep at bay randomness and disorder. And it is this tension – between order and disorder, between organization and entropy – that provides much of the narrative power of contemporary landscape architecture.

Long overshadowed by architecture and the fine arts, landscape architecture is producing remarkable transformations in our public environments. The profession is maturing, conceptually it is more complex. It is developing the artistic and technical tools to address extraordinary social and environmental demands. The ways in which we understand and

John Beardsley, from "A Word for Landscape Architecture," in *Harvard Design Magazine* 12 (Fall 2000), pp. 62–3.

represent our relationship with nature are enormously important in the expression of culture. The ways in which we meet the challenges of urban sprawl, open space preservation, resource consumption and waste, and environmental protection and restoration are crucial to the quality of our lives – maybe even to the survival of our species. It is landscape architecture that confronts these challenges. I wish to make an extreme statement, if only to make an emphatic one: landscape architecture will prove the most consequential art of our time.

323   ANTOINE PICON
from "Anxious Landscapes: From the Ruin to Rust" (2000)

This thoughtful essay, perhaps symptomatic of the broader disquiet evident in the years surrounding the change of millennia, opens with a description of the aerial images one sees on flying into Newark Airport (although almost any metropolitan center would do). In the distance shines the reflective and metallic visage of the distant metropolis, yet below one sees only a landscape filled with a chaotic display of rusting bridges, barges, tracks, cranes, container bins, and petroleum refineries. As much as the natural landscape or historical ruins make us happy and at ease with the world, Picon argues, the oxidizing technological landscape makes us apprehensive of our future well-being. The question that this French historian poses is "Why?" The answer is not simple, but it and the possibility of our re-enchantment seem to lie not just in the cyborg presentiment of our futuristic decayed human creations.

Why does rust frighten us so while the ruin is adorned with a reassuring character? It is very probably necessary to begin by replying to that question before we attempt to wrestle with "the inevitable ugliness of the technical universe." The ruin, as we have said, restores man to nature. Rust, on the other hand, confines him in the middle of his productions as if within a prison, a prison all the more terrible since he is its builder. Who other than he has built these cities which he practically never leaves anymore, these networks that keep him attached to his television or computer screen? The simple perspective of a destiny of this kind reveals what is inhuman in the work of man. The biggest fear suggested by the contemporary technological landscape is that of the death of humanity in the midst of the signs of its triumph over nature.

   Science fiction films describe this death to us in at least two different ways: extinction of the catastrophic sort, or extinction of a more insidious variety, in which a progressive denaturation of man occurs. The disappearance of the ozone layer on one side, the mechanization of man or his instrumentalization by means of genetic manipulation on the other – such are the two types of scenarios that haunt us. In the first instance, man and humanity disappear together. In the second, man witnesses himself being progressively dehumanized. He becomes an insensitive machine, capable of the worst monstrosities.

Antoine Picon, from "Anxious Landscapes: From the Ruin to Rust," trans. Karen Bates, in *Grey Room*, 01 (Fall 2000), pp. 79–81.

When perceived negatively, the cyborg – that amalgam of flesh and machine that recurs frequently in science fiction novels and films – constitutes one of the most extreme expressions of this second alternative.[1]

A Re-enchanted World

Nothing forces us, however, to envisage the becoming-cyborg of humanity as the shipwreck of civilization. More generally, it may very well be that the anxious character of many contemporary landscapes is the indication of profound transformations affecting the definition of the subject who contemplates them, without such transformations necessarily being synonymous with the irremediable degradation of the human condition. After all, this is not the first time that the look that we cast over our surroundings has been modified. Each time, such a transformation proves inseparable from a mutation of the ideal image we project of ourselves. When the categories of vision changed radically at the dawn of the Renaissance, for example, and perspective was invented, the figure of the modern man emerged to replace that of the faithful of the medieval period. Instead of embodying irretrievable degradation, the cyborg could well represent a new avatar of this ideal creature, this fiction that serves us simultaneously as reference and project.

Without resolving this new image that is about to be added to the long series of those that have allowed man to define himself and to act upon himself and his environment, one cannot help but be struck by the extent of the mutations that already affect the categories of vision. We see much further and much higher than our predecessors. Shortly after having invented perspective, Renaissance man was elevated by thought above his principal cities in order to portray them.[2] With the aid of satellites, we can now observe the entire earth like a tapestry of varied motifs. At the other end of the optic scale, we are now capable of observing even the most tenuous of phenomena, such as crystallizations and microfissures. We can be much more nearsighted, and, as Pascal suggested in his *Pensées* with his reflections on the two infinities,[3] there are entire worlds that reveal themselves to us in the folds of matter.

At the two extremities of this range of possible viewpoints, familiar forms seem to give way to luminous effects – scintillations, iridescence, reflections – as well as to textures often based upon contradictory impressions like smoothness, glossiness, or graininess. Configurations, both immediately perceptible by the senses and more abstract, substitute themselves for the contours of the world that is familiar. Seen by satellite, Los Angeles doesn't look much different from a section of matter observed in a microscope. The importance of the dominion of lights and textures in the contemporary technological landscape could well originate from this transformation in the categories of vision. Such a transformation leads us to suspend, if only provisionally, questions such as those of "far" and "near." Who tells us that it's Los Angeles we're contemplating, instead of a piece of sidewalk?

Rendered somewhat abstract by its functional character, the contemporary urban landscape is organized according to textures that owe more to woven design than to form in a traditional sense. It is perhaps this relationship with a universe more textile than sculptural or architectonic that remains for us to investigate and cultivate.

The abstract motifs that compose this landscape confer on it something mysterious, even magic. Like cyborgs and other intelligent robots of science fiction, new, fantastic creatures haunt its dark avenues forever after. We are possibly on the eve of a re-enchantment of the world. To live in an enchanted world, however, is not necessarily synonymous with ease. The people of the Middle Ages developed in a world populated by angels and demons, magic forests and supernatural animals. Yet this world was at the same time hard and cruel: in fairy tales, the children are almost always afraid and Tom Thumb is at the point of being eaten. No doubt it is for this reason that we feel at times lost and distressed in the middle of our cities, cities as large as the ogre's house.

NOTES

1   See Antoine Picon, *La Ville, territoire des cyborgs* (Paris: Éditions de l'Imprimeur, 1998).

2   See for example Antoine Picon and Jean-Paul Robert, *Un Atlas parisien: Le Dessus des cartes* (Paris: Éditions du Pavillon de l'Arsenal and Picard, 1999).

3   Blaise Pascal, *Pensées*, in *Œuvres complètes* (Paris: Gallimard, Collection de la Pléiade, 1954), 1106.

324   WILLIAM McDONOUGH AND MICHAEL BRAUNGART
from *Cradle to Cradle* (2000)

I n 1995 the architect William McDonough joined forces with the chemist Michael Braungart to create the firm MBDC. Not unlike McDonough's architectural office in New York City, the purpose of this firm, based in Charlottesville, Virginia, is "to create products and systems that contribute to economic, social, and environment prosperity." The firm also issues citations to products on the market that meet their high standards of environmentally friendly design criteria. *Cradle to Cradle* is the definitive statement of their design philosophy, and since its appearance in 2000 it has remained a bestseller. This passage on the "Industrial Re-Evolution" stands at the core of their beliefs.

An Industrial Re-Evolution

Design that deeply respects diversity on all the levels we have discussed brings about a process of *industrial re-evolution*. Our products and processes can be most deeply effective when they are resonant with information and responses – when they most resemble the

William McDonough and Michael Braungart, from *Cradle to Cradle: Remaking the Way We Make Things*. New York: North Point Press, 2000, pp. 154–6.

living world. Inventive machines that use the mechanisms of nature instead of harsh chemicals, concrete, or steel are a step in the right direction, but they are still *machines* – still a way of using technology (albeit benign technology) to harness nature to human purposes. The same could be said of our increasing use of cybertechnology, biotechnology, and nanotechnology to replace the functions of chemicals and brute force. The new technologies do not in themselves create industrial revolutions; unless we change their context, they are simply hyperefficient engines driving the steamship of the first Industrial Revolution to new extremes.

Even today, most cutting-edge environmental approaches are still based on the idea that human beings are inevitably destructive toward nature and must be curbed and contained. Even the idea of "natural capital" characterizes nature as a tool to be used for our benefit. This approach might have been valid two hundred years ago, when our species was developing its industrial systems, but now it cries out for rethinking. Otherwise, we are limited to efforts to slow the destruction of the natural world while we sustain the current industrial system of production and consumption for a few hundred years more. With human ingenuity and technological advances, we might even be able to create sustaining systems for our own species beyond that, after the natural world has greatly declined. But how exciting is sustainability? If a man characterized his relationship with his wife as sustainable, you might well pity them both.

Natural systems take from their environment, but they also give something back. The cherry tree drops its blossoms and leaves while it cycles water and makes oxygen; the ant community redistributes the nutrients throughout the soil. We can follow their cue to create a more inspiring engagement – a partnership – with nature. We can build factories whose products and by-products nourish the ecosystem with biodegradable material and recirculate technical materials instead of dumping, burning, or burying them. We can design systems that regulate themselves. Instead of using nature as a mere tool for human purposes, we can strive to become tools of nature who serve its agenda too. We can celebrate the fecundity in the world, instead of perpetuating a way of thinking and making that eliminates it. And there can be many of us and the things we make, because we have the right system – a creative, prosperous, intelligent, and fertile system – and, like the ants, we will be "effective."

325 MICHAEL BRAUNGART

from "Beyond the Limits of Sustainable Architecture" (2002)

With all the press statements, conferences, and books published on the "hot" issue of sustainability around the turn of the century, it was perhaps only to be expected that a more reflective period would ensue. Michael Braungart's contribution to the exhibition catalogue and book, *Big & Green: Toward Sustainable Architecture in the 21st Century*, is a case in point. Whereas the exhibition, which was held at the National Building Museum in Washington, DC, lauded the great strides that have been made in sustainable design, Braungart's note of caution suggests that the issues might be much more complex. Beyond the strategies of achieving energy efficiencies, recycling, the lessening of materials and weight of building – there remains the problem of the harvesting and processing of the materials themselves. Engineering this facet of the sustainability model remains an issue that will undoubtedly receive much future attention.

During the last decade of the twentieth century the high-rise building trades were booming. The traditional leaders in skyscraper construction, the urban centers of Europe and North America, were erecting tall building after tall building, reshaping the cityscape in typically energetic fashion. But the real boom was happening elsewhere. In Asia, nearly 1,800 skyscrapers were constructed during the 1990s, making the region the busiest builder of large-scale structures in the world. In Shanghai alone, where in 1969 there were only a dozen high-rises, 138 steel-and-concrete towers transformed the skyline in a single decade.

One might applaud these stunning feats of engineering. The recent building boom in East Asia transformed hundreds of thousands of tons of raw steel into dozens of potent symbols of technology, prosperity, and progress, celebrating the dynamism – short-lived, it turned out – of a late-twentieth-century economic force, the so-called Asian tigers. Yet these new skyscrapers also symbolized many of the environmental problems that have come to define contemporary building design. And they are only a fraction of massive stock of large-scale buildings that grows daily in industrialized nations and at an ever-quickening pace in the developing world.

So what's the problem with large-scale architecture? It's not just that buildings have gotten so big – it's more complex than that. We are quite capable of designing big, majestic, and inspiring buildings that celebrate human creativity and pleasure with enthusiasm *and* environmental sensitivity. Nevertheless, on a global scale, the physical impact of increasing building mass is undeniable. As we move into the second century of the skyscraper, the construction of buildings is consuming some *three billion tons* of raw materials each year. By most estimates, new construction accounts for 40 percent of the raw stone, gravel, and sand used each year; 40 percent of the processed materials, such as steel; and one-quarter of the world's wood harvest. Together, new and existing buildings account for two-fifths of the world's annual energy use, one-sixth of its water consumption, and one-half of its waste

Michael Braungart, from "Beyond the Limits of Sustainable Architecture: A New Material Sensibility for the Twenty-first Century," in *Big & Green: Toward Sustainable Architecture in the 21st Century*, ed. David Gissen. New York: Princeton Architectural Press, 2002, pp. 114–15, 120, 125.

stream. In fact, the construction and maintenance of modern buildings rivals the material and energy use of the entire manufacturing sector of the global economy.

[. . .]

Do these approaches to sustainability – efficiency, recycling, dematerialization, lightness – signal the decoupling of materials from economic growth that the World Resources Institute is hoping for? Perhaps. Does that mean we can now begin to feel more sanguine about architecture's effect on nature and human culture? Well, maybe not.

Each of these strategies has something to offer. Certainly, retrofitting an old building and reusing materials is a positive way to create new, pleasant spaces for office workers. And it's true that efficiently constructed buildings cut waste, and that light materials minimize resource consumption. But the overall design and material makeup of efficient buildings is very much like that of the skyscrapers of Shanghai and Berlin. While their designers may make material substitutions – superglass, triple glazing, recycled plastic surfaces – the chemistry of materials in efficient buildings tends to be largely the same as that in both their predecessors and their more gluttonous contemporaries. The same carcinogens, the same toxic heavy metals, the same endocrine disrupters – only now more tightly enclosed. Are these the kind of buildings we want all over the world?

[. . .]

Why not create buildings and systems that give more people more of what they want, need, and love? Cradle-to-cradle materials allow us to do so. And intelligent buildings allow us to leave an ever-larger ecological footprint, an imprint on the world that we can delight in rather than lament. Ultimately, it will be the delight buildings inspire, the way they enhance our feeling for life, that will move ecologically intelligent design from the agenda of a few to the demand of many. Imagine buildings so delightful, so expressive of the world's diverse interactions between nature and human culture, so comfortably affordable for so many, so able to inspire wonder in the living world, that the demand for them is driven by pleasure from the bottom up. Then perhaps, the newest skyscraper in Shanghai will be powered locally and remotely by the wind and the sun, and on a stroll down a wide, sunlit hallway you will feel a breeze from the East China Sea and know quite certainly just where you are and how it feels to inhabit that unique coastal land.

326 MASDAR, THE ABU DHABI FUTURE ENERGY COMPANY

press release, "WWF and Abu Dhabi's Masdar Initiative unveil plan for world's first carbon-neutral, waste-free, car-free city" (2008)

Norman Foster was one of the few architects throughout the last decades of the twentieth century who remained committed to technology and to the environmental ideals he learned in the 1960s. His Hongkong and Shanghai Bank (1986) is notable for its technologically sophisticated design, while the Swiss Re building in London (2004) not only became an instant global icon but also set a new standard for energy efficiency. Thus it was not surprising that in May of 2007 Foster + Partners unveiled the preliminary plans for the world first "zero-carbon, zero-waste city" in Abu Dhabi. This announcement by the Masdar, The Abu Dhabi Future Energy Company, quite possibly understates the city's global importance for the architecture of the future.

Abu Dhabi, United Arab Emirates, 13 January 2008 – The WWF and Masdar, The Abu Dhabi Future Energy Company, today launched a "Sustainability Action Plan" to deliver the world's greenest city – Masdar City. Located near Abu Dhabi International Airport, Masdar City will be the world's first zero-carbon, zero-waste, car-free city, aiming to exceed the 10 sustainability principles of "One Planet Living™"– a global initiative launched by the Worldwide Fund for Nature and environmental consultancy BioRegional.

Masdar City's electricity will be generated by photovoltaic panels, while cooling will be provided via concentrated solar power. Water will be provided through a solar-powered desalination plant. Landscaping within the city and crops grown outside the city will be irrigated with grey water and treated waste water produced by the city's water treatment plant.

The city is part of the Masdar Initiative, Abu Dhabi's multi-faceted investment in the exploration, development and commercialisation of future energy sources and clean technology solutions. The six-square kilometre city, growing eventually to 1,500 businesses and 50,000 residents, will be home to international business and top minds in the field of sustainable and alternative energy.

A model of the Masdar City will be unveiled on January 21, at the World Future Energy Summit in Abu Dhabi. Ground breaks for the construction of the city in the first quarter of 2008.

WWF and Abu Dhabi's Masdar Initiative unveil plan for world's first carbon-neutral, waste-free, car-free city
"Masdar City" to be flagship of WWF One Planet Living Programme

Jean-Paul Jeanrenaud, Director of WWF International's One Planet Living initiative, said: "Today Abu Dhabi is embarking on a journey to become the global capital of the renewable energy revolution. Abu Dhabi is the first hydrocarbon-producing nation to have taken such a significant step towards sustainable living.

"Masdar is an example of the paradigm shift that is needed. The strategic vision of the Abu Dhabi government is a case study in global leadership. We hope that Masdar City will prove that sustainable living can be affordable and attractive in all aspects of human living – from businesses and manufacturing facilities to universities and private homes," Jeanreneaud continued.

Dr. Sultan Al Jaber, CEO of the Masdar Initiative, said: "Masdar City will question conventional patterns of urban development, and set new benchmarks for sustainability and environmentally friendly design – the students, faculty and businesses located in Masdar City will not only be able to witness innovation first-hand, but they will also participate in its development."

"We are pleased to be able to work with One Planet Living to make our vision a reality," he said.

Pooran Desai OBE, co-founder of BioRegional and Technical Director of the One Planet Living Communities programme, said Masdar would be the largest and the most advanced sustainable communities in the world.

"The vision of One Planet Living is a world where people everywhere can lead happy, healthy lives within their fair share of the Earth's resources. Masdar gives us a breathtaking insight into this positive, alternative future.

"In realising the goal of a sustainable future, Masdar is committed to surpassing the One Planet Living Program's 10 Guiding Principles, covering issues that range from how waste is dealt with to the energy performance of the buildings."

The One Planet Living programme is based on 10 unique principles of sustainability. Masdar City will meet and exceed each of these, as detailed below.

These targets are to be achieved by the time the Masdar City is completed and fully functioning in 2015.

One Planet Living principle Masdar Target

ZERO CARBON: 100 per cent of energy supplied by renewable energy – Photovoltaics, concentrated solar power, wind, waste to energy and other technologies

ZERO WASTE: 99 per cent diversion of waste from landfill (includes waste reduction measures, re-use of waste wherever possible, recycling, composting, waste to energy)

SUSTAINABLE TRANSPORT: Zero carbon emissions from transport within the city; implementation of measures to reduce the carbon cost of journeys to the city boundaries (through facilitating and encouraging the use of public transport, vehicle sharing, supporting low emissions vehicle initiatives)

SUSTAINABLE MATERIALS: Specifying high recycled materials content within building products; tracking and encouraging the reduction of embodied energy within materials and throughout the construction process; specifying the use of sustainable materials such as Forest Stewardship Council certified timber, bamboo and other products

SUSTAINABLE FOOD: Retail outlets to meet targets for supplying organic food and sustainable and or fair trade products

SUSTAINABLE WATER: Per capita water consumption to be at least 50 per cent less than the national average; all waste water to be re-used

HABITATS AND WILDLIFE: All valuable species to be conserved or relocated with positive mitigation targets

CULTURE AND HERITAGE: Architecture to integrate local values.

EQUITY AND FAIR TRADE: Fair wages and working conditions for all workers (including construction) as defined by international labour standards

HEALTH AND HAPPINESS: Facilities and events for every demographic group

ACKNOWLEDGMENTS

We would like to thank Eric Ellingsen, Patrick Evans, Ralph Ghoche, and Louis Martin for their support and input on recent architectural debates. At the Canadian Centre for Architecture, we greatly appreciated the assistance of Alexis Sornin, Renata Guttman, Paul Chénier, Pierre Boisvert, and Suzie Quintal. At the Graham Resource Center of Illinois Institute of Technology, we wish to thank Matt Cook and Stuart MacRae. We also owe a huge debt of gratitude to Irina Nazarova and Orlando Barone for their help in translating Russian and Italian texts.

Text Acknowledgments

We and the publisher gratefully acknowledge the permission granted to reproduce the copyright material in this book:

1. John Ruskin, from *Fors Clavigera: Letters to the Workmen and Labourers of Great Britain*. Chicago and New York: Belford, Clarke & Co., n.d., pp. 72–3.

2. Christopher Dresser, from *Studies in Design*. London: Cassell, Petter & Galpin, 1874–6, pp. 11–12.

3. Richard Redgrave, from *Manual of Design* (1876), New York: Scribner, Welford & Armstrong, 1877, p. 15.

4. William Morris, from "The Prospects of Architecture in Civilization" (1881), in *Hopes and Fears for Art*. Boston: Roberts Bros., 1882, pp. 212–14.

5. Christopher Dresser, from *Japan: Its Architecture, Art, and Art Manufacturers*. London: Longmans, Green & Co, 1882, pp. 234–5, 237–8. Reprinted by permission of Garland Press.

6. Oscar Wilde, from "Art and the Handicraftsman" (1882), in *Essays and Lectures* (1888). London: Methuen & Co. Reprinted New York: Garland, 1978, pp. 185–8, 190–1. Reprinted by permission of Garland Press.

7. Arthur H. Mackmurdo, from "Arbitrary Conditions of Art," in *Hobby Horse*, II (1887), pp. 58–60.

8. William Morris, from "The Revival of Architecture" (1888), cited from Nikolaus Pevsner, *Some Architectural Writers of the Nineteenth Century*. Oxford: Clarendon Press, 1972, pp. 322–4.

9. Walter Crane, from *The Claims of Decorative Art*. London: Lawrence & Bullen, 1892, p. 12–15.

10. John D. Sedding, from "Design" (1891?), cited from *Arts and Crafts Essays*. London, 1893. Reprinted New York: Garland, 1977, pp. 409–12.

11. Charles Rennie Mackintosh, from "Architecture" (1893), in *Charles Rennie Mackintosh: The Architectural Papers*, ed. Pamela Robertson. Cambridge: MIT Press, 1990, pp. 206–7. Reprinted by permission of the Hunterian Museum and Art Gallery, University of Glasgow.

12. Charles Robert Ashbee, from *A Few Chapters in Workshop Re-Construction and Citizenship*. London: Guild and School of Handicraft, 1894, pp. 12–13.

13. Jacob von Falke, from *Art in the House* (1871). Trans. from *Die Kunst im Hause* by Charles C. Perkins. Boston: L. Prang & Co., 1878, pp. 170–2.

14. Georg Hirth, from *The German Renaissance Room* (1880). Trans. from *Das deutsche Zimmer der Renaissance* by Harry Francis Mallgrave. Munich: G. Hirth's Verlag, 1880, pp. 1–2.

15. Robert Dohme, from *The English House* (1888). Trans. from *Das englische Haus* by Harry Francis Mallgrave. Braunschweig: George Westermann, 1988, pp. 28, 42.

16. Cornelius Gurlitt, from *Inside the Middle-Class House* (1888). Trans. from *Im Bürgerhaus* by Harry Francis Mallgrave. Dresden: Gilbers'sche Köngl. Hof-Verlagsbuchhandlung, 1888, pp. 227–9.

17. Louis-Charles Boileau, from "Shops of the Bon Marché in Paris – Grand Staircase." Trans. from "Magasins du bon Marché, à Paris – grand Escalier" by Christina Contandriopoulos and Harry Francis Mallgrave, in *Encyclopédie d'architecture*. Paris: V. A. Morel, 1876, p. 120.

18. Charles Blanc, from *The Fine Arts at the Universal Exposition of 1878* (1878). Trans. from *Les Beaux-Arts à l'Exposition Universelle de 1878* by Christina Contandriopoulos and Harry Francis Mallgrave. Paris: Libraire Renocard, 1878, pp. 39–41.

19. Eugène-Emmanuel Viollet-le-Duc, "The Buildings of the Universal Exposition of 1878" (1878). Trans. from "Les bâtiments de l'Exposition Universelle de 1878" by Christina Contandriopoulos and Harry Francis Mallgrave, in *L'art: Revue hebdomadaire illustrée*. Paris: Ballue, 1878, p. 140.

20. Émile Zola, from *Au Bonheur des Dames* (1884). Trans. and ed. Robin Buss as *The Ladies' Delight*. London: Penguin Books, 2001, pp. 245–6. Reproduced by permission of Penguin Books Ltd.

21. Joris-Karl Huysmans, *À Rebours* (1884). Trans. Robert Baldick as *Against Nature*. London: Penguin, 2003, pp. 61–2. Reproduced by permission of Penguin Books Ltd.

22. Samuel Bing, from *Artistic Japan*. London, 1888, pp. 1–4.

23. Joseph Eugène Anatole de Baudot, from "The Universal Exposition of 1889 – first visit to the Champs de Mars" (1889), in *Encyclopédie d'architecture* 4 (1888–9), trans. Christina Contandriopoulos and Harry Francis Mallgrave, pp. 9–10.

24. Louis Gonse, from "The Architecture at the Universal Exposition of 1889," in *Gazette des Beaux-Arts*, trans. Christina Contandriopoulos and Harry Francis Mallgrave. Paris, 1889, pp. 476–8.

25. Edmond de Goncourt, from Edmond and Jules de Goncourt, *Journal, Mémoires de la vie littéraire, 1895–1896*, vol. 4, trans. Christina Contandriopoulos and Harry Francis Mallgrave. Monaco: Fasquelle & Flammarion, 1956, pp. 156–7.

26. Henry Hudson Holly, from "Modern Dwellings: Their Construction, Decoration, and Furniture," in *Harper's New Monthly Magazine* 52 (December 1875–May 1876), pp. 855–6.

27. Robert Swain Peabody, from "Georgian Homes of New England," in *The American Architect and Building News*, vol. II, 1877, p. 338.

28. Clarence Cook, from *The House Beautiful: Essays on Beds and Tables, Stools and Candlesticks* (1877). New York: Charles Scribner's Sons, 1895, pp. 19, 20.

29. Leopold Eidlitz, from *The Nature and Function of Art: More Especially of Architecture*. New York: A. C. Armstrong & Son, 1881, pp. 223–4.

30. Louis Sullivan, from "Characteristics and Tendencies of American Architecture" (1885). In *The Inland Architect and Builder*, vol. VI, #5, November 1885, pp. 58–9.

31 George William Sheldon, from *Artistic Country-Seats: Types of Recent American Villa and Cottage Architecture*. New York: D. Appleton & Co., 1886, p. 157.

32. John Root et al., from "What are the Present Tendencies of Architectural Design in America?," in *The Inland Architect and News Record* 9:3 (March 1887), pp. 23–4, 26.

33. Mariana Griswold Van Rensselaer, from *Henry Hobson Richardson and His Works* (1888). Reprint edition, New York: Dover Publications, 1969, p. 97.

34. Friedrich Baumann, from "Thoughts on Architecture," from "Thoughts on Style," in *The Inland Architect and News Record* XVI:5 (November 1890), p. 59.

35. Louis Sullivan, from "Ornament in Architecture," in *Louis Sullivan: The Public Papers*, ed. Robert Twombly. Chicago: University of Chicago Press, 1988, pp. 80–1.

36. Montgomery Schuyler, from "Last Words about the World's Fair" (1894), in *American Architecture and Other Writings*, ed. William H. Jordy and Ralph Coe. Cambridge, MA: Harvard University Press, 1961, pp. 571–3. Reprinted by permission of the publisher, The Belknap Press of Harvard University Press. Copyright © 1961 by the President and Fellows of Harvard College. Originally published in *Architectural Record, 3* (January–March 1894), 271–301.

37. Louis Sullivan, from "Emotional Architecture as Compared with Intellectual: A Study in Subjective and Objective," in *The Inland Architect and News Record* XXIV:4 (November 1894), p. 34.

38. Richard Lucae, "On the Aesthetic Development of Iron Constructions, especially its Use in Spaces of a Significant Span," from "Über die ästhetische Ausbildung der Eisen-Konstruktionen" trans. Harry Francis Mallgrave, in *Deutsche Bauzeitung* (January 13, 1870), pp. 10–13.

39. Friedrich Nietzsche, from *The Use and Abuse of History* (1872), trans. Adrian Collins. New York: Macmillan, 1967, pp. 14, 16–17.

40. Robert Vischer, "On the Optical Sense of Form: A Contribution to Aesthetics," from *Über das optische Formgefühl: Ein Beitrag zur Aesthetik* (1873), trans. Harry Francis Mallgrave and Eleftherios Ikonomou, in *Empathy, Form, and Space: Problems in German Aesthetics 1873–1893*. Santa Monica, CA: Getty Publication Programs, 1994, pp. 91–2. Reprinted by permission of the J. Paul Getty Trust ©.

41. Constantin Lipsius, "On the Aesthetic Treatment of Iron in Tall Buildings," from "Ueber die ästhetische Behandlung des Eisens in Hochbau," trans. Harry Francis Mallgrave, in *Deutsche Bauzeitung* 12 (1878), pp. 360–3.

42. Conrad Fiedler, from "Observations on the Nature and History of Architecture" (1878), trans. Harry Francis Mallgrave, in *Empathy, Form, and Space: Problems of German Aesthetics 1873–1893*, Santa Monica, CA: Getty Publication Programs, 1994, pp.142. Reprinted by permission of the J. Paul Getty Trust ©.

43. Hans Auer, "The Development of Space in Architecture," from "Die Entwickelung des Raumes in der Baukunst," trans. Harry Francis Mallgrave, in *Allgemeine Bauzeitung* 48 (1883), pp. 66, 74.

44. Josef Bayer, "Modern Building Types," from "Modernene Bautypen," trans. Harry Francis Mallgrave, in *Baustudien und Baubilder: Schriften zur Kunst*. Jena: Eugen Diederichs, 1919, pp. 282–3, 286–7.

45. Heinrich Wölfflin, "Prolegomena to a Psychology of Architecture," from "Prolegomena zu einer Psychologie der Architektur" (1886), trans. Harry Francis Mallgrave and Eleftherios Ikonomou, in *Empathy, Form, and Space: Problems of German Aesthetics 1873–1893*, Santa Monica, CA: Getty Publication Programs, 1994, pp. 151, 182–3. Reprinted by permission of the J. Paul Getty Trust ©.

46. Adolf Göller, "What is the Cause of Perpetual Style-Change in Architecture?," from "Was ist die Ursache der immerwährenden Stilveränderung in der Architektur?" trans. Harry Francis Mallgrave and Eleftherios Ikonomou, in *Empathy, Form, and Space: Problems of German Aesthetics 1873–1893*, Santa Monica, CA: Getty Publication Programs, 1994, pp. 194–5, 198. Reprinted by permission of the J. Paul Getty Trust ©.

47. Cornelius Gurlitt, "Göller's Aesthetic theory," from "Göller's ästhetische Lehre" trans. Harry Francis Mallgrave, in *Deutsche Bauzeitung* 21 (1887), pp. 603, 606.

48. Ferdinand Tönnies, from *Gemeinschaft und Gesellschaft* (1887), trans. Charles P. Loomis as *Community and Society*. New Brunswick, NJ: Transaction Books, 1988, pp. 234–5. Copyright © 1988 by Transaction Publishers. Reprinted by permission of the publisher.

49. Camillo Sitte, from *City Planning According to Its Artistic Principles*, from *Die Städtebau nach seinen künstlerischen Grundsätzen*, trans. George R. Collins and Christiane Crasemeann Collins, in *Camillo Sitte: The Birth of Modern City Planning*. New York: Rizzoli, 1986, pp. 224–5. Used with permission from Rizzoli International Publications, Inc.

50. August Schmarsow, *The Essence of Architectural Creation*, from *Das Wesen der architektonischen Schöpfung* (1893) trans. Harry Francis Mallgrave and Eleftherios Ikonomou, in *Empathy, Form, and Space: Problems of German Aesthetics 1873–1893*, Santa Monica, CA: Getty Publication Programs, 1994, pp. 286–7. Reprinted by permission of the J. Paul Getty Trust ©.

51. Otto Wagner, from "Inaugural Address to the Academy of Fine Arts," Santa Monica, CA: Getty Publication Programs, 1988, pp. 159–60. Reprinted by permission of the J. Paul Getty Trust ©.

52. Max Fabiani, "Out of the Wagner School," from "Aus der Wagner Schule," trans. Harry Francis Mallgrave, in *Der Architekt* 1 (1895), pp. 53–4.

53. Julius Lessing, "New Paths," from "Neue Wege" trans. Harry Francis Mallgrave, in *Kunstgewerbeblatt* 6 (1895), pp. 1–5.

54. Richard Streiter, "Out of Munich," from "Aus München," trans. Harry Francis Mallgrave, in *Pan* 2:3 (1896), p. 249.

55. Otto Wagner, from *Moderne Architektur* (1896), trans. Harry Francis Mallgrave as *Otto Wagner: Modern Architecture*, Santa Monica, CA: Getty Publication Programs, 1988, pp. 92–3, 96. Reprinted by permission of the J. Paul Getty Trust ©.

56. Richard Streiter, "Contemporary Architectural Questions" (1898), trans. from "Architektonische Zeitfragen: Eine Sammlung und Sichtung verschiedener Anschauungen mit besonderer Beziehung auf Profesor Otto Wagners Schrift 'Moderne Architektur'" (1898), trans. Harry Francis Mallgrave, in *Richard Streiter: Ausgewählte Schriften zur Aesthetik und Kunst-Geschichte*. Munich: Delphin, 1913, pp. 81–2.

57. Fritz Schumacher, "Style and Fashion" (1898), from "Stil und Mode," trans. Harry Francis Mallgrave, in *Im Kampfe um die Kunst*. Strasbourg: J. H. Heitz, 1902, pp. 23, 28–9.

58. August Endell, "On the Possibility and Goal of a New Architecture, from "Möglichkeit und Ziele einer neuen Architektur," trans. Harry Francis Mallgrave, in *Deutsche Kunst und Dekoration* 1 (March 1898), pp. 143–5.

59. Adolf Loos, "Potemkin City," from "Die Potemkin'sche Stadt" (1898), trans. Jane O. Newman and John H. Smith, in Adolf Loos, *Spoken into the Void: Collected Essays 1897–1900*. Cambridge, MA: MIT Press, 1982, pp. 95–6. © 1982 Massachusetts Institute of Technology, by permission of The MIT Press.

60. Hermann Muthesius, "New Ornament and New Art" (1901), from "Neues Ornament und neue Kunst," trans. Harry Francis Mallgrave, in *Dekorative Kunst* 4:9, pp. 364–5.

61. Hermann Muthesius, from *Stil-Architektur und Baukunst* (1902), trans. by Stanford Anderson as *Style-Architecture and Building-Art*. Santa Monica, CA: Getty Publication Programs, 1994, pp. 50, 79. Reprinted by permission of the J. Paul Getty Trust ©.

62. Fritz Schumacher, from "The Reconquest of a Harmonious Culture," inaugural address to the German Werkbund (October 1907), from excerpts published in Kurt Junghanns, *Der Deutsche Werkbund: Sein erstes Jahrzehnt*, trans. Harry Francis Mallgrave. Berlin: Henschelverlage Kunst und Gesellschaft, 1982, pp. 140–2.

63. Adolf Loos, "Ornament and Crime" (1908), from "Ornament und Verbrechen" trans. Wilfried Wang, in *The Architecture of Adolf Loos*. London: Arts Council Exhibition, 1985, pp. 100, 103.

64. Joseph August Lux, *Engineer-Aesthetic* (1910), from *Ingenieur-Aesthetik*, trans. Harry Francis Mallgrave. Munich: Gustav Lammers, 1910, pp. 14, 38.

65. Peter Behrens, "Art and Technology" (1910), trans. Iain Boyd Whyte, in *Industriekultur: Peter Behrens and the AEG*. Cambridge, MA: MIT Press, 1984, pp. 215, 219. © 1984 Massachusetts Institute of Technology, by permission of The MIT Press.

66. Hermann Muthesius and Henry van de Velde, from "theses" and "counter-theses" presented at the Cologne Werkbund Conference (1914), from Herman Muthesius, *Die Werkbund-Arbeit der Zukunft*, trans. Harry Francis Mallgrave. Jena: Eugen Diederichs, 1914, pp. 32, 49–50.

67. Camillo Boito, "On the Future Style of Italian Architecture" (1880), from *Architettura del Medio Evo in Italia*, trans. Maria Pia Smargiasso. Milan: Hoepli, 1880, pp. 26–7.

68. Hendrik Berlage, from "Baouwkunst en impressionisme" (1894), trans. Iain Boyd Whyte, as "Architecture and Impressionism," in *Hendrik Petrus Berlage: Thoughts on Style 1886–1909*. Santa Monica, CA: Getty Publication Programs, 1996, pp. 119–20. Reprinted by permission of the J. Paul Getty Trust ©.

69. Ebenezer Howard, from *To-morrow: A Peaceful Path to Real Reform*. London: Swan Sonnenschein & Co., pp. 14–16. Republished in 1902 as *Garden Cities of To-morrow*.

70. Henry van de Velde, "The New Ornament," from "Das neue Ornament," trans. Harry Francis Mallgrave, in *Die Renaissance im modernen Kunstgewserbe*. Berlin: Bruno & Paul Cassirer, 1901, pp. 97–8.

71. Henry van de Velde, "Clarification of Principles," from "Principielle Erklarungen," trans. Harry Francis Mallgrave, in *Kunstgewerbliche Laipredigten*. Leipzig: Hermann Seemann, 1902, pp. 175–6, 186–8.

72. Hedrik Berlage, *Thoughts on Style* (1905), from *Gedanken über Stil in der Baukunst* (1905), trans. Iain Boyd Whyte, in *Hendrik Petrus Berlage: Thoughts on Style 1886–1909*. Santa Monica, CA: Getty Publication Programs, 1996, pp. 139–40, 152. Reprinted by permission of the J. Paul Getty Trust ©.

73. Hendrik Berlage, *Foundations and Development of Architecture* (1908), from *Grundlagen und Entwicklung der Architektur*, trans. Iain Boyd Whyte, in *Hendrik Petrus Berlage: Thoughts on Style 1886–1909*. Santa Monica, CA: Getty Publication Programs, 1996, pp. 249–590. Reprinted by permission of the J. Paul Getty Trust ©.

74. Charles-Edouard Jeanneret (Le Corbusier), *Study of the Movement of Decorative Art in Germany* (1912), from *Étude sur le mouvement d'art décoratif en Allemagne*, trans. Christina Contandriopoulos and Harry Francis Mallgrave. New York: Da Capo, 1968, pp. 73–4.

75. Antonio Sant'Elia, "Message" (1914), from "Messaggio," trans. Esther da Costa Meyer, in *The Works of Antonio Sant'Elia: Retreat into the Future*. New Haven, CT: Yale University Press, 1995, p. 212. Reprinted by permission of the publisher Yale University Press.

76. Tony Garnier, from *Cité Industrielle* (1917), trans. Dora Wiebenson, in *Tony Garnier: The Cité Industrielle*. New York: George Braziller, 1969, pp. 107, 112.

77. Louis Sullivan, from "The Tall Office Building Artistically Considered," first published in *Lippincott's Magazine* (1896), cited here from Robert Twombly, *Louis Sullivan: The Public Papers*. Chicago: University of Chicago Press, 1988, pp. 105–6, 110–11.

78. Denkmar Adler, from "Function and Environment" (1896), in Lewis Mumford (ed.), *Roots of Contemporary American Architecture*. New York: Dover, 1972, pp. 243–4.

79. Oscar Lovell Triggs, from "A Proposal for a Guild and School of Handicraft," in *Chapters in the History of the Arts and Crafts Movement* (1901). Reprinted New York: Benjamin Blom, 1971, pp. 189–90.

80. Gustav Stickley, from foreword to *The Craftsman* 1:1 (1901), p. i.

81. Frank Lloyd Wright, from "The Art and Craft of the Machine," in *Frank Lloyd Wright: Collected Writings*, vol. 1, ed. Bruce Brooks Pfeiffer. New York: Rizzoli, 1992, pp. 68–9. Used with permission from Rizzoli International Publications, Inc.

82. Louis Sullivan, from "What is Architecture? A Study in the American People of Today" (1906), originally published in *The Craftsman*, but cited here from Robert Twombly, *Louis Sullivan: The Public Papers*. Chicago: University of Chicago Press, 1988, pp. 195–6.

83. Frank Lloyd Wright, from "In the Cause of Architecture" (1908), in *Frank Lloyd Wright: Collected Writings*, vol. 1, ed. Bruce Brooks Pfeiffer. New York: Rizzoli, 1992, pp. 89–90, 100. Used with permission from Rizzoli International Publications, Inc.

84. Gustav Stickley, from *Craftsman Homes* (1909), in facsimile edition. New York: Dover Publications, 1979, pp. 194–5.

85. Daniel Burnham and Edward H. Bennett, from *Plan for Chicago* (1909), in reprint edition. New York: Da Capo, 1970, pp. 1, 4.

86. Frank Lloyd Wright, from *Executed Buildings and Designs of Frank Lloyd Wright* (1911), originally *Ausgeführte Bauten und Entwürge von Frank Lloyd Wright*. Berlin: Wasmuth, 1911, cited from *Frank Lloyd*

Wright: Collected Writings, vol. 1, ed. Bruce Brooks Pfeiffer. New York: Rizzoli, 1992, p. 108. Used with permission from Rizzoli International Publications, Inc.

87. Irving Gill, from "The Home of the Future: The New Architecture of the West," in *The Craftsman* 30:2 (May 1916), pp. 141–2.

88. Frederick Winslow Taylor, from *The Principles of Scientific Management* (1911), in reprint edition. Mineola, New York: Dover, 1998, p. 1.

89. Claude Bragdon, from *Architecture and Democracy before, during and after the War* (1918), cited from *Architectural Record* 44:3 (September 1918), pp. 253–4. Reprinted with permission of the *Architectural Record*, The McGraw-Hill Companies, © 1918.

90. Irving Pond, "Zoning and the Architecture of High Buildings," in *Architectural Forum* 35:4 (October 1921), p. 133.

91. Hugh Ferris, from "The New Architecture," in *The New York Times* (March 19, 1922), pp. 8, 27.

92. *The Chicago Daily Tribune* (June 10, 1922), p. 11.

93. Lewis Mumford, from *Sticks and Stones: A Study of American Architecture and Civilization* (1924), in reprint edition. New York: Dover, 1955, pp. 9–10.

94. Lewis Mumford, from "The Search for 'Something More'" (1928), cited from *Architecture as a Home for Man: Essays for Architectural Record*, ed. Jeanne M. Daver. New York: Architectural Record Books, 1975, pp. 15, 18.

95. Hugh Ferriss, from *The Metropolis of Tomorrow.* New York: Ives Washburn, 1929, pp. 59–60. © 1986. Reprinted by permission of Princeton Architectural Press. All rights reserved.

96. R. Buckminster Fuller, "The Dymaxion House" (1929), from *Your Private Sky: Discourse*, ed. Joachim Krausse and Claude Lichtenstein. Zurich: Lars Müller, 2001, pp. 89–90. © 1929, 2001, The Estate of R. Buckminster Fuller. Reprinted by permission.

97. Henry-Russell Hitchcock, from *Modern Architecture* (1929), in reprint edition. New York: Hacker Art Books, 1970, pp. 195–6.

98. Frank Lloyd Wright, from "The Cardboard House," in *Collected Writings, 1930–1932*, ed. Bruce Brooks Pfeiffer. New York, Rizzoli, 1992, pp. 51–2. Used with permission from Rizzoli International Publications, Inc.

99. Alfred H. Barr, Jr., from preface to *Modern Architecture: International Exhibition* (1932), in the reprint edition. New York: Arno Press, pp. 13–16.

100. Henry-Russell Hitchcock and Philip Johnson, from *The International Style: Architecture since 1922* (1932), in paperback edition. New York: W. W. Norton & Co., 1966, pp. 19–20, 93–4. Copyright 1932 by W. W. Norton & Company, Inc., renewed © 1960 by Henry-Russell Hitchcock and Philip Johnson. Used by permission of W. W. Norton & Company, Inc.

101. V. I. Lenin, from *The State and Revolution*, in *Essential Works of Lenin*, ed. Henry M. Christman. New York: Bantam Books, 1966, pp. 338–9. Reprinted by permission of Bantam Books, Random House, Inc.

102. Vladimir Tatlin, T. Shapiro, I. Meyerzon, and Pavel Vinogradov, "The Work Ahead of Us" (1920), trans. Troelis Andersen, in The *Tradition of Constructivism*, ed. Stephen Bann. New York: Viking Press, 1974, pp. 12–13.

103. Alexander Rodchenko, "Slogans" (1921), trans. S.-O. Khan Magomedov, in *Rodchenko: The Complete Work*. London, 1986.

104. Aleksei Gan, from Constructivism (1922), trans. Troelis Andersen, in *The Tradition of Constructivism*, ed. Stephen Bann. New York: Viking Press, 1974, pp. 33–6.

105. Moisei Ginzburg, from *Style and Epoch* (1924), trans. Anatole Senkevitch, Jr. in *Moisei Ginzburg: Style and Epoch*. Cambridge, MA: MIT Press, 1982, pp. 70, 92. © 1983 Massachusetts Institute of Technology and IAUS, by permission of The MIT Press.

106. El Lissitzky, "Element and Invention" (1924), from "Element und Erfindung," trans. Harry Francis Mallgrave, in *ABC: Beiträge zum Bauen*, in facsimile edition. Baden: Lars Muller, 1993.

107. Nikolai Ladovsky and El Lissitzky, from *ASNOVA: Review of the Association of New Architects* (1926), trans. Irina Nazarova.

108. Theo van Doesburg et al., "Manifesto 1" (1918), trans. Nicholas Bullock, from *The Tradition of Constructivism*, ed. Stephen Bann. London, 1974, p. 65.

109. Amédée Ozenfant and Charles-Edouard Jeanneret, from preface to *L'Esprit Nouveau* 1 (1920), trans. Christina Contandriopoulos and Harry Francis Mallgrave, pp. 3–4.

110. Amédée Ozenfant and Charles-Edouard Jeanneret (Le Corbusier), from "Purism," in *L'Esprit Nouveau* 4 (1920), trans. R. L. Herbert, in *Modern Artists on Art*. Englewood Cliffs, NJ: Prentice-Hall, 1964, p. 73.

111. J. J. P. Oud, "On the Future Architecture and its Architectural Possibilities" (1921), from "Über die zukünftige Baukunst und ihre architektonische Möglichkeiten," trans. Harry Francis Mallgrave, German version in *Holländische Architektur*. Dessau: Bauhaus Press, 1926, pp. 67–8, 75–6.

112. Le Corbusier, *Toward an Architecture* (1923), from *Vers une Architecture*, trans. by Frederick Etchells as *Towards a New Architecture*. London: The Architectural Press, 1946, pp. 89, 104–5, 268–9. © FLC/ADAGP, Paris and DACS, London 2007 © Fondation Le Corbusier.

113. Le Corbusier, from *Toward an Architecture* (1923), from *Vers une Architecture* trans. by Frederick Etchells as *Towards a New Architecture*. London: The Architectural Press, 1946, pp. 268–9. © FLC/ADAGP, Paris and DACS, London 2007 © Fondation Le Corbusier.

114. Theo van Doesburg, "Towards Plastic Architecture," *De Stijl* 12:6–7 (1924), trans. Joost Baljeu, in *Theo van Doesburg*. New York: Macmillan, 1974, pp. 142, 144–5, 147.

115. Mart Stam, "Collective Design" (1924), from "Kollektive Gestaltung," trans. Catherine Schelbert and Michael Robinson, in *ABC: Beiträge zum Bauen*. Baden: Lars Muller, 1993, p. 10.

116. Le Corbusier, *Urbanism* (1925), from *Urbanisme*, trans. by Frederick Etchells as *The City of Tomorrow and its Planning*, 3rd ed. Cambridge, MA: MIT Press, 1971, pp. 5–6, 10–12. © 1971 Massachusetts Institute of Technology, by permission of The MIT Press.

117. Oswald Spengler, *The Decline of the West*, trans. Charles Francis Atkinson. New York: Alfred A. Knopf, 1926, reprinted as a one-volume edition in 1934, pp. 506–7.

118. Hans Poelzig, "Address to the Werkbund" (1919), from Julius Posener, *Hans Poelzig: Reflections on his Life and Work*, trans. Christine Charlesworth. New York: Architectural History Foundation, 1992, p. 130. © 1992 Architectural History Foundation and Massachusetts Institute of Technology, by permission of The MIT Press.

119. Manifesto for Arbeitsrat für Kunst (1919), trans. Michael Bullock, from *Programs and Manifestoes on 20th-Century Architecture*, ed. Ulrich Conrads. Cambridge, MA: MIT Press, 1975, pp. 44–5. © 1971 Lund Humphries Ltd. & MIT for English translation, by permission of The MIT Press.

120. Walter Gropius, "Program of the Staatliches Bauhaus in Weimar" (1919), from "Programm des staatlichen Bauhauses in Weimar," trans. Wolfgang Jabs and Basil Gilbert, in Hans M. Wingler, *The Bauhaus: Weimar, Dessau, Berlin, Chicago*. Cambridge, MA: MIT Press, 1978, pp. 31–2. © 1969 Massachusetts Institute of Technology for English translation, by permission of The MIT Press.

121. Bruno Taut, letter announcing the Crystal Chain (1919), from *The Crystal Chain Letter: Architectural Fantasies by Bruno Taut and His Circle*, trans. Iain Boyd Whyte. Cambridge, MA: MIT Press, 1985, p. 19. © 1985 Massachusetts Institute of Technology for English translation, by permission of The MIT Press.

122. Ludwig Mies van der Rohe, "Skyscrapers," from text published without title in *Frühlicht* 4 (1922), trans. Mark Jarzombek, in Fritz Neumeyer, *The Artless Word: Mies van der Rohe on the Building-Art*. Cambridge, MA: MIT Press, 1991, p. 240. © 1991 Massachusetts Institute of Technology for English translation, by permission of The MIT Press.

123. Ludwig Mies van der Rohe, "Office Building," from *G* 1 (July 1923), trans. Mark Jarzombek, in Fritz Neumeyer, *The Artless Word: Mies van der Rohe on the Building-Art*. Cambridge, MA: MIT Press,

1991, p. 241. © 1991 Massachusetts Institute of Technology for English translation, by permission of The MIT Press.

124. Walter Gropius, "The Viability of the Bauhaus Idea" (1922), from circular to Bauhaus Masters, trans. Wolfgang Jabs and Basil Gilbert, in Hans M. Wingler, *The Bauhaus: Weimar, Dessau, Berlin. Chicago.* Cambridge, MA: MIT Press, 1978, pp. 51–2. © 1969 Massachusetts Institute of Technology for English translation, by permission of The MIT Press.

125. Oscar Schlemmer, Manifesto in "The First Bauhaus Exhibition in Weimar," trans. Wolfgang Jabs and Basil Gilbert, in Hans M. Wingler, *The Bauhaus: Weimar, Dessau, Berlin. Chicago.* Cambridge, MA: MIT Press, 1978, 65–6. © 1969 Massachusetts Institute of Technology for English translation, by permission of The MIT Press.

126. Walter Gropius, *International Architecture* (1925), from *Internationale Architektur*, trans. Harry Francis Mallgrave. Dessau: Passavia Druckerei, 1925, pp. 7–8.

127. Hugo Häring, "Paths to Form" (1925), from "Wege zur Form," trans. Harry Francis Mallgrave, in *Hugo Häring: Schriften, Entwürfe, Bauten*, ed. Heinrich Lauterbach and Jürgens Joedicke. Stuttgart: Karl Krämer Verlag, 1956, p. 14.

128. Adolf Behne, *The Modern Functional Building* (1926), from *Die moderne Zweckbau*, trans. Michael Roberson. Santa Monica, CA: Getty Publication Programs, 1996, pp. 119–21. Reprinted by permission of the J. Paul Getty Trust ©.

129. Giuseppe Terragni et al., "Group 7" (1926), from "Il Gruppo 7," trans. Ellen R. Shapiro, in *Oppositions* 6 (Fall 1976), p. 89. © Massachusetts Institute of Technology and IAUS, by permission of the MIT Press.

130. Walter Curt Behrendt, *The Victory of the New Style* (1927), from *Das Sieg des neuen Baustils*, trans. Harry Francis Mallgrave. Los Angeles, CA: Getty Publication Programs, 2000, pp. 110, 114–15. Reprinted by permission of the J. Paul Getty Trust ©.

131. Ludwig Hilberseimer, *International New Architecture* (1927), from *Internationale Neue Baukunst*, trans. Harry Francis Mallgrave. Stuttgart: Julius Hoffmann, 1927, p. 5.

132. Le Corbusier and Pierre Jeanneret, "Five Points for a New Architecture" (1927), from Ulrich Conrads (ed.), *Programs and Manifestoes on 20th-Century Architecture*, ed. Ulrichs Conrad, trans. Michael Bullock. Cambridge: MIT Press, 1970, pp. 99–100. Originally published in *Bau und Wohnen*. Stuttgart: Fr. Wederkind & Co., 1927, pp. 27–28. © 1971 Lund Humphries Ltd. & MIT for English translation, by permission of The MIT Press.

133. Congrès Internationaux d'Architecture Moderne (CIAM), "The Declaration of La Sarraz" (1928), from Le Corbusier, *The Athens Charter*, trans. Anthony Eardley. New York: Grossman, 1973, pp. 6–8.

134. Sigfried Giedion, *Building in France, Building in Iron, Building in Ferro-Concrete* (1928), from *Bauen in Frankreich, Bauen in Eisen, Bauen in Eisenbeton*, trans. J. Duncan Berry. Santa Monica, CA: Getty Publication Programs, 1995, pp. 91–3. Reprinted by permission of the J. Paul Getty Trust ©.

135. Ernst May, "Housing Policy of Frankfort on the Main" (1928), published trilingually in the *International Housing Association* 2 (1929).

136. Walter Gropius, "The Sociological Foundations of the Minimum Dwelling" (1929), in Walter Gropius, *Scope of Total Architecture*. New York: Collier Books, 1962, pp. 98–100.

137. Sigfried Giedion, *Liberated Living* (1929), from *Befreites Wohnen*, trans. Harry Francis Mallgrave. Zurich: M. E. Häfeli, 1929, p. 7.

138. Lázló Moholy-Nagy, *From Material to Architecture* (1929), from *Von Material zu Architektur* (Dessau: Bauhaus, 1929), trans. by Daphne M. Hoffmann as *The New Vision: From Material to Architecture*. New York: Brewer, Warren & Putnam, 1932, pp. 159–60.

139. Erich Mendelsohn, from *Russia, Europe, America: An Architectural Cross Section* (1929), reprint edition (supplemented with English text) of *Russland, Europa, Amerika: Ein architektonischer Querschnitt*. Basel: Birkhäuser, 1989, p. 170. Reprinted by permission of Birkhäuser Verlag AG.

140. Karel Teige, *Modern Architecture in Czechoslovakia* (1930), from *Moderní architektura v Českoslo-vensku*, trans. Irena Žantovská and David Britt. Los Angeles, CA: Getty Publication Programs, 2000, pp. 297–8. Reprinted by permission of the J. Paul Getty Trust ©.

141. German Bestelmeyer et al., Manifesto of "Der Block" (1928). from Anna Teut, *Architektur im Dritten Reich*, trans. Harry Francis MaAllgrave. Frankfurt, 1967, p. 29.

142. Hannes Meyer, "An Open Letter to Lord Mayor Hesse of Dessau," in Hans M. Wingler, *The Bauhaus: Weimar, Dessau, Berlin, Chicago*, trans. Wolfgang Jabs and Basil Gilbert. Cambridge, MA: MIT Press, 1986, p. 165. © 1969 Massachusetts Institute of Technology for English translation, by permission of The MIT Press.

143. Mies van der Rohe, "Announcement to the Students of the Dissolution of the Bauhaus" (1933), in Hans M. Wingler, *The Bauhaus: Weimar, Dessau, Berlin, Chicago*, trans. Wolfgang Jabs and Basil Gilbert. Cambridge: MIT Press, 1986, p. 189. © 1969 Massachusetts Institute of Technology for English translation, by permission of The MIT Press.

144. Albert Speer, from *Inside the Third Reich: Memoirs by Albert Speer*, trans. Richard and Clara Winston. New York: Macmillan, 1970, pp. 48–50.

145. Marcel Breuer, from "Where Do We Stand?" in *The Rationalists: Theory and Design in the Modern Movement*, ed. Dennis Sharp. New York: Architectural Book Publishing Co., 1979, pp. 87–8.

146. Francis Yorke, from *The Modern House*, 2nd ed. London: The Architectural Press, 1936, pp. 1–3.

147. Nikolaus Pevsner, from *Pioneers of the Modern Movement: From William Morris to Walter Gropius*. London: Faber & Faber, 1936, pp. 41–3. Reprinted by permission of the publishers Faber & Faber Ltd.

148. J. M. Richards, from *An Introduction to Modern Architecture*. Harmondsworth: Penguin, 1940, pp. 9–10. Reproduced by permission of Penguin Books Ltd.

149. Sigfried Giedion, from *Space, Time and Architecture: The Growth of a New Tradition*. Cambridge, MA: Harvard University Press, 1949, pp. 13–14, 424–5. Reprinted by permission of the publisher, Copyright © 1941, 1949, 1954, 1962, 1967, 1969, by the President and Fellows of Harvard College, Copyright © 1977 by William J. Callaghan, Copyright © 1982 by Andreas Giedion and Verena Clay-Giedion.

150. Le Corbusier, *The Athens Charter* (1943), from *La Charte d'Athènes*, trans. Anthony Eardley. New York: Grossman, 1973, pp. 53–4, 57, 65, 105.

151. Sven Backström, from "A Swede Looks at Sweden," *The Architectural Review* 94:561 (September 1943), p. 80. Reprinted by permission of The Architectural Review.

152. Joseph Hudnut, from "The Education of an Architect," *Architectural Record* 69 (May 1931), pp. 412–14. Reprinted with permission of Architectural Record, The McGraw-Hill Companies, © 1931.

153. Frank Lloyd Wright, from *The Disappearing City*, in *Collected Writings, vol. 3, 1931–1939*, ed. Bruce Brooks Pfeiffer. New York, Rizzoli, 1993, pp. 78–80. Used with permission from Rizzoli International Publications, Inc.

154. Lewis Mumford, from *Techniques and Civilization*. New York: Harcourt, Brace & Co., 1934, pp. 404–5.

155. Catherine Bauer, from *Modern Housing*. Boston: Houghton Mifflin Co., 1934, pp. 188–9.

156. Frank Lloyd Wright, from "Jacobs House," *Architectural Forum* 68 (January 1938), pp. 78–9.

157. R. Buckminster Fuller, from *Nine Chains to the Moon: An Adventure Story of Thought*. Philadelphia, PA: Lippincott, 1938, p. 35.

158. Katherine Morrow Ford, from "Modern is Regional," *House & Garden* (March 1941), pp. 35, 79. Copyright © 1941 Condé Nast Publications. All rights reserved. Reprinted by permission.

159. Eliel Saarinen, from *The City: Its Growth, Its Decay, Its Future*. New York: Reinhold Publishing Corp., 1943, pp. 22–3.

160. György Kepes, from *Language of Vision*. Chicago: P. Theobald, 1944, reprint edition New York: Dover 1995, pp. 12–14.

161. Konrad Wachsmann, from *The Turning Point of Building: Structure and Design*. New York: Reinhold Publishing Corp., 1961, pp. 160–1.

162. John Entenza, Announcement of "The Case Study House Program" (1945), *Arts & Architecture* (January 1945), pp. 37–9. Reprinted by permission of Barbara Goldstein, editor, *Arts and Architecture: The Entenza Years*, © 1990, Massachusetts Institute of Technology, published by The MIT Press. Reprinted by permission of John Entenza.

163. Philip Johnson, from *Mies van der Rohe*. New York: Museum of Modern Art, 1947, pp. 138–40.

164. T. H. Robsjohn-Gibbings, from *Mona Lisa's Mustache: A Dissection of Modern Art*. New York: Alfred A. Knopf, 1947, pp. 211–13.

165. Lewis Mumford, "Status Quo," *The New Yorker* (11 October 1947), pp. 106, 109–10.

166. Alfred H. Barr, "What is Happening to Modern Architecture?," *Museum of Modern Art Bulletin* 15 (Spring 1948), pp. 6–8.

167. Philip Johnson, from "The Glass House," *Architectural Review* 108:645 (September 1950), in *Philip Johnson: The Glass House*, ed. David Whitney and Jeffrey Kipnis. New York: Pantheon Books, 1993, pp. 10–12.

168. Matthew Norwicki, from "Origin and Trends of Modern Architecture," *The Magazine of Art* (November 1951), cited from its revised title "Form and Function," in *Roots of Contemporary American Architecture*, ed. Lewis Mumford. New York: Dover, 1972, pp. 416–18.

169. Elizabeth Gordon, from "The Threat to the Next America," *House Beautiful* (April 1953), pp. 126–7. Courtesy of *House Beautiful*.

170. Harwell Hamilton Harris, from "Regionalism and Nationalism" (1954), cited from *Harwell Hamilton Harris: A Collection of his Writings*. Raleigh: University of North Carolina State at Raleigh, vol. 14, no. 5, 1965, pp. 26–8.

171. Richard Neutra, from *Survival through Design* (1954), cited from reprint edition, London: Oxford University Press, 1969, pp. 3–4, 91–2. Permissions courtesy Dion Neutra, Architect © and Richard and Dion Neutra Papers, Department of Special Collections, Charles E. Young Research Library, UCLA.

172. Louis I. Kahn, "Order and Form," *Perspecta 3: The Yale Architectural Journal* (1955), p. 57.

173. Bruno Zevi, from *Towards an Organic Architecture* (1945). London: Faber & Faber, 1950, pp. 47–8, 139. Originally published as *Verso un'architettura organica*. Reprinted by permission of the publishers Faber & Faber Ltd.

174. J. M. Richards, from "New Empiricism," *The Architectural Review* 101:606 (June 1947), pp. 199–200. Reprinted by permission of *The Architectural Review*.

175. Colin Rowe, from "The Mathematics of the Ideal Villa," *The Architectural Review* 101:603 (March 1947), p. 104. Reprinted by permission of *The Architectural Review*.

176. Bruno Zevi, *Architecture as Space* (1948), from *Sapere vedere l'architettura*, trans. Milton Gendel. New York: Horizon Press, 1957, pp. 143–4, 157–8, 191.

177. Rudolf Wittkower, *Architectural Principles in the Age of Humanism* (1949) 4th ed. London: Academy Editions, 1977, pp. 153–4. © FLC/ADAGP, Paris and DACS, London 2007.

178. Le Corbusier, *The Modular* (1950), from *Le Modular*, trans. Peter Francia and Anna Bostoack. Cambridge, MA: MIT Press, 1977, pp. 18–20. © Fondation Le Corbusier.

179. Alison and Peter Smithson, "House in Soho, London," *Architectural Design* (December 1953), p. 342.

180. Sigfried Giedion, from "The State of Contemporary Architecture," *Architectural Record* 115:1 (January 1954), p. 135–7. Reprinted with permission of *Architectural Record*, The McGraw-Hill Companies, © 1954.

181. Ernesto Nathan Rogers, inaugural editorial, trans. From *Casabella-Continuità* 199 (December 1953/January 1954), Addendum, p. I.

182. Reyner Banham, from "The New Brutalism," *The Architectural Review* 118:708 (December 1955), pp. 356, 361. Reprinted by permission of *The Architectural Review*.

183. Steen Eiler Rasmussen, from *Experiencing Architecture*. Cambridge, MA: MIT Press, 1964, pp. 33–4. © 1959 Massachusetts Institute of Technology, by permission of The MIT Press.

184. Peter Luigi Nervi, "The Foreseeable Future and the Training of Architects" (1962), in *Aesthetics and Technology in Building: The Charles Eliot Norton Lectures, 1961–1962*. Cambridge: Harvard University Press, 1965, pp. 186–7. Reprinted by permission of the publishers, Copyright © 1965 by the President and Fellow of Harvard College.

185. J. H. Forshaw and Patrick Abercrombie, from *County of London Plan*. London: Macmillan, 1944, pp. 7–8, 34–5.

186. Sigfried Giedion, "Reaffirmation of the Aims of CIAM: Bridgewater 1947," in *A Decade of New Architecture*. Zurich: Editions Girsberger, 1951, pp. 16–17.

187. J. M. Richards, from "Contemporary Architecture and the Common Man," in Sigfried Giedion, *A Decade of New Architecture*. Zurich: Editions Girsberger, 1951, p. 33.

188. Bruno Zevi, "A Message to the International Congress of Modern Architecture" (1949), from *Bruno Zevi on Modern Architecture*, trans. Andrea Oppenheimer Dean. New York: Rizzoli, 1983, pp. 127–8. Used with permission from Rizzoli International Publications, Inc.

189. Alison and Peter Smithson, Gillian and William Howell, and John Voelcker, from "Urban Reidentification" Grid, cited from Eric Mumford, *The CIAM Discourse on Urbanism, 1928–1960*. Cambridge, MA: MIT Press, 2000, p. 234–35. © 2000 Eric Mumford, by permission of The MIT Press.

190. Jacob Bakema, Aldo van Eyck, H. P. Daniel van Ginkel, Hans Hovens-Greve, Peter and Alison Smithson, and John Voelcker, "Statement on Habitat" (1954), *Forum* 7 (1959), p. 231.

191. Alison and Peter Smithson, "Open Letter to Sert and Team 10," in *The Emergence of Team 10 out of C.I.A.M.*, ed. Alison Smithson. London, Architectural Association, pp. 54–5.

192. Le Corbusier, "Message of Le Corbusier to the X Congress CIAM at Dubrovnik" (1956), manuscript copy of letter, July 23, 1956. Courtesy of Annie Pedret.

193. Ernesto Rogers, Peter Smithson, and Jacob Bakema, "Remarks on the Design of Torre Velasca, Milan" (1959), *CIAM '59 in Otterlo*, ed. Oscar Newman. Stuttgart: Karl Krämer Verlag, 1961, pp. 92–3, 96–7.

194. Team 10, "The Aim of Team 10 (1962), *Team 10 Primer*, ed. Alison Smithson. Cambridge, MA: MIT Press, 1968, p. 3.

195. Lewis Mumford, "Prefabricated Blight" (1948), reprinted in Lewis Mumford, *From the Ground Up: Observations on Contemporary Architecture, Housing, Highway Building, and Civic Design*. New York: Harcourt Brace Jovanovich, 1956, pp. 108–9. Compilation copyright © 1956 and renewed 1980 by Lewis Mumford.

196. Kevin Lynch, *The Image of the City* (1960), 7th printing. Cambridge, MA: MIT Press, 1971, pp. 46–8. © 1960 Massachusetts Institute of Technology, by permission of The MIT Press.

197. Jane Jacobs, from *The Life and Death of the American City*. New York: Random House, 1961, pp. 20–2, 202–3. Copyright © 1961, 1989 by Jane Jacobs. Used by permission of Random House, Inc.

198. Lewis Mumford, from "Mother Jacobs' Home Remedies" (1962), in *The Urban Prospect*. New York: Harcourt, Brace & World, 1968, pp. 194–5.

199. Herbert J. Gans, from *The Urban Villages: Group and Class in the Life of Italian-Americans*. New York: The Free Press, 1962, pp. ix–x.

200. Peter Blake, from *God's Own Junkyard: The Planned Deterioration of America's Landscape*. New York: Rinehart & Winston, 1964, p. 33.

201. Martin Anderson, from *The Federal Bulldozer: A Critical Analysis of Urban Renewal, 1949–1962*. Cambridge, MA: MIT Press, 1964, pp. 6–7. Reprinted by permission of Martin Anderson.

202. Melvin M. Webber, from "The Urban Place and the Nonplace Urban Realm" (1964), in Melvin M. Webber et al., *Explorations into Urban Structure*. Philadelphia: University of Pennsylvania Press, 1965, pp. 139–40, 146–7.

203. Charles Abrams, from "Housing in the Year 2000" (1967), in *Environment and Policy: The Next Fifty Years*, ed. William R. Ewald, Jr. Bloomington: Indiana University Press, 1968, pp. 214–15. Reprinted by permission of the publisher Indiana University Press.

204. Yona Friedman, *Mobile Architecture* (1959), from *L'architecture mobile*, trans. Christina Contandriopoulos and Harry Francis Mallgrave. Paris: Casterman, 1970.

205. Kiyonori Kikutake et al., from *Metabolism: The Proposals for New Urbanism*. Tokyo: Yasuko Kawazoe, 1960, pp. 22–3.

206. Reyner Banham, from *Theory and Design in the First Machine Age*. New York: Praeger, 1978, pp. 9–10.

207. Archigram, Manifesto, *Archigram* 1 (May 1961).

208. Rachel Carson, *Silent Spring* (1962), 2nd printing. oston: Houghton Mifflin, 1962, pp. 5–6, 246.

209. Constantino Doxiadis et al., "The Declaration of Delos," *Ekistics: Reviews on the Problems and Science of Human Settlements* 16:93.

210. R. Buckminster Fuller, from "World Design Initiative" (1963), in *The Design Initiative*, vol. 2 of *World Design Science Decade, 1965–1975*. Carbondale, IL, 1963. © The Estate of R. Buckminster Fuller. Reprinted by permission.

211. Kenneth E. Boulding, "Earth as a Space Ship" (1965), from Kenneth E. Boulding Papers, Archives (Box 8), University of Colorado at Boulder Libraries.

212. Ian McHarg, from *Design with Nature* (1969), paperback edition. Garden City, New York: American Museum of Natural History, Doubleday/Natural History, 1971, pp. 20–2. Copyright © 1969 John Wiley & Sons, Inc. Reprinted with permission of John Wiley & Sons, Inc.

213. R. Buckminster Fuller, from *Utopia or Oblivion: the Prospects for Humanity*. New York: Overlook Press, 1969, pp. 356–7. © 1969 The Estate of R. Buckminster Fuller. Reprinted by permission.

214. John McConnell, from "Earth Day Proclamation" (1970), United Nations Proclamation.

215. Reyner Banham, from "The Italian Retreat from Modern Architecture," *The Architectural Review* 125 (April 1959), pp. 231–2, 235. Reprinted by permission of *The Architectural Review*.

216. Ernesto Rogers, from "The Evolution of Architecture: An Answer to the Caretakers of Frigidaires," *Casabella-Continuità* 228 (June 1959), pp. VI–VII (addendum).

217. Aldo van Eyck, "Is Architecture Going to Reconcile Basic Values?," in *CIAM '59 in Otterlo*, ed. Oscar Newman. Stuttgart: Karl Krämer Verlag, 1961, p. 26–7.

218. Joseph Rykwert, from "Meaning in Building," *Zodiac* 6, pp. 193–5.

219. Tomás Maldonado, from "Notes on Communication," in *5 Uppercase*. London: Whitefriars Press, p. 5, 7.

220. Colin Rowe and Robert Slutzky, from "Transparency: Literal and Phenomenal" (1963), in *Transparency*. Basel: Birkhäuser, 1997, pp. 34–5, 37–8. Reprinted by permission of Birkhäuser Verlag AG.

221. Christian Norberg-Schulz, from *Intentions in Architecture*. Cambridge: MIT Press, 1965, pp. 22–3. © 1966 Massachusetts Institute of Technology, by permission of The MIT Press.

222. Christopher Alexander, *Notes on a Synthesis of Form* (1964), 1971 ed. Cambridge, MA: Harvard University Press, pp. 8–9. Reprinted by permission of the publisher, Harvard University Press. Copyright © 1964 by the President and Fellows of Harvard College. Copyright © renewed 1992 by Christopher Alexander.

223. Stanford Anderson, from "Architecture and Tradition That Isn't 'Trad, Dad'" (1964), in *The History, Theory and Criticism of Architecture*, ed. Marcus Whiffen. Cambridge., MA: MIT Press, 1965, pp. 71, 78–9. © 1966 American Institute of Architects, by permission of The MIT Press.

224. Robert Venturi, *Complexity and Contradiction in Architecture*. New York: Museum of Modern Art, pp. 22–3, 48–9.

225. Aldo Rossi, *The Architecture and the City* (1966), from *L'architettura della città*, trans. Diane Ghirado and Joan Ockman. Cambridge, MA: MIT Press, 1984, pp. 29, 32. © 1982 Massachusetts Institute of Technology & IAUS, by permission of The MIT Press.

226. Charles Moore, from "Plug it in Rameses, and See if it Lights Up, Because We Aren't Going to Keep it Unless it Works," *Perspecta 11: Yale Architectural Journa* (1967), pp. 42–3.

227. Denise Scott Brown and Robert Venturi, from "On Ducks and Decoration," *Architecture Canada* 45:10 (October 1968), p. 48. Reprinted by permission of the Royal Architectural Institute of Canada.

228. Manfredo Tafuri, "Toward a Critique of Architectural Ideology" (1969), from "Per una critica dell'ideologia architettonica," trans. Stephen Sartarelli, in *Architectural Theory since 1968*, ed. K. Michael Hays. Cambridge, MA: MIT Press, 2000, pp. 31–2. Originally appeared in *Contropiano*, #1, January–April, 1969. © 1998 Massachusetts Institite of Technology, by permission of The MIT Press.

229. Peter Eisenman, "Notes on Conceptual Architecture: Toward a Definition," *Design Quarterly* 78/79 (1970), cited from *Casabella* 359/360 (1971), pp. 51, 53. Reprinted by permission of Casabella and Peter Eisenman.

230. Colin Rowe, from Introduction to *Five Architects*. New York: Wittenborn, 1972, pp. 4, 7. Courtesy of Wittenborn Art Books, San Francisco. www.art-books.com.

231. Robert A. M. Stern and Jaquelin Robertson, from "Five on Five," *Architectural Forum* 138:4 (May 1973), pp. 46–7, 52–3.

232. Peter Eisenman, Kenneth Frampton, and Mario Gandelsonas, editorial statement of *Oppositions 1* (September 1973). n.p. © 1973 Massachusetts Institute of Technology and IAUS, by permission of The MIT Press.

233. Massimo Scolari, from "Avant Garde and the New Architecture," trans. Stephen Sartarelli, in *Architecture Theory since 1968*, ed. K. Michael Hays. Cambridge, MA: MIT Press, 2000, p. 140. © 1998 Massachusetts Institite of Technology, by permission of The MIT Press.

234. Joseph Rykwert, from "15a Triennale," *Domus*, 530 (January 1974), p. 3.

235. Manfredo Tafuri, from "L'Architecture dans le Boudoir: The Language of Criticism and the Criticism of Language," *Oppositions* 3 (May 1974), pp. 48, 52–3. © 1974 Massachusetts Institute of Technology and IAUS, by permission of The MIT Press.

236. Mario Gandelsonas, from "Neo-Functionalism," *Oppositions* 5 (Summer 1976). n.p. © 1976 Massachusetts Institute of Technology and IAUS, by permission of The MIT Press.

237. Peter Eisenmann, from "Post-Functionalism, *Oppositions* 6 (Fall 1976). n.p. © 1976 Massachusetts Institute of Technology and IAUS, by permission of The MIT Press.

238. Anthony Vidler, from "The Third Typology," *Oppositions* 7 (Winter 1976), pp. 3–4. © 1976 Massachusetts Institute of Technology and IAUS, by permission of The MIT Press.

239. Maurice Culot and Leon Krier, from "The Only Path for Architecture," *Oppositions* 14 (Fall 1978), pp. 41–3, trans. Christian Hubert. © 1976 Massachusetts Institute of Technology and IAUS by permission of The MIT Press.

240. Charles Jencks, from "Semiology in Architecture," in *Meaning in Architecture*. New York: George Braziller, 1969, pp. 11–13.

241. George Baird, from "La 'Dimension Amoureuse' in Architecture," in *Meaning in Architecture*. New York: George Braziller, 1970, pp. 81–2.

242. Christian Norberg-Schulz, from *Existence, Space & Architecture*. New York: Praeger, 1971, p. 11.

243. Alan Colquhoun, "Historicism and the Limits of Semiology" (1972), in Alan Colquhoun, *Essays in Architectural Criticism: Modern Architecture and Historical Change*. Cambridge, MA: MIT Press, 1985, pp. 130–1. © 1982 Massachusetts Institute of Technology and IAUS, by permission of The MIT Press.

244. Kenneth Frampton, "On Reading Heidegger," in *Oppositions* 4 (October 1974). n.p. © 1974 Massachusetts Institute of Technology and IAUS, by permission of The MIT Press.

245. Charles Jencks, from *The Language of Postmodern Architecture*. New York: Rizzoli International Publications, 1977, pp. 9–10. Used with permission from Rizzoli International Publications, Inc.

246. Juan Pablo Bonta, from *Architecture and its Interpretation: A Study of Expressive Systems in Architecture*. New York: Rizzoli International Publications, 1979, pp. 46–9. Used with permission from Rizzoli International Publications, Inc.

247. Denise Scott Brown, from "Learning from Pop," *Casabella* 359–360 (1971), pp. 15–17. Reprinted by permission of Casabella and Denise Scott Brown.

248. Kenneth Frampton, from "America 1960–1970: Notes on Urban Images and Theory," *Casabella* 359–360 (1971), p. 31. Reprinted by permission of Casabella and Kenneth Frampton.

249. Herman Hertzberger, from "Homework for more Hospitable Form," *Forum* XXIV:3 (1973), trans. (appearing with the original text) Angela Blom van Assendelft and Anne van Bladeren.

250. Hassan Fathy, from *Architecture for the Poor*. Chicago: University of Chicago Press, 1973, pp. 19–21. The book first appeared in 1969 under the title *Gourna: A Tale of Two Villages*.

251. Colin Rowe and Fred Koetter, from "Collage City," *The Architectural Review* 158:942 (August 1975), pp. 83–4. Reprinted by permission of *The Architectural Review*.

252. Arthur Drexler, from exhibition catalogue to *The Architecture of the École des Beaux-Arts*. New York: Museum of Modern Art, 1975, pp. 3–4.

253. Bernard Tschumi, from "Architecture and Transgression," *Oppositions* 7 (Winter 1976), p. 58–9. © 1976 Massachusetts Institute of Technology and IAUS, by permission of The MIT Press.

254. Christopher Alexander, from *A Pattern Language: Towns, Buildings, Construction*. New York: Oxford University Press, 1977, pp. 311–13. By permission of Oxford University Press, Inc.

255. Robert A. M. Stern, from "New Directions in Modern American Architecture: A Postscript at the Edge of Modernism," *AAQ* 9:2–3 (1977), p. 66.

256. Rem Koolhaas, from *Delirious New York*. New York: Oxford University Press, 1978, pp. 9–10.

257. François Lyotard, from *The Postmodern Condition: A Report on Knowledge* (1979). Trans. By Geoff Bennington and Brian Massumi as *Le Condition postmoderne: rapport sur le savoir*. Minneapolis: University of Minnesota Press, 1984, pp. xxiii–xxiv.

258. Coop Himmelblau, from *Architecture is Now: Projects, (Un)Buildings, Actions, Statements, Sketches, Commentaries, 1968–1983*, trans. Jo Steinbauer and Roswitha Prix. New York: Rizzoli, 1983, p. 90. Used with permission from Rizzoli International Publications, Inc.

259. Bernard Tschumi, *Manhattan Transcripts* (1981), from new edition. London: Academy Editions, 1994, pp. 7.

260. Daniel Libeskind, from "Symbol and Interpretation," in *Between Zero and Infinity: Selected Projects in Architecture*. New York: Rizzoli, 1981, 29. Used with permission from Rizzoli International Publications, Inc.

261. Jürgen Habermas, "Modern and Postmodern Architecture" (1981), in Jürgen Habermas, *The New Conservatism: Cultural Criticism and the Historians' Debate*, trans. Sherry Weber Nicholsen, intro. by Richard Wolin. Cambridge, MA: MIT Press, 1989, pp. 6–8. © 1989 Massachusetts Institute of Technology for English translation, by permission of The MIT Press.

262. Andreas Huyssen, from "Modernity and Postmodernity," *New German Critique* 33 (Autumn 1984), pp. 13–16. Reprinted by permission of New German Critique.

263. K. Michael Hays, from "Critical Architecture: Between Culture and Form," *Perspecta 21: The Yale Architectural Journal* (1984), pp. 47–9.

264. Peter Eisenman, "The End of the Classical: The End of the Beginning, the End of the End," *Perspecta 21: The Yale Architectural Journal* (1984), cited from *Architecture Theory since 1968*, ed. K. Michael Hays. Cambridge, MA: MIT Press, 2002, pp. 529–31.

265. Sanford Kwinter, from "La Città Nuova: Modernity and Continuity," *Zone 1/2*, ed. Jonathan Crary, Michel Feher, Hal Foster, and Sanford Kwinter. New York: Urzone, 1986, pp. 87–9.

266. Ignasi de Solà-Morales, from "Weak Architecture," in *Differences: Topographies of Contemporary Architecture*, trans. Graham Thompson. Cambridge, MA: MIT Press, 1995, pp. 62–3, 67–8. © 1997 Massachusetts Institute of Technology, by permission of The MIT Press.

267. Mark Wigley, from "Deconstructivist Architecture," in *Deconstructivist Architecture*. New York: Museum of Modern Art, 1988, pp. 10–11.

268. Catherine Ingraham, from "Milking Deconstruction, or Cow Was The Show?," *Inland Architect* 32:5 (September/October 1988), pp. 62–3.

269. "Beyond the Modern Movement" (1980), *Harvard Architecture Review* (Spring 1980), pp. 5–7. Reprinted by permission of MIT Press Journals.

270. Robert A. M. Stern, from "The Doubles of Post-Modern," *The Harvard Architectural Review* (Spring 1980), pp. 84–6. Reprinted by permission of Robert A. M. Stern.

271. Maurice Culot, "Nostalgia, Soul of the Revolution," *Architectural Design* 11–12 (1980), pp. 44.

272. Aldo van Eyck, from "Rats, Posts and Pests," *RIBA Journal* 88:4 (April 1981), pp. 48–9.

273. Geoffrey Broadbent, from "The Pests Strike Back!," *RIBA Journal* 88:11 (November 1981), pp. 33–4.

274. Rob Krier, "10 Theses on Architecture, in *On Architecture*. London: Academy Editions, 1982, p. 5.

275. Michael Graves, from "A Case for Figurative Architecture," in *Michael Graves: Buildings and Projects 1966–1981*. New York: Rizzoli, 1982, p. 11. Used with permission from Rizzoli International Publications, Inc.

276. Josef-Paul Kleihues, from "1984: The Berlin Exhibition, Architectural Dream or Reality?," *Architectural Association Quarterly* 13:23 (January–June 1982), p. 42.

277. Charles Jencks, from *What is Postmodern?* London: Academy Editions, 1982, pp. 12, 14.

278. Heinrich Klotz, "Postscript: Since 1980," in *The History of Postmodern Architecture*, trans. Radka Donnell. Cambridge, MA: MIT Press, 1988, pp. 433–4. © 1988 Massachusetts Institute of Technology for English translation, by permission of The MIT Press.

279. Colin Davies, from *High Tech Architecture*. New York: Rizzoli, 1987, pp. 6–7. Used with permission from Rizzoli International Publications, Inc.

280. Bruno Reichlin, from "Reflections – Interrelations between Concept, Representation and Built Architecture," *Daidalos: Berlin Architectural Journal* 1 (1981), pp. 60, 67, 69, 72.

281. Alexander Tzonis and Liane Lefaivre, from "The Grid and the Pathway," *Architecture in Greece*, 15 (1981), pp. 176–8.

282. Demietri Porphyrios, from "Classicism Is Not a Style," *Architectural Design* 52:5/6 (1982), pp. 52–6. Reprinted by permission of Dr. Demietri Porphyrios.

283. Vittorio Gregotti, "The Obsession with History," *Casabella* 478 (March 1982), p. 41. Reprinted by permission of *Casabella* and Vittorio Gregotti.

284. Alberto Pérez-Gómez, from *Architecture and the Crisis of Modern Science*. Cambridge, MA: MIT Press, 1983, pp. 10–12. © 1983 Massachusetts Institute of Technology, by permission of The MIT Press.

285. Kenneth Frampton, from "Towards a Critical Regionalism: Six Points for an Architecture of Resistance," in *The Anti-Aesthetic: Essays on Postmodern Culture*, ed. Hal Foster. Seattle, WA: Bay Press, 1983, pp. 20–1. © 1998 by Kenneth Frampton. Reprinted with the permission of The New Press. www.thenewpress.com and Reprinted by permission of Kenneth Frampton. ©

286. Marco Frascari, from "The Tell-the-Tale Detail," in *VIA 7, The Graduate School of Fine Arts*. University of Pennsylvania, 1984, pp. 30–1.

287. Rafael Moneo, from "The Idea of Lasting," *Perspecta 24: The Yale Architectural Journal* (1988), pp. 154–5.

288. Juhani Pallasmaa, from "Tradition & Modernity: The Feasibility of Regional Architecture in Post-Modern Society," *Architectural Review* 188:1095 (May 1988), pp. 32–3. Reprinted by permission of *The Architectural Review*.

289. Charles, Prince of Wales, "The Ten Commandments for Architecture," *Architectural Design* 59:11–12 (1989), p. XIV. An expanded version appears in *A Vision of Britain: A Personal View of Architecture*. London: Doubleday, 1989.

290. Andres Duany, Elizabeth Plater-Zyberk, and Chester E. Chellman, from "New Town Ordinances and Codes," *Architectural Design* 59:11–12 (1989), pp. 71–2.

291. Kenneth Frampton, from "*Rappel á l'ordre*: The Case for the Tectonic," *Architectural Design* 60 (1990), pp. 19–21. Reprinted by permission of Kenneth Frampton.

292. Toyo Ito, "Vortex and Current: On Architecture as Phenomenalism," *Architectural Design* 62:9–10 (September/October 1992), pp. 22–3.

293. Gilles Deleuze, from *The Fold: Leibniz and the Baroque* (1993), in *Le Pli: Leibniz et le baroque*, trans. Tom Conley. Minneapolis: University of Minnesota Press, pp. 4–6.

294. Greg Lynn, "Architectural Curvilinearity: The Folded, the Pliant and the Supple," *Architectural Design* 102 (March/April 1993), pp. 8–9.

295. Peter Eisenman, from "Folding in Time: The Singularity of Rebstock," *Architectural Design* 102 (March/April 1993), pp. 24–5. Reprinted by permission of Peter Eisenman.

296. Jeffrey Kipnis, from "Towards a New Architecture," *Architectural Design* 102 (March/April 1993), p. 43. Reprinted by permission of Jeffrey Kipnis.

297. Mark C. Taylor, from "Seaming," *Newsline: Columbia Architecture, Planning, Preservation* 6:1 (September/October), p. 5.

298. Gevork Hartoonian, from *Ontology of Construction: On Nihilism of Technology in Theories of Modern Architecture*. New York: Cambridge University Press, 1994, pp. 26–7.

299. Mitchell Schwarzer, from "Tectonics of the Unforeseen," *ANY* 14 (1994), p. 65. Reprinted by permission of Mitchell Schwarzer.

300. Lindy Roy, "Geometry as a Nervous System," *ANY* 17 (1997), p. 27. Reprinted by permission of Lindy Roy.

301. Stan Allen, "From Object to Field," *Architectural Design* 67:5/6 (May–June 1997), p. 24. Reprinted by permission of Stan Allen.

302. Cecil Balmond, from "New Structure and the Informal," *Lotus International* 98 (1998), pp. 76–9, 83. Reprinted by permission of Editoriale Lotus srl.

303. Bernard Cache, from "Digital Semper," in *Anymore*, ed. Cynthia C. Davidson. New York: Anyone Corporation, 2000, p. 191.

304. Moshen Mostarfavi and David Leatherbarrow, from *On Weathering: The Life of Buildings in Time*. Cambridge, MA: MIT Press, 1993, pp. 112–20. © 1993 Massachusetts Institute of Technology, by permission of The MIT Press.

305. Juhani Pallasmaa, from "An Architecture of the Seven Senses," *a+u* (July 1994), pp. 29, 41.

306. OMA, Rem Koolhaas, and Bruce Mau, from "Bigness, or the problem of Large" in *S, M, L, XL*. New York: Monacelli Press, 1995, pp. 509–11, 513–15. Reprinted by permission of the Office of Metropolitan Architecture. Copyright © 1995 by Rem Koolhaas and The Monacelli Press, Inc. Published by kind permission of the author and the publisher.

307. Winy Maas, from "Datascape," in *Farmax: Excursions on Density*, ed. Winy Maas and Jacob van Rijs with Richard Koek. Rotterdam: 010 Publishers, 1998, pp. 100–3. All rights reserved. Reproduced by permission of 010 Publishers www.010publishers.nl.

308. Michael Speaks, "It's out there ... the Formal Limits of the American Avant-Garde," *Architectural Design* 68:5/6 (May–June 1998), pp. 30–1.

309. John Rajchman, from "A New Pragmatism?," in *Anyhow*, ed. Cynthia C. Davidson. Cambridge, MA: MIT Press, 1998, p. 217. © 1998 Cynthia Davidson, by permission of The MIT Press.

310. Cynthia C. Davidson, from "Architecture between Theory and Ideology," *archis* 7 (1998), pp. 10–11. Reprinted by permission of Stichting Archis www.archis.org.

311. K. Michael Hays, from *Introduction to Architectural Theory since 1968*. Cambridge, MA: MIT Press, 1998, xi–xii. © 1998 Massachusetts Institute of Technology, by permission of The MIT Press.

312. Sanford Kwinter, from "FFE: Le Trahison des Clercs (and other Travesties of the Modern)," *ANY* 24 (1999), pp. 61–62.

313. William J. Mitchell, from *e-topia: "Urban Life, Jim – But Not As We Know It."* Cambridge, MA: MIT Press, 1999, pp. 148–9. © 1999 Massachusetts Institute of Technology, by permission of The MIT Press.

314. Ben van Berkel and Caroline Bos, "The New Concept of the Architect," *Move: Imagination*, vol. 1. Amsterdam: UN Studio & Goose Press, 1999, pp. 27–8.

315. James Wines, "Green Dreams," *Art Forum* (October 1991), pp. 83–4. © *Artforum*.

316. William McDonough, "Hannover Principles," in *The Hannover Principles: Design for Sustainability* (1992). Reprinted by permission of William McDonough + Partners.

317. Bernard Cache, from *Earth Moves* (1995), in *Terre Meuble*, trans. Anne Boyman. Cambridge, MA: MIT Press, 1995, pp. 13–15. © 1995 Massachusetts Institute of Technology, by permission of The MIT Press.

318. Ken Yeang, *Designing with Nature*. New York: McGraw-Hill, 1995, pp. 190–1.

319. Victor Papanek, from *The Green Imperative: Natural Design for the Real World*. New York: Thames & Hudson, 1995, pp. 235–6.

320. James Corner, from "Eidetic Operations and New Landscape" in *Recovering Landscape: Essays in Contemporary Landscape Architecture*, ed. James Corner. New York: Princeton Architectural Press, 1999, pp. 158–60, 162. Reprinted by permission of James Corner. © 1999. Reprinted by permission of Princeton Architectural Press. All rights reserved.

321. Kenneth Frampton, "Seven Points for the Millennium: An Untimely Manifesto" (1999), *The Journal of Architecture* 5 (Spring 2000), pp. 26–9.

322. John Beardsley, from "A Word for Landscape Architecture," *Harvard Design Magazine* 12 (Fall 2000), pp. 62–3. Copyright, John Beardsley.

323. Antoine Picon, from "Anxious Landscapes: From the Ruin to Rust," trans. Karen Bates, *Grey Room* 01 (Fall 2000), pp. 79–81. Reprinted by permission of MIT Press Journals.

324. William McDonough and Michael Braungart, from *Cradle to Cradle: Remaking the Way We Make Things*. New York: North Point Press, 2002, pp. 154–6. Reprinted by permission of William McDonough and Michael Braungart.

325. Michael Braungart, "Beyond the Limits of Sustainable Architecture," in *Big & Green: Toward Sustainable Architecture in the 21st Century*, ed. David Gissen. New York: Princeton Architectural Press, 2002, pp. 114–15, 120, 125. Reprinted by permission of Michael Braungart.

326. Masdar, The Abu Dhabi Future Energy Company press release, "WWF and Abu Dhabi's Masdar Initiative unveil plan for world's first carbon-neutral, waste-free, car-free city," 2008.